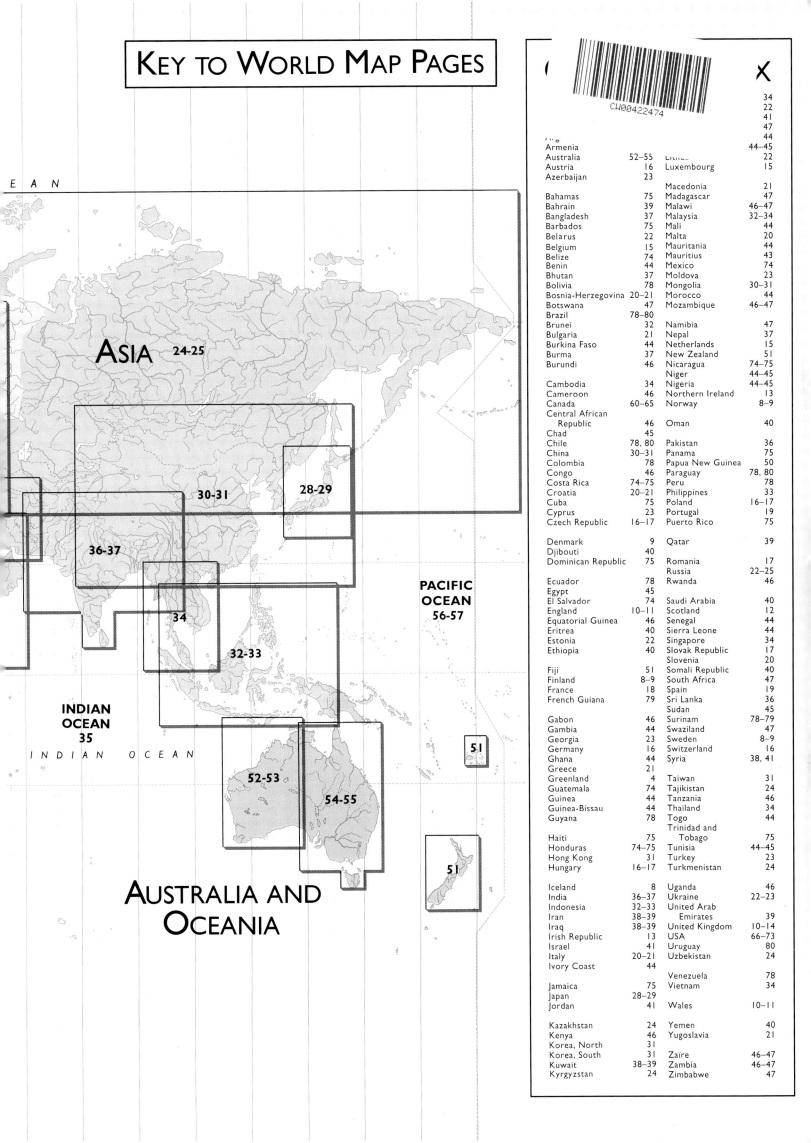

KEY TO WORLD MAP PAGES

ASIA 24-25

30-31

36-37

28-29

34

32-33

PACIFIC OCEAN 56-57

INDIAN OCEAN 35

INDIAN OCEAN

52-53

54-55

51

51

AUSTRALIA AND OCEANIA

E A N

X

		34
		22
		41
		47
		44
Armenia		44–45
Australia	52–55	22
Austria	16	Luxembourg 15
Azerbaijan	23	
		Macedonia 21
Bahamas	75	Madagascar 47
Bahrain	39	Malawi 46–47
Bangladesh	37	Malaysia 32–34
Barbados	75	Mali 44
Belarus	22	Malta 20
Belgium	15	Mauritania 44
Belize	74	Mauritius 43
Benin	44	Mexico 74
Bhutan	37	Moldova 23
Bolivia	78	Mongolia 30–31
Bosnia-Herzegovina	20–21	Morocco 44
Botswana	47	Mozambique 46–47
Brazil	78–80	
Brunei	32	Namibia 47
Bulgaria	21	Nepal 37
Burkina Faso	44	Netherlands 15
Burma	37	New Zealand 51
Burundi	46	Nicaragua 74–75
		Niger 44–45
Cambodia	34	Nigeria 44–45
Cameroon	46	Northern Ireland 13
Canada	60–65	Norway 8–9
Central African		
Republic	46	Oman 40
Chad	45	
Chile	78, 80	Pakistan 36
China	30–31	Panama 75
Colombia	78	Papua New Guinea 50
Congo	46	Paraguay 78, 80
Costa Rica	74–75	Peru 78
Croatia	20–21	Philippines 33
Cuba	75	Poland 16–17
Cyprus	23	Portugal 19
Czech Republic	16–17	Puerto Rico 75
Denmark	9	Qatar 39
Djibouti	40	
Dominican Republic	75	Romania 17
		Russia 22–25
Ecuador	78	Rwanda 46
Egypt	45	
El Salvador	74	Saudi Arabia 40
England	10–11	Scotland 12
Equatorial Guinea	46	Senegal 44
Eritrea	40	Sierra Leone 44
Estonia	22	Singapore 34
Ethiopia	40	Slovak Republic 17
		Slovenia 20
Fiji	51	Somali Republic 40
Finland	8–9	South Africa 47
France	18	Spain 19
French Guiana	79	Sri Lanka 36
		Sudan 45
Gabon	46	Surinam 78–79
Gambia	44	Swaziland 47
Georgia	23	Sweden 8–9
Germany	16	Switzerland 16
Ghana	44	Syria 38, 41
Greece	21	
Greenland	4	Taiwan 31
Guatemala	74	Tajikistan 24
Guinea	44	Tanzania 46
Guinea-Bissau	44	Thailand 34
Guyana	78	Togo 44
		Trinidad and
Haiti	75	Tobago 75
Honduras	74–75	Tunisia 44–45
Hong Kong	31	Turkey 23
Hungary	16–17	Turkmenistan 24
Iceland	8	Uganda 46
India	36–37	Ukraine 22–23
Indonesia	32–33	United Arab
Iran	38–39	Emirates 39
Iraq	38–39	United Kingdom 10–14
Irish Republic	13	USA 66–73
Israel	41	Uruguay 80
Italy	20–21	Uzbekistan 24
Ivory Coast	44	
		Venezuela 78
Jamaica	75	Vietnam 34
Japan	28–29	
Jordan	41	Wales 10–11
Kazakhstan	24	Yemen 40
Kenya	46	Yugoslavia 21
Korea, North	31	
Korea, South	31	Zaïre 46–47
Kuwait	38–39	Zambia 46–47
Kyrgyzstan	24	Zimbabwe 47

CW00422474

PHILIP'S

NEW
WORLD
ATLAS

This 1995 edition published by Chancellor Press,
an imprint of Reed Books
Michelin House, 81 Fulham Road, London SW3 6RB,
and Auckland, Melbourne, Singapore and Toronto

Copyright © 1995 Reed International Books Limited

Cartography by Philip's

ISBN 1-85152-897-0

A CIP catalogue record for this book is available
from the British Library

Printed in Hong Kong

PHILIP'S

NEW
WORLD
ATLAS

CHANCELLOR
PRESS

CONTENTS

WORLD MAPS

Map Symbols
1

The World: Political
1:80 000 000
2–3

Arctic Ocean
1:35 000 000
4

Antarctica
1:35 000 000
5

EUROPE

Europe: Physical
1:20 000 000
6

Europe: Political
1:20 000 000
7

Scandinavia
1:5 000 000
8–9

England and Wales
1:2 000 000
10–11

Scotland
1:2 000 000
12

Ireland
1:2 000 000
13

British Isles
1:5 000 000
14

Netherlands, Belgium and Luxembourg
1:2 500 000
15

Middle Europe
1:5 000 000
16–17

France
1:5 000 000
18

Spain and Portugal
1:5 000 000
19

Italy and the Balkan States
1:5 000 000
20–21

Eastern Europe and Turkey
1:10 000 000
22–23

ASIA

Russia and Central Asia
1:20 000 000
24–25

Asia: Physical
1:50 000 000
26

Asia: Political
1:50 000 000
27

Japan
1:5 000 000
28–29

China and Korea
1:15 000 000
30–31

Indonesia and the Philippines
1:12 500 000
32–33

Mainland South-east Asia
1:10 000 000
34

Indian Ocean
1:50 000 000
35

South Asia
1:10 000 000
36–37

The Middle East
1:7 000 000
38–39

Arabia and the Horn of Africa
1:15 000 000
40

The Near East
1:2 500 000
41

AFRICA

Africa: Physical
1:42 000 000
42

Africa: Political
1:42 000 000
43

Northern Africa
1:15 000 000
44–45

Central and Southern Africa
1:15 000 000
46–47

Southern Africa
1:8 000 000
Madagascar 1:8 000 000
48–49

AUSTRALIA AND OCEANIA

Australia and Oceania: Physical and Political
1:50 000 000
50

New Zealand
1:6 000 000
51

Western Australia
1:8 000 000
52–53

Eastern Australia
1:8 000 000
54–55

Pacific Ocean
1:54 000 000
56–57

NORTH AMERICA

North America: Physical
1:35 000 000
58

North America: Political
1:35 000 000
59

Canada
1:15 000 000
Alaska 1:30 000 000
60–61

Eastern Canada
1:7 000 000
62–63

Western Canada
1:7 000 000
64–65

United States
1:12 000 000
Hawaii 1:10 000 000
66–67

Eastern United States
1:6 000 000
68–69

Middle United States
1:6 000 000
70–71

Western United States
1:6 000 000
72–73

Mexico, Central America and the West Indies
1:15 000 000
74–75

SOUTH AMERICA

South America: Physical
1:35 000 000
76

South America: Political
1:35 000 000
77

South America – North
1:16 000 000
78–79

South America – South
1:16 000 000
80

INDEX TO WORLD MAPS

81–128

World: Regions in the News **129**

WORLD MAPS

SETTLEMENTS

◻ PARIS ◼ Berne ◉ Livorno ◉ Brugge ◎ Algeciras ○ Fréjus ○ Oberammergau ○ Thira

Settlement symbols and type styles vary according to the scale of each map and indicate the importance
of towns on the map rather than specific population figures

∴ Ruins or Archæological Sites ˇ Wells in Desert

ADMINISTRATION

——— International Boundaries

— — — International Boundaries
(Undefined or Disputed)

·········· Internal Boundaries

National Parks

Country Names

NICARAGUA

Administrative
Area Names

KENT

CALABRIA

International boundaries show the *de facto* situation where there are rival claims to territory

COMMUNICATIONS

——— Principal Roads

⌒ Other Roads

-·--·· Trails and Seasonal Roads

≍ Passes

✧ Airfields

⌢ Principal Railways

·--·-· Railways
Under Construction

⌢ Other Railways

⊐---⊏ Railway Tunnels

············ Principal Canals

PHYSICAL FEATURES

⌁ Perennial Streams

········ Intermittent Streams

⬭ Perennial Lakes

⬭ Intermittent Lakes

Swamps and Marshes

Permanent Ice
and Glaciers

▲ 8848 Elevations in metres

▾ 8050 Sea Depths in metres

1134 Height of Lake Surface
Above Sea Level
in metres

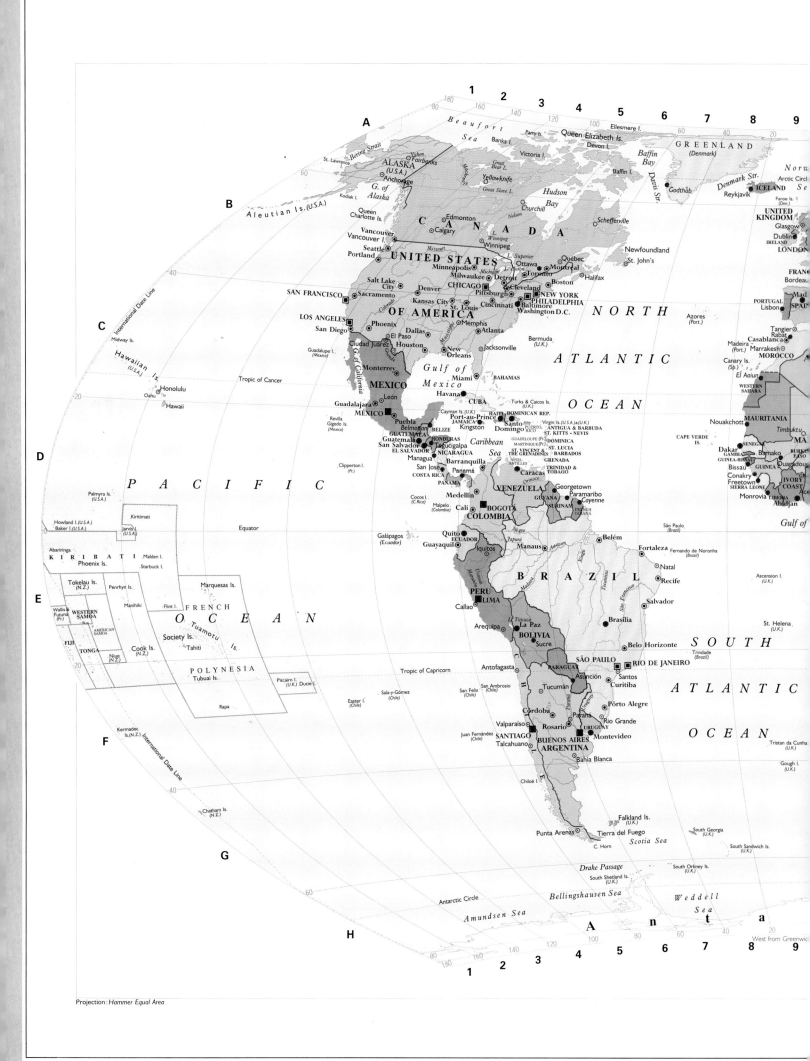

Projection: *Hammer Equal Area*

Hanoi ● Capital Cities

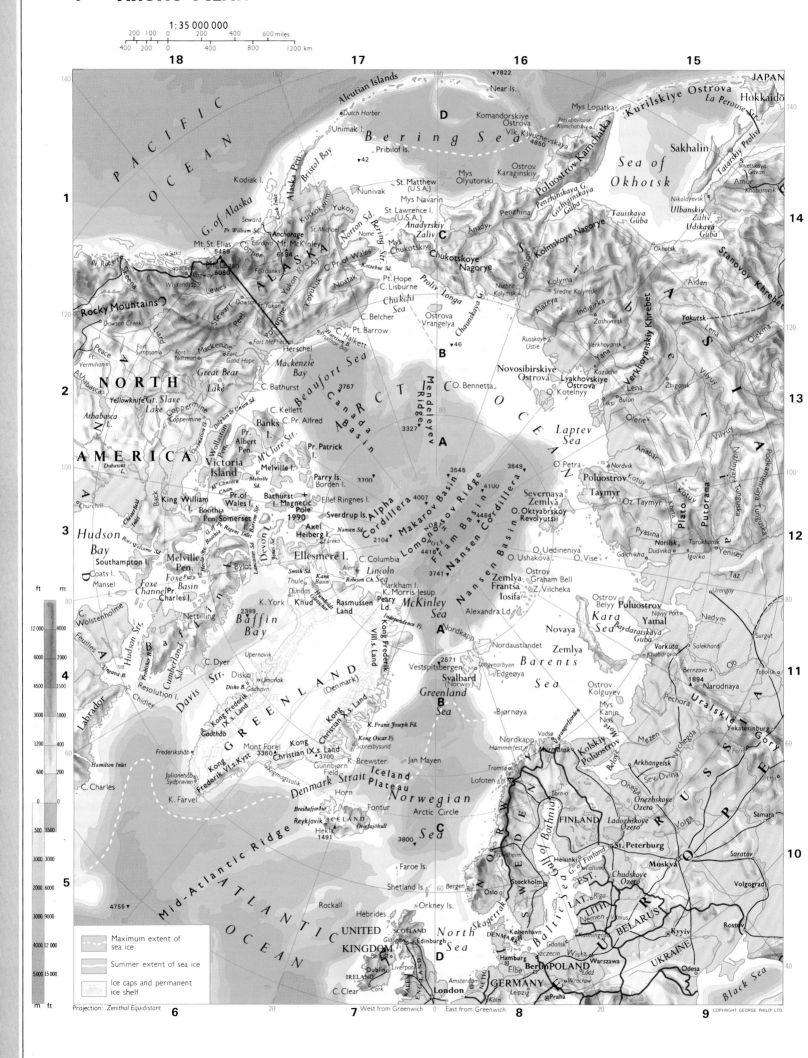

1:35 000 000

Projection: Zenithal Equidistant

West from Greenwich   East from Greenwich

COPYRIGHT GEORGE PHILIP LTD.

Maximum extent of sea ice

Summer extent of sea ice

Ice caps and permanent ice shelf

1:35 000 000

400 200 0 400 800 1200 km
200 100 0 200 400 600 miles

West from Greenwich | East from Greenwich

1 **2** **3** **4**

ATLANTIC OCEAN

INDIAN OCEAN

Atlantic - Indian Basin

SOUTHERN OCEAN

Antarctic Circle

▼8265
Zavodovski I.
Visokoi I.
Leskov I. Candlemas I.
Saunders I. S. Sandwich Is. (U.K.)
Montagu I. Bristol I.

South Georgia
Bird I. (U.K.)

Bases on
King George Island:
Jubany (Argentina)
Com. Ferraz (Brazil)
Ten. Rodolfo Marsh (Chile)
Great Wall (China)
King Sejong (Korea)
Arctowski (Poland)
Artigas (Uruguay)

Stanley (U.K.)
Falkland Is.
(U.K.)

6739▼

▼5552
Orcadas (Arg.)
Signy I. (U.K.) South
Coronation I. Orkney Is.
(U.K.)

Georg Forster
(Germany)
Dakshin Gangotri
(India)

Georg von
Neumayer
(Germany)

Sanae (S. Afr.)

Prinsesse Astrid Kyst Prinsesse Ragnhild
Kyst

Riiser-
Larsen-halvøya

Lützow Holmbukta
Syowa (Japan)

ARGENTINA
Tierra
del
Fuego C. de Hornos
CHILE
I. Hoste

Clarence I.
Elephant I.
South
Kg. George I.
Gen. Bernardo
O'Higgins (Chile)
Joinville I.
Esperanza (Arg.)
Capitan Arturo Prat
(Chile)
Marambio (Arg.)
James Ross I.
Robertson I.

Shetland Is.
Deception I.
Palmer Arch.
Graham Land
Palmer (U.S.A.)
Anvers I.
Faraday (U.K.)
Biscoe Is.
Adelaide I.
Rothera (U.K.)

Alexander
I.

Charcot I.

Peter I Øy
(Nor.)

Antarctic
Peninsula
Palmer
Land

Halley Bay
(U.K.)

Weddell
Sea

Vahsel Bay

Berkner
I.

Ronne
Ice
Shelf

Larsen Ice Shelf
San Martin
(Arg.) Dyer
Plateau 4191
George VI Sound
▲3658
2987
2896▲

Coats Land
Caird Coast
Kronprinsesse Martha
Kyst 2717
Mühlig Hofmann
fjell

Sør-Rondane
3630 Kyst

Prins Harald
Kyst

Kronprins
Olav Kyst

Mizuho
(Japan)

Enderby Ld.
Kemp
Land
2260

C. Borley

Stefansson B.

Mawson
(Austr.)

3212
3039
3318
2990
2311
1431
3556
2600

3355

Mac-
Robertson
Land

2645

C. Darnley

Prince Charles Mts.
Lambert
Glacier

Amery
Ice Shelf

Prydz Bay
Zhongshan (China)
Davis (Austr.)

Queen Maud Land

D

E

975
158
131

Pensacola
Mountains
3657

South
Pole
(U.S.A.)

Amundsen-Scott
(U.S.A.)

2773
2407

4030
1040

American
Highland

1800

Interior
Christensen
Coast

East
Antarctica

West
Ice
Shelf

Ellsworth Mts.
4897▲
Vinson
Massif

Abbot
Ice Shelf

Thiel
Mts.

Horlick Mts.

3810

4176

Queen
Maud Mts.

Beardmore
Glacier

4528

Queen
Alexandra Ra.
Mt. Markham
4349

2801
3491

3488
3700

3030
2570

Wilhelm II
Coast

Queen
Mary
Land

Drygalski I.
Davis Sea
Masson I.

Shackleton
Ice Shelf

Denman Gl.

Mill I.

Thurston I.

C. Flying Fish

1036

Hudson Mts.

Walgreen
Coast

West
Antarctica

Marie Byrd Land

Kohler
Ra.

Mt. Sidley
▲4181

Bakutis Coast

C.
Dart

3109

Getz
Ice Shelf

Hobbs Coast

3496

1797
4335

3022

Edward VII
Land

Rockefeller
Plateau
666
2080

Sulzberger
Ice Shelf

Biscoe B.

Bay of Whales
Roosevelt
I.

Ross Ice Shelf

2407
3087

Scott Gl.

Knox Coast

Casey (Austr.)

Budd
Coast
Sabrina
Coast

Totten Glacier

Dalton Iceberg
Tongue

C. Poinsett

Bowman I.

Banzare
Coast

2216
2798

Shackleton Inlet

Mt. Erebus
4023
McMurdo
3743
Scott (N.Z.) McMurdo
(U.S.A.)
Ross
I.

Mt. Lister

Victoria

Pr. Albert Mts.

Wilkes Land

2435
4776

Clarie
Coast

Porpoise Bay

Blodgett Iceberg
Tongue

Dumont d'Urville (Fr.)

Terre Adélie

George V
Land

C. Colbeck

Ross
Sea

Franklin I.

Coulman I.

Mt.
Murchison
3502

Land

Possession I.

C. Adare

3719

Oates Land

Bellingshausen
Sea

Amundsen
Sea

C. Byrd

Siple (U.S.A.)

C. Freshfield

Commonwealth B.
+
Magnetic Pole 1990

Southeast
Pacific
Basin

Pacific
Basin

Southeast
Pacific

Antarctic Circle

Scott I.

Balleny Is.

Antarctic Ridge

Southeast Indian Rise

Southwestern
Pacific Basin

▼6240

Macquarie Is.
(Austr.)

Tasman
Plat.

Campbell I.
(N.Z.)

Auckland Is.
(N.Z.)

Tasman
Sea

Tasmania

Hobart

Bass
Strait

Antipodes Is.

Campbell
Plateau

Bounty Is.
Dunedin

Stewart I.

NEW ZEALAND

Melbourne

AUSTRALIA

ft m
12000 4000
6000 2000
4500 1500
3000 1000
1200 400
600 200
0 0
500 1500
1000 3000
2000 6000
3000 9000
4000 12000
5000 15000
m ft

Legend

Ice cap

Permanent ice shelf

Maximum extent of
sea ice

March (Summer) extent
of sea ice

▲3488 Surface elevation and
3700 depth of ice (in metres)

• Stanley
(U.K.) Permanent bases

Projection: Zenithal Equidistant

COPYRIGHT GEORGE PHILIP LTD.

The Antarctic Treaty was signed in Washington in
1959 so that scientific and technical research could
continue unhampered by international politics.

All territorial claims covering land areas south
of latitude 60°S have been suspended. Those
claims were:

Norwegian claim 45°E - 20°W
Australian claims { 45°E - 136°E
{ 142°E - 160°E

French claim 136°E - 142°E
New Zealand claim 160°E - 150°W
Chilean claim 90°W - 53°W

British claim 80°W - 20°W
Argentine claim 74°W - 53°W

1:20 000 000

100 0 100 200 300 400 miles
100 0 100 200 300 400 500 600 km

ATLANTIC OCEAN

Norwegian Sea

North Sea

Baltic Sea

White Sea

Black Sea

Caspian Sea

Mediterranean Sea

Adriatic Sea

Tyrrhenian Sea

Ligurian Sea

Ionian Sea

Aegean Sea

Sea of Marmara

Sea of Azov

Ural Mountains

Caspian Depression

Obschi Syrt

Volga Hts.

Central Russian Uplands

European Plain

Scandinavia

Lapland

Finland

Ukraine

Carpathians

Alps

Pyrenees

Apennines

Dinaric Alps

Balkans

Pindus

Caucasus

Anatolia (Asia Minor)

Kurdistan

Armenia

Mesopotamia

Pontine Mts.

Taurus Mts.

Plain of Hungary

Wallachia

Transylvanian Alps

Rhodope

Iberian Peninsula

Sierra Morena

Sierra Nevada

Andalusia

Old Castile

New Castile

Cantabrian Mts.

Massif Central

Black Forest

Vosges

Jura

Ardennes

Bohemian Forest

Erzgebirge

Harz

Sudeten Hts.

Moravian Hts.

Jutland

Great Britain

Ireland

British Isles

Hebrides

Orkney Is.

Shetland Is.

Faroe Is.

Iceland

Rockall

Vesterålen

Lofoten

Gotland

Öland

Bornholm

Åland

Saaremaa

Corsica

Sardinia

Sicily

Crete

Cyprus

Rhodes

Malta

Balearic Is.

Ibiza

Majorca

Minorca

Kola Pen.

Kanin Pen.

North Cape

Nordkinn

Kebnekaise 2117

Galdhøpiggen 2468

Ben Nevis 1343

Snowdon 1085

Mont Blanc 4807

Gran Sasso d'Italia 2914

Vesuvius 1277

Etna 3340

Mulhacén 3478

Pico de Aneto 3404

Puy de Sancy 1886

Elbrus 5633

Ararat 5165

Kazbek 5047

Hekla 1491

Öraefajökull 2119

Olympus 2971

Volga

Don

Donets

Dnieper

Dniester

Bug

Prut

Danube

Tisza

Sava

Drava

Oder

Vistula

Elbe

Weser

Rhine

Meuse

Seine

Loire

Garonne

Gironde

Ebro

Duero

Guadiana

Guadalquivir

Po

Tiber

Rhône

Saône

Tigris

Euphrates

Kura

Aras

Terek

Kuban

Manych

Ural

Kama

Pechora

Mezen

N. Dvina

Onega

Neva

Svir

W. Dvina

Niemen

Oka

Kama

Torne

Ume

Indals

Klar

Göta

Dal

Vänern

Vättern

Mälaren

L. Ladoga

L. Onega

L. Chudskoye

L. Van

L. Urmia

Rybinsk Res.

Tsimlyansk Res.

G. of Bothnia

G. of Finland

G. of Riga

English Channel

Irish Sea

Celtic Sea

Kattegat

Skagerrak

Bay of Biscay

G. of Lions

Str. of Gibraltar

Str. of Messina

Str. of Bonifacio

Str. of Otranto

Dardanelles

Bosporus

Str. of Kerch

Crimea

Brittany

Channel Is.

Ushant

Land's End

Lindesnes

Helgoland

Jutland

C. Finisterre

C. da Roca

C. de São Vicente

C. Trafalgar

C. Clear

C. Bon

C. Matapan

Morea

Calabria

Plateau of the Shotts

Atlas

Afr ica

Mts. of Kurdistan

Arctic Circle

West from Greenwich 0 East from Greenwich

Projection Bonne

CARTOGRAPHY BY PHILIP'S. COPYRIGHT REED INTERNATIONAL BOOKS LTD.

ft m
15 000 5000
12 000 4000
6000 2000
3000 1000
1200 400
600 200
0
0
600 200
4000 2000
12 000 4000
m ft

1 : 20 000 000

100 0 100 200 300 400 miles
100 0 100 200 300 400 500 600 km

CARTOGRAPHY BY PHILIPS. COPYRIGHT REED INTERNATIONAL BOOKS LTD.

■ LONDON Capital Cities

Projection: Bonne   West from Greenwich   0   East from Greenwich

Seas and Oceans

ATLANTIC OCEAN
Norwegian Sea
North Sea
White Sea
Baltic Sea
Gulf of Bothnia
Kattegat
Skagerrak
English Channel
Bay of Biscay
Mediterranean Sea
Tyrrhenian Sea
Adriatic Sea
Ionian Sea
Aegean Sea
Black Sea
Caspian Sea

Countries and regions

ICELAND — Reykjavik
IRELAND — Dublin
UNITED KINGDOM — SCOTLAND, ENGLAND, WALES, London, Cardiff, Belfast
NORWAY — Oslo, Bergen, Trondheim, Narvik, Tromsø, Hammerfest, Stavanger
SWEDEN — Stockholm, Gothenburg, Malmö, Uppsala, Örebro, Kiruna, Luleå
FINLAND — Helsinki, Turku, Tampere, Vaasa, Oulu
DENMARK — Copenhagen, Århus, Aalborg, Kiel
ESTONIA — Tallinn
LATVIA — Riga
LITHUANIA — Vilnius, Kaunas, Kaliningrad (Russia)
BELARUS — Minsk, Vitebsk, Mogilev, Gomel, Brest
RUSSIA — MOSCOW, ST. PETERSBURG, Murmansk, Arkhangelsk
POLAND — Warsaw, Kraków, Łódź, Wrocław, Poznań, Gdańsk, Szczecin, Bydgoszcz, Lublin, Katowice
GERMANY — Berlin, Hamburg, Munich, Cologne, Frankfurt am Main, Hanover, Bremen, Dresden, Leipzig, Stuttgart, Dortmund, Essen, Magdeburg, Nuremberg, Bonn, Chemnitz, Halle, Wiesbaden
NETHERLANDS — Amsterdam, The Hague, Rotterdam
BELGIUM — Brussels, Antwerp
LUX. — Luxembourg
FRANCE — PARIS, Lyons, Marseilles, Bordeaux, Toulouse, Nantes, Lille, Nice, Strasbourg, Rouen, Le Havre, Dijon, Limoges, St-Étienne, Grenoble, Brest
SWITZERLAND — Bern, Zürich, Geneva, Basle
AUSTRIA — Vienna, Salzburg, Linz, Graz, Innsbruck
LIECH.
CZECH REP. — Prague, Brno, Ostrava
SLOVAK REP. — Bratislava
HUNGARY — Budapest, Miskolc, Debrecen
SLOVENIA — Ljubljana
CROATIA — Zagreb, Split
BOSNIA-HERZ. — Sarajevo
YUGOSLAVIA — SERBIA, Belgrade, Niš, MONTENEGRO
MACEDONIA — Skopje
ALBANIA — Tirana
ROMANIA — Bucharest, Cluj-Napoca, Timişoara, Braşov, Galaţi, Ploieşti
MOLDOVA — Kishinev
BULGARIA — Sofia, Plovdiv, Varna
GREECE — Athens, Thessaloníki, Patras, Corfu
ITALY — Rome, Milan, Naples, Turin, Genoa, Florence, Bologna, Venice, Palermo, Bari, Catania, Messina, Taranto, Cagliari
MONACO
SAN MARINO
MALTA — Valletta
SPAIN — Madrid, Barcelona, Valencia, Seville, Zaragoza, Málaga, Bilbao, Murcia, Alicante, Córdoba, Valladolid, Granada, La Coruña, Vigo
PORTUGAL — Lisbon, Porto
ANDORRA — Andorra-la-Vella
GIBRALTAR (U.K.)

UKRAINE — Kiev, Kharkov, Donetsk, Odessa, Dnepropetrovsk, Zaporozhye, Krivoy Rog, Lvov, Nikolayev, Kherson, Zhitomir, Chernigov
KAZAKHSTAN
GEORGIA — Tbilisi
ARMENIA — Yerevan
AZERBAIJAN — Baku
TURKEY — Ankara, Istanbul, İzmir, Bursa, Konya, Adana, Antalya, Kayseri, Samsun, Erzurum, Diyarbakir, Tabriz
IRAN — Tabriz
IRAQ — Baghdad, Mosul
SYRIA — Aleppo
CYPRUS — Nicosia
ALGERIA — Algiers, Oran, Constantine, Annaba
TUNISIA — Tunis
MOROCCO — Tangier
Africa

Physical features / islands

Shetland Is.
Orkney Is.
Hebrides
Faroe Is. (Den.)
Gotland
Öland
Corsica
Sardinia
Sicily
Balearic Is. — Majorca, Minorca, Ibiza
Crete
Rhodes
Crimea

Rivers and lakes

Ob
Volga
Don
Dnieper
Dniester
Danube
Rhine
Rhône
Seine
Loire
Garonne
Ebro
Tagus
Vistula
Oder
Elbe
L. Ladoga
L. Onega
Arctic Circle

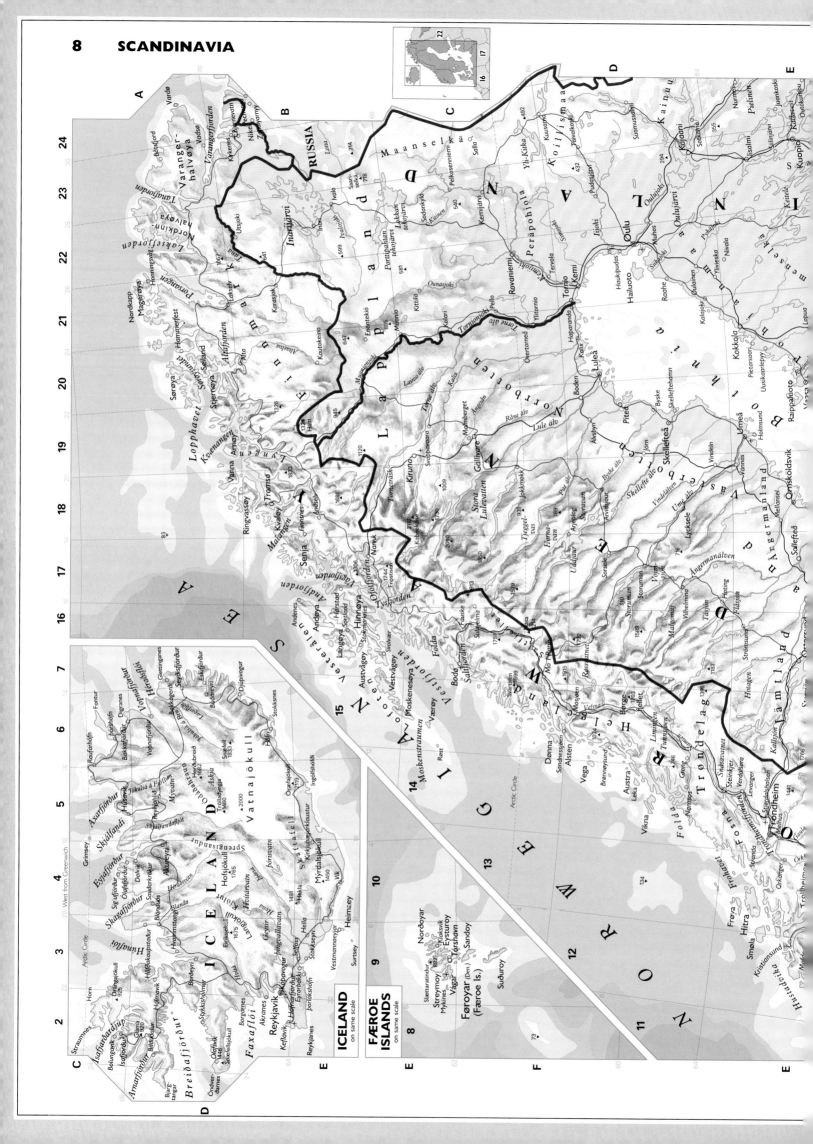

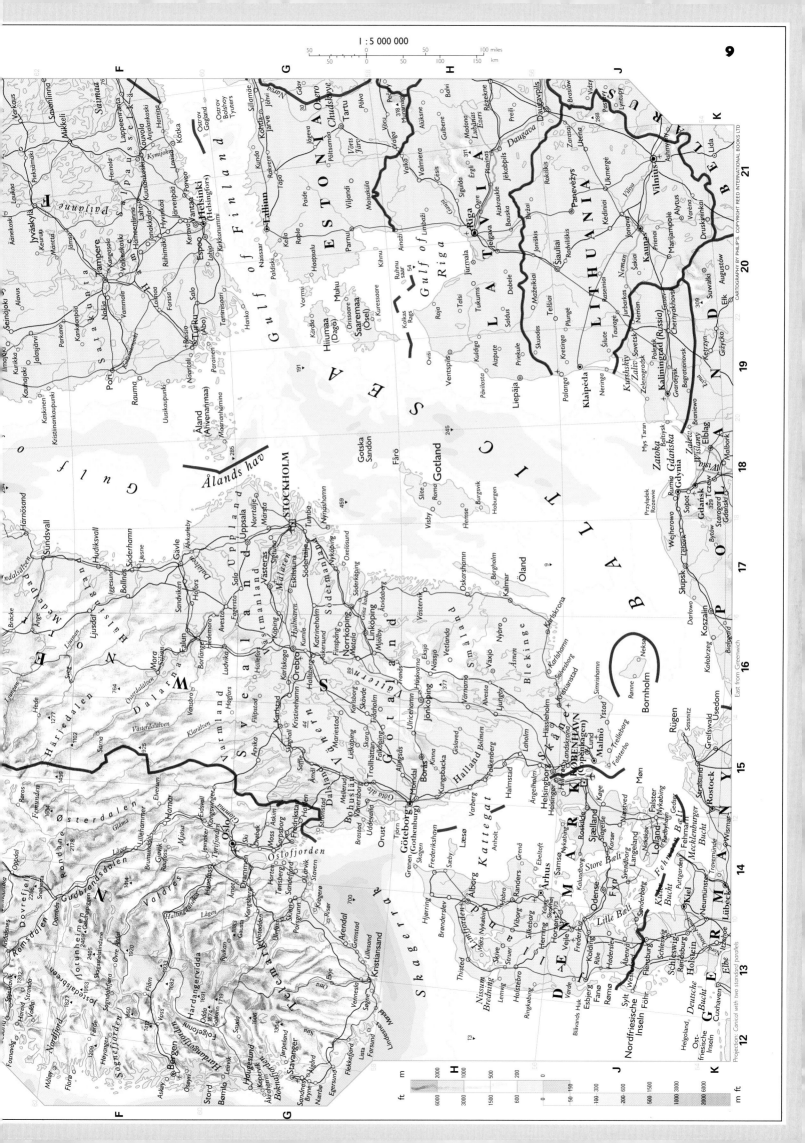

NORTH SEA

IRISH SEA

North Channel

SCOTLAND

Southern Uplands

Cheviot Hills

NORTHUMBERLAND

CUMBRIA

Cumbrian Mts.

Pennines

NORTH YORKSHIRE

DURHAM

TYNE & WEAR

CLEVELAND (Teesside)

HUMBERSIDE

LINCOLN Wolds

LANCASHIRE

W. YORKSHIRE

SOUTH YORKSHIRE

GREATER MANCHESTER

MERSEYSIDE

CHESHIRE

DERBY

NOTT

STAFFORD

GWYNEDD

CLWYD

Anglesey

Isle of Man

Kintyre

Jura

Arran

Sound of Jura

Firth of Clyde

Galloway

Solway Firth

Morecambe Bay

The Wash

The Broads

Inveraray
Lochgilphead
Campbeltown
Gigha I.
Mull of Kintyre
Ailsa Craig
Girvan
Stranraer
Portpatrick
Wigtown
Wigtown Bay
Newton Stewart
Luce Bay
Whithorn
Mull of Galloway
Port Erin
Calf of Man
Peel
Castletown
Douglas
Ramsey
Snaefell 620
Pt. of Ayre
Maryport
Workington
Whitehaven
St. Bee's Hd.
Seascale
Millom
Barrow
Walney I.
Fleetwood
Cleveleys
Blackpool
Lytham St. Annes
Southport
Formby Pt.
Bootle
Wallasey
Birkenhead
Liverpool
St. Helens
Wigan
Bolton
Bury
Rochdale
Oldham
Manchester
Salford
Stockport
Macclesfield
Crewe
Nantwich
Northwich
Stoke-on-Trent
Newcastle-under-Lyme
Leek
Buxton
Chesterfield
Sheffield
Rotherham
Barnsley
Huddersfield
Halifax
Bradford
Leeds
Wakefield
Harrogate
Knaresborough
Ripon
York
Selby
Goole
Doncaster
Scunthorpe
Gainsborough
Retford
Worksop
Mansfield
Nottingham
Derby
Burton on Trent
Stafford
Lincoln
Louth
Mablethorpe
Skegness
Boston
Grantham
Sleaford
Newark
Grimsby
Cleethorpes
Immingham
Barton upon Humber
Kingston upon Hull
Beverley
Hornsea
Withernsea
Spurn Hd.
Holderness
Bridlington
Flamborough Hd.
Filey
Scarborough
Whitby
Pickering
Malton
Driffield
Thirsk
Northallerton
Richmond
Darlington
Stockton
Middlesbrough
Redcar
Hartlepool
Houghton-le-Spring
Peterlee
Sunderland
South Shields
Tynemouth
Newcastle
Gateshead
Blyth
Ashington
Morpeth
Hexham
Consett
Durham
Bishop Auckland
Barnard Castle
Appleby
Penrith
Carlisle
Brampton
Gretna Green
Alston
Cross Fell 893
Keswick
Skiddaw 931
Helvellyn 950
Scafell Pike 978
Ambleside
Windermere
Kendal
Ulverston
Sedbergh
Settle
Pen-y-Ghent 693
Whernside 736
Ingleborough 723
Great Whernside 704
Lancaster
Morecambe
Heysham
Forest of Bowland
Preston
Chorley
Leyland
Blackburn
Accrington
Burnley
Nelson
Colne
Skipton
Keighley
Berwick-upon-Tweed
Holy I.
Farne Is.
Bamburgh
Alnwick
Coquet

SCOTLAND place names:
Fife Ness
Anstruther
North Berwick
No. Bass Rock
Dunbar
St. Abb's Hd.
Eyemouth
Kirkcaldy
Kinross
L. Leven
Dunfermline
Leith
Edinburgh
Musselburgh
Haddington
Lammermuir Hills
Moorfoot Hills
Pentland Hills
Peebles
Coldstream
Kelso
Jedburgh
The Cheviot 816
Flodden
Galashiels
Selkirk
Hawick
Langholm
Annan
Dumfries
Dalbeattie
Kirkcudbright
Castle Douglas
Merrick 843
Ayr
Irvine
Kilmarnock
Saltcoats
Largs
Greenock
Port Glasgow
Gourock
Helensburgh
Dumbarton
Clydebank
Glasgow
Rutherglen
Paisley
Hamilton
Motherwell
Wishaw
Coatbridge
Airdrie
Falkirk
Stirling
Alloa
Ochil Hills
B. Lomond 974
L. Lomond
L. Katrine
Trossachs
Loch Awe
Crinan
Katrine
Forth
Dunoon

WALES place names:
Holyhead
Holy I.
Amlwch
Beaumaris
Bangor
Caernarfon
Menai Strait
Pwllheli
Nefyn
Criccieth
Portmadoc
Harlech
Barmouth
Dolgellau
Bala
Llangollen
Wrexham
Llandudno
Colwyn Bay
Rhyl
Conwy
Denbigh
Ruthin
Mold
Snowdon 1085
Snowdonia
Cadair Idris 893
Gt. Orme's Hd.

Ireland:
Belfast
Bangor
Newtownards
Strangford L.
Downpatrick
Ardglass
Donaghadee
Larne
Carrickfergus
Belfast Lough
Pt. of Magee
Portaferry

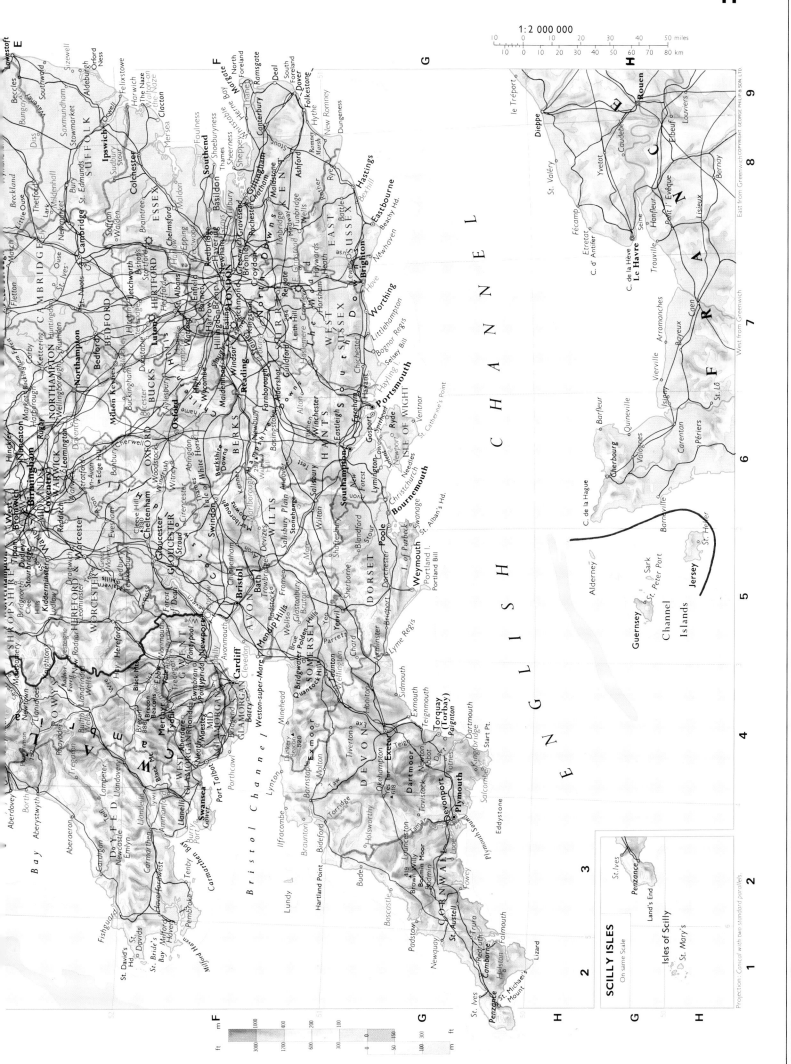

11

1:2 000 000

SCILLY ISLES
On same Scale

Isles of Scilly

Projection: Conical with two standard parallels.

East from Greenwich   West from Greenwich   COPYRIGHT GEORGE PHILIP & SON LTD.

1 : 2 000 000

10 0 10 20 30 40 50 miles
10 0 10 20 30 40 50 60 70 80 km

ORKNEY IS.
On same scale

Scapa Flow
Hoy
South Ronaldsay
Orkney Is.
Pentland Firth
Dunnet Hd.
Strathy Pt.
C. Wrath
Durness
Thurso
Dounreay
John o'Groats
Halladale
Noss Hd.
L. Eriboll
Tongue
Ben Hope 927
Wick
Naver
Reay Forest
L. Loyal
Eddrachillis Bay
Lochinver
Enard Bay
L. Assynt
B. More Assynt
Lybster
Ord of Caithness
Helmsdale
Brora
Shin
Lairg
Oykel
Dornoch Firth
Golspie
Brora
Dornoch
Tarbat Ness
Tain
Westray
North Ronaldsay
Rousay
Eday
Sanday
Stronsay
Mainland
Shapinsay
ORKNEY
Stromness
Kirkwall
Scapa Flow
Hoy
South Ronaldsay
Pentland Firth
Dunnet Hd.
John o'Groats

Butt of Lewis
Flannan Is.
L. Roag
Stornoway
Broad Bay
Eye Pen.
Lewis
Tarbert
Harris
L. Seaforth
WESTERN ISLES
Sound of Harris
North Uist
Lochmaddy
Monach Is.
Benbecula
South Uist
Ben More 620
Lochboisdale
Sound of Barra
Barra
Barra Hd.

OUTER HEBRIDES
NORTH MINCH
Little Minch
INNER HEBRIDES

Rubha Hunish
Snizort
Trotternish
Sound of Raasay
Rona
Raasay
Portree
Skye
Scalpay
Cuillin Hills
Cuillin Sound
Canna
Rhum
Eigg
Muck
Coll
Tiree
Staffa
Iona
Mull
Ben More 966
Colonsay

L. Gairloch
Rubha Reidh
L. Ewe
L. Maree
L. Torridon
L. Bracadale
Sound of Sleat
L. Hourn
Mallaig
Morar
L. Moidart
L. Shiel
L. Eil
Arisaig
L. Arkaig
Ardgour
Pt. of Ardnamurchan
Loch Sunart
MORVERN
Tobermory
Sound of Mull
L. Linnhe

L. Broom
Ullapool
B. Dearg 1081
Ben Wyvis 1046
Strathpeffer
Dingwall
Cromarty
Fortrose
Beauly
INVERNESS
Culloden Moor
HIGHLAND
WEST HIGHLANDS
NORTH WEST HIGHLANDS
Glen Affric
Glen Moriston
Fort Augustus
Glen Garry
Glen Spean
Loch Ness
L. Oich
Newtonmore
Kingussie
Aviemore
Monadhliath Mts.
Cairn Gorm 1245
Cairngorm Mts.
Cairn Toul 1292
Ben Macdhui 1311
GRAMPIAN HIGHLANDS
BADENOCH
Fort William
Ben Nevis 1343
Glen Nevis
Ballachulish
Rannoch Moor
L. Rannoch
L. Laggan
Forest of Atholl
Blair Atholl
Pass of Killiecrankie
Pitlochry
Lochnagar 1154
Balmoral
Braemar

Nairn
Forres
Elgin
Lossiemouth
Buckie
Cullen
Portsoy
Banff
Macduff
Fraserburgh
Kinnaird's Head
Rattray Head
Peterhead
Buchan Ness
Ellon
Keith
Rothes
Dufftown
Huntly
Turriff
BUCHAN
Deveron
Ythan
GRAMPIAN
Tomintoul
Alford
Inverurie
Don
Aberdeen
Girdle Ness
Ballater
Aboyne
Dee
Banchory
Stonehaven
Inverbervie
Laurencekirk
Braes of Angus
N. Esk
Brechin
Montrose
Strathmore
Kirriemuir
Forfar
Isla
S. Esk
Blairgowrie
Alyth
Aberfeldy
Ben Lawers 1214
L. Tay
Dunkeld
Breadalbane
Killin
Sidlaw Hills
TAYSIDE
Dundee
Broughty Ferry
Firth of Tay
Tayport
St. Andrews
Fife Ness
Crieff
Perth
Scone
Earn
L. Earn
B. Vorlich 983
Ben More 1174
Callander
Trossachs
L. Katrine
Ben Lomond 974
CENTRAL
Dunblane
Doune
L. Lomond
Stirling
Bannockburn
Alloa
Kinross
L. Leven
FIFE
Glenrothes
Lochgelly
Leven
Buckhaven
Kirkcaldy
Dunfermline
Rosyth
Firth of Forth
Leith
Prestonpans
North Berwick
Bass Rock
Dunbar
St. Abbs Hd.
Eyemouth

NORTH SEA

ATLANTIC OCEAN

Oban
L. Etive
Ben Cruachan 1124
L. Awe
Inveraray
L. Fyne
B. Vorlich 943
Lochgilphead
Crinan
Jura
Sound of Jura
Rubh a' Mhail
Islay
Bowmore
Port Ellen
Gigha
KINTYRE
Tarbert
Kilberry
Helensburgh
Dunoon
Dumbarton
Clydebank
Port Glasgow
Greenock
Renfrew
Paisley
Johnstone
GLASGOW
Clyde
Cumbernauld
Kirkintilloch
Airdrie
Coatbridge
Rutherglen
E. Kilbride
Motherwell
Wishaw
Hamilton
Falkirk
Grangemouth
Bo'ness
Linlithgow
Livingston
Bathgate
LOTHIAN
EDINBURGH
Musselburgh
Dalkeith
Penicuik
Haddington
Duns
Lammermuir Hills
Coldstream
Kelso
Berwick-upon-Tweed
Holy I.
Flodden
Till
The Cheviot 816
CHEVIOT HILLS
Jedburgh
Hawick
Galashiels
Melrose
Moorfoot Hills
Peebles
Biggar
Lanark
Carstairs
Pentland Hills
Tweed
Ettrick
BORDERS
Broad Law 840
SOUTHERN UPLANDS
Leadhills
Moffat
N. Tyne
ENGLAND
HADRIAN'S WALL
Hexham
Alston

STRATHCLYDE
Bute
Rothesay
Largs
Ardrossan
Saltcoats
Goat Fell 874
Arran
Brodick
Troon
Prestwick
Ayr
Irvine
Kilmarnock
Cumnock
Sanquhar
Nith
Dalmellington
Doon
Girvan
Ailsa Craig
Campbeltown
Mull of Kintyre
North Channel
Fair Hd.
Ballycastle
Rathlin
Merrick 843
Ken
Newton Stewart
Galloway
Stranraer
Portpatrick
L. Ryan
Luce Bay
Whithorn
Wigtown
Wigtown Bay
Mull of Galloway
DUMFRIES AND GALLOWAY
Dumfries
Dalbeattie
Castle Douglas
Kirkcudbright
Gatehouse of Fleet
Creetown
Solway Firth
Annan
Gretna Green
Lockerbie
Langholm
Esk
Carlisle
Workington
Derwent
Skiddaw 931
Ullswater
Cross Fell 893
Penrith
Wear
S. Tyne
Cumbrian Mts.
Tees
Barnard Castle

SHETLAND IS.
On same scale
Unst
Fetlar
Yell
Yell Sound
SHETLAND
Mainland
Foula
Scalloway
Whalsay
Bressay
Lerwick
Sumburgh Hd.

NORTHERN IRELAND
Belfast
Belfast Lough
Bangor
Newtownards
Ballymena
Larne

ft m
3000 1000
1200 400
600 200
300 100
0 0
50 150
100 300
m ft

Projection: Conical with two standard parallels.

West from Greenwich

COPYRIGHT. GEORGE PHILIP & SON. LTD.

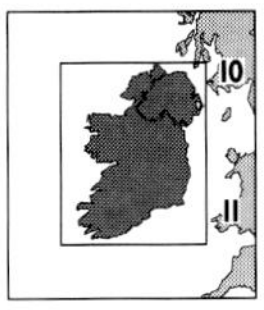

1 : 2 000 000

10 0 10 20 30 40 50 miles
10 0 10 20 30 40 50 60 70 80 km

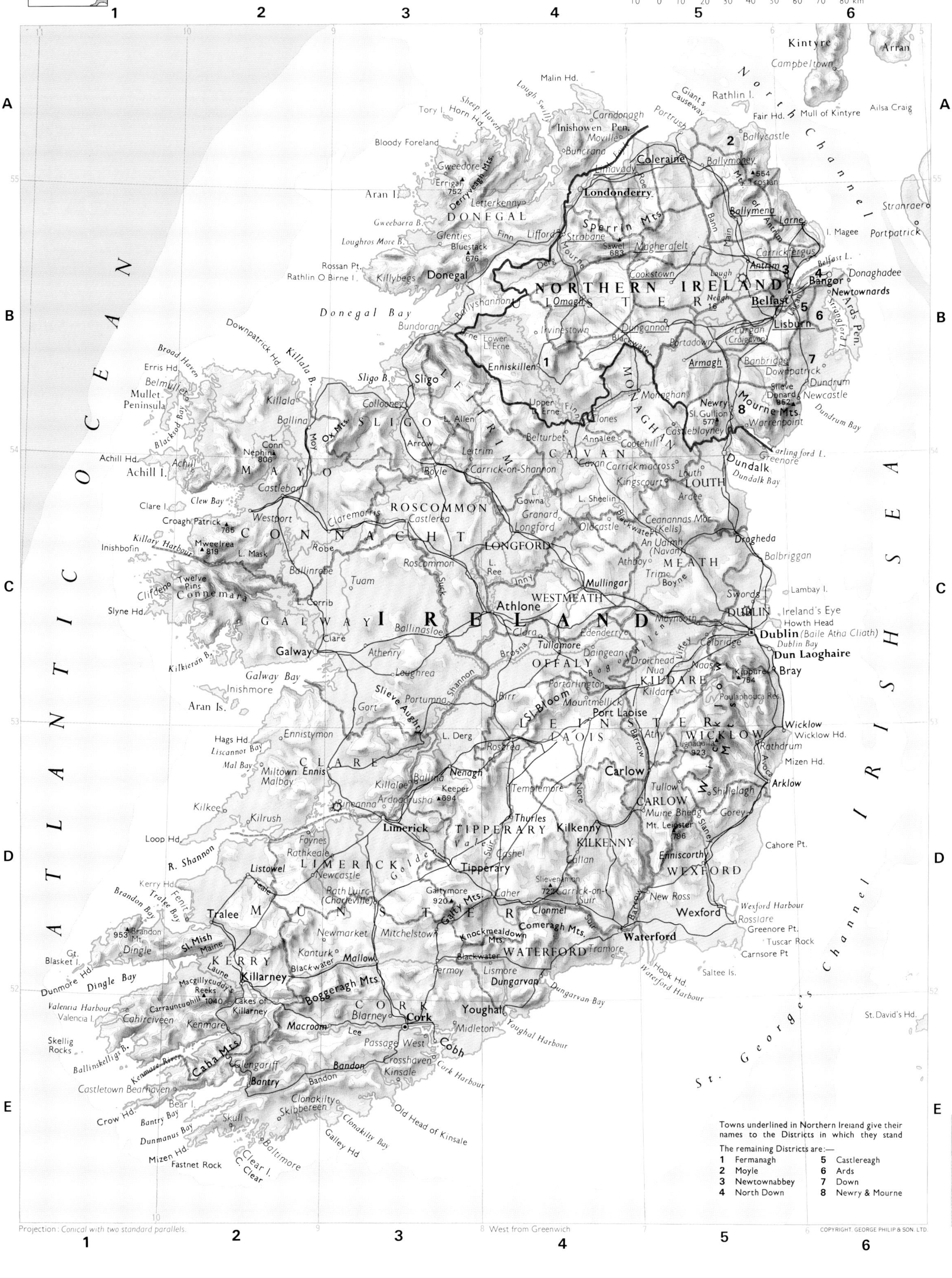

ATLANTIC OCEAN

NORTHERN IRELAND

ULSTER

DONEGAL
Londonderry
Coleraine
Ballymena
Larne
Belfast
Lisburn
Armagh
Newry
Dundalk

Sligo
LEITRIM
CAVAN
MONAGHAN
LOUTH
Drogheda

MAYO
Achill I.
Castlebar
Westport
ROSCOMMON
LONGFORD
MEATH
Dublin (Baile Átha Cliath)
Dun Laoghaire
Bray

CONNACHT
Galway
GALWAY
Connemara
Aran Is.

IRELAND
Athlone
WESTMEATH
OFFALY
KILDARE
LEINSTER
WICKLOW
Wicklow
Arklow

CLARE
Ennis
Limerick
TIPPERARY
LAOIS
Carlow
CARLOW
KILKENNY
Kilkenny
WEXFORD
Wexford
New Ross
Rosslare

KERRY
Tralee
Killarney
MUNSTER
LIMERICK
Tipperary
Clonmel
WATERFORD
Waterford
Dungarvan
Youghal

CORK
Cork
Blarney
Bantry
Skibbereen
Clonakilty
Kinsale

IRISH SEA

St. George's Channel

North Channel

Kintyre
Arran

Towns underlined in Northern Ireland give their names to the Districts in which they stand
The remaining Districts are:—
1 Fermanagh 5 Castlereagh
2 Moyle 6 Ards
3 Newtownabbey 7 Down
4 North Down 8 Newry & Mourne

Projection: Conical with two standard parallels.
West from Greenwich
COPYRIGHT GEORGE PHILIP & SON. LTD.

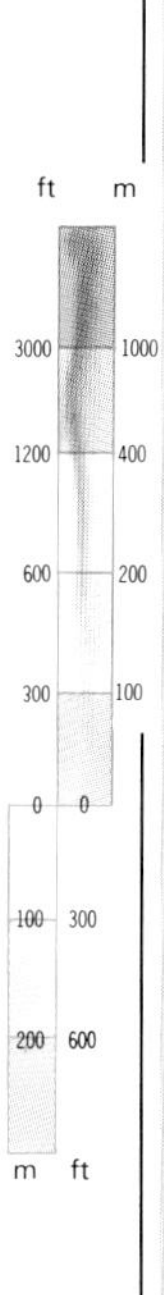

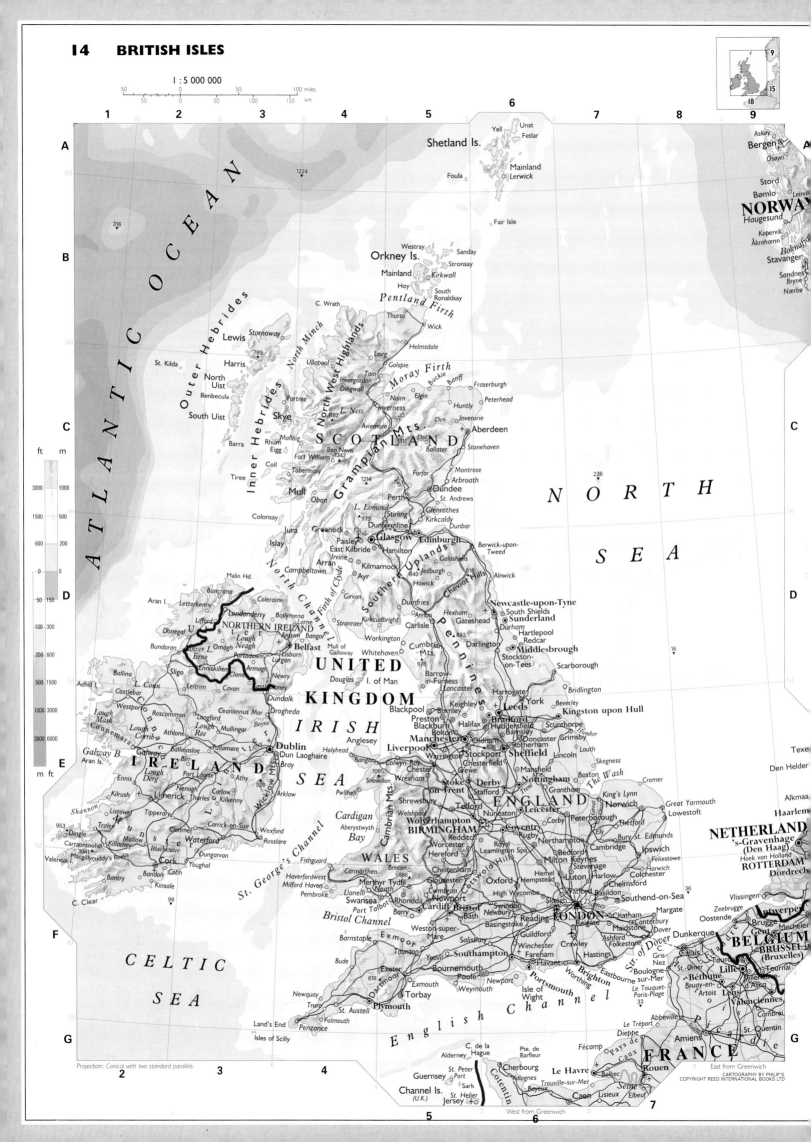

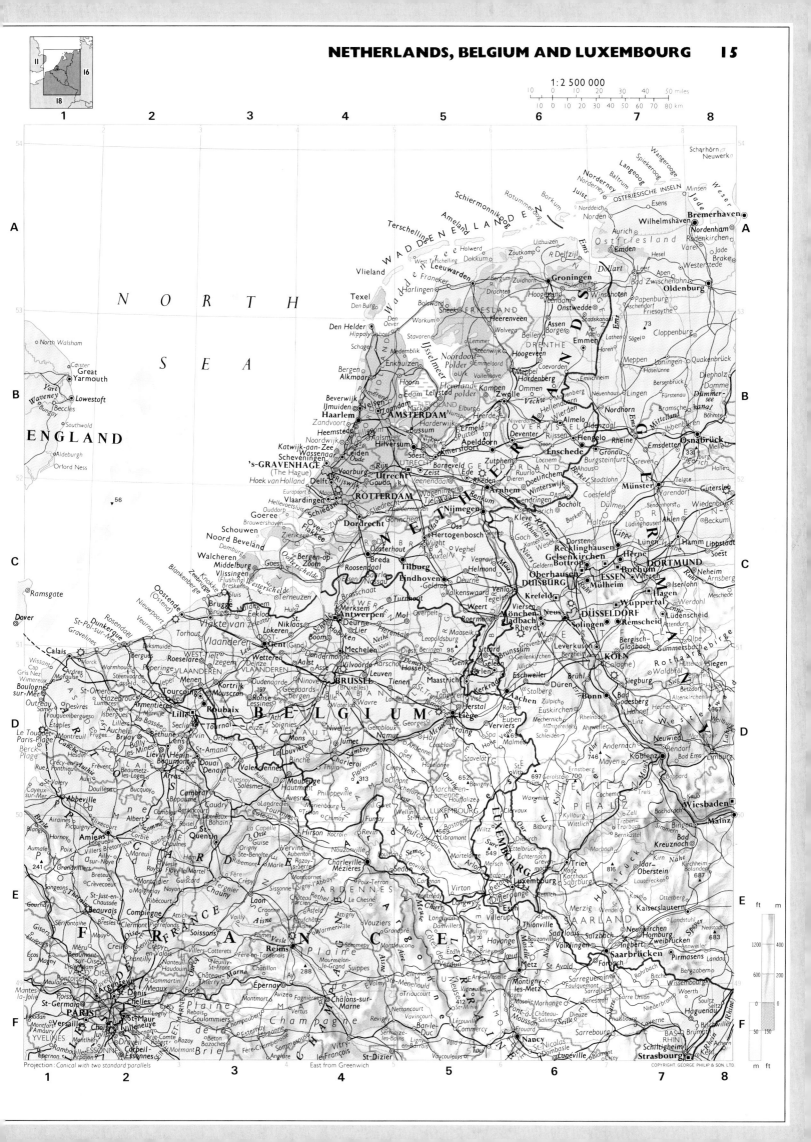

NORTH SEA

BALTIC SEA

DENMARK

UNITED KINGDOM

NETHERLANDS

BELGIUM

LUXEMBOURG

GERMANY

FRANCE

SWITZERLAND

LIECHTENSTEIN

AUSTRIA

CZECH

ITALY

SLOVENIA

ADRIATIC SEA

Sylt, Westerland, Föhr, Flensburg, Sønderborg, Åbenrå, Svendborg, Næstved, Møn, Nordfriesische Inseln, Schleswig, Nakskov, Falster, Nykøbing, Rügen, Sassnitz, Helgoland, Deutsche Bucht, Husum, Heide, Rendsburg, Kiel, Kieler Bucht, Lolland, Rødbyhavn, Gedser, Kołobrzeg, Darłowo, Ost-friesische Inseln, Norderney, Wangerooge, Cuxhaven, Neumünster, Lübeck, Travemünde, Wismar, Rostock, Stralsund, Greifswald, Wolin, Świnoujście, Koszalin

Norwich, Cromer, Great Yarmouth, Lowestoft, Ipswich, Felixstowe, Harwich, Margate, Dover, Dunkerque

Den Helder, Texel, Leeuwarden, Groningen, Emden, Oldenburg, Bremerhaven, Buxtehude, HAMBURG, Norderstedt, Schwerin, Neubrandenburg, Mecklenburg, Güstrow, Parchim, Neustrelitz, Szczecin, Stettiner Haff, Usedom, Police, Goleniów, Stargard, Szczeciński

Haarlem, AMSTERDAM, 's-Gravenhage (Den Haag), Leiden, Gouda, Hilversum, Utrecht, ROTTERDAM, Dordrecht, Arnhem, Nijmegen, Zwolle, Apeldoorn, Deventer, Enschede, Münster, Osnabrück, Minden, Hannover, Wolfsburg, Braunschweig, Magdeburg, BERLIN, Potsdam, Brandenburg, Frankfurt, Świebodzin, Zielona Góra, Gorzów Wielkopolski, Kostrzyn, Eberswalde-Finow, Oranienburg, Rathenow

Breda, Tilburg, 's-Hertogenbosch, Eindhoven, Venlo, Krefeld, Duisburg, Essen, Dortmund, Hagen, Bochum, Wuppertal, Hamm, Paderborn, Hildesheim, Salzgitter, Goslar, Halberstadt, Bernburg, Dessau, Wittenberg, Anhalt, Halle, Leipzig, Cottbus, Forst, Nowa Sól, Żagań, Głogów

Antwerpen, Gent, Brugge, Mechelen, BRUSSEL (Bruxelles), Leuven, Maastricht, Heerlen, Aachen, Mönchengladbach, Köln (Cologne), Düsseldorf, Solingen, Bonn, Koblenz, Siegen, Marburg, Kassel, Göttingen, Nordhausen, Sangerhausen, Merseburg, Zeitz, Gera, Chemnitz, Dresden, Görlitz, Zgorzelec, Legnica, Bautzen, Hoyerswerda, Meissen, Riesa

Lille, Roubaix, Tournai, Mons, Namur, Charleroi, Liège, Verviers, Dinant, Bastogne, Trier, Wiesbaden, Mainz, Frankfurt, Hanau, Offenbach, Darmstadt, Würzburg, Bamberg, Coburg, Suhl, Erfurt, Weimar, Jena, Zwickau, Plauen, Hof, Bayreuth, Weiden, Karlovy Vary, Kladno, PRAHA (Prague), Kolín, Hradec Králové, Pardubice, Liberec, Jablonec, Walbrzych, Jelenia Góra

Calais, Boulogne-sur-Mer, Saint-Omer, Béthune, Lens, Douai, Arras, Cambrai, Valenciennes, Maubeuge, Charleville-Mézières, Sedan, Luxembourg, Saarbrücken, Kaiserslautern, Neunkirchen, Pirmasens, Worms, Mannheim, Ludwigshafen, Heidelberg, Karlsruhe, Pforzheim, Heilbronn, Stuttgart, Esslingen, Göppingen, Aalen, Ansbach, Nürnberg, Fürth, Erlangen, Schwabach, Amberg, Regensburg, Straubing, Plzeň, Beroun, Příbram, Tábor, České Budějovice, Jihlava

Amiens, Beauvais, Compiègne, Laon, Soissons, Reims, Châlons-sur-Marne, Épernay, Meaux, PARIS, Créteil, Melun, Provins, Nancy, Metz, Verdun, Bar-le-Duc, Toul, Lunéville, Épinal, Saint-Dizier, Troyes, Strasbourg, Offenburg, Baden-Baden, Tübingen, Reutlingen, Ulm, Augsburg, Ingolstadt, Donauwörth, Landshut, Dachau, MÜNCHEN (Munich), Freising, Passau, Linz, Freistadt, Krems, Gmünd, Znojmo

Sens, Auxerre, Fontainebleau, Chaumont, Langres, Dijon, Besançon, Belfort, Mulhouse, Freiburg, Villingen-Schwenningen, Konstanz, Memmingen, Kempten, Rosenheim, Garmisch-Partenkirchen, Salzburg, Bad Ischl, Kufstein, Innsbruck, Wels, Steyr, Amstetten, Sankt Pölten, Wiener Neustadt

Nevers, Moulins, Autun, Chalon-sur-Saône, Montceau-les-Mines, Mâcon, Lons-le-Saunier, Bourg-en-Bresse, Neuchâtel, Biel, Solothurn, Aarau, Zürich, Winterthur, Sankt Gallen, Bregenz, Feldkirch, Vaduz, Landeck, Merano, Bolzano, Bressanone, Lienz, Villach, Klagenfurt, Wolfsberg, Graz, Maribor

Roanne, Thiers, Vichy, Lyonnais, LYON, Aix-les-Bains, Chambéry, Annecy, Genève, Lausanne, Montreux, Sion, Fribourg, Bern, Thun, Interlaken, Luzern, Zug, Schwyz, Chur, Davos, St. Moritz, Bellinzona, Locarno, Lugano, Como, Lecco, Sondrio, Trento, Rovereto, Belluno, Vittório Véneto, Udine, Gorizia, Ljubljana, Trieste, Koper, Novo Mesto, Celje, Zagreb

Saint-Étienne, Le Puy-en-Velay, Tournon, Grenoble, Voiron, Romans-sur-Isère, Valence, Chamonix, Mont Blanc, Aosta, Ivrea, Biella, Novara, Vercelli, Vigevano, Pavia, Milano, Monza, Bérgamo, Brescia, Verona, Vicenza, Pádova, Venézia (Venice), Treviso, Mantova, Cremona, Rovigo, Golfo di Venézia, Pula, Rovinj

Montélimar, Privas, Gap, Briançon, Cuneo, Fossano, Mondovì, Savona, Génova, Alba, Asti, Alessándria, Piacenza, Parma, Reggio nell'Emília, Módena, Ferrara, Bologna, Imola, Faenza, Ravenna, Comácchio

Nîmes, Avignon, Orange, Carpentras, Aix-en-Provence, Salon-de-Provence, Draguignan, Grasse, Cannes, Antibes, Nice, MONACO, Monte-Carlo, Menton, San Remo, Impéria, La Spézia, Massa, Carrara, Pistóia, Lucca, Prato, Firenze (Florence), SAN MARINO, Rímini, Cesena, Forlì, Pésaro, Fano, Pisa, Livorno, Scandicci

MARSEILLE, Toulon, La Seyne-sur-Mer, Hyères, Fréjus, St-Tropez

Projection: Conical with two standard parallels

ft m 12000 4000 9000 3000 6000 2000 3000 1000 1500 500 600 200 0 0 50 150 100 300 200 600 500 1500 1000 3000 2000 6000 m ft

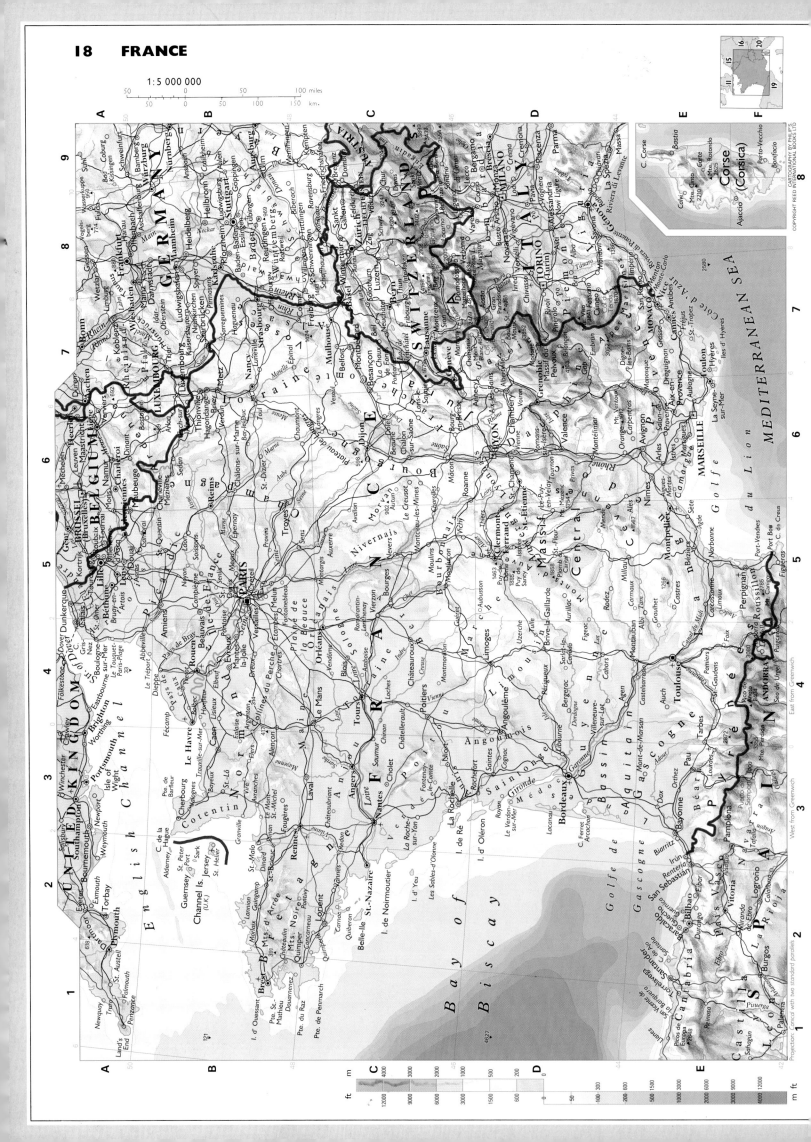

1 : 5 000 000

CARTOGRAPHY BY PHILIP'S
COPYRIGHT REED INTERNATIONAL BOOKS LTD

Corse (Corsica)

MEDITERRANEAN SEA

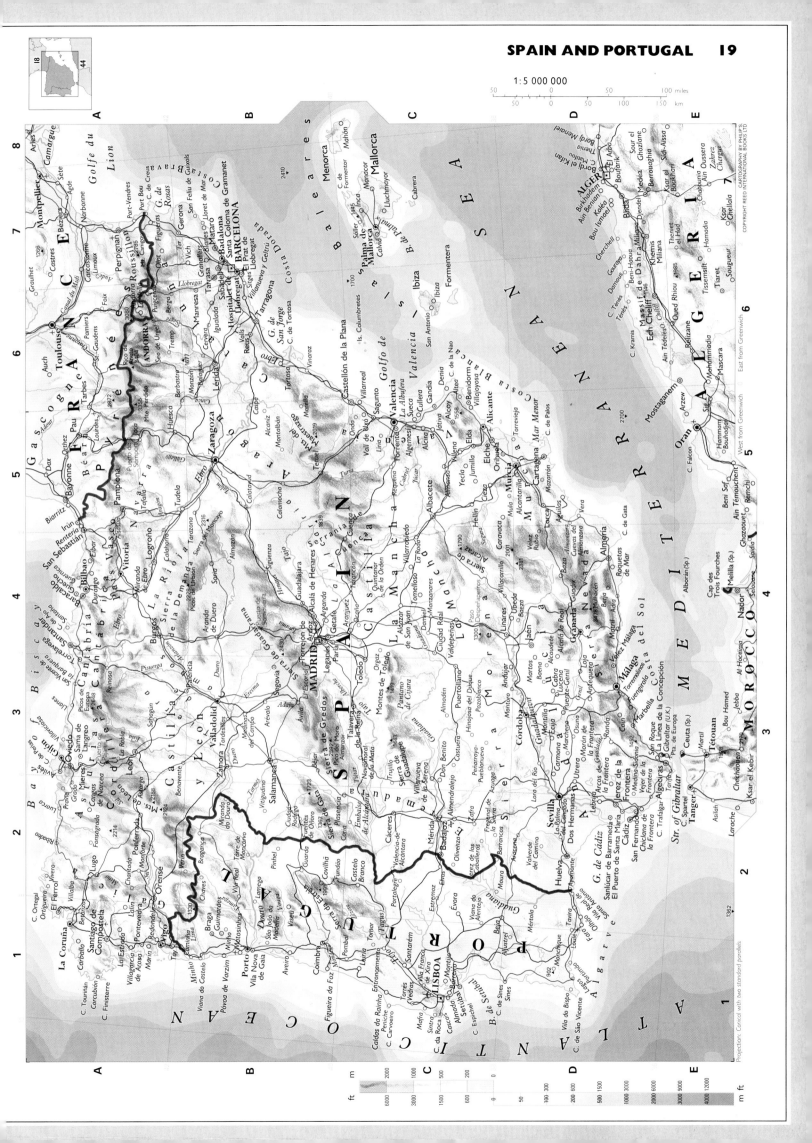

SWITZERLAND

AUSTRIA

FRANCE

SLOVENIA

CROATIA

MONACO

LYON
Chambéry
Aix-les-Bains
Grenoble
Valence
Montélimar
Avignon
Orange
Carpentras
Salon-de-Provence
Aix-en-Provence
MARSEILLE
Toulon
La Seyne-sur-Mer
Hyères
Cannes
Antibes
Nice
Menton
Monte-Carlo
San Remo
Imperia

TORINO (Turin)
Pinerolo
Cuneo
Savona
Génova
La Spezia
Carrara
Massa
Viaréggio
Pisa
Livorno

MILANO
Novara
Vercelli
Monza
Bérgamo
Brescia
Como
Lecco
Pavia
Piacenza
Cremona
Mantova
Verona
Vicenza
Pádova
Venézia (Venice)
Treviso
Trieste
Udine
Trento
Rovereto
Bolzano
Merano

Ljubljana
Maribor
Zagréb
Karlovac

Bologna
Parma
Módena
Réggio nell'Emilia
Ferrara
Ravenna
Forlì
Rímini
Cesena
Faenza
Imola

Firenze (Florence)
Prato
Pistoia
Lucca
Siena
Arezzo
Perúgia
Assisi
Foligno
Terni
Viterbo
Grosseto
Orvieto

SAN MARINO
Pésaro
Fano
Ancona
Urbino
Macerata
Fermo
Ascoli Piceno
Téramo
Pescara
Chieti
L'Áquila

Civitavécchia
VATICAN CITY
ROMA
Tívoli
Latina
Ánzio
Frosinone
Cassino
Formia
Terracina

NÁPOLI
Caserta
Avellino
Salerno
Torre del Greco
Castellammare di Stábia
Capri
Ischia
Pozzuoli

Campobasso
Isérnia
Foggia
Manfredónia
San Severo
Cerignola
Barletta
Andria
Trani
Bari
Molfetta
Monópoli
Altamura
Matera
Potenza

Táranto
Corigliano Cálabro
Rossano Cálabro
Cosenza
Catanzaro
Crotone
Vibo Valéntia
Nicastro

Messina
Réggio di Calábria

Palermo
Trápani
Marsala
Mazara del Vallo
Sciacca
Agrigento
Caltanissetta
Enna
Catánia
Siracusa
Augusta
Ragusa
Gela
Vittória
Módica
Avola
Lentini
Acireale
Giarre

SICILIA
Etna 3340

LIGURIAN SEA

TYRRHENIAN SEA

ADRIATIC SEA

MEDITERRANEAN

Corse
Ajaccio
Bastia
Calvi
Bonifacio
Porto-Vecchio

Sardegna
Sássari
Olbia
Alghero
Oristano
Nuoro
Cágliari
Iglésias
Carbonia
Sant' Antioco
Quartu Sant' Elena

Golfo di Génova
Golfo dell' Asinara
Golfo di Cágliari
Golfo di Oristano

ALGERIA
Annaba
Constantine
Skikda
Guelma
Souk-Ahras
El Milia
Collo

TUNISIA
Tunis
Bizerte
Tabarka
Béja
Jendouba
Kairouan
Sousse
Monastir
Mahdia
Nabeul
Hammamet
Golfe de Tunis
Golfe de Hammamet

MALTA
Valletta
Gozo
Rabat

Pantelleria (Italy)
Lampedusa
Ísole Pelagie (Italy)
Ísole Égadi
Ísole Eólie
Strómboli
Lípari
Ustica (Italy)

Projection: Conical with two standard parallels

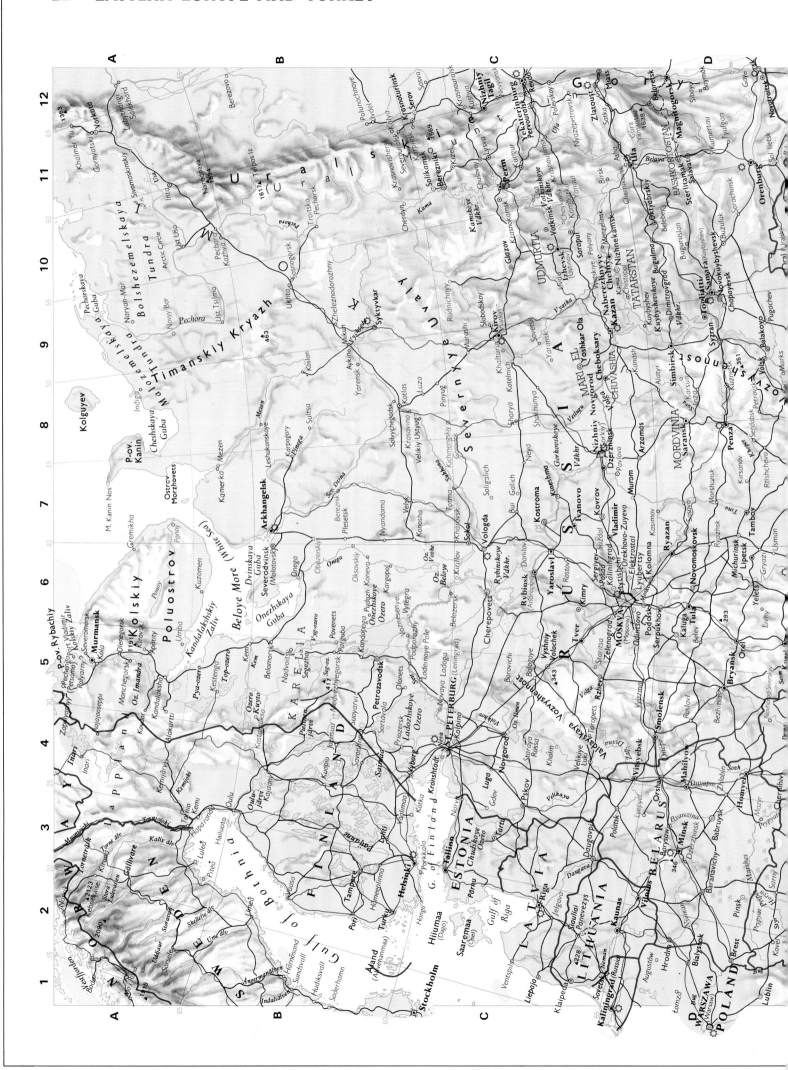

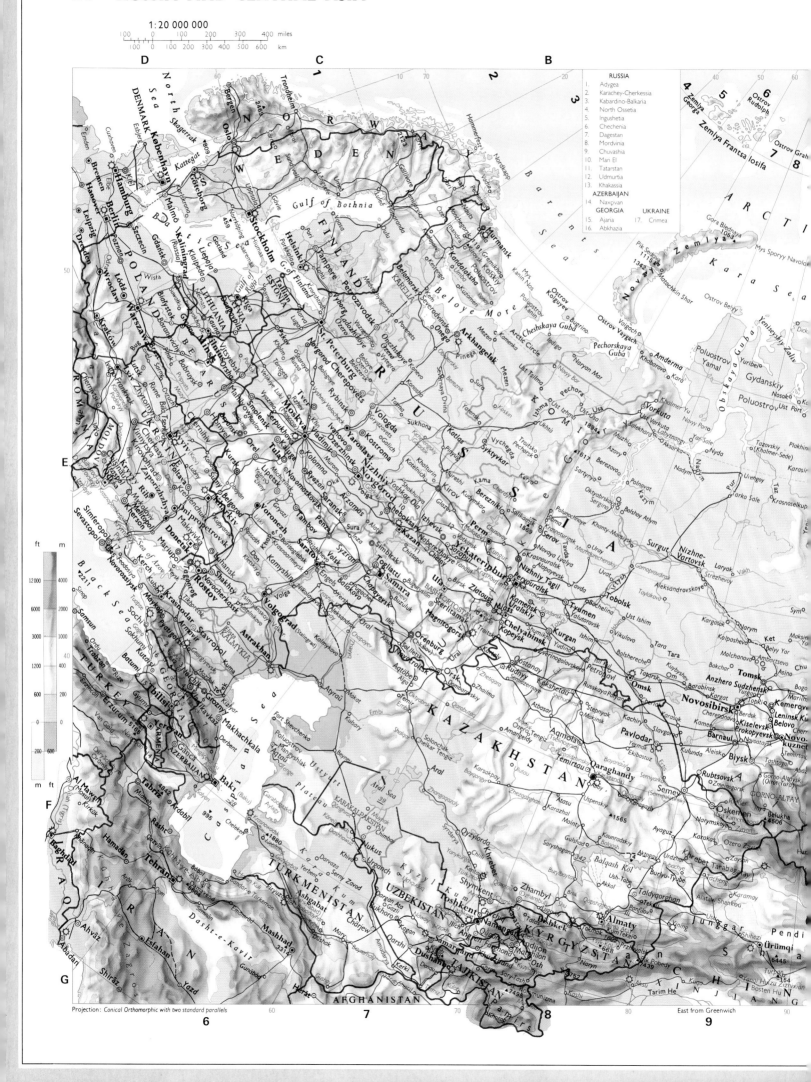

1:20 000 000

Projection: *Conical Orthomorphic with two standard parallels*

East from Greenwich

	RUSSIA
1.	Adygea
2.	Karachey-Cherkessia
3.	Kabardino-Balkaria
4.	North Ossetia
5.	Ingushetia
6.	Chechenia
7.	Dagestan
8.	Mordvinia
9.	Chuvashia
10.	Man El
11.	Tatarstan
12.	Udmurtia
13.	Khakassia

AZERBAIJAN
14. Naxçivan

GEORGIA   **UKRAINE**
15. Ajaria   17. Crimea
16. Abkhazia

C

Mys Dezhneva
(East C.)

19

St. Lawrence I.
(U.S.A.)

Chukchi
Sea

Ostrov Vrangelya

Ostrov
Henrietta
Ostrova Delong
Ostrov
Jeanette
Ostrov Zhokhova

East Siberian Sea

OCEAN

Ostrov
Bennett
Ostrova
Ostrov
Faddeyevskiy
Ostrov
Novaya Sibir

Laptev Novosibirskiye Ostrova

Ostrov
Medvezhi

Bering
Sea

Severnaya
Zemlya

Ostrov Shmidta

Mys Arkticheskiy

10 11

9   Ostrov
    Pioner   Ostrov
             Komsomolets

12

Ostrov Oktyabrskoy
Revolyutsii

965

Ostrov Bolshevik

13 14 3800
        15
    16
        17

18

D

Kolymskoye Nagorye

Koryakskoye Nagorye

2562

Srediny

Poluostrov
Kamchatka

Kanandorskiye Ostrova

Proliv Vilkitskogo

PoluoByrranga
GoryuOstrov 146

Taymyr Taymyr
         Nordvik

Ostrov Bolshoy
Begichev

Tiksi

Srednekolymsk

Khrebet Cherskogo

Okhotsk

3147

Gora Chen

Magadan

Petropavlovsk-
Kamchatskiy

3456

Norilsk
Gory
Putorana
1701

962 Arctic Circle

Y
A
K
U
T
S
K
A
Y
A

Verkhoyansk
2389

Sea of Okhotsk

50

RUSSIA

Yakutsk

Vilyuysk

Olekminsk

Sakhalin

Sakhalinskiy
Zaliv

1790

Okha

Nikolayevsk-
na-Am.

Kirensk

2999

Bratsk

Komsomolsk

Khrebet Sikhote Alin

Sovetskaya
Gavan

Yuzhno-Sakhalinsk

Kurilskiye Ostrova

E

Krasnoyarsk

Nizhneudinsk

Stanovoy Khrebet

Chita

Blagoveshchensk

Khabarovsk

Hokkaidō

Sapporo

Hakodate

Irkutsk

Ulan Ude

1620

Ondorhaan

Ulaanbaatar
(Ulan Bator)

2800

Hentiyn
Nuruu

Da Hinggan Ling

Dong bei

Qiqihar

Harbin

Jiamusi

Ussuriysk
Vladivostok
Nakhodka

Sea of
JAPAN

Honshū

40

MONGOLIA

Jilin

Changchun

Siping

Chongjin

Niigata

1949

Shenyang Fushun
Anshan

NORTH
KOREA

Wŏnsan

Kanazawa

To-yama

CHINA REPUBLIC

Baotou Hohhot
Zhangjiakou

Beijing

Dandong

Dalian

P'yŏngyang

Inch'on

Sŏul

SOUTH KOREA
Taejŏn

Taegu

Pusan

Boundaries of
Republics

10   11   12   13   14

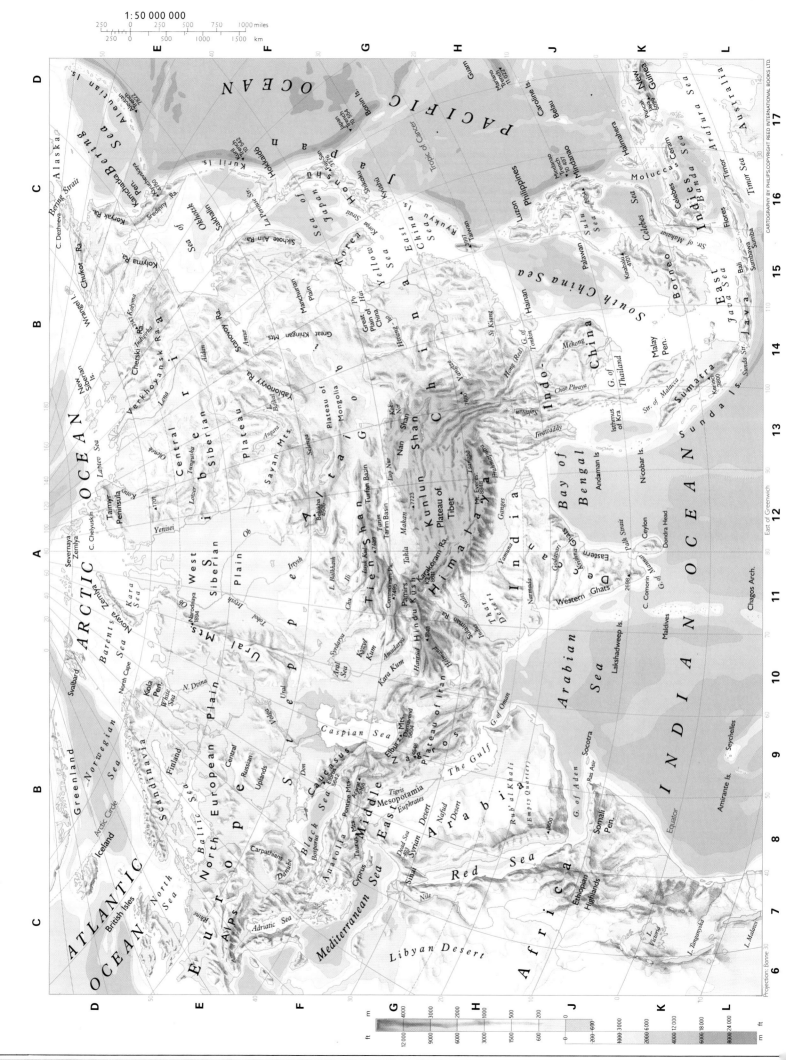

1:50 000 000

250   0   250   500   750   1000 miles
250   0   500   1000   1500 km

CARTOGRAPHY BY PHILIP'S COPYRIGHT REED INTERNATIONAL BOOKS LTD.

PACIFIC OCEAN

ARCTIC OCEAN

ATLANTIC OCEAN

INDIAN OCEAN

R U S S I A

C H I N A

MONGOLIA

KAZAKHSTAN

INDIA

I N D O N E S I A

AUSTRALIA

JAPAN
TOKYO
Honshu
Hokkaido
Sapporo
Kuril Is.
Sakhalin

NORTH KOREA
SOUTH KOREA
SEOUL
Pusan

BEIJING
SHENYANG
TIANJIN
SHANGHAI
HANGZHOU
GUANGZHOU
HONG KONG (U.K.)

TAIWAN
Taipei

PHILIPPINES
MANILA
Luzon
Mindanao

VIETNAM
Hanoi
Ho Chi Minh City
LAOS
Vientiane
CAMBODIA
Phnom Penh
THAILAND
BANGKOK
BURMA (MYANMAR)
Rangoon

MALAYSIA
Kuala Lumpur
SINGAPORE
Borneo
SARAWAK
SABAH
BRUNEI
Sumatra
JAKARTA
Java
Bandung
Surabaya

BENGAL
Bay of Bengal
CALCUTTA
BOMBAY
MADRAS
Bangalore
SRI LANKA
Colombo
MALDIVES
Male

NEPAL
Kathmandu
BHUTAN
Thimphu
BANGLADESH
DACCA
Chittagong

New Delhi
DELHI
PAKISTAN
KARACHI
Islamabad
Lahore

AFGHANISTAN
Kabul
Qandahar
Herat

IRAN
TEHRAN
Esfahan
Shiraz
Tabriz
Mashhad

TURKMENISTAN
Ashkhabad
UZBEKISTAN
Tashkent
TAJIKISTAN
Dushanbe
KIRGYZSTAN
Bishkek
Alma Ata

OMAN
Muscat
UNITED ARAB EMIRATES
Abu Dhabi
QATAR
Doha
BAHRAIN
Manamah
KUWAIT

SAUDI ARABIA
Riyadh
Mecca
Medina
Jedda

YEMEN
Sana
Aden

IRAQ
Baghdad
Basra
Mosul

SYRIA
Damascus
Aleppo
LEBANON
Beirut
ISRAEL
Jerusalem
JORDAN
Amman
CYPRUS
Nicosia

TURKEY
Ankara
ISTANBUL
Izmir
Adana
Konya
Bursa

GEORGIA
Tbilisi
ARMENIA
Yerevan
AZERBAIJAN
Baku

EGYPT
CAIRO
Alexandria
Suez
Aswan

SUDAN
Khartoum
Port Sudan

ETHIOPIA
Addis Ababa
ERITREA
DJIBOUTI
SOMALI REP.
Mogadishu

KENYA
Nairobi
Mombasa
UGANDA
TANZANIA
Dar es Salaam
ZAIRE
ZAMBIA
MALAWI

SEYCHELLES
Victoria

MOSCOW
ST. PETERSBURG
FINLAND
SWEDEN
NORWAY
ICELAND
GREENLAND
UNITED KINGDOM
LONDON
FRANCE
PARIS
GERMANY
Berlin
ITALY
Rome
Athens
Belgrade
Warsaw
Prague
UKRAINE
Odessa
Danube

Caspian Sea
Black Sea
Mediterranean Sea
Red Sea
Arabian Sea
The Gulf
G. of Aden
G. of Oman
Str. of Malacca
South China Sea
East China Sea
Yellow Sea
Sea of Japan
Sea of Okhotsk
Bering Sea
Barents Sea
Kara Sea
Laptev Sea
Java Sea
Banda Sea
Celebes Sea
Sulu Sea
Arafura Sea
Timor Sea
Andaman Is. (India)
Nicobar Is. (India)
Lakshadweep Is. (India)
Chagos Arch. (U.K.)
Socotra (Yemen)

Hanoi ● Capital Cities

East from Greenwich

Projection: Bonne

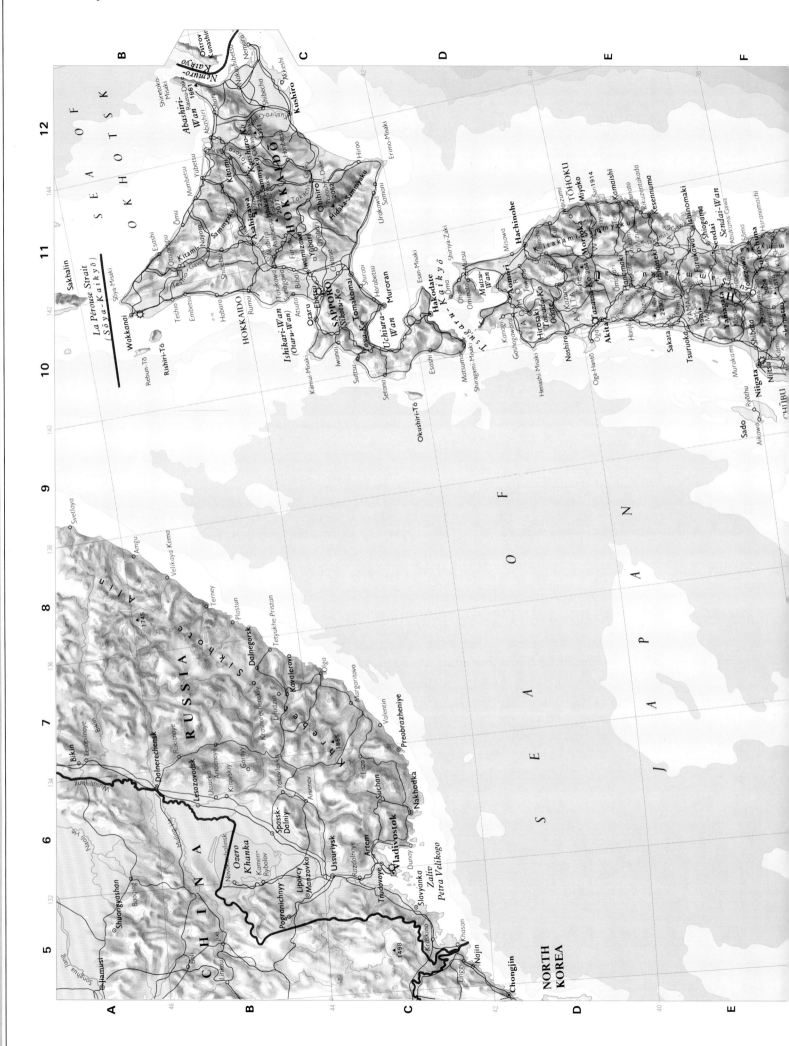

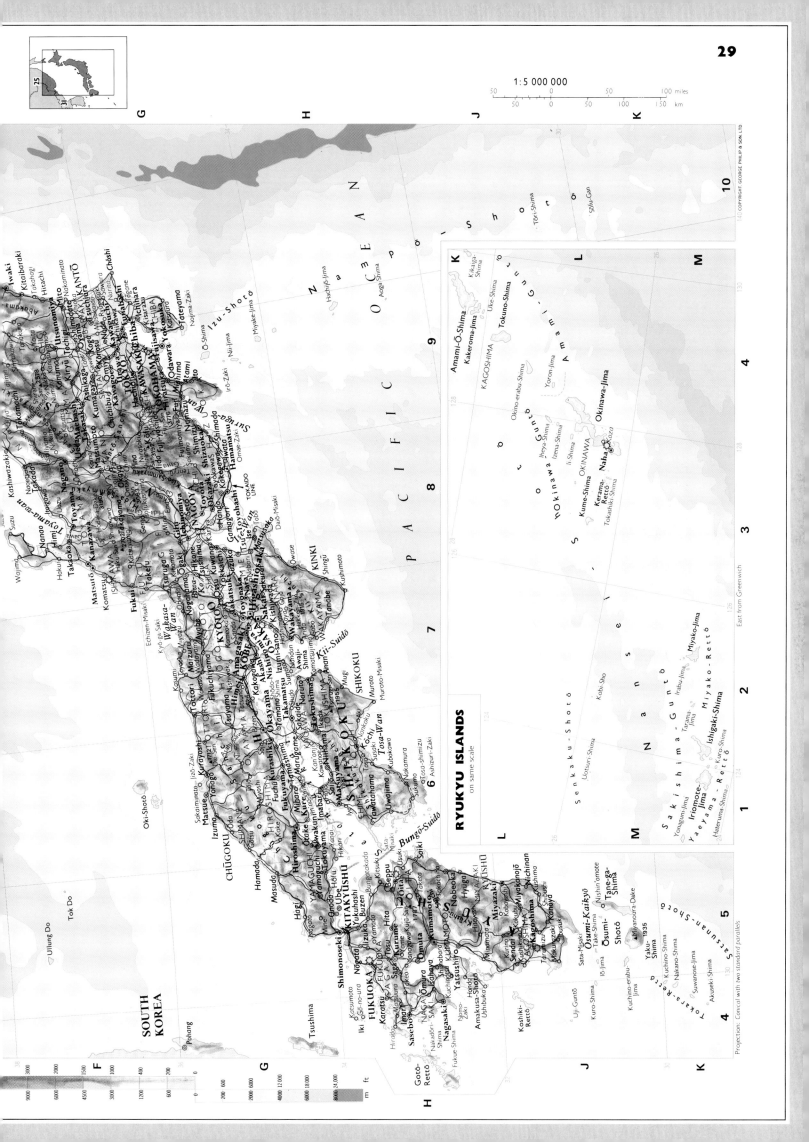

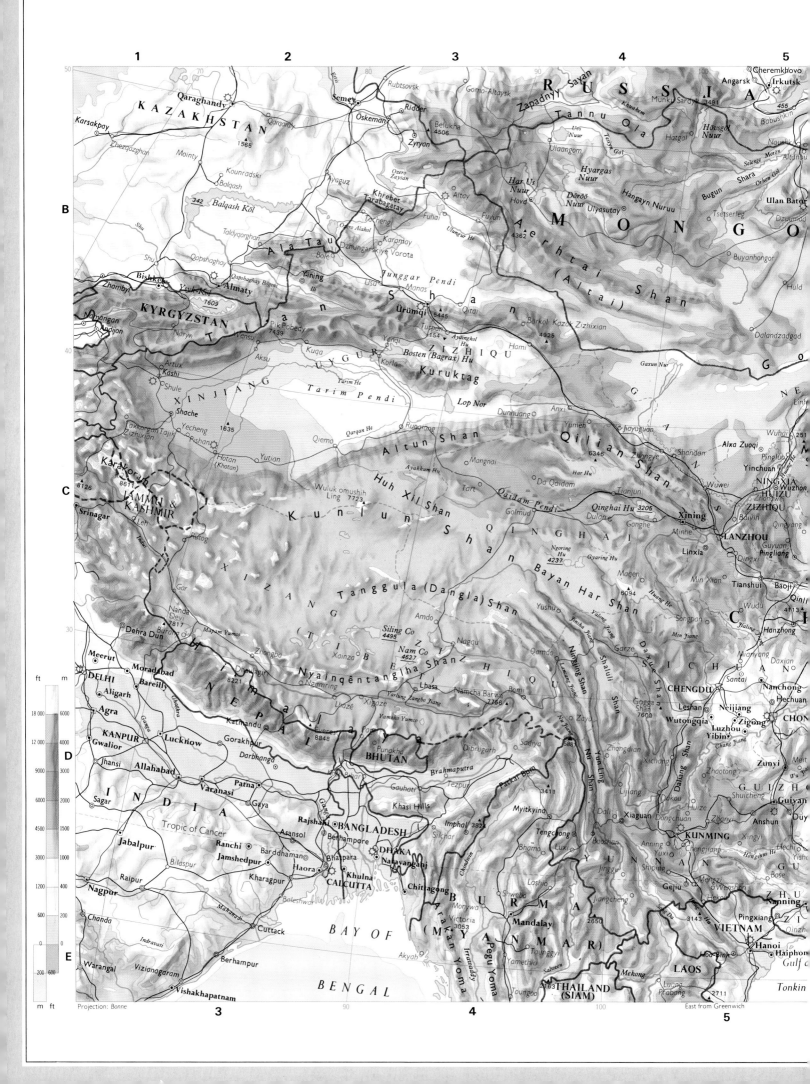

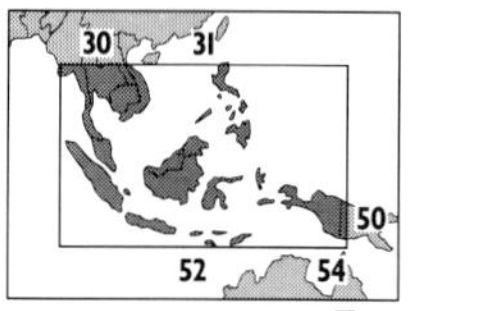

THAILAND

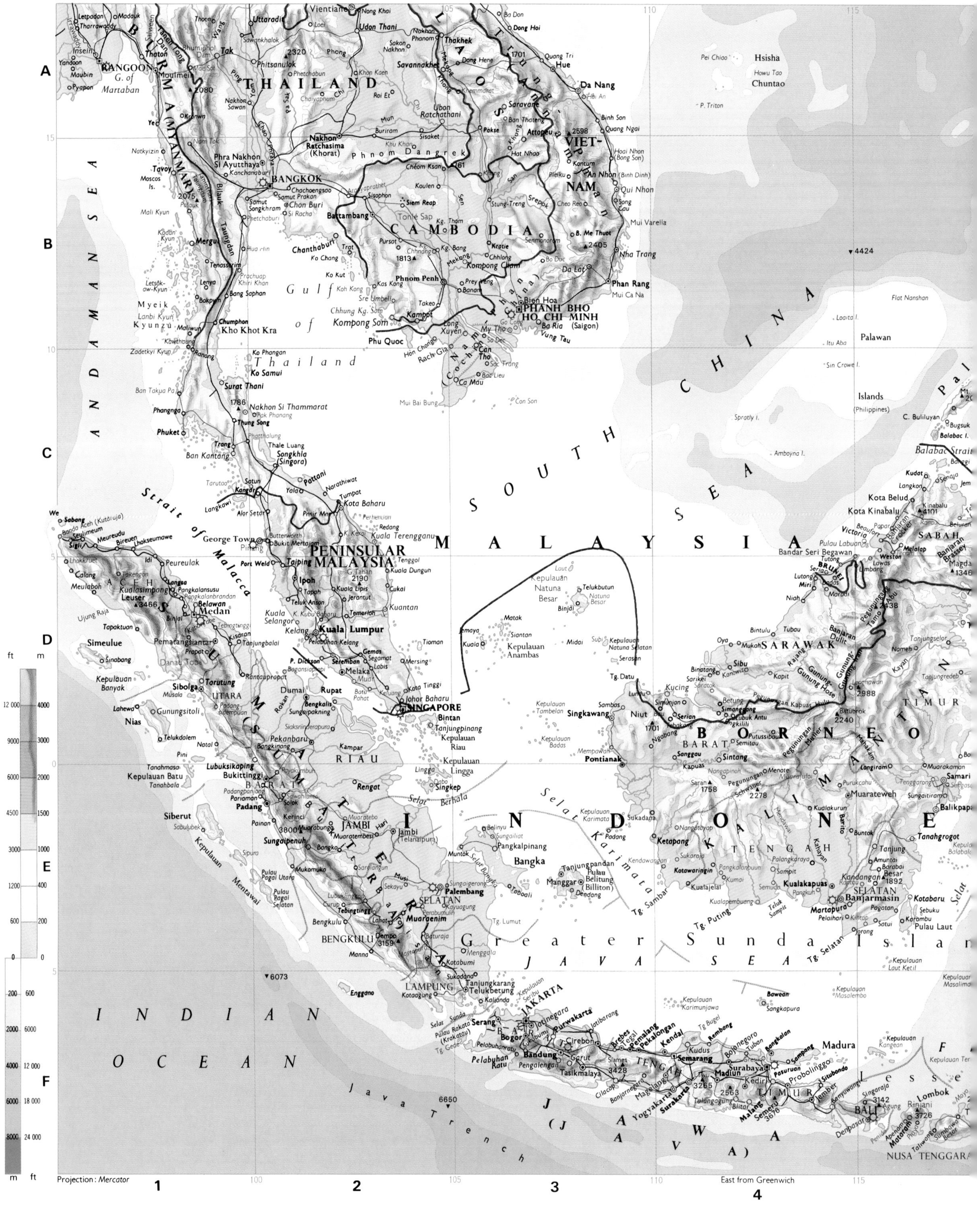

BURMA / MYANMAR

LAOS

VIET-NAM

CAMBODIA

BANGKOK

Phnom Penh

PHANH BHO HO CHI MINH (Saigon)

Gulf of Thailand

ANDAMAN SEA

SOUTH CHINA SEA

MALAYSIA

PENINSULAR MALAYSIA

Kuala Lumpur

SINGAPORE

Strait of Malacca

SUMATRA

RIAU

BARAT

SELATAN

UTARA

Medan

Padang

Palembang

Jambi

BENGKULU

LAMPUNG

JAKARTA

Bandung

Semarang

Surabaya

Madura

BALI

SARAWAK

SABAH

BRUNEI

Bandar Seri Begawan

Kota Kinabalu

BORNEO

KALIMANTAN

BARAT

TENGAH

SELATAN

TIMUR

Pontianak

Banjarmasin

Balikpapan

INDONESIA

GREATER SUNDA ISLANDS

JAVA SEA

Greater Sunda Islands

INDIAN OCEAN

Java Trench

J A V A (J A W A)

NUSA TENGGARA

Palawan

Islands (Philippines)

Projection: Mercator

East from Greenwich

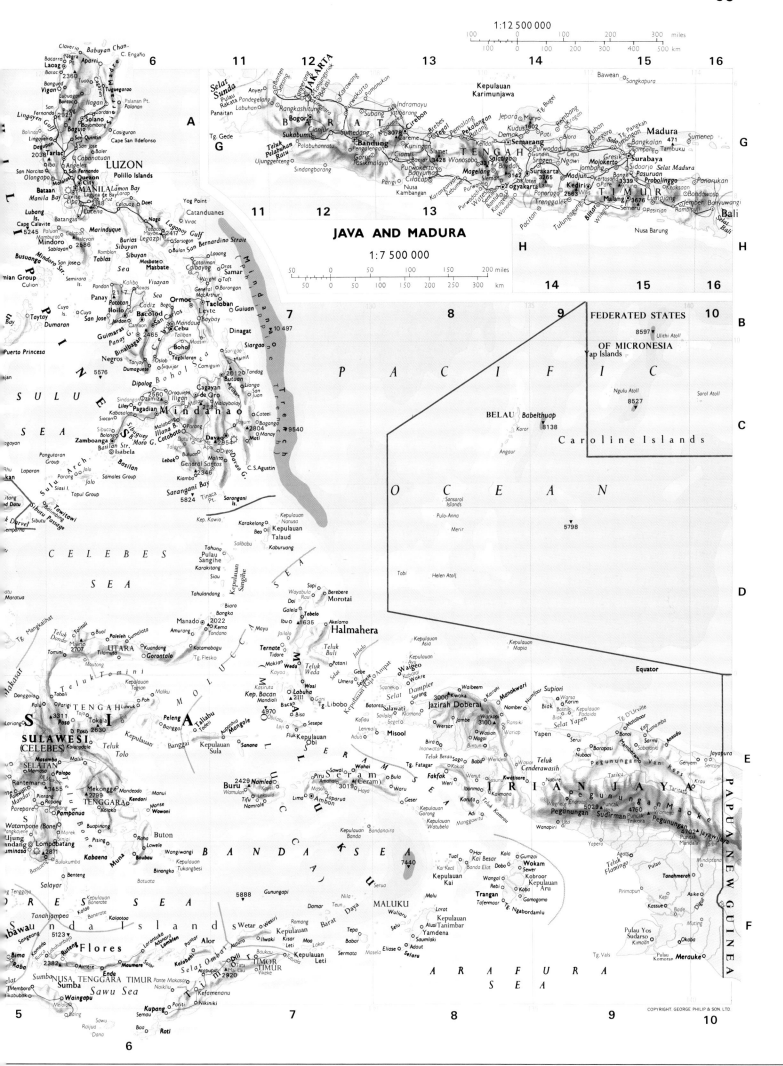

1:12 500 000

100   0   100   200   300   miles
100   0   100   200   300   400   500 km

6   11   12   JAKARTA   13   14   15   16

A

Selat Sunda
Pulau Rakata

Anyer
Bonten
Serang
Rangkashtung

B   B A R A T

Bogor
Sukabumi
Bandung

G   **Teluk Pelabuhan Ratu**

Panaitan
Tg. Gede
Ujunggenteng

Sindangbarang
Pameungpeuk   Nusa Kambangan

Kepulauan Karimunjawa

Indramayu   Brebes
Subang   **Cirebon**   Tegal   Pekalongan
Sumedang   Kendal   1602   Rembang
3078   Gareme   Demak   Kudus   Blora   Tuban
Ciamis   Slamet   **Semarang**   Pati
Tasikmalaya   3428   Wonosobo   Salatigo   Ngawi
Purwokerto   Banyumas   3142   Sragen
Cilacap   Kebumen   Magelang   Boyolali   **Surakarta**   Madjun
Parigi   Purworejo   Sleman   3265   Klaten   3339
Yogyakarta   Lawu   Blitar
Wonosari   Poporogo   2563   Trenggalek
Paciton   Tulungagung

Bawean   Sangkapura

Tg. Bugel

Tg. Pangkah

Madura
Bangkalan   471   Sumenep
Sampang   Tambuku

Gresik   **Surabaya**
Mojokerto   Sidoarjo   **Selat Madura**
Pasuruan   **Probolinggo**   Panarukan
Bangil   Kertosono   Bondowoso
Malang   3676   Lumajang   Jember   Banyuwangi
Semeru   Pasirian   Rambipuji

T I M U R

Bali
Selat Bali

Nusa Barung

G

H

JAVA AND MADURA

1:7 500 000

50   0   50   100   150   miles
50   0   50   100   150   200   250   300 km

11   12   13   14   15   16

7   8   9   **FEDERATED STATES**   10   B

8597   Ulithi Atoll

OF MICRONESIA
Yap Islands

Ngulu Atoll   Sorol Atoll
8527

BELAU   Babelthuap
Koror   8138   **Caroline Islands**

Angaur

Sonsorol Islands

Pulo-Anna

Merir   5798

Tobi   Helen Atoll

Claveria   Babuyan Chan.
Bacarra   Negra   Aparri   C. Engaño
Laoag   Batac   Tuao   Tuguegarao
Bangued   2360   Ilagan   Palanan Pt.
Vigan   Lubuagan   Palanan
Bontoc   Solano   Casiguran
Lingayen   2929   Cordon
Baguio   Bayombong   Baler
Bolinao   Bambang   San Jose
Lingayen   **San Quintin**   San Jose
Dagupan   Cabanatuan
Tarlac   Celauag   Daet
Angeles   Laguna de Bay
Batan   **Quezon**   Lamon Bay
Olongapo   **City**   Celaoag
Manila Bay   Cavite   Lucena
Lubang   Batangas   Naga   2417
Is.   5245   Calapan   Legazpi
Cape Calavite   Marinduque   Tabaco
Mindoro   Burias   Sibuyan   Sorsogon
Sablayan   2586   Romblon   Sibuyan   San Bernardino Strait
Busuanga   Tablas   Sea   Bulan
Semirara Is.   Catarman   Oras
Group   Culion   Masbate   Wright   Taft
Cuyo   Panay   **Masbate**   Calbayog   General MacArthur
Pandan   2117   **Iloilo**   Catbalogan   Borongan
Bacolod   Roxas   Samar
Cuyo Is.   Cadiz   Guiuan
San Jose   **Panay** G.   San Carlos   **Leyte**
Taytay   Jordan   Mandaue   Baybay
Dumaran   **Guimaras**   2465   **Cebu**   Dinagat
Binalbagan   Taliban   Siargao
Puerto Princesa   Negros   **Bohol**   Siquijor   10 497
Tanjoy   Tagbilaran   Camiguin   Surigao
Dipolog   Oroquieta   Iligan   2012   Tandag
5576   Dumaguete   2560   Cagayan   Lianga
Sindangan   Ozamiz   de Oro   2889   San
Zamboanga   Iligan   Malaybalay   Bislig   9540
Sibuco   Shuguey   Illana B.   **Davao**
Bolong   Moro G.   Cotabato   2804
Isabela   Talayan   Butu   2854
Basilan   Lebok   Malita   9540
Jolo   Buluan   Digos
Samales   General Santos   2346   C. S. Agustin
Group   Kiamba   **Davao**
Topul Group   Sarangani Bay   Davao G.
5824   Tinaca   Sarangani
Pt.   Is.

LUZON
Polillo Islands
Yog Point
Catanduanes
Virac

Mayon 2417

Mindoro Str.
Sibuyan
Sea
Visayan
Sea

Pototan

Bohol Sea
Dinagat

Mati

K A L I M A N T A N

Sandakan
Lahad Datu
Darvel

Pangutaran
Group
Basilan Str.
Siasi I.

S U L U   S E A

Sibutu Passage

Mangkalihat
Tg.

Maratua

P A C I F I C

O C E A N

C

D

Equator

Kep. Kawio
Karakelong   Kepulauan
Beo   Nanusa
Kepulauan   Salibabu
Talaud   Kaburuang

C E L E B E S

S E A

Tahuna
Pulau
Sanghe
Karakitang
Siau
Kepulauan
Sanghe
Tahulandang

Biaro
Bangka

Manado   2022   **Tobelo**
Kema   Wayabula   Rau   Sopi
Amurang   Tondano   Galela   Berebere
Paleleh   Kuandang   Doi   **Morotai**
Gorontalo   Kotamobagu   Ibu   1635
Tilamuta   Tg. Flesko   Jailolo   Akelamo
Mautong   **Ternate**   **Halmahera**
UTARA   Tidore   Teluk Buli
Toli-Toli   2707   Makian   Weda
Buol   Weda   Teluk Weda
Kwandang   Wosi   Patani
Paguat   Kasiruta   Gebe
Parigi   **Kep. Bacan**   Gani   Tg. Libobo
Poso   Mandioli   Bacan   4970
Poso   3311   Bacan   2111   Obilatu   Loji
Tokala   Banggai   Obira   Bisa
Kolonodale   Peleng   **Taliabu**   Sesepe
Tomini   Banggai   **Mangole**   Amophia   Sanana
Toboli   Kepulauan   Obilatu
TENGAH   Luwuk   Banggai   Kepulauan Obi
Donggala   Toboli   Kepulauan Togian   Kepulauan
Teluk Tomini   Maliku   Sula
Teluk Tolo   Kepulauan Sula

Tg. D'Urville
Sarmi
Kepulauan
Mapia

Kepulauan
Asia
Kepulauan
Mapia

Kepulauan   3000   Kwoka   Manokwari   Numfoor   Supiori
Waigeo   Kabare   Biak   Warsa
Wakre   Waibeem   Karoti   Number   Korim
Dampier   Saonek   Bosnik   Kepulauan
Sorong   **Jazirah Doberai**   Warkopi   Biak   Padaido
Salawati   Kofiau   3100   Ransiki   Bonoi
Sailolo   Segat   Wasian   Wariap   Serui   Barapasi
Misool   Adua   Mogoi   Yapen   Sarmi
Wersar   Lenmalu   Bintuni   **Yapen**   Mamberamo   Saberompi   Taritatu
Bira   Inanwatan   Berau   Wasior   Teluk   Genyem   Sentani
Kokas   Babo   Weriden   Cenderawasih   **Jayapura**
Fakfak   Wenut   Sagun   Nabire   Pegunungan Van Rees   Krau   Tariku
Teluk Berau   Goras   Kwatisore   Tariku
Kaimana   Ibonmaoi   Uta   **IRIAN JAYA**   Taritatu
Weri   Karufa   Wanapiri   Pegunungan Maoke
Kepulauan   Urak   5029   Puncak   4760   Pegunungan
Gorong   Manggawitu   Pegunungan Sudirman   4702   Puncak
Kepulauan   Watubela   Sudirman   Trikora   **Jayawijaya**
Banda   Bandanaira   Mandala   Sibil
Kepulauan   Tual   Kola   Gumzai   Agats   Mindiptanah
Banda   Kai Besar   Banda Elat   **Wokam**   Teluk   Tanahmerah
Kai Kecil   Dobo   Flamingo   Pulau   Kepi
7440   **Kepulauan**   Sewer   Kepulauan   Asike
Gunungapi   **Kai**   Wangal   **Aru**   Bade   Digul
5888   Nila   Kobroor   Pirimapun   Kassue   Muting
Serua   Molu   Kobo   Okaba
Damar   Teun   **Trangan**   Kola   Pulau Yos   **Merauke**
Tafermaar   Tg. Ngabordamlu   Sudarso   Komoran
Daya   **MALUKU**   Kimaan
Wuliaru   Lorat   Kepulauan   Pulau
Tepa   Selu   **Yamdena**   Komoran
Babar   Masela   Adaut   Tg. Vals

S U L A W E S I
(CELEBES)

Masamba
Palopo
Mamasa   3455
Rantemario
SELATAN
Pinrang   3455
Rapang   2799
Parepare   **Pampanua**
TENGGARA   Mekongga   Mondeodo   Kendari
Watampone   Buapinang   Monse
(Bone)   Manui   Wowoni
Sinjai   Marek   **Buton**
Ujung Pandang   Lompobatang   Pising
(Makasar)   2871   Raha   Lawele
Bulukumba   Kabaena   Baubau
Muna   Wangiwangi
Benteng   Bonerate   Binongko   Tukangbesi
Salayar   Batuata

Mandar
Teluk   Mandar
Pinrang

Namlea
2429   Amahai
Buru   Wamulan   Kayeli   Masohi   3019
Tifu   Leksula   Haya   Taparura
Namrole   Lima   **Ambon**
Wotai

BURU

Wahai   Tg. Fatagar   Manggawitu
Piru   Amahai   **Bula**   Kepulauan
Seram (Ceram)   Geser   Gorong
3019   Haya   Kepulauan
Watubela

M A L U K U

B A N D A   S E A

5888   Gunungapi   7440

N U S A   T E N G G A R A   T I M U R

Flores
5123   2382
Ende   Maumere
Bima   Aimere   Larantuka   Lomblen
Raba   Adonara   Pantar   Alor   **Alor**
Sumba   Waikabubak   Kalabahi   Pontar
Sumba   Ruteng   2920   Selat Ombai   Maubara
Waingapu   Kefamenanu   **Dili**   Baukau
Kupang   Naikliu   **TIMOR TIMUR**
Soe   Niki-niki   Viqueque
Semau   **Roti**   Baa   Masela

S U M B A

S A W U   S E A

B A N D A   S E A

A R A F U R A

S E A

S
U
L
A
W
E
S
I

M
I
N
D
A
N
A
O

M
i
n
d
a
n
a
o
   T
r
e
n
c
h

P
A
P
U
A
   N
E
W
   G
U
I
N
E
A

E

F

5   6   7   8   9   10

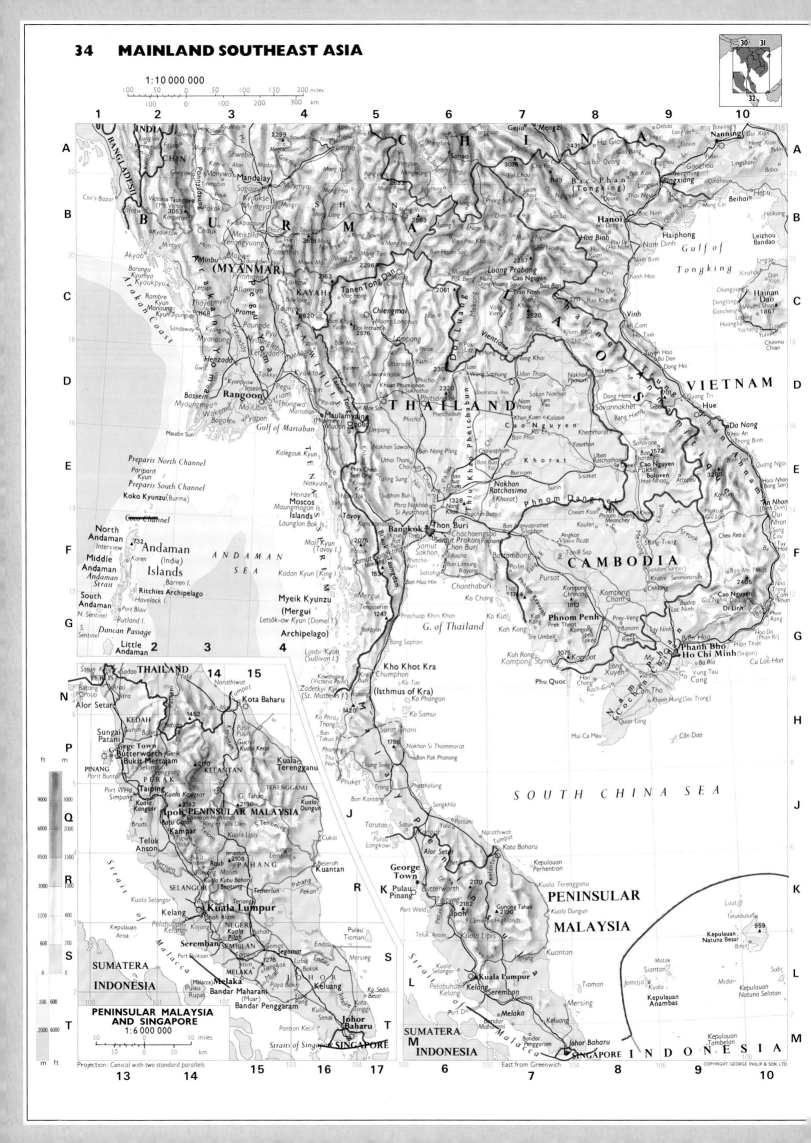

Equatorial Scale 1:50 000 000

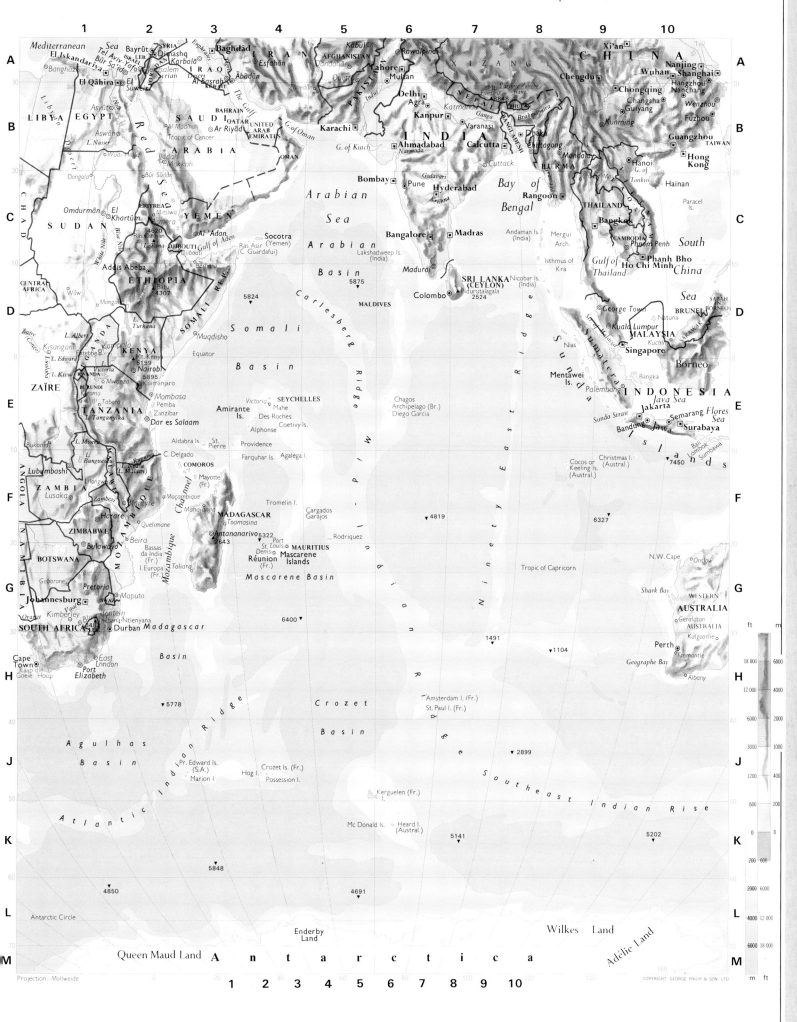

Projection: Mollweide

COPYRIGHT GEORGE PHILIP & SON LTD.

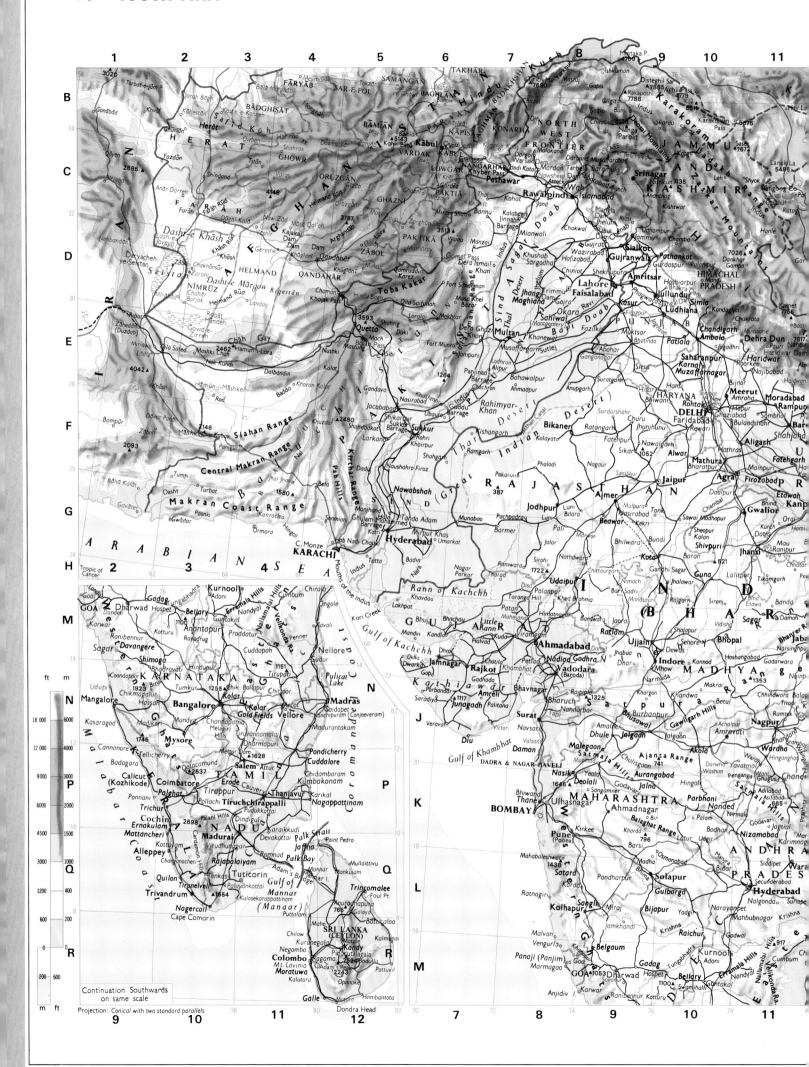

Continuation Southwards
on same scale

Projection: Conical with two standard parallels

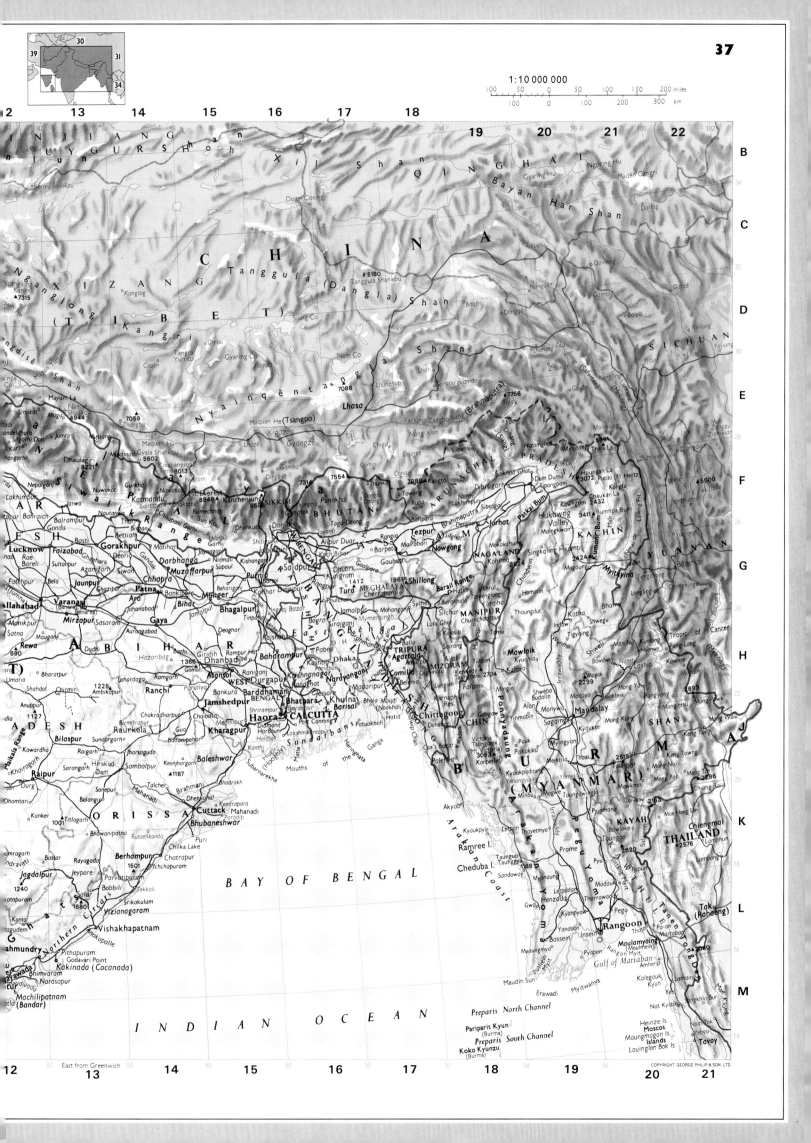

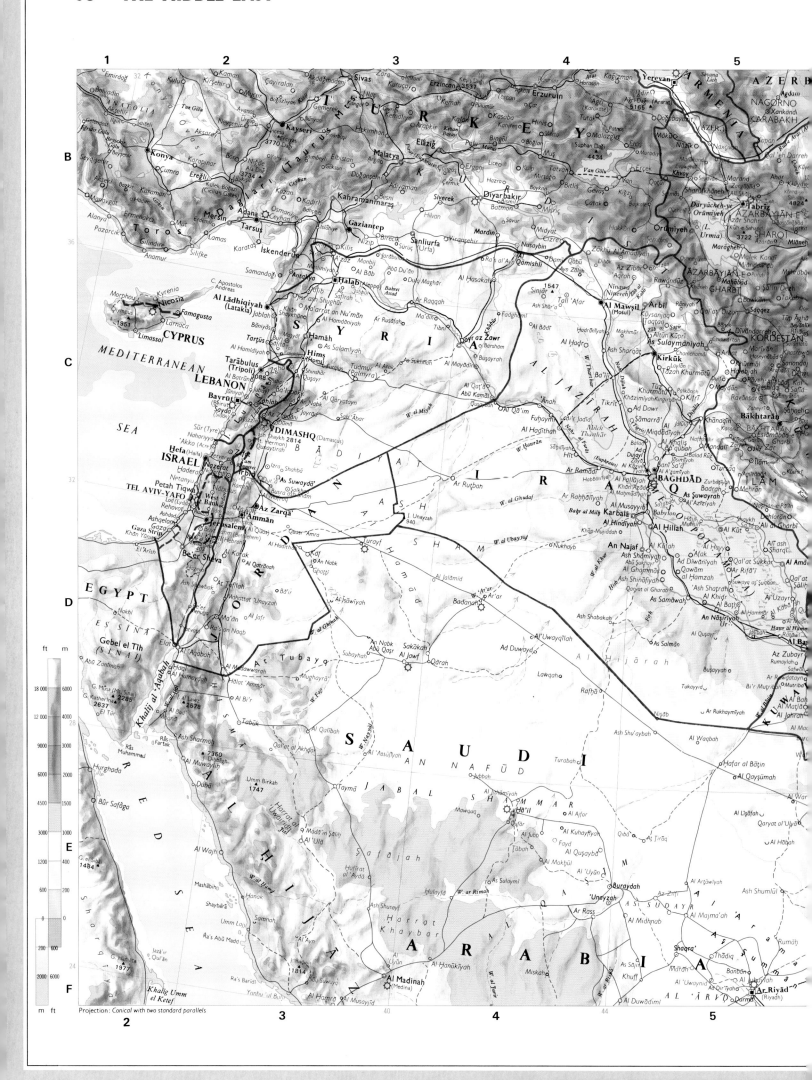

1:7 000 000

50 0 50 100 150 200 miles

50 0 50 100 150 200 250 300 km

6 7 8 9 10

TURKMENISTAN

KARA KUM

BAKÎ (Baku)

Qazimämmäd

Älät

Krasnowodsk

Khrebet Bolshoy Balkhan

Nebitdag

26 Bakinskikh Komissarov

Krasnovodskiy Zaliv

Poluostrov Cheleken

Ostrov Ogurchinskiy

Kizyl Atrek

Gyzylarbat

Chärjew

Amudarya

Mary

Bayramaly

Iolotan

Ashgabat

Dushak

Tejen

Serakhs

Tashkepri

Bälä Morghäb

Qal'eh-ye Vali

CASPIAN SEA

Astara

Ardabil

Kurinskaya Kosa

995

Neftsala

Talesh

Bandar-e Anzali

Rasht

Lāhījān

Rāmsar

Tonekābon

Now Shahr

Bābol Sar

Behshahr

Neka

Sārī

Gorgān

Bandar-e Torkeman

Gomīshān

Gonbad-e Kāvus

MAZANDARAN

Qazvin

Karaj

Tajrish

TEHRĀN

Rey

Eslāmshahr

Damāvand

Semnān

SEMNĀN

Dāmghān

Shāhrūd

Bastām

Emāmrūd

Māmey

Torbat-e Heydarīyeh

Torbat-e Jām

HERĀT

Herāt

BĀDGHISAT

Qal'eh-ye Now

Safīd Kūh

Mashhad (Meshed)

Kūh-e Binālūd 3314

Neyshābūr

Sabzevār

Quchān

Bojnūrd

Shīrvān

Bajgīrān

Kūh-e Sorkh 3020

KHORĀSĀN

Kavīr-e Namak

Bejestān

Gonābād

Ferdows

Birjand

Qāyen

Tabas

AFGHANISTAN

FARĀH

Farāh

Zābol

Dasht-e Margow

NĪMRŪZ

Zaranj

Qom

Daryācheh-ye Namak

Kāshān

Naṭanz

Ardestān

DASHT-E KAVĪR

Chāh Kavīr

Jandaq

Khvor

Tabas

HAMADĀN

Arāk

MARKAZĪ

Khomeyn

Borūjerd

Khorramābād

Golpāyegān

Khomeyni Shahr

ESFAHĀN

Eṣfahān

Nā'īn

Ardakān

YAZD

Yazd

Taft

Mehrīz

Dezfūl

Shūshtar

CHAHĀR MAHĀLL VA BAKHTĪARĪ

Shahr Kord

4548

Ahvāz

KHŪZESTĀN

Rāmhormoz

Behbahān

KOHKĪLŪYEH VA BŪYER AHMADĪ

Kūh-e Dīnār 4431

FĀRS

Shīrāz

Marvdasht

Neyrīz

Fasā

Dārāb

Estahbānāt

Kerman 3314

KERMĀN

Kermān

Bam

Sīrjān

Bāft

Rafsanjān

Zarand

Shahdād

Namakzār-e Shahdād

Zābol

SĪSTĀN VA BALŪCHESTĀN

Zāhedān (Duzdāb)

PAKISTAN

Mīrjāveh

Khāsh

Īrānshahr

Bampūr

Sarbāz

Khārk

Būshehr (Bushire)

BŪSHEHR

Borāzjān

Kāzerūn

Fīrūzābād

Jahrom

Lār

Bandar-e 'Abbās

HORMOZGĀN

Mīnāb

Qeshm

Bandar-e Lengeh

Qeys

Jāsk

Kūhhā-ye Bashākerd

Nīkshahr

Chāh Bahār

Gwātar

Str. of Hormuz

Ra's Musandam

Khasab

OMAN

Ra's al Khaymah

Dībā

Al Fujayrah

Umm al Qaywayn

Ajmān

Ash Shāriqah (Sharjah)

Dubayy (Dubai)

Abū Zaby (Abu Dhabi)

UNITED ARAB EMIRATES

OMAN

GULF of OMAN

THE GULF

Kuwayt (Kuwait)

Mīnā al Ahmadī

Al Khafjī

Ra's al Mish'āb

As Saffānīyah

Al Jubayl

Ad Dammām

Az Zahrān (Dhahran)

BAHRAIN

Al Manāmah

Al Muharraq

Al Hufūf

Al Mubarraz

QATAR

Ad Dawhah (Doha)

Dukhān

Umm Sa'īd

AD DAFRAH

East from Greenwich

COPYRIGHT GEORGE PHILIP & SON LTD.

6 7 8 9

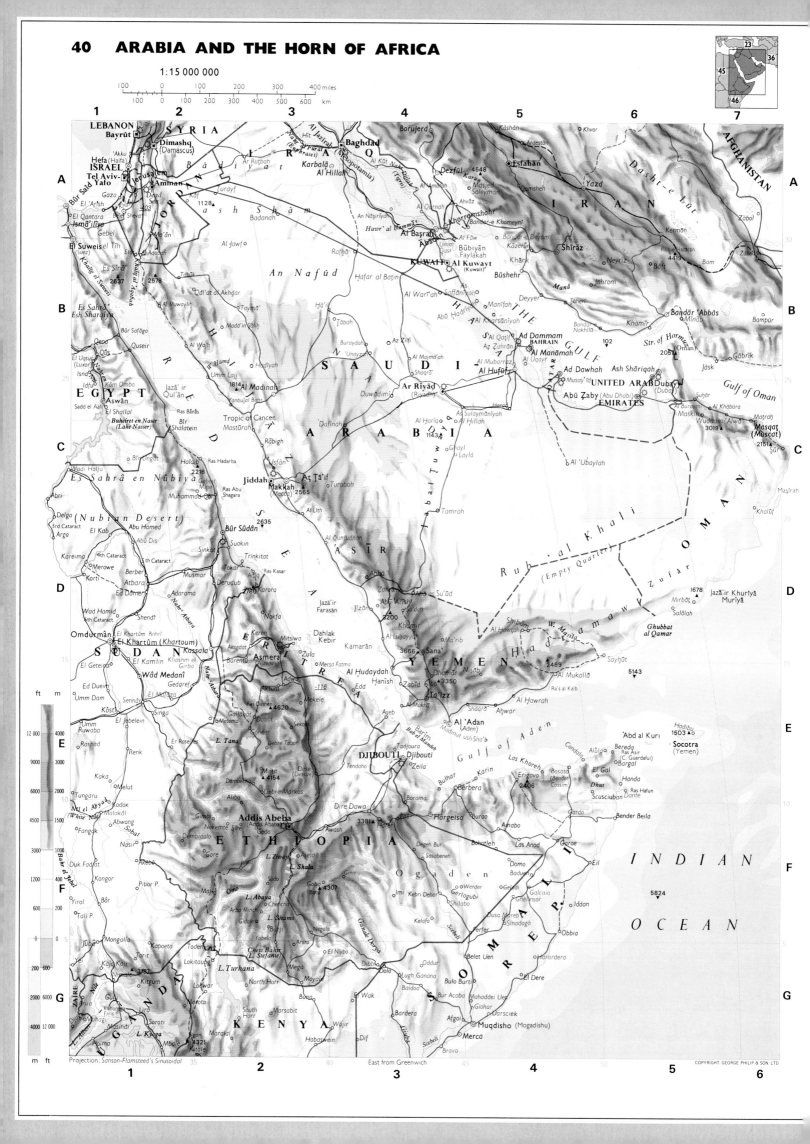

1:15 000 000

Projection: Sanson-Flamsteed's Sinusoidal

East from Greenwich

1 : 2 500 000

10 0 10 20 30 40 50 miles
10 0 10 20 30 40 50 60 70 80 km

CYPRUS

Paphos
Episkopi
Episkopi Bay
Akrotiri Bay
Limassol
C. Gata

M E D I T E R R A N E A N

S E A

SYRIA

Ḥimṣ (Homs)
Al Ḥamīdīyah
Tall Kalakh
Shinshār
Furqlus
1075
ASH SHAMĀL
Al Mīnā'
Tarābulus (Tripoli)
Al Ḥirmil
Al Quṣayr
Al Qaryatayn
 Az Zgharta
Qurnat as Sawdā' 3088
Al Baṭrūn
Dūmā
Al Labwah 2464
Al Buray
Bi'r Ghadīr
Jubayl
Qarṭabā
An Nabk
Ibrāhīm
2616
Ba'labakk
An Nabk
Sānnin 2828
Yabrūd
Jūniyah
Biqya'ya
Sharqī
BAYRŪT (Beirut)
Zahlah
'Jaz Zubaydīyah 1406
Ash Shuwayfāt
Ḥawsh Ḥassa 2420
LEBANON
Khirbat Qanāfār
Al Barūk 1942
Az Zabdānī
Al Quṭayfah
Khān Abū Shāmat
Saydā (Sidon)
Jazzīn
Qaṭanā
Darayyā
Al Kiswah
DIMASHQ (Damascus)
Dūmā
Al A'waj
Al Ḥijānah
An Nabaṭīyah at Taḥtā
Jabal ash Shaykh (Mt. Hermon) 2814
Būrāq
Ad Ṣafā
Sūr (Tyre)
AL JANŪB
Qiryat Shemona
Al Qunayṭirah 1197
Ḥadbat Golan (Golan Heights)
As Sanamayn
Naharīyya
Me'ona
Rafīd
Burda
DAR'Ā
HAZOR
Zefat
'Akko (Acre)
Sakhnīn
Miqdal
Izra'
Shahba
Mifraz Hefa
Qiryat Yam
Yam
Soham al Jawlan
As Suwayda 1800
Ṣafah
Hefa (Haifa)
Qiryat Ata Teverya (Tiberias)
Nazerat (Nozeret)
Kinneret
Dar'ā
Busrá ash Sham
AS SUWAYDĀ'
Tirat Karme
Dāliyat el Karmel
Afula
Yarmūk
Jaba
HEFA
HAZAFON
Salkhad
TEL MEGIDDO
Bet She'an
AD DURŪZ
CAESAREA
Shōmrōn
Janīn
Irbid
Al Ramthā
Umm al Qiṭṭayn
Hadera
Umm el Fahm
SAMARIA
Al Mafraq
IRBID
ISRAEL
Netanya
Ṭūlkarm
Nāblus
Allūn 1247
'Ajlūn
Jarash
HAMERKAZ
Herzliyya
Azzūn
Zarqā'
Benē Beraq
SHILO
Tel Aviv-Yafo
Peraḥ Tiqwa
Tall 'Aṣūr 1016
AL BALQĀ'
Az Zarqā'
Ramat Gan
West
As Salt
Bat Yam
Rishon le Ziyyon
Lod
Ramla
Bank
Wādī as S
AMMĀN
N. Soreq
Rehovot
Rām Allāh
289
Al Arīḥā (Jericho)
Naʿūr
At Tunayb
Ashdod
Yavne
Jerusalem (Yerushalayim) (Al Quds)
Maʿdaba
Qiryat Mal'akhi
Bet Shemesh
Bayt Laḥm (Bethlehem)
AL ʿĀṢIMAH
Ashqelon
Qiryat Gat
TEL LAKHISH
Al Khalīl (Hebron)
Wādī al Ḥaydān
Dhibān
Gaza
Gaza
N. Shiqma
Az Zāhiriya
W. al Mūjib
Strip
Sederot
Arad
1065
Khān Yūnis
Rafah
Al Qaṭrānah
Be'er Sheva
Al Karak
W. al Ghadaf
Bûr Sa'id (Port Said)
Bor Mashash
981
Bûr Fu'ad
El Daheir
403
Khalīg el Tîna
Rās Burūn
Sabkhet el Bardawîl
Dimona
Al Mazār 1305
Bir Sa'id
Romāni
El 'Arîsh
W. el Lahfān
682
W. al Ḥasā
JORDAN
Bir el 'Abd
Bir el Garārât
Bir Kaseiba
-333
HADAROM
AL KARAK
Bir Qaṭia
W. al 'Arīsh
Qezi'ot
At Ṭafīlah
W. al Bātir
El Qanṭara
Bir el Duweidar
Bir el Jafir
Birein
Bā'ir
Wāḥid
Bir Madkūr
-121
Ha 'Arava
Ismâ'ilîya
Ṭalaṭa
Muweilih
El Quseima
1072
J. ash Shawmari
Mizpe Ramon
Khamsa
El Buheirat el Murrat el Kubra (Gt. Bitter L.)
G. Yi 'Allaq 1094
Bir el Mālḥi
Bir Beida
Ha Negev (Negev Desert)
Bi'r ad Dabbāghāt
Rujm Tal'at al Jamā'ah 1736
W. Abu Ṣafāt
Gineifa
EL SUWEIS
Bir el Thamāda
W. el Brūk
W. Qiratya
El Agrūd
N. Paran
N. Ḥiyyon
PETRA
Qa' el Jafr
E GY P T
875
W. el Saheira
Wādi el 'Arîsh
W. Mahashim
Al Jafr
Ma'ān
El Suweis (Suez)
Bir Taufiq
Bir Gebel Hisn
'En Avrona
Bi'r al Mārī
MAʿĀN
Uyūn Mūsa
'Ain Sudr
W. Varga
Nakhl
W. el 'Aqaba
N. Hiyyon
El Kuntilla
Yotvata
Bir al Butayyihāt
Ras an Naqb
Mahaṭṭat ash Shidīyah
SAUDI
Bir Bad
W. el Tamarīng
Bir Abu Muhammad
Ra's an Naqb 1435
Khalīg el Suweis
G. el Kabrît 948
ET Thamad
W. Raqq
W. Giraf
Bir al Qaṭṭa
Ghubbet el Bûs
S î n â i   P e n i n s u l a
Bir el Biarât
1592
Aṭ Ṭubayq
Ras Matarma
W. Abu Ga'da
Gebel el Tîh
Al 'Aqabah
952
A R A B I A
1272
W. Abu el Gairi
Bir el Hesi
Elat
Bir Taba
Khalīj al 'Aqaba
1165
Ḥaql
W. an Nuwaybi'

ft   m
9000 3000
6000 2000
4500 1500
3000 1000
1200   400
600   200
0   0
200   600
2000 6000
m   ft

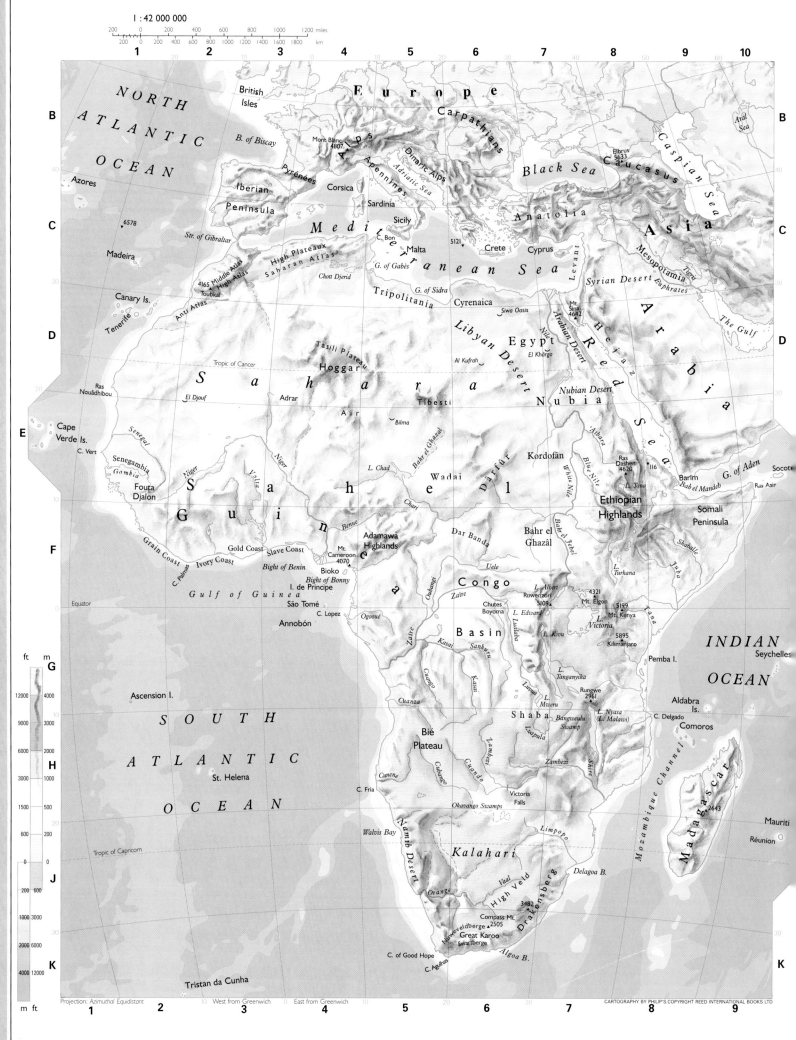

1 : 42 000 000

Projection: Azimuthal Equidistant

West from Greenwich   East from Greenwich

CARTOGRAPHY BY PHILIP'S. COPYRIGHT REED INTERNATIONAL BOOKS LTD

1 : 42 000 000

200 0 200 400 600 800 1000 1200 miles
200 0 200 400 600 800 1000 1200 1400 1600 1800 km

NORTH

ATLANTIC

OCEAN

Azores
(Port.)

Madeira
(Port.)

Canary Is.
(Sp.)

PE VERDE IS.

Praia

St-Louis
C. Vert
Dakar
GAMBIA
GUINEA-
BISSAU
Conakry
Freetown
SIERRA
LEONE
Monrovia
LIBERIA

UNITED
KINGDOM
LONDON

NETH.
BELG.
PARIS
FRANCE

B. of Biscay

PORTUGAL
Lisbon
SPAIN
Madrid

Rabat
Casablanca
Fès
Tétouan
MOROCCO
Marrakech

Algiers
Annaba
Constantine
TUNISIA
Tunis
Sfax

Corsica
Rome
Sardinia
ITALY

Sicily
MALTA
Tripoli
Misrātah

Chott Djerid

GERMANY
Prague
CZECH REP.
Vienna
SWITZ. AUSTRIA
CROATIA
BOS.
HERZ.

POLAND
Warsaw
SLOVAK REP.
HUNGARY
YUG.
ALB.
MAC.

Kiev

UKRAINE

ROMANIA
Odessa
BULGARIA

GREECE
Athens
Crete

RUSSIA

Volgograd

KAZAKHSTAN

Aral
Sea

GEORGIA
ARM. AZER.
Baku

Caspian Sea

TURKMEN.

Ankara
TURKEY

CYPRUS

Aleppo
SYRIA
LEB.
Damascus
Tel Aviv-
Jaffa
ISRAEL
Jerusalem
JORDAN

Mosul
Tigris
Baghdād

Euphrates

IRAQ

Basra

KUWAIT

TEHRĀN
Eşfahān

IRAN

The Gulf
BAHRAIN
QATAR

Black Sea

Mediterranean Sea

ALGERIA
In Salah

Sahara

LIBYA
Marzūq
Al Jawf

Tropic of Cancer

EGYPT
El Faiyûm
Asyût
Aswân
Wādi Halfa

Alexandria
Port Said
CAIRO
Suez

Benghazi

Red Sea

SAUDI
ARABIA
Medina
Mecca
Jedda

Riyadh

WESTERN SAHARA
El Aaiún
Dakhla
Fdérik

Ras
Nouâdhibou

MAURITANIA
Nouakchott

Tombouctou

MALI
Bamako

SENEGAL
Senegal
Banjul
Bissau
GUINEA

NIGER
Agadès
Niamey

BURKINA
FASO
Ouagadougou
Bobo-
Dioulasso

Kano

NIGERIA
Abuja

CHAD
Abéché
Ndjamena
L. Chad

SUDAN
El Fâsher
El Obeid

Omdurmân
Khartoum
Atbara

Wād Medani

Port Sudan

ERITREA
Asmera
Mesewa

YEMEN
Socotra
(Yemen)

G. of Aden

Ras Asir

IVORY
COAST
Bouaké
Yamoussoukro
Abidjan

GHANA
Kumasi
Accra
Sekondi-
Takoradi

TOGO
BENIN
Lomé
Porto
Novo
Lagos
Ibadan
Enugu

Benue

Chari

CENTRAL
AFRICAN REP.
Bangui

Bight of Benin
Port
Harcourt
Douala
CAMEROON
Yaoundé
Malabo
EQUATORIAL
GUINEA
SÃO TOMÉ & PRINCIPE

Wau
Bahr el Jebel
Malakâl

L. Tana
Addis Ababa
ETHIOPIA
Harer
Berbera

DJIBOUTI
Djibouti

SOMALI REP.
Mogadishu

L. Turkana

White Nile
Blue Nile

Gulf of Guinea
C. Lopez
Annobón

Libreville
GABON

CONGO
Brazzaville
Pointe Noire
CABINDA
(Angola)
Matadi

Zaïre
Mbandaka
Kisangani

ZAÏRE
Kananga
Kasai
Kwango

L. Albert
L. Edward
RWANDA
Kigali
BURUNDI
Bujumbura
L. Kivu

UGANDA
Kampala
L. Victoria

KENYA
Kisumu
Nairobi
Mombasa

Kismayu
Juba
Tana

INDIAN

OCEAN

SEYCHELLES

Equator

Kinshasa

Ascension I.
(U.K.)

SOUTH

ATLANTIC

OCEAN

St. Helena
(U.K.)

Luanda
Lobito
Namibe

ANGOLA
Huambo

Cunene

Cubango

TANZANIA
Dodoma
Zanzibar
Dar es Salaam
L. Tanganyika
L. Mweru
Likasi
Lubumbashi
Ndola
Kitwe

ZAMBIA
Lusaka
Livingstone

L. Malawi
L. Malawi
MALAWI
Lilongwe
Blantyre

C. Delgado

COMOROS
Mayotte
(Fr.)

Aldabra
Is.

Antsiranana

Moçambique
Mahajanga

Toamasina

C. Fria

NAMIBIA
Windhoek

BOTSWANA
Gaborone

Limpopo

ZIMBABWE
Harare
Bulawayo
Beira

MOZAMBIQUE
Zambezi

Mozambique Channel

MADAGASCAR
Antananarivo
Fianarantsoa

MAURITIUS
Réunion
(Fr.)

Tropic of Capricorn

Orange
Vaal

Johannesburg
Kimberley
Pretoria
Mbabane
SWAZ.
Maputo

LESOTHO
Maseru
Durban

SOUTH AFRICA

Cape Town
C. of Good Hope
C. Agulhas
Port
Elizabeth
East
London

West from Greenwich   East from Greenwich

Tristan da Cunha
(U.K.)

Projection: Azimuthal Equidistant

Dakar   Capital Cities

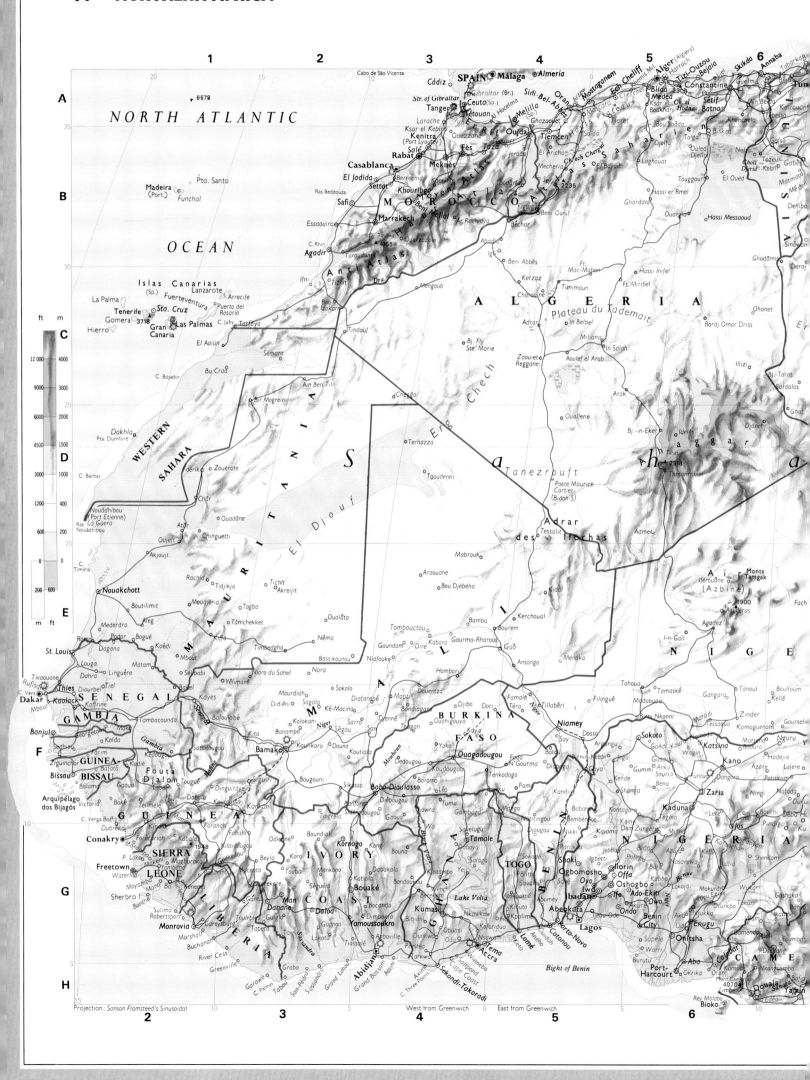

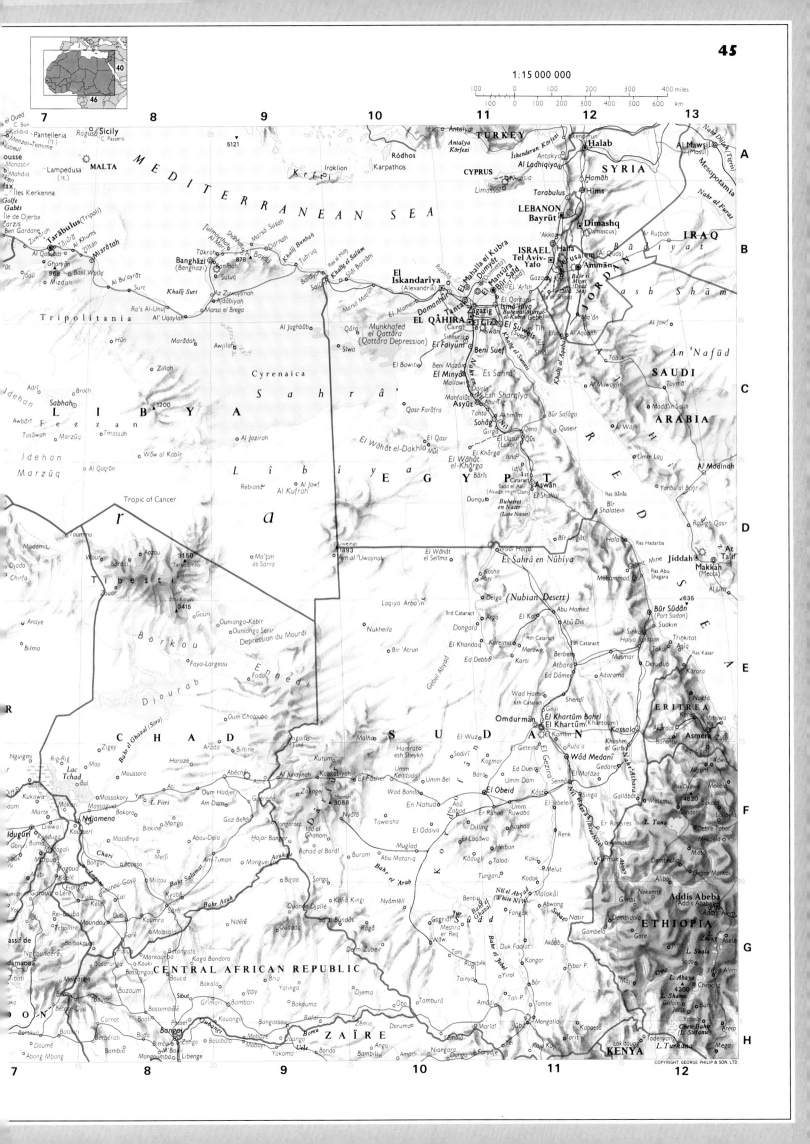

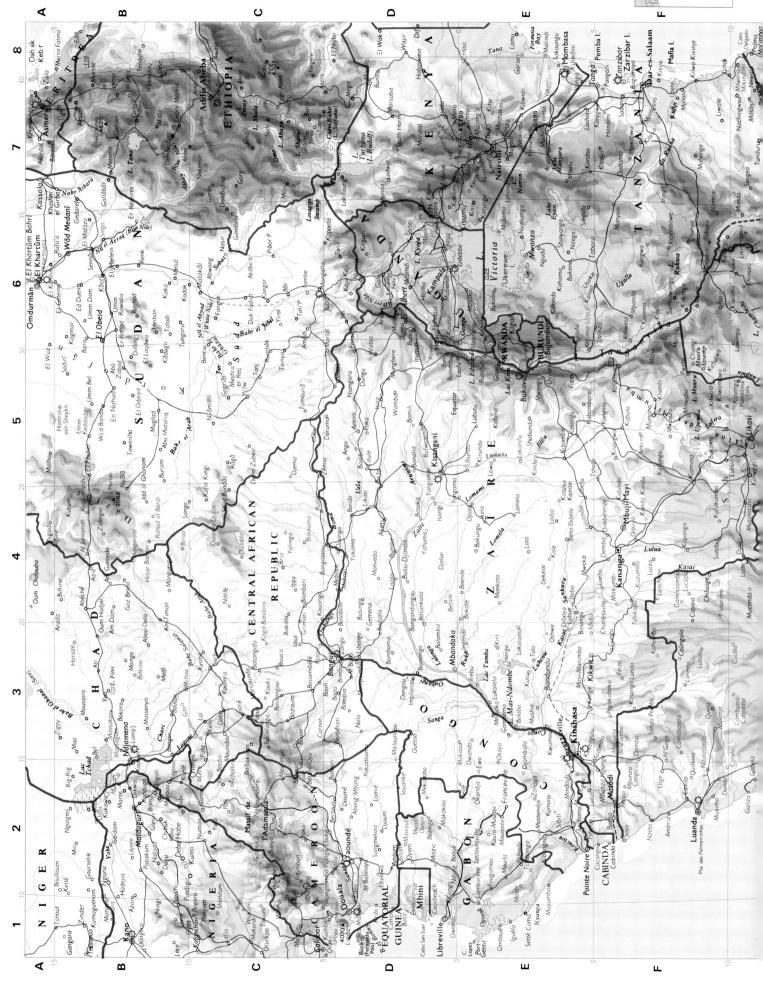

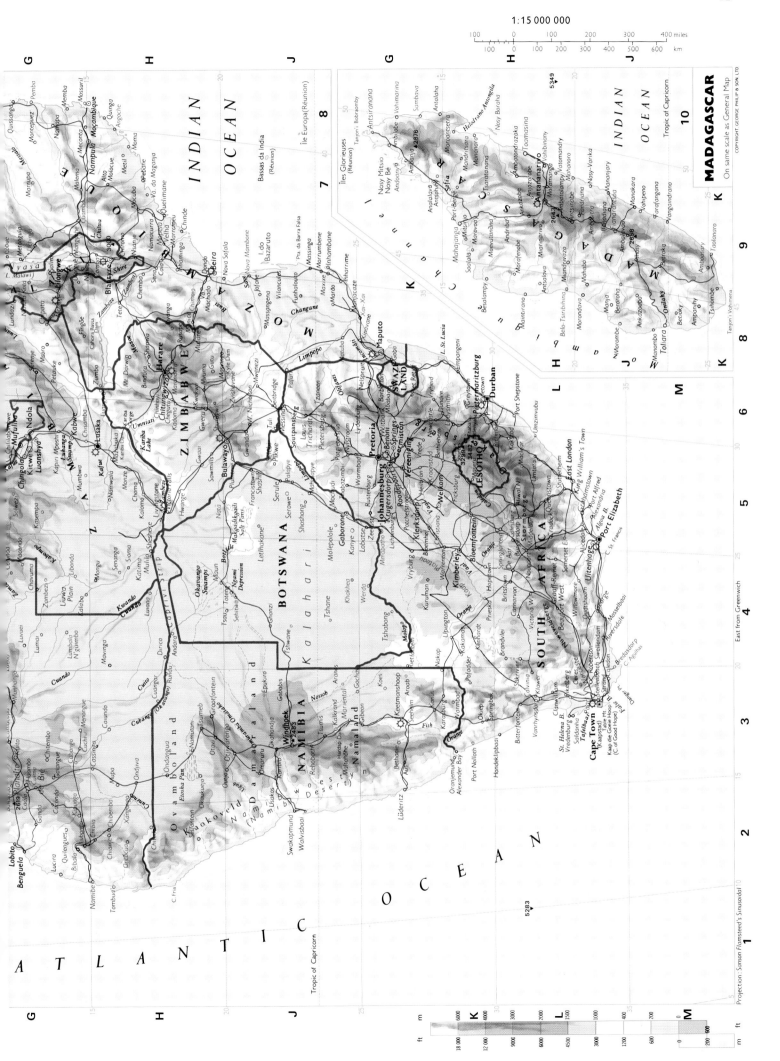

1:15 000 000

100   0   100   200   300   400 miles
100   0   100 200 300 400 500 600 km

MADAGASCAR
On same scale as General Map
COPYRIGHT GEORGE PHILIP & SON LTD

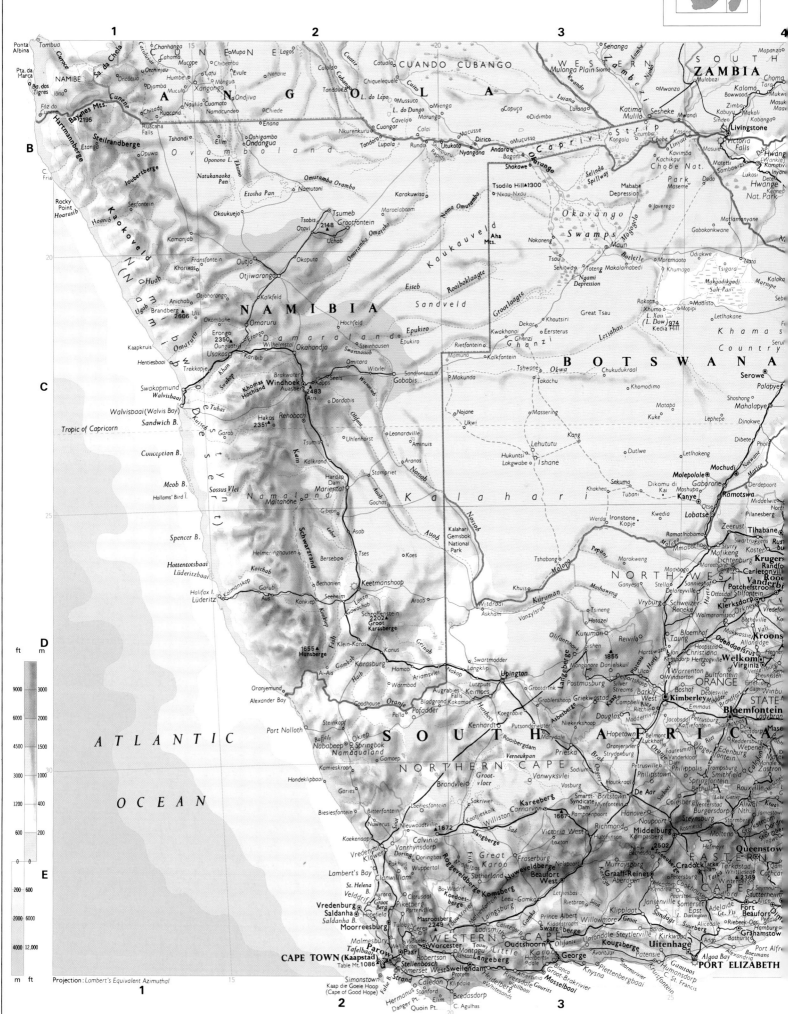

Projection: Lambert's Equivalent Azimuthal

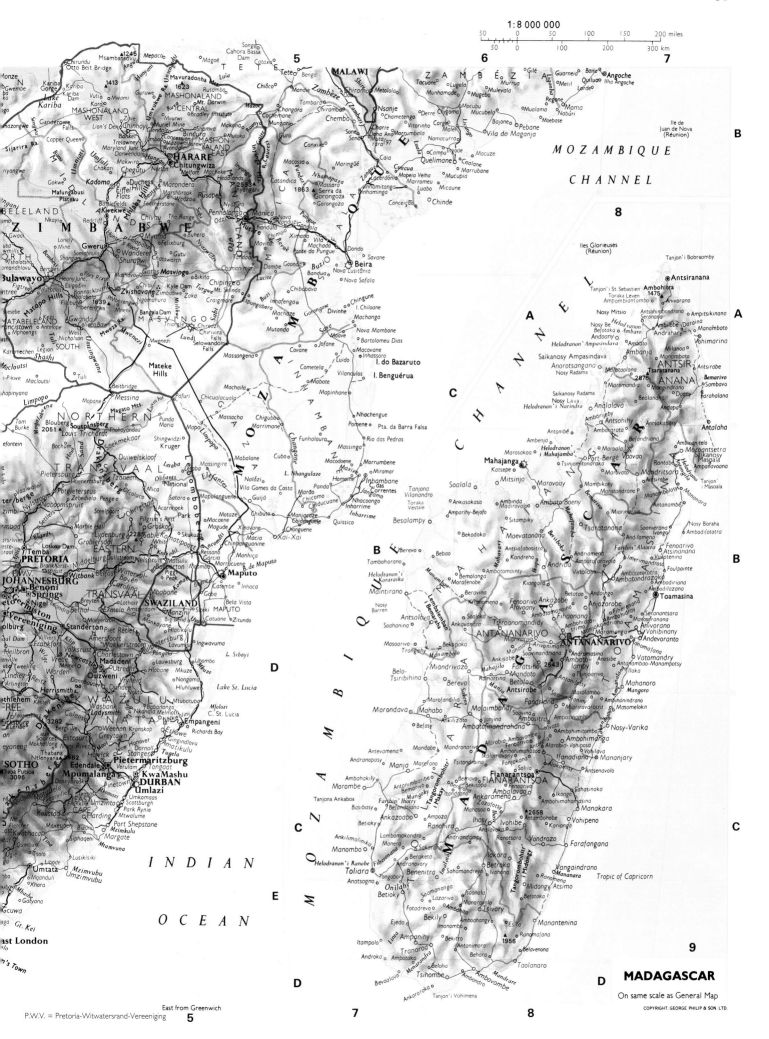

1:8 000 000

50   0   50   100   150   200 miles
50   0   100   200   300 km

5   6   7

MALAWI

Z A M B É Z I A

M O Z A M B I Q U E

C H A N N E L

Ile de Juan de Nova (Réunion)

B

8

Iles Glorieuses (Réunion)

Tanjon' i Bobraomby

Antsiranana

Tanjon' i St. Sebastien   Ambohitra 1475
Toraka Leven   Anivorano
Ampombintambo

Nosy Mitsio   Antsohimbondrona
veranana   Ampitsikinana

Nosy Be   Helodranon   Ambilobe   Daraina   Manambato
Befotaka   Ambaro   Andrahary   Vohimarina
Andoany

Helodranon' Ampasindava   Ambato

Saikanosy Ampasindava   Ambanja   Milanoa

Anorotsangana   Maromandia   Dogny   ANTSIR   Antsirabe
Nosy Radama   Bealanana   Bemarivo   Sambava
Saikanosy Radama   2876   ANANA

Nosy Lava   Analalava   Andapa   Farahalana
Helodranon' i Narindra   Antsohihy   Antsakabary   Antalaha

Antonibé   Ambodimotso   Mandritsara   Tanjon' i Masoala
Ambenja   Ambaratra   Befandriana   Rantabé
Port-Bergé   Vaovao   Ambinanitelo   Masoasoy
Marosakoa   Tsinjomitondraka   Marovato   Mananara

Mahajanga   Helodranon'   Mampikony   Amparafaravola   Ampanavoana
i Mahajamba   Morotandrano

Katsepe   Tsaratanana   Mamaintsetra

Soalala   Mitsinjo   Marovoay   Miarinarivo   Nosy Boraha

Ankasakasa   Ambinda   Ambato Boeny   Mariarano   Soanierana
Amparihy-Bejofo   Madirovalo   Ivongo
Sitampiky   Tsaratanana   Fenoarivo
Besalampy   Bekodoka   Maevatanana   Atsinanana
Andilamena   Vohibinany

Berevo   Beboo   Antsalovabositra   Andriamena   Foulpointe
Tambohorano   Kandreho   Vatomandry   Ambatosoratra   Ambodiriana
Helodranon' i   Bemolanga   Kiangara   Betaoo   Andingo   Ambodilazana
Koraraika   Morafenobe   Beravina   Ankazobe   Anjozorobe

Maintirano   Antsalova   Ankavandra   Tsiroanomandidy   Amboasary   Toamasina

Nosy   Soahanina   Ankavandra   Bekopaka   Mahabo   Andramasina   Maramanga
Barren   ANTANANARIVO   Fihaonana
Masoarivo   Trangahy   ANTANANARIVO   Manjakandriana   Anivorano
Trabonjy   Manambolo   Andramasina   Vatomandry   Andevoranto

Belo-   Miandrivazo   Ankisabe   Antanetibe   Moramanga
Tsiribihina   Mahajilo   Mandoto   2643   Ambato   Ilaka
Berevo   Betafo   Antanambao-Manampotsy   Ilaka

Antsirabe   Fandriana   Mananjary

Morondava   Mahabo   Malaimbandy   Soavina   Marovoay   Mahanoro
Ambositra   Ambohimanga   Mangoro

Ankilizato   Ambatofinandrahana

Befasy   Mahabo   Marofandilia   Ambohimahasoa   Nosy-Varika
Amboasary

Antevamena   Mandabe   Mandronarivo   Alarobia-Ambovombe
Andranopasy   Fenoarivo   Alarobia-Vohiposa   Vohilava
Manja   Marerano   Tsitondroina   Ambalavao   Vohilava

Tsitondroina   FIANARANTSOA   Ifanadiana   Mananjary

Morombe   Fanjakana   Ikongo
Tanjona Ankaboa   Antanimbaribe   Bevato   Ambalavao   Sahasinaka
Mahaboboka   Bekisopa   Ankaramena
Betroka   Manakara

Helodranon'i Ranobe   Ankazoabo   Amboropotsy   Iakora   Ihosy   Ivohibe   Vohipeno
Toliara   Fenoarivo   Andranovory   Zazafotsy   Antambohobe   Karianga
Benenitra   Ihosy   Ivohibe   Vondrozo   Farafangana

Sakaraha   Betraka   Vangaindrano
Lambomakondro   Manera   Beraketa   Ankarana   Ranotsara
Manombo   Andriandampy   Vondrozo
Betioky   Ranohira   Andriandampy   Mananara

Ankilimalinika   Ambohimahasoa   Ikalamavony   Midongy Atsimo
Betioky   Sahambano   Ranomafana   Midongy Atsimo   Manantenina

Soananga   Ivato   Isivory

Onilahy   Bekily   Maniranta
Ejeda   Ampanihy   Ambalavao   Esira
Ampanihy   Behara   Belevona

Itampolo   Tranoroo   Antanimora   1956

Androka   Bekitro

Tsihombe   Behola   Tranoroo   Taolanaro

Ambovombe   Mandrare

Bevoalavo   Ambondro

Ankaroaka   Tanjon' i Vohimena   9

I N D I A N

O C E A N

M O Z A M B I Q U E

East from Greenwich

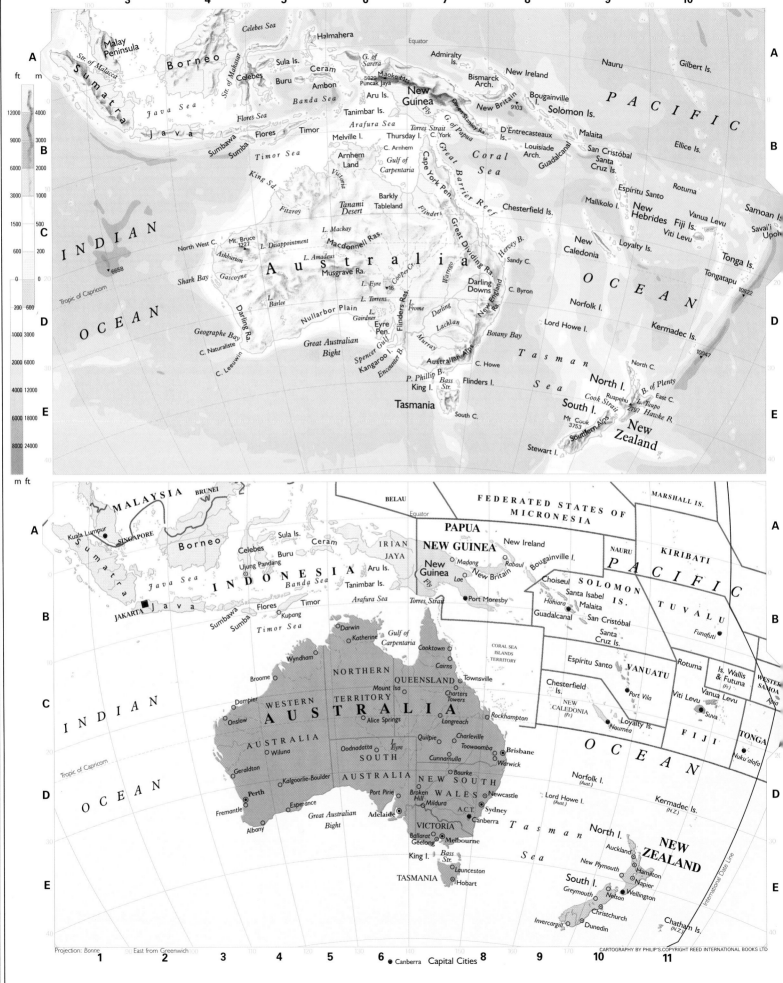

1 : 50 000 000

Projection: Bonne   East from Greenwich

Canberra   Capital Cities

CARTOGRAPHY BY PHILIP'S. COPYRIGHT REED INTERNATIONAL BOOKS LTD

1:6 000 000

20 0 20 40 60 80 100 miles
20 0 40 80 120 160 km

KIRIBATI

TUVALU (Ellice Is.)
Tokelau Is. (N.Z.)
Tongareva (Penrhyn) I.
Pukapuka
Rakahanga
Manihiki
WESTERN SAMOA
Savaii Upolu
Nassau
Suwarrow
Northern Group
Wallis & Futuna (Fr.)
Rotuma
Tutuila
AMER. SAMOA (U.S.)
Cook Is. (N.Z.)
Îles de la Société
Vanua Levu
Lau or Eastern Group
FIJI
Viti Levu
TONGA (Friendly Is.)
Niue (N.Z.)
Palmerston Atoll
Aitutaki
Mitiaro
Mauke
Lower Group
Rarotonga
Mangaia
FRENCH POLYNESIA
VANUATU
Tropic of Capricorn

PACIFIC OCEAN

Macauley
Raoul (Sunday) I.
Kermadec Is. (N.Z.)
Curtis
Three Kings Is.
Auckland
NORTH I.
Cook Strait
NEW ZEALAND
Wellington
Christchurch
SOUTH I.
Chatham I.
Chatham Is.
Pitt I.
Tasman Sea
Dunedin
Bounty Is.
Stewart I.
Antipodes Is.
Snares
Auckland Is.
Campbell I.
Macquarie I. (Austr.)
SOUTHERN OCEAN

NEW ZEALAND & S.W. PACIFIC
1:60 000 000

200 0 200 400 600 800 miles
200 0 400 800 1200 km

NORTH ISLAND

Three Kings Is.
C. Reinga
North C.
C. Maria van Diemen
Houhora
Rangaunu Bay
Doubtless Bay
Mangonui
Whangaroa Bay
Ahipara B.
Kaitaia
B. of Islands
C. Brett
Tauroa Pt.
Opua
Rawene
Kaikohe
Hikurangi
Hokianga Harb.
Whangarei
Donnelly's Crossing
Whangarei Harb.
Bream Hd.
Dargaville
Bream Bay
Waipu
Lit. Barrier I.
Gt. Barrier I.
Kaipara Harb.
C. Rodney
Warkworth
C. Colville
Cuvier I.
Helensville
Hauraki Gulf
Coromandel
Takapuna **Devonport**
Whitianga
Onehunga
AUCKLAND
Manukau
Papakura
Thames
Waiuku
Mercer
Pukekohe
Waihi
Mayor I.
Waikato
Paeroa
Tauranga Harb.
Huntly
Te Aroha
Mt. Maunganui
White I.
C. Runaway
Morrinsville
Tauranga
Bay of Plenty
Raglan
Hamilton
Cambridge
Te Puke
Whakatane
Opotiki
Kawhia Harb.
Te Awamutu
Putaruru
Rotorua
Kawerau
Raukumara Ra.
Hikurangi
Otorohanga
Kinleith
Tarawera
Waipiro
Te Kuiti
Makai
L. Tarawera
Murupara
Motu
Tolaga Bay
North Taranaki Bight
Waikato
KAINGAROA FOREST
Waikaremoana
Ormond
Gisborne
Waitara
Ongarue
Up. Taupo
Poverty Bay
New Plymouth
Taumarunui
Nuhaka
Waikokopu
Mt. Egmont (Taranaki)
Inglewood
Kaimanawa Mts.
Tarawera
Mahia Peninsula
Stratford
Raetihi
Ruahine
Wairoa
Opunake
Eltham
Ruapehu
Waiour
Hawke Bay
Kapuni
Hawera
Taihape
View
Waverley
Mangaweka
Napier
South Taranaki Bight
Taihape
C. Kidnappers
Pateo
Waipawa
Hastings
Wanganui
Marton
Holcombe
Waipukurau
Bulls
Feilding
Dannevirke
Foxton
Palmerston N.
Shannon
Woodville
Pahiatua
Levin
Eketahuna
Otaki
C. Turnagain
Paraparaumu
Kapiti I.
Masterton
Carterton
Pacific Ocean
Up. Hutt
Greytown
Featherston
Lr. Hutt
Martinborough
Petone
WELLINGTON
Eastbourne
Cook Strait

SOUTH ISLAND

C. Farewell
Golden Bay
D'Urville I.
Collingwood
Takaka
Tasman Bay
Tasman Mts.
Motueka
Pelorus Sd.
Karamea Bight
Tadmor
Nelson
Picton
Seddonville
Havelock
Wairau
Granity
Wakefield
Blenheim
Westport
Murchison
Richmond
Inangahua Junction
Blenheim
Seddon
Mt. Travers 2338
Ward
Lyell
Rotoroa
Reefton
Spenser Mts.
Hanmer
Kaikoura
Blackball
Runanga
Amuri B.
Springs
Waiau
Greymouth
Stillwater
Culverden
Kumara
L. Brunner
Hurunui
Waipara
Jacksons
Amberley
Hokitika
Arthur's
Waikari
Oxford
Pegasus Bay
Ross
Rangiora
Kaiapoi
Abut Hd.
Okarito
Springfield
New Brighton
Whitecliffs
Christchurch
Mt. Cook 3753
Riccarton
Lyttelton
Springs
Methven
Lincoln
Banks Peninsula
Stavely
Coalgate
L. Ellesmere
Akaroa
LittleRiver
Mt. Aspiring 3027
Geraldine
Fairlie
Rakaia
Ashburton
Jackson B.
Okuru
Mt. Cook
Pukaki
Timaru
Temuka
St. Andrews
Milford Sd.
Mt. Earnslaw 2819
Hawea
Waitaki
Waimate
Bligh Sd.
Wanaka
Kurow
George Sd.
Arrowtown
Cromwell
Tokarahi
Ngapara
Oamaru
Secretary I.
Queenstown
Clyde
Naseby
Hampden
Doubtful Sd.
Wakatipu
Alexandra
Dunback
Breaksea Sd.
Kingston
Roxburgh
Palmerston
Resolution I.
Te Anau
Waikouaiti
Dusky Sd.
Manapouri
Edievale
Kelso
Otago Harbour
Lumsden
Lawrence
Port Chalmers
Mossburn
Ohai
Nightcaps
Tapanui
Dunedin
Mosgiel
Poteriteri
Clifden
Tuatapere
St. Kilda
Orepuki
Winton
Clinton
Mataura
Milton
Fairfield
Riverton
Edendale
Gore
Balclutha
Te Woewae B.
Kaitangata
Nugget Pt.
Invercargill
Wyndham
Tokanui
Owaka
Bluff
Ruapuke I.
Waikawa
Tahakopa
Foveaux Str.
Stewart I.
Halfmoon Bay
Port Pegasus
S.W. Cape

TASMAN SEA

WESTLAND
Westland Bight
Southern Alps
Canterbury Plains
Eyre Mts.
Garvie Mts.
Umbrella Mts.
Southland

Projection: Conical with two standard parallels

SAMOA ISLANDS
1:12 000 000

WESTERN SAMOA
AMERICAN SAMOA
Savai'i
Apia
Upolu
Pago Pago
Manua Is.
Tutuila
Rose I.
Wallis & Futuna (Fr.)
Futuna
WESTERN SAMOA

FIJI AND TONGA ISLANDS
1:12 000 000

50 0 50 100 150 miles
50 0 50 100 150 200 250 km

Thikombia
Niuafo'ou (Tonga)
Lambasa
Yakawa Group
Vanua Levu
Vanua Levu
FIJI
Vanua Balavu
Taveuni
Koro
Lautoka
Levuka
Lau or Eastern Group
Nandi
Viti Levu
Ovalau
TONGA (Friendly Is.)
Vava'u
Suva
Ngau
Koro Sea
Lakemba
Moala
Vatoa
Tofua I.
Kandavu
Tongatapu
Nuku'alofa

ft m
12 000 4000
9000 3000
6000 2000
3000 1000
1200 400
600 200
0
200 600
m ft

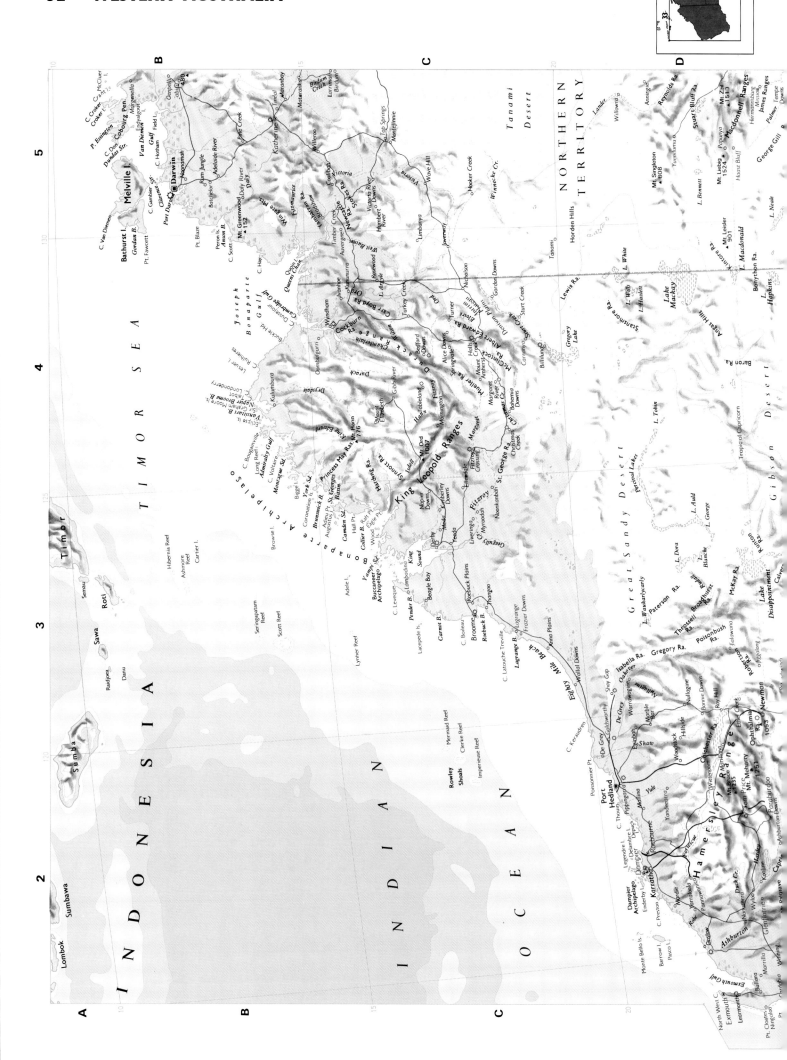

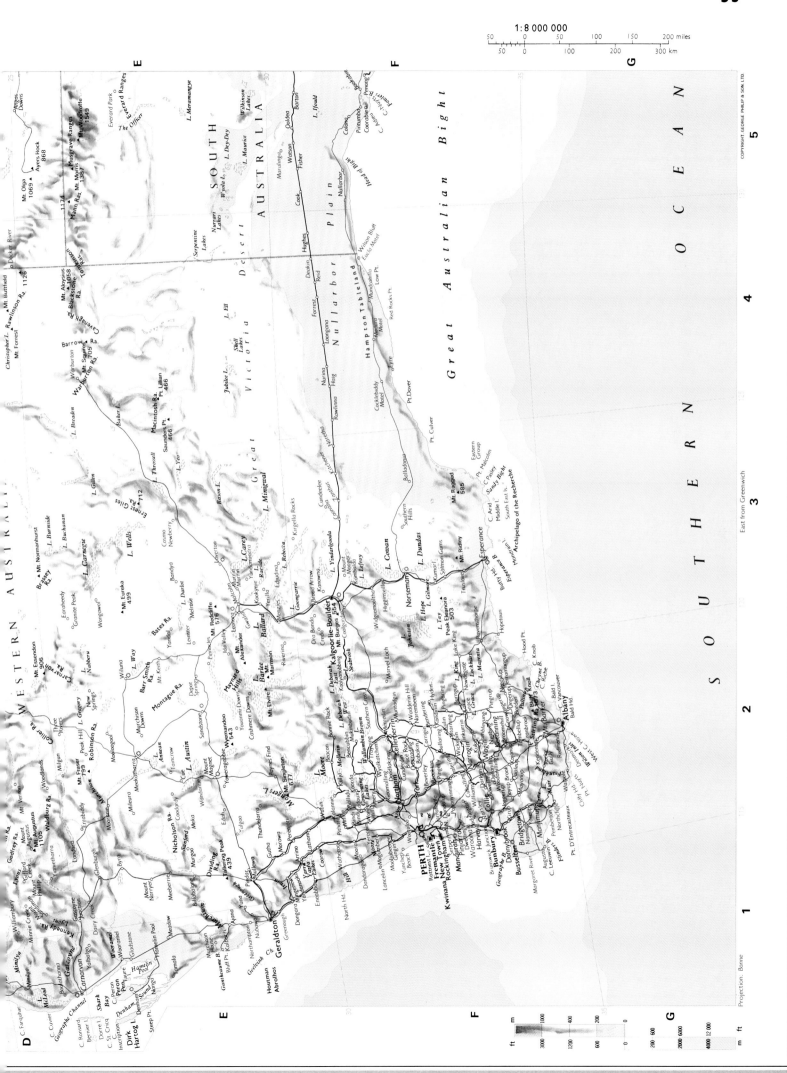

1:8 000 000

50   0   50   100   150   200 miles
50   0   100   200   300 km

D

E

WESTERN AUSTRALIA

SOUTH AUSTRALIA

Everard Ranges
Ayers Rock
868

Mt. Olga
1069

Mt. Woodroffe
1549

Mann Ras. Mt. Morris
1387

Musgrave Ranges

1174

The Officer

Tomkinson Mountains

Mt. Buttfield

Mt. Aloysius
1058

Blackstone
Ra.

Rawlinson Ra.   1126

Cavenagh Ra.

Christopher L.

Mt. Forest

Barrow
Ra.

Warburton   Mt. Squires
705

Warburton Ra.

Mt. Lillian
466

Macintosh Ra.
466

Saunders Pt.

Throssell

L. Breaden

Baker L.

L. Gillen

L. Yeo

L. Ell

Jubilee L.

Shell
Lakes

Great

Victoria

Desert

L. Meramangye

Wilkinson
Lakes

L. Maurice   L. Dey-Dey

Serpentine
Lakes

Nurrari
Lakes

Ooldea

Barton

Watson

Fisher

C. Nuyts
Frontier

Penong

Coorabie

Coombra

Pintumbo

Colona

Wynbring

Wyola L.

Hesper of Bight

Cook

Hughes

Deakin

Reid

Forrest

Loongana

Nurina

Haig

Naretha

Kitchener

Zanthus

Cundeelee

Kingella Rocks

Rawlinna

Nullarbor Plain

Nullarbor

Wilson Bluff

Eucla Motel

Mandrabilla

Low Pt.

Eyre

Cocklebiddy
Motel

Madura
Motel

Hampton Tableland

Red Rocks Pt.

Pt. Dover

Pt. Culver

Great   Australian   Bight

SOUTHERN   OCEAN

East from Greenwich

COPYRIGHT. GEORGE PHILIP & SON LTD.

5

4

3

2

1

Projection. Bonne

m   ft
3000   12 000
2000   6000
1200   4000
600   2000
400   1200
200   600
0   0

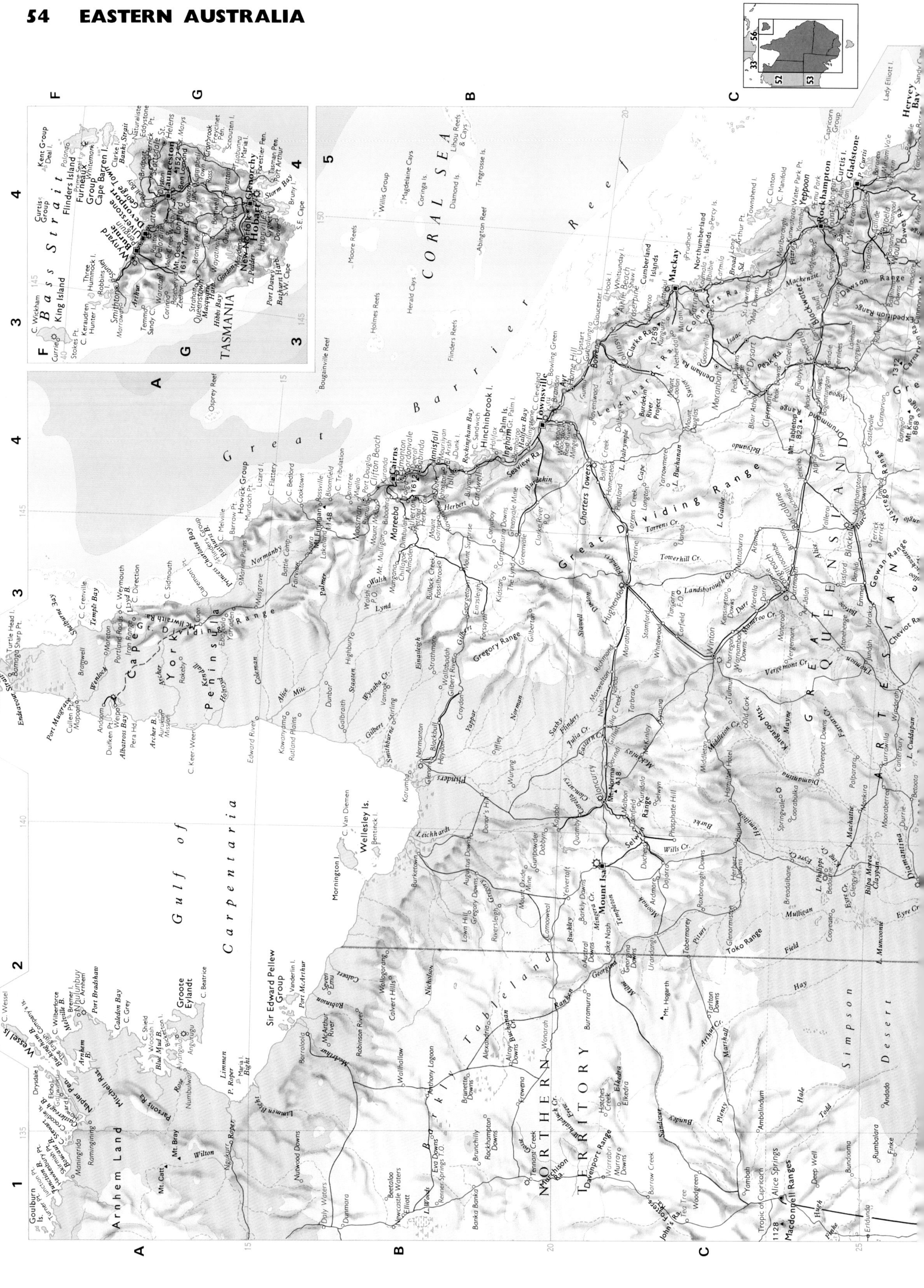

TASMANIA

Bass Strait

CORAL SEA

Great Barrier Reef

Gulf of Carpentaria

Cape York Peninsula

Great Dividing Range

ARNHEM LAND

NORTHERN TERRITORY

QUEENSLAND

Simpson Desert

Barkly Tableland

Wessel Is.

Groote Eylandt

Sir Edward Pellew Group

Wellesley Is.

Mornington I.

Thursday I.

Prince of Wales

Cairns

Townsville

Mackay

Rockhampton

Gladstone

Mount Isa

Cloncurry

Charters Towers

Mareeba

Winton

Alice Springs

Macdonnell Ranges

Tropic of Capricorn

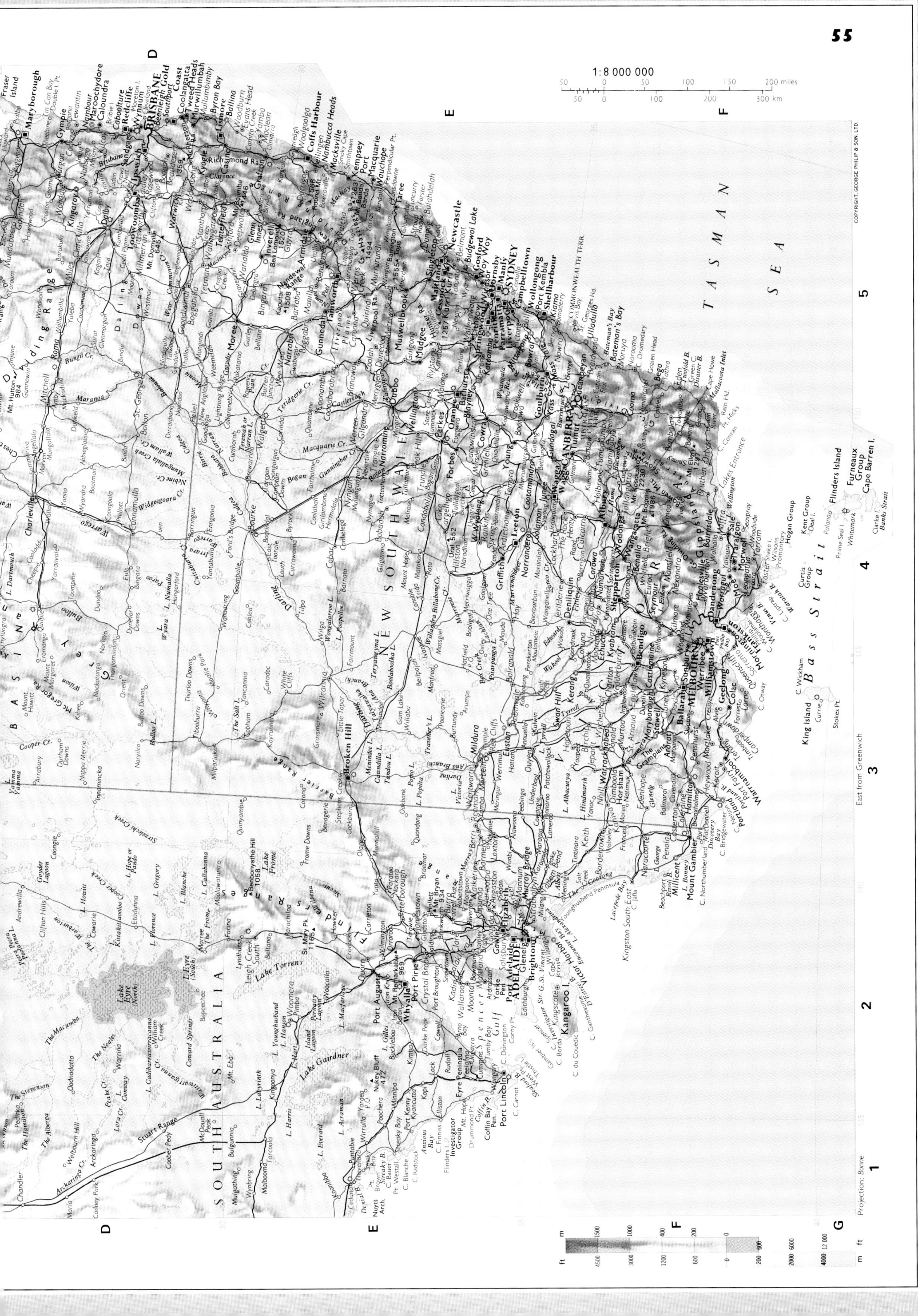

1:8 000 000

50   0   50   100   150   200 miles
50   0   50   100   150   200   300 km

NEW SOUTH WALES

SOUTH AUSTRALIA

VICTORIA

AUSTRALIAN CAPITAL TERR.

GREAT DIVIDING RANGE

GREY RANGE

BARRIER RANGE

FLINDERS RANGE

ARTESIAN BASIN

TASMAN SEA

Bass Strait

Spencer Gulf

Lake Eyre North
Lake Eyre (South)
Lake Torrens
Lake Gairdner
Lake Frome
Lake Blanche

BRISBANE
SYDNEY
CANBERRA
MELBOURNE
ADELAIDE
Newcastle
Wollongong
Geelong
Ballarat
Bendigo
Broken Hill
Port Augusta
Whyalla
Port Pirie
Coffs Harbour
Maryborough

King Island
Flinders Island
Cape Barren I.
Furneaux Group
Kangaroo Island
Fraser Island

East from Greenwich

Projection: Bonne

COPYRIGHT GEORGE PHILIP & SON LTD.

m   ft
4500 15 000
3000 10 000
1200 4000
600   2000
200   600
0   0

D   E   F

1   2   3   4   5

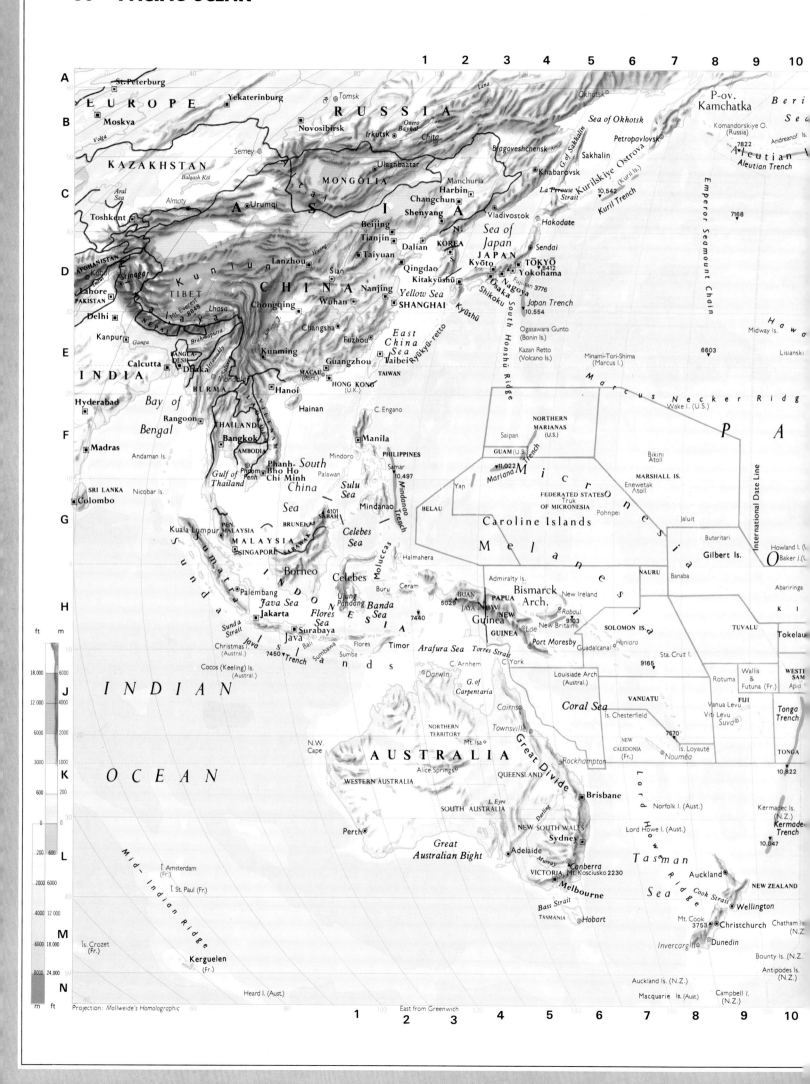

11 12 13 14 15 16 17 18 19 20

A L A S K A
(U.S.) ▲5959
Bristol Bay
Gulf of Alaska
Juneau
Prince of Wales I.
Prince Rupert
Queen Charlotte Is.
Kitimat
Edmonton
R O C A N A D A
Hudson Bay
GREENLAND C. Farewell

N O R T H A M E R I C A
Labrador
Newfoundland
N O R T H

Vancouver
Vancouver I.
Calgary
Regina
Winnipeg
L. Winnipeg
Victoria
Seattle
Portland
Boise
Snake
Montréal
Quebec
St. Lawrence
Pr. Edward I.
Saint John

L. Superior
L. Huron
Ottawa
Toronto
L. Ontario
Buffalo
Boston
C. Sable
Pittsburgh **NEW YORK**
Philadelphia
Baltimore
Washington

Minneapolis
L. Michigan
L. Erie
CHICAGO
Detroit
Cincinnati

C. Mendocino
Salt Lake City
Denver
Kansas City
St. Louis
Memphis
Appalachian Mts.

San Francisco
4418
U N I T E D S T A T E S
Oklahoma
Dallas
Atlanta
C. Hatteras

Los Angeles
San Diego
Ciudad Juarez
Mississippi
Jacksonville
Bermuda (U.K.)

▼6741
Mountains
Rocky

A T L A N T I C

Colorado

Sierra Madre
San Antonio
New Orleans
Houston
O C E A N

Hawaiian Is.
(U.S.)
Oahu
Honolulu
Tropic of Cancer
I. Guadalupe
(Mexico)
6225
M E X I
Monterrey
Gulf of Mexico
Miami
Florida Strait
BAHAMAS

Ridge
San I.
nston I. (U.S.)
4205 ▲ Hawaii
Is. Revilla Gigedo
(Mexico)
Guadalajara
Gulf of California
México
Puebla 5700
Acapulco
Mérida
Yucatan Channel
La Habana
C U B A
West Indies
Hispaniola 9200
DOM. REP.
HAITI
7680
JAMAICA
Kingston
PUERTO RICO
(U.S.)
Leeward Is.

C I F I C
P A C I F I C
Christmas Island Ridge
Palmyra Is. (U.S.)
Teraina
Tabuaeran
Kiritimati
Jarvis I.
(U.S.)
BELIZE
GUATEMALA
Guatemala
San Salvador
EL SALVADOR
HONDURAS
NICARAGUA
Managua
CENTRAL AMERICA
Caribbean Sea
Barranquilla
San José
COSTA RICA
Colón
PANAMA
Panama Canal
Maracaibo
Windward Is.
BARBADOS
TRINIDAD & TOBAGO
Caracas
Orinoco
VENEZUELA

E A N
O
bury I.
enix Is.
I B A T I
Malden I.
Starbuck I.
Î. Clipperton (Fr.)
I. del Coco
(Costa Rica)
Medellín
Bogota
Cali
COLOMBIA

Equator
Galápagos
(Ecuador)
I. de Malpelo
(Colombia)
Quito
ECUADOR
Guayaquil
Iquitos
Manaus
Amazonas
C. Pariñas
B R A Z I L
S O U T H

Î. Marquises
Tongareva
Penrhyn Is.
Manihiki
Suwarrow Is.
Vostok I.
Flint I.
Caroline I.
Trujillo
P E R U
6369 ▼
Lima
A M E R I C A
Cuzco

Cook Islands
(N.Z.)
Manuae
Î. de la Société
Tahiti
Î. Tuamotu
FRENCH POLYNESIA
L. Titicaca
Illampu & Ancohuma
6550
Arequipa
La Paz
▼6866
BOLIVIA
Peru–
Iquique
Chile
Tropic of Capricorn
8050
Antofagasta
Trench
PARAGUAY
Asunción

Rarotonga
Seamount Chain
Tuamotu Ridge
Î. Tubuai
(Îs. Australes)
Rapa
Austral
Pitcairn I. (U.K.)
Ducie I.
(U.K.)
I. de Pascua
(Easter I.)
(Chile)
Sala-y-Gomez
(Chile)
San Félix (Chile)
San Ambrosio (Chile)
Tucumán
Pto. Alegre

East Pacific Ridge
Arch. de Juan Fernández
(Chile)
6960
Córdoba
Rosario
URUGUAY
Valparaíso
Santiago
Buenos Aires
Montevideo

Pacific–Antarctic Ridge
Chile Rise
Concepción
A R G E N T I N A
Río de la Plata

Patagonia
SOUTH

ATLANTIC

6212 ▼
OCEAN
Falkland Is. (U.K.)

Punta Arenas
Str. of Magellan
Tierra del Fuego
C. Horn
West from Greenwich
South Georgia (U.K.)
COPYRIGHT. GEORGE PHILIP & SON. LTD.

11 12 13 14 15 16 17 18 19 20

A B C D E F G H J K L M N

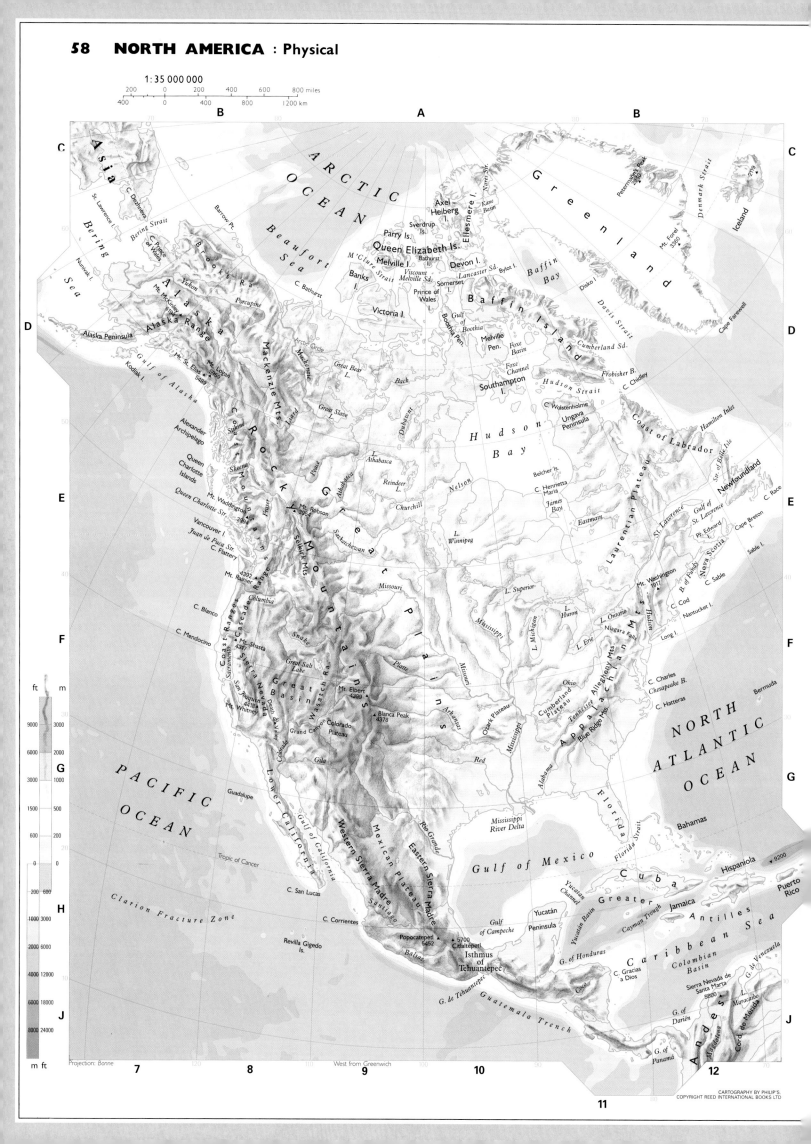

1:35 000 000

Projection: Bonne

West from Greenwich

1 : 35 000 000

| 200 | 0 | 200 | 400 | 600 | 800 miles |
| 400 | 0 | 400 | 800 | 1200 km |

B   A   B

C

RUSSIA

Asia

St. Lawrence

Bering Strait

International Date Line

ARCTIC

OCEAN

GREENLAND

(Denmark)

ICELAND

Denmark Strait

Reykjavík

C

Bering

Sea

Beaufort

Sea

Queen Elizabeth Is.

Ellesmere I.

Baffin

Bay

Davis Strait

D

Kodiak I.

Gulf of Alaska

ALASKA

(USA)

Yukon

Porcupine

Anchorage

Fairbanks

Arctic Circle

YUKON

TERRITORY

Whitehorse

Juneau

Victoria I.

NORTHWEST TERRITORIES

Great Bear

L.

Mackenzie

Back

Hudson Strait

Baffin Island

Godthåb

Cape Farewell

D

Skeena

Fraser

BRITISH

COLUMBIA

Peace

Liard

Great

Slave L.

Yellowknife

Thelon

Dubawnt

Hudson

Bay

Churchill

Nelson

Eastmain

NEWFOUNDLAND

Labrador

St. John's

E

Victoria

Vancouver

Olympia

Portland

Salem

WASHINGTON

Seattle

Columbia

OREGON

Edmonton

ALBERTA

Calgary

Athabasca

Saskatchewan

L.

Athabasca

SASKATCHEWAN

Regina

MANITOBA

L.

Winnipeg

Winnipeg

ONTARIO

L. Superior

QUÉBEC

St. Lawrence

Québec

PRINCE

EDWARD

I.

Charlottetown

NEW

BRUNSWICK

Fredericton

NOVA

SCOTIA

Halifax

St-Pierre

Et Miquelon

(Fr.)

C. Sable

E

F

Sacramento

SAN FRANCISCO

San Jose

Carson

City

Salem

IDAHO

Boise

Snake

MONTANA

Helena

Missouri

Bismarck

NORTH

DAKOTA

SOUTH

DAKOTA

MINNESOTA

Minneapolis

WISCONSIN

Madison

Milwaukee

MICHIGAN

Lansing

L. Michigan

L. Huron

Toronto

Detroit

L. Erie

Cleveland

Buffalo

NEW YORK

Ottawa

Montréal

VER.

N.H.

Concord

MAINE

Augusta

MASS.

Boston

Providence

Hartford

NEW YORK CITY

PHILADELPHIA

F

Phoenix

WYOMING

Cheyenne

Salt Lake

City

UTAH

NEVADA

CALIFORNIA

Las Vegas

LOS ANGELES

San Diego

Colorado

ARIZONA

NEBRASKA

Lincoln

Denver

COLORADO

Santa Fe

Albuquerque

NEW MEXICO

KANSAS

Topeka

Kansas City

IOWA

MISSOURI

St.

Louis

ILLINOIS

Springfield

CHICAGO

INDIANA

Indianapolis

OHIO

Columbus

Cincinnati

KENTUCKY

Nashville

TENNESSEE

PA.

Pittsburgh

W.V.

Washington D.C.

Richmond

VIRGINIA

NORTH

CAROLINA

Raleigh

Charlotte

DE.

Baltimore

MD.

N.J.

G

PACIFIC

OCEAN

Guadalupe

(Mex.)

Tucson

El Paso

TEXAS

Dallas

Austin

OKLAHOMA

Oklahoma

City

ARKANSAS

Little Rock

Memphis

MISSISSIPPI

Birmingham

ALABAMA

Jackson

Montgomery

GEORGIA

Atlanta

Columbia

SOUTH

CAROLINA

Charleston

Jacksonville

NORTH

ATLANTIC

OCEAN

Bermuda

(U.K.)

G

Hermosillo

Rio Grande

Houston

Baton

Rouge

LOUISIANA

New

Orleans

Tallahassee

FLORIDA

Tampa

Miami

Gulf of Mexico

Florida Str.

Nassau

BAHAMAS

Turks & Caicos Is.

(U.K.)

H

Tropic of Cancer

Culiacán

Monterrey

MEXICO

Mérida

Havana

CUBA

Cayman Is.

(U.K.)

JAMAICA

Kingston

HAITI

Port-au-

Prince

DOMINICAN

REP.

Santo

Domingo

PUERTO

RICO

(U.S.A.)

San Juan

Caribbean Sea

H

Revilla Gigedo Is.

(Mex.)

Guadalajara

MÉXICO

Puebla

Acapulco

Belmopan

BELIZE

GUATEMALA

Guatemala

Maracaibo

VENEZUELA

Barranquilla

J

Projection: Bonne

El Salvador

EL SALVADOR

San Salvador

HONDURAS

Tegucigalpa

NICARAGUA

Managua

L. Nicaragua

COSTA

RICA

San José

PANAMA

Panamá

COLOMBIA

Medellín

South

America

J

West from Greenwich

7 ■ MÉXICO Capital Cities **8**   **9**   **10**   **12**

11

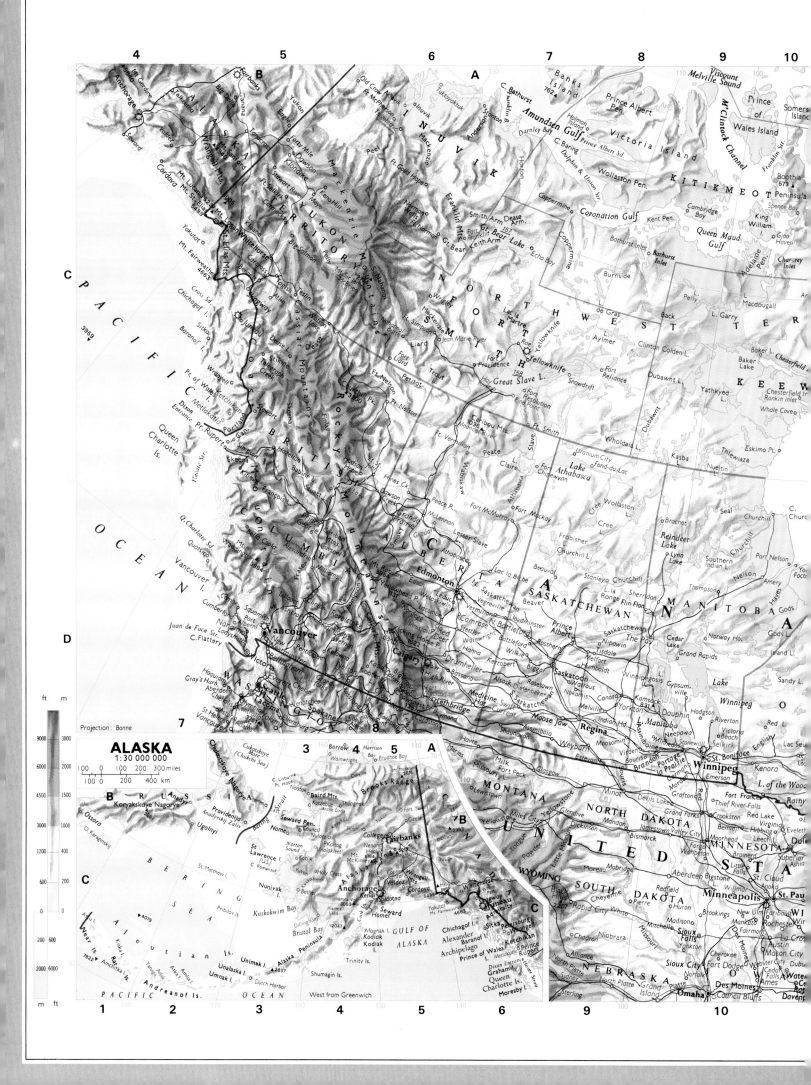

Projection: Bonne

ALASKA
1:30 000 000
100 0 100 200 300 miles
100 0 200 400 km

West from Greenwich

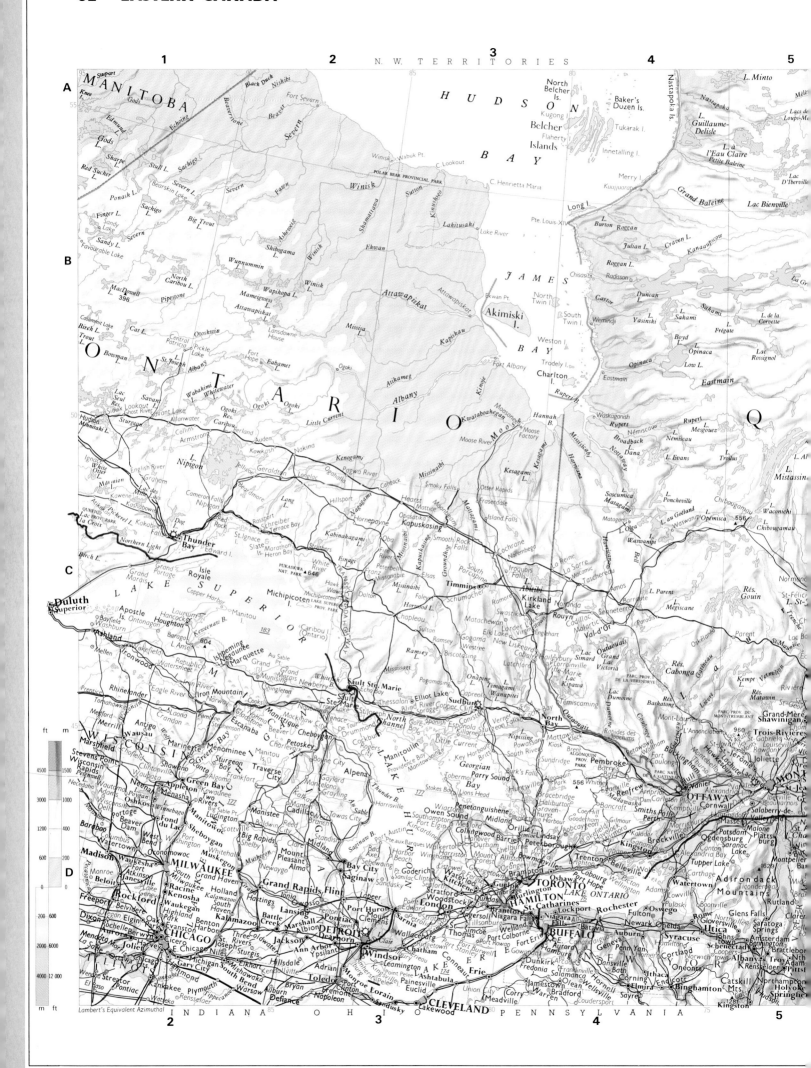

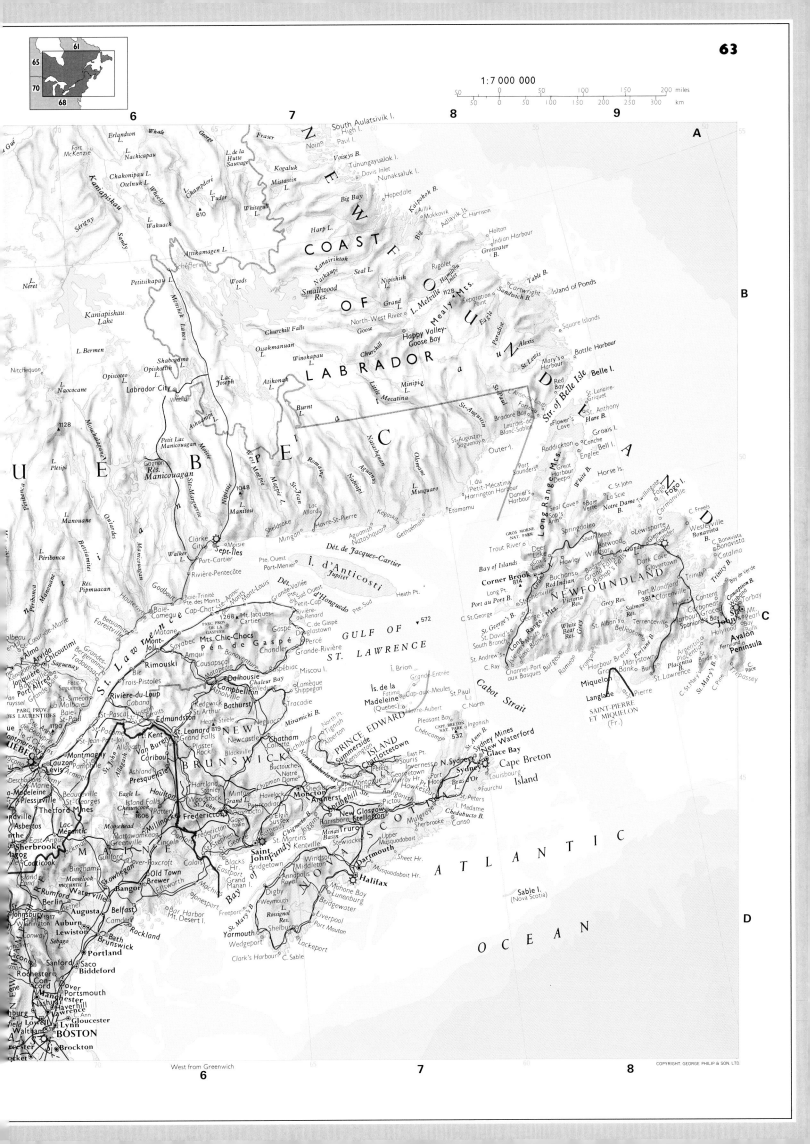

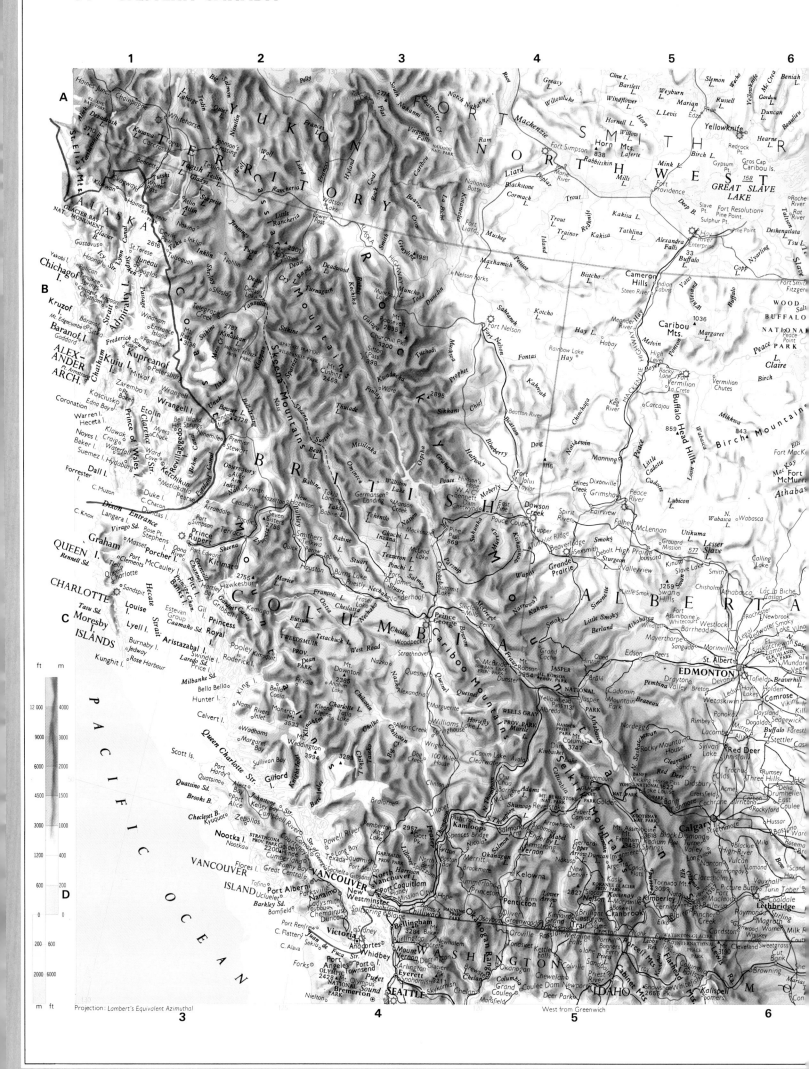

Projection: Lambert's Equivalent Azimuthal

West from Greenwich

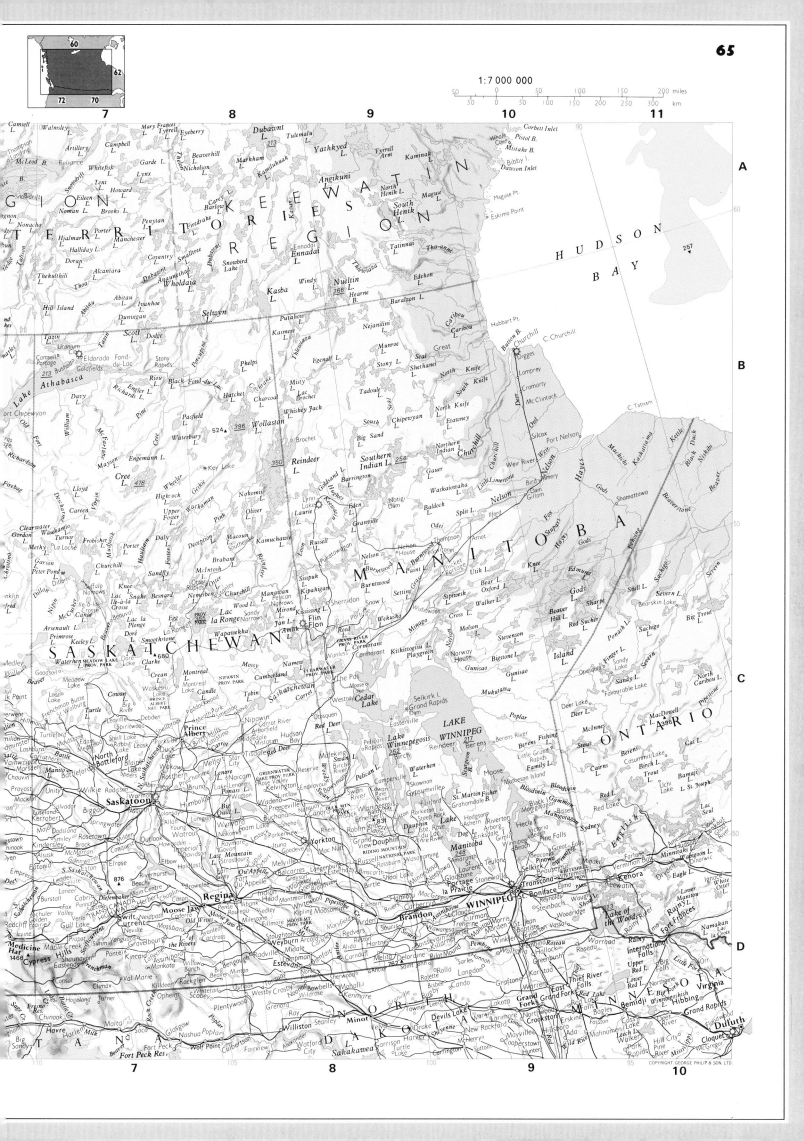

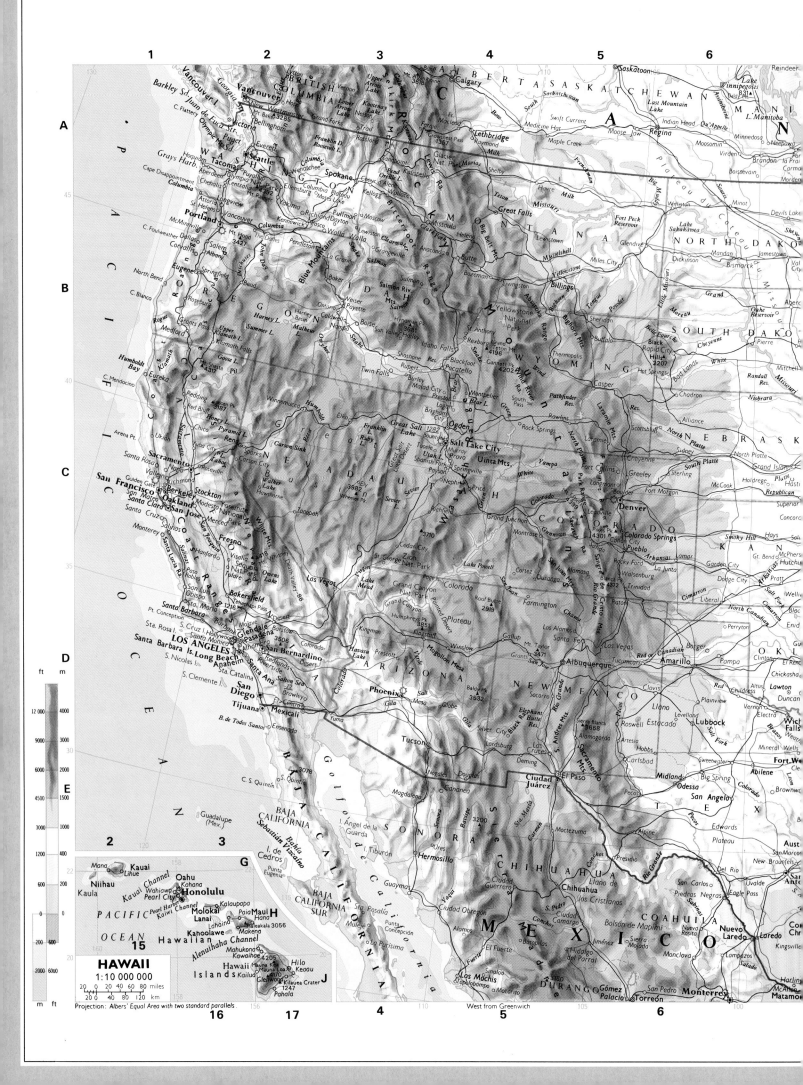

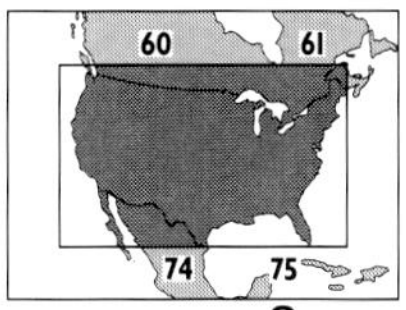

1:12 000 000

50 0 50 100 150 200 250 300 miles
50 0 50 100 150 200 250 300 350 400 450 km

60 | 61
74 | 75

8 9 10 11 12 13

Map of the Eastern United States and Southeastern Canada

CANADA

Lake Winnipeg
Winnipeg
Lake of the Woods
Thunder Bay
Lake Superior
Duluth
MINNESOTA
Minneapolis · St. Paul
WISCONSIN
Madison
Milwaukee
IOWA
Des Moines
Council Bluffs
MISSOURI
Kansas City
St. Louis
OKLAHOMA
Oklahoma City
Tulsa
ARKANSAS
Little Rock
TEXAS
Dallas
Houston
Galveston
LOUISIANA
Baton Rouge
New Orleans
MISSISSIPPI
ALABAMA
Birmingham
Montgomery
Mobile
TENNESSEE
Memphis
Nashville
Chattanooga
Knoxville
KENTUCKY
Louisville
ILLINOIS
Chicago
Springfield
INDIANA
Indianapolis
OHIO
Columbus
Cincinnati
Dayton
Cleveland
MICHIGAN
DETROIT
Grand Rapids
Lansing
Lake Michigan
Lake Huron
Lake Erie
Lake Ontario
TORONTO
Buffalo
Rochester
NEW YORK
PENNSYLVANIA
Pittsburgh
PHILADELPHIA
Baltimore
Washington D.C.
WEST VIRGINIA
VIRGINIA
Richmond
Norfolk
NORTH CAROLINA
Raleigh
Charlotte
Winston Salem
Greensboro
Asheville
SOUTH CAROLINA
Columbia
Charleston
GEORGIA
Atlanta
Savannah
Macon
Columbus
FLORIDA
Jacksonville
Orlando
Tampa
St. Petersburg
Miami
MONTRÉAL
Ottawa
Quebec
MAINE
NEW BRUNSWICK
NEW HAMPSHIRE
VERMONT
Boston
MASS.
Providence
Hartford
New Haven
NEW YORK
NEW JERSEY

GULF OF MEXICO
ATLANTIC OCEAN
BAHAMAS
Eleuthera I.
Key West
Florida Keys

Grid references (top): B C D E F G
Left/right scale rows: 10 9 8 7 6 5 4 3 2 1

QUEBEC

ONTARIO

NEW YORK

PENNSYLVANIA

OHIO

INDIANA

KENTUCKY

WEST VIRGINIA

VIRGINIA

MARYLAND

NEW JERSEY

DELAWARE

VERMONT

NEW HAMPSHIRE

MASS.

CONN.

R.I.

MICHIGAN

WISCONSIN

ILLINOIS

LAKE SUPERIOR

LAKE HURON

LAKE MICHIGAN

LAKE ERIE

LAKE ONTARIO

Georgian Bay

Green Bay

Chesapeake Bay

Montreal

Ottawa

Toronto

Hamilton

Buffalo

Rochester

Syracuse

Albany

Boston

New York

Newark

Elizabeth

Philadelphia

Baltimore

Washington D.C.

Pittsburgh

Cleveland

Columbus

Cincinnati

Detroit

Milwaukee

Chicago

Indianapolis

Richmond

Quebec

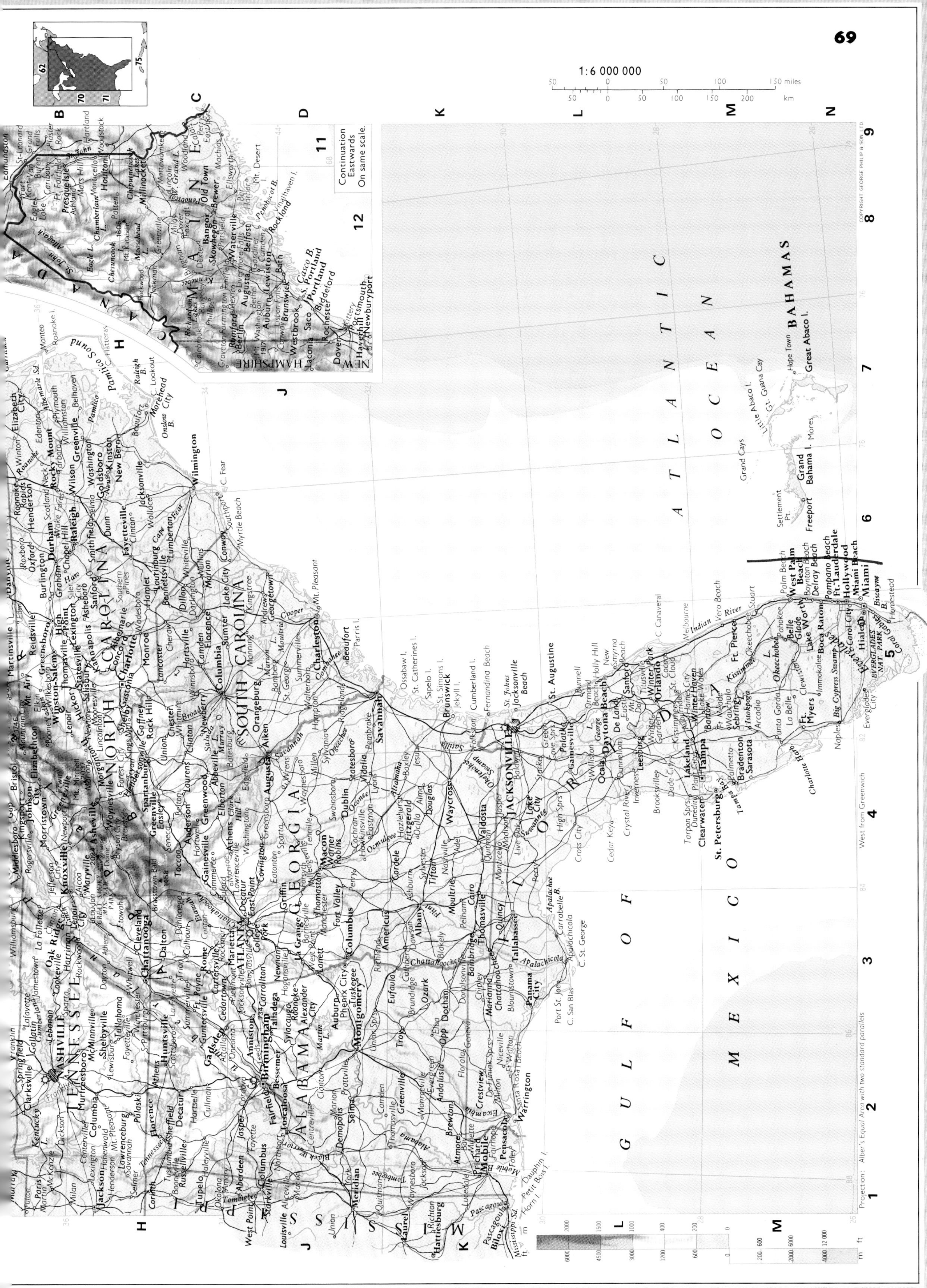

1:6 000 000

MAINE

NEW HAMPSHIRE

NORTH CAROLINA

SOUTH CAROLINA

GEORGIA

ALABAMA

TENNESSEE

MISSISSIPPI

FLORIDA

GULF OF MEXICO

ATLANTIC OCEAN

BAHAMAS

Great Abaco I.

Grand Bahama I.

ATLANTA

Miami

Jacksonville

Tampa

Nashville

Mobile

Birmingham

Columbia

Raleigh

Charlotte

Savannah

Tallahassee

Montgomery

West from Greenwich

Projection: Alber's Equal Area with two standard parallels

COPYRIGHT GEORGE PHILIP & SON LTD

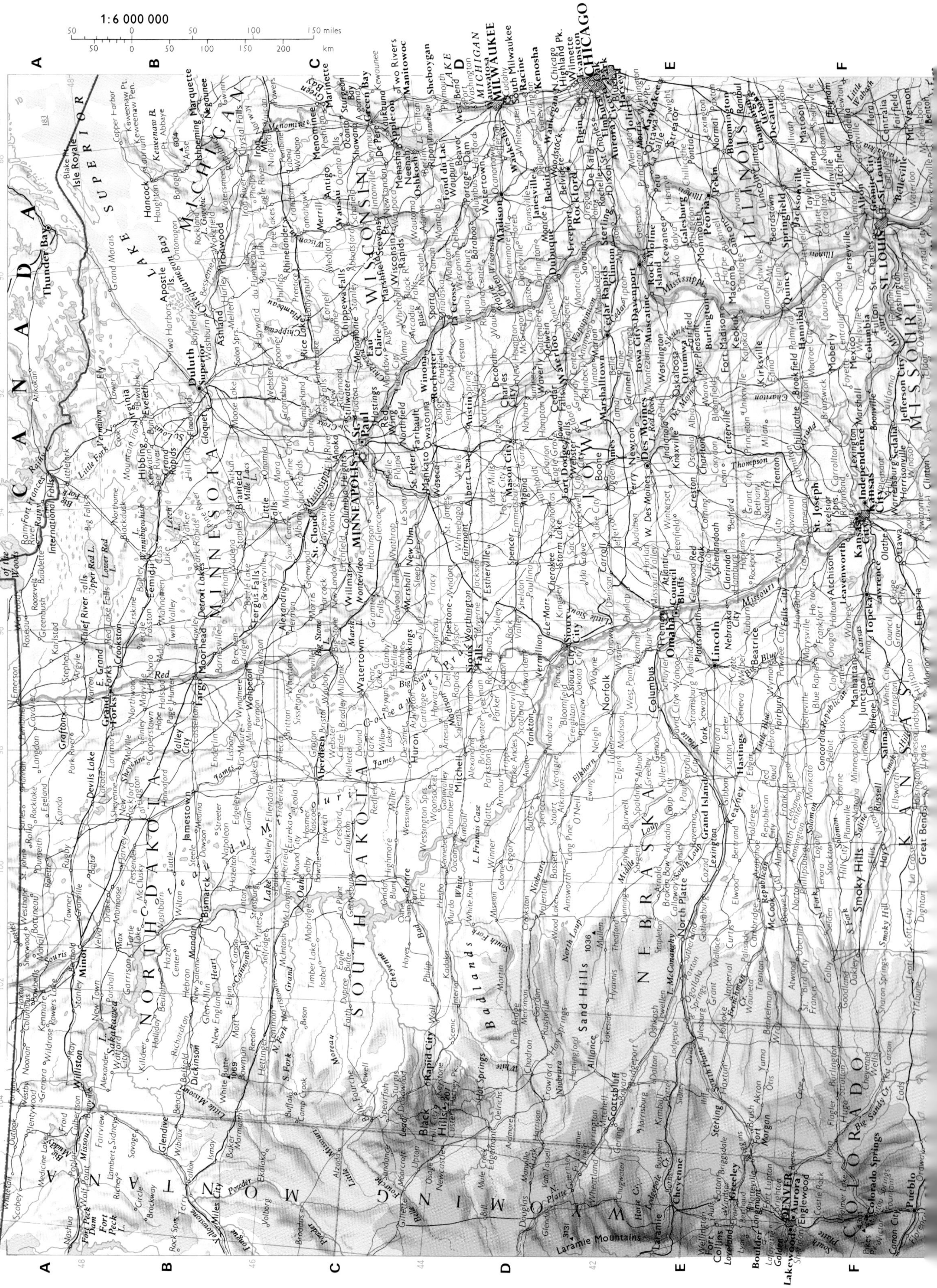

1:6 000 000

50 0 50 100 150 miles

50 0 50 100 150 200 km

CANADA

LAKE SUPERIOR

MICHIGAN

WISCONSIN

MINNESOTA

NORTH DAKOTA

SOUTH DAKOTA

NEBRASKA

KANSAS

IOWA

ILLINOIS

MISSOURI

WYOMING

COLORADO

MONTANA

LAKE MICHIGAN

CHICAGO

MILWAUKEE

Green Bay

Duluth

Minneapolis

St. Paul

Fargo

Grand Forks

Bismarck

Sioux Falls

Sioux City

Omaha

Lincoln

Des Moines

Cedar Rapids

Davenport

Rock Island

Kansas City

St. Joseph

Topeka

St. Louis

Springfield

Peoria

Rockford

Madison

Denver

Colorado Springs

Pueblo

Rapid City

Black Hills

Badlands

Sand Hills

Laramie Mountains

Lake of the Woods

Thunder Bay

Isle Royale

OKLAHOMA
ARKANSAS
MISSISSIPPI
LOUISIANA
TENNESSEE
TEXAS
NEW MEXICO
MEXICO
COAHUILA
CHIHUAHUA
GULF OF MEXICO
Llano Estacado
Edwards Plateau
Balcones Escarpment
Sangre de Cristo Mts.
Boston Mts.
Ouachita Mts.
Stockton Plateau
Rio Grande
Rio Bravo del Norte
DALLAS
HOUSTON
SAN ANTONIO
MEMPHIS
NEW ORLEANS
Oklahoma City
Little Rock
Jackson
Baton Rouge
Austin
Fort Worth
Shreveport
Tulsa
Wichita
Amarillo
Lubbock
Corpus Christi
Laredo
Brownsville
Continuation Southwards on same scale
Projection: Albers' Equal Area with two standard parallels
West from Greenwich
COPYRIGHT GEORGE PHILIP & SON, LTD.

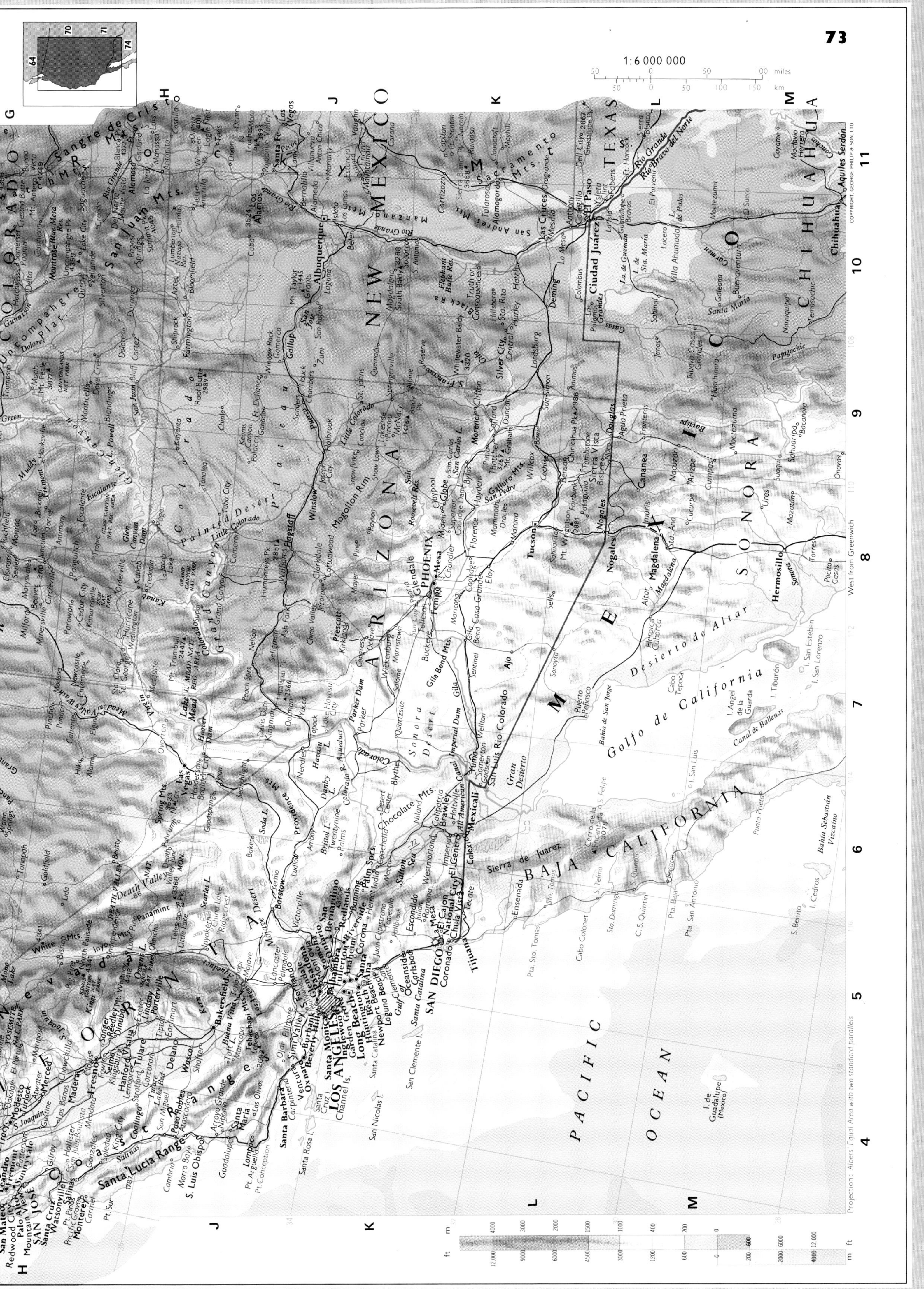

1:6 000 000

50 0 50 100 miles

50 0 50 100 150 km

COLORADO

NEW MEXICO

TEXAS

CHIHUAHUA

ARIZONA

SONORA

MEXICO

CALIFORNIA

BAJA CALIFORNIA

PACIFIC OCEAN

Golfo de California

Sangre de Cristo Mts.

San Juan Mts.

Colorado Plateau

Painted Desert

Mogollon Rim

Grand Canyon

Sonora Desert

Gran Desierto

Desierto de Altar

Sierra de Juarez

Santa Lucia Range

Death Valley

LOS ANGELES

PHOENIX

Tucson

SAN DIEGO

Albuquerque

Santa Fe

El Paso

Ciudad Juárez

Hermosillo

Las Vegas

Bakersfield

Fresno

SAN JOSE

Long Beach

Santa Barbara

Flagstaff

Mexicali

Tijuana

Chihuahua

Magdalena

Nogales

West from Greenwich

Projection: Albers' Equal Area with two standard parallels

COPYRIGHT GEORGE PHILIP & SON LTD

ft 12,000 9000 6000 4500 3000 1500 600 0

m 4000 3000 2000 1500 1000 600 200 0 200 2000 4000 12,000 ft

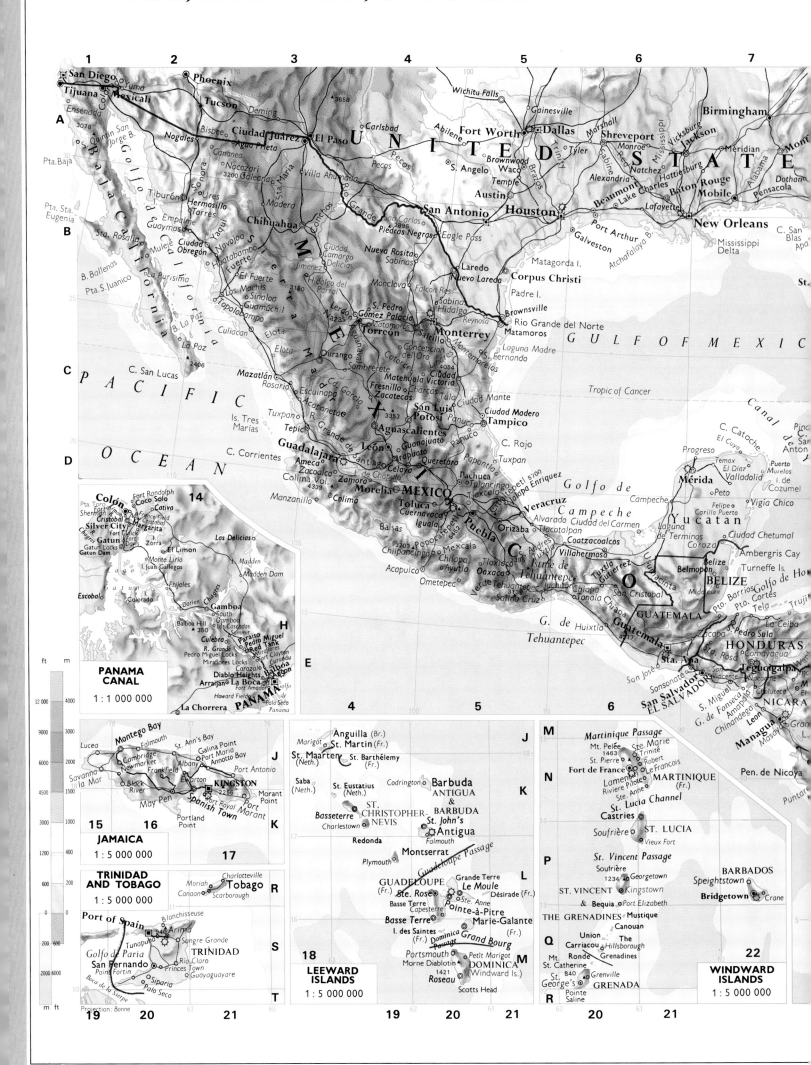

66 67
78 79

8 9 10 11 12 13

1:15 000 000

100   0   100   200   300   400 miles
100   0   100   200   300   400   500   600 km

A

Columbia
Atlanta
Augusta
Macon
lumbus
Savannah
Albany
Altamaha
llahassee
Jacksonville

C. Fear
Long Bay
C. Royal
Charleston

Bermuda
Hamilton

ATLANTIC OCEAN

B

Daytona Beach
Orlando
C. Canaveral
Tampa
rsburg
Lakeland
Sarasota
L. Okeechobee
West Palm Beach
Grand Bahama
Fort Lauderdale
Freeport
Gt. Abaco I.
New Providence I.
Miami
C. Sable
Eleuthera I.
Nassau
Cat I.
S. Salvador or Watlings I.
Tropic of Cancer

C

Key West
Florida Str.
Andros I.
BAHAMAS
Long I.

a Habana
(Havana)
rianao
Matanzas
Cárdenas
Colón
Sagua la Grande
Caibarién
STA. CLARA
Mayaguana
Acklins
Gt. Inagua I.
Caicos I. (Br.)
Turks Is.(Br.)

Río
G. de Guane
Batabanó
Batabanó
Cienfuegos
Trinidad
Sancti Spíritus
Júcaro
Ciego de Ávila
Morón
Camagüey
Nuevitas
Holguin
Antilla
Martí
Manzanillo
Campechuela
Guantánamo
Baracoa
Port de Paix
Cap Haitien
Monte Cristi
Valverde
Santiago
Pto. Plata
S. Francisco de Macoris
Sánchez

Grand Cayman
(Br.)
Santiago de Cuba
Bay
2000
Paso de los Vientos
Gonaïves
St. Marc
Jérémie
Leogane
La Vega
DOMINICAN REP.
La Roman
S. Pedro de Macoris

PUERTO RICO (U.S.A.)
Aguadilla
Arecibo
San Juan
1338
Caguas
Ponce
Mayagüez
Guayama

St. Thomas (U.S.A.)
Charlotte Amalie
Virgin Is. (Br.)
Sombrero (Br.)
Anguilla
St. Martin (Fr. & Neth.)
ST. CHRISTOPHER-
NEVIS
ANTIGUA & BARBUDA
St. John's
Basseterre
St. Croix (U.S.A.)
Christiansted
Charlestown
Plymouth Montserrat
Guadeloupe (Fr.)
Pointe à Pitre
Marie Galante (Fr.)

D

Montego Bay
Savanna la Mar
St. Ann's Bay
P. Antonio
JAMAICA
Kingston
Spanish Town
Les Cayes
Port au Prince
Jacmel
2680
Bani
Barahona
Azua
Hispaniola
Santo Domingo

GREATER
ANTILLES
LESSER
Leeward Islands
DOMINICA
Roseau

E

L. Caratasca
C. Gracias á Dios
Puerto Cabezas
CARIBBEAN SEA
Martinique (Fr.)
Fort de France
Castries
ST. LUCIA
BARBADOS
Kingstown
Bridgetown
ANTILLES
Windward
ST. VINCENT
&
THE GRENADINES Islands
GRENADA
St. George's
La Blanquilla (Ven.)
The Grenadines
Tobago
Port of Spain

Providencia (Col.)
San Andrés (Col.)
Bluefields
agua
Irazú
Pta. Gallinas
Pen. de la Guajira
Aruba (Neth.)
Curaçao (Neth.)
Willemstad
Bonaire (Neth.)
NETH. ANTILLES
Golfo de Venezuela
Maiquetía
Margarita
La Asunción
Carúpano
San Fernando
TRINIDAD & TOBAGO
Delta of the Orinoco

F

Santa Marta
Ríohacha
Barranquilla
5800
Sierra Nevada de Santa Marta
Soledad
Cartagena
Calamar
Plato
Mompós
El Banco
Ocaña
Corozal
Sincelejo
G. del Darién
Turbo
Atrato
Pto. Wilches
San Cristóbal
Cúcuta
Pamplona
Cord. de Mérida
2598
5007
Valera
Trujillo
L. de Maracaibo
Maracaibo
Cabimas
Dabajuro
Coro
Pto. Cabello
Maracay
Valencia
San Felipe
Barquisimeto
Calabozo
Portuguesa
Guanare
Apure
San Fernando de Apure
Caracas
Barcelona
Cariaco
El Tigre
Maturín
Tucupita
Los Mercedes
Caicara
Cumaná
La Tortuga (Ven.)
G. de Paria
Cúcuta
Ciudad Guayana
Ciudad Bolívar
El Callao
Tumeremo
Georgetown
New Amsterdam
Wismare

Rica
Vol. Chiriqui
3442
Limón
Colón
Panama
3374
3883
David
Chitré
Arch. de las Perlas
El Real
La Palma
Coiba
Pen. de Azuero
G. de Panama
G. de Cupica
Pta. Charambirá
Buenaventura

Quibdó
Medellín
Barrancabermeja
Berrío
El Dorado
Manizales
Pereira
Cartago
Buga
Palmira
Cali
Neiva
Popayán
2646
Armenia
Ibagué
1410
Tolima 5215
Girardot
Zipaquirá
Honda
Tunja
Bogotá
Pto. Páez
Meta
Pto. Carreño
2285
Pto. Ayacucho
COLOMBIA
VENEZUELA
Arauca
Arauca
Caura
Caroní
Parágua
2560
Roraima
2810
Sierra Pacaraima
Sa. Parima
1280
GUYANA
SURINAM

G

Guaviare
Casiquiare
BRAZIL

West from Greenwich

9 10 11 12

COPYRIGHT. GEORGE PHILIP & SON. LTD

1 : 35 000 000

200   0   200   400   600   800 miles
400   0   400   800   1200 km

North Atlantic Ocean

Tropic of Cancer

Yucatán Channel
Yucatán Peninsula
Gulf of Campeche
Isthmus of Tehuantepec
G. de Honduras
Guatemala Trench
Coco
C. Gracias a Dios
L. Nicaragua
Panama Canal
Gulf of Panamá
G. of Darién

Cuba
Greater Antilles
Jamaica
Turks & Caicos Is.
Hispaniola
9200
Puerto Rico
Lesser Antilles
Guadeloupe
Dominica
Martinique
St. Lucia
St. Vincent
Barbados
Grenada
Tobago
Trinidad

Caribbean Sea

NORTH ATLANTIC OCEAN

I. Margarita

C. de la Aguja
5800
Sierra Nevada de Santa Marta
L. Maracaibo
C. de Mérida
Cord. de Mérida
Orinoco
Meta
Llanos
Guaviare
Caquetá

Guiana Highlands
Mt. Roraima 2810
Sierra Pacaraima
Serra Tumucumaque
C. Orange
Branco
Negro

Cordillera Occidental
Cordillera Central
Cordillera Oriental
C. de San Francisco
Cotopaxi 5897
Chimborazo 6267

Galapagos Is.

G. of Guayaquil
Pta. Pariñas
Pta. Negra

Putumayo
Napo
Marañón
Japurá
Juruá
Purus
Ucayali

Selvas
Amazon
Amazon

Marajó I.
Equator

C. de São Roque

Madeira
Aripuanã
Roosevelt
Tapajós
Teles Pires
Xingu
Tocantins
Araguaia
Parnaíba
São Francisco

Plat. of Borborema

Huascarán 6768
Chincha Alta
L. Titicaca
Nevada Ancohuma 6650

Madre de Dios
Mamoré
Guaporé
Beni

Plateau of Mato Grosso

Brazilian Highlands

PACIFIC

OCEAN

Bolivian Plateau
L. de Poopó

Chile Peru Trench

Gran Chaco

Paraguay
Pilcomayo

Abrolhos Bank

Serra da Mantiqueira 2890
Pico da Bandeira
Serra do Mar
C. Frio

Tropic of Capricorn
San Félix
San Ambrosio

8050
Atacama Desert
Cerro Ojos del Salado 6863

Andes

Salinas Grandes

Salado

Paraná

Iguaçu Falls
Uruguay

Entre Ríos

Arch. de Juan Fernández

Mt. Aconcagua 6960

Sierra de Córdoba
L. Mar Chiquita

Pampas

Paraná

Rio de la Plata
L. dos Patos

SOUTH

ATLANTIC

OCEAN

Chile Rise
Chiloé I.

Colorado
Negro
Bahía Blanca
G. San Matías
Valdés Peninsula
40

Argentine Basin

Chonos Archipelago
Mte. San Valentin 4058
Taitao Peninsula
Gulf of Penas
Wellington I.
Madre de Dios I.

Chubut
Patagonia
Gulf of San Jorge

6212

Magellan's Str.
Santa Inés I.
Canal Cockburn
Canal Beagle
Tierra del Fuego
Staten I.
C. Horn

West Falkland
East Falkland
Falkland Is.

South Georgia

ft   m
12000 4000
9000   3000
6000   2000
3000   1000
1500   500
600   200
0   0
200   600
1000   3000
2000   6000
4000   12000
6000   18000
8000   24000
m   ft

Projection: Lambert's Azimuthal Equal Area

CARTOGRAPHY BY PHILIP'S.
COPYRIGHT REED INTERNATIONAL BOOKS LTD

West from Greenwich

1 : 35 000 000

200   0   200   400   600   800 miles
400   0   400   800   1200 km

1   **2**   **3**   **4**   **5**   **6**   **7**

Tropic of Cancer

A

Havana   BAHAMAS
C U B A
Turks & Caicos Is.
(U.K.)

N O R T H

B

MEXICO
BELIZE
GUATEMALA
Guatemala
HONDURAS
Tegucigalpa
San Salvador
EL SALVADOR
NICARAGUA
Managua
COSTA San José
RICA
Panamá
P A N A M A

HAITI
Port-au-Prince
JAMAICA Kingston
DOMINICAN REP.
San Juan
PUERTO RICO
(U.S.A.)
Virgin Is.
(U.K.)
ST. KITTS-NEVIS
ANTIGUA & BARBUDA
Basse-Terre GUADELOUPE (Fr.)
DOMINICA
Fort-de-France
Castries MARTINIQUE (Fr.)
ST. LUCIA
ST. VINCENT BARBADOS
Kingstown Bridgetown
GRENADA St. George's
TRINIDAD & TOBAGO

A T L A N T I C

Caribbean Sea

Aruba Curaçao
Port of Spain

O C E A N

Barranquilla
Cartagena
C. de la Aguja
G. of Darién
Cúcuta
Maracaibo
Barquisimeto
Valencia
Caracas
San Cristóbal
Medellín
Bucaramanga
VENEZUELA
Orinoco
Ciudad Guayana
Georgetown
GUYANA
Paramaribo
SURINAM
Cayenne
C. Orange
FRENCH GUIANA

C

Cali
Bogotá
COLOMBIA
RORAIMA
Branco
Essequibo

North Atlantic Ocean

Galapagos Is.
(Ecuador)
Quito
ECUADOR
Guayaquil
G. of Guayaquil
Napo
Putumayo
Japurá
Amazon
Manaus
Santarém
Marajó I.
Belém
Equator
AMAPÁ

D

Marañón
Iquitos
AMAZONAS
Juruá
Purus
Madeira
Tapajós
Xingu
PARÁ
Tocantins
MARANHÃO
Teresina
São Luís
Fortaleza
C. de São Roque
RIO G. DO NORTE
Natal
CEARÁ
PIAUÍ
Parnaíba
PERNAMBUCO
Campina Grande
Recife
PARAÍBA
Chiclayo
Trujillo
Chimbote
Ucayali
ACRE
Pôrto Velho
RONDÔNIA

E

P E R U
Callao LIMA
Cuzco
Madre de Dios
L. Titicaca
Arequipa
La Paz
BOLIVIA
Cochabamba
Santa Cruz
Sucre
Mamoré
Paraguay
B R A Z I L
MATO GROSSO
TOCANTINS
GOIÁS
Brasília
DIS. FED.
Goiânia
Cuiabá
BAHÍA
São Francisco
Salvador
Aracaju
SERGIPE
ALAGOAS
Maceió
MINAS GERAIS
Belo Horizonte
ESPÍRITO SANTO
Vitória

P A C I F I C

Iquique
MATO GROSSO DO SUL
Paraná
Ribeirão Prêto
SÃO PAULO
Campinas
Juiz de Fora
Niterói
R. DE J.
RIO DE JANEIRO
Campos

F

Antofagasta
Salta
PARAGUAY
Pilcomayo
Asunción
PARANÁ
SÃO PAULO
Curitiba
SANTA CATARINA
San Félix (Chile)
San Ambrosio (Chile)
San Miguel de Tucumán
Resistencia
Corrientes
Uruguay
RIO GRANDE DO SUL
Pôrto Alegre

O C E A N

Tropic of Capricorn

G

Arch. de Juan Fernández (Chile)
Córdoba
San Juan
Santa Fe
Paraná
Pelotas
URUGUAY
Viña del Mar
Valparaíso
SANTIAGO
Mendoza
Rosario
A R G E N T I N A
C H I L E
Talca
BUENOS AIRES
Montevideo
La Plata
Río de la Plata
Concepción
Bahía Blanca
Colorado
Mar del Plata
Valdivia
Negro
Viedma

S O U T H

A T L A N T I C

H

Puerto Montt
Chubut
Comodoro Rivadavia
Gulf of San Jorge
Gulf of Penas
Magellan's Str.
Punta Arenas
Tierra del Fuego
C. Horn
West Falkland FALKLAND IS. (U.K.)
Stanley
East Falkland
South Georgia (U.K.)

O C E A N

Projection: Lambert's Azimuthal Equal Area

1 LIMA Capital Cities **2**

West from Greenwich

CARTOGRAPHY BY PHILIP'S
COPYRIGHT REED INTERNATIONAL BOOKS LTD

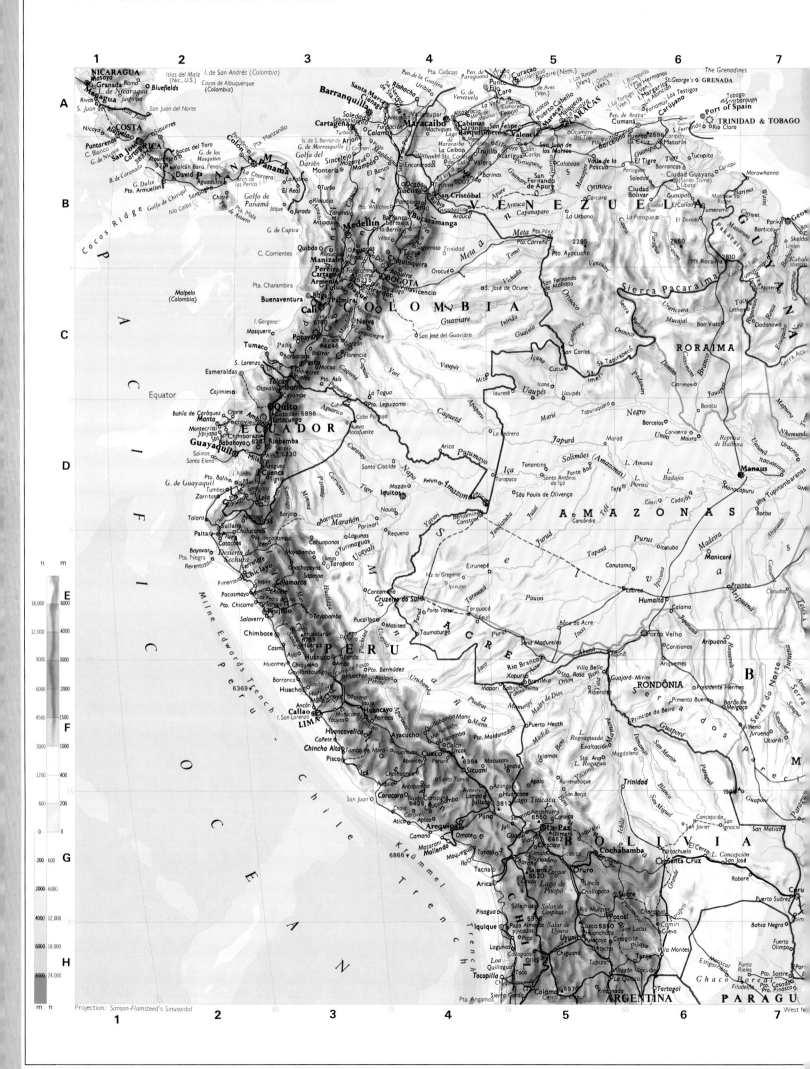

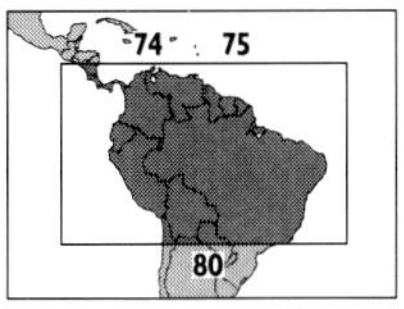

1:16 000 000

100 50 0   100   200   300 miles
100   0   100 200 300 400 km

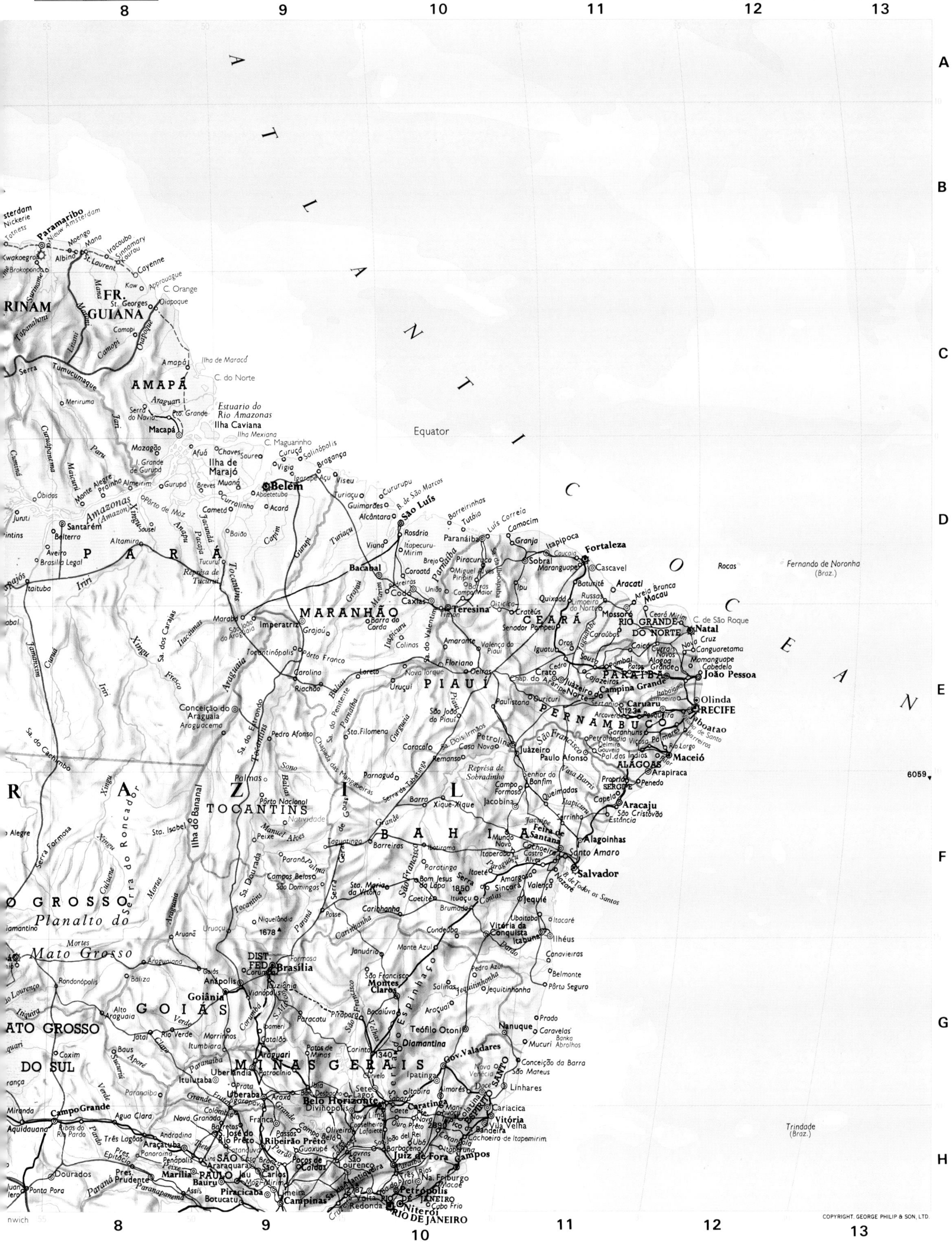

8   9   10   11   12   13

A

B

ATLANTIC

C

RINAM
FR. GUIANA
Paramaribo
Nieuw Amsterdam
Totness
Kwakoegron
Albina
St. Laurent
Cayenne
Brokopondo
Mana
Iracoubo
Sinnamary
Kourou
Approuague
C. Orange
St. Georges
Oiapoque
Kaw

AMAPÁ
Amapá
Ilha de Maracá
C. do Norte
Macapá
Estuário do Rio Amazonas
Ilha Caviana
Ilha Mexiana
C. Maguarinho

Equator

Mazagão
Afuá
Chaves
Soure
Curuçá
Salinópolis
Ilha de Marajó
Vigia
Bragança
I. Grande de Gurupá
Breves
Muaná
Igarapé-Açu
Viseu
Belém
Abaetetuba
Acará
Cametá
Curralinho
Turiaçu
Cururupu
Alcântara
São Luís
Barreirinhas
Tutóia
Luís Correia
Camocim
Granja
Isapipoca
Fortaleza

D

PARÁ
Santarém
Altamira
Tocantins
Marabá
Imperatriz
MARANHÃO
Bacabal
Codó
Caxias
Teresina
CEARÁ
Sobral
Maranguape
Cascavel
Baturité
Aracati
Russas
Mossoró
Macau
RIO GRANDE DO NORTE
Natal

BRAZIL
TOCANTINS
Palmas
Pôrto Nacional
Natividade
Paranã
Correntina
PIAUÍ
Floriano
Oeiras
Picos
Crateús
Senador Pompeu
Quixadá
Iguatu
Crato
Juàzeiro do Norte
PARAÍBA
Campina Grande
João Pessoa
Caruaru
PERNAMBUCO
Olinda
RECIFE

E

Conceição do Araguaia
Araguacema
Xingu
Sono
Petrolina
Juàzeiro
Paulo Afonso
ALAGOAS
Maceió
Arapiraca
Penedo
SERGIPE
Aracaju
São Cristóvão
Estância

6059

F

GOIÁS
Goiânia
Anápolis
DIST. FED.
Brasília
BAHIA
Barreiras
Xique-Xique
Jacobina
Feira de Santana
Alagoinhas
Santo Amaro
Salvador
B. de Todos os Santos
Valença
Jequié
Vitória da Conquista
Itabuna
Ilhéus

G

MATO GROSSO
Planalto do Mato Grosso
Montes Claros
Diamantina
Teófilo Otoni
Nanuque
Caravelas
Prado
Pôrto Seguro
Belmonte
Canavieiras

MATO GROSSO DO SUL
Campo Grande
Três Lagoas
Araçatuba
Marília
MINAS GERAIS
Araguari
Uberlândia
Uberaba
Araxá
Belo Horizonte
Divinópolis
Gov. Valadares
Ipatinga
ESPÍRITO SANTO
Linhares
Vitória
Vila Velha
Cariacica

H

Dourados
Presidente Prudente
SÃO PAULO
Bauru
Piracicaba
Campinas
Ribeirão Prêto
São José do Rio Prêto
Poços de Caldas
Juiz de Fora
Campos
Petrópolis
Nova Friburgo
RIO DE JANEIRO
Niterói
Volta Redonda
Cabo Frio

COPYRIGHT. GEORGE PHILIP & SON, LTD.

8   9   10   11   12   13

Fernando de Noronha (Braz.)

Rocas

Trindade (Braz.)

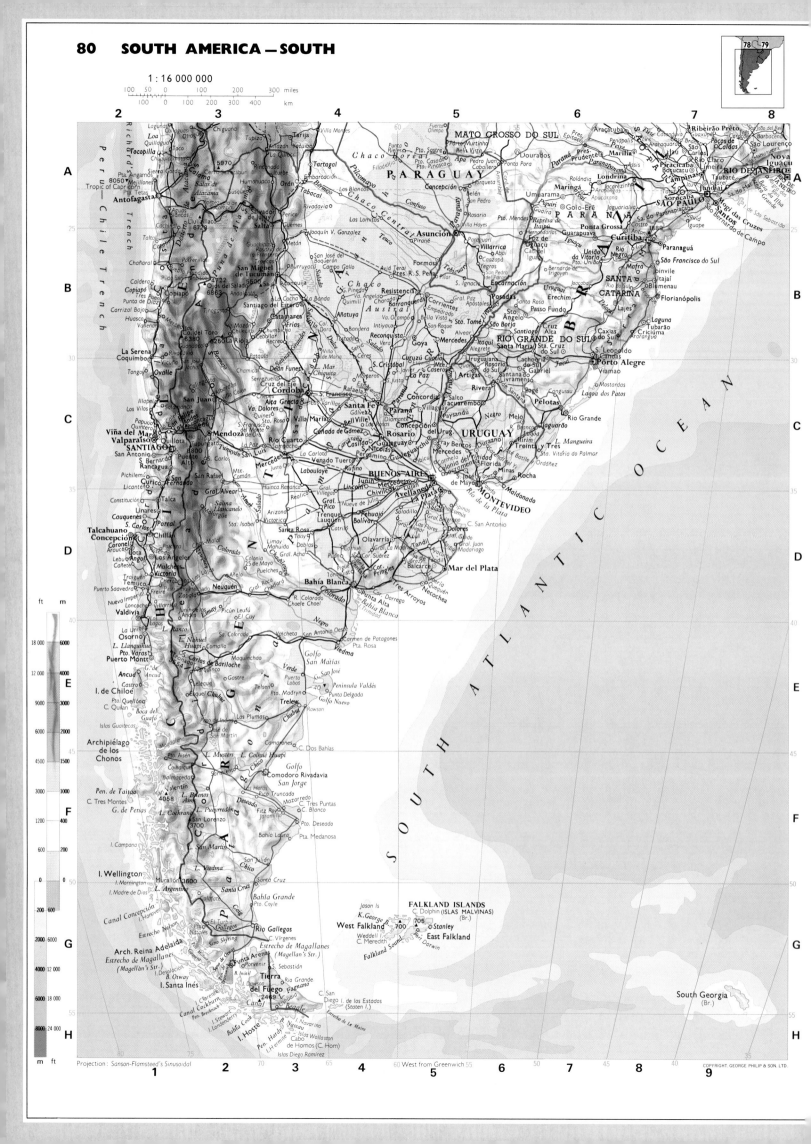

INDEX

The index contains the names of all the principal places and features shown on the World Maps. Each name is followed by an additional entry in italics giving the country or region within which it is located. The alphabetical order of names composed of two or more words is governed primarily by the first word and then by the second. This is an example of the rule:

Mīr Kūh, *Iran* **39 E8**
Mīr Shahdād, *Iran* **39 E8**
Miraj, *India* **36 L9**
Miram Shah, *Pakistan* . . **36 C7**
Miramar, *Mozam.* **49 C6**

Physical features composed of a proper name (Erie) and a description (Lake) are positioned alphabetically by the proper name. The description is positioned after the proper name and is usually abbreviated:

Erie, L., *N. Amer.* **68 D5**

Where a description forms part of a settlement or administrative name however, it is always written in full and put in its true alphabetic position:

Mount Morris, *U.S.A.* . . . **68 D7**

Names beginning with M' and Mc are indexed as if they were spelled Mac. Names beginning St. are alphabetised under Saint, but Sankt, Sint, Sant', Santa and San are all spelt in full and are alphabetised accordingly. If the same place name occurs two or more times in the index and all are in the same country, each is followed by the name of the administrative subdivision in which it is located. The names are placed in the alphabetical order of the subdivisions. For example:

Jackson, *Ky., U.S.A.* **68 G4**
Jackson, *Mich., U.S.A.* . . **68 D3**
Jackson, *Minn., U.S.A.* . . . **70 D7**

The number in bold type which follows each name in the index refers to the number of the map page where that feature or place will be found. This is usually the largest scale at which the place or feature appears. The letter and figure which are in bold type immediately after the page number give the grid square on the map page, within which the feature is situated. The letter represents the latitude and the figure the longitude.

In some cases the feature itself may fall within the specified square, while the name is outside. This is usually the case only with features which are larger than a grid square. Rivers are indexed to their mouths or confluences, and carry the symbol → after their names. A solid square ■ follows the name of a country while, an open square □ refers to a first order administrative area.

Abbreviations used in the index

A.C.T. — Australian Capital Territory
Afghan. — Afghanistan
Ala. — Alabama
Alta. — Alberta
Amer. — America(n)
Arch. — Archipelago
Ariz. — Arizona
Ark. — Arkansas
Atl. Oc. — Atlantic Ocean
B. — Baie, Bahia, Bay, Bucht, Bugt
B.C. — British Columbia
Bangla. — Bangladesh
Barr. — Barrage
C. — Cabo, Cap, Cape, Coast
C.A.R. — Central African Republic
C. Prov. — Cape Province
Calif. — California
Cent. — Central
Chan. — Channel
Colo. — Colorado
Conn. — Connecticut
Cord. — Cordillera
Cr. — Creek
Czech. — Czech Republic
D.C. — District of Columbia
Del. — Delaware
Dep. — Dependency
Des. — Desert
Dist. — District
Dj. — Djebel
Domin. — Dominica
Dom. Rep. — Dominican Republic
E. — East
El Salv. — El Salvador

Eq. Guin. — Equatorial Guinea
Fla. — Florida
Falk. Is. — Falkland Is.
G. — Golfe, Golfo, Gulf, Guba, Gebel
Ga. — Georgia
Gt. — Great, Greater
Guinea-Biss. — Guinea-Bissau
H.K. — Hong Kong
H.P. — Himachal Pradesh
Hants. — Hampshire
Harb. — Harbor, Harbour
Hd. — Head
Hts. — Heights
I.(s). — Île, Ilha, Insel, Isla, Island, Isle
Ill. — Illinois
Ind. — Indiana
Ind. Oc. — Indian Ocean
Ivory C. — Ivory Coast
J. — Jabal, Jebel, Jazira
Junc. — Junction
K. — Kap, Kapp
Kans. — Kansas
Kep. — Kepulauan
Ky. — Kentucky
L. — Lac, Lacul, Lago, Lagoa, Lake, Limni, Loch, Lough
La. — Louisiana
Liech. — Liechtenstein
Lux. — Luxembourg
Mad. P. — Madhya Pradesh
Madag. — Madagascar
Man. — Manitoba
Mass. — Massachusetts

Md. — Maryland
Me. — Maine
Medit. S. — Mediterranean Sea
Mich. — Michigan
Minn. — Minnesota
Miss. — Mississippi
Mo. — Missouri
Mont. — Montana
Mozam. — Mozambique
Mt.(e). — Mont, Monte, Monti, Montaña, Mountain
N. — Nord, Norte, North, Northern, Nouveau
N.B. — New Brunswick
N.C. — North Carolina
N. Cal. — New Caledonia
N. Dak. — North Dakota
N.H. — New Hampshire
N.I. — North Island
N.J. — New Jersey
N. Mex. — New Mexico
N.S. — Nova Scotia
N.S.W. — New South Wales
N.W.T. — North West Territory
N.Y. — New York
N.Z. — New Zealand
Nebr. — Nebraska
Neths. — Netherlands
Nev. — Nevada
Nfld. — Newfoundland
Nic. — Nicaragua
O. — Oued, Ouadi
Occ. — Occidentale
O.F.S. — Orange Free State
Okla. — Oklahoma

Ont. — Ontario
Or. — Orientale
Oreg. — Oregon
Os. — Ostrov
Oz. — Ozero
P. — Pass, Passo, Pasul, Pulau
P.E.I. — Prince Edward Island
Pa. — Pennsylvania
Pac. Oc. — Pacific Ocean
Papua N.G. — Papua New Guinea
Pass. — Passage
Pen. — Peninsula, Péninsule
Phil. — Philippines
Pk. — Park, Peak
Plat. — Plateau
P-ov. — Poluostrov
Prov. — Province, Provincial
Pt. — Point
Pta. — Ponta, Punta
Pte. — Pointe
Qué. — Québec
Queens. — Queensland
R. — Rio, River
R.I. — Rhode Island
Ra.(s). — Range(s)
Raj. — Rajasthan
Reg. — Region
Rep. — Republic
Res. — Reserve, Reservoir
S. — San, South, Sea
Si. Arabia — Saudi Arabia
S.C. — South Carolina
S. Dak. — South Dakota
S.I. — South Island
S. Leone — Sierra Leone

Sa. — Serra, Sierra
Sask. — Saskatchewan
Scot. — Scotland
Sd. — Sound
Sev. — Severnaya
Sib. — Siberia
Sprs. — Springs
St. — Saint, Sankt, Sint
Sta. — Santa, Station
Ste. — Sainte
Sto. — Santo
Str. — Strait, Stretto
Switz. — Switzerland
Tas. — Tasmania
Tenn. — Tennessee
Tex. — Texas
Tg. — Tanjung
Trin. & Tob. — Trinidad & Tobago
U.A.E. — United Arab Emirates
U.K. — United Kingdom
U.S.A. — United States of America
Ut. P. — Uttar Pradesh
Va. — Virginia
Vdkhr. — Vodokhranilishche
Vf. — Vîrful
Vic. — Victoria
Vol. — Volcano
Vt. — Vermont
W. — Wadi, West
W. Va. — West Virginia
Wash. — Washington
Wis. — Wisconsin
Wlkp. — Wielkopolski
Wyo. — Wyoming
Yorks. — Yorkshire

A Coruña

A

A Coruña = La Coruña,
 Spain 19 A1
Aachen, Germany 16 C4
Aalborg = Ålborg,
 Denmark 9 H13
Aalen, Germany 16 D6
Aalsmeer, Neths. 15 B4
Aalst, Belgium 15 D4
Aalten, Neths. 15 C6
Äänekoski, Finland . . . 9 E21
Aarau, Switz. 16 E5
Aare ➤, Switz. 16 E5
Aarhus = Århus,
 Denmark 9 H14
Aarschot, Belgium . . . 15 D4
Aba, Nigeria 44 G6
Åbådån, Iran 39 D6
Åbådeh, Iran 39 D7
Abadla, Algeria 44 B4
Abaetetuba, Brazil . . . 79 D9
Abakan, Russia 25 D10
Abancay, Peru 78 F4
Abariringa, Kiribati . . . 56 H10
Abarqŭ, Iran 39 D7
Abashiri, Japan 28 B12
Abashiri-Wan, Japan . . 28 B12
Abay, Kazakhstan . . . 24 E8
Abaya, L., Ethiopia . . . 45 G12
Abaza, Russia 24 D10
'Abbåsåbåd, Iran 39 C8
Abbay = Nîl el
 Azraq ➤, Sudan . . 45 E11
Abbaye, Pt., U.S.A. . . 68 B1
Abbeville, France 18 A4
Abbeville, La., U.S.A. . 71 K8
Abbeville, S.C., U.S.A. 69 H4
Abbieglassie, Australia 55 D4
Abbot Ice Shelf,
 Antarctica 5 D16
Abbotsford, Canada . . 64 D4
Abbotsford, U.S.A. . . . 70 C9
Abbottabad, Pakistan . 36 B8
Abd al Kŭrî, Ind. Oc. . . 40 E5
Åbdar, Iran 39 D7
'Abdolåbåd, Iran 39 C8
Abéché, Chad 45 F9
Åbenrå, Denmark . . . 9 J13
Abeokuta, Nigeria . . . 44 G5
Aberaeron, U.K. 11 E3
Aberayron =
 Aberaeron, U.K. . . . 11 E3
Abercorn = Mbala,
 Zambia 46 F6
Abercorn, Australia . . . 55 D5
Aberdare, U.K. 11 F4
Aberdeen, Australia . . 55 E5
Aberdeen, Canada . . . 65 C7
Aberdeen, S. Africa . . 48 E3
Aberdeen, U.K. 12 D6
Aberdeen, Ala., U.S.A. 69 J1
Aberdeen, Idaho,
 U.S.A. 72 E7
Aberdeen, S. Dak.,
 U.S.A. 70 C5
Aberdeen, Wash.,
 U.S.A. 72 C2
Aberdovey = Aberdyfi,
 U.K. 11 E3
Aberdyfi, U.K. 11 E3
Aberfeldy, U.K. 12 E5
Abergavenny, U.K. . . . 11 F4
Abernathy, U.S.A. . . . 71 J4
Abert, L., U.S.A. 72 E3
Aberystwyth, U.K. . . . 11 E3
Abhar, Iran 39 B6
Abidjan, Ivory C. 44 G4
Abilene, Kans., U.S.A. 70 F6
Abilene, Tex., U.S.A. . 71 J5
Abingdon, U.K. 11 F6
Abingdon, Ill., U.S.A. . 70 E9
Abingdon, Va., U.S.A. 69 G5
Abington Reef,
 Australia 54 B4
Abitau ➤, Canada . . . 65 B7
Abitau L., Canada . . . 65 A7
Abitibi L., Canada . . . 62 C4
Abkhaz Republic =
 Abkhazia □, Georgia 23 F7
Abkhazia □, Georgia . 23 F7
Abkit, Russia 25 C16
Abminga, Australia . . . 55 D1
Åbo = Turku, Finland . 9 F20
Abohar, India 36 D9
Aboméy, Benin 44 G5
Abong-Mbang,
 Cameroon 46 D2
Abou-Deïa, Chad 45 F8
Aboyne, U.K. 12 D6
Abri, Sudan 45 D11
Abrolhos, Banka, Brazil 79 G11
Abrud, Romania 17 E12
Absaroka Range, U.S.A. 72 D9
Abŭ al Khaṣîb, Iraq . . 39 D6
Abŭ 'Alî, Si. Arabia . . 39 E6
Abŭ 'Alî ➤, Lebanon . 41 A4
Abu 'Arîsh, Si. Arabia . 40 D3
Abu Dhabi = Abŭ Żåby,
 U.A.E. 39 E7
Abŭ Dîs, Sudan 45 E11
Abŭ Du'ån, Syria 38 B3
Abu el Gairi, W. ➤,
 Egypt 41 F2
Abu Ga'da, W. ➤,
 Egypt 41 F1
Abŭ Ḩadrîyah,
 Si. Arabia 39 E6
Abu Hamed, Sudan . . 45 E11
Abŭ Kamål, Syria . . . 38 C4
Abŭ Madd, Ra's,
 Si. Arabia 38 E3

Abu Matariq, Sudan . . 45 F10
Abu Ṣafåt, W. ➤,
 Jordan 41 E5
Abŭ Ṣukhayr, Iraq . . . 38 D5
Abu Tig, Egypt 45 C11
Abŭ Zabad, Sudan . . . 45 F10
Abŭ Żåby, U.A.E. 39 E7
Abŭ Zeydåbåd, Iran . . 39 C6
Abuja, Nigeria 44 G6
Abukuma-Gawa ➤,
 Japan 28 E10
Abukuma-Sammyaku,
 Japan 28 F10
Abunå, Brazil 78 E5
Abunå ➤, Brazil 78 E5
Abut Hd., N.Z. 51 K3
Abwong, Sudan 45 G11
Acaponeta, Mexico . . 74 C3
Acapulco, Mexico . . . 74 D5
Acarigua, Venezuela . 78 B5
Accomac, U.S.A. 68 G8
Accra, Ghana 44 G4
Accrington, U.K. 10 D5
Aceh □, Indonesia . . . 32 D1
Achalpur, India 36 J10
Achill, Ireland 13 C2
Achill Hd., Ireland . . . 13 C1
Achill I., Ireland 13 C1
Achill Sd., Ireland . . . 13 C2
Achinsk, Russia 25 D10
Acireale, Italy 20 F6
Ackerman, U.S.A. . . . 71 J10
Acklins I., Bahamas . . 75 C10
Acme, Canada 64 C6
Aconcagua, Cerro,
 Argentina 80 C3
Aconquija, Mt.,
 Argentina 80 B3
Açores, Is. dos =
 Azores, Atl. Oc. . . . 2 C8
Acraman, L., Australia 55 E2
Acre = 'Akko, Israel . 41 C4
Acre □, Brazil 78 E4
Acre ➤, Brazil 78 E5
Ad Dammåm,
 Si. Arabia 39 E6
Ad Dawhah, Qatar . . . 39 E6
Ad Dawr, Iraq 38 C4
Ad Dir'îyah, Si. Arabia 38 E5
Ad Dîwåniyah, Iraq . . 38 D5
Ad Dujayl, Iraq 38 C5
Ad Durŭz, J., Jordan . 41 C5
Ada, Minn., U.S.A. . . 70 B6
Ada, Okla., U.S.A. . . . 71 H6
Adaja ➤, Spain 19 B3
Adamaoua, Massif de
 l', Cameroon 45 G7
Adamawa Highlands =
 Adamaoua, Massif de
 l', Cameroon 45 G7
Adamello, Mte., Italy . 20 A4
Adaminaby, Australia . 55 F4
Adams, Wis., U.S.A. . 70 D10
Adam's Bridge,
 Sri Lanka 36 Q11
Adams, L., Canada . . 64 C5
Adams Mt., U.S.A. . . . 72 C3
Adam's Peak, Sri Lanka 36 R12
Adana, Turkey 23 G6
Adarama, Sudan 45 E11
Adare, C., Antarctica . 5 D11
Adaut, Indonesia 33 F8
Adavale, Australia . . . 55 D3
Adda ➤, Italy 20 B3
Addis Ababa = Addis
 Abeba, Ethiopia . . . 45 G12
Addis Abeba, Ethiopia 45 G12
Addis Alem, Ethiopia . 45 G12
Addo, S. Africa 48 E4
Ådeh, Iran 38 B5
Adel, U.S.A. 69 K4
Adelaide, Australia . . 55 E2
Adelaide, S. Africa . . 48 E4
Adelaide I., Antarctica 5 C17
Adelaide Pen., Canada 60 B10
Adelaide River,
 Australia 52 B5
Adele I., Australia . . . 52 C3
Adélie, Terre,
 Antarctica 5 C10
Adélie Land = Adélie,
 Terre, Antarctica . . 5 C10
Aden = Al 'Adan,
 Yemen 40 E4
Aden, G. of, Asia 40 E4
Adendorp, S. Africa . . 48 E3
Adh Dhayd, U.A.E. . . . 39 E7
Adi, Indonesia 33 E8
Adi Ugri, Eritrea 45 F12
Adieu, C., Australia . . 53 F5
Adieu Pt., Australia . . 52 C3
Adige ➤, Italy 20 B5
Adilabad, India 36 K11
Adin, U.S.A. 72 F3
Adin Khel, Afghan. . . . 36 C6
Adirondack Mts., U.S.A. 68 D8
Adlavik Is., Canada . . 63 B8
Admer, Algeria 44 D6
Admiralty G., Australia 52 B4
Admiralty I., U.S.A. . . 60 C6
Admiralty Inlet, U.S.A. 72 C2
Admiralty Is.,
 Papua N. G. 56 H6
Ado-Ekiti, Nigeria . . . 44 G6
Adonara, Indonesia . . 33 F6
Adoni, India 36 M10
Adour ➤, France 18 E3
Adra, Spain 19 D4
Adrano, Italy 20 F6
Adrar, Algeria 44 C4
Adré, Chad 45 F9

Adri, Libya 45 C7
Adrian, Mich., U.S.A. . 68 E3
Adrian, Tex., U.S.A. . . 71 H3
Adriatic Sea, Medit. S. 20 C6
Adua, Indonesia 33 E7
Adwa, Ethiopia 45 F12
Adzhar Republic =
 Ajaria □, Georgia . . 23 F7
Ægean Sea, Medit. S. 21 E11
Æolian Is. = Eólie, Ís.,
 Italy 20 E6
Aerhtai Shan, Mongolia 30 B4
'Afak, Iraq 38 C5
Afars & Issas, Terr. of
 = Djibouti ■, Africa . 40 E3
Afghanistan ■, Asia . . 36 C4
Afgoi, Somali Rep. . . . 40 G3
Afognak I., U.S.A. . . . 60 C4
'Afrîn, Syria 38 B3
Afuá, Brazil 79 D8
Afula, Israel 41 C4
Afyonkarahisar, Turkey 23 G5
Agadès = Agadez,
 Niger 44 E6
Agadez, Niger 44 E6
Agadir, Morocco 44 B3
Agapa, Russia 25 B9
Agartala, India 37 H17
Agassiz, Canada 64 D4
Agats, Indonesia 33 F9
Agboville, Ivory C. . . . 44 G4
Agde, France 18 E5
Agen, France 18 D4
Ågh Kand, Iran 39 B6
Aginskoye, Russia . . . 25 D12
Agra, India 36 F10
Agri ➤, Italy 20 D7
Ağri Dağl, Turkey 23 G7
Ağri Karakose, Turkey 23 G7
Agrigento, Italy 20 F5
Agrinion, Greece 21 E9
Agua Clara, Brazil . . . 79 H8
Agua Prieta, Mexico . . 74 A3
Aguadas, Colombia . . 78 B3
Aguadilla, Puerto Rico 75 D11
Aguanish ➤, Canada . 63 B7
Aguanus ➤, Canada . 63 B7
Aguarico ➤, Ecuador . 78 D3
Aguas Blancas, Chile . 80 A3
Aguascalientes, Mexico 74 C4
Aguilas, Spain 19 D5
Agulhas, C., S. Africa . 48 E3
Agung, Indonesia 32 F5
Agusan ➤, Phil. 33 C7
Aha Mts., Botswana . . 48 B3
Ahaggar, Algeria 44 D6
Ahar, Iran 38 B5
Ahipara B., N.Z. 51 F4
Ahiri, India 36 K12
Ahmadåbåd, Khorâsân,
 Iran 39 C9
Ahmadåbåd, Khorâsân,
 Iran 39 C8
Aḩmadî, Iran 39 E8
Ahmadnagar, India . . 36 K9
Ahmadpur, Pakistan . 36 E7
Ahmedabad =
 Ahmadåbåd, India . . 36 H8
Ahmednagar =
 Ahmadnagar, India . 36 K9
Ahome, Mexico 74 B3
Åhŭ, Iran 39 C6
Ahvåz, Iran 39 D6
Ahvenanmaa = Åland,
 Finland 9 F19
Aḩwar, Yemen 40 E4
Aichi □, Japan 29 G8
Aigues-Mortes, France 18 E6
Aihui, China 31 A7
Aija, Peru 78 E3
Aikawa, Japan 28 E9
Aiken, U.S.A. 69 J5
Aillik, Canada 63 A8
Ailsa Craig, U.K. 12 F3
'Ailŭn, Jordan 41 C4
Aim, Russia 25 D14
Aimere, Indonesia . . . 33 F6
Aimorés, Brazil 79 G10
Aïn Beïda, Algeria . . . 44 A6
Aïn Ben Tili, Mauritania 44 C3
Aïn-Sefra, Algeria . . . 44 B4
'Ain Sudr, Egypt 41 F2
Ainabo, Somali Rep. . 40 F4
Ainaži, Latvia 9 H21
Ainsworth, U.S.A. . . . 70 D5
Aïr, Niger 44 E6
Airdrie, U.K. 12 F5
Aire ➤, U.K. 10 D7
Airlie Beach, Australia 54 C4
Aisne ➤, France 18 B5
Aitkin, U.S.A. 70 B8
Aiud, Romania 17 E12
Aix-en-Provence,
 France 18 E6
Aix-la-Chapelle =
 Aachen, Germany . . 16 C4
Aix-les-Bains, France . 18 D6
Aiyansh, Canada 64 B3
Aiyion, Greece 21 E10
Aizawl, India 37 H18
Aizkraukle, Latvia . . . 9 H21
Aizpute, Latvia 9 H19
Aizuwakamatsu, Japan 28 F9
Ajaccio, France 18 F8
Ajanta Ra., India 36 J9
Ajari Rep. = Ajaria □,
 Georgia 23 F7
Ajaria □, Georgia 23 F7
Ajdåbiyah, Libya 45 B9
Ajka, Hungary 17 E9
'Ajmån, U.A.E. 39 E7
Ajmer, India 36 F9

Ajo, U.S.A. 73 K7
Ajo, C. de, Spain 19 A4
Akabira, Japan 28 C11
Akaroa, N.Z. 51 K4
Akashi, Japan 29 G7
Akelamo, Indonesia . . 33 D7
Aketi, Zaïre 46 D4
Akharnaí, Greece 21 E10
Akhelóös ➤, Greece . . 21 E9
Akhisar, Turkey 21 E12
Akhmîm, Egypt 45 C11
Aki, Japan 29 H6
Akimiski I., Canada . . 62 B3
Akita, Japan 28 E10
Akita □, Japan 28 E10
Akjoujt, Mauritania . . 44 E2
'Akko, Israel 41 C4
Akkol, Kazakhstan . . . 24 E8
Aklavik, Canada 60 B6
Akmolinsk = Aqmola,
 Kazakhstan 24 D8
Akô, Japan 29 G7
Akobo ➤, Ethiopia . . . 45 G11
Akola, India 36 J10
Akordat, Eritrea 45 E12
Akpatok I., Canada . . 61 B13
Åkrahamn, Norway . . 9 G11
Akranes, Iceland 8 D2
Akreïjit, Mauritania . . 44 E3
Akron, Colo., U.S.A. . 70 E3
Akron, Ohio, U.S.A. . . 68 E5
Aksai Chin, India 36 B11
Aksarka, Russia 24 C7
Aksay, Kazakhstan . . 22 D9
Aksenovo Zilovskoye,
 Russia 25 D12
Aksu, China 30 B3
Aksum, Ethiopia 45 F12
Aktogay, Kazakhstan . 24 E8
Aktsyabrski, Belarus . 17 B15
Aktyubinsk = Aqtöbe,
 Kazakhstan 23 D10
Aku, Nigeria 44 G6
Akure, Nigeria 44 G6
Akureyri, Iceland 8 D4
Akuseki-Shima, Japan 29 K4
Akyab = Sittwe, Burma 37 J18
Al 'Adan, Yemen 40 E4
Al Aḩså, Si. Arabia . . 39 E6
Al Ajfar, Si. Arabia . . 38 E4
Al Amådîyah, Iraq . . . 38 B4
Al Amårah, Iraq 38 D5
Al 'Aqabah, Jordan . . 41 F4
Al Arak, Syria 38 C3
Al 'Aramah, Si. Arabia 38 E5
Al Arṭåwîyah, Si. Arabia 38 E5
Al 'Åsimah □, Jordan . 41 D5
Al 'Azamîyah, Iraq . . . 38 C5
Al 'Azîzîyah, Iraq 38 C5
Al Båb, Syria 38 B3
Al Bad', Si. Arabia . . 38 D2
Al Bådî, Iraq 38 C4
Al Baḩrah, Kuwait . . . 38 D5
Al Balqå □, Jordan . . 41 C4
Al Bårŭk, J., Lebanon 41 B4
Al Başrah, Iraq 38 D5
Al Baṭḩå, Iraq 38 D5
Al Batrŭn, Lebanon . . 41 A4
Al Baydå, Libya 45 B9
Al Biqå □, Lebanon . . 41 A5
Al Bi'r, Si. Arabia . . . 38 D3
Al Burayj, Syria 41 A5
Al Fallŭjah, Iraq 38 C4
Al Fåw, Iraq 39 D6
Al Fujayrah, U.A.E. . . 39 E8
Al Ghadaf, W. ➤,
 Jordan 41 D4
Al Ghammås, Iraq . . . 38 D5
Al Ḩåbah, Si. Arabia . 38 E5
Al Ḩadîthah, Iraq . . . 38 C4
Al Ḩadîthah, Si. Arabia 38 D3
Al Ḩåjånah, Syria . . . 41 B5
Al Ḩåmad, Si. Arabia . 38 D3
Al Ḩamdånîyah, Syria 38 C3
Al Ḩamîdîyah, Syria . 41 A4
Al Ḩammår, Iraq 38 D5
Al Ḩarîr, W. ➤, Syria . 41 C4
Al Ḩaså, W. ➤,
 Jordan 41 D4
Al Ḩasakah, Syria . . . 38 B4
Al Ḩawrah, Yemen . . 40 E4
Al Ḩaydån, W. ➤,
 Jordan 41 D4
Al Ḩayy, Iraq 38 C5
Al Ḩijåz, Si. Arabia . . 40 B2
Al Ḩillah, Iraq 38 C5
Al Ḩillah, Si. Arabia . 40 C4
Al Ḩirmil, Lebanon . . 41 A5
Al Hoceïma, Morocco 44 A4
Al Ḩudaydah, Yemen . 40 E3
Al Ḩufŭf, Si. Arabia . . 39 E6
Al Ḩumaydah,
 Si. Arabia 38 D2
Al Ḩunayy, Si. Arabia . 39 E6
Al Ittiḩåd = Madînat
 ash Sha'b, Yemen . 40 E3
Al Jafr, Jordan 41 E5
Al Jaghbŭb, Libya . . . 45 C9
Al Jahrah, Kuwait . . . 38 D5
Al Jalåmîd, Si. Arabia 38 D3
Al Jamalîyah, Qatar . 39 E6
Al Janŭb □, Lebanon . 41 B4
Al Jawf, Libya 45 D9
Al Jawf, Si. Arabia . . 38 D3
Al Jazirah, Iraq 38 C5

Al Jazirah, Libya 45 C9
Al Jithåmîyah,
 Si. Arabia 38 E4
Al Jubayl, Si. Arabia . 39 E6
Al Jubaylah, Si. Arabia 38 E5
Al Jubb, Si. Arabia . . 38 E4
Al Junaynah, Sudan . . 45 F9
Al Kabå'ish, Iraq 38 D5
Al Karak, Jordan 41 D4
Al Karak □, Jordan . . 41 E5
Al Kåzim Tyah, Iraq . . 38 C5
Al Khalîl, West Bank . 41 D4
Al Khawr, Qatar 39 E6
Al Khidr, Iraq 38 D5
Al Khiyåm, Lebanon . 41 B4
Al Kiswah, Syria 41 B5
Al Kufrah, Libya 45 D9
Al Kŭt, Iraq 38 C5
Al Kuwayt, Kuwait . . . 38 D5
Al Labwah, Lebanon . 41 A5
Al Lådhiqîyah, Syria . 38 C2
Al Liwå', Oman 39 E8
Al Luḩayyah, Yemen . 40 D3
Al Madînah, Iraq 38 D5
Al Madînah, Si. Arabia 40 C2
Al-Mafraq, Jordan . . . 41 C5
Al Maḩmŭdîyah, Iraq . 38 C5
Al Majma'ah, Si. Arabia 38 E5
Al Makhruq, W. ➤,
 Jordan 41 D6
Al Makhŭl, Si. Arabia . 38 E4
Al Manåmah, Bahrain 39 E6
Al Maqwa', Kuwait . . 38 D5
Al Marj, Libya 45 B9
Al Maṭlå, Kuwait 38 D5
Al Mawjib, W. ➤,
 Jordan 41 D4
Al Mawṣil, Iraq 38 B4
Al Mayådin, Syria . . . 38 C4
Al Mazår, Jordan 41 D4
Al Midhnab, Si. Arabia 38 E5
Al Minå', Lebanon . . . 41 A4
Al Miqdådîyah, Iraq . . 38 C5
Al Mubarraz, Si. Arabia 39 E6
Al Mughayrå', U.A.E. . 39 E7
Al Muḩarraq, Bahrain 39 E6
Al Mukallå, Yemen . . 40 E4
Al Mukhå, Yemen . . . 40 E3
Al Musayjid, Si. Arabia 38 E3
Al Musayyib, Iraq . . . 38 C5
Al Muwaylih, Si. Arabia 38 E2
Al Qå'im, Iraq 38 C4
Al Qalîbah, Si. Arabia 38 D3
Al Qaryatayn, Syria . . 41 A6
Al Qaṭ'å, Syria 38 C4
Al Qaṭîf, Si. Arabia . . 39 E6
Al Qaṭrånah, Jordan . 41 D5
Al Qaṭrŭn, Libya 45 D8
Al Qayṣŭmah,
 Si. Arabia 38 D5
Al Quds = Jerusalem,
 Israel 41 D4
Al Qunaytirah, Syria . 41 C4
Al Qurnah, Iraq 38 D5
Al Quṣayr, Iraq 38 D5
Al Quṣayr, Syria 41 A5
Al Qutayfah, Syria . . . 41 B5
Al 'Udayliyah,
 Si. Arabia 39 E6
Al 'Ulå, Si. Arabia . . . 38 E3
Al Uqaylah ash
 Sharqigah, Libya . . 45 B8
Al Uqayr, Si. Arabia . 39 E6
Al 'Uwaynid, Si. Arabia 38 E5
Al 'Uwayqilah,
 Si. Arabia 38 D4
Al 'Uyŭn, Si. Arabia . 38 E4
Al 'Uyŭn, Si. Arabia . 38 E3
Al Wajh, Si. Arabia . . 38 E3
Al Wakrah, Qatar . . . 39 E6
Al Wannån, Si. Arabia 38 E6
Al Waqbah, Si. Arabia 38 D5
Al Wari'åh, Si. Arabia 38 E5
Al Wusayl, Qatar 39 E6
Ala Tau Shankou =
 Dzhungarskiye
 Vorota, Kazakhstan . 30 B3
Alabama □, U.S.A. . . 69 J2
Alabama ➤, U.S.A. . . 69 K2
Alaçam Dağlari, Turkey 21 E13
Alagoa Grande, Brazil 79 E11
Alagoas □, Brazil . . . 79 E11
Alagoinhas, Brazil . . . 79 F11
Alajuela, Costa Rica . 75 E8
Alakamisy, Madag. . . 49 C8
Alakurtti, Russia 22 A5
Alameda, U.S.A. 73 H4
Alamo, U.S.A. 73 H6
Alamogordo, U.S.A. . 73 K11
Alamosa, U.S.A. 73 H11
Åland, Finland 9 F19
Ålands hav, Sweden . 9 F19
Alandur, India 36 N12
Alania = North
 Ossetia □, Russia . 23 F7
Alanya, Turkey 23 G5
Alaotra, Farihin',
 Madag. 49 B8
Alapayevsk, Russia . . 24 D7
Alaşehir, Turkey 21 E13
Alaska □, U.S.A. 60 B5
Alaska, G. of, Pac. Oc. 60 C5
Alaska Highway,
 Canada 64 B3
Alaska Peninsula,
 U.S.A. 60 C4
Alaska Range, U.S.A. 60 B4
Älät, Azerbaijan 23 G8
Alatyr, Russia 22 D8
Alausi, Ecuador 78 D3

Alava, C., U.S.A. 72 B1
Alavus, Finland 9 E20
Alawoona, Australia . . 55 E3
'Alayh, Lebanon 41 B4
Alba, Italy 20 B3
Alba-Iulia, Romania . . 17 E12
Albacete, Spain 19 C5
Albacutya, L., Australia 55 F3
Albania ■, Europe . . . 21 D9
Albany, Australia 53 G2
Albany, Ga., U.S.A. . . 69 K3
Albany, Minn., U.S.A. 70 C7
Albany, N.Y., U.S.A. . 68 D9
Albany, Oreg., U.S.A. 72 D2
Albany, Tex., U.S.A. . 71 J5
Albany ➤, Canada . . . 62 B3
Albardón, Argentina . 80 C3
Albatross B., Australia 54 A3
Albemarle, U.S.A. . . . 69 H5
Albemarle Sd., U.S.A. 69 H7
Alberche ➤, Spain . . 19 C3
Albert, L., Australia . . 55 F2
Albert Canyon, Canada 64 C5
Albert Edward Ra.,
 Australia 52 C4
Albert L., Africa 46 D6
Albert Lea, U.S.A. . . . 70 D8
Albert Nile ➤,
 Uganda 46 D6
Alberta □, Canada . . . 64 C6
Albertinia, S. Africa . . 48 E3
Alberton, Canada . . . 63 C7
Albertville = Kalemie,
 Zaïre 46 F5
Albertville, France . . . 18 D7
Albi, France 18 E5
Albia, U.S.A. 70 E8
Albina, Surinam 79 B8
Albina, Ponta, Angola 48 B1
Albion, Idaho, U.S.A. . 72 E7
Albion, Mich., U.S.A. . 68 D3
Albion, Nebr., U.S.A. . 70 E5
Alborán, Medit. S. . . . 19 E4
Ålborg, Denmark 9 H13
Alborz, Reshteh-ye
 Kŭhha-ye, Iran 39 C7
Albreda, Canada 64 C5
Albuquerque, U.S.A. . 73 J10
Albury, Australia 55 F4
Alcalá de Henares,
 Spain 19 B4
Alcalá la Real, Spain . 19 D4
Alcamo, Italy 20 F5
Alcañiz, Spain 19 B5
Alcântara, Brazil 79 D10
Alcántara, Embalse de,
 Spain 19 C2
Alcantara L., Canada . 65 A7
Alcantarilla, Spain . . . 19 D5
Alcaraz, Sierra de,
 Spain 19 C4
Alcaudete, Spain 19 D3
Alcázar de San Juan,
 Spain 19 C4
Alchevsk, Ukraine . . . 23 E6
Alcira, Spain 19 C5
Alcoa, U.S.A. 69 H4
Alcova, U.S.A. 72 E10
Alcoy, Spain 19 C5
Aldabra Is., Seychelles 43 G8
Aldan, Russia 25 D13
Aldan ➤, Russia 25 C13
Aldeburgh, U.K. 11 E9
Alder, U.S.A. 72 D7
Alderney, U.K. 11 H5
Aldershot, U.K. 11 F7
Aledo, U.S.A. 70 E9
Aleg, Mauritania 44 E2
Alegrete, Brazil 80 B5
Aleisk, Russia 24 D9
Aleksandriya =
 Oleksandriya, Ukraine 17 C14
Aleksandrovsk-
 Sakhalinskiy, Russia 25 D15
Aleksandrovskiy Zavod,
 Russia 25 D12
Aleksandrovskoye,
 Russia 24 C8
Alemania, Argentina . 80 B3
Alençon, France 18 B4
Alenuihaha Channel,
 U.S.A. 66 H17
Aleppo = Ḩalab, Syria 38 B3
Alert Bay, Canada . . . 64 C3
Alès, France 18 D6
Alessándria, Italy . . . 20 B3
Ålesund, Norway 9 E12
Aleutian Is., Pac. Oc. . 60 C2
Aleutian Trench,
 Pac. Oc. 56 B10
Alexander, U.S.A. . . . 70 B3
Alexander, Mt.,
 Australia 53 E3
Alexander Arch., U.S.A. 64 B2
Alexander Bay,
 S. Africa 48 D2
Alexander City, U.S.A. 69 J3
Alexander I., Antarctica 5 C17
Alexandra, Australia . 55 F4
Alexandra, N.Z. 51 L2
Alexandra Falls,
 Canada 64 A5
Alexandretta =
 Iskenderun, Turkey . 23 G6
Alexandria = El
 Iskandarîya, Egypt . 45 B10
Alexandria, B.C.,
 Canada 64 C4
Alexandria, Ont.,
 Canada 62 C5
Alexandria, Romania . 17 G13
Alexandria, S. Africa . 48 E4

Alexandria, *Ind., U.S.A.* 68 E3
Alexandria, *La., U.S.A.* 71 K8
Alexandria, *Minn.,*
U.S.A. 70 C7
Alexandria, *S. Dak.,*
U.S.A. 70 D6
Alexandria, *Va., U.S.A.* 68 F7
Alexandria Bay, *U.S.A.* 68 C8
Alexandrina, L.,
Australia 55 F2
Alexandroúpolis,
Greece 21 D11
Alexis ➔, *Canada* . . 63 B8
Alexis Creek, *Canada* . 64 C4
Alford, *U.K.* 12 D6
Alfreton, *U.K.* 10 D6
Alga, *Kazakhstan* . . . 23 E10
Algård, *Norway* 9 G11
Algarve, *Portugal* . . . 19 D1
Algeciras, *Spain* . . . 19 D3
Algemesí, *Spain* . . . 19 C5
Alger, *Algeria* 44 A5
Algeria ■, *Africa* . . . 44 C5
Alghero, *Italy* 20 D3
Algiers = Alger, *Algeria* 44 A5
Algoa B., *S. Africa* . . 48 E4
Algoma, *U.S.A.* 68 C2
Algona, *U.S.A.* 70 D7
Alhambra, *U.S.A.* . . . 73 J4
Alhucemas = Al
Hoceima, *Morocco* . 44 A4
'Alī al Gharbī, *Iraq* . . 38 C5
'Alī ash Sharqī, *Iraq* . 38 C5
'Alī Khēl, *Afghan.* . . 36 C6
'Alī Shāh, *Iran* 38 B5
'Alīābād, *Khorāsān, Iran* 39 C8
'Alīābād, *Kordestān,*
Iran 38 C5
'Alīābād, *Yazd, Iran* . 39 D7
Aliağa, *Turkey* 21 E12
Aliákmon ➔, *Greece* 21 D10
Alibo, *Ethiopia* 45 G12
Alicante, *Spain* 19 C5
Alice, *S. Africa* 48 E4
Alice, *U.S.A.* 71 M5
Alice ➔, *Queens.,*
Australia 54 C3
Alice ➔, *Queens.,*
Australia 54 B3
Alice Arm, *Canada* . . 64 B3
Alice Downs, *Australia* 52 C4
Alice Springs, *Australia* 54 C1
Alicedale, *S. Africa* . . 48 E4
Aliceville, *U.S.A.* . . . 69 J1
Alick Cr. ➔, *Australia* 54 C3
Alida, *Canada* 65 D8
Aligarh, *India* 36 F11
Alīgūdarz, *Iran* 39 C6
Alingsås, *Sweden* . . . 9 H15
Alipur, *Pakistan* . . . 36 E7
Alipur Duar, *India* . . 37 F16
Aliquippa, *U.S.A.* . . . 68 E5
Alitus = Alytus,
Lithuania 9 J21
Aliwal North, *S. Africa* 48 E4
Alix, *Canada* 64 C6
Aljustrel, *Portugal* . . 19 D1
Alkmaar, *Neths.* . . . 15 B4
All American Canal,
U.S.A. 73 K6
Allahabad, *India* . . . 37 G12
Allakh-Yun, *Russia* . . 25 C14
Allan, *Canada* 65 C7
Allanmyo, *Burma* . . . 37 K19
Allanridge, *S. Africa* . 48 D4
Allanwater, *Canada* . . 62 B1
Allegan, *U.S.A.* 68 D3
Allegheny ➔, *U.S.A.* 68 E6
Allegheny Plateau,
U.S.A. 68 G6
Allen, Bog of, *Ireland* . 13 C4
Allen, L., *Ireland* . . . 13 B3
Allentown, *U.S.A.* . . . 68 E8
Alleppey, *India* 36 Q10
Aller ➔, *Germany* . . 16 B5
Alliance, *Nebr., U.S.A.* 70 D3
Alliance, *Ohio, U.S.A.* 68 E5
Allier ➔, *France* . . . 18 C5
Alliston, *Canada* . . . 62 D4
Alloa, *U.K.* 12 E5
Allora, *Australia* . . . 55 D5
Alluitsup Paa =
Sydprøven,
Greenland 4 C5
Alma, *Canada* 63 C5
Alma, *Ga., U.S.A.* . . 69 K4
Alma, *Kans., U.S.A.* . 70 F6
Alma, *Mich., U.S.A.* . 68 D3
Alma, *Nebr., U.S.A.* . 70 E5
Alma, *Wis., U.S.A.* . . 70 C9
Alma Ata = Almaty,
Kazakhstan 24 E8
Almada, *Portugal* . . . 19 C1
Almaden, *Australia* . . 54 B3
Almadén, *Spain* 19 C3
Almanor, L., *U.S.A.* . 72 F3
Almansa, *Spain* 19 C5
Almanzor, Pico del
Moro, *Spain* 19 B3
Almanzora ➔, *Spain* 19 D5
Almaty, *Kazakhstan* . 24 E8
Almazán, *Spain* 19 B4
Almeirim, *Brazil* . . . 79 D8
Almelo, *Neths.* 15 B6
Almendralejo, *Spain* . 19 C2
Almería, *Spain* 19 D4
Almora, *India* 36 E11
Alnwick, *U.K.* 10 B6
Alon, *Burma* 37 H19
Alor, *Indonesia* 33 F6
Alor Setar, *Malaysia* . 34 N13
Aloysius, Mt., *Australia* 53 E4
Alpena, *U.S.A.* 68 C4

Alpha, *Australia* 54 C4
Alphonse, *Seychelles* . 35 E4
Alpine, *Ariz., U.S.A.* . 73 K9
Alpine, *Tex., U.S.A.* . 71 K3
Alps, *Europe* 16 E5
Alroy Downs, *Australia* 54 B2
Alsace, *France* 18 B7
Alsask, *Canada* 65 C7
Alsásua, *Spain* 19 A4
Alsten, *Norway* 8 D15
Alta, *Norway* 8 B20
Alta Gracia, *Argentina* 80 C4
Alta Lake, *Canada* . . 64 C4
Altaelva ➔, *Norway* . 8 B20
Altafjorden, *Norway* . 8 A20
Altagracia, *Venezuela* 78 A4
Altai = Aerhtai Shan,
Mongolia 30 B4
Altamaha ➔, *U.S.A.* 69 K5
Altamira, *Brazil* 79 D8
Altamura, *Italy* 20 D7
Altanbulag, *Mongolia* . 30 A5
Altavista, *U.S.A.* . . . 68 G6
Altay, *China* 30 B3
Altea, *Spain* 19 C5
Alto Araguaia, *Brazil* . 79 G8
Alto Molocue, *Mozam.* 47 H7
Alton, *U.S.A.* 70 F9
Alton Downs, *Australia* 55 D2
Altoona, *U.S.A.* 68 E6
Altún Küprī, *Iraq* . . . 38 C5
Altun Shan, *China* . . 30 C3
Alturas, *U.S.A.* 72 F3
Altus, *U.S.A.* 71 H5
Alūksne, *Latvia* 9 H22
Alùla, *Somali Rep.* . . 40 E5
Alusi, *Indonesia* . . . 33 F8
Al'Uzayr, *Iraq* 38 D5
Alva, *U.S.A.* 71 G5
Alvarado, *Mexico* . . . 74 D5
Alvarado, *U.S.A.* . . . 71 J6
Alvear, *Argentina* . . . 80 B5
Alvesta, *Sweden* . . . 9 H16
Alvie, *Australia* 55 F3
Alvin, *U.S.A.* 71 L7
Álvkarleby, *Sweden* . . 9 F17
Älvsbyn, *Sweden* . . . 8 D19
Alwar, *India* 36 F10
Alxa Zuoqi, *China* . . 30 C5
Alyaskitovyy, *Russia* . 25 C15
Alyata = Älät,
Azerbaijan 23 G8
Alyth, *U.K.* 12 E5
Alytus, *Lithuania* . . . 9 J21
Alzada, *U.S.A.* 70 C2
Am Dam, *Chad* 45 F9
Am-Timan, *Chad* . . . 45 F9
Amadeus, L., *Australia* 53 D5
Amâdi, *Sudan* 45 G11
Amadi, *Zaïre* 46 D5
Amadjuak, *Canada* . . 61 B12
Amadjuak L., *Canada* . 61 B12
Amagasaki, *Japan* . . 29 G7
Amakusa-Shotō, *Japan* 29 H5
Åmål, *Sweden* 9 G15
Amaliás, *Greece* . . . 21 F9
Amalner, *India* 36 J9
Amambay, Cordillera
de, *S. Amer.* 80 A5
Amami-Guntō, *Japan* . 29 L4
Amami-Ō-Shima, *Japan* 29 L4
Amangeldy, *Kazakhstan* 24 D7
Amapá, *Brazil* 79 C8
Amapá □, *Brazil* . . . 79 C8
Amarante, *Brazil* . . . 79 E10
Amaranth, *Canada* . . 65 C9
Amargosa, *Brazil* . . . 79 F11
Amarillo, *U.S.A.* . . . 71 H4
Amaro, Mte., *Italy* . . 20 C6
Amatikulu, *S. Africa* . 49 D5
Amazon =
Amazonas ➔,
S. Amer. 79 C9
Amazonas □, *Brazil* . 78 E6
Amazonas ➔,
S. Amer. 79 C9
Ambahikily, *Madag.* . . 49 C7
Ambala, *India* 36 D10
Ambalavao, *Madag.* . 49 C8
Ambalindum, *Australia* 54 C2
Ambam, *Cameroon* . . 46 D2
Ambanja, *Madag.* . . . 49 A8
Ambarchik, *Russia* . . 25 C17
Ambarijeby, *Madag.* . 49 A8
Ambaro, Helodranon',
Madag. 49 A8
Ambartsevo, *Russia* . . 24 D9
Ambato, *Ecuador* . . . 78 D3
Ambato Boeny, *Madag.* 49 B8
Ambatofinandrahana,
Madag. 49 C8
Ambatolampy, *Madag.* 49 B8
Ambatondrazaka,
Madag. 49 B8
Ambatosoratra, *Madag.* 49 B8
Ambenja, *Madag.* . . . 49 B8
Amberg, *Germany* . . . 16 D6
Ambergris Cay, *Belize* 74 D7
Amberley, *N.Z.* 51 K4
Ambikapur, *India* . . . 37 H13
Ambilobé, *Madag.* . . 49 A8
Ambinanindrano,
Madag. 49 C8
Ambleside, *U.K.* . . . 10 C5
Ambo, *Peru* 78 F3
Ambodifototra, *Madag.* 49 B8
Ambodilazana, *Madag.* 49 B8
Ambohimahasoa,
Madag. 49 C8
Ambohimanga, *Madag.* 49 C8
Ambohitra, *Madag.* . . 49 A8
Amboise, *France* . . . 18 C4
Ambon, *Indonesia* . . 33 E7

Ambositra, *Madag.* . . . 49 C8
Ambovombé, *Madag.* . 49 D8
Amboy, *U.S.A.* 73 J6
Amboyna I.,
S. China Sea 32 C4
Ambriz, *Angola* 46 F2
Amby, *Australia* 55 D4
Amchitka I., *U.S.A.* . . 60 C1
Amderma, *Russia* . . . 24 C7
Ameca, *Mexico* 74 C4
Ameland, *Neths.* . . . 15 A5
Amen, *Russia* 25 C18
American Falls, *U.S.A.* 72 E7
American Falls
Reservoir, *U.S.A.* . . 72 E7
American Highland,
Antarctica 5 D6
American Samoa ■,
Pac. Oc. 51 B13
Americus, *U.S.A.* . . . 69 J3
Amersfoort, *Neths.* . . 15 B5
Amersfoort, *S. Africa* . 49 D4
Amery, *Australia* . . . 53 F2
Amery, *Canada* 65 B10
Amery Ice Shelf,
Antarctica 5 C6
Ames, *U.S.A.* 70 E8
Amga, *Russia* 25 C14
Amga ➔, *Russia* . . . 25 C14
Amgu, *Russia* 25 E14
Amgun ➔, *Russia* . . 25 D14
Amherst, *Burma* . . . 37 L20
Amherst, *Canada* . . . 63 C7
Amherst, *U.S.A.* . . . 71 H3
Amherstburg, *Canada* . 62 D3
Amiata, Mte., *Italy* . . 20 C4
Amiens, *France* 18 B5
Amīrābād, *Iran* 38 C5
Amirante Is., *Seychelles* 35 E4
Amisk L., *Canada* . . . 65 C8
Amite, *U.S.A.* 71 K9
Amlwch, *U.K.* 10 D3
'Ammān, *Jordan* . . . 41 D4
Ammanford, *U.K.* . . . 11 F3
Ammassalik =
Angmagssalik,
Greenland 4 C6
Åmol, *Iran* 39 B7
Amorgós, *Greece* . . . 21 F11
Amory, *U.S.A.* 69 J1
Amos, *Canada* 62 C4
Åmot, *Norway* 9 G13
Amoy = Xiamen, *China* 31 D6
Ampanihy, *Madag.* . . 49 C7
Ampasinda,
Helodranon', *Madag.* 49 A8
Ampasindava,
Saikanosy, *Madag.* . 49 A8
Ampenan, *Indonesia* . 32 F5
Amper ➔, *Germany* . 16 D6
Ampotaka, *Madag.* . . 49 D7
Ampoza, *Madag.* . . . 49 C7
Amqui, *Canada* 63 C6
Amravati, *India* 36 J10
Amreli, *India* 36 J7
Amritsar, *India* 36 D9
Amroha, *India* 36 E11
Amsterdam, *Neths.* . . 15 B4
Amsterdam, *U.S.A.* . . 68 D8
Amsterdam, I., *Ind. Oc.* 35 H6
Amstetten, *Austria* . . 16 D8
Amudarya ➔,
Uzbekistan 24 E6
Amundsen Gulf,
Canada 60 A7
Amundsen Sea,
Antarctica 5 D15
Amuntai, *Indonesia* . . 32 E5
Amur ➔, *Russia* . . . 25 D15
Amurang, *Indonesia* . 33 D6
Amuri Pass, *N.Z.* . . . 51 K4
Amursk, *Russia* 25 D14
Amurzet, *Russia* 25 E14
Amyderya =
Amudarya ➔,
Uzbekistan 24 E6
An Nabatīyah at Tahta,
Lebanon 41 B4
An Nabk, *Si. Arabia* . 38 D3
An Nabk, *Syria* 41 A5
An Nabk Abū Qaşr,
Si. Arabia 38 D3
An Nafūd, *Si. Arabia* . 38 D4
An Najaf, *Iraq* 38 C5
An Nāşirīyah, *Iraq* . . 38 D5
An Nhon, *Vietnam* . . 34 F10
An Nu'ayrīyah,
Si. Arabia 39 E6
An Nuwaybi', W. ➔,
Si. Arabia 41 F3
An Uaimh, *Ireland* . . 13 C5
Anabar ➔, *Russia* . . 25 B12
'Anabtā, *West Bank* . 41 C4
Anaconda, *U.S.A.* . . . 72 C7
Anacortes, *U.S.A.* . . . 72 B2
Anadarko, *U.S.A.* . . . 71 H5
Anadolu, *Turkey* . . . 23 G5
Anadyr, *Russia* 25 C18
Anadyr ➔, *Russia* . . 25 C18
Anadyrskiy Zaliv,
Russia 25 C19
'Ānah, *Iraq* 38 C4
Anaheim, *U.S.A.* . . . 73 K5
Anahim Lake, *Canada* 64 C3
Anakapalle, *India* . . . 37 L13
Anakie, *Australia* . . . 54 C4
Analalava, *Madag.* . . 49 A8
Anambas, Kepulauan,
Indonesia 32 D3
Anambas Is. =
Anambas, Kepulauan,
Indonesia 32 D3
Anamoose, *U.S.A.* . . . 70 B4

Anamosa, *U.S.A.* . . . 70 D9
Anamur, *Turkey* . . . 23 G5
Anan, *Japan* 29 H7
Anantnag, *India* . . . 36 C9
Anápolis, *Brazil* 79 G9
Anār, *Iran* 39 D7
Anārak, *Iran* 39 C7
Anatolia = Anadolu,
Turkey 23 G5
Anatone, *U.S.A.* . . . 72 C5
Anatsogno, *Madag.* . . 49 C7
Añatuya, *Argentina* . . 80 B4
Anaye, *Niger* 45 E7
Anchorage, *U.S.A.* . . 60 B5
Ancohuma, Nevada,
Bolivia 78 G5
Ancón, *Peru* 78 F3
Ancona, *Italy* 20 C5
Ancud, *Chile* 80 E2
Ancud, G. de, *Chile* . 80 E2
Anda, *China* 31 B7
Andado, *Australia* . . . 54 D2
Andalgalá, *Argentina* . 80 B3
Åndalsnes, *Norway* . . 9 E12
Andalucia □, *Spain* . 19 D3
Andalusia, *U.S.A.* . . . 69 K2
Andalusia =
Andalucía □, *Spain* . 19 D3
Andaman Is., *Ind. Oc.* 34 F2
Andaman Sea, *Ind. Oc.* 34 F3
Andaman Str., *India* . 34 F2
Andara, *Namibia* . . . 48 B3
Andenes, *Norway* . . . 8 B17
Andenne, *Belgium* . . 15 D5
Anderson, *Calif., U.S.A.* 72 F2
Anderson, *Ind., U.S.A.* 68 E3
Anderson, *Mo., U.S.A.* 71 G7
Anderson, *S.C., U.S.A.* 69 H4
Anderson ➔, *Canada* 60 B7
Andes = Andes, Cord.
de los, *S. Amer.* . . 78 F4
Andes, Cord. de los,
S. Amer. 78 F4
Andfjorden, *Norway* . 8 B17
Andhra Pradesh □,
India 36 L11
Andijon, *Uzbekistan* . 24 E8
Andikíthira, *Greece* . . 21 G10
Andīmeshk, *Iran* . . . 39 C6
Andizhan = Andijon,
Uzbekistan 24 E8
Andoany, *Madag.* . . . 49 A8
Andong, *S. Korea* . . . 31 C7
Andorra ■, *Europe* . . 19 A6
Andorra La Vella,
Andorra 19 A6
Andover, *U.K.* 11 F6
Andøya, *Norway* . . . 8 B16
Andrahary, Mt., *Madag.* 49 A8
Andramasina, *Madag.* 49 B8
Andranopasy, *Madag.* 49 C7
Andreanof Is., *U.S.A.* . 60 C2
Andrewilla, *Australia* . 55 D2
Andrews, *S.C., U.S.A.* 69 J6
Andrews, *Tex., U.S.A.* 71 J3
Ándria, *Italy* 20 D7
Andriba, *Madag.* . . . 49 B8
Androka, *Madag.* . . . 49 C7
Andropov = Rybinsk,
Russia 22 C6
Ándros, *Greece* 21 F11
Andros I., *Bahamas* . 75 C9
Andselv, *Norway* . . . 8 B18
Andújar, *Spain* 19 C3
Andulo, *Angola* 46 G3
Anéfo, *Togo* 44 G5
Aneto, Pico de, *Spain* 19 A6
Ang Thong, *Thailand* . 34 E6
Angamos, Punta, *Chile* 80 A2
Angara ➔, *Russia* . . 25 D10
Angarsk, *Russia* . . . 25 D11
Angas Downs, *Australia* 53 E5
Angas Hills, *Australia* . 52 D4
Angaston, *Australia* . . 55 E2
Ånge, *Sweden* 9 E16
Angeles, *Phil.* 33 A6
Ängelholm, *Sweden* . 9 H15
Angellala, *Australia* . . 55 D4
Angels Camp, *U.S.A.* . 73 G3
Ångermanälven ➔,
Sweden 8 E17
Ångermanland,
Sweden 8 E18
Angers, *France* 18 C3
Ångesån ➔, *Sweden* 8 C20
Angikuni L., *Canada* . 65 A9
Angkor, *Cambodia* . . 34 F7
Anglesey, *U.K.* 10 D3
Angleton, *U.S.A.* . . . 71 L7
Angmagssalik,
Greenland 4 C6
Ango, *Zaïre* 46 D5
Angoche, *Mozam.* . . 47 H7
Angol, *Chile* 80 D2
Angola, *U.S.A.* 68 E3
Angola ■, *Africa* . . . 47 G3
Angoon, *U.S.A.* 64 B2
Angoulême, *France* . . 18 D4
Angoumois, *France* . . 18 D3
Angra dos Reis, *Brazil* 80 A8
Angren, *Uzbekistan* . 24 E8
Anguilla ■, *W. Indies* 74 J18
Angurugu, *Australia* . . 54 A2
Angus, Braes of, *U.K.* 12 E5
Anholt, *Denmark* . . . 9 H14
Anhui □, *China* 31 C6
Anhwei = Anhui □,
China 31 C6
Anin, *Burma* 34 E4
Anivorano, *Madag.* . . 49 B8
Anjalankoski, *Finland* . 9 F22

Anjidiv I., *India* 36 M9
Anjou, *France* 18 C3
Anjozorobe, *Madag.* . 49 B8
Anka, *Nigeria* 44 F6
Ankaboa, Tanjona,
Madag. 49 C7
Ankang, *China* 31 C5
Ankara, *Turkey* 23 G5
Ankaramena, *Madag.* . 49 C8
Ankazoabo, *Madag.* . 49 C7
Ankazobe, *Madag.* . . 49 B8
Ankisabe, *Madag.* . . 49 B8
Ankoro, *Zaïre* 46 F5
Ann, C., *U.S.A.* 68 D10
Ann Arbor, *U.S.A.* . . . 68 D4
Anna, *U.S.A.* 71 G10
Anna Plains, *Australia* 52 C3
Annaba, *Algeria* 44 A6
Annalee ➔, *Ireland* . 13 B4
Annam = Trung-Phan,
Vietnam 34 D10
Annamitique, Chaîne,
Asia 34 D9
Annan, *U.K.* 12 G5
Annan ➔, *U.K.* 12 G5
Annapolis, *U.S.A.* . . . 68 F7
Annapolis Royal,
Canada 63 D6
Annean, L., *Australia* . 53 E2
Annecy, *France* 18 D7
Anning, *China* 30 D5
Anningie, *Australia* . . 52 D5
Anniston, *U.S.A.* . . . 69 J3
Annobón, *Atl. Oc.* . . 43 G4
Annotto Bay, *Jamaica* 74 J17
Annuello, *Australia* . . 55 E3
Anoka, *U.S.A.* 70 C8
Anorotsangana, *Madag.* 49 A8
Anqing, *China* 31 C6
Ansbach, *Germany* . . 16 D6
Anshan, *China* 31 B7
Anshun, *China* 30 D5
Ansirabe, *Madag.* . . . 49 B8
Ansley, *U.S.A.* 70 E5
Anson, *U.S.A.* 71 J5
Anson B., *Australia* . . 52 B5
Ansongo, *Mali* 44 E5
Anstruther, *U.K.* . . . 12 E6
Ansudu, *Indonesia* . . 33 E9
Antabamba, *Peru* . . . 78 F4
Antakya, *Turkey* . . . 23 G6
Antalaha, *Madag.* . . . 49 A9
Antalya, *Turkey* 23 G5
Antalya Körfezi, *Turkey* 23 G5
Antananarivo, *Madag.* 49 B8
Antananarivo □,
Madag. 49 B8
Antarctic Pen.,
Antarctica 5 C18
Antarctica 5 E3
Antequera, *Spain* . . . 19 D3
Antero, Mt., *U.S.A.* . . 73 G10
Anthony, *Kans., U.S.A.* 71 G5
Anthony, *N. Mex.,*
U.S.A. 73 K10
Anthony Lagoon,
Australia 54 B2
Anti Atlas, *Morocco* . . 44 C3
Anti-Lebanon = Ash
Sharqi, Al Jabal,
Lebanon 41 B5
Antibes, *France* 18 E7
Anticosti, I. d', *Canada* 63 C7
Antigo, *U.S.A.* 70 C10
Antigonish, *Canada* . 63 C7
Antigua, *W. Indies* . . 74 L20
Antigua & Barbuda ■,
W. Indies 74 K20
Antilla, *Cuba* 75 C9
Antimony, *U.S.A.* . . . 73 G8
Antioch, *U.S.A.* 72 G3
Antioquia, *Colombia* . 78 B3
Antipodes Is., *Pac. Oc.* 56 M9
Antler, *U.S.A.* 70 A4
Antler ➔, *Canada* . . 65 D8
Antlers, *U.S.A.* 71 H7
Antofagasta, *Chile* . . 80 A2
Antofagasta de la
Sierra, *Argentina* . . 80 B3
Antofalla, *Argentina* . 80 B3
Anton, *U.S.A.* 71 J3
Anton Chico, *U.S.A.* . 73 J11
Antongila, Helodrano,
Madag. 49 B8
Antonibé, *Madag.* . . . 49 B8
Antonibé, Presqu'île d',
Madag. 49 A8
Antonina, *Brazil* 80 B7
Antonito, *U.S.A.* . . . 73 H10
Antrim, *U.K.* 13 B5
Antrim □, *U.K.* 13 B5
Antrim, Mts. of, *U.K.* . 13 A5
Antrim Plateau,
Australia 52 C4
Antsalova, *Madag.* . . 49 B7
Antsiranana, *Madag.* . 49 A8
Antsohihy, *Madag.* . . 49 A8
Antsohimbondrona
Seranana, *Madag.* . 49 A8
Antwerp = Antwerpen,
Belgium 15 C4
Antwerpen, *Belgium* . 15 C4
Antwerpen □, *Belgium* 15 C4
Anupgarh, *India* 36 E8
Anuradhapura,
Sri Lanka 36 Q12
Anveh, *Iran* 39 E7
Anvers = Antwerpen,
Belgium 15 C4
Anvers I., *Antarctica* . 5 C17
Anxi, *China* 30 B4
Anxious B., *Australia* . 55 E1
Anyang, *China* 31 C6

Anzhero-Sudzhensk,
Russia 24 D9
Ánzio, *Italy* 20 D5
Aoga-Shima, *Japan* . 29 H9
Aomori, *Japan* 28 D10
Aomori □, *Japan* . . . 28 D10
Aosta, *Italy* 20 B2
Aoudéras, *Niger* . . . 44 E6
Aoulef el Arab, *Algeria* 44 C5
Apache, *U.S.A.* 71 H5
Apalachee B., *U.S.A.* . 69 L3
Apalachicola, *U.S.A.* . 69 L3
Apalachicola ➔,
U.S.A. 69 L3
Apaporis ➔,
Colombia 78 D5
Aparri, *Phil.* 33 A6
Apatity, *Russia* 22 A5
Apeldoorn, *Neths.* . . 15 B5
Apennines =
Appennini, *Italy* . . 20 B4
Apia, *W. Samoa* . . . 51 A13
Apiacás, Serra dos,
Brazil 78 E7
Aplao, *Peru* 78 G4
Apo, Mt., *Phil.* 33 C7
Apollonia = Marsá
Susah, *Libya* 45 B9
Apolo, *Bolivia* 78 F5
Apostle Is., *U.S.A.* . . 70 B9
Apostolos Andreas, C.,
Cyprus 38 C2
Apoteri, *Guyana* . . . 78 C7
Appalachian Mts.,
U.S.A. 68 G6
Appennini, *Italy* . . . 20 B4
Appleby-in-
Westmorland, *U.K.* . 10 C5
Appleton, *U.S.A.* . . . 68 C1
Approuague, *Fr. Guiana* 79 C8
Aprília, *Italy* 20 D5
Apucarana, *Brazil* . . . 80 A6
Apure ➔, *Venezuela* 78 B5
Apurimac ➔, *Peru* . . 78 F4
Aqabah = Al 'Aqabah,
Jordan 41 F4
'Aqabah, Khalij al,
Red Sea 38 D2
'Aqdā, *Iran* 39 C7
Aqiq, *Sudan* 45 E12
Aqmola, *Kazakhstan* . 24 D8
Aqrah, *Iraq* 38 B4
Aqtöbe, *Kazakhstan* . 23 D10
Aquidauana, *Brazil* . . 79 H7
Aquitain, Bassin,
France 18 D3
Ar Rachidiya, *Morocco* 44 B4
Ar Rafid, *Syria* 41 C4
Ar Raḥḥālīyah, *Iraq* . 38 C4
Ar Ramādī, *Iraq* . . . 38 C4
Ar Ramthā, *Jordan* . . 41 C5
Ar Raqqah, *Syria* . . . 38 C3
Ar Rass, *Si. Arabia* . . 38 E4
Ar Rifā'ī, *Iraq* 38 D5
Ar Riyāḍ, *Si. Arabia* . 40 C4
Ar Ru'ays, *Qatar* . . . 39 E6
Ar Rukhaymīyah, *Iraq* . 38 D5
Ar Ruqayyidah,
Si. Arabia 39 E6
Ar Ruşāfah, *Syria* . . . 38 C3
Ar Ruţbah, *Iraq* 38 C4
'Arab, Bahr el ➔,
Sudan 45 G10
'Arabābād, *Iran* 39 C8
Arabia, *Asia* 40 C4
Arabian Desert = Es
Sahrâ' Esh Sharqîya,
Egypt 45 C11
Arabian Gulf = Gulf,
The, *Asia* 39 E6
Arabian Sea, *Ind. Oc.* 27 H10
Aracaju, *Brazil* 79 F11
Aracataca, *Colombia* . 78 A4
Aracati, *Brazil* 79 D11
Araçatuba, *Brazil* . . . 79 H8
Aracena, *Spain* 19 D2
Araçuaí, *Brazil* 79 G10
'Arad, *Israel* 41 D4
Arad, *Romania* 17 E11
Arada, *Chad* 45 F9
Arafura Sea, *E. Indies* 33 F8
Aragón □, *Spain* . . . 19 B5
Aragón ➔, *Spain* . . 19 A5
Araguacema, *Brazil* . 79 E9
Araguaia ➔, *Brazil* . 79 E9
Araguari, *Brazil* 79 G9
Araguari ➔, *Brazil* . 79 C9
Arak, *Algeria* 44 C5
Arāk, *Iran* 39 C6
Arakan Coast, *Burma* 37 K19
Arakan Yoma, *Burma* 37 K19
Araks = Aras, Rūd-
e ➔, *Azerbaijan* . . 38 B5
Aral, *Kazakhstan* . . . 24 E7
Aral Sea, *Asia* 24 E7
Aral Tengizi = Aral Sea
, *Asia* 24 E7
Aralsk = Aral,
Kazakhstan 24 E7
Aralskoye More = Aral
Sea , *Asia* 24 E7
Aramac, *Australia* . . 54 C4
Aran I., *Ireland* 13 B3
Aran Is., *Ireland* . . . 13 C2
Aranda de Duero,
Spain 19 B4
Aranjuez, *Spain* 19 B4
Aranos, *Namibia* . . . 48 C2
Aransas Pass, *U.S.A.* 71 M6
Araouane, *Mali* 44 E4
Arapahoe, *U.S.A.* . . . 70 E5

Arapiraca, *Brazil* 79 E11
Arapongas, *Brazil* 80 A6
Ar'ar, *Si. Arabia* 38 D4
Araranguá, *Brazil* 80 B7
Araraquara, *Brazil* 79 H9
Ararat, *Australia* 55 F3
Ararat, Mt. = Ağrı Dağı,
 Turkey 23 G7
Araripe, Chapada do,
 Brazil 79 E11
Aras, Rūd-e →,
 Azerbaijan 38 B5
Arauca, *Colombia* 78 B4
Arauca →, *Venezuela* 78 B5
Arauco, *Chile* 80 D2
Araxá, *Brazil* 79 G9
Araya, Pen. de,
 Venezuela 78 A6
Arbat, *Iraq* 38 C5
Arbatax, *Italy* 20 E3
Arbīl, *Iraq* 38 B5
Arborfield, *Canada* .. 65 C8
Arborg, *Canada* 65 C9
Arbroath, *U.K.* 12 E6
Arbuckle, *U.S.A.* 72 G2
Arcachon, *France* 18 D3
Arcadia, *Fla., U.S.A.* 69 M5
Arcadia, *La., U.S.A.* . 71 J8
Arcadia, *Nebr., U.S.A.* 70 E5
Arcadia, *Wis., U.S.A.* 70 C9
Arcata, *U.S.A.* 72 F1
Archangel =
 Arkhangelsk, *Russia* 22 B7
Archer →, *Australia* . 54 A3
Archer B., *Australia* . 54 A3
Arcila = Asilah,
 Morocco 44 A3
Arckaringa, *Australia* . 55 D1
Arckaringa Cr. →,
 Australia 55 D2
Arco, *U.S.A.* 72 E7
Arcola, *Canada* 65 D8
Arcos de la Frontera,
 Spain 19 D3
Arcot, *India* 36 N11
Arcoverde, *Brazil* ... 79 E11
Arctic Bay, *Canada* . 61 A11
Arctic Ocean, *Arctic* . 4 B18
Arctic Red River,
 Canada 60 B6
Arda →, *Bulgaria* .. 21 D12
Ardabīl, *Iran* 39 B6
Ardakān = Sepīdān,
 Iran 39 D7
Ardee, *Ireland* 13 C5
Ardenne, *Belgium* ... 15 E5
Ardennes = Ardenne,
 Belgium 15 E5
Ardestān, *Iran* 39 C7
Ardgour, *U.K.* 12 E3
Ardlethan, *Australia* . 55 E4
Ardmore, *Australia* .. 54 C2
Ardmore, *Okla., U.S.A.* 71 H6
Ardmore, *S. Dak.,
 U.S.A.* 70 D3
Ardnacrusha, *Ireland* . 13 D3
Ardnamurchan, Pt. of,
 U.K. 12 E2
Ardrossan, *Australia* . 55 E2
Ardrossan, *U.K.* 12 F4
Ards □, *U.K.* 13 B6
Ards Pen., *U.K.* 13 B6
Arecibo, *Puerto Rico* . 75 D11
Areia Branca, *Brazil* . 79 D11
Arendal, *Norway* 9 G13
Arequipa, *Peru* 78 G4
Arero, *Ethiopia* 45 H12
Arévalo, *Spain* 19 B3
Arezzo, *Italy* 20 C4
Argamakmur, *Indonesia* 32 E2
Arganda, *Spain* 19 B4
Argentan, *France* ... 18 B3
Argentário, Mte., *Italy* 20 C4
Argentia, *Canada* ... 63 C9
Argentina ■, *S. Amer.* 80 D3
Argentina Is., *Antarctica* 5 C17
Argentino, L., *Argentina* 80 G2
Argeș →, *Romania* . 17 F14
Arghandab →,
 Afghan. 36 D4
Argo, *Sudan* 45 E11
Argolikós Kólpos,
 Greece 21 F10
Árgos, *Greece* 21 F10
Argostólion, *Greece* . 21 E9
Arguello, Pt., *U.S.A.* . 73 J3
Argun →, *Russia* .. 25 D13
Argungu, *Nigeria* ... 44 F5
Argyle, *U.S.A.* 70 A6
Argyle, L., *Australia* . 52 C4
Århus, *Denmark* 9 H14
Ariadnoye, *Russia* .. 28 B7
Ariamsvlei, *Namibia* . 48 D2
Arica, *Chile* 78 G4
Arica, *Colombia* 78 D4
Arid, C., *Australia* .. 53 F3
Arida, *Japan* 29 G7
Arīḥā, *Syria* 38 C3
Arima, *Trin. & Tob.* .. 74 S20
Arinos →, *Brazil* ... 78 F7
Aripuanã, *Brazil* 78 E6
Aripuanã →, *Brazil* . 78 E6
Ariquemes, *Brazil* ... 78 E6
Arisaig, *U.K.* 12 E3
Aristazabal I., *Canada* . 64 C3
Arivaca, *U.S.A.* 73 L8
Arivonimamo, *Madag.* 49 B8
Arizona, *Argentina* .. 80 D3
Arizona □, *U.S.A.* .. 73 J8
Arjeplog, *Sweden* ... 8 D18
Arjona, *Colombia* ... 78 A3
Arjuno, *Indonesia* .. 33 G15
Arka, *Russia* 25 C15

Arkadelphia, *U.S.A.* . 71 H8
Arkaig, L., *U.K.* 12 E3
Arkalyk = Arqalyq,
 Kazakhstan 24 D7
Arkansas □, *U.S.A.* . 71 H8
Arkansas →, *U.S.A.* . 71 J9
Arkansas City, *U.S.A.* . 71 G6
Arkhangelsk, *Russia* . 22 B7
Arklow, *Ireland* 13 D5
Arkticheskiy, Mys,
 Russia 25 A10
Arlanzón →, *Spain* . 19 A3
Arlberg P., *Austria* .. 16 E6
Arlee, *U.S.A.* 72 C6
Arles, *France* 18 E6
Arlington, *S. Africa* .. 49 D4
Arlington, *Oreg., U.S.A.* 72 D3
Arlington, *S. Dak.,
 U.S.A.* 70 C6
Arlington, *Va., U.S.A.* 68 F7
Arlington, *Wash.,
 U.S.A.* 72 B2
Arlon, *Belgium* 15 E5
Armagh, *U.K.* 13 B5
Armagh □, *U.K.* 13 B5
Armavir, *Russia* 23 E7
Armenia, *Colombia* .. 78 C3
Armenia ■, *Asia* ... 23 F7
Armidale, *Australia* .. 55 E5
Armour, *U.S.A.* 70 D5
Armstrong, *B.C.,
 Canada* 64 C5
Armstrong, *Ont.,
 Canada* 62 B2
Armstrong, *U.S.A.* .. 71 M6
Armstrong →,
 Australia 52 C5
Arnarfjörður, *Iceland* . 8 D2
Arnaud →, *Canada* . 61 B12
Arnauti, C., *Cyprus* .. 38 C2
Arnett, *U.S.A.* 71 G5
Arnhem, *Neths.* 15 C5
Arnhem, C., *Australia* 54 A2
Arnhem B., *Australia* . 54 A2
Arnhem Land, *Australia* 54 A1
Arno →, *Italy* 20 C4
Arno Bay, *Australia* . 55 E2
Arnold, *U.S.A.* 70 E4
Arnot, *Canada* 65 B9
Arnøy, *Norway* 8 A19
Arnprior, *Canada* ... 62 C4
Arnsberg, *Germany* . 16 C5
Aroab, *Namibia* 48 D2
Arqalyq, *Kazakhstan* . 24 D7
Arrabury, *Australia* .. 55 D3
Arrah = Ara, *India* .. 37 G14
Arraijän, *Panama* ... 74 H14
Arran, *U.K.* 12 F3
Arrandale, *Canada* .. 64 C3
Arras, *France* 18 A5
Arrecife, *Canary Is.* .. 44 C2
Arrée, Mts. d', *France* . 18 B2
Arrilalah P.O., *Australia* 54 C3
Arrino, *Australia* ... 53 E2
Arrow, L., *Ireland* ... 13 B3
Arrow Rock Res.,
 U.S.A. 72 E6
Arrowhead, *Canada* . 64 C5
Arrowtown, *N.Z.* ... 51 L2
Arroyo Grande, *U.S.A.* 73 J3
Ars, *Iran* 38 B5
Arsenault L., *Canada* . 65 B7
Arsenev, *Russia* 28 B6
Árta, *Greece* 21 E9
Artem, *Russia* 28 C6
Artemovsk = Mosomane,
 Botswana 48 C4
Artesia, *U.S.A.* 71 J2
Artesia Wells, *U.S.A.* . 71 L5
Artesian, *U.S.A.* ... 70 C6
Arthur →, *Australia* . 54 G3
Arthur Cr. →,
 Australia 54 C2
Arthur Pt., *Australia* . 54 C5
Arthur's Pass, *N.Z.* .. 51 K3
Artigas, *Uruguay* ... 80 C5
Artillery L., *Canada* .. 65 A7
Artois, *France* 18 A5
Artsyz, *Ukraine* 17 E15
Artvin, *Turkey* 23 F7
Aru, Kepulauan,
 Indonesia 33 F8
Aru Is. = Aru,
 Kepulauan, *Indonesia* 33 F8
Arua, *Uganda* 46 D6
Aruanã, *Brazil* 79 F8
Aruba ■, *W. Indies* . 75 E11
Arumpo, *Australia* .. 55 E3
Arunachal Pradesh □,
 India 37 E19
Arusha, *Tanzania* ... 46 E7
Aruwimi →, *Zaïre* .. 46 D4
Arvada, *U.S.A.* 72 D10
Arvida, *Canada* 63 C5
Arvidsjaur, *Sweden* . 8 D18
Arvika, *Sweden* 9 G15
Arxan, *China* 31 B6
Arys, *Kazakhstan* ... 24 E7
Arzamas, *Russia* ... 22 C7
Arzew, *Algeria* 44 A4
Aş Şafā, *Syria* 41 B6
'As Saffānīyah,
 Si. Arabia 39 D6
As Safirah, *Syria* ... 38 B3
As Salamīyah, *Si. Arabia* 38 C3
As Salţ, *Jordan* 41 C4
As Sal'w'a, *Qatar* ... 39 E6
As Samāwah, *Iraq* .. 38 D5
As Sanamayn, *Syria* . 41 B5

As Sukhnah, *Syria* .. 38 C3
As Sulaymānīyah, *Iraq* 38 C5
As Sulaymī, *Si. Arabia* 38 E4
As Summān, *Si. Arabia* 38 E5
As Suwaydā', *Syria* . 41 C5
As Suwaydā □, *Syria* 41 C5
As Şuwayrah, *Iraq* .. 38 C5
Asab, *Namibia* 48 D2
Asahi-Gawa →, *Japan* 29 G6
Asahigawa, *Japan* .. 28 C11
Asansol, *India* 37 H15
Asbesberge, *S. Africa* . 48 D3
Asbestos, *Canada* .. 63 C5
Asbury Park, *U.S.A.* . 68 E8
Ascension I., *Atl. Oc.* . 2 E9
Aschaffenburg,
 Germany 16 D5
Aschersleben, *Germany* 16 C6
Áscoli Piceno, *Italy* .. 20 C5
Ascope, *Peru* 78 E3
Aseb, *Eritrea* 40 E3
Asela, *Ethiopia* 45 G12
Asenovgrad, *Bulgaria* 21 C11
Asgata →, *Lebanon* 41 A5
Ash Shāmīyah, *Iraq* . 38 D5
Ash Shāriqah, *U.A.E.* 39 E7
Ash Sharmah,
 Si. Arabia 38 D2
Ash Sharqāt, *Iraq* ... 38 C4
Ash Sharqi, Al Jabal,
 Lebanon 41 B5
Ash Shaţrah, *Iraq* ... 38 D5
Ash Shawbak, *Jordan* 38 D2
Ash Shawmari, J.,
 Jordan 41 E5
Ash Shaykh, J.,
 Lebanon 41 B4
Ash Shināfiyah, *Iraq* . 38 D5
Ash Shu'aybah,
 Si. Arabia 38 E5
Ash Shumlūl, *Si. Arabia* 38 E5
Ash Shūr'a, *Iraq* 38 C4
Ash Shurayf, *Si. Arabia* 38 E3
Ash Shuwayfāt,
 Lebanon 41 B4
Asha, *Russia* 22 D10
Ashburn, *U.S.A.* 69 K4
Ashburton, *N.Z.* 51 K3
Ashburton →,
 Australia 52 D1
Ashburton Downs,
 Australia 52 D2
Ashby de la Zouch,
 U.K. 10 E6
Ashcroft, *Canada* ... 64 C4
Ashdod, *Israel* 41 D3
Asheboro, *U.S.A.* ... 69 H6
Asherton, *U.S.A.* ... 71 L5
Asheville, *U.S.A.* ... 69 H4
Asheweig →, *Canada* 62 B2
Ashford, *Australia* .. 55 D5
Ashford, *U.K.* 11 F8
Ashford, *U.S.A.* 72 C2
Ashgabat,
 Turkmenistan 24 F6
Ashibetsu, *Japan* ... 28 C11
Ashikaga, *Japan* ... 29 F9
Ashizuri-Zaki, *Japan* . 29 H6
Ashkhabad =
 Ashgabat,
 Turkmenistan 24 F6
Ashland, *Kans., U.S.A.* 71 G5
Ashland, *Ky., U.S.A.* . 68 F4
Ashland, *Maine, U.S.A.* 63 C6
Ashland, *Mont., U.S.A.* 72 D10
Ashland, *Nebr., U.S.A.* 70 E6
Ashland, *Ohio, U.S.A.* 68 E4
Ashland, *Oreg., U.S.A.* 72 E2
Ashland, *Va., U.S.A.* . 68 G7
Ashland, *Wis., U.S.A.* 70 B9
Ashley, *N. Dak., U.S.A.* 70 B5
Ashley, *Pa., U.S.A.* .. 68 E8
Ashmont, *Canada* .. 64 C6
Ashmore Reef,
 Australia 52 B3
Ashmyany, *Belarus* . 9 J21
Ashqelon, *Israel* 41 D3
Ashtabula, *U.S.A.* .. 68 E5
Ashton, *S. Africa* ... 48 E3
Ashton, *U.S.A.* 72 D8
Ashton under Lyne,
 U.K. 10 D5
Ashuanipi, L., *Canada* 63 B6
Asia, Kepulauan,
 Indonesia 33 D8
Asifabad, *India* 36 K11
Asike, *Indonesia* ... 33 F10
Asilah, *Morocco* 44 A3
Asinara, *Italy* 20 D3
Asinara, G. dell', *Italy* 20 D3
Asino, *Russia* 24 D9
Asipovichy, *Belarus* . 17 B15
'Asir □, *Si. Arabia* .. 40 D3
Asir, Ras, *Somali Rep.* 40 E5
Askersund, *Sweden* . 9 G16
Askham, *S. Africa* .. 48 D3
Askim, *Norway* 9 G14
Askja, *Iceland* 8 D5
Askøy, *Norway* 9 F11
Asmara = Asmera,
 Eritrea 45 E12
Asmera, *Eritrea* 45 E12
Åsnen, *Sweden* 9 H16
Asotin, *U.S.A.* 72 C5
Aspen, *U.S.A.* 73 G10
Aspermont, *U.S.A.* .. 71 J4
Aspiring, Mt., *N.Z.* .. 51 L2
Asquith, *Canada* ... 65 C7
Assad, Bahret, *Syria* . 38 C3
Assam □, *India* 37 F18

Asse, *Belgium* 15 D4
Assen, *Neths.* 15 B6
Assini, *Ivory C.* 44 G4
Assiniboia, *Canada* . 65 D7
Assiniboine →,
 Canada 65 D9
Assis, *Brazil* 80 A6
Assisi, *Italy* 20 C5
Assynt, L., *U.K.* 12 C3
Astara, *Azerbaijan* .. 23 G8
Asti, *Italy* 20 B3
Astipálaia, *Greece* .. 21 F12
Astorga, *Spain* 19 A2
Astoria, *U.S.A.* 72 C2
Astrakhan, *Russia* .. 23 E8
Astrakhan-Bazàr,
 Azerbaijan 23 G8
Asturias □, *Spain* .. 19 A3
Asunción, *Paraguay* . 80 B5
Aswân, *Egypt* 45 D11
Aswân High Dam =
 Sadd el Aali, *Egypt* . 45 D11
Asyût, *Egypt* 45 C11
At Ţafilah, *Jordan* .. 41 E4
At Ţā'if, *Si. Arabia* .. 40 C3
Aţ Ţirāq, *Si. Arabia* . 38 E5
Atacama, Desierto de,
 Chile 80 A3
Atacama, Salar de,
 Chile 80 A3
Atakpamé, *Togo* 44 G5
Atalaya, *Peru* 78 F4
Atami, *Japan* 29 G9
Atapupu, *Indonesia* . 33 F6
Atâr, *Mauritania* ... 44 D2
Atascadero, *U.S.A.* .. 73 J3
Atasu, *Kazakhstan* .. 24 E8
Atauro, *Indonesia* .. 33 F7
Atbara, *Sudan* 45 E11
'Atbara →, *Sudan* .. 45 E11
Atbasar, *Kazakhstan* . 24 D7
Atchafalaya B., *U.S.A.* 71 L9
Atchison, *U.S.A.* ... 70 F7
Ath, *Belgium* 15 D3
Athabasca, *Canada* . 64 C6
Athabasca →, *Canada* 65 B6
Athabasca, L., *Canada* 65 B7
Athboy, *Ireland* 13 C5
Athenry, *Ireland* ... 13 C3
Athens = Athínai,
 Greece 21 F10
Athens, *Ala., U.S.A.* . 69 H2
Athens, *Ga., U.S.A.* . 69 J4
Athens, *Ohio, U.S.A.* 68 F4
Athens, *Tenn., U.S.A.* 69 H3
Athens, *Tex., U.S.A.* . 71 J7
Athínai, *Greece* 21 F10
Athlone, *Ireland* ... 13 C4
Atholl, Forest of, *U.K.* 12 E5
Atholville, *Canada* .. 63 C6
Áthos, *Greece* 21 D11
Athy, *Ireland* 13 D5
Ati, *Chad* 45 F8
Atico, *Peru* 78 G4
Atikokan, *Canada* .. 62 C1
Atikonak L., *Canada* . 63 B7
Atka, *Russia* 25 C16
Atkinson, *U.S.A.* ... 70 D5
Atlanta, *Ga., U.S.A.* . 69 J3
Atlanta, *Tex., U.S.A.* . 71 J7
Atlantic, *U.S.A.* 70 E7
Atlantic City, *U.S.A.* . 68 F8
Atlantic Ocean 2 E9
Atlas Mts. = Haut
 Atlas, *Morocco* 44 B3
Atlin, *Canada* 64 B2
Atlin, L., *Canada* ... 64 B2
Atmore, *U.S.A.* 69 K2
Atoka, *U.S.A.* 71 H6
Atrak →,
 Turkmenistan 39 B8
Atrek →,
 Turkmenistan 39 B8
Atsuta, *Japan* 28 C10
Attalla, *U.S.A.* 69 H2
Attawapiskat, *Canada* 62 B3
Attawapiskat →,
 Canada 62 B3
Attawapiskat, L.,
 Canada 62 B2
Attica, *U.S.A.* 68 E2
Attikamagen L., *Canada* 63 A6
Attleboro, *U.S.A.* ... 68 E10
Attock, *Pakistan* ... 36 C8
Attopeu, *Laos* 34 E9
Attur, *India* 36 P11
Atuel →, *Argentina* . 80 D3
Atwater, *U.S.A.* 73 H3
Atwood, *U.S.A.* 70 F4
Atyraū, *Kazakhstan* . 23 E9
Au Sable →, *U.S.A.* . 68 C4
Au Sable Pt., *U.S.A.* . 62 C2
Aubagne, *France* ... 18 E6
Aube →, *France* 18 B5
Auburn, *Ala., U.S.A.* . 69 J3
Auburn, *Calif., U.S.A.* 72 G3
Auburn, *Ind., U.S.A.* 68 E3
Auburn, *N.Y., U.S.A.* 68 D7
Auburn, *Nebr., U.S.A.* 70 E7
Auburn Ra., *Australia* 55 D5
Auburndale, *U.S.A.* . 69 L5
Aubusson, *France* .. 18 D5
Auch, *France* 18 E4
Auckland, *N.Z.* 51 G5
Auckland Is., *Pac. Oc.* 56 N8
Aude →, *France* 18 E5
Auden, *Canada* 62 B2
Audubon, *U.S.A.* ... 70 E7
Augathella, *Australia* . 55 D4
Augrabies Falls,
 S. Africa 48 D3

Augsburg, *Germany* . 16 D6
Augusta, *Italy* 20 F6
Augusta, *Ark., U.S.A.* 71 H9
Augusta, *Ga., U.S.A.* 69 J5
Augusta, *Kans., U.S.A.* 71 G6
Augusta, *Maine, U.S.A.* 63 D6
Augusta, *Mont., U.S.A.* 72 C7
Augusta, *Wis., U.S.A.* 70 C9
Augustów, *Poland* .. 17 B12
Augustus, Mt.,
 Australia 52 D2
Augustus Downs,
 Australia 54 B2
Augustus I., *Australia* 52 C3
Auld, L., *Australia* .. 52 D3
Ault, *U.S.A.* 70 E2
Aunis, *France* 18 C3
Auponhia, *Indonesia* 33 E7
Aurangabad, *Bihar,
 India* 37 G14
Aurangabad,
 Maharashtra, India . 36 K9
Aurich, *Germany* ... 16 B4
Aurillac, *France* 18 D5
Aurora, *S. Africa* ... 48 E2
Aurora, *Colo., U.S.A.* 70 F2
Aurora, *Ill., U.S.A.* .. 68 E1
Aurora, *Mo., U.S.A.* . 71 G8
Aurora, *Nebr., U.S.A.* 70 E6
Aurukun Mission,
 Australia 54 A3
Aus, *Namibia* 48 D2
Auschwitz = Oświęcim,
 Poland 17 C10
Austin, *Minn., U.S.A.* 70 D8
Austin, *Nev., U.S.A.* . 72 G5
Austin, *Tex., U.S.A.* . 71 K6
Austin, L., *Australia* . 53 E2
Austra, *Norway* 8 D14
Austral Downs,
 Australia 54 C2
Austral Is. = Tubuai Is.,
 Pac. Oc. 57 K12
Austral Seamount
 Chain, *Pac. Oc.* ... 57 K13
Australia ■, *Oceania* 56 K5
Australian Alps,
 Australia 55 F4
Australian Capital
 Territory □, *Australia* 55 F4
Austria ■, *Europe* .. 16 E8
Austvågøy, *Norway* . 8 B16
Autun, *France* 18 C6
Auvergne, *Australia* . 52 C5
Auvergne, *France* ... 18 D5
Auvergne, Mts. d',
 France 18 D5
Auxerre, *France* 18 C5
Avallon, *France* 18 C5
Avalon Pen., *Canada* 63 C9
Aveiro, *Brazil* 79 D7
Aveiro, *Portugal* 19 B1
Åvej, *Iran* 39 C6
Avellaneda, *Argentina* 80 C5
Avellino, *Italy* 20 D6
Aversa, *Italy* 20 D6
Avery, *U.S.A.* 72 C6
Avesta, *Sweden* 9 F17
Avezzano, *Italy* 20 C5
Aviá Terai, *Argentina* 80 B4
Avignon, *France* 18 E6
Ávila, *Spain* 19 B3
Avilés, *Spain* 19 A3
Avoca, *Ireland* 13 D5
Avoca →, *Australia* . 55 F3
Avola, *Canada* 64 C5
Avola, *Italy* 20 F6
Avon →, *U.S.A.* ... 70 D5
Avon □, *U.K.* 11 F5
Avon →, *Australia* . 53 F2
Avon →, *Avon, U.K.* 11 F5
Avon →, *Hants., U.K.* 11 G6
Avon →, *Warks., U.K.* 11 F5
Avonlea, *Canada* ... 65 D7
Avonmouth, *U.K.* ... 11 F5
Avranches, *France* .. 18 B3
A'waj →, *Syria* 41 B5
Awash, *Ethiopia* ... 40 F3
Awatere →, *N.Z.* ... 51 J5
Awbārī, *Libya* 45 C7
Awe, L., *U.K.* 12 E3
Awjilah, *Libya* 45 C9
Axarfjörður, *Iceland* . 8 C5
Axel Heiberg I., *Canada* 4 B3
Axim, *Ghana* 44 H4
Axiós →, *Greece* .. 21 D10
Axminster, *U.K.* 11 G4
Ayabaca, *Peru* 78 D3
Ayabe, *Japan* 29 G7
Ayacucho, *Argentina* 80 D5
Ayacucho, *Peru* 78 F4
Ayaguz, *Kazakhstan* . 24 E9
Ayamonte, *Spain* ... 19 D2
Ayan, *Russia* 25 D14
Ayaviri, *Peru* 78 F4
Aydın, *Turkey* 21 F12
Ayeritam, *Malaysia* . 34 P13
Ayers Rock, *Australia* 53 E5
Áyios Evstrátios,
 Greece 21 E11
Aykino, *Russia* 22 B8
Aylesbury, *U.K.* 11 F7
Aylmer, L., *Canada* . 60 B8
Ayon, Ostrov, *Russia* 25 C17
Ayr, *Australia* 54 B4
Ayr, *U.K.* 12 F4
Ayr →, *U.K.* 12 F4
Ayre, Pt. of, *U.K.* ... 10 C3
Aytos, *Bulgaria* 21 C12
Ayu, Kepulauan,
 Indonesia 33 D8

Ayutla, *Mexico* 74 D5
Ayvacık, *Turkey* 21 E12
Ayvalık, *Turkey* 21 E12
Az Zabdānī, *Syria* .. 41 B5
Aẕ Ẕāhirīyah,
 West Bank 41 D3
Aẕ Ẕahrān, *Si. Arabia* 39 E6
Az Zarqā, *Jordan* ... 41 C5
Az Zibār, *Iraq* 38 B5
Az Zubayr, *Iraq* 38 D5
Az Zuwaytinah, *Libya* 45 B9
Azamgarh, *India* ... 37 F13
Azar Shahr, *Iran* ... 38 B5
Āẕarbāyjān =
 Azerbaijan ■, *Asia* . 23 F8
Āẕarbāyjān-e Gharbī □,
 Iran 38 B5
Āẕarbāyjān-e Sharqī □,
 Iran 38 B5
Azare, *Nigeria* 44 F7
A'zāz, *Syria* 38 B3
Azbine = Aïr, *Niger* . 44 E6
Azerbaijan ■, *Asia* . 23 F8
Azerbaijchan =
 Azerbaijan ■, *Asia* . 23 F8
Azogues, *Ecuador* .. 78 D3
Azores, *Atl. Oc.* 2 C8
Azov, *Russia* 23 E6
Azov, Sea of, *Europe* 23 E6
Azovskoye More =
 Azov, Sea of, *Europe* 23 E6
Azovy, *Russia* 24 C7
Aztec, *U.S.A.* 73 H10
Azúa, *Dom. Rep.* ... 75 D10
Azuaga, *Spain* 19 C3
Azuero, Pen. de,
 Panama 75 F8
Azul, *Argentina* 80 D5
'Azzūn, *West Bank* . 41 C4

B

Ba Don, *Vietnam* 34 D9
Ba Ngoi = Cam Lam,
 Vietnam 34 G10
Ba Ria, *Vietnam* 34 G9
Baa, *Indonesia* 33 F6
Baarle Nassau, *Belgium* 15 C4
Baarn, *Neths.* 15 B5
Bab el Mandeb,
 Red Sea 40 E3
Baba Burnu, *Turkey* . 21 E12
Bābā Kalū, *Iran* 39 D6
Babadag, *Romania* . 17 F15
Babadayhan,
 Turkmenistan 24 F7
Babaeski, *Turkey* ... 21 D12
Babahoyo, *Ecuador* . 78 D3
Babakin, *Australia* .. 53 F2
Babana, *Nigeria* 44 F5
Babar, *Indonesia* ... 33 F7
Babb, *U.S.A.* 72 B7
Babinda, *Australia* .. 54 B4
Babine, *Canada* 64 B3
Babine →, *Canada* . 64 B3
Babine L., *Canada* .. 64 C3
Babo, *Indonesia* ... 33 E8
Bābol, *Iran* 39 B7
Bābol Sar, *Iran* 39 B7
Baboua, *C.A.R.* 46 C2
Babruysk, *Belarus* .. 17 B15
Babura, *Nigeria* 44 F6
Babuyan Chan., *Phil.* 33 A6
Babylon, *Iraq* 38 C5
Bac Kan, *Vietnam* .. 34 A8
Bac Ninh, *Vietnam* .. 34 B9
Bac Phan, *Vietnam* . 34 A8
Bac Quang, *Vietnam* 34 A8
Bacabal, *Brazil* 79 D10
Bacan, Kepulauan,
 Indonesia 33 E7
Bacan, Pulau, *Indonesia* 33 E7
Bacarra, *Phil.* 33 A6
Bacău, *Romania* 17 E14
Bachelina, *Russia* .. 24 D7
Back →, *Canada* ... 60 B9
Backstairs Passage,
 Australia 55 F2
Bacolod, *Phil.* 33 B6
Bād, *Iran* 39 C7
Bad →, *U.S.A.* 70 C4
Bad Axe, *U.S.A.* 68 D4
Bad Ischl, *Austria* .. 16 E7
Bad Kissingen,
 Germany 16 C6
Bad Lands, *U.S.A.* .. 70 D3
Badagara, *India* 36 P9
Badajoz, *Spain* 19 C2
Badalona, *Spain* 19 B7
Badalzai, *Afghan.* .. 36 E4
Badampahar, *India* . 37 H15
Badanah, *Si. Arabia* . 38 D4
Badarinath, *India* ... 36 D11
Badas, *Brunei* 32 D4
Badas, Kepulauan,
 Indonesia 32 D3
Baddo →, *Pakistan* . 36 F4
Bade, *Indonesia* 33 F9
Baden, *Austria* 16 D9
Baden-Baden, *Germany* 16 D5
Baden-Württemberg □,
 Germany 16 D5
Badenoch, *U.K.* 12 E4
Badgastein, *Austria* . 16 E7
Badger, *Canada* 63 C8
Bādghīsāt □, *Afghan.* 36 B3
Badin, *Pakistan* 36 G6
Baduen, *Somali Rep.* 40 F4
Badulla, *Sri Lanka* .. 36 R12

Baena, *Spain* 19   D3
Baeza, *Spain* 19   D4
Bafatá, *Guinea-Biss.* . . 44   F2
Baffin B., *Canada* 4   B4
Baffin I., *Canada* 61   B12
Bafia, *Cameroon* 44   H7
Bafing →, *Mali* 44   F2
Bafoulabé, *Mali* 44   F2
Bâfq, *Iran* 39   D7
Bâft, *Iran* 39   D8
Bafwasende, *Zaïre* . . . 46   D5
Bagamoyo, *Tanzania* . . 46   F7
Baganga, *Phil.* 33   C7
Bagani, *Namibia* 48   B3
Bagansiapiapi,
   Indonesia 32   D2
Bagdarin, *Russia* 25   D12
Bagé, *Brazil* 80   C6
Bagenalstown = Muine
   Bheag, *Ireland* 13   D5
Baggs, *U.S.A.* 72   F10
Baghdâd, *Iraq* 38   C5
Bagheria, *Italy* 20   E5
Baghlân, *Afghan.* 36   A6
Bagley, *U.S.A.* 70   B7
Bagotville, *Canada* . . . 63   C5
Bagrationovsk, *Russia* . 9   J19
Baguio, *Phil.* 33   A6
Bahamas ■, *N. Amer.* 75   C10
Baharampur, *India* . . 37   G16
Bahau, *Malaysia* 34   S15
Bahawalpur, *Pakistan* . 36   E7
Bahía = Salvador,
   Brazil 79   F11
Bahía □, *Brazil* 79   F10
Bahía Blanca, *Argentina* 80   D4
Bahía de Caráquez,
   Ecuador 78   D2
Bahía Laura, *Argentina* 80   F3
Bahía Negra, *Paraguay* 78   H7
Bahmanzād, *Iran* 39   D6
Bahr Aouk →, *C.A.R.* 46   C3
Bahr Salamat →,
   Chad 45   G8
Bahraich, *India* 37   F12
Bahrain ■, *Asia* 39   E6
Bāhū Kalāt, *Iran* 39   E9
Bai Bung, Mui, *Vietnam* 34   H8
Baia Mare, *Romania* . . 17   E12
Baïbokoum, *Chad* 45   G8
Baidoa, *Somali Rep.* . . 40   G3
Baie Comeau, *Canada* . 63   C6
Baie-St-Paul, *Canada* . 63   C5
Baie Trinité, *Canada* . . 63   C6
Baie Verte, *Canada* . . . 63   C8
Ba'ijī, *Iraq* 38   C4
Baikal, L. = Baykal, Oz.,
   Russia 25   D11
Baile Atha Cliath =
   Dublin, *Ireland* 13   C5
Băileşti, *Romania* 17   F12
Bailundo, *Angola* 47   G3
Bainbridge, *U.S.A.* . . . 69   K3
Baing, *Indonesia* 33   F6
Bainville, *U.S.A.* 70   A2
Bā'ir, *Jordan* 41   E5
Baird, *U.S.A.* 71   J5
Baird Mts., *U.S.A.* . . . 60   B3
Bairnsdale, *Australia* . . 55   F4
Baïtadi, *Nepal* 37   E12
Baiyin, *China* 30   C5
Baja, *Hungary* 17   E10
Baja, Pta., *Mexico* . . . 74   B1
Baja California, *Mexico* 74   B2
Bājgīrān, *Iran* 39   B8
Bajimba, Mt., *Australia* 55   D5
Bajool, *Australia* 54   C5
Bakala, *C.A.R.* 45   G9
Bakchar, *Russia* 24   D9
Bakel, *Senegal* 44   F2
Baker, *Calif., U.S.A.* . . 73   J5
Baker, *Mont., U.S.A.* . . 70   B2
Baker, *Oreg., U.S.A.* . . 72   D5
Baker, L., *Canada* . . . 60   B10
Baker I., *Pac. Oc.* . . . 56   G10
Baker L., *Australia* . . . 53   E4
Baker Lake, *Canada* . . 60   B10
Baker Mt., *U.S.A.* 72   B3
Bakers Creek, *Australia* 54   C4
Baker's Dozen Is.,
   Canada 62   A4
Bakersfield, *U.S.A.* . . . 73   J4
Bākhtarān, *Iran* 38   C5
Bakhtārān □, *Iran* . . . 38   C5
Bakı, *Azerbaijan* 23   F8
Bakkafjörður, *Iceland* . 8   C6
Bakkagerði, *Iceland* . . 8   D7
Bakony Forest =
   Bakony Hegyseg,
   Hungary 17   E9
Bakony Hegyseg,
   Hungary 17   E9
Bakouma, *C.A.R.* 45   G9
Baku = Bakı, *Azerbaijan* 23   F8
Bakutis Coast,
   Antarctica 5   D15
Baky = Bakı, *Azerbaijan* 23   F8
Bala, L., *U.K.* 10   E4
Balabac I., *Phil.* 32   C5
Balabac Str., *E. Indies* 32   C5
Ba'labakk, *Lebanon* . . 41   A5
Balabalangan,
   Kepulauan, *Indonesia* 32   E5
Balad, *Iraq* 38   C5
Balad Rūz, *Iraq* 38   C5
Bālādeh, *Fārs, Iran* . . 39   D6
Bālādeh, *Māzandarān,
   Iran* 39   B6
Balaghat, *India* 36   J12
Balaghat Ra., *India* . . 36   K10
Balaguer, *Spain* 19   B6
Balaklava, *Australia* . . 55   E2

Balaklava, *Ukraine* . . . 23   F5
Balakovo, *Russia* 22   D8
Balashov, *Russia* 22   D7
Balasore = Baleshwar,
   India 37   J15
Balaton, *Hungary* 17   E9
Balbina, Reprêsa de,
   Brazil 78   D7
Balboa, *Panama* 74   H14
Balboa Hill, *Panama* . 74   H14
Balbriggan, *Ireland* . . 13   C5
Balcarce, *Argentina* . . 80   D5
Balcarres, *Canada* . . . 65   C8
Balchik, *Bulgaria* 21   C13
Balclutha, *N.Z.* 51   M2
Bald Hd., *Australia* . . . 53   G2
Bald I., *Australia* 53   F2
Bald Knob, *U.S.A.* . . . 71   H9
Baldock L., *Canada* . . 65   B9
Baldwin, *Fla., U.S.A.* . . 69   K4
Baldwin, *Mich., U.S.A.* . 68   D3
Baldwinsville, *U.S.A.* . . 68   D7
Baldy Peak, *U.S.A.* . . . 73   K9
Baleares, Is. = Baleares,
   Is., *Spain* 19   C7
Balearic Is. = Baleares,
   Is., *Spain* 19   C7
Baler, *Phil.* 33   A6
Baleshwar, *India* 37   J15
Balfe's Creek, *Australia* 54   C4
Bali, *Cameroon* 44   G7
Bali, *Indonesia* 32   F5
Bali □, *Indonesia* 32   F5
Bali, Selat, *Indonesia* . 33   H16
Balıkeşir, *Turkey* 21   E12
Balikpapan, *Indonesia* 32   E5
Balimbing, *Phil.* 33   C5
Baling, *Malaysia* 34   P13
Balipara, *India* 37   F18
Baliza, *Brazil* 79   G8
Balkan Mts. = Stara
   Planina, *Bulgaria* . . 21   C10
Balkhash = Balqash,
   Kazakhstan 24   E8
Balkhash, Ozero =
   Balqash Köl,
   Kazakhstan 24   E8
Balla, *Bangla.* 37   G17
Ballachulish, *U.K.* 12   E3
Balladonia, *Australia* . 53   F3
Ballarat, *Australia* . . . 55   F3
Ballard, L., *Australia* . . 53   E3
Ballater, *U.K.* 12   D5
Balleny Is., *Antarctica* . 5   C11
Ballidu, *Australia* 53   F2
Ballina, *Australia* 55   D5
Ballina, *Mayo, Ireland* . 13   B2
Ballina, *Tipp., Ireland* . 13   D3
Ballinasloe, *Ireland* . . 13   C3
Ballinger, *U.S.A.* 71   K5
Ballinrobe, *Ireland* . . . 13   C2
Ballinskelligs B., *Ireland* 13   E1
Ballycastle, *U.K.* 13   A5
Ballymena, *U.K.* 13   B5
Ballymena □, *U.K.* . . . 13   B5
Ballymoney, *U.K.* 13   A5
Ballymoney □, *U.K.* . . 13   A5
Ballyshannon, *Ireland* . 13   B3
Balmaceda, *Chile* 80   F2
Balmoral, *Australia* . . . 55   F3
Balmoral, *U.K.* 12   D5
Balmorhea, *U.S.A.* . . . 71   K3
Balonne →, *Australia* . 55   D4
Balqash, *Kazakhstan* . 24   E8
Balqash Köl,
   Kazakhstan 24   E8
Balrampur, *India* 37   F13
Balranald, *Australia* . . 55   E3
Balsas →, *Mexico* . . . 74   D4
Balta, *Ukraine* 17   D15
Balta, *U.S.A.* 70   A4
Bălți, *Moldova* 17   E14
Baltic Sea, *Europe* . . . 9   H18
Baltimore, *Ireland* 13   E2
Baltimore, *U.S.A.* 68   F7
Baltiysk, *Russia* 9   J18
Baluchistan □, *Pakistan* 36   F4
Balvi, *Latvia* 9   H22
Balya, *Turkey* 21   E12
Balygychan, *Russia* . . 25   C16
Bam, *Iran* 39   D8
Bama, *Nigeria* 45   F7
Bamako, *Mali* 44   F3
Bamba, *Mali* 44   E4
Bambari, *C.A.R.* 45   G9
Bambaroo, *Australia* . . 54   B4
Bamberg, *Germany* . . 16   D6
Bamberg, *U.S.A.* 69   J5
Bambili, *Zaïre* 46   D5
Bamenda, *Cameroon* . 44   G7
Bamfield, *Canada* . . . 64   D3
Bāmiān □, *Afghan.* . . 36   B5
Bampūr, *Iran* 39   E9
Ban Aranyaprathet,
   Thailand 34   F7
Ban Ban, *Laos* 34   C7
Ban Bua Chum,
   Thailand 34   E6
Ban Don = Surat Thani,
   Thailand 34   H5
Ban Houei Sai, *Laos* . 34   B6
Ban Khe Bo, *Vietnam* . 34   C8
Ban Khun Yuam,
   Thailand 34   C4
Ban Mê Thuôt = Buon
   Me Thuot, *Vietnam* . 34   F10
Ban Phai, *Thailand* . . 34   D7
Ban Thateng, *Laos* . . 34   E9
Banaba, *Kiribati* 56   H8
Banalia, *Zaïre* 46   D5
Banam, *Cambodia* . . . 34   G8
Banamba, *Mali* 44   F3
Banana, *Australia* . . . 54   C5
Banana, I. do, *Brazil* . 79   F8

Banaras = Varanasi,
   India 37   G13
Banbān, *Si. Arabia* . . 38   E5
Banbridge, *U.K.* 13   B5
Banbridge □, *U.K.* . . 13   B5
Banbury, *U.K.* 11   E6
Banchory, *U.K.* 12   D6
Bancroft, *Canada* . . . 62   C4
Band Boni, *Iran* 39   E8
Band Qīr, *Iran* 39   D6
Banda, *India* 36   G12
Banda, Kepulauan,
   Indonesia 33   E7
Banda Aceh, *Indonesia* 32   C1
Banda Banda, Mt.,
   Australia 55   E5
Banda Elat, *Indonesia* . 33   F8
Banda Is. = Banda,
   Kepulauan, *Indonesia* 33   E7
Banda Sea, *Indonesia* . 33   F7
Bandai-San, *Japan* . . 28   F10
Bandān, *Iran* 39   D9
Bandanaira, *Indonesia* 33   E7
Bandar =
   Machilipatnam, *India* 37   L12
Bandār 'Abbās, *Iran* . . 39   E8
Bandar-e Anzalī, *Iran* . 39   B6
Bandar-e Bushehr =
   Būshehr, *Iran* 39   D6
Bandar-e Chārak, *Iran* 39   E7
Bandar-e Deylam, *Iran* 39   D6
Bandar-e Khomeynı,
   Iran 39   D6
Bandar-e Lengeh, *Iran* 39   E7
Bandar-e Maqām, *Iran* 39   E7
Bandar-e Ma'shur, *Iran* 39   D6
Bandar-e Nakhīlū, *Iran* 39   E7
Bandar-e Rīg, *Iran* . . 39   D6
Bandar-e Torkeman,
   Iran 39   B7
Bandar Maharani =
   Muar, *Malaysia* . . . 34   S15
Bandar Penggaram =
   Batu Pahat, *Malaysia* 34   T15
Bandar Seri Begawan,
   Brunei 32   C4
Bandawe, *Malawi* . . . 47   G6
Bandeira, Pico da,
   Brazil 79   H10
Bandera, *Argentina* . . 80   B4
Bandera, *U.S.A.* 71   L5
Bandiagara, *Mali* . . . 44   F4
Bandırma, *Turkey* . . . 21   D13
Bandon, *Ireland* 13   E3
Bandon →, *Ireland* . . 13   E3
Bandundu, *Zaïre* 46   E3
Bandung, *Indonesia* . . 33   G12
Bandya, *Australia* . . . 53   E3
Bāneh, *Iran* 38   C5
Banes, *Cuba* 75   C10
Banff, *Canada* 64   C5
Banff, *U.K.* 12   D6
Banff Nat. Park, *Canada* 64   C5
Banfora, *Burkina Faso* 44   F4
Bang Hieng →, *Laos* . 34   D8
Bang Lamung, *Thailand* 34   F6
Bang Saphan, *Thailand* 34   G5
Bangalore, *India* 36   N10
Bangassou, *C.A.R.* . . 46   D4
Banggai, Kepulauan,
   Indonesia 33   E6
Banggi, P., *Malaysia* . 32   C5
Banghāzī, *Libya* 45   B9
Bangil, *Indonesia* . . . 33   G15
Bangka, P., *Sulawesi,
   Indonesia* 33   D7
Bangka, P., *Sumatera,
   Indonesia* 32   E3
Bangka, Selat,
   Indonesia 32   E3
Bangkalan, *Indonesia* . 33   G15
Bangkinang, *Indonesia* 32   D2
Bangko, *Indonesia* . . 32   E2
Bangkok, *Thailand* . . 34   F6
Bangladesh ■, *Asia* . . 37   H17
Bangong Co, *India* . . 36   B11
Bangor, *Down, U.K.* . . 13   B6
Bangor, *Gwynedd, U.K.* 10   D3
Bangor, *U.S.A.* 63   D6
Bangued, *Phil.* 33   A6
Bangui, *C.A.R.* 46   D3
Bangweulu, L., *Zambia* 46   G6
Bani, *Dom. Rep.* 75   D10
Banī Sa'd, *Iraq* 38   C5
Banī Walīd, *Libya* . . . 45   B7
Banīnah, *Libya* 45   B9
Bāniyās, *Syria* 38   C3
Banja Luka, *Bos.-H.* . . 20   B7
Banjar, *Indonesia* . . . 33   G13
Banjarmasin, *Indonesia* 32   E4
Banjarnegara,
   Indonesia 33   G13
Banjul, *Gambia* 44   F1
Banka Banka, *Australia* 54   B1
Bankipore, *India* 37   G14
Banks I., *B.C., Canada* 64   C3
Banks I., *N.W.T.,
   Canada* 60   A7
Banks Pen., *N.Z.* 51   K4
Banks Str., *Australia* . 54   G4
Bann →, *L'derry., U.K.* 13   A5
Bann →, *Tyrone, U.K.* 13   B5
Banning, *U.S.A.* 73   K5
Banningville =
   Bandundu, *Zaïre* . . 46   E3
Bannockburn, *U.K.* . . 12   E5
Bannu, *Pakistan* 36   C7
Banská Bystrica,
   Slovak Rep. 17   D10
Banswara, *India* 36   H9
Banten, *Indonesia* . . . 33   G12
Bantry, *Ireland* 13   E2
Bantry B., *Ireland* . . . 13   E2
Banda, *Brazil* 79   F10

Bantul, *Indonesia* . . . 33   G14
Banu, *Afghan.* 36   B6
Banyak, Kepulauan,
   Indonesia 32   D1
Banyo, *Cameroon* . . . 44   G7
Banyumas, *Indonesia* 33   G13
Banyuwangi, *Indonesia* 33   H16
Banzare Coast,
   Antarctica 5   C9
Banzyville = Mobayi,
   Zaïre 46   D4
Baoding, *China* 31   C6
Baoji, *China* 30   C5
Baoshan, *China* 30   D4
Baotou, *China* 31   B6
Bapatla, *India* 37   M12
Ba'qūbah, *Iraq* 38   C5
Bar, *Montenegro, Yug.* 21   C8
Bar, *Ukraine* 17   D14
Bar Harbor, *U.S.A.* . . 63   D6
Bar-le-Duc, *France* . . 18   B6
Barabai, *Indonesia* . . 32   E5
Baraboo, *U.S.A.* 70   D10
Baracaldo, *Spain* . . . 19   A4
Baracoa, *Cuba* 75   C10
Baraga, *U.S.A.* 70   B10
Barahona, *Dom. Rep.* 75   D10
Barail Range, *India* . . 37   G18
Barakaldo = Baracaldo,
   Spain 19   A4
Barakhola, *India* 37   G18
Barakpur, *India* 37   H16
Barakula, *Australia* . . 55   D5
Baralaba, *Australia* . . 54   C4
Baralzon L., *Canada* . 65   B9
Baramula, *India* 36   B9
Baran, *India* 36   G10
Baranavichy, *Belarus* . 17   B14
Baranof I., *U.S.A.* . . . 64   B1
Barão de Melgaço,
   Brazil 78   F6
Barapasi, *Indonesia* . 33   E9
Barat Daya, Kepulauan,
   Indonesia 33   F7
Barataria B., *U.S.A.* . 71   L10
Barbacena, *Brazil* . . . 79   H10
Barbacoas, *Colombia* . 78   C3
Barbados ■, *W. Indies* 74   P22
Barbastro, *Spain* 19   A6
Barberton, *S. Africa* . . 49   D5
Barberton, *U.S.A.* . . . 68   E5
Barbourville, *U.S.A.* . . 69   G4
Barbuda, *W. Indies* . . 74   K20
Barcaldine, *Australia* . 54   C4
Barcellona Pozzo di
   Gotto, *Italy* 20   E6
Barcelona, *Spain* 19   B7
Barcelona, *Venezuela* . 78   A6
Barcelos, *Brazil* 78   D6
Barcoo →, *Australia* . 54   D3
Bardai, *Chad* 45   D8
Barddhaman, *India* . . 37   H15
Bardejov, *Slovak Rep.* 17   D11
Bardera, *Somali Rep.* . 40   G3
Bardīyah, *Libya* 45   B9
Bardsey I., *U.K.* 10   E3
Bardstown, *U.S.A.* . . 68   G3
Bareilly, *India* 36   E11
Barents Sea, *Arctic* . . 4   B9
Barentu, *Eritrea* 45   E12
Barfleur, Pte. de, *France* 18   B3
Bargal, *Somali Rep.* . 40   E5
Bargara, *Australia* . . 54   C5
Barguzin, *Russia* . . . 25   D11
Barhi, *India* 37   G14
Bari, *Italy* 20   D7
Bari Doab, *Pakistan* . 36   D8
Barīm, *Yemen* 40   E3
Barinas, *Venezuela* . . 78   B4
Baring, C., *Canada* . . 60   B8
Barisal, *Bangla.* 37   H17
Barisan, Bukit,
   Indonesia 32   E2
Barito →, *Indonesia* . 32   E4
Barkley Sound, *Canada* 64   D3
Barkly Downs, *Australia* 54   C2
Barkly East, *S. Africa* . 48   E4
Barkly Tableland,
   Australia 54   B2
Barkly West, *S. Africa* 48   D3
Barkol, *China* 30   B4
Barksdale, *U.S.A.* . . . 71   L4
Barlee, L., *Australia* . . 53   E2
Barlee, Mt., *Australia* . 53   D4
Barletta, *Italy* 20   D7
Barlow L., *Canada* . . 65   A8
Barmedman, *Australia* 55   E4
Barmer, *India* 36   G7
Barmera, *Australia* . . 55   E3
Barmouth, *U.K.* 10   E3
Barnard Castle, *U.K.* . 10   C6
Barnato, *Australia* . . . 55   E3
Barnaul, *Russia* 24   D9
Barnesville, *U.S.A.* . . 69   J3
Barnet, *U.K.* 11   F7
Barneveld, *Neths.* . . . 15   B5
Barnhart, *U.S.A.* 71   K4
Barnsley, *U.K.* 10   D6
Barnstaple, *U.K.* 11   F3
Barnsville, *U.S.A.* . . . 70   B6
Baro, *Nigeria* 44   G6
Baroda = Vadodara,
   India 36   H8
Baroe, *S. Africa* 48   E3
Baron Ra., *Australia* . 52   D4
Barpeta, *India* 37   F17
Barques, Pt. Aux,
   U.S.A. 68   C4
Barquísimeto,
   Venezuela 78   A5
Barra, *Brazil* 79   F10

Barra, *U.K.* 12   E1
Barra, Sd. of, *U.K.* . . 12   D1
Barra do Corda, *Brazil* 79   E9
Barra do Piraí, *Brazil* . 79   H10
Barra Falsa, Pta. da,
   Mozam. 49   C6
Barra Hd., *U.K.* 12   E1
Barraba, *Australia* . . . 55   E5
Barrackpur = Barakpur,
   India 37   H16
Barraigh = Barra, *U.K.* 12   E1
Barranca, *Lima, Peru* 78   F3
Barranca, *Loreto, Peru* 78   D3
Barrancabermeja,
   Colombia 78   B4
Barrancas, *Venezuela* . 78   B6
Barrancos, *Portugal* . 19   C2
Barranqueras,
   Argentina 80   B5
Barranquilla, *Colombia* 78   A4
Barras, *Brazil* 79   D10
Barraute, *Canada* . . . 62   C4
Barre, *U.S.A.* 68   C9
Barreiras, *Brazil* 79   F10
Barreirinhas, *Brazil* . . 79   D10
Barreiro, *Portugal* . . . 19   C1
Barreiros, *Brazil* 79   E11
Barren, Nosy, *Madag.* 49   B7
Barren I., *India* 34   F2
Barretos, *Brazil* 79   H9
Barrhead, *Canada* . . 64   C6
Barrie, *Canada* 62   D4
Barrier Ra., *Australia* . 55   E3
Barrière, *Canada* . . . 64   C4
Barrington, L., *Canada* 65   B8
Barrington Tops,
   Australia 55   E5
Barringun, *Australia* . 55   D4
Barrow, *U.S.A.* 60   A4
Barrow →, *Ireland* . . 13   D4
Barrow Creek, *Australia* 54   C1
Barrow I., *Australia* . . 52   D2
Barrow-in-Furness, *U.K.* 10   C4
Barrow Pt., *Australia* . 54   A3
Barrow Ra., *Australia* . 53   E4
Barrow Str., *Canada* . 4   B3
Barry, *U.K.* 11   F4
Barry's Bay, *Canada* . 62   C4
Barsham, *Syria* 38   C4
Barsi, *India* 36   K9
Barsoi, *India* 37   G15
Barstow, *Calif., U.S.A.* 73   J5
Barstow, *Tex., U.S.A.* 71   K3
Bartica, *Guyana* 78   B7
Bartlesville, *U.S.A.* . . 71   G7
Bartlett, *U.S.A.* 71   K6
Bartlett, L., *Canada* . 64   A5
Barton, *Australia* 53   F5
Barton upon Humber,
   U.K. 10   D7
Bartow, *U.S.A.* 69   M5
Barysaw, *Belarus* . . . 17   A15
Barzān, *Iraq* 38   B5
Bāsa'idū, *Iran* 39   E7
Basankusa, *Zaïre* . . . 46   D3
Basarabeasca, *Moldova* 17   E15
Basel, *Switz.* 16   E4
Bāshī, *Iran* 39   D6
Bashkir Republic =
   Bashkortostan □,
   Russia 22   D10
Bashkortostan □,
   Russia 22   D10
Basilan, *Phil.* 33   C6
Basilan Str., *Phil.* . . . 33   C6
Basildon, *U.K.* 11   F8
Basim = Washim, *India* 36   J10
Basin, *U.S.A.* 72   D9
Basingstoke, *U.K.* . . . 11   F6
Baskatong, Rés.,
   Canada 62   C4
Basle = Basel, *Switz.* . 16   E4
Basoka, *Zaïre* 46   D4
Basongo, *Zaïre* 46   E4
Basque Provinces =
   Pais Vasco □, *Spain* 19   A4
Basra = Al Başrah, *Iraq* 38   D5
Bass Rock, *U.K.* 12   E6
Bass Str., *Australia* . . 54   F4
Bassano, *Canada* . . . 64   C6
Bassano del Grappa,
   Italy 20   B4
Bassas da India,
   Ind. Oc. 47   J7
Basse-Terre,
   Guadeloupe 74   M20
Bassein, *Burma* 37   L19
Basseterre,
   St. Christopher-Nevis 74   K19
Bassett, *Nebr., U.S.A.* 70   D5
Bassett, *Va., U.S.A.* . 69   G6
Bassikounou,
   Mauritania 44   E3
Bastak, *Iran* 39   E7
Baştām, *Iran* 39   B7
Bastar, *India* 37   K12
Basti, *India* 37   F13
Bastia, *France* 18   E8
Bastogne, *Belgium* . . 15   D5
Bastrop, *U.S.A.* 71   K6
Bat Yam, *Israel* 41   C3
Bata, *Eq. Guin.* 46   D1
Bataan, *Phil.* 33   B6
Batabanó, *Cuba* 75   C8
Batabanó, G. de, *Cuba* 75   C8
Batac, *Phil.* 33   A6
Batagoy, *Russia* 25   C14
Batamay, *Russia* 25   C13
Batang, *Indonesia* . . 33   G13
Batangafo, *C.A.R.* . . . 45   G8
Batangas, *Phil.* 33   B6
Batanta, *Indonesia* . . 33   E8
Batavia, *U.S.A.* 68   D6

Batchelor, *Australia* . . 52   B5
Bateman's B., *Australia* 55   F5
Batemans Bay,
   Australia 55   F5
Bates Ra., *Australia* . . 53   E3
Batesburg, *U.S.A.* . . . 69   J5
Batesville, *Ark., U.S.A.* 71   H9
Batesville, *Miss., U.S.A.* 71   H10
Batesville, *Tex., U.S.A.* 71   L5
Bath, *U.K.* 11   F5
Bath, *Maine, U.S.A.* . 63   D6
Bath, *N.Y., U.S.A.* . . 68   D7
Bathgate, *U.K.* 12   F5
Bathurst = Banjul,
   Gambia 44   F1
Bathurst, *Australia* . . 55   E4
Bathurst, *Canada* . . . 63   C6
Bathurst, *S. Africa* . . 48   E4
Bathurst, C., *Canada* . 60   A7
Bathurst B., *Australia* . 54   A3
Bathurst Harb.,
   Australia 54   G4
Bathurst I., *Australia* . 52   B5
Bathurst I., *Canada* . . 4   B2
Bathurst Inlet, *Canada* 60   B9
Batlow, *Australia* 55   F4
Batna, *Algeria* 44   A6
Baton Rouge, *U.S.A.* . 71   K9
Batouri, *Cameroon* . . 46   D2
Båtsfjord, *Norway* . . . 8   A23
Battambang, *Cambodia* 34   F7
Batticaloa, *Sri Lanka* . 36   R12
Battipáglia, *Italy* 20   D6
Battle, *U.K.* 11   G8
Battle →, *Canada* . . . 65   C7
Battle Camp, *Australia* 54   B3
Battle Creek, *U.S.A.* . 68   D3
Battle Harbour, *Canada* 63   B8
Battle Lake, *U.S.A.* . . 70   B7
Battle Mountain, *U.S.A.* 72   F5
Battleford, *Canada* . . 65   C7
Batu, *Ethiopia* 40   F2
Batu, Kepulauan,
   Indonesia 32   E1
Batu Gajah, *Malaysia* . 34   Q14
Batu Is. = Batu,
   Kepulauan, *Indonesia* 32   E1
Batu Pahat, *Malaysia* . 34   T15
Batuata, *Indonesia* . . 33   F6
Batumi, *Georgia* 23   F7
Baturaja, *Indonesia* . . 32   E2
Baturité, *Brazil* 79   D11
Bau, *Malaysia* 32   D4
Baubau, *Indonesia* . . 33   F6
Bauchi, *Nigeria* 44   F6
Baudette, *U.S.A.* 70   A7
Bauer, C., *Australia* . . 55   E1
Bauhinia Downs,
   Australia 54   C4
Baukau, *Indonesia* . . 33   F7
Bauru, *Brazil* 79   H9
Baús, *Brazil* 79   G8
Bauska, *Latvia* 9   H21
Bautzen, *Germany* . . 16   C8
Bavānāt, *Iran* 39   D7
Bavaria = Bayern □,
   Germany 16   D6
Bawdwin, *Burma* 37   H20
Bawean, *Indonesia* . . 32   F4
Bawku, *Ghana* 44   F4
Bawlake, *Burma* 37   K20
Baxley, *U.S.A.* 69   K4
Baxter Springs, *U.S.A.* 71   G7
Bay, L. de, *Phil.* 33   B6
Bay Bulls, *Canada* . . 63   C9
Bay City, *Mich., U.S.A.* 68   D4
Bay City, *Oreg., U.S.A.* 72   D2
Bay City, *Tex., U.S.A.* 71   L7
Bay de Verde, *Canada* 63   C9
Bay Minette, *U.S.A.* . 69   K2
Bay St. Louis, *U.S.A.* . 71   K10
Bay Springs, *U.S.A.* . 71   K10
Bay View, *N.Z.* 51   H6
Bayamo, *Cuba* 75   C9
Bayamón, *Puerto Rico*
Bayan Har Shan, *China* 30   C4
Bayan Hot = Alxa
   Zuoqi, *China* 30   C5
Bayanaūyl, *Kazakhstan* 24   D8
Bayanhongor,
   Mongolia 30   B5
Bayard, *U.S.A.* 70   E3
Baybay, *Phil.* 33   B6
Bayern □, *Germany* . 16   D6
Bayeux, *France* 18   B3
Bayfield, *U.S.A.* 70   B9
Bayındır, *Turkey* 21   E12
Baykal, Oz., *Russia* . . 25   D11
Baykit, *Russia* 25   C10
Baykonur = Bayqongyr,
   Kazakhstan 24   E7
Baymak, *Russia* 22   D10
Baynes Mts., *Namibia* 48   B1
Bayombong, *Phil.* . . . 33   A6
Bayonne, *France* . . . 18   E3
Bayovar, *Peru* 78   E2
Bayqongyr, *Kazakhstan* 24   E7
Bayram-Ali =
   Bayramaly,
   Turkmenistan 24   F7
Bayramaly,
   Turkmenistan 24   F7
Bayramiç, *Turkey* . . . 21   E12
Bayreuth, *Germany* . . 16   D6
Bayrūt, *Lebanon* 41   B4
Bayt Lahm, *West Bank* 41   D4
Baytown, *U.S.A.* 71   L7
Baza, *Spain* 19   D4
Bazaruto, I. do, *Mozam.* 49   C6
Bazmān, Kūh-e, *Iran* . 39   D9
Beach, *U.S.A.* 70   B3
Beachport, *Australia* . 55   F2
Beachy Hd., *U.K.* . . . 11   G8
Beacon, *Australia* . . . 53   F2

Beacon

Beacon, *U.S.A.* 68 E9
Beaconia, *Canada* .. 65 C9
Beagle, Canal, *S. Amer.* 80 G3
Beagle Bay, *Australia* . 52 C3
Bealanana, *Madag.* ... 49 A8
Bear I., *Ireland* 13 E2
Bear L., *B.C., Canada* .. 64 B3
Bear L., *Man., Canada* 65 B9
Bear L., *U.S.A.* 72 E8
Bearcreek, *U.S.A.* 72 D9
Beardmore, *Canada* .. 62 C2
Beardmore Glacier,
  Antarctica 5 E11
Beardstown, *U.S.A.* ... 70 F9
Béarn, *France* 18 E3
Bearpaw Mts., *U.S.A.* . 72 B9
Bearskin Lake, *Canada* 62 B1
Beatrice, *U.S.A.* 70 E6
Beatrice, C., *Australia* . 54 A2
Beatton →, *Canada* .. 64 B4
Beatton River, *Canada* 64 B4
Beatty, *U.S.A.* 73 H5
Beauce, Plaine de la,
  France 18 B4
Beauceville, *Canada* .. 63 C5
Beaudesert, *Australia* . 55 D5
Beaufort, *Malaysia* ... 32 C5
Beaufort, *N.C., U.S.A.* . 69 H7
Beaufort, *S.C., U.S.A.* . 69 J5
Beaufort Sea, *Arctic* .. 4 B1
Beaufort West, *S. Africa* 48 E3
Beauharnois, *Canada* . 62 C5
Beaulieu →, *Canada* .. 64 A6
Beauly →, *U.K.* 12 D4
Beauly →, *U.K.* 12 D4
Beaumaris, *U.K.* 10 D3
Beaumont, *U.S.A.* 71 K7
Beaune, *France* 18 C6
Beauséjour, *Canada* .. 65 C9
Beauvais, *France* 18 B5
Beauval, *Canada* 65 B7
Beaver, *Okla., U.S.A.* . 71 G4
Beaver, *Utah, U.S.A.* . 73 G7
Beaver →, *B.C.,
  Canada* 64 B4
Beaver →, *Ont.,
  Canada* 62 A2
Beaver →, *Sask.,
  Canada* 65 B7
Beaver City, *U.S.A.* ... 70 E5
Beaver Dam, *U.S.A.* .. 70 D10
Beaver Falls, *U.S.A.* .. 68 E5
Beaver Hill L., *Canada* 65 C10
Beaver I., *U.S.A.* 68 C3
Beaverhill L., *Alta.,
  Canada* 64 C6
Beaverhill L., *N.W.T.,
  Canada* 65 A8
Beaverlodge, *Canada* . 64 B5
Beavermouth, *Canada* 64 C5
Beaverstone →,
  Canada 62 B2
Beawar, *India* 36 F9
Beboa, *Madag.* 49 B7
Beccles, *U.K.* 11 E9
Bečej, *Serbia, Yug.* .. 21 B9
Béchar, *Algeria* 44 B4
Beckley, *U.S.A.* 68 G5
Bedford, *Canada* 62 C5
Bedford, *S. Africa* 48 E4
Bedford, *U.K.* 11 E7
Bedford, *Ind., U.S.A.* . 68 F2
Bedford, *Iowa, U.S.A.* . 70 E7
Bedford, *Ohio, U.S.A.* . 68 E5
Bedford, *Va., U.S.A.* . 68 G6
Bedford, C., *Australia* . 54 B4
Bedford Downs,
  Australia 52 C4
Bedfordshire □, *U.K.* . 11 E7
Bedourie, *Australia* ... 54 C2
Beech Grove, *U.S.A.* .. 68 F2
Beechy, *Canada* 65 C7
Beenleigh, *Australia* .. 55 D5
Be'er Menuha, *Israel* . 38 D2
Be'er Sheva, *Israel* .. 41 D3
Beersheba = Be'er
  Sheva, *Israel* 41 D3
Beeston, *U.K.* 10 E6
Beetaloo, *Australia* ... 54 B1
Beeville, *U.S.A.* 71 L6
Befale, *Zaïre* 46 D4
Befandriana, *Madag.* . 49 C7
Befotaka, *Madag.* 49 C8
Bega, *Australia* 55 F4
Behbahān, *Iran* 39 C8
Behara, *Madag.* 49 C8
Behbehān, *Iran* 39 D6
Behshahr, *Iran* 39 B7
Bei Jiang →, *China* .. 31 D6
Bei'an, *China* 31 B7
Beihai, *China* 31 D5
Beijing, *China* 31 C6
Beilen, *Neths.* 15 B6
Beilpajah, *Australia* .. 55 E3
Beinn na Faoghla =
  Benbecula, *U.K.* .. 12 D1
Beira, *Mozam.* 47 H6
Beirut = Bayrūt,
  Lebanon 41 B4
Beitbridge, *Zimbabwe* 47 J6
Beja, *Portugal* 19 C2
Béja, *Tunisia* 44 A6
Bejaia, *Algeria* 44 A6
Béjar, *Spain* 19 B3
Bejestān, *Iran* 39 C8
Bekaa Valley = Al
  Biqā □, *Lebanon* .. 41 A5
Bekasi, *Indonesia* 33 G12
Békéscsaba, *Hungary* . 17 E11
Bekily, *Madag.* 49 C8
Bekok, *Malaysia* 34 S16
Bela, *India* 37 G13

Bela, *Pakistan* 36 F5
Bela Crkva,
  Serbia, Yug. 21 B9
Bela Vista, *Brazil* 80 A5
Bela Vista, *Mozam.* .. 49 D5
Belarus ■, *Europe* ... 17 B14
Belau □, *Pac. Oc.* 56 G5
Belavenona, *Madag.* . 49 C8
Belawan, *Indonesia* .. 32 D1
Belaya →, *Russia* ... 22 C9
Belaya Tserkov = Bila
  Tserkva, *Ukraine* .. 17 D16
Belcher Is., *Canada* .. 61 C12
Belebey, *Russia* 22 D9
Belém, *Brazil* 79 D9
Belén, *Paraguay* 80 A5
Belen, *U.S.A.* 73 J10
Belet Uen, *Somali Rep.* 40 G4
Belev, *Russia* 22 D6
Belfast, *S. Africa* 49 D5
Belfast, *U.K.* 13 B6
Belfast, *U.S.A.* 63 D6
Belfast □, *U.K.* 13 B6
Belfast L., *U.K.* 13 B6
Belfield, *U.S.A.* 70 B3
Belfort, *France* 18 C7
Belfry, *U.S.A.* 72 D9
Belgaum, *India* 36 M9
Belgium ■, *Europe* ... 15 D5
Belgorod, *Russia* 23 D6
Belgorod-Dnestrovskiy
  = Bilhorod-
  Dnivstrovskyy,
  Ukraine 23 E5
Belgrade = Beograd,
  Serbia, Yug. 21 B9
Belgrade, *U.S.A.* 72 D8
Belhaven, *U.S.A.* 69 H7
Beli Drim →, *Europe* 21 C9
Belinga, *Gabon* 46 D2
Belinyu, *Indonesia* ... 32 E3
Beliton Is. = Belitung,
  Indonesia 32 E3
Belitung, *Indonesia* .. 32 E3
Belize ■, *Cent. Amer.* . 74 D7
Belize City, *Belize* 74 D7
Belkovskiy, Ostrov,
  Russia 25 B14
Bell →, *Canada* 62 C4
Bell Bay, *Australia* ... 54 G4
Bell I., *Canada* 63 B8
Bell-Irving →, *Canada* 64 B3
Bell Peninsula, *Canada* 61 B11
Bell Ville, *Argentina* .. 80 C4
Bella Bella, *Canada* .. 64 C3
Bella Coola, *Canada* . 64 C3
Bella Unión, *Uruguay* . 80 C5
Bella Vista, *Argentina* . 80 B5
Bellaire, *U.S.A.* 68 E5
Bellary, *India* 36 M10
Bellata, *Australia* 55 D4
Belle Fourche, *U.S.A.* . 70 C3
Belle Fourche →,
  U.S.A. 70 C3
Belle Glade, *U.S.A.* .. 69 M5
Belle-Ile, *France* 18 C2
Belle Isle, *Canada* ... 63 B8
Belle Isle, Str. of,
  Canada 63 B8
Belle Plaine, *Iowa,
  U.S.A.* 70 E8
Belle Plaine, *Minn.,
  U.S.A.* 70 C8
Belledune, *Canada* ... 63 C6
Bellefontaine, *U.S.A.* . 68 E4
Bellefonte, *U.S.A.* ... 68 E7
Belleoram, *Canada* ... 63 C8
Belleville, *Canada* ... 62 D4
Belleville, *Ill., U.S.A.* . 70 F10
Belleville, *Kans., U.S.A.* 70 F6
Bellevue, *Canada* 64 D6
Bellevue, *U.S.A.* 72 E6
Bellin = Kangirsuk,
  Canada 61 B13
Bellingen, *Australia* .. 55 E5
Bellingham, *U.S.A.* .. 72 B2
Bellingshausen Sea,
  Antarctica 5 C17
Bellinzona, *Switz.* ... 16 E5
Bellows Falls, *U.S.A.* . 68 D9
Belluno, *Italy* 20 A5
Bellville, *U.S.A.* 71 L6
Belmont, *Australia* ... 55 E5
Belmont, *S. Africa* ... 48 D3
Belmonte, *Brazil* 79 G11
Belmopan, *Belize* 74 D7
Belmullet, *Ireland* ... 13 B2
Belo Horizonte, *Brazil* 79 G10
Belo-sur-Mer, *Madag.* 49 C7
Belo-Tsiribihina,
  Madag. 49 B7
Belogorsk, *Russia* ... 25 D13
Beloha, *Madag.* 49 D8
Beloit, *Kans., U.S.A.* . 70 F5
Beloit, *Wis., U.S.A.* .. 70 D10
Belokorovichi, *Ukraine* 17 C15
Belomorsk, *Russia* ... 22 B5
Belonia, *India* 37 H17
Beloretsk, *Russia* 22 D10
Belorussia = Belarus ■,
  Europe 17 B14
Belovo, *Russia* 24 D9
Beloye, Ozero, *Russia* 22 B6
Beloye More, *Russia* . 22 A6
Belozersk, *Russia* 22 B6
Beltana, *Australia* ... 55 E2
Belterra, *Brazil* 79 D8
Belton, *S.C., U.S.A.* .. 69 H4
Belton, *Tex., U.S.A.* .. 71 K6
Belton Res., *U.S.A.* .. 71 K6
Beltsy = Bălți, *Moldova* 17 E14
Belturbet, *Ireland* ... 13 B4
Belukha, *Russia* 24 E9

Beluran, *Malaysia* 32 C5
Belvidere, *U.S.A.* 70 D10
Belyando →, *Australia* 54 C4
Belyy, Ostrov, *Russia* . 24 B8
Belyy Yar, *Russia* 24 D9
Belzoni, *U.S.A.* 71 J9
Bemaraha,
  Lembalemban' i,
  Madag. 49 B7
Bemarivo, *Madag.* ... 49 C7
Bemarivo →, *Madag.* 49 B8
Bemavo, *Madag.* 49 C8
Bembéréke, *Benin* ... 44 F5
Bemidji, *U.S.A.* 70 B7
Ben, *Iran* 39 C6
Ben Cruachan, *U.K.* . 12 E3
Ben Dearg, *U.K.* 12 D4
Ben Gardane, *Tunisia* . 45 B7
Ben Hope, *U.K.* 12 C4
Ben Lawers, *U.K.* ... 12 E4
Ben Lomond, *N.S.W.,
  Australia* 55 E5
Ben Lomond, *Tas.,
  Australia* 54 G4
Ben Lomond, *U.K.* ... 12 E4
Ben Macdhui, *U.K.* .. 12 D5
Ben Mhor, *U.K.* 12 D1
Ben More, *Central, U.K.* 12 E4
Ben More, *Strath., U.K.* 12 E2
Ben More Assynt, *U.K.* 12 C4
Ben Nevis, *U.K.* 12 E4
Ben Vorlich, *U.K.* 12 E4
Ben Wyvis, *U.K.* 12 D4
Bena, *Nigeria* 44 F6
Bena Dibele, *Zaïre* .. 46 E4
Benagerie, *Australia* . 55 E3
Benalla, *Australia* ... 55 F4
Benambra, Mt.,
  Australia 55 F4
Benares = Varanasi,
  India 37 G13
Benavente, *Spain* ... 19 A3
Benavides, *U.S.A.* ... 71 M5
Benbecula, *U.K.* 12 D1
Benbonyathe, *Australia* 55 E2
Bencubbin, *Australia* . 53 F2
Bend, *U.S.A.* 72 D3
Bender Beila,
  Somali Rep. 40 F5
Bendering, *Australia* . 53 F2
Bendery = Tighina,
  Moldova 17 E15
Bendigo, *Australia* ... 55 F3
Benē Beraq, *Israel* .. 41 C3
Benenitra, *Madag.* ... 49 C8
Benevento, *Italy* 20 D6
Bengal, Bay of, *Ind. Oc.* 37 K16
Bengbu, *China* 31 C6
Benghazi = Banghāzī,
  Libya 45 B9
Bengkalis, *Indonesia* . 32 D2
Bengkulu, *Indonesia* . 32 E2
Bengkulu □, *Indonesia* 32 E2
Bengough, *Canada* .. 65 D7
Benguela, *Angola* ... 47 G2
Benguérua, I., *Mozam.* 49 C6
Beni, *Zaïre* 46 D5
Beni →, *Bolivia* 78 F5
Beni Mazâr, *Egypt* .. 45 C11
Beni Abbès, *Algeria* . 44 B4
Beni Mellal, *Morocco* . 44 B3
Beni Ounif, *Algeria* .. 44 B4
Beni Suef, *Egypt* 45 C11
Beniah L., *Canada* ... 64 A6
Benidorm, *Spain* 19 C5
Benin ■, *Africa* 44 G5
Benin, Bight of, *W. Afr.* 44 H5
Benin City, *Nigeria* .. 44 G6
Benjamin Constant,
  Brazil 78 D4
Benkelman, *U.S.A.* .. 70 E4
Benlidi, *Australia* 54 C3
Bennett, *Canada* 64 B2
Bennett, L., *Australia* . 52 D5
Bennett, Ostrov, *Russia* 25 B15
Bennettsville, *U.S.A.* . 69 H6
Bennington, *U.S.A.* .. 68 D9
Benoni, *S. Africa* 49 D4
Benson, *U.S.A.* 73 L8
Bent, *Iran* 39 E8
Benteng, *Indonesia* .. 33 F6
Bentinck I., *Australia* . 54 B2
Benton, *Ark., U.S.A.* . 71 H8
Benton, *Ill., U.S.A.* .. 70 F10
Benton Harbor, *U.S.A.* 68 D2
Bentung, *Malaysia* .. 34 R14
Benue →, *Nigeria* ... 44 G6
Benxi, *China* 31 B7
Beo, *Indonesia* 33 D7
Beograd, *Serbia, Yug.* 21 B9
Beowawe, *U.S.A.* 72 F5
Beppu, *Japan* 29 H5
Beqaa Valley = Al
  Biqā □, *Lebanon* .. 41 A5
Berati, *Albania* 21 D8
Berau, Teluk, *Indonesia* 33 E8
Berber, *Sudan* 45 E11
Berbera, *Somali Rep.* . 40 E4
Berbérati, *C.A.R.* 46 D3
Berbice →, *Guyana* .. 78 B7
Berdichev = Berdychiv,
  Ukraine 17 D15
Berdsk, *Russia* 24 D9
Berdyansk, *Ukraine* .. 23 E6
Berdychiv, *Ukraine* .. 17 D15
Berea, *U.S.A.* 68 G3
Berebere, *Indonesia* . 33 D7
Bereda, *Somali Rep.* . 40 E5
Berehove, *Ukraine* .. 17 D12
Berekum, *Ghana* 44 G4
Berens →, *Canada* .. 65 C9
Berens I., *Canada* ... 65 C9
Berens River, *Canada* 65 C9

Berestechko, *Ukraine* . 17 C13
Berevo, *Mahajanga,
  Madag.* 49 B7
Berevo, *Toliara, Madag.* 49 B7
Bereza, *Belarus* 17 B13
Berezhany, *Ukraine* .. 17 D13
Berezina =
  Byarezina →,
  Belarus 17 B16
Berezniki, *Russia* 24 D6
Berezovo, *Russia* 22 B11
Berga, *Spain* 19 A6
Bergama, *Turkey* 21 E12
Bérgamo, *Italy* 20 B3
Bergen, *Neths.* 15 B4
Bergen, *Norway* 9 F11
Bergen-op-Zoom,
  Neths. 15 C4
Bergerac, *France* ... 18 D4
Bergum, *Neths.* 15 A5
Bergville, *S. Africa* ... 49 D4
Berhala, Selat,
  Indonesia 32 E2
Berhampore =
  Baharampur, *India* 37 G16
Berhampur, *India* ... 37 K14
Bering Sea, *Pac. Oc.* . 60 C1
Bering Strait, *U.S.A.* . 60 B3
Beringen, *Belgium* .. 15 C5
Beringovskiy, *Russia* . 25 C18
Berja, *Spain* 19 D4
Berkeley, *U.K.* 11 F5
Berkeley, *U.S.A.* 72 H2
Berkeley Springs,
  U.S.A. 68 F6
Berkner I., *Antarctica* . 5 D18
Berkshire □, *U.K.* ... 11 F6
Berland →, *Canada* . 64 C5
Berlin, *Germany* 16 B7
Berlin, *Md., U.S.A.* .. 68 F8
Berlin, *N.H., U.S.A.* .. 68 C10
Berlin, *Wis., U.S.A.* .. 68 D1
Bermejo →, *Formosa,
  Argentina* 80 B5
Bermejo →, *San Juan,
  Argentina* 80 C3
Bermuda ■, *Atl. Oc.* . 75 A12
Bern, *Switz.* 16 E4
Bernado, *U.S.A.* 73 J10
Bernalillo, *U.S.A.* ... 73 J10
Bernam →, *Malaysia* 34 R14
Bernardo de Irigoyen,
  Argentina 80 B6
Bernburg, *Germany* . 16 C6
Berne = Bern, *Switz.* . 16 E4
Bernier I., *Australia* .. 53 D1
Bernina, Piz, *Switz.* .. 16 E5
Beroroha, *Madag.* ... 49 C8
Beroun, *Czech.* 16 D8
Berrechid, *Morocco* .. 44 B3
Berri, *Australia* 55 E3
Berry, *Australia* 55 E5
Berry, *France* 18 C5
Berryville, *U.S.A.* ... 71 G8
Bershad, *Ukraine* ... 17 D15
Berthold, *U.S.A.* 70 A4
Berthoud, *U.S.A.* 70 E2
Bertoua, *Cameroon* . 46 D2
Bertrand, *U.S.A.* 70 E5
Berwick, *U.S.A.* 68 E7
Berwick-upon-Tweed,
  U.K. 10 B5
Berwyn Mts., *U.K.* ... 10 E4
Besalampy, *Madag.* . 49 B7
Besançon, *France* ... 18 C7
Besar, *Indonesia* 32 E5
Beserah, *Malaysia* .. 34 R16
Besnard L., *Canada* . 65 B7
Besor, N. →, *Egypt* .. 41 D3
Bessarabka =
  Basarabeasca,
  Moldova 17 E15
Bessemer, *Ala., U.S.A.* 69 J2
Bessemer, *Mich.,
  U.S.A.* 70 B9
Bet She'an, *Israel* ... 41 C4
Bet Shemesh, *Israel* . 41 D3
Betafo, *Madag.* 49 B8
Betanzos, *Spain* 19 A1
Bétaré Oya, *Cameroon* 46 C2
Bethal, *S. Africa* 49 D4
Bethanien, *Namibia* . 48 D2
Bethany, *U.S.A.* 70 E7
Bethel, *U.S.A.* 60 B3
Bethlehem = Bayt
  Lahm, *West Bank* . 41 D4
Bethlehem, *S. Africa* . 49 D4
Bethlehem, *U.S.A.* ... 68 E8
Bethulie, *S. Africa* ... 48 E4
Béthune, *France* 18 A5
Bethungra, *Australia* . 55 E4
Betioky, *Madag.* 49 C7
Betong, *Thailand* ... 34 P14
Betoota, *Australia* ... 54 D3
Betroka, *Madag.* 49 C8
Betsiamites, *Canada* . 63 C6
Betsiamites →,
  Canada 63 C6
Betsiboka →, *Madag.* 49 B8
Bettiah, *India* 37 F14
Betul, *India* 36 J10
Betung, *Malaysia* ... 32 D4
Beulah, *U.S.A.* 70 B4
Beverley, *Australia* .. 53 F2
Beverley, *U.K.* 10 D7
Beverly, *U.S.A.* 72 C4
Beverly Hills, *U.S.A.* . 73 J4
Beverwijk, *Neths.* ... 15 B4
Beya, *Russia* 25 D10
Beyānlū, *Iran* 38 C5
Beyla, *Guinea* 44 G3
Beyneu, *Kazakhstan* . 23 E10

Beypazarı, *Turkey* ... 23 F5
Beyşehir Gölü, *Turkey* 23 G5
Bezhitsa, *Russia* 22 D5
Béziers, *France* 18 E5
Bezwada = Vijayawada,
  India 37 L12
Bhachau, *India* 36 H7
Bhadrakh, *India* 37 J15
Bhadravati, *India* ... 36 N9
Bhagalpur, *India* 37 G15
Bhakra Dam, *India* .. 36 D10
Bhamo, *Burma* 37 G20
Bhandara, *India* 36 J11
Bhanrer Ra., *India* .. 36 H11
Bharat = India ■, *Asia* 36 K11
Bharatpur, *India* 36 F10
Bhatpara, *India* 37 H16
Bhaunagar =
  Bhavnagar, *India* . 36 J8
Bhavnagar, *India* ... 36 J8
Bhawanipatna, *India* . 37 K12
Bhilsa = Vidisha, *India* 36 H10
Bhilwara, *India* 36 G9
Bhima →, *India* 36 L10
Bhimavaram, *India* .. 37 L12
Bhind, *India* 36 F11
Bhiwandi, *India* 36 K8
Bhiwani, *India* 36 E10
Bhola, *Bangla.* 37 H17
Bhopal, *India* 36 H10
Bhubaneshwar, *India* 37 J14
Bhuj, *India* 36 H6
Bhumiphol Dam =
  Phumiphon, Khuan,
  Thailand 32 A1
Bhusaval, *India* 36 J9
Bhutan ■, *Asia* 37 F17
Biafra, B. of = Bonny,
  Bight of, *Africa* ... 46 D1
Biak, *Indonesia* 33 E9
Biała Podlaska, *Poland* 17 B12
Białogard, *Poland* ... 16 A8
Białystok, *Poland* 17 B12
Biārjmand, *Iran* 39 B7
Biaro, *Indonesia* 33 D7
Biarritz, *France* 18 E3
Bibai, *Japan* 28 C10
Bibala, *Angola* 47 G2
Bibby I., *Canada* 65 A10
Biberach, *Germany* .. 16 D5
Bibiani, *Ghana* 44 G4
Biboohra, *Australia* .. 54 B4
Bic, *Canada* 63 C6
Bickerton I., *Australia* . 54 A2
Bicknell, *Ind., U.S.A.* . 68 F2
Bicknell, *Utah, U.S.A.* . 73 G8
Bida, *Nigeria* 44 G6
Bidar, *India* 36 L10
Biddeford, *U.S.A.* ... 63 D10
Bideford, *U.K.* 11 F3
Bidon 5 = Poste
  Maurice Cortier,
  Algeria 44 D5
Bidor, *Malaysia* 34 Q14
Bié, Planalto de, *Angola* 47 G3
Bieber, *U.S.A.* 72 F3
Biel, *Switz.* 16 E4
Bielé Karpaty, *Europe* 17 D9
Bielefeld, *Germany* .. 16 B5
Biella, *Italy* 20 B3
Bielsk Podlaski, *Poland* 17 B12
Bielsko-Biała, *Poland* 17 D10
Bien Hoa, *Vietnam* .. 34 G9
Bienfait, *Canada* 65 D8
Bienne = Biel, *Switz.* . 16 E4
Bienville, L., *Canada* . 62 A5
Biesiesfontein, *S. Africa* 48 E2
Big →, *Canada* 63 B8
Big B., *Canada* 63 A7
Big Beaver, *Canada* . 65 D7
Big Belt Mts., *U.S.A.* . 72 C8
Big Bend, *Swaziland* . 49 D5
Big Bend National Park,
  U.S.A. 71 L3
Big Black →, *U.S.A.* . 71 J9
Big Blue →, *U.S.A.* .. 70 F6
Big Cr. →, *Canada* .. 64 C4
Big Cypress Swamp,
  U.S.A. 69 M5
Big Falls, *U.S.A.* 70 A8
Big Fork →, *U.S.A.* .. 70 A8
Big Horn Mts. =
  Bighorn Mts., *U.S.A.* 72 D10
Big Lake, *U.S.A.* 71 K4
Big Muddy Cr. →,
  U.S.A. 70 A2
Big Pine, *U.S.A.* 73 H4
Big Piney, *U.S.A.* ... 72 E8
Big Quill L., *Canada* . 65 C8
Big Rapids, *U.S.A.* .. 68 D3
Big River, *Canada* ... 65 C7
Big Sable Pt., *U.S.A.* . 68 C2
Big Sand L., *Canada* . 65 B9
Big Sandy, *U.S.A.* ... 72 B8
Big Sandy Cr. →,
  U.S.A. 70 F3
Big Sioux →, *U.S.A.* . 70 D6
Big Spring, *U.S.A.* ... 71 J4
Big Springs, *U.S.A.* .. 70 E3
Big Stone City, *U.S.A.* 70 C6
Big Stone Gap, *U.S.A.* 69 G4
Big Stone L., *U.S.A.* . 70 C6
Big Timber, *U.S.A.* .. 72 D9
Big Trout L., *Canada* . 62 B1
Biğa, *Turkey* 21 D12
Bigadiç, *Turkey* 21 E13
Bigfork, *U.S.A.* 72 B6
Biggar, *Canada* 65 C7
Biggar, *U.K.* 12 F5
Bigge I., *Australia* ... 52 B4
Biggenden, *Australia* . 55 D5
Bighorn, *U.S.A.* 72 C10
Bighorn →, *U.S.A.* .. 72 C10

Bighorn Mts., *U.S.A.* . 72 D10
Bigstone L., *Canada* . 65 C9
Bihać, *Bos.-H.* 16 F8
Bihar, *India* 37 G14
Bihar □, *India* 37 G14
Bihor, Munții, *Romania* 17 E12
Bijagós, Arquipélago
  dos, *Guinea-Biss.* . 44 F1
Bijapur, *Karnataka,
  India* 36 L9
Bijapur, *Mad. P., India* 37 K12
Bijār, *Iran* 38 C5
Bijeljina, *Bos.-H.* 21 B8
Bijnor, *India* 36 E11
Bikaner, *India* 36 E8
Bikfayyā, *Lebanon* .. 41 B4
Bikin, *Russia* 25 E14
Bikin →, *Russia* 28 A7
Bikini Atoll, *Pac. Oc.* . 56 F8
Bila Tserkva, *Ukraine* 17 D16
Bilara, *India* 36 F8
Bilaspur, *India* 37 H13
Bilauk Taungdan,
  Thailand 34 F5
Bilbao, *Spain* 19 A4
Bilbo = Bilbao, *Spain* 19 A4
Bildudalur, *Iceland* .. 8 D2
Bilecik, *Turkey* 23 F5
Bilhorod-Dnivstrovskyy,
  Ukraine 23 E5
Bilibino, *Russia* 25 C17
Bilir, *Russia* 25 C14
Bill, *U.S.A.* 70 D2
Billabalong, *Australia* . 53 E2
Billiluna, *Australia* ... 52 C4
Billingham, *U.K.* 10 C6
Billings, *U.S.A.* 72 D9
Billiton Is. = Belitung,
  Indonesia 32 E3
Bilma, *Niger* 45 E7
Biloela, *Australia* ... 54 C5
Biloxi, *U.S.A.* 71 K10
Bilpa Morea Claypan,
  Australia 54 D2
Biltine, *Chad* 45 F9
Bilyana, *Australia* ... 54 B4
Bima, *Indonesia* 33 F5
Bimbo, *C.A.R.* 46 D3
Bina-Etawah, *India* .. 36 G11
Bināb, *Iran* 39 B8
Binalbagan, *Phil.* ... 33 B6
Binalong, *Australia* .. 55 E4
Bīnālūd, Kūh-e, *Iran* . 39 B8
Binatang, *Malaysia* .. 32 D4
Binbee, *Australia* ... 54 C4
Binche, *Belgium* 15 D4
Binda, *Australia* 55 D4
Bindle, *Australia* 55 D4
Bindura, *Zimbabwe* . 47 H6
Bingara, *N.S.W.,
  Australia* 55 D5
Bingara, *Queens.,
  Australia* 55 D3
Bingham, *U.S.A.* 63 C6
Bingham Canyon,
  U.S.A. 72 F7
Binghamton, *U.S.A.* . 68 D8
Binh Dinh = An Nhon,
  Vietnam 34 F10
Binh Son, *Vietnam* .. 34 E10
Binjai, *Indonesia* 32 D1
Binnaway, *Australia* . 55 E4
Binongko, *Indonesia* . 33 F6
Binscarth, *Canada* ... 65 C8
Bintan, *Indonesia* ... 32 D2
Bintulu, *Malaysia* ... 32 D4
Bintuni, *Indonesia* .. 33 E8
Binzert = Bizerte,
  Tunisia 44 A6
Bioko, *Eq. Guin.* 44 H6
Bir, *India* 36 K9
Bîr Abu Muhammad,
  Egypt 41 F3
Bi'r ad Dabbāghāt,
  Jordan 41 E4
Bi'r al Butayyihāt,
  Jordan 41 F4
Bi'r al Mārī, *Jordan* .. 41 E4
Bi'r al Qattār, *Jordan* . 41 F4
Bir Autrun, *Sudan* ... 45 E10
Bîr Beida, *Egypt* 41 E3
Bîr el 'Abd, *Egypt* ... 41 D2
Bîr el Biarât, *Egypt* .. 41 F3
Bîr el Duweidar, *Egypt* 41 E1
Bîr el Garârât, *Egypt* . 41 D2
Bîr el Heisi, *Egypt* ... 41 F3
Bîr el Jafir, *Egypt* ... 41 E1
Bîr el Mālhi, *Egypt* .. 41 E2
Bîr el Thamâda, *Egypt* 41 E2
Bîr Gebeil Hisn, *Egypt* 41 E2
Bi'r Ghadīr, *Syria* ... 41 A6
Bîr Hasana, *Egypt* ... 41 E2
Bi'r Jadīd, *Iraq* 38 C4
Bîr Kaseiba, *Egypt* .. 41 E2
Bîr Madkûr, *Egypt* .. 41 E1
Bir Mogrein, *Mauritania* 44 C2
Bi'r Mutribah, *Kuwait* . 38 D5
Bîr Qatia, *Egypt* 41 E1
Bîr Ungât, *Egypt* 45 D11
Bira, *Indonesia* 33 E9
Birao, *C.A.R.* 45 F9
Birch Hills, *Canada* .. 65 C7
Birch I., *Canada* 65 C9
Birch L., *N.W.T.,
  Canada* 64 A5
Birch L., *Ont., Canada* 62 C1
Birch Mts., *Canada* .. 64 B6
Birch River, *Canada* . 65 C8
Birchip, *Australia* ... 55 F3
Bird, *Canada* 65 B10
Bird City, *U.S.A.* 70 F4

Birdlip, *U.K.* 11 F5
Birdsville, *Australia* . . 54 D2
Birdum, *Australia* . . . 52 C5
Birein, *Israel* 41 E3
Bireuen, *Indonesia* . . 32 C1
Birkenhead, *U.K.* 10 D4
Bîrlad, *Romania* 17 E14
Bîrlad →, *Romania* . . 17 F14
Birmingham, *U.K.* . . . 11 E6
Birmingham, *U.S.A.* . . 69 J2
Birmitrapur, *India* . . . 37 H14
Birni Nkonni, *Niger* . . 44 F6
Birnin Kebbi, *Nigeria* . 44 F5
Birobidzhan, *Russia* . . 25 E14
Birr, *Ireland* 13 C4
Birrie →, *Australia* . . 55 D4
Birsk, *Russia* 22 C10
Birtle, *Canada* 65 C8
Birur, *India* 36 N9
Biržai, *Lithuania* 9 H21
Bisa, *Indonesia* 33 E7
Bisbee, *U.S.A.* 73 L9
Biscay, B. of, *Atl. Oc.* . 18 D1
Biscayne B., *U.S.A.* . . 69 N5
Biscoe Bay, *Antarctica* . 5 D13
Biscoe Is., *Antarctica* . 5 C17
Biscostasing, *Canada* . 62 C3
Bishkek, *Kyrgyzstan* . 24 E8
Bisho, *S. Africa* 49 E4
Bishop, *Calif., U.S.A.* . 73 H4
Bishop, *Tex., U.S.A.* . 71 M6
Bishop Auckland, *U.K.* . 10 C6
Bishop's Falls, *Canada* . 63 C8
Bishop's Stortford, *U.K.* 11 F8
Biskra, *Algeria* 44 B6
Bislig, *Phil.* 33 C7
Bismarck, *U.S.A.* 70 B4
Bismarck Arch.,
  Papua N. G. 56 H6
Bison, *U.S.A.* 70 C3
Bisotûn, *Iran* 38 C5
Bissagos = Bijagós,
  Arquipélago dos,
  Guinea-Biss. 44 F1
Bissau, *Guinea-Biss.* . 44 F1
Bissett, *Canada* 65 C9
Bistcho L., *Canada* . . 64 B5
Bistriţa, *Romania* . . . 17 E13
Bistriţa →, *Romania* . . 17 E14
Bitam, *Gabon* 46 D2
Bitkine, *Chad* 45 F8
Bitlis, *Turkey* 23 G7
Bitola, *Macedonia* . . . 21 D9
Bitolj = Bitola,
  Macedonia 21 D9
Bitter Creek, *U.S.A.* . . 72 F9
Bitter L. = Buheirat-
  Murrat-el-Kubra,
  Egypt 45 B11
Bitterfontein, *S. Africa* 48 E2
Bitterroot →, *U.S.A.* . 72 C6
Bitterroot Range, *U.S.A.* 72 D6
Biu, *Nigeria* 45 F7
Biwa-Ko, *Japan* 29 G8
Biwabik, *U.S.A.* 70 B8
Biysk, *Russia* 24 D9
Bizana, *S. Africa* 49 E4
Bizen, *Japan* 29 G7
Bizerte, *Tunisia* 44 A6
Bjargtangar, *Iceland* . 8 D1
Bjelovar, *Croatia* 20 B7
Bjørnevatn, *Norway* . . 8 B23
Bjørnøya, *Arctic* 4 B8
Black = Da →,
  Vietnam 34 B8
Black →, *Ark., U.S.A.* 71 H9
Black →, *Wis., U.S.A.* 70 D9
Black Diamond, *Canada* 64 C6
Black Forest =
  Schwarzwald,
  Germany 16 D5
Black Hills, *U.S.A.* . . . 70 C3
Black I., *Canada* 65 C9
Black L., *Canada* 65 B7
Black L., *U.S.A.* 68 C3
Black Mesa, *U.S.A.* . . 71 G3
Black Mt. = Mynydd
  Du, *U.K.* 11 F4
Black Mts., *U.K.* 11 F4
Black Range, *U.S.A.* . 73 K10
Black River, *Jamaica* . 74 K16
Black River Falls, *U.S.A.* 70 C9
Black Sea, *Eurasia* . . 23 F6
Black Volta →, *Africa* 44 G4
Black Warrior →,
  U.S.A. 69 J2
Blackall, *Australia* . . . 54 C4
Blackball, *N.Z.* 51 K3
Blackbull, *Australia* . . 54 B3
Blackburn, *U.K.* 10 D5
Blackduck, *U.S.A.* . . . 70 B7
Blackfoot, *U.S.A.* . . . 72 E7
Blackfoot →, *U.S.A.* . 72 C7
Blackfoot River
  Reservoir, *U.S.A.* . . 72 E8
Blackie, *Canada* 64 C6
Blackpool, *U.K.* 10 D4
Blacks Harbour, *Canada* 63 C6
Blacksburg, *U.S.A.* . . 68 G5
Blacksod B., *Ireland* . 13 B2
Blackstone, *U.S.A.* . . 68 G6
Blackstone →, *Canada* 64 A4
Blackstone Ra.,
  Australia 53 E4
Blackville, *Canada* . . . 63 C6
Blackwater, *Australia* . 54 C4
Blackwater →, *Ireland* 13 E4
Blackwater →, *U.K.* . 13 B5
Blackwater Cr. →,
  Australia 55 D3
Blackwell, *U.S.A.* . . . 71 G6
Blaenau Ffestiniog, *U.K.* 10 E4

Blagodarnoye =
  Blagodarnyy, *Russia* 23 E7
Blagodarnyy, *Russia* . . 23 E7
Blagoevgrad, *Bulgaria* 21 C10
Blagoveshchensk,
  Russia 25 D13
Blaine, *U.S.A.* 72 B2
Blaine Lake, *Canada* . 65 C7
Blair, *U.S.A.* 70 E6
Blair Athol, *Australia* . 54 C4
Blair Atholl, *U.K.* 12 E5
Blairgowrie, *U.K.* 12 E5
Blairmore, *Canada* . . . 64 D6
Blake Pt., *U.S.A.* 70 A10
Blakely, *U.S.A.* 69 K3
Blanc, *Mont, Alps* . . . 18 D7
Blanc, B., *Argentina* . . 80 D4
Blanca Peak, *U.S.A.* . 73 H11
Blanchard, *U.S.A.* . . . 71 H6
Blanche, C., *Australia* . 55 E1
Blanche, L., *S. Austral.*,
  Australia 55 D2
Blanche, L., *W. Austral.*,
  Australia 52 D3
Blanco, *S. Africa* 48 E3
Blanco, *U.S.A.* 71 K5
Blanco, C., *U.S.A.* . . . 72 E1
Blanda →, *Iceland* . . 8 D3
Blandford Forum, *U.K.* 11 G5
Blanding, *U.S.A.* 73 H9
Blanes, *Spain* 19 B7
Blankenberge, *Belgium* 15 C3
Blantyre, *Malawi* 47 H6
Blarney, *Ireland* 13 E3
Blåvands Huk, *Denmark* 9 J13
Blaydon, *U.K.* 10 C6
Blayney, *Australia* . . . 55 E4
Blaze, Pt., *Australia* . . 52 B5
Blednaya, Gora, *Russia* 24 B7
Blekinge, *Sweden* . . . 9 H16
Blenheim, *N.Z.* 51 J4
Blida, *Algeria* 44 A5
Bligh Sound, *N.Z.* . . . 51 L1
Blind River, *Canada* . . 62 C3
Blitar, *Indonesia* 33 H15
Blitta, *Togo* 44 G5
Block I., *U.S.A.* 68 E10
Blodgett Iceberg
  Tongue, *Antarctica* . 5 C9
Bloemfontein, *S. Africa* 48 D4
Bloemhof, *S. Africa* . . 48 D4
Blois, *France* 18 C4
Blönduós, *Iceland* . . . 8 D3
Bloodvein →, *Canada* 65 C9
Bloody Foreland,
  Ireland 13 A3
Bloomer, *U.S.A.* 70 C9
Bloomfield, *Australia* . 54 B4
Bloomfield, *Iowa*,
  U.S.A. 70 E8
Bloomfield, *N. Mex.*,
  U.S.A. 73 H10
Bloomfield, *Nebr.*,
  U.S.A. 70 D6
Bloomington, *Ill.*,
  U.S.A. 70 E10
Bloomington, *Ind.*,
  U.S.A. 68 F2
Bloomsburg, *U.S.A.* . . 68 E7
Blora, *Indonesia* 33 G14
Blouberg, *S. Africa* . . 49 C4
Blountstown, *U.S.A.* . 69 K3
Blue Island, *U.S.A.* . . 68 E2
Blue Lake, *U.S.A.* . . . 72 F2
Blue Mesa Reservoir,
  U.S.A. 73 G10
Blue Mts., *Oreg., U.S.A.* 72 D4
Blue Mts., *Pa., U.S.A.* 68 E7
Blue Mud B., *Australia* 54 A2
Blue Nile = Nîl el
  Azraq →, *Sudan* . . 45 E11
Blue Rapids, *U.S.A.* . . 70 F6
Blue Ridge Mts., *U.S.A.* 69 G5
Blue Stack Mts., *Ireland* 13 B3
Blueberry →, *Canada* 64 B4
Bluefield, *U.S.A.* 68 G5
Bluefields, *Nic.* 75 E8
Bluff, *Australia* 54 C4
Bluff, *N.Z.* 51 M2
Bluff, *U.S.A.* 73 H9
Bluff Knoll, *Australia* . 53 F2
Bluff Pt., *Australia* . . 53 E1
Blufffton, *U.S.A.* 68 E3
Blumenau, *Brazil* 80 B7
Blunt, *U.S.A.* 70 C4
Bly, *U.S.A.* 72 E3
Blyth, *U.K.* 10 B6
Blyth Bridge, *U.K.* . . . 10 E5
Blythe, *U.S.A.* 73 K6
Bo, *S. Leone* 44 G2
Bo Duc, *Vietnam* 34 G9
Bo Hai, *China* 31 C6
Boa Vista, *Brazil* 78 C6
Boatman, *Australia* . . 55 D4
Bobadah, *Australia* . . 55 E4
Bobbili, *India* 37 K13
Bobcaygeon, *Canada* . 62 D4
Bobo-Dioulasso,
  Burkina Faso 44 F4
Bóbr →, *Poland* 16 B8
Bobraomby, Tanjon' i,
  Madag. 49 A8
Bobruysk = Babruysk,
  Belarus 17 B15
Bôca do Acre, *Brazil* . 78 E5
Boca Raton, *U.S.A.* . . 69 M5
Bocaiúva, *Brazil* 79 G10
Bocanda, *Ivory C.* . . . 44 G4
Bocaranga, *C.A.R.* . . . 45 G8
Bochnia, *Poland* 17 D11
Bochum, *Germany* . . . 16 C4
Boda, *C.A.R.* 46 D3

Bodaybo, *Russia* 25 D12
Boddington, *Australia* . 53 F2
Boden, *Sweden* 8 D19
Bodensee, *Europe* . . . 16 E5
Bodhan, *India* 36 K10
Bodmin, *U.K.* 11 G3
Bodmin Moor, *U.K.* . . 11 G3
Bodø, *Norway* 8 C16
Bodrog →, *Hungary* . 17 D11
Bodrum, *Turkey* 21 F12
Boende, *Zaïre* 46 E4
Boerne, *U.S.A.* 71 L5
Boffa, *Guinea* 44 F2
Bogalusa, *U.S.A.* 71 K10
Bogan Gate, *Australia* 55 E4
Bogantungan, *Australia* 54 C4
Bogata, *U.S.A.* 71 J7
Boggabilla, *Australia* . 55 D5
Boggabri, *Australia* . . 55 E5
Boggeragh Mts.,
  Ireland 13 D3
Bognor Regis, *U.K.* . . 11 G7
Bogo, *Phil.* 33 B6
Bogong, Mt., *Australia* 55 F4
Bogor, *Indonesia* 33 G12
Bogorodskoye, *Russia* 25 D15
Bogotá, *Colombia* . . . 78 C4
Bogotol, *Russia* 24 D9
Bogra, *Bangla.* 37 G16
Boguchany, *Russia* . . 25 D10
Bogué, *Mauritania* . . 44 E2
Bohemia Downs,
  Australia 52 C4
Bohemian Forest =
  Böhmerwald,
  Germany 16 D7
Bohena Cr. →,
  Australia 55 E4
Böhmerwald, *Germany* 16 D7
Bohol, *Phil.* 33 C6
Bohol Sea, *Phil.* 33 C6
Bohotleh, *Somali Rep.* 40 F4
Bohuslän, *Sweden* . . . 9 G14
Boileau, C., *Australia* . 52 C3
Boise, *U.S.A.* 72 E5
Boise City, *U.S.A.* . . . 71 G3
Boissevain, *Canada* . . 65 D8
Bojador C., *W. Sahara* 44 C2
Bojana →, *Albania* . . 21 D8
Bojnûrd, *Iran* 39 B8
Bojonegoro, *Indonesia* 33 G14
Boké, *Guinea* 44 F2
Bokhara →, *Australia* 55 D4
Boknafjorden, *Norway* 9 G11
Bokoro, *Chad* 45 F8
Bokote, *Zaïre* 46 E4
Bokpyin, *Burma* 34 G5
Bokungu, *Zaïre* 46 E4
Bol, *Chad* 45 F7
Bolama, *Guinea-Biss.* 44 F1
Bolan Pass, *Pakistan* . 36 E5
Bolbec, *France* 18 B4
Boldâjî, *Iran* 39 D6
Bole, *China* 30 B3
Bolekhiv, *Ukraine* . . . 17 D12
Bolekhov = Bolekhiv,
  Ukraine 17 D12
Bolesławiec, *Poland* . 16 C8
Bolgrad = Bolhrad,
  Ukraine 17 F15
Bolhrad, *Ukraine* 17 F15
Bolinao C., *Phil.* 33 A5
Bolívar, *Argentina* . . . 80 D4
Bolívar, *Colombia* . . . 78 C3
Bolivar, *Mo., U.S.A.* . 71 G8
Bolivar, *Tenn., U.S.A.* 71 H10
Bolivia ■, *S. Amer.* . . 78 G6
Bolivian Plateau,
  S. Amer. 76 E4
Bollnäs, *Sweden* 9 F17
Bollon, *Australia* 55 D4
Bolmen, *Sweden* 9 H15
Bolobo, *Zaïre* 46 E3
Bologna, *Italy* 20 B4
Bologoye, *Russia* . . . 22 C5
Bolomba, *Zaïre* 46 D3
Bolong, *Phil.* 33 C6
Boloven, Cao Nguyen,
  Laos 34 E9
Bolsena, L. di, *Italy* . . 20 C4
Bolshereche, *Russia* . 24 D8
Bolshevik, Ostrov,
  Russia 25 B11
Bolshezemelskaya
  Tundra, *Russia* 22 A10
Bolshoi Kavkas =
  Caucasus Mountains,
  Eurasia 23 F7
Bolshoy Anyuy →,
  Russia 25 C17
Bolshoy Atlym, *Russia* 24 C7
Bolshoy Begichev,
  Ostrov, *Russia* 25 B12
Bolshoy Lyakhovskiy,
  Ostrov, *Russia* 25 B15
Bolshoy Tyuters,
  Ostrov, *Russia* 9 G22
Bolsward, *Neths.* 15 A5
Bolton, *U.K.* 10 D5
Bolu, *Turkey* 23 F5
Bolungavík, *Iceland* . 8 C2
Bolvadin, *Turkey* 23 G5
Bolzano, *Italy* 20 A4
Bom Jesus da Lapa,
  Brazil 79 F10
Boma, *Zaïre* 46 F2
Bomaderry, *Australia* . 55 E5
Bombala, *Australia* . . 55 F4
Bombay, *India* 36 K8
Bomboma, *Zaïre* 46 D3
Bomili, *Zaïre* 46 D5
Bømlo, *Norway* 9 G11

Bomongo, *Zaïre* 46 D3
Bomu →, *C.A.R.* 46 D4
Bon, C., *Tunisia* 45 A7
Bonaire, *Neth. Ant.* . . 75 E11
Bonang, *Australia* . . . 55 F4
Bonaparte Arch.,
  Australia 52 B3
Bonaventure, *Canada* . 63 C6
Bonavista, *Canada* . . 63 C9
Bonavista, C., *Canada* 63 C9
Bondo, *Zaïre* 46 D4
Bondoukou, *Ivory C.* . 44 G4
Bondowoso, *Indonesia* 33 G15
Bone, Teluk, *Indonesia* 33 E6
Bonerate, *Indonesia* . 33 F6
Bonerate, Kepulauan,
  Indonesia 33 F6
Bo'ness, *U.K.* 12 E5
Bong Son = Hoai
  Nhon, *Vietnam* 34 E10
Bongandanga, *Zaïre* . 46 D4
Bongor, *Chad* 45 F8
Bonham, *U.S.A.* 71 J6
Bonifacio, *France* . . . 18 F8
Bonin Is. = Ogasawara
  Gunto, *Pac. Oc.* . . . 56 E6
Bonn, *Germany* 16 C4
Bonne Terre, *U.S.A.* . 71 G9
Bonners Ferry, *U.S.A.* 72 B5
Bonney, L., *Australia* . 55 F3
Bonnie Downs,
  Australia 54 C3
Bonnie Rock, *Australia* 53 F2
Bonny, Bight of, *Africa* 46 D1
Bonnyville, *Canada* . . 65 C6
Bonoi, *Indonesia* 33 E9
Bontang, *Indonesia* . . 32 D5
Bonthain, *Indonesia* . 33 F5
Bonthe, S. *Leone* 44 G2
Bontoc, *Phil.* 33 A6
Bonython Ra., *Australia* 52 D4
Bookabie, *Australia* . . 53 F5
Booker, *U.S.A.* 71 G4
Boolaboolka L.,
  Australia 55 E3
Booligal, *Australia* . . . 55 E3
Boom, *Belgium* 15 C4
Boonah, *Australia* . . . 55 D5
Boone, *Iowa, U.S.A.* . 70 D8
Boone, *N.C., U.S.A.* . 69 G5
Booneville, *Ark., U.S.A.* 71 H8
Booneville, *Miss.*,
  U.S.A. 69 H1
Boonville, *Ind., U.S.A.* 68 F2
Boonville, *Mo., U.S.A.* 70 F8
Boonville, *N.Y., U.S.A.* 68 D8
Boorindal, *Australia* . . 55 E4
Boorowa, *Australia* . . 55 E4
Boothia, Gulf of,
  Canada 61 A11
Boothia Pen., *Canada* . 60 A10
Bootle, *U.K.* 10 D4
Booué, *Gabon* 46 E2
Bor, *Serbia, Yug.* . . . 21 B10
Bôr, *Sudan* 45 G11
Bor Mashash, *Israel* . 41 D3
Borâdâ →, *Syria* . . . 41 B5
Borah Peak, *U.S.A.* . . 72 D7
Borama, *Somali Rep.* . 40 F3
Borås, *Sweden* 9 H15
Borâzjân, *Iran* 39 D6
Borba, *Brazil* 78 D7
Bord Khûn-e Now, *Iran* 39 D6
Borda, C., *Australia* . . 55 F2
Bordeaux, *France* . . . 18 D3
Borden, *Australia* . . . 53 F2
Borden, *Canada* 63 C7
Borden I., *Canada* . . . 4 B2
Borders □, *U.K.* 12 F6
Bordertown, *Australia* 55 F3
Borðeyri, *Iceland* . . . 8 D3
Bordj Fly Ste. Marie,
  Algeria 44 C4
Bordj-in-Eker, *Algeria* 44 D6
Bordj Omar Driss,
  Algeria 44 C6
Bordj-Tarat, *Algeria* . 44 C6
Borgå = Porvoo,
  Finland 9 F21
Borgarnes, *Iceland* . . 8 D3
Børgefjell, *Norway* . . 8 D15
Borger, *Neths.* 15 B6
Borger, *U.S.A.* 71 H4
Borgholm, *Sweden* . . 9 H17
Borikhane, *Laos* . . . . (not present)
Borisoglebsk, *Russia* . 23 D7
Borisov = Barysaw,
  Belarus 17 A15
Borja, *Peru* 78 D3
Borkou, *Chad* 45 E8
Borkum, *Germany* . . . 16 B4
Borlänge, *Sweden* . . . 9 F16
Borley, C., *Antarctica* . 5 C5
Borneo, E. *Indies* . . . 32 D5
Bornholm, *Denmark* . . 9 J16
Borobudur, *Indonesia* 33 G14
Borogontsy, *Russia* . . 25 C14
Boromo, *Burkina Faso* 44 F4
Borongan, *Phil.* 33 B7
Bororen, *Australia* . . . 54 C5
Borovichi, *Russia* . . . 22 C5
Borroloola, *Australia* . 54 B2
Borşa, *Romania* 17 E13
Borth, *U.K.* 11 E3
Borûjerd, *Iran* 39 C6
Boryslav, *Ukraine* . . . 17 D12
Borzya, *Russia* 25 D12
Bosa, *Italy* 20 D3
Bosanska Gradiška,
  Bos.-H. 20 B7
Bosaso, *Somali Rep.* . 40 E4
Boscastle, *U.K.* 11 G3
Boshof, *S. Africa* 48 D4
Boshrûyeh, *Iran* 39 C8

Bosna →, *Bos.-H.* . . . 21 B8
Bosna i Hercegovina =
  Bosnia-
  Herzegovina ■,
  Europe 20 B7
Bosnia-Herzegovina ■,
  Europe 20 B7
Bosnik, *Indonesia* . . . 33 E9
Bosobolo, *Zaïre* 46 D3
Bosporus = Karadeniz
  Boğazı, *Turkey* 21 D13
Bossangoa, *C.A.R.* . . 45 G8
Bossembélé, *C.A.R.* . 45 G8
Bossier City, *U.S.A.* . 71 J8
Bosso, *Niger* 45 F7
Bostan Hu, *China* . . . 30 B3
Boston, *U.K.* 10 E7
Boston, *U.S.A.* 68 D10
Boston Bar, *Canada* . 64 D4
Boswell, *Canada* 64 D5
Boswell, *U.S.A.* 71 H7
Botany B., *Australia* . 55 E5
Bothaville, *S. Africa* . 48 D4
Bothnia, G. of, *Europe* 8 E19
Bothwell, *Australia* . . 54 G4
Botletle →, *Botswana* 48 C3
Botoşani, *Romania* . . 17 E14
Botswana ■, *Africa* . 48 C3
Bottineau, *U.S.A.* . . . 70 A4
Bottrop, *Germany* . . . 15 C6
Botucatu, *Brazil* 80 A7
Botwood, *Canada* . . . 63 C8
Bou Djébéha, *Mali* . . 44 E4
Bou Izakarn, *Morocco* 44 C3
Bouaké, *Ivory C.* 44 G3
Bouar, *C.A.R.* 46 C3
Bouârfa, *Morocco* . . . 44 B4
Bouca, *C.A.R.* 45 G8
Boucaut B., *Australia* 54 A1
Bougainville, C.,
  Australia 52 B4
Bougainville Reef,
  Australia 54 B4
Bougie = Bejaia,
  Algeria 44 A6
Bougouni, *Mali* 44 F3
Bouillon, *Belgium* . . . 15 E5
Boulder, *Colo., U.S.A.* 70 E2
Boulder, *Mont., U.S.A.* 72 C7
Boulder City, *U.S.A.* . 73 J6
Boulder Dam = Hoover
  Dam, *U.S.A.* 73 J6
Boulia, *Australia* 54 C2
Boulogne-sur-Mer,
  France 18 A4
Boultoum, *Niger* 44 F7
Bouna, *Ivory C.* 44 G4
Boundali, *Ivory C.* . . . 44 G3
Bountiful, *U.S.A.* 72 F8
Bounty Is., *Pac. Oc.* . 56 M9
Bourbonnais, *France* . 18 C5
Bourem, *Mali* 44 E4
Bourg-en-Bresse,
  France 18 C6
Bourg-St.-Maurice,
  France 18 D7
Bourges, *France* 18 C5
Bourgogne, *France* . . 18 C6
Bourke, *Australia* . . . 55 E4
Bournemouth, *U.K.* . . 11 G6
Bousso, *Chad* 45 F8
Boutilimit, *Mauritania* 44 E2
Bouvet I. = Bouvetøya,
  Antarctica 3 G10
Bouvetøya, *Antarctica* 3 G10
Bovigny, *Belgium* . . . 15 D5
Bovill, *U.S.A.* 72 C5
Bow Island, *Canada* . 64 D6
Bowbells, *U.S.A.* . . . 70 A3
Bowdle, *U.S.A.* 70 C5
Bowelling, *Australia* . 53 F2
Bowen, *Australia* 54 C4
Bowen Mts., *Australia* 55 F4
Bowie, *Ariz., U.S.A.* . 73 K9
Bowie, *Tex., U.S.A.* . 71 J6
Bowkân, *Iran* 38 B5
Bowland, Forest of,
  U.K. 10 D5
Bowling Green, *Ky.*,
  U.S.A. 68 G2
Bowling Green, *Ohio*,
  U.S.A. 68 E4
Bowling Green, C.,
  Australia 54 B4
Bowman, *U.S.A.* 70 B3
Bowman I., *Antarctica* 5 C8
Bowmans, *Australia* . 55 E2
Bowmanville, *Canada* . 62 D4
Bowmore, *U.K.* 12 F2
Bowral, *Australia* . . . 55 E5
Bowraville, *Australia* . 55 E5
Bowron →, *Canada* . 64 C4
Bowser L., *Canada* . . 64 B3
Bowsman, *Canada* . . 65 C8
Boxtel, *Neths.* 15 C5
Boyce, *U.S.A.* 71 K8
Boyer →, *Canada* . . 64 B5
Boyle, *Ireland* 13 C3
Boyne →, *Ireland* . . . 13 C5
Boyne City, *U.S.A.* . . 68 C3
Boynton Beach, *U.S.A.* 69 M5
Boyup Brook, *Australia* 53 F2
Boz Dağları, *Turkey* . 21 E13
Bozburun, *Turkey* . . . 21 F13
Bozcaada, *Turkey* . . . 21 E12
Bozdoğan, *Turkey* . . . 21 F13
Bozeman, *U.S.A.* . . . 72 D8
Bozen = Bolzano, *Italy* 20 A4
Bozoum, *C.A.R.* 45 G8

Brač, *Croatia* 20 C7
Bracadale, L., *U.K.* . . 12 D2
Bracciano, L. di, *Italy* . 20 C5
Bracebridge, *Canada* . 62 C4
Brach, *Libya* 45 C7
Bräcke, *Sweden* 9 E16
Brackettville, *U.S.A.* . 71 L4
Brad, *Romania* 17 E12
Bradenton, *U.S.A.* . . . 69 M4
Bradford, *U.K.* 10 D6
Bradford, *U.S.A.* 68 E6
Bradley, *Ark., U.S.A.* 71 J8
Bradley, *S. Dak., U.S.A.* 70 C5
Bradore Bay, *Canada* 63 B8
Bradshaw, *Australia* . 52 C5
Brady, *U.S.A.* 71 K5
Braemar, *Australia* . . 55 E2
Braga, *Portugal* 19 B1
Bragança, *Brazil* 79 D9
Bragança, *Portugal* . . 19 B2
Brahmanbaria, *Bangla.* 37 H17
Brahmani →, *India* . . 37 J15
Brahmaputra →, *India* 37 H16
Braich-y-pwll, *U.K.* . . 10 E3
Braidwood, *Australia* . 55 F4
Bräila, *Romania* 17 F14
Brainerd, *U.S.A.* 70 B7
Braintree, *U.K.* 11 F8
Brak →, *S. Africa* . . . 48 D3
Brakwater, *Namibia* . 48 C2
Bralorne, *Canada* . . . 64 C4
Brampton, *Canada* . . 62 D4
Bramwell, *Australia* . 54 A3
Branco →, *Brazil* . . . 78 D6
Brandenburg =
  Neubrandenburg,
  Germany 16 B7
Brandenburg, *Germany* 16 B7
Brandenburg □,
  Germany 16 B6
Brandfort, *S. Africa* . . 48 D4
Brandon, *Canada* . . . 65 D9
Brandon B., *Ireland* . . 13 D1
Brandon Mt., *Ireland* . 13 D1
Brandvlei, *S. Africa* . . 48 E3
Braniewo, *Poland* . . . 17 A10
Bransfield Str.,
  Antarctica 5 C18
Branson, *Colo., U.S.A.* 71 G3
Branson, *Mo., U.S.A.* 71 G8
Brantford, *Canada* . . 62 D3
Branxholme, *Australia* 55 F3
Bras d'Or, L., *Canada* 63 C7
Brasiléia, *Brazil* 78 F5
Brasília, *Brazil* 79 G9
Braslaw, *Belarus* . . . 9 J22
Braşov, *Romania* . . . 17 F13
Brasschaat, *Belgium* . 15 C4
Brassey, Banjaran,
  Malaysia 32 D5
Brassey Ra., *Australia* 53 E3
Brasstown Bald, *U.S.A.* 69 H4
Brastad, *Sweden* 9 G14
Bratislava, *Slovak Rep.* 17 D9
Bratsk, *Russia* 25 D11
Brattleboro, *U.S.A.* . . 68 D9
Braunau, *Austria* . . . 16 D7
Braunschweig,
  Germany 16 B6
Braunton, *U.K.* 11 F3
Brava, *Somali Rep.* . . 40 G3
Bravo del Norte, R. =
  Grande, Rio →,
  U.S.A. 71 N6
Brawley, *U.S.A.* 73 K6
Bray, *Ireland* 13 C5
Bray, Mt., *Australia* . . 54 A1
Bray, Pays de, *France* 18 B4
Brazeau →, *Canada* . 64 C5
Brazil, *U.S.A.* 68 F2
Brazil ■, *S. Amer.* . . . 79 F9
Brazos →, *U.S.A.* . . . 71 L7
Brazzaville, *Congo* . . 46 E3
Brčko, *Bos.-H.* 21 B8
Breadalbane, *Australia* 54 C2
Breadalbane, *U.K.* . . 12 E4
Breaden, L., *Australia* 53 E4
Breaksea Sd., *N.Z.* . . 51 L1
Bream B., *N.Z.* 51 F5
Bream Hd., *N.Z.* 51 F5
Brebes, *Indonesia* . . . 33 G13
Brechin, *U.K.* 12 E6
Breckenridge, *Colo.*,
  U.S.A. 72 G10
Breckenridge, *Minn.*,
  U.S.A. 70 B6
Breckenridge, *Tex.*,
  U.S.A. 71 J5
Breckland, *U.K.* 11 E8
Brecon, *U.K.* 11 F4
Brecon Beacons, *U.K.* 11 F4
Breda, *Neths.* 15 C4
Bredasdorp, *S. Africa* 48 E3
Bredbo, *Australia* . . . 55 F4
Bregenz, *Austria* . . . 16 E5
Breiðafjörður, *Iceland* 8 D2
Brejo, *Brazil* 79 D10
Bremen, *Germany* . . . 16 B5
Bremer I., *Australia* . . 54 A2
Bremerhaven, *Germany* 16 B5
Bremerton, *U.S.A.* . . 72 C2
Brenham, *U.S.A.* 71 K6
Brenner P., *Austria* . . 16 E6
Brent, *Canada* 62 C4
Brent, *U.K.* 11 F7
Brentwood, *U.K.* 11 F8
Bréscia, *Italy* 20 B4
Breskens, *Neths.* . . . 15 C3
Breslau = Wrocław,
  Poland 17 C9
Bressanone, *Italy* . . . 20 A4
Bressay, *U.K.* 12 A7
Brest, *Belarus* 17 B12

Brest

Brest, France 18 B1
Brest-Litovsk = Brest, Belarus 17 B12
Bretagne, France 18 B2
Breton, Canada 64 C6
Breton Sd., U.S.A. 71 L10
Brett, C., N.Z. 51 F5
Brevard, U.S.A. 69 H4
Brewarrina, Australia 55 D4
Brewer, U.S.A. 63 D6
Brewster, U.S.A. 72 B4
Brewster, Kap, Greenland 4 B6
Brewton, U.S.A. 69 K2
Breyten, S. Africa 49 D4
Brezhnev = Naberezhnyye Chelny, Russia 22 C9
Bria, C.A.R. 45 G9
Briançon, France 18 D7
Bribie I., Australia 55 D5
Bridgend, U.K. 11 F4
Bridgeport, Calif., U.S.A. 73 G4
Bridgeport, Conn., U.S.A. 68 E9
Bridgeport, Nebr., U.S.A. 70 E3
Bridgeport, Tex., U.S.A. 71 J6
Bridger, U.S.A. 72 D9
Bridgeton, U.S.A. 68 F8
Bridgetown, Australia 53 F2
Bridgetown, Barbados 74 P22
Bridgetown, Canada 63 D6
Bridgewater, Canada 63 D7
Bridgewater, U.S.A. 70 D6
Bridgewater, C., Australia 55 F3
Bridgnorth, U.K. 11 E5
Bridgwater, U.K. 11 F4
Bridlington, U.K. 10 C7
Bridport, Australia 54 G4
Bridport, U.K. 11 G5
Brig, Switz. 16 E4
Brigg, U.K. 10 D7
Briggsdale, U.S.A. 70 E2
Brigham City, U.S.A. 72 F7
Bright, Australia 55 F4
Brighton, Australia 55 F2
Brighton, Canada 62 D4
Brighton, U.K. 11 G7
Brighton, U.S.A. 70 F2
Brilliant, Canada 64 D5
Bríndisi, Italy 21 D7
Brinkley, U.S.A. 71 H9
Brinkworth, Australia 55 E2
Brion, I., Canada 63 C7
Brisbane, Australia 55 D5
Brisbane →, Australia 55 D5
Bristol, U.K. 11 F5
Bristol, Conn., U.S.A. 68 E9
Bristol, S. Dak., U.S.A. 70 C6
Bristol, Tenn., U.S.A. 69 G4
Bristol B., U.S.A. 60 C4
Bristol Channel, U.K. 11 F3
Bristol I., Antarctica 5 B1
Bristol L., U.S.A. 73 J5
Bristow, U.S.A. 71 H6
British Columbia □, Canada 64 C3
British Isles, Europe 6 E5
Brits, S. Africa 49 D4
Britstown, S. Africa 48 E3
Britt, Canada 62 C3
Brittany = Bretagne, France 18 B2
Britton, U.S.A. 70 C6
Brive-la-Gaillarde, France 18 D4
Brixen = Bressanone, Italy 20 A4
Brixton, Australia 54 C3
Brlik, Kazakhstan 24 E8
Brno, Czech. 17 D9
Broad →, U.S.A. 69 J5
Broad Arrow, Australia 53 F3
Broad B., U.K. 12 C2
Broad Haven, Ireland 13 B2
Broad Law, U.K. 12 F5
Broad Sd., Australia 54 C4
Broadhurst Ra., Australia 52 D3
Broads, The, U.K. 10 E9
Broadus, U.S.A. 70 C2
Broadview, Canada 65 C8
Brochet, Canada 65 B8
Brochet, L., Canada 65 B8
Brock, Canada 65 C7
Brocken, Germany 16 C6
Brockport, U.S.A. 68 D7
Brockville, Canada 62 D4
Brockway, U.S.A. 70 B2
Brodeur Pen., Canada 61 A11
Brodick, U.K. 12 F3
Brodnica, Poland 17 B10
Brody, Ukraine 17 C13
Brogan, U.S.A. 72 D5
Broken Bow, Nebr., U.S.A. 70 E5
Broken Bow, Okla., U.S.A. 71 H7
Broken Hill = Kabwe, Zambia 47 G5
Broken Hill, Australia 55 E3
Bromfield, U.K. 11 E5
Bromley, U.K. 11 F8
Brønderslev, Denmark 9 H13
Bronkhorstspruit, S. Africa 49 D4
Brønnøysund, Norway 8 D15
Bronte, U.S.A. 71 K4
Bronte Park, Australia 54 G4
Brookfield, U.S.A. 70 F8
Brookhaven, U.S.A. 71 K9
Brookings, Oreg., U.S.A. 72 E1
Brookings, S. Dak., U.S.A. 70 C6
Brookmere, Canada 64 D4
Brooks, Canada 64 C6
Brooks B., Canada 64 C3
Brooks L., Canada 65 A7
Brooks Ra., U.S.A. 60 B5
Brooksville, U.S.A. 69 L4
Brookville, U.S.A. 68 F3
Brooloo, Australia 55 D5
Broom, L., U.K. 12 D3
Broome, Australia 52 C3
Broomehill, Australia 53 F2
Brora, U.K. 12 C5
Brora →, U.K. 12 C5
Brosna →, Ireland 13 C4
Brothers, U.S.A. 72 E3
Brough, U.K. 10 C5
Broughton Island, Canada 61 B13
Broughty Ferry, U.K. 12 E6
Brouwershaven, Neths. 15 C3
Browerville, U.S.A. 70 B7
Brown, Pt., Australia 55 E1
Brown Willy, U.K. 11 G3
Brownfield, U.S.A. 71 J3
Browning, U.S.A. 72 B7
Brownlee, Canada 65 C7
Brownsville, Oreg., U.S.A. 72 D2
Brownsville, Tenn., U.S.A. 71 H10
Brownsville, Tex., U.S.A. 71 N6
Brownwood, U.S.A. 71 K5
Brownwood, L., U.S.A. 71 K5
Browse I., Australia 52 B3
Bruas, Malaysia 34 Q13
Bruay-en-Artois, France 18 A5
Bruce, Mt., Australia 52 D2
Bruce Rock, Australia 53 F2
Bruck an der Leitha, Austria 17 D9
Bruck an der Mur, Austria 16 E8
Brue →, U.K. 11 F5
Bruges = Brugge, Belgium 15 C3
Brugge, Belgium 15 C3
Brûlé, Canada 64 C5
Brumado, Brazil 79 F10
Brumunddal, Norway 9 F14
Brunchilly, Australia 54 B1
Brundidge, U.S.A. 69 K3
Bruneau, U.S.A. 72 E6
Bruneau →, U.S.A. 72 E6
Brunei = Bandar Seri Begawan, Brunei 32 C4
Brunei ■, Asia 32 D4
Brunette Downs, Australia 54 B2
Brunner, L., N.Z. 51 K3
Bruno, Canada 65 C7
Brunswick = Braunschweig, Germany 16 B6
Brunswick, Ga., U.S.A. 69 K5
Brunswick, Maine, U.S.A. 63 D6
Brunswick, Md., U.S.A. 68 F7
Brunswick, Mo., U.S.A. 70 F8
Brunswick, Pen. de, Chile 80 G2
Brunswick B., Australia 52 C3
Brunswick Junction, Australia 53 F2
Bruny I., Australia 54 G4
Brush, U.S.A. 70 E3
Brusque, Brazil 80 B7
Brussel, Belgium 15 D4
Brussels = Brussel, Belgium 15 D4
Bruthen, Australia 55 F4
Bruxelles = Brussel, Belgium 15 D4
Bryan, Ohio, U.S.A. 68 E3
Bryan, Tex., U.S.A. 71 K6
Bryan, Mt., Australia 55 E2
Bryansk, Russia 22 D5
Bryant, U.S.A. 70 C6
Bryne, Norway 9 G11
Bryson City, U.S.A. 69 H4
Bsharri, Lebanon 41 A5
Bū Baqarah, U.A.E. 39 E8
Bu Craa, W. Sahara 44 C2
Bū Ḥasā, U.A.E. 39 F7
Bua Yai, Thailand 34 E7
Buapinang, Indonesia 33 E6
Buayan, Phil. 33 C7
Būbiyān, Kuwait 39 D6
Bucaramanga, Colombia 78 B4
Buccaneer Arch., Australia 52 C3
Buchach, Ukraine 17 D13
Buchan, U.K. 12 D6
Buchan Ness, U.K. 12 D7
Buchanan, Canada 65 C8
Buchanan, Liberia 44 G2
Buchanan, L., Queens., Australia 54 C4
Buchanan, L., W. Austral., Australia 53 E3
Buchanan, L., U.S.A. 71 K5
Buchanan Cr. →, Australia 54 B2
Buchans, Canada 63 C8
Bucharest = Bucureşti, Romania 17 F14
Buckeye, U.S.A. 73 K7
Buckhannon, U.S.A. 68 F5
Buckhaven, U.K. 12 E5
Buckie, U.K. 12 D6
Buckingham, Canada 62 C4
Buckingham, U.K. 11 F7
Buckingham B., Australia 54 A2
Buckinghamshire □, U.K. 11 F7
Buckle Hd., Australia 52 B4
Buckleboo, Australia 55 E2
Buckley, U.S.A. 72 C2
Buckley →, Australia 54 C2
Bucklin, U.S.A. 71 G5
Buctouche, Canada 63 C7
Bucureşti, Romania 17 F14
Bucyrus, U.S.A. 68 E4
Budalin, Burma 37 H19
Budapest, Hungary 17 E10
Budd Coast, Antarctica 5 C8
Bude, U.K. 11 G3
Budennovsk, Russia 23 F7
Budgewoi, Australia 55 E5
Búðareyri, Iceland 8 D6
Budjala, Zaïre 46 D3
Buena Vista, Colo., U.S.A. 73 G10
Buena Vista, Va., U.S.A. 68 G6
Buena Vista L., U.S.A. 73 J4
Buenaventura, Colombia 78 C3
Buenos Aires, Argentina 80 C5
Buenos Aires, L., Chile 80 F2
Buffalo, Mo., U.S.A. 71 G8
Buffalo, N.Y., U.S.A. 68 D6
Buffalo, Okla., U.S.A. 71 G5
Buffalo, S. Dak., U.S.A. 70 C3
Buffalo, Wyo., U.S.A. 72 D10
Buffalo →, Canada 64 A5
Buffalo Head Hills, Canada 64 B5
Buffalo L., Canada 64 C6
Buffalo Narrows, Canada 65 B7
Buffels →, S. Africa 48 D2
Buford, U.S.A. 69 H4
Bug = Buh →, Ukraine 23 E5
Bug →, Poland 17 B11
Buga, Colombia 78 C3
Bugel, Tanjung, Indonesia 32 F4
Bugsuk, Phil. 32 C5
Bugulma, Russia 22 D9
Bugun Shara, Mongolia 30 B6
Buguruslan, Russia 22 D9
Buh →, Ukraine 23 E5
Buheirat-Murrat-el-Kubra, Egypt 45 B11
Buhl, Idaho, U.S.A. 72 E6
Buhl, Minn., U.S.A. 70 B8
Buick, U.S.A. 71 G9
Builth Wells, U.K. 11 E4
Buir Nur, Mongolia 31 B6
Bujumbura, Burundi 46 E5
Bukachacha, Russia 25 D12
Bukama, Zaïre 46 F5
Bukavu, Zaïre 46 E5
Bukene, Tanzania 46 E6
Bukhara = Bukhoro, Uzbekistan 24 F7
Bukhoro, Uzbekistan 24 F7
Bukittinggi, Indonesia 32 E2
Bukoba, Tanzania 46 E6
Bula, Indonesia 33 E8
Bulahdelah, Australia 55 E5
Bulan, Phil. 33 B6
Bulandshahr, India 36 E10
Bulawayo, Zimbabwe 47 J5
Buldan, Turkey 21 E13
Bulgaria ■, Europe 21 C11
Bulgroo, Australia 55 D3
Bulgunnia, Australia 55 E1
Bulhar, Somali Rep. 40 E3
Buli, Teluk, Indonesia 33 D7
Buliluyan, C., Phil. 32 C5
Bulkley →, Canada 64 B3
Bull Shoals L., U.S.A. 71 G8
Bullara, Australia 52 D1
Bullaring, Australia 53 F2
Bulli, Australia 55 E5
Bullock Creek, Australia 54 B3
Bulloo →, Australia 55 D3
Bulloo Downs, Queens., Australia 55 D3
Bulloo Downs, W. Austral., Australia 52 D2
Bulloo L., Australia 55 D3
Bulls, N.Z. 51 J5
Bulo Burti, Somali Rep. 40 G4
Bulsar = Valsad, India 36 J8
Bultfontein, S. Africa 48 D4
Bulu Karakelong, Indonesia 33 D7
Bulukumba, Indonesia 33 F6
Bulun, Russia 25 B13
Bulus, Russia 25 C13
Bumba, Zaïre 46 D4
Bumhpa Bum, Burma 37 F20
Buna, Kenya 46 D7
Bunbah, Khalīj, Libya 45 B9
Bunbury, Australia 53 F2
Buncrana, Ireland 13 A4
Bundaberg, Australia 55 C5
Bundey →, Australia 54 C2
Bundi, India 36 G9
Bundooma, Australia 54 C1
Bundoran, Ireland 13 B3
Bungatakada, Japan 29 H5
Bungil Cr. →, Australia 54 D4
Bungo-Suidō, Japan 29 H6
Bunia, Zaïre 46 D6
Bunji, Pakistan 36 B9
Bunkie, U.S.A. 71 K8
Bunnell, U.S.A. 69 L5
Buntok, Indonesia 32 E4
Bunyu, Indonesia 32 D5
Buol, Indonesia 33 D6
Buon Me Thuot, Vietnam 34 F10
Buorkhaya, Mys, Russia 25 B14
Buqayq, Si. Arabia 39 E6
Bur Acaba, Somali Rep. 40 G3
Bûr Safâga, Egypt 45 C11
Bûr Sa'îd, Egypt 45 B11
Bûr Sûdân, Sudan 45 E12
Burao, Somali Rep. 40 F4
Burâq, Syria 41 B5
Buras, U.S.A. 71 L10
Buraydah, Si. Arabia 38 E5
Burbank, U.S.A. 73 J4
Burcher, Australia 55 E4
Burdekin →, Australia 54 B4
Burdett, Canada 64 D6
Burdur, Turkey 23 G5
Burdwan = Barddhaman, India 37 H15
Bure →, U.K. 10 E9
Bureya →, Russia 25 E13
Burgas, Bulgaria 21 C12
Burgeo, Canada 63 C8
Burgersdorp, S. Africa 48 E4
Burges, Mt., Australia 53 F3
Burgos, Spain 19 A4
Burgsvik, Sweden 9 H18
Burgundy = Bourgogne, France 18 C6
Burhaniye, Turkey 21 E12
Burhanpur, India 36 J10
Burias, Phil. 33 B6
Burin, Canada 63 C8
Buriram, Thailand 34 E7
Burj Sāfitā, Syria 38 C3
Burji, Ethiopia 45 G12
Burkburnett, U.S.A. 71 H5
Burke, U.S.A. 72 C6
Burke →, Australia 54 C2
Burketown, Australia 54 B2
Burkina Faso ■, Africa 44 F4
Burk's Falls, Canada 62 C4
Burley, U.S.A. 72 E7
Burlington, Colo., U.S.A. 70 F3
Burlington, Iowa, U.S.A. 70 E9
Burlington, Kans., U.S.A. 70 F7
Burlington, N.C., U.S.A. 69 G6
Burlington, N.J., U.S.A. 68 E8
Burlington, Vt., U.S.A. 68 C9
Burlington, Wash., U.S.A. 72 B2
Burlington, Wis., U.S.A. 68 D1
Burlyu-Tyube, Kazakhstan 24 E8
Burma ■, Asia 37 J20
Burnaby I., Canada 64 C2
Burnet, U.S.A. 71 K5
Burney, U.S.A. 72 F3
Burngup, Australia 53 F2
Burnie, Australia 54 G4
Burnley, U.K. 10 D5
Burns, Oreg., U.S.A. 72 E4
Burns, Wyo., U.S.A. 70 E2
Burns Lake, Canada 64 C3
Burnside →, Canada 60 B9
Burnside, L., Australia 53 E3
Burntwood →, Canada 65 B9
Burntwood L., Canada 65 B8
Burqān, Kuwait 38 D5
Burra, Australia 55 E2
Burramurra, Australia 54 C2
Burren Junction, Australia 55 E4
Burrendong Dam, Australia 55 E4
Burrinjuck Res., Australia 55 F4
Burruyacú, Argentina 80 B4
Burry Port, U.K. 11 F3
Bursa, Turkey 21 D13
Burstall, Canada 65 C7
Burton L., Canada 62 B4
Burton upon Trent, U.K. 10 E6
Burtundy, Australia 55 E3
Buru, Indonesia 33 E7
Burûn, Râs, Egypt 41 D2
Burundi ■, Africa 46 E5
Burutu, Nigeria 44 G6
Burwell, U.S.A. 70 E5
Bury, U.K. 10 D5
Bury St. Edmunds, U.K. 11 E8
Buryatia □, Russia 25 D11
Buşayrah, Syria 38 C4
Buşayyah, Iraq 38 D5
Būshehr, Iran 39 D6
Būshehr □, Iran 39 D6
Bushell, Canada 65 B7
Bushire = Būshehr, Iran 39 D6
Bushnell, Ill., U.S.A. 70 E9
Bushnell, Nebr., U.S.A. 70 E3
Businga, Zaïre 46 D4
Busra ash Shām, Syria 41 C5
Busselton, Australia 53 F2
Bussum, Neths. 15 B5
Busto Arsízio, Italy 20 B3
Busu-Djanoa, Zaïre 46 D4
Busuanga, Phil. 33 B5
Buta, Zaïre 46 D4
Butare, Rwanda 46 E5
Butaritari, Kiribati 56 G9
Bute, U.K. 12 F3
Bute Inlet, Canada 64 C4
Butembo, Zaïre 46 D5
Butha Qi, China 31 B7
Butler, Mo., U.S.A. 70 F7
Butler, Pa., U.S.A. 68 E6
Buton, Indonesia 33 E6
Butte, Mont., U.S.A. 72 C7
Butte, Nebr., U.S.A. 70 D5
Butterworth = Gcuwa, S. Africa 49 E4
Butterworth, Malaysia 34 P13
Buttfield, Mt., Australia 53 D4
Button B., Canada 65 B10
Butty Hd., Australia 53 F3
Butuan, Phil. 33 C7
Butung = Buton, Indonesia 33 E6
Buturlinovka, Russia 23 D7
Buxtehude, Germany 16 B5
Buxton, U.K. 10 D6
Buy, Russia 22 C7
Büyük Menderes →, Turkey 21 F12
Büyükçekmece, Turkey 21 D13
Buzău, Romania 17 F14
Buzău →, Romania 17 F14
Buzen, Japan 29 H5
Buzi →, Mozam. 47 H6
Buzuluk, Russia 22 D9
Buzzards Bay, U.S.A. 68 E10
Byarezina →, Belarus 17 B16
Bydgoszcz, Poland 17 B9
Byelarus = Belarus ■, Europe 17 B14
Byelorussia = Belarus ■, Europe 17 B14
Byers, U.S.A. 70 F2
Byhalia, U.S.A. 71 H10
Bykhaw, Belarus 17 B16
Bykhov = Bykhaw, Belarus 17 B16
Bylas, U.S.A. 73 K8
Bylot I., Canada 61 A12
Byrd, C., Antarctica 5 C17
Byro, Australia 53 E2
Byrock, Australia 55 E4
Byron Bay, Australia 55 D5
Byrranga, Gory, Russia 25 B11
Byrranga Mts. = Byrranga, Gory, Russia 25 B11
Byske, Sweden 8 D19
Byske älv →, Sweden 8 D19
Bytom, Poland 17 C10
Bytów, Poland 17 A9

C

Ca Mau = Quan Long, Vietnam 34 H8
Ca Mau, Mui = Bai Bung, Mui, Vietnam 34 H8
Caála, Angola 47 G3
Caamano Sd., Canada 64 C3
Cabanatuan, Phil. 33 A6
Cabano, Canada 63 C6
Cabedelo, Brazil 79 E12
Cabimas, Venezuela 78 A4
Cabinda, Angola 46 F2
Cabinda □, Angola 46 F2
Cabinet Mts., U.S.A. 72 C6
Cabo Blanco, Argentina 80 F3
Cabo Frio, Brazil 79 H10
Cabo Pantoja, Peru 78 D3
Cabonga, Réservoir, Canada 62 C4
Cabool, U.S.A. 71 G8
Caboolture, Australia 55 D5
Cabora Bassa Dam = Cahora Bassa Dam, Mozam. 47 H6
Cabot Str., Canada 63 C8
Cabra, Spain 19 D3
Cabrera, Spain 19 C7
Cabri, Canada 65 C7
Cabriel →, Spain 19 C5
Čačak, Serbia, Yug. 21 C9
Cáceres, Brazil 78 G7
Cáceres, Spain 19 C2
Cache Bay, Canada 62 C4
Cachimbo, Serra do, Brazil 79 E7
Cachoeira, Brazil 79 F11
Cachoeira de Itapemirim, Brazil 79 H10
Cachoeira do Sul, Brazil 80 C6
Cacólo, Angola 46 G3
Caconda, Angola 47 G3
Cacongo, Angola 46 F2
Caddo, U.S.A. 71 H6
Cadell Cr. →, Australia 54 C3
Cader Idris, U.K. 10 E4
Cadibarrawirracanna, L., Australia 55 D2
Cadillac, Canada 62 C4
Cadillac, U.S.A. 68 C3
Cadiz, Phil. 33 B6
Cádiz, Spain 19 D2
Cádiz, G. de, Spain 19 D2
Cadney Park, Australia 55 D1
Cadomin, Canada 64 C5
Cadotte →, Canada 64 B5
Cadoux, Australia 53 F2
Caen, France 18 B3
Caernarfon, U.K. 10 D3
Caernarfon B., U.K. 10 D3
Caernarvon = Caernarfon, U.K. 10 D3
Caerphilly, U.K. 11 F4
Caesarea, Israel 41 C3
Caeté, Brazil 79 G10
Caetité, Brazil 79 F10
Cafu, Angola 48 B2
Cagayan →, Phil. 33 A6
Cagayan de Oro, Phil. 33 C6
Cágliari, Italy 20 E3
Cágliari, G. di, Italy 20 E3
Caguas, Puerto Rico 75 D11
Caha Mts., Ireland 13 E2
Cahama, Angola 48 B1
Caher, Ireland 13 D4
Cahersiveen, Ireland 13 E1
Cahora Bassa Dam, Mozam. 47 H6
Cahore Pt., Ireland 13 D5
Cahors, France 18 D4
Cahuapanas, Peru 78 E3
Cahul, Moldova 17 F15
Caia, Mozam. 47 H7
Caibarién, Cuba 75 C9
Caicara, Venezuela 78 B5
Caicó, Brazil 79 E11
Caicos Is., W. Indies 75 C10
Caird Coast, Antarctica 5 D1
Cairn Gorm, U.K. 12 D5
Cairn Toul, U.K. 12 D5
Cairngorm Mts., U.K. 12 D5
Cairns, Australia 54 B4
Cairo = El Qâhira, Egypt 45 B11
Cairo, Ga., U.S.A. 69 K3
Cairo, Ill., U.S.A. 71 G10
Caithness, Ord of, U.K. 12 C5
Caiundo, Angola 47 H3
Caiza, Bolivia 78 H5
Cajamarca, Peru 78 E3
Cajàzeiras, Brazil 79 E11
Calabar, Nigeria 44 H6
Calábria □, Italy 20 E7
Calafate, Argentina 80 G2
Calahorra, Spain 19 A5
Calais, France 18 A4
Calais, U.S.A. 63 C6
Calama, Brazil 78 E6
Calama, Chile 80 A3
Calamar, Bolívar, Colombia 78 A4
Calamar, Vaupés, Colombia 78 C4
Calamian Group, Phil. 33 B5
Calamocha, Spain 19 B5
Calang, Indonesia 32 D1
Calapan, Phil. 33 B6
Călăraşi, Romania 17 F14
Calatayud, Spain 19 B5
Calauag, Phil. 33 B6
Calavite, C., Phil. 33 B6
Calbayog, Phil. 33 B6
Calca, Peru 78 F4
Calcasieu L., U.S.A. 71 L8
Calcutta, India 37 H16
Caldas da Rainha, Portugal 19 C1
Calder →, U.K. 10 D6
Caldera, Chile 80 B2
Caldwell, Idaho, U.S.A. 72 E5
Caldwell, Kans., U.S.A. 71 G6
Caldwell, Tex., U.S.A. 71 K6
Caledon, S. Africa 48 E2
Caledon →, S. Africa 48 E4
Caledon B., Australia 54 A2
Calemba, Angola 48 B2
Calexico, U.S.A. 73 K6
Calf of Man, U.K. 10 C3
Calgary, Canada 64 C6
Calhoun, U.S.A. 69 H3
Cali, Colombia 78 C3
Calicut, India 36 P9
Caliente, U.S.A. 73 H6
California, U.S.A. 70 F8
California □, U.S.A. 73 H4
California, G. de, Mexico 74 B2
Calingasta, Argentina 80 C3
Calipatria, U.S.A. 73 K6
Calistoga, U.S.A. 72 G2
Calitzdorp, S. Africa 48 E3
Callabonna, L., Australia 55 D3
Callan, Ireland 13 D4
Callander, U.K. 12 E4
Callao, Peru 78 F3
Callaway, U.S.A. 70 E5
Callide, Australia 54 C5
Calling Lake, Canada 64 B6
Calliope, Australia 54 C5
Calola, Angola 48 B2
Caloundra, Australia 55 D5
Calstock, Canada 62 C3
Caltagirone, Italy 20 F6
Caltanissetta, Italy 20 F6
Calulo, Angola 46 G2
Calumet, U.S.A. 68 B1
Calunda, Angola 47 G4
Calvert, U.S.A. 71 K6
Calvert →, Australia 54 B2
Calvert Hills, Australia 54 B2
Calvert I., Canada 64 C3
Calvert Ra., Australia 52 D3
Calvi, France 18 E8
Calviá, Spain 19 C7
Calvinia, S. Africa 48 E2
Cam →, U.K. 11 E8
Cam Lam, Vietnam 34 G10
Cam Ranh, Vietnam 34 G10
Camabatela, Angola 46 F3
Camacupa, Angola 47 G3
Camagüey, Cuba 75 C9
Camaná, Peru 78 G4
Camargo, Bolivia 78 H5
Camargue, France 18 E6
Camarones, Argentina 80 E3

Camas, *U.S.A.* 72 D2
Camas Valley, *U.S.A.* . 72 E2
Cambay = Khambhat,
India 36 H8
Cambay, G. of =
Khambat, G. of, *India* 36 J8
Cambodia ■, *Asia* ... 34 F8
Camborne, *U.K.* 11 G2
Cambrai, *France* 18 A5
Cambria, *U.S.A.* 73 J3
Cambrian Mts., *U.K.* . 11 E4
Cambridge, *Canada* .. 62 D3
Cambridge, *N.Z.* 51 G5
Cambridge, *U.K.* 11 E8
Cambridge, *Idaho,*
U.S.A. 72 D5
Cambridge, *Mass.,*
U.S.A. 68 D10
Cambridge, *Md., U.S.A.* 68 F7
Cambridge, *Minn.,*
U.S.A. 70 C8
Cambridge, *Nebr.,*
U.S.A. 70 E4
Cambridge, *Ohio,*
U.S.A. 68 E5
Cambridge Bay,
Canada 60 B9
Cambridge G., *Australia* 52 B4
Cambridgeshire □, *U.K.* 11 E8
Cambundi-Catembo,
Angola 46 G3
Camden, *Ala., U.S.A.* . 69 K2
Camden, *Ark., U.S.A.* . 71 J8
Camden, *Maine, U.S.A.* 63 D11
Camden, *N.J., U.S.A.* . 68 F8
Camden, *S.C., U.S.A.* . 69 H5
Camden Sd., *Australia* . 52 C3
Camdenton, *U.S.A.* ... 71 F8
Cameron, *Ariz., U.S.A.* 73 J8
Cameron, *La., U.S.A.* . 71 L8
Cameron, *Mo., U.S.A.* 70 F7
Cameron, *Tex., U.S.A.* 71 K6
Cameron Falls, *Canada* 62 C2
Cameron Highlands,
Malaysia 34 Q14
Cameron Hills, *Canada* 64 B5
Cameroon ■, *Africa* .. 45 G7
Cameroun, Mt.,
Cameroon 44 H6
Cametá, *Brazil* 79 D9
Caminha, *Portugal* ... 19 B1
Camino, *U.S.A.* 72 G3
Camira Creek, *Australia* 55 D5
Camissombo, *Angola* . 46 F4
Camocim, *Brazil* 79 D10
Camooweal, *Australia* . 54 B2
Camopi →, *Fr. Guiana* 79 C8
Camp Crook, *U.S.A.* .. 70 C3
Camp Wood, *U.S.A.* .. 71 L4
Campana, *I., Chile* ... 80 F1
Campánia □, *Italy* 20 D6
Campbell, *S. Africa* ... 48 D3
Campbell I., *Pac. Oc.* . 56 N8
Campbell L., *Canada* . 65 A7
Campbell River, *Canada* 64 C3
Campbell Town,
Australia 54 G4
Campbellsville, *U.S.A.* 68 G3
Campbellton, *Canada* . 63 C6
Campbelltown,
Australia 55 E5
Campbeltown, *U.K.* .. 12 F3
Campeche, *Mexico* ... 74 D6
Campeche, B. de,
Mexico 74 D6
Camperdown, *Australia* 55 F3
Camperville, *Canada* . 65 C8
Campina Grande, *Brazil* 79 E11
Campinas, *Brazil* 80 A7
Campo, *Cameroon* ... 46 D1
Campo Belo, *Brazil* ... 79 H9
Campo Formoso, *Brazil* 79 F10
Campo Grande, *Brazil* 79 H8
Campo Maior, *Brazil* . 79 D10
Campo Mourão, *Brazil* 79 H8
Campoalegre,
Colombia 78 C3
Campobasso, *Italy* ... 20 D6
Campos, *Brazil* 79 H10
Campos Belos, *Brazil* . 79 F9
Campuya →, *Peru* ... 78 D4
Camrose, *Canada* 64 C6
Camsell Portage,
Canada 65 B7
Çan, *Turkey* 21 D12
Can Tho, *Vietnam* ... 34 G8
Canada ■, *N. Amer.* .. 60 C10
Cañada de Gómez,
Argentina 80 C4
Canadian, *U.S.A.* 71 H4
Canadian →, *U.S.A.* . 71 H7
Canadian Shield,
Canada 61 C10
Çanakkale, *Turkey* ... 21 D12
Çanakkale Boğazı,
Turkey 21 D12
Canal Flats, *Canada* .. 64 C5
Canandaigua, *U.S.A.* . 68 D7
Cananea, *Mexico* 74 A2
Canarias, Is., *Atl. Oc.* . 44 C1
Canary Is. = Canarias,
Is., *Atl. Oc.* 44 C1
Canaveral, C., *U.S.A.* . 69 L5
Canavieiras, *Brazil* ... 79 G11
Canbelego, *Australia* . 55 E4
Canberra, *Australia* ... 55 F4
Canby, *Calif., U.S.A.* . 72 F3
Canby, *Minn., U.S.A.* . 70 C6
Canby, *Oreg., U.S.A.* . 72 D2
Candala, *Somali Rep.* . 40 E4
Candelo, *Australia* ... 55 F4
Candia = Iráklion,
Greece 21 G11

Candle L., *Canada* 65 C7
Candlemas I.,
Antarctica 5 B1
Cando, *U.S.A.* 70 A5
Canea = Khaniá,
Greece 21 G11
Canelones, *Uruguay* .. 80 C5
Cañete, *Chile* 80 D2
Cañete, *Peru* 78 F3
Cangas de Narcea,
Spain 19 A2
Canguaretama, *Brazil* . 79 E11
Canguçu, *Brazil* 80 C6
Canicattì, *Italy* 20 F5
Canigou, Mt., *France* . 18 E5
Canim Lake, *Canada* . 64 C4
Canipaan, *Phil.* 32 C5
Çankırı, *Turkey* 23 F5
Cann River, *Australia* . 55 F4
Canna, *U.K.* 12 D2
Cannanore, *India* 36 P9
Cannes, *France* 18 E7
Cannock, *U.K.* 10 E5
Cannon Ball →, *U.S.A.* 70 B4
Cannondale Mt.,
Australia 54 D4
Canoas, *Brazil* 80 B6
Canoe L., *Canada* 65 B7
Canon City, *U.S.A.* .. 70 F2
Canora, *Canada* 65 C8
Canowindra, *Australia* 55 E4
Canso, *Canada* 63 C7
Cantabria □, *Spain* ... 19 A4
Cantabrian Mts. =
Cantábrica,
Cordillera, *Spain* .. 19 A3
Cantábrica, Cordillera,
Spain 19 A3
Cantal, Plomb du,
France 18 D5
Canterbury, *Australia* . 54 D3
Canterbury, *U.K.* 11 F9
Canterbury □, *N.Z.* .. 51 K3
Canterbury Bight, *N.Z.* 51 L3
Canterbury Plains, *N.Z.* 51 K3
Canton = Guangzhou,
China 31 D6
Canton, *Ga., U.S.A.* .. 69 H3
Canton, *Ill., U.S.A.* ... 70 E9
Canton, *Miss., U.S.A.* . 71 J9
Canton, *Mo., U.S.A.* . 70 E9
Canton, *N.Y., U.S.A.* . 68 C8
Canton, *Ohio, U.S.A.* . 68 E5
Canton, *Okla., U.S.A.* 71 G5
Canton, *S. Dak., U.S.A.* 70 D6
Canton L., *U.S.A.* 71 G5
Canudos, *Brazil* 78 E7
Canutama, *Brazil* 78 E6
Canutillo, *U.S.A.* 73 L10
Canyon, *Tex., U.S.A.* . 71 H4
Canyon, *Wyo., U.S.A.* 72 D8
Canyonlands National
Park, *U.S.A.* 73 G9
Canyonville, *U.S.A.* .. 72 E2
Cap-aux-Meules,
Canada 63 C7
Cap-Chat, *Canada* ... 63 C6
Cap-de-la-Madeleine,
Canada 62 C5
Cap-Haïtien, *Haiti* ... 75 D10
Cap St-Jacques =
Vung Tau, *Vietnam* . 34 G9
Capaia, *Angola* 46 F4
Capanaparo →,
Venezuela 78 B5
Cape →, *Australia* ... 54 C4
Cape Barren I.,
Australia 54 G4
Cape Breton Highlands
Nat. Park, *Canada* . 63 C7
Cape Breton I., *Canada* 63 C7
Cape Charles, *U.S.A.* . 68 G8
Cape Coast, *Ghana* .. 44 G4
Cape Dorset, *Canada* . 61 B12
Cape Dyer, *Canada* .. 61 B13
Cape Fear →, *U.S.A.* . 69 H6
Cape Girardeau, *U.S.A.* 71 G10
Cape Jervis, *Australia* . 55 F2
Cape May, *U.S.A.* 68 F8
Cape May Point, *U.S.A.* 67 C12
Cape Tormentine,
Canada 63 C7
Cape Town, *S. Africa* . 48 E2
Cape Verde Is. ■,
Atl. Oc. 2 D8
Cape York Peninsula,
Australia 54 A3
Capela, *Brazil* 79 F11
Capella, *Australia* 54 C4
Capim →, *Brazil* 79 D9
Capitan, *U.S.A.* 73 K11
Capoeira Group,
Australia 54 C4
Capricorn Ra., *Australia* 52 D2
Caprivi Strip, *Namibia* 48 B3
Captain's Flat, *Australia* 55 F4
Caquetá →, *Colombia* 78 D5
Caracal, *Romania* 17 F13
Caracas, *Venezuela* .. 78 A5
Caracol, *Brazil* 79 E10
Caradoc, *Australia* ... 55 E3
Carajás, Serra dos,
Brazil 79 E8
Carangola, *Brazil* 79 H10
Carani, *Australia* 53 F2
Caransebeş, *Romania* . 17 F12
Caratasca, L., *Honduras* 75 D7
Caratinga, *Brazil* 79 G10
Caraúbas, *Brazil* 79 E11

Caravaca, *Spain* 19 C5
Caravelas, *Brazil* 79 G11
Caraveli, *Peru* 78 G4
Carballo, *Spain* 19 A1
Carberry, *Canada* 65 D9
Carbon, *Canada* 64 C6
Carbonara, C., *Italy* .. 20 E3
Carbondale, *Colo.,*
U.S.A. 72 G10
Carbondale, *Ill., U.S.A.* 71 G10
Carbondale, *Pa., U.S.A.* 68 E8
Carbonear, *Canada* .. 63 C9
Carboneras, *Spain* ... 19 D5
Carbonia, *Italy* 20 E3
Carcajou, *Canada* 64 B5
Carcassonne, *France* . 18 E5
Carcross, *Canada* 60 B6
Cardabia, *Australia* .. 52 D1
Cardamon Hills, *India* . 36 Q10
Cárdenas, *Cuba* 75 C8
Cardiff, *U.K.* 11 F4
Cardigan, *U.K.* 11 E3
Cardigan B., *U.K.* 11 E3
Cardross, *Canada* 65 D7
Cardston, *Canada* 64 D6
Cardwell, *Australia* ... 54 B4
Careen L., *Canada* ... 65 B7
Carei, *Romania* 17 E12
Careme, *Indonesia* ... 33 G13
Carey, *Idaho, U.S.A.* . 72 E7
Carey, *Ohio, U.S.A.* .. 68 E4
Carey, L., *Australia* ... 53 E3
Carey, L., *Canada* 65 A8
Careysburg, *Liberia* .. 44 G2
Cargados Garajos,
Ind. Oc. 35 F4
Carhué, *Argentina* ... 80 D4
Caria, *Turkey* 21 F13
Cariacica, *Brazil* 79 H10
Caribbean Sea,
W. Indies 75 E10
Cariboo Mts., *Canada* 64 C4
Caribou, *U.S.A.* 63 C6
Caribou →, *Man.,*
Canada 65 B10
Caribou →, *N.W.T.,*
Canada 64 A3
Caribou I., *Canada* ... 62 C2
Caribou Is., *Canada* .. 64 A6
Caribou L., *Man.,*
Canada 65 B9
Caribou L., *Ont.,*
Canada 62 B2
Caribou Mts., *Canada* 64 B5
Carinda, *Australia* 55 E4
Carinhanha, *Brazil* ... 79 F10
Carinthia = Kärnten □,
Austria 16 E8
Caripito, *Venezuela* .. 78 A6
Caritianas, *Brazil* 78 E6
Carleton Place, *Canada* 62 C4
Carletonville, *S. Africa* 48 D4
Carlin, *U.S.A.* 72 F5
Carlingford L., *U.K.* .. 13 B5
Carlinville, *U.S.A.* 70 F10
Carlisle, *U.K.* 10 C5
Carlisle, *U.S.A.* 68 E7
Carlow, *Ireland* 13 D5
Carlow □, *Ireland* 13 D5
Carlsbad, *Calif., U.S.A.* 73 K5
Carlsbad, *N. Mex.,*
U.S.A. 71 J2
Carlyle, *Canada* 65 D8
Carlyle, *U.S.A.* 70 F10
Carmacks, *Canada* ... 60 B6
Carman, *Canada* 65 D9
Carmangay, *Canada* . 64 C6
Carmanville, *Canada* . 63 C9
Carmarthen, *U.K.* 11 F3
Carmarthen B., *U.K.* . 11 F3
Carmaux, *France* 18 D5
Carmel-by-the-Sea,
U.S.A. 73 H3
Carmelo, *Uruguay* ... 80 C5
Carmen, *Colombia* ... 78 B3
Carmen de Patagones,
Argentina 80 E4
Carmi, *U.S.A.* 68 F1
Carmila, *Australia* 54 C4
Carmona, *Spain* 19 D3
Carnac, *France* 18 C2
Carnarvon, *Queens.,*
Australia 54 C4
Carnarvon, *W. Austral.,*
Australia 53 D1
Carnarvon, *S. Africa* . 48 E3
Carnarvon Ra.,
Queens., Australia . 54 D4
Carnarvon Ra.,
W. Austral., Australia 53 E3
Carndonagh, *Ireland* . 13 A4
Carnduff, *Canada* 65 D8
Carnegie, *Canada* 62 C3
Carnegie, L., *Australia* 53 E3
Carnic Alps =
Karnische Alpen,
Europe 16 E7
Carniche Alpi =
Karnische Alpen,
Europe 16 E7
Carnot, *C.A.R.* 46 D3
Carnot, *Australia* 55 E2
Carnot B., *Australia* .. 52 C3
Carnsore Pt., *Ireland* . 13 D5
Caro, *U.S.A.* 68 D4
Carol City, *U.S.A.* ... 69 N5
Carolina, *Brazil* 79 E9
Carolina, *S. Africa* ... 49 D5
Caroline I., *Kiribati* ... 57 H12
Caroline Is., *Pac. Oc.* . 56 G6
Caroní →, *Venezuela* 78 B6
Caroníe = Nébrodi,
Monti, *Italy* 20 F6
Caroona, *Australia* ... 55 E5

Carpathians, *Europe* .. 17 D11
Carpaţii Meridionali,
Romania 17 F13
Carpentaria, G. of,
Australia 54 A2
Carpentaria Downs,
Australia 54 B3
Carpentras, *France* ... 18 D6
Carpi, *Italy* 20 B4
Carpinteria, *U.S.A.* ... 73 J4
Carpolac = Morea,
Australia 55 F3
Carr Boyd Ra., *Australia* 52 C4
Carrabelle, *U.S.A.* 69 L3
Carranya, *Australia* ... 52 C4
Carrara, *Italy* 20 B4
Carrauntoohill, *Ireland* 13 E2
Carrick-on-Shannon,
Ireland 13 C3
Carrick-on-Suir, *Ireland* 13 D4
Carrickfergus, *U.K.* ... 13 B6
Carrickfergus □, *U.K.* . 13 B6
Carrickmacross, *Ireland* 13 C5
Carrieton, *Australia* .. 55 E2
Carrington, *U.S.A.* ... 70 B5
Carrizal Bajo, *Chile* .. 80 B2
Carrizo Cr. →, *U.S.A.* 71 G3
Carrizo Springs, *U.S.A.* 71 L5
Carrizozo, *U.S.A.* 73 K11
Carroll, *U.S.A.* 70 D7
Carrollton, *Ga., U.S.A.* 69 J3
Carrollton, *Ill., U.S.A.* . 70 F9
Carrollton, *Ky., U.S.A.* 68 F3
Carrollton, *Mo., U.S.A.* 70 F8
Carron →, *U.K.* 12 D3
Carron, L., *U.K.* 12 D3
Carrot →, *Canada* ... 65 C8
Carrot River, *Canada* . 65 C8
Carruthers, *Canada* .. 65 C7
Carse of Gowrie, *U.K.* 12 E5
Carson, *U.S.A.* 70 B4
Carson City, *U.S.A.* .. 72 G4
Carson Sink, *U.S.A.* .. 72 G4
Carstairs, *U.K.* 12 F5
Cartagena, *Colombia* . 78 A3
Cartagena, *Spain* 19 D5
Cartago, *Colombia* ... 78 C3
Cartago, *Costa Rica* . 75 F8
Cartersville, *U.S.A.* ... 69 H3
Carterton, *N.Z.* 51 J5
Carthage, *Ark., U.S.A.* 71 H8
Carthage, *Ill., U.S.A.* . 70 E9
Carthage, *Mo., U.S.A.* 71 G7
Carthage, *S. Dak.,*
U.S.A. 70 C6
Carthage, *Tex., U.S.A.* 71 J7
Cartier I., *Australia* ... 52 B3
Cartwright, *Canada* .. 63 B8
Caruaru, *Brazil* 79 E11
Carúpano, *Venezuela* 78 A6
Caruthersville, *U.S.A.* 71 G10
Carvoeiro, *Brazil* 78 D6
Carvoeiro, C., *Portugal* 19 C1
Casa Grande, *U.S.A.* . 73 K8
Casablanca, *Morocco* . 44 B3
Cascade, *Idaho, U.S.A.* 72 D5
Cascade, *Mont., U.S.A.* 72 C8
Cascade Locks, *U.S.A.* 72 D3
Cascade Ra., *U.S.A.* .. 72 C3
Cascais, *Portugal* 19 C1
Cascavel, *Brazil* 80 A6
Cáscina, *Italy* 20 C4
Caserta, *Italy* 20 D6
Cashel, *Ireland* 13 D4
Cashmere, *U.S.A.* 72 C3
Cashmere Downs,
Australia 53 E2
Casiguran, *Phil.* 33 A6
Casilda, *Argentina* ... 80 C4
Casino, *Australia* 55 D5
Casiquiare →,
Venezuela 78 C5
Caslan, *Canada* 64 C6
Casma, *Peru* 78 E3
Caspe, *Spain* 19 B5
Casper, *U.S.A.* 72 E10
Caspian Depression,
Eurasia 23 E8
Caspian Sea, *Eurasia* 23 F9
Cass City, *U.S.A.* 68 D4
Cass Lake, *U.S.A.* 70 B7
Casselton, *U.S.A.* 70 B6
Cassiar, *Canada* 64 B3
Cassiar Mts., *Canada* 64 B2
Cassinga, *Angola* 47 H3
Cassino, *Italy* 20 D5
Cassville, *U.S.A.* 71 G8
Castellammare di
Stábia, *Italy* 20 D6
Castellón de la Plana,
Spain 19 C5
Castelo Branco,
Portugal 19 C2
Castelsarrasin, *France* 18 E4
Castelvetrano, *Italy* .. 20 F5
Castilla La Mancha □,
Spain 19 C4
Castilla y Leon □,
Spain 19 B3
Castle Dale, *U.S.A.* .. 72 G8
Castle Douglas, *U.K.* . 12 G5
Castle Rock, *Colo.,*
U.S.A. 70 F2
Castle Rock, *Wash.,*
U.S.A. 72 C2
Castlebar, *Ireland* 13 C2
Castleblaney, *Ireland* . 13 B5
Castlegar, *Canada* 64 D5
Castlemaine, *Australia* 55 F3
Castlereagh, *Ireland* .. 13 C3
Castlereagh □, *U.K.* .. 13 B6

Castlereagh →,
Australia 55 E4
Castlereagh B.,
Australia 54 A2
Castletown, *U.K.* 10 C3
Castletown Bearhaven,
Ireland 13 E2
Castlevale, *Australia* .. 54 C4
Castor, *Canada* 64 C6
Castres, *France* 18 E5
Castries, *St. Lucia* ... 74 N21
Castro, *Chile* 80 E2
Castro Alves, *Brazil* .. 79 F11
Castroville, *U.S.A.* ... 71 L5
Castuera, *Spain* 19 C3
Casummit Lake,
Canada 62 B1
Cat I., *Bahamas* 75 C9
Cat I., *U.S.A.* 71 K10
Cat L., *Canada* 62 B1
Catacáos, *Peru* 78 E2
Catahoula L., *U.S.A.* . 71 K8
Catalão, *Brazil* 79 G9
Catalca, *Turkey* 21 D13
Catalina, *Canada* 63 C9
Catalonia =
Cataluña □, *Spain* . 19 B6
Cataluña □, *Spain* ... 19 B6
Catamarca, *Argentina* 80 B3
Catanduanes, *Phil.* ... 33 B6
Catanduva, *Brazil* 79 H9
Catánia, *Italy* 20 F6
Catanzaro, *Italy* 20 E7
Cataruban, *Phil.* 33 B6
Cateel, *Phil.* 33 C7
Cathcart, *S. Africa* ... 48 E4
Cathlamet, *U.S.A.* ... 72 C2
Cativa, *Panama* 74 H14
Catlettsburg, *U.S.A.* . 68 F4
Catoche, C., *Mexico* . 74 C7
Catrimani, *Brazil* 78 C6
Catskill, *U.S.A.* 68 D9
Catskill Mts., *U.S.A.* . 68 D8
Catt, Mt., *Australia* ... 54 A1
Catuala, *Angola* 48 B2
Cauca →, *Colombia* . 78 B4
Caucaia, *Brazil* 79 D11
Caucasus Mountains,
Eurasia 23 F7
Caúngula, *Angola* 46 F3
Cauquenes, *Chile* 80 D2
Caura →, *Venezuela* . 78 B6
Causapscal, *Canada* . 63 C6
Cauvery →, *India* ... 36 P11
Caux, Pays de, *France* 18 B4
Cavalier, *U.S.A.* 70 A6
Cavan, *Ireland* 13 C4
Cavan □, *Ireland* 13 C4
Cave City, *U.S.A.* 68 G3
Cavenagh Ra., *Australia* 53 E4
Cavendish, *Australia* .. 55 F3
Caviana, I., *Brazil* 79 C8
Cavite, *Phil.* 33 B6
Cawndilla L., *Australia* 55 E3
Cawnpore = Kanpur,
India 36 F12
Caxias, *Brazil* 79 D10
Caxias do Sul, *Brazil* . 80 B6
Caxito, *Angola* 46 F2
Cayambe, *Ecuador* ... 78 C3
Cayenne, *Fr. Guiana* . 79 B8
Cayuga L., *U.S.A.* 68 D7
Cazombo, *Angola* 47 G4
Ceadâr-Lunga =
Ceadâr-Lunga,
Moldova 17 E15
Ceanannus Mor, *Ireland* 13 C5
Ceará = Fortaleza,
Brazil 79 D11
Ceará □, *Brazil* 79 E11
Ceará Mirim, *Brazil* .. 79 E11
Cebollar, *Argentina* .. 80 B3
Cebu, *Phil.* 33 B6
Cecil Plains, *Australia* 55 D5
Cedar →, *U.S.A.* 70 E9
Cedar City, *U.S.A.* ... 73 H7
Cedar Creek Reservoir,
U.S.A. 71 J6
Cedar Falls, *U.S.A.* ... 70 D8
Cedar Key, *U.S.A.* ... 69 L4
Cedar L., *Canada* 65 C8
Cedar Rapids, *U.S.A.* 70 E9
Cedartown, *U.S.A.* ... 69 H3
Cedarvale, *Canada* ... 64 B3
Cedarville, *S. Africa* .. 49 E4
Cedarville, *U.S.A.* 72 F3
Cedro, *Brazil* 79 E11
Ceduna, *Australia* 55 E1
Cefalù, *Italy* 20 E6
Cegléd, *Hungary* 17 E10
Celaya, *Mexico* 74 C4
Celbridge, *Ireland* 13 C5
Celebes = Sulawesi □,
Indonesia 33 E6
Celebes Sea, *Indonesia* 33 D6
Celina, *U.S.A.* 68 E3
Celje, *Slovenia* 16 E8
Celle, *Germany* 16 B6
Cement, *U.S.A.* 71 H5
Center, *N. Dak., U.S.A.* 70 B4
Center, *Tex., U.S.A.* . 71 K7
Centerfield, *U.S.A.* ... 73 G8
Centerville, *Iowa,*
U.S.A. 70 E8
Centerville, *S. Dak.,*
U.S.A. 70 D6
Centerville, *Tenn.,*
U.S.A. 69 H2
Centerville, *Tex., U.S.A.* 71 K7
Central, *U.S.A.* 73 K9
Central □, *U.K.* 12 E4
Central, Cordillera,
Colombia 78 C4
Central African Rep. ■,
Africa 45 G9

Central City, *Ky., U.S.A.* 68 G2
Central City, *Nebr.,*
U.S.A. 70 E5
Central Makran Range,
Pakistan 36 F4
Central Patricia, *Canada* 62 B1
Central Russian
Uplands, *Europe* .. 6 E13
Centralia, *Ill., U.S.A.* . 70 F10
Centralia, *Mo., U.S.A.* 70 F8
Centralia, *Wash., U.S.A.* 72 C2
Centreville, *Ala., U.S.A.* 69 J2
Centreville, *Miss.,*
U.S.A. 71 K9
Cephalonia =
Kefallinía, *Greece* . 21 E9
Cepu, *Indonesia* 33 G14
Ceram = Seram,
Indonesia 33 E7
Ceram Sea = Seram
Sea, *Indonesia* 33 E7
Ceres, *Argentina* 80 B4
Ceres, *S. Africa* 48 E2
Cerignola, *Italy* 20 D6
Cerigo = Kíthira,
Greece 21 F10
Çerkeşköy, *Turkey* ... 21 D12
Cervera, *Spain* 19 B6
Cesena, *Italy* 20 B5
Cēsis, *Latvia* 9 H21
Česka Republika =
Czech Rep. ■, *Europe* 16 D8
České Budějovice,
Czech. 16 D8
Ceskomoravska
Vrchovina, *Czech.* . 16 D8
Çeşme, *Turkey* 21 E12
Cessnock, *Australia* .. 55 E5
Cetinje,
Montenegro, Yug. . 21 C8
Cetraro, *Italy* 20 E6
Ceuta, *N. Afr.* 19 E3
Cévennes, *France* 18 D5
Ceyhan →, *Turkey* .. 23 G6
Ceylon = Sri Lanka ■,
Asia 36 R12
Cha I., *Vietnam* 34 A7
Chachapoyas, *Peru* .. 78 E3
Chachran, *Pakistan* .. 36 E7
Chad ■, *Africa* 45 E8
Chad, L. = Tchad, L.,
Chad 45 F7
Chadan, *Russia* 25 D10
Chadileuvú →,
Argentina 80 D3
Chadron, *U.S.A.* 70 D3
Chadyr-Lunga =
Ceadâr-Lunga,
Moldova 17 E15
Chagai Hills, *Afghan.* . 36 E3
Chagda, *Russia* 25 D14
Chagos Arch., *Ind. Oc.* 26 K11
Chágres →, *Panama* . 74 H14
Chāh Ākhvor, *Iran* ... 39 C8
Chāh Bahār, *Iran* 39 E9
Chāh-e-Malek, *Iran* .. 39 D8
Chāh Kavīr, *Iran* 39 D7
Chahar Burjak, *Afghan.* 36 D3
Chaïbasa, *India* 37 H14
Chakhānsūr, *Afghan.* . 36 D3
Chakonipau, L., *Canada* 63 A6
Chakradharpur, *India* . 37 H14
Chakwal, *Pakistan* ... 36 C8
Chala, *Peru* 78 G4
Chalcis = Khalkís,
Greece 21 E10
Chaleur B., *Canada* .. 63 C6
Chalhuanca, *Peru* 78 F4
Chalisgaon, *India* 36 J9
Chalky Inlet, *N.Z.* 51 M1
Challapata, *Bolivia* ... 78 G5
Challis, *U.S.A.* 72 D6
Chalon-sur-Saône,
France 18 C6
Châlons-sur-Marne,
France 18 B6
Chama, *U.S.A.* 73 H10
Chaman, *Pakistan* ... 36 D5
Chamba, *India* 36 C10
Chamba, *Tanzania* ... 47 G7
Chambal →, *India* ... 36 F11
Chamberlain, *U.S.A.* . 70 D5
Chamberlain →,
Australia 52 C4
Chambers, *U.S.A.* ... 73 J9
Chambersburg, *U.S.A.* 68 F7
Chambéry, *France* ... 18 D6
Chambord, *Canada* .. 63 C5
Chamchamal, *Iraq* ... 38 C5
Chamical, *Argentina* . 80 C3
Chamonix-Mont Blanc,
France 18 D7
Champagne, *Canada* . 64 A1
Champagne, *France* .. 18 B6
Champaign, *U.S.A.* ... 68 E1
Champlain, *Canada* .. 68 B9
Champlain, *U.S.A.* ... 68 C9
Champlain, L., *U.S.A.* 68 C9
Chañaral, *Chile* 80 B2
Chanārān, *Iran* 39 B8
Chandeleur Is., *U.S.A.* 71 L10
Chandeleur Sd., *U.S.A.* 71 L10
Chandigarh, *India* ... 36 D10
Chandler, *Australia* .. 55 D1
Chandler, *Canada* 63 C7
Chandler, *Ariz., U.S.A.* 73 K8
Chandler, *Okla., U.S.A.* 71 H6
Chandpur, *Bangla.* ... 37 H17
Chandrapur, *India* ... 36 K11
Chānf, *Iran* 39 E9

Ch'ang Chiang

Ch'ang Chiang = Chang Jiang →, China 31 C7
Chang Jiang →, China 31 C7
Changanacheri, India 36 Q10
Changane →, Mozam. 49 C5
Changchiak'ou = Zhangjiakou, China 31 B6
Ch'angchou = Changzhou, China 31 C6
Changchun, China 31 B7
Changde, China 31 D6
Changhai = Shanghai, China 31 C7
Changsha, China 31 D6
Changzhi, China 31 C6
Changzhou, China 31 C6
Chanhanga, Angola 48 B1
Channapatna, India 36 N10
Channel Is., U.K. 11 H5
Channel Is., U.S.A. 73 K4
Channel-Port aux Basques, Canada 63 C8
Channing, Mich., U.S.A. 68 B1
Channing, Tex., U.S.A. 71 H3
Chantada, Spain 19 A2
Chanthaburi, Thailand 34 F7
Chantrey Inlet, Canada 60 B10
Chanute, U.S.A. 71 G7
Chao Phraya →, Thailand 34 F6
Chao'an, China 31 D6
Chapala, L. de, Mexico 74 C4
Chapayev, Kazakhstan 23 D9
Chapayevsk, Russia 22 D8
Chapel Hill, U.S.A. 69 H6
Chapleau, Canada 62 C3
Chaplin, Canada 65 C7
Chapra = Chhapra, India 37 G14
Châr, Mauritania 44 D2
Chara, Russia 25 D12
Charadai, Argentina 80 B5
Charagua, Bolivia 78 G6
Charaña, Bolivia 78 G5
Charcoal L., Canada 65 B8
Chard, U.K. 11 G5
Chardara, Kazakhstan 24 E7
Chardzhou = Chärjew, Turkmenistan 24 F7
Charente →, France 18 D3
Chari →, Chad 45 F7
Chārīkār, Afghan. 36 B6
Chariton →, U.S.A. 70 F8
Chärjew, Turkmenistan 24 F7
Charleroi, Belgium 15 D4
Charles, C., U.S.A. 68 G8
Charles City, U.S.A. 70 D8
Charles L., Canada 65 B6
Charles Town, U.S.A. 68 F7
Charleston, Ill., U.S.A. 68 F1
Charleston, Miss., U.S.A. 71 H9
Charleston, Mo., U.S.A. 71 G10
Charleston, S.C., U.S.A. 69 J6
Charleston, W. Va., U.S.A. 68 F5
Charlestown, S. Africa 49 D4
Charlestown, U.S.A. 68 F3
Charlesville, Zaïre 46 F4
Charleville = Rath Luirc, Ireland 13 D3
Charleville, Australia 55 D4
Charleville-Mézières, France 18 B6
Charlevoix, U.S.A. 68 C3
Charlotte, Mich., U.S.A. 68 D3
Charlotte, N.C., U.S.A. 69 H5
Charlotte Amalie, Virgin Is. 75 D12
Charlotte Harbor, U.S.A. 69 M4
Charlottesville, U.S.A. 68 F6
Charlottetown, Canada 63 C7
Charlton, Australia 55 F3
Charlton, U.S.A. 70 E8
Charlton I., Canada 62 B4
Charny, Canada 63 C5
Charolles, France 18 C6
Charouine, Algeria 44 C4
Charters Towers, Australia 54 C4
Chartres, France 18 B4
Chascomús, Argentina 80 D5
Chasovnya-Uchurskaya, Russia 25 D14
Chât, Iran 39 B7
Châteaubriant, France 18 C3
Châteaulin, France 18 B1
Châteauroux, France 18 C4
Châtellerault, France 18 C4
Chatfield, U.S.A. 70 D9
Chatham, N.B., Canada 63 C6
Chatham, Ont., Canada 62 D3
Chatham, U.K. 11 F8
Chatham, U.S.A. 71 J8
Chatham Is., Pac. Oc. 56 M10
Chatham Str., U.S.A. 64 B2
Chatrapur, India 37 K14
Chattahoochee →, U.S.A. 69 K3
Chattanooga, U.S.A. 69 H3
Chauk, Burma 37 J19
Chaukan La, Burma 37 F20
Chaumont, France 18 B6
Chauvin, Canada 65 C6
Chaves, Brazil 79 D9
Chaves, Portugal 19 B2
Chavuma, Zambia 47 G4
Chaykovskiy, Russia 22 C9
Cheb, Czech. 16 C7
Cheboksary, Russia 22 C8
Cheboygan, U.S.A. 68 C3
Chech, Erg, Africa 44 D4
Chechenia □, Russia 23 F8
Checheno-Ingush Republic = Chechenia □, Russia 23 F8
Chechnya = Chechenia □, Russia 23 F8
Checleset B., Canada 64 C3
Checotah, U.S.A. 71 H7
Chedabucto B., Canada 63 C7
Cheduba I., Burma 37 K18
Cheepie, Australia 55 D4
Chegdomyn, Russia 25 D14
Chegga, Mauritania 44 C3
Chegutu, Zimbabwe 47 H6
Chehalis, U.S.A. 72 C2
Cheju Do, S. Korea 31 C7
Chekiang = Zhejiang □, China 31 D7
Chela, Sa. da, Angola 48 B1
Chelan, U.S.A. 72 C4
Chelan, L., U.S.A. 72 C3
Cheleken, Turkmenistan 23 G9
Chelforó, Argentina 80 D3
Chelkar = Shalqar, Kazakhstan 24 E6
Chelkar Tengiz, Solonchak, Kazakhstan 24 E7
Chełm, Poland 17 C12
Chełmno, Poland 17 B10
Chelmsford, U.K. 11 F8
Chelsea, U.S.A. 71 G7
Cheltenham, U.K. 11 F5
Chelyabinsk, Russia 24 D7
Chelyuskin, C., Russia 26 B14
Chemainus, Canada 64 D4
Chemnitz, Germany 16 C7
Chemult, U.S.A. 72 E3
Chen, Gora, Russia 25 C15
Chenab →, Pakistan 36 D7
Chencha, Ethiopia 45 G12
Cheney, U.S.A. 72 C5
Chengchou = Zhengzhou, China 31 C6
Chengde, China 31 B6
Chengdu, China 30 C5
Chengjiang, China 30 D5
Ch'engtu = Chengdu, China 30 C5
Cheo Reo, Vietnam 34 F10
Cheom Ksan, Cambodia 34 E8
Chepén, Peru 78 E3
Chepes, Argentina 80 C3
Chequamegon B., U.S.A. 70 B9
Cher →, France 18 C4
Cheraw, U.S.A. 69 H6
Cherbourg, France 18 B3
Cherchell, Algeria 44 A5
Cherdyn, Russia 22 B10
Cheremkhovo, Russia 25 D11
Cherepanovo, Russia 24 D9
Cherepovets, Russia 22 C6
Chergui, Chott ech, Algeria 44 B5
Cherikov = Cherykaw, Belarus 17 B16
Cherkasy, Ukraine 23 E5
Cherlak, Russia 24 D8
Chernaya, Russia 25 B9
Chernigov = Chernihiv, Ukraine 22 D5
Chernihiv, Ukraine 22 D5
Chernikovsk, Russia 22 D10
Chernivtsi, Ukraine 17 D13
Chernobyl = Chornobyl, Ukraine 17 C16
Chernogorsk, Russia 25 D10
Chernovtsy = Chernivtsi, Ukraine 17 D13
Chernyakhovsk, Russia 9 J19
Chernyshovskiy, Russia 25 C12
Cherokee, Iowa, U.S.A. 70 D7
Cherokee, Okla., U.S.A. 71 G5
Cherokees, Lake O' The, U.S.A. 71 G7
Cherquenco, Chile 80 D2
Cherrapunji, India 37 G17
Cherry Creek, U.S.A. 72 G6
Cherryvale, U.S.A. 71 G7
Cherskiy, Russia 25 C17
Cherskogo Khrebet, Russia 25 C15
Cherven, Belarus 17 B15
Chervonohrad, Ukraine 17 C13
Cherwell →, U.K. 11 F6
Cherykaw, Belarus 17 B16
Chesapeake, U.S.A. 68 G7
Chesapeake B., U.S.A. 68 F7
Cheshire □, U.K. 10 D5
Cheshskaya Guba, Russia 22 A8
Cheslatta L., Canada 64 C3
Chester, U.K. 10 D5
Chester, Calif., U.S.A. 72 F3
Chester, Ill., U.S.A. 71 G10
Chester, Mont., U.S.A. 72 B8
Chester, Pa., U.S.A. 68 F8
Chester, S.C., U.S.A. 69 H5
Chesterfield, U.K. 10 D6
Chesterfield, Is., N. Cal. 56 J7
Chesterfield Inlet, Canada 60 B10
Chesterton Ra., Australia 55 D4
Chesuncook L., U.S.A. 63 C6
Chéticamp, Canada 63 C7
Chetwynd, Canada 64 B4
Cheviot, The, U.K. 10 B5
Cheviot Hills, U.K. 10 B5
Cheviot Ra., Australia 54 D3
Chew Bahir, Ethiopia 45 H12
Chewelah, U.S.A. 72 B5
Cheyenne, Okla., U.S.A. 71 H5
Cheyenne, Wyo., U.S.A. 70 E2
Cheyenne →, U.S.A. 70 C4
Cheyenne Wells, U.S.A. 70 F3
Cheyne B., Australia 53 F2
Chhapra, India 37 G14
Chhatarpur, India 36 G11
Chhindwara, India 36 H11
Chhlong, Cambodia 34 F8
Chi →, Thailand 34 E8
Chiai, Taiwan 31 D7
Chiamis, Indonesia 33 G13
Chiamussu = Jiamusi, China 31 B8
Chiang Mai, Thailand 34 C5
Chiange, Angola 47 H2
Chiapa →, Mexico 74 D6
Chiávari, Italy 20 B3
Chiavenna, Italy 20 A3
Chiba, Japan 29 G10
Chibabava, Mozam. 49 C5
Chibatu, Indonesia 33 G12
Chibemba, Cunene, Angola 47 H2
Chibemba, Huila, Angola 48 B2
Chibia, Angola 47 H2
Chibougamau, Canada 62 C5
Chibougamau L., Canada 62 C5
Chibuk, Nigeria 45 F7
Chic-Chocs, Mts., Canada 63 C6
Chicacole = Srikakulam, India 37 K13
Chicago, U.S.A. 68 E2
Chicago Heights, U.S.A. 68 E2
Chichagof I., U.S.A. 64 B1
Chichester, U.K. 11 G7
Chichibu, Japan 29 F9
Ch'ich'ihaerh = Qiqihar, China 25 E13
Chickasha, U.S.A. 71 H5
Chiclana de la Frontera, Spain 19 D2
Chiclayo, Peru 78 E3
Chico, U.S.A. 72 G3
Chico →, Chubut, Argentina 80 E3
Chico →, Santa Cruz, Argentina 80 G3
Chicomo, Mozam. 49 C5
Chicopee, U.S.A. 68 D9
Chicoutimi, Canada 63 C5
Chicualacuala, Mozam. 49 C5
Chidambaram, India 36 P11
Chidenguele, Mozam. 49 C5
Chidley, C., Canada 61 B13
Chiede, Angola 48 B2
Chiemsee, Germany 16 E7
Chiengi, Zambia 46 F5
Chiengmai = Chiang Mai, Thailand 34 C5
Chiese →, Italy 20 B4
Chieti, Italy 20 C6
Chignecto B., Canada 63 C7
Chiguana, Bolivia 78 H5
Chihli, G. of = Bo Hai, China 31 C6
Chihuahua, Mexico 74 B3
Chiili, Kazakhstan 24 E7
Chik Bollapur, India 36 N10
Chikmagalur, India 36 N9
Chilako →, Canada 64 C4
Chilapa, Mexico 74 D5
Chilas, Pakistan 36 B9
Chilaw, Sri Lanka 36 R11
Chilcotin →, Canada 64 C4
Childers, Australia 55 D5
Childress, U.S.A. 71 H4
Chile ■, S. Amer. 80 D2
Chile Rise, Pac. Oc. 57 L18
Chilete, Peru 78 E3
Chililabombwe, Zambia 47 G5
Chilin = Jilin, China 31 B7
Chilka L., India 37 K14
Chilko →, Canada 64 C4
Chilko, L., Canada 64 C4
Chillagoe, Australia 54 B3
Chillán, Chile 80 D2
Chillicothe, Ill., U.S.A. 70 E10
Chillicothe, Mo., U.S.A. 70 F8
Chillicothe, Ohio, U.S.A. 68 F4
Chilliwack, Canada 64 D4
Chiloane, I., Mozam. 49 C5
Chiloé, I. de, Chile 80 E2
Chilpancingo, Mexico 74 D5
Chiltern Hills, U.K. 11 F7
Chilton, U.S.A. 68 C1
Chiluage, Angola 46 F4
Chilung, Taiwan 31 D7
Chilwa, L., Malawi 47 H7
Chimay, Belgium 15 D4
Chimbay, Uzbekistan 24 E6
Chimborazo, Ecuador 78 D3
Chimbote, Peru 78 E3
Chimkent = Shymkent, Kazakhstan 24 E7
Chimoio, Mozam. 47 H6
Chin □, Burma 37 J18
China ■, Asia 31 C6
Chinan = Jinan, China 31 C6
Chinandega, Nic. 74 E7
Chinati Peak, U.S.A. 71 K2
Chincha Alta, Peru 78 F3
Chinchilla, Australia 55 D5
Chinchou = Jinzhou, China 31 B7
Chincoteague, U.S.A. 68 G8
Chinde, Mozam. 47 H7
Chindwin →, Burma 37 J19
Chingola, Zambia 47 G5
Ch'ingtao = Qingdao, China 31 C7
Chinguetti, Mauritania 44 D2
Chingune, Mozam. 49 C5
Chinhanguanine, Mozam. 49 D5
Chinhoyi, Zimbabwe 47 H6
Chiniot, Pakistan 36 D8
Chinle, U.S.A. 73 H9
Chino, Japan 29 G9
Chino Valley, U.S.A. 73 J7
Chinon, France 18 C4
Chinook, Canada 65 C6
Chinook, U.S.A. 72 B9
Chinsali, Zambia 46 G6
Chióggia, Italy 20 B5
Chíos = Khíos, Greece 21 E12
Chipata, Zambia 47 G6
Chipewyan L., Canada 65 B9
Chipley, U.S.A. 69 K3
Chipman, Canada 63 C6
Chippenham, U.K. 11 F5
Chippewa →, U.S.A. 70 C8
Chippewa Falls, U.S.A. 70 C9
Chiquián, Peru 78 F3
Chiquinquira, Colombia 78 B4
Chirala, India 36 M12
Chirchiq, Uzbekistan 24 E7
Chiricahua Peak, U.S.A. 73 L9
Chirmiri, India 37 H13
Chiromo, Malawi 47 H7
Chisamba, Zambia 47 G5
Chisapani Garhi, Nepal 37 F14
Chisasibi, Canada 62 B4
Chisholm, Canada 64 C6
Chişinău, Moldova 17 E15
Chisos Mts., U.S.A. 71 L3
Chistopol, Russia 22 C9
Chita, Russia 25 D12
Chitado, Angola 47 H2
Chitembo, Angola 47 G3
Chitose, Japan 28 C10
Chitral, Pakistan 36 B7
Chitré, Panama 75 F8
Chittagong, Bangla. 37 H17
Chittagong □, Bangla. 37 G17
Chittaurgarh, India 36 G9
Chittoor, India 36 N11
Chiusi, Italy 20 C4
Chivasso, Italy 20 B2
Chivilcoy, Argentina 80 D4
Chkalov = Orenburg, Russia 22 D10
Chobe National Park, Botswana 48 B3
Choctawhatchee B., U.S.A. 67 D9
Choele Choel, Argentina 80 D3
Chojnice, Poland 17 B9
Chōkai-San, Japan 28 E10
Chokurdakh, Russia 25 B15
Cholet, France 18 C3
Choluteca, Honduras 74 E7
Choma, Zambia 47 H5
Chomutov, Czech. 16 C7
Chon Buri, Thailand 34 F6
Chone, Ecuador 78 D2
Chŏngjin, N. Korea 31 B7
Chongqing, China 30 D5
Chonos, Arch. de los, Chile 80 F2
Chop, Ukraine 17 D12
Chorley, U.K. 10 D5
Chornobyl, Ukraine 17 C16
Chorregon, Australia 54 C3
Chortkiv, Ukraine 17 D13
Chorzów, Poland 17 C10
Chos-Malal, Argentina 80 D2
Choszczno, Poland 16 B8
Choteau, U.S.A. 72 C7
Chotila, India 36 H7
Chowchilla, U.S.A. 73 H3
Choybalsan, Mongolia 31 B6
Christchurch, N.Z. 51 K4
Christchurch, U.K. 11 G6
Christiana, S. Africa 48 D4
Christie B., Canada 65 A6
Christina →, Canada 65 B6
Christmas Cr. →, Australia 52 C4
Christmas Creek, Australia 52 C4
Christmas I. = Kiritimati, Kiribati 57 G12
Christmas I., Ind. Oc. 35 F9
Christopher L., Australia 53 D4
Chu = Shu, Kazakhstan 24 E8
Chu →, Vietnam 34 C8
Chu Chua, Canada 64 C4
Ch'uanchou = Quanzhou, China 31 D6
Chūbu □, Japan 29 F8
Chubut →, Argentina 80 E3
Chuchi L., Canada 64 B4
Chudskoye, Oz., Russia 9 G22
Chūgoku □, Japan 29 G6
Chūgoku-Sanchi, Japan 29 G6
Chugwater, U.S.A. 70 E2
Chukchi Sea, Russia 25 C19
Chukotskoye Nagorye, Russia 25 C18
Chula Vista, U.S.A. 73 K5
Chulman, Russia 25 D13
Chulucanas, Peru 78 E2
Chulym →, Russia 24 D9
Chumbicha, Argentina 80 B3
Chumikan, Russia 25 D14
Chumphon, Thailand 34 G5
Chuna →, Russia 25 D10
Chungking = Chongqing, China 30 D5
Chunya, Tanzania 46 F6
Chuquibamba, Peru 78 G4
Chuquicamata, Chile 80 A3
Chur, Switz. 16 E5
Churachandpur, India 37 G18
Churchill, Canada 65 B10
Churchill →, Man., Canada 65 B10
Churchill →, Nfld., Canada 63 B7
Churchill, C., Canada 65 B10
Churchill Falls, Canada 63 B7
Churchill L., Canada 65 B7
Churchill Pk., Canada 64 B3
Churu, India 36 E9
Chushal, India 36 C11
Chusovoy, Russia 22 C10
Chuvash Republic = Chuvashia □, Russia 22 C8
Chuvashia □, Russia 22 C8
Chuwārtah, Iraq 38 C5
Cianjur, Indonesia 33 G12
Cibadok, Indonesia 33 G12
Cibatu, Indonesia 33 G12
Cicero, U.S.A. 68 E2
Ciechanów, Poland 17 B11
Ciego de Avila, Cuba 75 C9
Ciénaga, Colombia 78 A4
Cienfuegos, Cuba 75 C8
Cieszyn, Poland 17 D10
Cieza, Spain 19 C5
Cijara, Pantano de, Spain 19 C3
Cijulang, Indonesia 33 G13
Cikajang, Indonesia 33 G12
Cikampek, Indonesia 33 G12
Cilacap, Indonesia 33 G13
Cill Chainnigh = Kilkenny, Ireland 13 D4
Cimahi, Indonesia 33 G12
Cimarron, Kans., U.S.A. 71 G4
Cimarron, N. Mex., U.S.A. 71 G2
Cimarron →, U.S.A. 71 G6
Cimişlia, Moldova 17 E15
Cimone, Mte., Italy 20 B4
Cîmpina, Romania 17 F13
Cîmpulung, Romania 17 F13
Cinca →, Spain 19 B6
Cincar, Bos.-H. 20 C7
Cincinnati, U.S.A. 68 F3
Çine, Turkey 21 F13
Ciney, Belgium 15 D5
Cinto, Mte., France 18 E8
Circle, Alaska, U.S.A. 60 B5
Circle, Mont., U.S.A. 70 B2
Circleville, Ohio, U.S.A. 68 F4
Circleville, Utah, U.S.A. 73 G7
Cirebon, Indonesia 33 G13
Cirencester, U.K. 11 F6
Cisco, U.S.A. 71 J5
Citlaltépetl, Mexico 74 D5
Citrusdal, S. Africa 48 E2
Città di Castello, Italy 20 C5
Ciudad Bolívar, Venezuela 78 B6
Ciudad Chetumal, Mexico 74 D7
Ciudad del Carmen, Mexico 74 D6
Ciudad Delicias = Delicias, Mexico 74 B3
Ciudad Guayana, Venezuela 78 B6
Ciudad Juárez, Mexico 74 A3
Ciudad Madero, Mexico 74 C5
Ciudad Mante, Mexico 74 C5
Ciudad Obregón, Mexico 74 B3
Ciudad Real, Spain 19 C4
Ciudad Rodrigo, Spain 19 B2
Ciudad Trujillo = Santo Domingo, Dom. Rep. 75 D11
Ciudad Victoria, Mexico 74 C5
Civitanova Marche, Italy 20 C5
Civitavécchia, Italy 20 C4
Cizre, Turkey 23 G7
Clacton-on-Sea, U.K. 11 F9
Claire, L., Canada 64 B6
Clairemont, U.S.A. 71 J4
Clanton, U.S.A. 69 J2
Clanwilliam, S. Africa 48 E2
Clara, Ireland 13 C4
Clara →, Australia 54 B3
Clare, Australia 55 E2
Clare, U.S.A. 68 D3
Clare □, Ireland 13 D3
Clare →, Ireland 13 C2
Clare I., Ireland 13 C2
Claremont, U.S.A. 68 D9
Claremont Pt., Australia 54 A3
Claremore, U.S.A. 71 G7
Claremorris, Ireland 13 C3
Clarence →, Australia 55 D5
Clarence →, N.Z. 51 K4
Clarence, I., Chile 80 G2
Clarence I., Antarctica 5 C18
Clarence Str., Australia 52 B5
Clarence Str., U.S.A. 64 B2
Clarendon, Ark., U.S.A. 71 H9
Clarendon, Tex., U.S.A. 71 H4
Clarenville, Canada 63 C9
Claresholm, Canada 64 C6
Clarie Coast, Antarctica 5 C9
Clarinda, U.S.A. 70 E7
Clarion, U.S.A. 70 D8
Clark, U.S.A. 70 C6
Clark Fork, U.S.A. 72 B5
Clark Fork →, U.S.A. 72 B5
Clark Hill Res., U.S.A. 69 J4
Clarkdale, U.S.A. 73 J7
Clarke City, Canada 63 B6
Clarke I., Australia 54 G4
Clarke L., Canada 65 C7
Clarke Ra., Australia 54 C4
Clark's Fork →, U.S.A. 72 D9
Clark's Harbour, Canada 63 D6
Clarksburg, U.S.A. 68 F5
Clarksdale, U.S.A. 71 H9
Clarkston, U.S.A. 72 C5
Clarksville, Ark., U.S.A. 71 H8
Clarksville, Tenn., U.S.A. 69 G2
Clarksville, Tex., U.S.A. 71 J7
Clatskanie, U.S.A. 72 C2
Claude, U.S.A. 71 H4
Claveria, Phil. 33 A6
Clay Center, U.S.A. 70 F6
Claypool, U.S.A. 73 K8
Clayton, Idaho, U.S.A. 72 D6
Clayton, N. Mex., U.S.A. 71 G3
Cle Elum, U.S.A. 72 C3
Clear, C., Ireland 13 E2
Clear I., Ireland 13 E2
Clear L., U.S.A. 72 G2
Clear Lake, S. Dak., U.S.A. 70 C6
Clear Lake, Wash., U.S.A. 72 B2
Clear Lake Reservoir, U.S.A. 72 F3
Clearfield, Pa., U.S.A. 68 E6
Clearfield, Utah, U.S.A. 72 F7
Clearmont, U.S.A. 72 D10
Clearwater, Canada 64 C4
Clearwater, U.S.A. 69 M4
Clearwater →, Alta., Canada 64 C6
Clearwater →, Alta., Canada 65 B6
Clearwater Cr. →, Canada 64 A3
Clearwater Mts., U.S.A. 72 C6
Clearwater Prov. Park, Canada 65 C8
Cleburne, U.S.A. 71 J6
Cleethorpes, U.K. 10 D7
Cleeve Hill, U.K. 11 F6
Clerke Reef, Australia 52 C2
Clermont, Australia 54 C4
Clermont-Ferrand, France 18 D5
Clervaux, Lux. 15 D6
Cleveland, Australia 55 D5
Cleveland, Miss., U.S.A. 71 J9
Cleveland, Ohio, U.S.A. 68 E5
Cleveland, Okla., U.S.A. 71 G6
Cleveland, Tenn., U.S.A. 69 H3
Cleveland, Tex., U.S.A. 71 K7
Cleveland □, U.K. 10 C9
Cleveland, C., Australia 54 B4
Clew B., Ireland 13 C2
Clewiston, U.S.A. 69 M5
Clifden, Ireland 13 C1
Clifden, N.Z. 51 M1
Clifton, Australia 55 D5
Clifton, Ariz., U.S.A. 73 K9
Clifton, Tex., U.S.A. 71 K6
Clifton Beach, Australia 54 B4
Clifton Forge, U.S.A. 68 G6
Clifton Hills, Australia 55 D2
Climax, Canada 65 D7
Clinch →, U.S.A. 69 H3
Clingmans Dome, U.S.A. 69 H4
Clint, U.S.A. 73 L10
Clinton, B.C., Canada 64 C4
Clinton, Ont., Canada 62 D3
Clinton, N.Z. 51 M2
Clinton, Ark., U.S.A. 71 H8
Clinton, Ill., U.S.A. 70 E10
Clinton, Ind., U.S.A. 68 F2
Clinton, Iowa, U.S.A. 70 E9
Clinton, Mass., U.S.A. 68 D10
Clinton, Mo., U.S.A. 70 F8
Clinton, N.C., U.S.A. 69 H6
Clinton, Okla., U.S.A. 71 H5
Clinton, S.C., U.S.A. 69 H5
Clinton, Tenn., U.S.A. 69 G3
Clinton C., Australia 54 C5
Clinton Colden L., Canada 60 B9
Clintonville, U.S.A. 70 C10
Clipperton, I., Pac. Oc. 57 F17
Clive L., Canada 64 A5
Cloates, Pt., Australia 52 D1
Clocolan, S. Africa 49 D4
Clonakilty, Ireland 13 E3
Clonakilty B., Ireland 13 E3
Cloncurry, Australia 54 C3
Cloncurry →, Australia 54 B3
Clones, Ireland 13 B4
Clonmel, Ireland 13 D4
Cloquet, U.S.A. 70 B8
Cloud Peak, U.S.A. 72 D10
Cloudcroft, U.S.A. 73 K11
Cloverdale, U.S.A. 72 G2
Clovis, Calif., U.S.A. 73 H4
Clovis, N. Mex., U.S.A. 71 H3
Cluj-Napoca, Romania 17 E12
Clunes, Australia 55 F3
Clutha →, N.Z. 51 M2
Clwyd □, U.K. 10 D4
Clwyd →, U.K. 10 D4
Clyde, N.Z. 51 L2
Clyde →, U.K. 12 F4
Clyde, Firth of, U.K. 12 F4
Clyde River, Canada 61 A13
Clydebank, U.K. 12 F4

Cuenca

Coachella, *U.S.A.* 73 K5
Coahoma, *U.S.A.* 71 J4
Coal →, *Canada* 64 B3
Coaldale, *Canada* 64 D6
Coalgate, *U.S.A.* 71 H6
Coalinga, *U.S.A.* 73 H3
Coalville, *U.K.* 10 E6
Coalville, *U.S.A.* 72 F8
Coari, *Brazil* 78 D6
Coast Mts., *Canada* 64 C3
Coast Ranges, *U.S.A.* 72 F2
Coatbridge, *U.K.* 12 F4
Coatesville, *U.S.A.* 68 F8
Coaticook, *Canada* 63 C5
Coats I., *Canada* 61 B11
Coats Land, *Antarctica* 5 D1
Coatzacoalcos, *Mexico* 74 D6
Cobalt, *Canada* 62 C4
Cobar, *Australia* 55 E4
Cóbh, *Ireland* 13 E3
Cobham, *Australia* 55 E3
Cobija, *Bolivia* 78 F5
Cobleskill, *U.S.A.* 68 D8
Cobourg, *Canada* 62 D4
Cobourg Pen., *Australia* 52 B5
Cobram, *Australia* 55 F4
Cobre, *U.S.A.* 72 F6
Cóbué, *Mozam.* 47 G6
Coburg, *Germany* 16 C6
Cocanada = Kakinada, *India* 37 L13
Cochabamba, *Bolivia* 78 G5
Cochin, *India* 36 Q10
Cochin China = Nam-Phan, *Vietnam* 34 G9
Cochise, *U.S.A.* 73 K9
Cochran, *U.S.A.* 69 J4
Cochrane, *Alta., Canada* 64 C6
Cochrane, *Ont., Canada* 62 C3
Cochrane →, *Canada* 65 B8
Cochrane, L., *Chile* 80 F2
Cockburn, *Australia* 55 E3
Cockburn, Canal, *Chile* 80 G2
Cockburn I., *Canada* 62 C3
Cockburn Ra., *Australia* 52 C4
Cocklebiddy Motel, *Australia* 53 F4
Coco →, *Cent. Amer.* 75 E8
Coco Chan., *India* 34 F2
Coco Solo, *Panama* 74 H14
Cocoa, *U.S.A.* 69 L5
Cocobeach, *Gabon* 46 D1
Cocos, I. del, *Pac. Oc.* 57 G19
Cocos Is., *Ind. Oc.* 35 F8
Cod, C., *U.S.A.* 67 B13
Codajás, *Brazil* 78 D6
Coderre, *Canada* 65 C7
Codó, *Brazil* 79 D10
Cody, *U.S.A.* 72 D9
Coe Hill, *Canada* 62 D4
Coen, *Australia* 54 A3
Coetivy Is., *Seychelles* 35 E4
Cœur d'Alene, *U.S.A.* 72 C5
Cœur d'Alene L., *U.S.A.* 72 C5
Coevorden, *Neths.* 15 B6
Coffeyville, *U.S.A.* 71 G7
Coffin B., *Australia* 55 E2
Coffin Bay Peninsula, *Australia* 55 E2
Coffs Harbour, *Australia* 55 E5
Cognac, *France* 18 D3
Cohagen, *U.S.A.* 72 C10
Cohoes, *U.S.A.* 68 D9
Cohuna, *Australia* 55 F3
Coiba, I., *Panama* 75 F8
Coig →, *Argentina* 80 G3
Coihaique, *Chile* 80 F2
Coimbatore, *India* 36 P10
Coimbra, *Brazil* 78 G7
Coimbra, *Portugal* 19 B1
Coin, *Spain* 19 D3
Cojimies, *Ecuador* 78 C2
Cokeville, *U.S.A.* 72 E8
Colac, *Australia* 55 F3
Colatina, *Brazil* 79 G10
Colbeck, C., *Antarctica* 5 D13
Colbinabbin, *Australia* 55 F3
Colby, *U.S.A.* 70 F4
Colchester, *U.K.* 11 F8
Coldstream, *U.K.* 12 F6
Coldwater, *U.S.A.* 71 G5
Colebrook, *Australia* 54 G4
Colebrook, *U.S.A.* 68 C10
Coleman, *Canada* 64 D6
Coleman, *U.S.A.* 71 K5
Coleman →, *Australia* 54 B3
Colenso, *S. Africa* 49 D4
Coleraine, *Australia* 55 F3
Coleraine, *U.K.* 13 A5
Coleraine □, *U.K.* 13 A5
Coleridge, L., *N.Z.* 51 K3
Colesberg, *S. Africa* 48 E4
Colfax, *La., U.S.A.* 71 K8
Colfax, *Wash., U.S.A.* 72 C5
Colhué Huapi, L., *Argentina* 80 F3
Coligny, *S. Africa* 49 D4
Colima, *Mexico* 74 D4
Colinas, *Brazil* 79 E10
Coll, *U.K.* 12 E2
Collaguasi, *Chile* 78 H5
Collarenebri, *Australia* 55 D4
Collbran, *U.S.A.* 73 G10
College Park, *U.S.A.* 69 J3
Collette, *Canada* 63 C6
Collie, *Australia* 53 F2
Collier B., *Australia* 52 C3
Collier Ra., *Australia* 52 D2
Collingwood, *Canada* 62 D3
Collingwood, *N.Z.* 51 J4
Collins, *Canada* 62 B2
Collinsville, *Australia* 54 C4
Collooney, *Ireland* 13 B3
Colmar, *France* 18 B7
Colne, *U.K.* 10 D5
Colo →, *Australia* 55 E5
Cologne = Köln, *Germany* 16 C4
Colomb-Béchar = Béchar, *Algeria* 44 B4
Colômbia, *Brazil* 79 H9
Colombia ■, *S. Amer.* 78 C4
Colombo, *Sri Lanka* 36 R11
Colome, *U.S.A.* 70 D5
Colón, *Cuba* 75 C8
Colón, *Panama* 74 H14
Colona, *Australia* 53 F5
Colonia, *Uruguay* 80 C5
Colonia Dora, *Argentina* 80 B4
Colonial Heights, *U.S.A.* 68 G7
Colonsay, *Canada* 65 C7
Colonsay, *U.K.* 12 E2
Colorado □, *U.S.A.* 73 G10
Colorado →, *Argentina* 80 D4
Colorado →, *N. Amer.* 73 L6
Colorado →, *U.S.A.* 71 L7
Colorado, I., *Panama* 74 H14
Colorado City, *U.S.A.* 71 J4
Colorado Desert, *U.S.A.* 66 D3
Colorado Plateau, *U.S.A.* 73 H8
Colorado River Aqueduct, *U.S.A.* 73 J6
Colorado Springs, *U.S.A.* 70 F2
Colton, *U.S.A.* 72 C5
Columbia, *La., U.S.A.* 71 J8
Columbia, *Miss., U.S.A.* 71 K10
Columbia, *Mo., U.S.A.* 70 F8
Columbia, *Pa., U.S.A.* 68 E7
Columbia, *S.C., U.S.A.* 69 H5
Columbia, *Tenn., U.S.A.* 69 H2
Columbia →, *U.S.A.* 72 C1
Columbia, C., *Canada* 4 A4
Columbia, District of □, *U.S.A.* 68 F7
Columbia, Mt., *Canada* 64 C5
Columbia Basin, *U.S.A.* 72 C4
Columbia Falls, *U.S.A.* 72 B6
Columbia Heights, *U.S.A.* 70 C8
Columbretes, Is., *Spain* 19 C6
Columbus, *Ga., U.S.A.* 69 J3
Columbus, *Ind., U.S.A.* 68 F3
Columbus, *Kans., U.S.A.* 71 G7
Columbus, *Miss., U.S.A.* 69 J1
Columbus, *Mont., U.S.A.* 72 D9
Columbus, *N. Dak., U.S.A.* 70 A3
Columbus, *N. Mex., U.S.A.* 73 L10
Columbus, *Nebr., U.S.A.* 70 E6
Columbus, *Ohio, U.S.A.* 68 F4
Columbus, *Tex., U.S.A.* 71 L6
Columbus, *Wis., U.S.A.* 70 D10
Colusa, *U.S.A.* 72 G2
Colville, *U.S.A.* 72 B5
Colville →, *U.S.A.* 60 A4
Colville, C., *N.Z.* 51 G5
Colwyn Bay, *U.K.* 10 D4
Comácchio, *Italy* 20 B5
Comallo, *Argentina* 80 E2
Comanche, *Okla., U.S.A.* 71 H6
Comanche, *Tex., U.S.A.* 71 K5
Combahee →, *U.S.A.* 69 J5
Comblain-au-Pont, *Belgium* 15 D5
Comeragh Mts., *Ireland* 13 D4
Comet, *Australia* 54 C4
Comilla, *Bangla.* 37 H17
Comino, C., *Italy* 20 D3
Commerce, *Ga., U.S.A.* 69 H4
Commerce, *Tex., U.S.A.* 71 J7
Committee B., *Canada* 61 B11
Commonwealth B., *Antarctica* 5 C10
Commoron Cr. →, *Australia* 55 D5
Communism Pk. = Kommunizma, Pik, *Tajikistan* 24 F8
Como, *Italy* 20 B3
Como, L. di, *Italy* 20 B3
Comodoro Rivadavia, *Argentina* 80 F3
Comorin, C., *India* 36 Q10
Comoro Is. = Comoros ■, *Ind. Oc.* 43 H8
Comoros ■, *Ind. Oc.* 43 H8
Comox, *Canada* 64 D4
Compiègne, *France* 18 B5
Compton Downs, *Australia* 55 E4
Comrat, *Moldova* 17 E15
Côn Dao, *Vietnam* 34 H9
Conakry, *Guinea* 44 G2
Conara Junction, *Australia* 54 G4
Concarneau, *France* 18 C2
Conceição da Barra, *Brazil* 79 G11
Conceição do Araguaia, *Brazil* 79 E9
Concepción, *Bolivia* 78 G6
Concepción, *Chile* 80 D2
Concepción, *Paraguay* 80 A5
Concepción, L., *Bolivia* 78 G6
Concepción del Oro, *Mexico* 74 C4
Concepción del Uruguay, *Argentina* 80 C5
Conception, Pt., *U.S.A.* 73 J3
Conception B., *Namibia* 48 C1
Conchas Dam, *U.S.A.* 71 H2
Conche, *Canada* 63 B8
Concho, *U.S.A.* 73 J9
Concho →, *U.S.A.* 71 K5
Conchos →, *Mexico* 74 B3
Concord, *Calif., U.S.A.* 72 H2
Concord, *N.C., U.S.A.* 69 H5
Concord, *N.H., U.S.A.* 68 D10
Concordia, *Argentina* 80 C5
Concórdia, *Brazil* 78 D5
Concordia, *U.S.A.* 70 F6
Concrete, *U.S.A.* 72 B3
Condamine, *Australia* 55 D5
Conde, *U.S.A.* 70 C5
Condeúba, *Brazil* 79 F10
Condobolin, *Australia* 55 E4
Condon, *U.S.A.* 72 D3
Conegliano, *Italy* 20 B5
Confuso →, *Paraguay* 80 B5
Congleton, *U.K.* 10 D5
Congo = Zaïre →, *Africa* 46 F2
Congo (Kinshasa) = Zaïre ■, *Africa* 46 E4
Congo ■, *Africa* 46 E3
Congo Basin, *Africa* 42 G6
Congress, *U.S.A.* 73 J7
Coniston, *Canada* 62 C3
Conjeeveram = Kanchipuram, *India* 36 N11
Conjuboy, *Australia* 54 B3
Conklin, *Canada* 65 B6
Conlea, *Australia* 55 E3
Conn, L., *Ireland* 13 B2
Connacht □, *Ireland* 13 C3
Conneaut, *U.S.A.* 68 E5
Connecticut □, *U.S.A.* 68 E9
Connecticut →, *U.S.A.* 68 E9
Connell, *U.S.A.* 72 C4
Connellsville, *U.S.A.* 68 E6
Connemara, *Ireland* 13 C2
Connersville, *U.S.A.* 68 F3
Connors Ra., *Australia* 54 C4
Conoble, *Australia* 55 E3
Cononaco →, *Ecuador* 78 D3
Cononbridge, *U.K.* 12 D4
Conquest, *Canada* 65 C7
Conrad, *U.S.A.* 72 B8
Conran, C., *Australia* 55 F4
Conroe, *U.S.A.* 71 K7
Conselheiro Lafaiete, *Brazil* 79 H10
Consort, *Canada* 65 C6
Constance = Konstanz, *Germany* 16 E5
Constance, L. = Bodensee, *Europe* 16 E5
Constanța, *Romania* 17 F15
Constantine, *Algeria* 44 A6
Constitución, *Chile* 80 D2
Consul, *Canada* 65 D7
Contact, *U.S.A.* 72 F6
Contai, *India* 37 J15
Contamana, *Peru* 78 E4
Contas →, *Brazil* 79 F11
Contra Costa, *Mozam.* 49 D5
Conway = Conwy, *U.K.* 10 D4
Conway = Conwy →, *U.K.* 10 D4
Conway, *Ark., U.S.A.* 71 H8
Conway, *N.H., U.S.A.* 68 D10
Conway, *S.C., U.S.A.* 69 J6
Conway, L., *Australia* 55 D2
Conwy, *U.K.* 10 D4
Conwy →, *U.K.* 10 D4
Coober Pedy, *Australia* 55 D1
Cooch Behar = Koch Bihar, *India* 37 F16
Coodardy, *Australia* 53 E2
Cook, *Australia* 53 F5
Cook, *U.S.A.* 70 B8
Cook, B., *Chile* 80 H3
Cook, Mt., *N.Z.* 51 K3
Cook Inlet, *U.S.A.* 60 C4
Cook Is., *Pac. Oc.* 57 J11
Cook Strait, *N.Z.* 51 J5
Cookeville, *U.S.A.* 69 G3
Cookhouse, *S. Africa* 48 E4
Cookstown, *U.K.* 13 B5
Cookstown □, *U.K.* 13 B5
Cooktown, *Australia* 54 B4
Coolabah, *Australia* 55 E4
Cooladdi, *Australia* 55 D4
Coolah, *Australia* 55 E4
Coolamon, *Australia* 55 E4
Coolangatta, *Australia* 55 D5
Coolgardie, *Australia* 53 F3
Coolibah, *Australia* 52 C5
Coolidge, *U.S.A.* 73 K8
Coolidge Dam, *U.S.A.* 73 K8
Cooma, *Australia* 55 F4
Coonabarabran, *Australia* 55 E4
Coonamble, *Australia* 55 E4
Coonana, *Australia* 53 F3
Coondapoor, *India* 36 N9
Coongie, *Australia* 55 D3
Coongoola, *Australia* 55 D4
Cooninie, L., *Australia* 55 D2
Cooper, *U.S.A.* 71 J7
Cooper →, *U.S.A.* 69 J6
Cooper Cr. →, *Australia* 55 D2
Cooperstown, *N. Dak., U.S.A.* 70 B5
Cooperstown, *N.Y., U.S.A.* 68 D8
Coorabie, *Australia* 53 F5
Coorabulka, *Australia* 54 C3
Coorow, *Australia* 53 E2
Cooroy, *Australia* 55 D5
Coos Bay, *U.S.A.* 72 E1
Cootamundra, *Australia* 55 E4
Cootehill, *Ireland* 13 B4
Cooyar, *Australia* 55 D5
Cooyeana, *Australia* 54 C2
Cope, *U.S.A.* 70 F3
Copenhagen = København, *Denmark* 9 J15
Copiapó, *Chile* 80 B2
Copiapó →, *Chile* 80 B2
Copley, *Australia* 55 E2
Copp L., *Canada* 64 A6
Copper Center, *U.S.A.* 60 B5
Copper Cliff, *Canada* 62 C3
Copper Harbor, *U.S.A.* 68 B2
Coppermine, *Canada* 60 B8
Coppermine →, *Canada* 60 B8
Coquet →, *U.K.* 10 B6
Coquilhatville = Mbandaka, *Zaïre* 46 D3
Coquille, *U.S.A.* 72 E1
Coquimbo, *Chile* 80 C2
Corabia, *Romania* 17 G13
Coracora, *Peru* 78 G4
Coral Gables, *U.S.A.* 69 N5
Coral Harbour, *Canada* 61 B11
Coral Sea, *Pac. Oc.* 56 J7
Corato, *Italy* 20 D7
Corbin, *U.S.A.* 68 G3
Corby, *U.K.* 11 E7
Corby Glen, *U.K.* 11 E7
Corcaigh = Cork, *Ireland* 13 E3
Corcoran, *U.S.A.* 73 H4
Corcubión, *Spain* 19 A1
Cordele, *U.S.A.* 69 K4
Cordell, *U.S.A.* 71 H5
Córdoba, *Argentina* 80 C4
Córdoba, *Spain* 19 D3
Córdoba, Sierra de, *Argentina* 80 C4
Cordon, *Phil.* 33 A6
Cordova, *Ala., U.S.A.* 69 J2
Cordova, *Alaska, U.S.A.* 60 B5
Corella →, *Australia* 54 B3
Corfield, *Australia* 54 C3
Corfu = Kérkira, *Greece* 21 E8
Coria, *Spain* 19 C2
Corigliano Cálabro, *Italy* 20 E7
Coringa Is., *Australia* 54 B4
Corinna, *Australia* 54 G4
Corinth = Kórinthos, *Greece* 21 F10
Corinth, *U.S.A.* 69 H1
Corinth, G. of = Korinthiakós Kólpos, *Greece* 21 E10
Corinto, *Brazil* 79 G10
Cork, *Ireland* 13 E3
Cork □, *Ireland* 13 E3
Cork Harbour, *Ireland* 13 E3
Çorlu, *Turkey* 21 D12
Cormack L., *Canada* 64 A4
Cormorant, *Canada* 65 C8
Cormorant L., *Canada* 65 C8
Cornell, *U.S.A.* 70 C9
Corner Brook, *Canada* 63 C8
Cornești, *Moldova* 17 E15
Corning, *Ark., U.S.A.* 71 G9
Corning, *Calif., U.S.A.* 72 G2
Corning, *Iowa, U.S.A.* 70 E7
Corning, *N.Y., U.S.A.* 68 D7
Cornwall, *Canada* 62 C5
Cornwall □, *U.K.* 11 G3
Corny Pt., *Australia* 55 E2
Coro, *Venezuela* 78 A5
Coroatá, *Brazil* 79 D10
Corocoro, *Bolivia* 78 G5
Coroico, *Bolivia* 78 G5
Coromandel, *N.Z.* 51 G5
Coromandel Coast, *India* 36 N12
Corona, *Australia* 55 E3
Corona, *Calif., U.S.A.* 73 K5
Corona, *N. Mex., U.S.A.* 73 J11
Coronado, *U.S.A.* 73 K5
Coronation, *Canada* 64 C6
Coronation Gulf, *Canada* 60 B8
Coronation I., *Antarctica* 5 C18
Coronation I., *U.S.A.* 64 B2
Coronation Is., *Australia* 52 B3
Coronel, *Chile* 80 D2
Coronel Dorrego, *Argentina* 80 D4
Coronel Pringles, *Argentina* 80 D4
Coronel Suárez, *Argentina* 80 D4
Corowa, *Australia* 55 F4
Corozal, *Panama* 74 H14
Corpus Christi, *U.S.A.* 71 M6
Corpus Christi, L., *U.S.A.* 71 L6
Corque, *Bolivia* 78 G5
Correntes, C. das, *Mozam.* 49 C6
Corrib, L., *Ireland* 13 C2
Corrientes, *Argentina* 80 B5
Corrientes →, *Peru* 78 D4
Corrientes, C., *Colombia* 78 B3
Corrientes, C., *Mexico* 74 C3
Corrigan, *U.S.A.* 71 K7
Corrigin, *Australia* 53 F2
Corry, *U.S.A.* 68 E6
Corse, *France* 18 F8
Corse, C., *France* 18 E8
Corsica = Corse, *France* 18 F8
Corsicana, *U.S.A.* 71 J6
Corte, *France* 18 E8
Cortez, *U.S.A.* 73 H9
Cortland, *U.S.A.* 68 D7
Çorum, *Turkey* 23 F5
Corumbá, *Brazil* 78 G7
Corumbá de Goiás, *Brazil* 79 G9
Corunna = La Coruña, *Spain* 19 A1
Corvallis, *U.S.A.* 72 D2
Corvette, L. de la, *Canada* 62 B5
Corydon, *U.S.A.* 70 E8
Cosenza, *Italy* 20 E7
Coshocton, *U.S.A.* 68 E5
Cosmo Newberry, *Australia* 53 E3
Costa Blanca, *Spain* 19 C5
Costa Brava, *Spain* 19 B7
Costa del Sol, *Spain* 19 D3
Costa Dorada, *Spain* 19 B6
Costa Rica ■, *Cent. Amer.* 75 F8
Costilla, *U.S.A.* 73 H11
Cotabato, *Phil.* 33 C6
Cotagaita, *Bolivia* 78 H5
Côte d'Azur, *France* 18 E7
Côte-d'Ivoire = Ivory Coast ■, *Africa* 44 G3
Coteau des Prairies, *U.S.A.* 70 C6
Coteau du Missouri, *U.S.A.* 70 B4
Cotentin, *France* 18 B3
Cotonou, *Benin* 44 G5
Cotopaxi, *Ecuador* 78 D3
Cotswold Hills, *U.K.* 11 F5
Cottage Grove, *U.S.A.* 72 E2
Cottbus, *Germany* 16 C8
Cottingham, *U.K.* 10 C5
Cottonwood, *U.S.A.* 73 J7
Cotulla, *U.S.A.* 71 L5
Coudersport, *U.S.A.* 68 E6
Couedic, C. du, *Australia* 55 F2
Coulee City, *U.S.A.* 72 C4
Coulman I., *Antarctica* 5 D11
Coulonge →, *Canada* 62 C4
Council, *Alaska, U.S.A.* 60 B3
Council, *Idaho, U.S.A.* 72 D5
Council Bluffs, *U.S.A.* 70 E7
Council Grove, *U.S.A.* 70 F6
Courantyne →, *S. Amer.* 78 B7
Courtenay, *Canada* 64 D3
Courtrai = Kortrijk, *Belgium* 15 D3
Coushatta, *U.S.A.* 71 J8
Coutts, *Canada* 64 D6
Coventry, *U.K.* 11 E6
Coventry L., *Canada* 65 A7
Covilhã, *Portugal* 19 B2
Covington, *Ga., U.S.A.* 69 J4
Covington, *Ky., U.S.A.* 68 F3
Covington, *Okla., U.S.A.* 71 G6
Covington, *Tenn., U.S.A.* 71 H10
Cowal, L., *Australia* 55 E4
Cowan, *Canada* 65 C8
Cowan, L., *Australia* 53 F3
Cowan L., *Canada* 65 C7
Cowangie, *Australia* 55 F3
Cowarie, *Australia* 55 D2
Cowcowing Lakes, *Australia* 53 F2
Cowdenbeath, *U.K.* 12 E5
Cowell, *Australia* 55 E2
Cowes, *U.K.* 11 G6
Cowra, *Australia* 55 E4
Coxim, *Brazil* 79 G8
Cox's Bazar, *Bangla.* 37 J17
Cox's Cove, *Canada* 63 C8
Cozad, *U.S.A.* 70 E5
Cozumel, I. de, *Mexico* 74 C7
Craboon, *Australia* 55 E4
Cracow = Kraków, *Poland* 17 C10
Cracow, *Australia* 55 D5
Cradock, *S. Africa* 48 E4
Craig, *Alaska, U.S.A.* 64 B2
Craig, *Colo., U.S.A.* 72 F10
Craigavon, *U.K.* 13 B5
Crailsheim, *Germany* 16 D6
Craiova, *Romania* 17 F12
Cramsie, *Australia* 54 C3
Cranberry Portage, *Canada* 65 C8
Cranbrook, *Tas., Australia* 54 G4
Cranbrook, *W. Austral., Australia* 53 F2
Cranbrook, *Canada* 64 D5
Crandon, *U.S.A.* 70 C10
Crane, *Oreg., U.S.A.* 72 E4
Crane, *Tex., U.S.A.* 71 K3
Crater L., *U.S.A.* 72 E2
Crateús, *Brazil* 79 E10
Crato, *Brazil* 79 E11
Crawford, *U.S.A.* 70 D3
Crawfordsville, *U.S.A.* 68 E2
Crawley, *U.K.* 11 F7
Crazy Mts., *U.S.A.* 72 C8
Crean L., *Canada* 65 C7
Credo, *Australia* 53 F3
Cree →, *Canada* 65 B7
Cree →, *U.K.* 12 G4
Cree L., *Canada* 65 B7
Creede, *U.S.A.* 73 H10
Creighton, *U.S.A.* 70 D6
Crema, *Italy* 20 B3
Cremona, *Italy* 20 B4
Cres, *Croatia* 16 F8
Cresbard, *U.S.A.* 70 C5
Crescent, *Okla., U.S.A.* 71 H6
Crescent, *Oreg., U.S.A.* 72 E3
Crescent City, *U.S.A.* 72 F1
Cressy, *Australia* 55 F3
Crested Butte, *U.S.A.* 73 G10
Creston, *Canada* 64 D5
Creston, *Iowa, U.S.A.* 70 E7
Creston, *Wash., U.S.A.* 72 C4
Crestview, *U.S.A.* 69 K2
Crete = Kríti, *Greece* 21 G11
Crete, *U.S.A.* 70 E6
Créteil, *France* 18 B5
Creus, C. de, *Spain* 19 A7
Creuse →, *France* 18 C4
Crewe, *U.K.* 10 D5
Criciúma, *Brazil* 80 B7
Crieff, *U.K.* 12 E5
Crimean Pen. = Krymskyy Pivostriv, *Ukraine* 23 E5
Cristóbal, *Panama* 74 H14
Crișul Alb →, *Romania* 17 E11
Crișul Negru →, *Romania* 17 E11
Crna Gora = Montenegro □, *Yugoslavia* 21 C8
Crna Gora, *Serbia, Yug.* 21 C9
Crna Reka →, *Macedonia* 21 D9
Croagh Patrick, *Ireland* 13 C2
Croatia ■, *Europe* 16 F9
Crocker, Banjaran, *Malaysia* 32 C5
Crockett, *U.S.A.* 71 K7
Crocodile = Krokodil →, *Mozam.* 49 D5
Crocodile Is., *Australia* 54 A1
Croix, L. La, *Canada* 62 C1
Croker, C., *Australia* 52 B5
Croker I., *Australia* 52 B5
Cromarty, *Canada* 65 B10
Cromarty, *U.K.* 12 D4
Cromer, *U.K.* 10 E9
Cromwell, *N.Z.* 51 L2
Cronulla, *Australia* 55 E5
Crooked →, *Canada* 64 C4
Crooked →, *U.S.A.* 72 D3
Crookston, *Minn., U.S.A.* 70 B6
Crookston, *Nebr., U.S.A.* 70 D4
Crooksville, *U.S.A.* 68 F4
Crookwell, *Australia* 55 E4
Crosby, *Minn., U.S.A.* 70 B8
Crosby, *N. Dak., U.S.A.* 65 D8
Crosbyton, *U.S.A.* 71 J4
Cross City, *U.S.A.* 69 L4
Cross Fell, *U.K.* 10 C5
Cross L., *Canada* 65 C9
Cross Plains, *U.S.A.* 71 J5
Cross Sound, *U.S.A.* 60 C6
Crossett, *U.S.A.* 71 J9
Crossfield, *Canada* 64 C6
Crosshaven, *Ireland* 13 E3
Crotone, *Italy* 20 E7
Crow →, *Canada* 64 B4
Crow Agency, *U.S.A.* 72 D10
Crow Hd., *Ireland* 13 E1
Crowell, *U.S.A.* 71 J5
Crowley, *U.S.A.* 71 K8
Crown Point, *U.S.A.* 68 E2
Crows Nest, *Australia* 55 D5
Crowsnest Pass, *Canada* 64 D6
Croydon, *Australia* 54 B3
Croydon, *U.K.* 11 F7
Crozet Is., *Ind. Oc.* 35 J4
Cruz Alta, *Brazil* 80 B6
Cruz del Eje, *Argentina* 80 C4
Cruzeiro, *Brazil* 79 H10
Cruzeiro do Sul, *Brazil* 78 E4
Cry L., *Canada* 64 B3
Crystal Brook, *Australia* 55 E2
Crystal City, *Mo., U.S.A.* 70 F9
Crystal City, *Tex., U.S.A.* 71 L5
Crystal Falls, *U.S.A.* 68 B1
Crystal River, *U.S.A.* 69 L4
Crystal Springs, *U.S.A.* 71 K9
Csongrád, *Hungary* 17 E11
Cu Lao Hon, *Vietnam* 34 G10
Cuamato, *Angola* 48 B2
Cuamba, *Mozam.* 47 G7
Cuando →, *Angola* 47 H4
Cuando Cubango □, *Angola* 48 B3
Cuangar, *Angola* 48 B2
Cuanza →, *Angola* 42 G5
Cuarto →, *Argentina* 80 C4
Cuba, *U.S.A.* 73 J10
Cuba ■, *W. Indies* 75 C9
Cuballing, *Australia* 53 F2
Cubango →, *Africa* 48 B3
Cuchi, *Angola* 47 G3
Cúcuta, *Colombia* 78 B4
Cudahy, *U.S.A.* 68 D2
Cuddalore, *India* 36 P11
Cuddapah, *India* 36 M11
Cuddapan, L., *Australia* 54 D3
Cudgewa, *Australia* 55 F4
Cue, *Australia* 53 E2
Cuenca, *Ecuador* 78 D3
Cuenca, *Spain* 19 B4

Cuenca, Serranía de

Cuenca, Serranía de, Spain 19 C5
Cuernavaca, Mexico .. 74 D5
Cuero, U.S.A. 71 L6
Cuervo, U.S.A. 71 H2
Cuevas del Almanzora, Spain 19 D5
Cuevo, Bolivia 78 H6
Cuiabá, Brazil 79 G7
Cuiabá →, Brazil 79 G7
Cuillin Hills, U.K. 12 D2
Cuillin Sd., U.K. 12 D2
Cuima, Angola 47 G3
Cuito →, Angola 48 B3
Cukai, Malaysia 34 Q16
Culbertson, U.S.A. ... 70 A2
Culcairn, Australia ... 55 F4
Culgoa →, Australia .. 55 D4
Culiacán, Mexico 74 C3
Culion, Phil. 33 B6
Cullarin Ra., Australia 55 E4
Cullen, U.K. 12 D6
Cullen Pt., Australia .. 54 A3
Cullera, Spain 19 C5
Cullman, U.S.A. 69 H2
Culloden, U.K. 12 D4
Culpeper, U.S.A. 68 F7
Culuene →, Brazil ... 79 F8
Culverden, N.Z. 51 K4
Culver, Pt., Australia . 53 F3
Cumaná, Venezuela .. 78 A6
Cumberland, Canada . 64 D3
Cumberland, Md., U.S.A. 68 F6
Cumberland, Wis., U.S.A. 70 C8
Cumberland →, U.S.A. 69 G2
Cumberland I., U.S.A. 69 K5
Cumberland Is., Australia 54 C4
Cumberland L., Canada 65 C8
Cumberland Pen., Canada 61 B13
Cumberland Plateau, U.S.A. 69 H3
Cumberland Sd., Canada 61 B13
Cumborah, Australia . 55 D4
Cumbria □, U.K. 10 C5
Cumbrian Mts., U.K. . 10 C4
Cumbum, India 36 M11
Cummins, Australia .. 55 E2
Cumnock, Australia .. 55 E4
Cumnock, U.K. 12 F4
Cundeelee, Australia . 53 F3
Cunderdin, Australia . 53 F2
Cunene →, Angola .. 48 B1
Cúneo, Italy 20 B2
Cunnamulla, Australia 55 D4
Cupar, Canada 65 C8
Cupar, U.K. 12 E5
Cupica, G. de, Colombia 78 B3
Curaçao, Neth. Ant. . 75 E11
Curaray →, Peru ... 78 D4
Curiapo, Venezuela .. 78 B6
Curicó, Chile 80 C2
Curitiba, Brazil 80 B7
Currabubula, Australia 55 E5
Currais Novos, Brazil 79 E11
Curralinho, Brazil ... 79 D9
Currant, U.S.A. 72 G6
Curraweena, Australia 55 E4
Currawilla, Australia . 54 D3
Current →, U.S.A. .. 71 G9
Currie, Australia 54 F3
Currie, U.S.A. 72 F6
Currituck Sd., U.S.A. 69 G8
Curtea de Argeş, Romania 17 F13
Curtis, U.S.A. 70 E4
Curtis Group, Australia 54 F4
Curtis I., Australia ... 54 C5
Curuápanema →, Brazil 79 D7
Curuçá, Brazil 79 D9
Çürüksu Çayi →, Turkey 23 G4
Curup, Indonesia 32 E2
Cururupu, Brazil 79 D10
Curuzú Cuatiá, Argentina 80 B5
Cushing, U.S.A. 71 H6
Cushing, Mt., Canada 64 B3
Custer, U.S.A. 70 D3
Cut Bank, U.S.A. ... 72 B7
Cuthbert, U.S.A. 69 K3
Cuttaburra →, Australia 55 D3
Cuttack, India 37 J14
Cuvier, C., Australia . 53 D1
Cuvier I., N.Z. 51 G5
Cuxhaven, Germany . 16 B5
Cuyahoga Falls, U.S.A. 68 E3
Cuyo, Phil. 33 B6
Cuzco, Bolivia 78 H5
Cuzco, Peru 78 F4
Cwmbran, U.K. 11 F4
Cyclades = Kikládhes, Greece 21 F11
Cygnet, Australia ... 54 G4
Cynthiana, U.S.A. .. 68 F3
Cypress Hills, Canada 65 D7
Cyprus ■, Asia 38 C2
Cyrenaica, Libya 45 C9
Cyrene = Shaḥḥāt, Libya 45 B9
Czar, Canada 65 C6
Czech Rep. ■, Europe 16 D8
Częstochowa, Poland . 17 C10

D

Da →, Vietnam 34 B8
Da Hinggan Ling, China 31 B7
Da Lat, Vietnam 34 G10
Da Nang, Vietnam ... 34 D10
Da Qaidam, China .. 30 C4
Daba Shan, China .. 31 C5
Dabakala, Ivory C. .. 44 G4
Dabo, Indonesia 32 E2
Dabola, Guinea 44 F2
Daboya, Ghana 44 G4
Dacca = Dhaka, Bangla. 37 H17
Dacca = Dhaka □, Bangla. 37 G17
Dachau, Germany ... 16 D6
Dadanawa, Guyana .. 78 C7
Dade City, U.S.A. ... 69 L4
Dadra and Nagar Haveli □, India .. 36 J8
Dadu, Pakistan 36 F5
Daet, Phil. 33 B6
Dagana, Senegal ... 44 E1
Dagestan □, Russia . 23 F8
Daghestan Republic = Dagestan □, Russia . 23 F8
Dagö = Hiiumaa, Estonia 9 G20
Dagupan, Phil. 33 A6
Dahlak Kebir, Eritrea . 40 D3
Dahlonega, U.S.A. .. 69 H4
Dahod, India 36 H9
Dahomey = Benin ■, Africa 44 G6
Dahra, Senegal 44 E1
Dai-Sen, Japan 29 G6
Daingean, Ireland ... 13 C4
Daió-Misaki, Japan .. 29 G8
Dairût, Egypt 45 C11
Daisetsu-Zan, Japan . 28 C11
Dajarra, Australia ... 54 C2
Dakar, Senegal 44 F1
Dakhla, W. Sahara .. 44 D1
Dakhla, El Wâhât el-, Egypt 45 C10
Dakhovskaya, Russia . 23 F7
Dakota City, U.S.A. . 70 D6
Dakovica, Serbia, Yug. 21 C9
Dālakī, Iran 39 D6
Dalälven, Sweden ... 9 F17
Dalaman →, Turkey . 21 F13
Dalandzadgad, Mongolia 30 B5
Dalarna, Sweden ... 9 F16
Dālbandīn, Pakistan . 36 E4
Dalbeattie, U.K. 12 G5
Dalby, Australia 55 D5
Dalgán, Iran 39 E8
Dalhart, U.S.A. 71 G3
Dalhousie, Canada .. 63 C6
Dali, China 30 D5
Dalian, China 31 C7
Daliang Shan, China . 30 D5
Dāliyat el Karmel, Israel 41 C4
Dalkeith, U.K. 12 F5
Dall I., U.S.A. 64 C2
Dallarnil, Australia .. 55 D5
Dallas, Oreg., U.S.A. 72 D2
Dallas, Tex., U.S.A. . 71 J6
Dalmacija, Croatia .. 20 C7
Dalmatia = Dalmacija, Croatia 20 C7
Dalmellington, U.K. . 12 F4
Dalnegorsk, Russia .. 25 E14
Dalnerechensk, Russia 25 E14
Daloa, Ivory C. 44 G3
Dalsland, Sweden ... 9 G14
Dalton, Canada 62 C3
Dalton, Ga., U.S.A. . 69 H3
Dalton, Nebr., U.S.A. 70 E3
Dalton Iceberg Tongue, Antarctica 5 C9
Dalvík, Iceland 8 D4
Daly →, Australia .. 52 B5
Daly L., Canada 65 B7
Daly Waters, Australia 54 B1
Daman, India 36 J8
Dāmaneh, Iran 39 C6
Damanhûr, Egypt ... 45 B11
Damar, Indonesia ... 33 F7
Damaraland, Namibia 48 C2
Damascus = Dimashq, Syria 41 B5
Damāvand, Iran 39 C7
Damāvand, Qolleh-ye, Iran 39 C7
Damba, Angola 46 F3
Dāmghān, Iran 39 B7
Damiel, Spain 19 C4
Damietta = Dumyât, Egypt 45 B11
Damīr Qābū, Syria .. 38 B4
Dammam = Ad Dammām, Si. Arabia 39 E6
Damoh, India 36 H11
Dampier, Australia .. 52 D2
Dampier, Selat, Indonesia 33 E8
Dampier Arch., Australia 52 D2
Dana, L., Canada ... 62 B4
Danbury, U.S.A. 68 E9
Danby L., U.S.A. ... 73 J6
Dandaragan, Australia 53 F2
Dandeldhura, Nepal . 37 E12
Dandeli, India 36 M9
Dandenong, Australia 55 F4
Dandong, China 31 B7
Danforth, U.S.A. ... 63 C6

Danger Is. = Pukapuka, Cook Is. 57 J11
Danger Pt., S. Africa . 48 E2
Dangora, Nigeria ... 44 F6
Daniel, U.S.A. 72 E8
Daniel's Harbour, Canada 63 B8
Danielskuil, S. Africa . 48 D3
Danilov, Russia 22 C7
Dankhar Gompa, India 36 C11
Dannemora, U.S.A. .. 68 C9
Dannevirke, N.Z. ... 51 J6
Dannhauser, S. Africa 49 D5
Dansville, U.S.A. ... 68 D7
Dante, Somali Rep. .. 40 E5
Danube = Dunărea →, Europe 17 F15
Danville, Ill., U.S.A. . 68 E2
Danville, Ky., U.S.A. . 68 G3
Danville, Va., U.S.A. . 69 G6
Danzig = Gdańsk, Poland 17 A10
Dao, Phil. 33 B6
Daoud = Aïn Beïda, Algeria 44 A6
Dar el Beida = Casablanca, Morocco 44 B3
Dar es Salaam, Tanzania 46 F7
Dar Mazār, Iran 39 D8
Dar'ā, Syria 41 C5
Dar'ā □, Syria 41 C5
Dārāb, Iran 39 D7
Daraj, Libya 44 B7
Dārān, Iran 39 C6
Dārayyā, Syria 41 B5
Darband, Pakistan .. 36 B8
Darband, Kūh-e, Iran . 39 D8
Darbhanga, India ... 37 F14
Darby, U.S.A. 72 C6
Dardanelle, U.S.A. .. 71 H8
Dardanelles = Çanakkale Boğazı, Turkey 21 D12
Dārestān, Iran 39 D8
Dārfūr, Sudan 45 F9
Dargai, Pakistan ... 36 B7
Dargan Ata, Uzbekistan 24 E7
Dargaville, N.Z. 51 F4
Darica, Turkey 21 D13
Darién, G. del, Colombia 78 B3
Darjeeling = Darjiling, India 37 F16
Darjiling, India 37 F16
Dark Cove, Canada .. 63 C9
Darkan, Australia ... 53 F2
Darkhazineh, Iran .. 39 D6
Darling →, Australia . 55 E3
Darling Downs, Australia 55 D5
Darling Ra., Australia 53 F2
Darlington, U.K. 10 C6
Darlington, S.C., U.S.A. 69 H6
Darlington, Wis., U.S.A. 70 D9
Darlington, L., S. Africa 48 E4
Darlot, L., Australia . 53 E3
Darłowo, Poland ... 16 A9
Darmstadt, Germany . 16 D5
Darnah, Libya 45 B9
Darnall, S. Africa ... 49 D5
Darnley, C., Antarctica 5 C6
Darnley B., Canada .. 60 B7
Darr →, Australia .. 54 C3
Darr →, Australia .. 54 C3
Darrington, U.S.A. .. 72 B3
Dart →, U.K. 11 G4
Dart, C., Antarctica . 5 D14
Dartmoor, U.K. 11 G4
Dartmouth, Australia 54 C3
Dartmouth, Canada .. 63 D7
Dartmouth, U.K. 11 G4
Dartmouth, L., Australia 55 D4
Darvaza, Turkmenistan 24 E6
Darvel, Teluk, Malaysia 33 D5
Darwha, India 36 J10
Darwin, Australia ... 52 B5
Darwin River, Australia 52 B5
Daryoi Amu = Amudarya →, Uzbekistan 24 E6
Dās, U.A.E. 39 E7
Dashhowuz, Turkmenistan ... 24 E6
Dasht, Iran 39 B8
Dasht →, Pakistan . 36 G2
Dasht-e Mārgow, Afghan. 36 D3
Datça, Turkey 21 F12
Datia, India 36 G11
Datong, China 31 B6
Datu, Tanjung, Indonesia 32 D3
Datu Piang, Phil. ... 33 C6
Daugava →, Latvia . 9 H21
Daugavpils, Latvia .. 9 J22
Daulpur, India 36 F10
Dauphin, Canada ... 65 C8
Dauphin I., U.S.A. .. 69 K1
Dauphin L., Canada . 65 C9
Dauphiné, France ... 18 D6
Davangere, India ... 36 M9
Davao, Phil. 33 C7
Davao, G. of, Phil. .. 33 C7
Dāvar Panāh, Iran .. 39 E9
Davenport, Iowa, U.S.A. 70 E9
Davenport, Wash., U.S.A. 72 C4
Davenport Downs, Australia 54 C3
Davenport Ra., Australia 54 C1

David, Panama 75 F8
David City, U.S.A. .. 70 E6
David Gorodok = Davyd Haradok, Belarus 17 B14
Davidson, Canada .. 65 C7
Davis, U.S.A. 72 G3
Davis Dam, U.S.A. .. 73 J6
Davis Inlet, Canada . 63 A7
Davis Mts., U.S.A. .. 71 K2
Davis Sea, Antarctica 5 C7
Davis Str., N. Amer. . 61 B14
Davos, Switz. 16 E5
Davy L., Canada 65 B7
Davyd Haradok, Belarus 17 B14
Dawes Ra., Australia 54 C5
Dawson, Canada 60 B6
Dawson, Ga., U.S.A. 69 K3
Dawson, N. Dak., U.S.A. 70 B5
Dawson, I., Chile ... 80 G2
Dawson Creek, Canada 64 B4
Dawson Inlet, Canada 65 A10
Dawson Ra., Australia 54 C4
Dax, France 18 E3
Daxian, China 30 C5
Daxue Shan, China .. 30 C5
Daylesford, Australia 55 F3
Dayr az Zawr, Syria . 38 C4
Daysland, Canada .. 64 C6
Dayton, Ohio, U.S.A. 68 F3
Dayton, Tenn., U.S.A. 69 H3
Dayton, Wash., U.S.A. 72 C4
Daytona Beach, U.S.A. 69 L5
Dayville, U.S.A. 72 D4
De Aar, S. Africa ... 48 E3
De Funiak Springs, U.S.A. 69 K2
De Grey, Australia .. 52 D2
De Grey →, Australia 52 D2
De Kalb, U.S.A. 70 E10
De Land, U.S.A. 69 L5
De Leon, U.S.A. 71 J5
De Pere, U.S.A. 68 C1
De Queen, U.S.A. ... 71 H7
De Quincy, U.S.A. .. 71 K8
De Ridder, U.S.A. .. 71 K8
De Smet, U.S.A. ... 70 C6
De Soto, U.S.A. 70 F9
De Tour Village, U.S.A. 68 C4
De Witt, U.S.A. 71 H9
Dead Sea, Asia 41 D4
Deadwood, U.S.A. .. 70 C3
Deadwood L., Canada 64 B3
Deakin, Australia ... 53 F4
Deal, U.K. 11 F9
Deal I., Australia ... 54 F4
Dealesville, S. Africa 48 D4
Dean, Forest of, U.K. 11 F5
Deán Funes, Argentina 80 C4
Dearborn, U.S.A. ... 62 D3
Dease →, Canada .. 64 B3
Dease L., Canada ... 64 B2
Dease Lake, Canada . 64 B2
Death Valley, U.S.A. 73 H5
Death Valley Junction, U.S.A. 73 H5
Death Valley National Monument, U.S.A. 73 H5
Deba Habe, Nigeria . 44 F7
Debar, Macedonia .. 21 D9
Debden, Canada 65 C7
Dębica, Poland 17 C11
Debolt, Canada 64 B5
Deborah East, L., Australia 53 F2
Deborah West, L., Australia 53 F2
Debre Markos, Ethiopia 45 F12
Debre Tabor, Ethiopia 45 F12
Debrecen, Hungary . 17 E11
Decatur, Ala., U.S.A. 69 H2
Decatur, Ga., U.S.A. 69 J3
Decatur, Ill., U.S.A. . 70 F10
Decatur, Ind., U.S.A. 68 E3
Decatur, Tex., U.S.A. 71 J6
Deccan, India 36 M10
Deception L., Canada 65 B8
Děčín, Czech. 16 C8
Decorah, U.S.A. ... 70 D9
Dedéagach = Alexandroúpolis, Greece 21 D11
Dédougou, Burkina Faso 44 F4
Dee →, Clwyd, U.K. 10 D4
Dee →, Gramp., U.K. 12 D6
Deep B., Canada ... 64 A5
Deep Well, Australia 54 C1
Deepwater, Australia 55 D5
Deer →, Canada ... 65 B10
Deer Lake, Nfld., Canada 63 C8
Deer Lake, Ont., Canada 65 C10
Deer Lodge, U.S.A. . 72 C7
Deer Park, U.S.A. .. 72 C5
Deer River, U.S.A. .. 70 B8
Deeral, Australia ... 54 B4
Deerdepoort, S. Africa 48 C4
Defiance, U.S.A. ... 68 E3
Degeh Bur, Ethiopia . 40 F3
Deggendorf, Germany 16 D7
Deh Bid, Iran 39 D7
Deh-e Shīr, Iran 39 D7
Dehaj, Iran 39 D7
Dehdez, Iran 39 D6
Dehestān, Iran 39 D7
Dehgolān, Iran 38 C5
Dehi Titan, Afghan. . 36 C3
Dehibat, Tunisia ... 44 B7
Dehlorān, Iran 38 C5

Dehnow-e Kūhestān, Iran 39 E8
Deinze, Belgium 15 D3
Dej, Romania 17 E12
Dekese, Zaïre 46 E4
Del Norte, U.S.A. ... 73 H10
Del Rio, U.S.A. 71 L4
Delano, U.S.A. 73 J4
Delareyville, S. Africa 48 D4
Delavan, U.S.A. 70 D10
Delaware, U.S.A. ... 68 E4
Delaware □, U.S.A. . 68 F8
Delaware →, U.S.A. 68 F8
Delaware B., U.S.A. . 67 C12
Delegate, Australia .. 55 F4
Delft, Neths. 15 B4
Delfzijl, Neths. 15 A6
Delgado, C., Mozam. 46 G8
Delgo, Sudan 45 D11
Delhi, India 36 E10
Delia, Canada 64 C6
Delice →, Turkey .. 23 G5
Delicias, Mexico 74 B3
Delījān, Iran 39 C6
Dell City, U.S.A. ... 73 L11
Dell Rapids, U.S.A. . 70 D6
Delmenhorst, Germany 16 B5
Delong, Ostrova, Russia 25 B15
Deloraine, Australia . 54 G4
Deloraine, Canada .. 65 D8
Delphi, U.S.A. 68 E2
Delphos, U.S.A. 68 E3
Delportshoop, S. Africa 48 D3
Delray Beach, U.S.A. 69 M5
Delta, Colo., U.S.A. . 73 G9
Delta, Utah, U.S.A. . 72 G7
Delungra, Australia . 55 D5
Delvinë, Albania ... 21 E9
Demanda, Sierra de la, Spain 19 A4
Demavend = Damāvand, Iran .. 39 C7
Demba, Zaïre 46 F4
Dembecha, Ethiopia . 45 F12
Dembidolo, Ethiopia . 45 G11
Demer →, Belgium . 15 D4
Deming, U.S.A. 73 K10
Demini →, Brazil ... 78 D6
Demirci, Turkey 21 E13
Demirköy, Turkey ... 21 D12
Demopolis, U.S.A. .. 69 J2
Dempo, Indonesia .. 32 E2
Den Burg, Neths. ... 15 A4
Den Haag = 's-Gravenhage, Neths. 15 B4
Den Helder, Neths. . 15 B4
Den Oever, Neths. .. 15 B5
Denain, France 15 D3
Denau, Uzbekistan .. 24 F7
Denbigh, U.K. 10 D4
Dendang, Indonesia . 32 E3
Dendermonde, Belgium 15 C4
Denham, Australia .. 53 E1
Denham Ra., Australia 54 C4
Denham Sd., Australia 53 E1
Denia, Spain 19 C6
Denial B., Australia . 55 E1
Deniliquin, Australia 55 F3
Denison, Iowa, U.S.A. 70 D7
Denison, Tex., U.S.A. 71 J6
Denison Plains, Australia 52 C4
Denizli, Turkey 23 G4
Denman Glacier, Antarctica 5 C7
Denmark, Australia . 53 F2
Denmark ■, Europe . 9 J13
Denmark Str., Atl. Oc. 4 C6
Denpasar, Indonesia 32 F5
Denton, Mont., U.S.A. 72 C9
Denton, Tex., U.S.A. 71 J6
D'Entrecasteaux, Pt., Australia 53 F2
Denver, U.S.A. 70 F2
Denver City, U.S.A. . 71 J3
Deoghar, India 37 G15
Deolali, India 36 K8
Deoli, India 36 G9
Deosai Mts., Pakistan 36 B9
Depot Springs, Australia 53 E3
Deputatskiy, Russia . 25 C14
Dera Ghazi Khan, Pakistan 36 D7
Dera Ismail Khan, Pakistan 36 D7
Derbent, Russia 23 F8
Derby, Australia 52 C3
Derby, U.K. 10 E6
Derbyshire □, U.K. . 10 E6
Derg →, U.K. 13 B4
Derg, L., Ireland ... 13 D3
Dergaon, India 37 F19
Dernieres, Isles, U.S.A. 71 L9
Derry = Londonderry, U.K. 13 B4
Derryveagh Mts., Ireland 13 B3
Derudub, Sudan 45 E12
Derwent, Canada ... 65 C6
Derwent →, Derby, U.K. 10 E6
Derwent →, N. Yorks., U.K. 10 D7
Derwent Water, U.K. 10 C4
Des Moines, Iowa, U.S.A. 70 E8
Des Moines, N. Mex., U.S.A. 71 G3
Des Moines →, U.S.A. 70 E9

Desaguadero →, Bolivia 78 G5
Deschaillons, Canada 63 C5
Descharme →, Canada 65 B7
Deschutes →, U.S.A. 72 D3
Dese, Ethiopia 40 E2
Desert Center, U.S.A. 73 K6
Deskenatlata L., Canada 64 A6
Desna →, Ukraine . 17 C16
Desolación, I., Chile . 80 G2
Despeñaperros, Paso, Spain 19 C4
Dessau, Germany ... 16 C7
Dessye = Dese, Ethiopia 40 E2
Detmold, Germany .. 16 C5
Detour, Pt., U.S.A. . 68 C2
Detroit, Mich., U.S.A. 62 D3
Detroit, Tex., U.S.A. 71 J7
Detroit Lakes, U.S.A. 70 B7
Deurne, Belgium ... 15 C4
Deurne, Neths. 15 C5
Deutsche Bucht, Germany 16 A5
Deva, Romania 17 F12
Devakottai, India ... 36 Q11
Deventer, Neths. ... 15 B6
Deveron →, U.K. ... 12 D6
Devils Lake, U.S.A. . 70 A5
Devils Paw, Canada . 64 B2
Devizes, U.K. 11 F6
Devon, Canada 64 C6
Devon □, U.K. 11 G4
Devon I., Canada ... 4 B3
Devonport, Australia 54 G4
Devonport, N.Z. 51 G5
Devonport, U.K. 11 G3
Dewas, India 36 H10
Dewetsdorp, S. Africa 48 D4
Dewsbury, U.K. 10 D6
Dexter, Mo., U.S.A. . 71 G9
Dexter, N. Mex., U.S.A. 71 J2
Dey-Dey, L., Australia 53 E5
Deyhūk, Iran 39 C8
Deyyer, Iran 39 E6
Dezadeash L., Canada 64 A1
Dezfūl, Iran 39 C6
Dezhneva, Mys, Russia 25 C19
Dhahiriya = Zāhirīyah, West Bank 41 D3
Dhahran = Az Zahrān, Si. Arabia ... 39 E6
Dhaka, Bangla. 37 H17
Dhaka □, Bangla. .. 37 G17
Dhamar, Yemen 40 E3
Dhamtari, India 37 J12
Dhanbad, India 37 H15
Dhangarhi, Nepal ... 37 E12
Dhankuta, Nepal ... 37 F15
Dhar, India 36 H9
Dharmapuri, India .. 36 N11
Dharwad, India 36 M9
Dhaulagiri, Nepal ... 37 E13
Dhenkanal, India ... 37 J14
Dhībān, Jordan 41 D4
Dhíkti Óros, Greece . 21 G11
Dhirfis, Greece 21 E10
Dhodhekánisos, Greece 21 F12
Dhrol, India 36 H7
Dhuburi, India 37 F16
Dhule, India 36 J9
Dhut →, Somali Rep. 40 E5
Di Linh, Cao Nguyen, Vietnam 34 G10
Diablo Heights, Panama 74 H14
Diafarabé, Mali 44 F4
Diamante, Brazil ... 79 G10
Diamantina, Australia 55 D2
Diamantino, Brazil .. 79 F7
Diamond Harbour, India 37 H16
Diamond Is., Australia 54 B5
Diamond Mts., U.S.A. 72 G6
Diamondville, U.S.A. 72 F8
Diapaga, Burkina Faso 44 F5
Dībā, Oman 39 E8
Dibaya, Zaïre 46 F4
Dibaya-Lubue, Zaïre . 46 E3
Dibbi, Ethiopia 40 G3
Dibete, Botswana ... 48 C4
Dibrugarh, India ... 37 F19
Dickinson, U.S.A. ... 70 B3
Dickson, Russia 24 B9
Dickson, U.S.A. 69 G2
Didiéni, Mali 44 F3
Didsbury, Canada .. 64 C6
Diébougou, Burkina Faso 44 F4
Diefenbaker L., Canada 65 C7
Diego Garcia, Ind. Oc. 3 E13
Diekirch, Lux. 15 E6
Dien Bien, Vietnam . 34 B7
Dieppe, France 18 B4
Dieren, Neths. 15 B6
Dierks, U.S.A. 71 H7
Diest, Belgium 15 D5
Differdange, Lux. ... 15 E5
Digby, Canada 63 D6
Digges, Canada 65 B10
Digges Is., Canada .. 61 B12
Dighinala, Bangla. .. 37 H18
Dighton, U.S.A. 70 F4
Digne-les-Bains, France 18 D7
Digos, Phil. 33 C7
Digranes, Iceland ... 8 C6
Digul →, Indonesia . 33 F9
Dihang →, India ... 37 F19
Dīhōk, Iraq 38 B3
Dijlah, Nahr →, Asia 38 D5
Dijon, France 18 C6

Dikimdya, *Russia*	25	D13
Dikomu di Kai, *Botswana*	48	C3
Diksmuide, *Belgium*	15	C2
Dikson = Dickson, *Russia*	24	B9
Dikwa, *Nigeria*	45	F7
Dili, *Indonesia*	33	F7
Dilley, *U.S.A.*	71	L5
Dilling, *Sudan*	45	F10
Dillingham, *U.S.A.*	60	C4
Dillon, *Canada*	65	B7
Dillon, *Mont., U.S.A.*	72	D7
Dillon, *S.C., U.S.A.*	69	H6
Dillon →, *Canada*	65	B7
Dilolo, *Zaïre*	46	G4
Dilston, *Australia*	54	G4
Dimashq, *Syria*	41	B5
Dimashq □, *Syria*	41	B5
Dimbaza, *S. Africa*	49	E4
Dimbokro, *Ivory C.*	44	G4
Dimboola, *Australia*	55	F3
Dîmbovița →, *Romania*	17	F14
Dimbulah, *Australia*	54	B4
Dimitrovgrad, *Bulgaria*	21	C11
Dimitrovgrad, *Russia*	22	D8
Dimitrovo = Pernik, *Bulgaria*	21	C10
Dimmitt, *U.S.A.*	71	H3
Dimona, *Israel*	41	D4
Dinagat, *Phil.*	33	B7
Dinajpur, *Bangla.*	37	G16
Dinan, *France*	18	B2
Dīnān Āb, *Iran*	39	C8
Dinant, *Belgium*	15	D4
Dīnār, Kūh-e, *Iran*	39	D6
Dinara Planina, *Croatia*	20	C7
Dinard, *France*	18	B2
Dinaric Alps = Dinara Planina, *Croatia*	20	C7
Dindigul, *India*	36	P11
Dingle, *Ireland*	13	D1
Dingle B., *Ireland*	13	D1
Dingo, *Australia*	54	C4
Dinguiraye, *Guinea*	44	F2
Dingwall, *U.K.*	12	D4
Dinokwe, *Botswana*	48	C4
Dinosaur National Monument, *U.S.A.*	72	F9
Dinuba, *U.S.A.*	73	H4
Diourbel, *Senegal*	44	F1
Dipolog, *Phil.*	33	C6
Dir, *Pakistan*	36	B7
Diré, *Mali*	44	E4
Dire Dawa, *Ethiopia*	40	F3
Dirico, *Angola*	47	H4
Dirk Hartog I., *Australia*	53	E1
Dirranbandi, *Australia*	55	D4
Disa, *India*	36	G8
Disappointment, C., *U.S.A.*	72	C1
Disappointment, L., *Australia*	52	D3
Disaster B., *Australia*	55	F4
Discovery B., *Australia*	55	F3
Disko, *Greenland*	4	C5
Disko Bugt, *Greenland*	4	C5
Disteghil Sar, *Pakistan*	36	A9
Distrito Federal □, *Brazil*	79	G9
Diu, *India*	36	J7
Dīvāndarreh, *Iran*	38	C5
Divide, *U.S.A.*	72	D7
Dividing Ra., *Australia*	53	E2
Divinópolis, *Brazil*	79	H10
Divnoye, *Russia*	23	E7
Dīwāl Kol, *Afghan.*	36	B5
Dixon, *Ill., U.S.A.*	70	E10
Dixon, *Mont., U.S.A.*	72	C7
Dixon, *N. Mex., U.S.A.*	73	H11
Dixon Entrance, *U.S.A.*	64	C2
Dixonville, *Canada*	64	B5
Diyarbakır, *Turkey*	23	G7
Djado, *Niger*	45	D7
Djakarta = Jakarta, *Indonesia*	33	G12
Djamba, *Angola*	48	B1
Djambala, *Congo*	46	E2
Djanet, *Algeria*	44	D6
Djawa = Jawa, *Indonesia*	33	G14
Djelfa, *Algeria*	44	B5
Djema, *C.A.R.*	46	C5
Djenné, *Mali*	44	F4
Djerba, I. de, *Tunisia*	45	B7
Djerid, Chott, *Tunisia*	44	B6
Djibo, *Burkina Faso*	44	F4
Djibouti, *Djibouti*	40	E3
Djibouti ■, *Africa*	40	E3
Djolu, *Zaïre*	46	D4
Djougou, *Benin*	44	G5
Djoum, *Cameroon*	46	D2
Djourab, *Chad*	45	E8
Djugu, *Zaïre*	46	D6
Djúpivogur, *Iceland*	8	D6
Dmitriya Lapteva, Proliv, *Russia*	25	B15
Dnepr = Dnipro →, *Ukraine*	23	E5
Dneprodzerzhinsk = Dniprodzerzhynsk, *Ukraine*	23	E5
Dnepropetrovsk = Dnipropetrovsk, *Ukraine*	23	E5
Dnestr = Dnister →, *Europe*	17	E16
Dnestrovski = Belgorod, *Russia*	23	D6
Dnieper = Dnipro →, *Ukraine*	23	E5

Dniester = Dnister →, *Europe*	17	E16
Dnipro →, *Ukraine*	23	E5
Dniprodzerzhynsk, *Ukraine*	23	E5
Dnipropetrovsk, *Ukraine*	23	E5
Dnister →, *Europe*	17	E16
Dnistrovskyy Lyman, *Ukraine*	17	E16
Dnyapro = Dnipro →, *Ukraine*	23	E5
Doba, *Chad*	45	G8
Dobbyn, *Australia*	54	B3
Dobele, *Latvia*	9	H20
Doberai, Jazirah, *Indonesia*	33	E8
Doblas, *Argentina*	80	D4
Dobo, *Indonesia*	33	F8
Doboj, *Bos.-H.*	21	B8
Dobreta-Turnu-Severin, *Romania*	17	F12
Dobrich, *Bulgaria*	21	C12
Dobruja, *Romania*	17	F15
Dobrush, *Belarus*	17	B16
Dodecanese = Dhodhekánisos, *Greece*	21	F12
Dodge Center, *U.S.A.*	70	C8
Dodge City, *U.S.A.*	71	G5
Dodge L., *Canada*	65	B7
Dodgeville, *U.S.A.*	70	D9
Dodoma, *Tanzania*	46	F7
Dodsland, *Canada*	65	C7
Dodson, *U.S.A.*	72	B9
Doetinchem, *Neths.*	15	C6
Dog Creek, *Canada*	64	C4
Dog L., *Man., Canada*	65	C9
Dog L., *Ont., Canada*	62	C2
Dogi, *Afghan.*	36	C3
Doha = Ad Dawḥah, *Qatar*	39	E6
Dohazari, *Bangla.*	37	H18
Doi, *Indonesia*	33	D7
Doi Luang, *Thailand*	34	C6
Doig →, *Canada*	64	B4
Dois Irmãos, Sa., *Brazil*	79	E10
Dokkum, *Neths.*	15	A5
Doland, *U.S.A.*	70	C5
Dolbeau, *Canada*	63	C5
Dole, *France*	18	C6
Dolgellau, *U.K.*	10	E4
Dolgelley = Dolgellau, *U.K.*	10	E4
Dollart, *Neths.*	15	A7
Dolomites = Dolomiti, *Italy*	20	A4
Dolomiti, *Italy*	20	A4
Dolores, *Argentina*	80	D5
Dolores, *U.S.A.*	73	H9
Dolores →, *U.S.A.*	73	G9
Dolphin, C., *Falk. Is.*	80	G5
Dolphin and Union Str., *Canada*	60	B8
Dombarovskiy, *Russia*	24	D6
Dombås, *Norway*	9	E13
Domburg, *Neths.*	15	C3
Domel I. = Letsôk-aw Kyun, *Burma*	34	G5
Dominica ■, *W. Indies*	74	M20
Dominican Rep. ■, *W. Indies*	75	D10
Domo, *Ethiopia*	40	F4
Domodóssola, *Italy*	20	A3
Domville, Mt., *Australia*	55	D5
Don →, *Russia*	23	E6
Don →, *Gramp., U.K.*	12	D6
Don →, *Humber., U.K.*	10	D7
Don, C., *Australia*	52	B5
Don Benito, *Spain*	19	C3
Donaghadee, *U.K.*	13	B6
Donald, *Australia*	55	F3
Donalda, *Canada*	64	C6
Donaldsonville, *U.S.A.*	71	K9
Donalsonville, *U.S.A.*	69	K3
Donau = Dunărea →, *Europe*	17	F15
Donauwörth, *Germany*	16	D6
Doncaster, *U.K.*	10	D6
Dondo, *Angola*	46	F2
Dondo, *Mozam.*	47	H6
Dondo, Teluk, *Indonesia*	33	D6
Dondra Head, *Sri Lanka*	36	S12
Donegal, *Ireland*	13	B3
Donegal □, *Ireland*	13	B4
Donegal B., *Ireland*	13	B3
Donets →, *Russia*	23	E7
Donetsk, *Ukraine*	23	E6
Dongara, *Australia*	53	E1
Dongbei, *China*	31	B7
Dongchuan, *China*	30	D5
Donggala, *Indonesia*	33	E5
Dongola, *Sudan*	45	E11
Dongou, *Congo*	46	D3
Dongting Hu, *China*	31	D6
Donington, C., *Australia*	55	E2
Doniphan, *U.S.A.*	71	G9
Dønna, *Norway*	8	C15
Donna, *U.S.A.*	71	M5
Donnaconna, *Canada*	63	C5
Donnelly's Crossing, *N.Z.*	51	F4
Donnybrook, *Australia*	53	F2
Donnybrook, *S. Africa*	49	D4
Donor's Hill, *Australia*	54	B3
Donostia = San Sebastián, *Spain*	19	A5
Doon →, *U.K.*	12	F4
Dora, L., *Australia*	52	D3
Dora Báltea →, *Italy*	20	B3
Doran L., *Canada*	65	A7
Dorchester, *U.K.*	11	G5

Dorchester, C., *Canada*	61	B12
Dordogne →, *France*	18	D3
Dordrecht, *Neths.*	15	C4
Dordrecht, *S. Africa*	48	E4
Doré L., *Canada*	65	C7
Doré Lake, *Canada*	65	C7
Dori, *Burkina Faso*	44	F4
Doring →, *S. Africa*	48	E2
Doringbos, *S. Africa*	48	E2
Dorion, *Canada*	62	C5
Dornbirn, *Austria*	16	E5
Dornoch, *U.K.*	12	D4
Dornoch Firth, *U.K.*	12	D4
Dorohoi, *Romania*	17	E14
Döröö Nuur, *Mongolia*	30	B4
Dorr, *Iran*	39	C6
Dorre I., *Australia*	53	E1
Dorrigo, *Australia*	55	E5
Dorris, *U.S.A.*	72	F3
Dorset □, *U.K.*	11	G5
Dortmund, *Germany*	16	C4
Doruma, *Zaïre*	46	D5
Dorüneh, *Iran*	39	C8
Dos Bahías, C., *Argentina*	80	E3
Dos Hermanas, *Spain*	19	D3
Dosso, *Niger*	44	F5
Dothan, *U.S.A.*	69	K3
Douai, *France*	18	A5
Douala, *Cameroon*	44	H6
Douarnenez, *France*	18	B1
Double Island Pt., *Australia*	55	D5
Doubs →, *France*	18	C6
Doubtful Sd., *N.Z.*	51	L1
Doubtless B., *N.Z.*	51	F4
Douentza, *Mali*	44	F4
Douglas, *S. Africa*	48	D3
Douglas, *U.K.*	10	C3
Douglas, *Alaska, U.S.A.*	64	B2
Douglas, *Ariz., U.S.A.*	73	L9
Douglas, *Ga., U.S.A.*	69	K4
Douglas, *Wyo., U.S.A.*	70	D2
Douglastown, *Canada*	63	C7
Douglasville, *U.S.A.*	69	J3
Doumé, *Cameroon*	46	D2
Dounreay, *U.K.*	12	C5
Dourados, *Brazil*	80	A6
Douro →, *Europe*	19	B1
Dove →, *U.K.*	10	E6
Dove Creek, *U.S.A.*	73	H9
Dover, *Australia*	54	G4
Dover, *U.K.*	11	F9
Dover, *Del., U.S.A.*	68	F8
Dover, *N.H., U.S.A.*	68	D10
Dover, *Ohio, U.S.A.*	68	E5
Dover, Pt., *Australia*	53	F4
Dover, Str. of, *Europe*	18	A4
Dover-Foxcroft, *U.S.A.*	63	C6
Dovey = Dyfi →, *U.K.*	11	E4
Dovrefjell, *Norway*	9	E13
Dow Rūd, *Iran*	39	C6
Dowagiac, *U.S.A.*	68	E2
Dowgha'i, *Iran*	39	B8
Dowlatābād, *Iran*	39	D8
Down □, *U.K.*	13	B6
Downey, *U.S.A.*	72	E7
Downham Market, *U.K.*	11	E8
Downieville, *U.S.A.*	72	G3
Downpatrick, *U.K.*	13	B6
Downpatrick Hd., *Ireland*	13	B2
Dowsāri, *Iran*	39	D8
Draa, Oued →, *Morocco*	44	C2
Drachten, *Neths.*	15	A6
Drăgăşani, *Romania*	17	F13
Dragoman, Prokhod, *Bulgaria*	21	C10
Draguignan, *France*	18	E7
Drain, *U.S.A.*	72	E2
Drake, *Australia*	55	D5
Drake, *U.S.A.*	70	B4
Drake Passage, *S. Ocean*	5	B17
Drakensberg, *S. Africa*	49	E4
Dráma, *Greece*	21	D11
Drammen, *Norway*	9	G14
Drangajökull, *Iceland*	8	C2
Drau = Drava →, *Croatia*	21	B8
Drava →, *Croatia*	21	B8
Drayton Valley, *Canada*	64	C6
Drenthe □, *Neths.*	15	B6
Dresden, *Germany*	16	C7
Dreux, *France*	18	B4
Driffield, *U.K.*	10	C7
Driggs, *U.S.A.*	72	E8
Drin →, *Bos.-H.*	21	B8
Drina →, *Albania*	21	C8
Drøbak, *Norway*	9	G14
Drochia, *Moldova*	17	D14
Drogheda, *Ireland*	13	C5
Drogichin = Dragichyn, *Belarus*	17	B13
Drogobych = Drohobych, *Ukraine*	17	D12
Drohobych, *Ukraine*	17	D12
Droichead Atha = Drogheda, *Ireland*	13	C5
Droichead Nua, *Ireland*	13	C5
Droitwich, *U.K.*	11	E5
Dromedary, C., *Australia*	55	F5
Dronfield, *Australia*	54	C3
Dronten, *Neths.*	15	B5
Drumheller, *Canada*	64	C6
Drummond, *U.S.A.*	72	C7
Drummond I., *U.S.A.*	62	C3
Drummond Pt., *Australia*	55	E2
Drummond Ra., *Australia*	54	C4

Drummondville, *Canada*	62	C5
Drumright, *U.S.A.*	71	H6
Drut →, *Belarus*	17	B16
Druzhina, *Russia*	25	C15
Dryden, *Canada*	65	D10
Dryden, *U.S.A.*	71	K3
Drygalski I., *Antarctica*	5	C7
Drysdale →, *Australia*	52	B4
Drysdale I., *Australia*	54	A2
Dschang, *Cameroon*	44	G7
Du Bois, *U.S.A.*	68	E6
Du Quoin, *U.S.A.*	70	G10
Duaringa, *Australia*	54	C4
Dubā, *Si. Arabia*	38	E2
Dubai = Dubayy, *U.A.E.*	39	E7
Dubāsari, *Moldova*	17	E15
Dubāsari Vdkhr., *Moldova*	17	E15
Dubawnt →, *Canada*	65	A8
Dubawnt, L., *Canada*	65	A8
Dubayy, *U.A.E.*	39	E7
Dubbo, *Australia*	55	E4
Dublin, *Ireland*	13	C5
Dublin, *Ga., U.S.A.*	69	J4
Dublin, *Tex., U.S.A.*	71	J5
Dublin □, *Ireland*	13	C5
Dublin B., *Ireland*	13	C5
Dubno, *Ukraine*	17	C13
Dubois, *U.S.A.*	72	D7
Dubossary = Dubāsari, *Moldova*	17	E15
Dubossary Vdkhr. = Dubāsari Vdkhr., *Moldova*	17	E15
Dubovka, *Russia*	23	E7
Dubréka, *Guinea*	44	G2
Dubrovitsa = Dubrovytsya, *Ukraine*	17	C14
Dubrovnik, *Croatia*	21	C8
Dubrovskoye, *Russia*	25	D12
Dubrovytsya, *Ukraine*	17	C14
Dubuque, *U.S.A.*	70	D9
Duchesne, *U.S.A.*	72	F8
Duchess, *Australia*	54	C2
Ducie I., *Pac. Oc.*	57	K15
Duck Cr. →, *Australia*	52	D2
Duck Lake, *Canada*	65	C7
Duck Mountain Prov. Park, *Canada*	65	C8
Dudhi, *India*	37	G13
Dudinka, *Russia*	25	C9
Dudley, *U.K.*	11	E5
Duero = Douro →, *Europe*	19	B1
Dufftown, *U.K.*	12	D5
Dugi Otok, *Croatia*	16	G8
Duifken Pt., *Australia*	54	A3
Duisburg, *Germany*	16	C4
Duiwelskloof, *S. Africa*	49	C5
Dūkdamīn, *Iran*	39	C8
Duke I., *U.S.A.*	64	C2
Dukelský Průsmyk, *Slovak Rep.*	17	D11
Dukhān, *Qatar*	39	E6
Duki, *Pakistan*	36	D6
Duku, *Nigeria*	44	F7
Dulce, *Argentina*	80	C4
Dulf, *Iraq*	38	C5
Dulit, Banjaran, *Malaysia*	32	D4
Dulq Maghār, *Syria*	38	B3
Dululu, *Australia*	54	C5
Duluth, *U.S.A.*	70	B8
Dum Dum, *India*	37	H16
Dum Hadjer, *Chad*	45	F8
Dūmā, *Lebanon*	41	A4
Dūmā, *Syria*	41	B5
Dumaguete, *Phil.*	33	C6
Dumai, *Indonesia*	32	D2
Dumaran, *Phil.*	33	B5
Dumas, *Ark., U.S.A.*	71	J9
Dumas, *Tex., U.S.A.*	71	H4
Dumbarton, *U.K.*	12	F4
Dumbleyung, *Australia*	53	F2
Dumfries, *U.K.*	12	F5
Dumfries & Galloway □, *U.K.*	12	F5
Dumoine →, *Canada*	62	C4
Dumoine L., *Canada*	62	C4
Dumyât, *Egypt*	45	B11
Dún Dealgan = Dundalk, *Ireland*	13	B5
Dun Laoghaire, *Ireland*	13	C5
Duna = Dunărea →, *Europe*	17	F15
Dunaj = Dunărea →, *Europe*	17	F15
Dunakeszi, *Hungary*	17	E10
Dunărea →, *Europe*	17	F15
Dunaújváros, *Hungary*	17	E10
Dunav = Dunărea →, *Europe*	17	F15
Dunay, *Russia*	28	C6
Dunback, *N.Z.*	51	L3
Dunbar, *Australia*	54	B3
Dunbar, *U.K.*	12	E6
Dunblane, *U.K.*	12	E5
Duncan, *Canada*	64	D4
Duncan, *Ariz., U.S.A.*	73	K9
Duncan, *Okla., U.S.A.*	71	H6
Duncan, L., *Canada*	62	B4
Duncan L., *Canada*	64	A6
Duncan Passage, *Ind. Oc.*	34	G2
Dundalk, *Ireland*	13	B5
Dundalk Bay, *Ireland*	13	C5
Dundas, *Canada*	62	D4
Dundas, L., *Australia*	53	F3
Dundas I., *Canada*	64	C2
Dundas Str., *Australia*	52	B5
Dundee, *S. Africa*	49	D5

Dundee, *U.K.*	12	E6
Dundoo, *Australia*	55	D3
Dundrum, *U.K.*	13	B6
Dundrum B., *U.K.*	13	B6
Dunedin, *N.Z.*	51	L3
Dunedin, *U.S.A.*	69	L4
Dunedin →, *Canada*	64	B4
Dunfermline, *U.K.*	12	E5
Dungannon, *U.K.*	13	B5
Dungannon □, *U.K.*	13	B5
Dungarvan, *Ireland*	13	D4
Dungarvan Harbour, *Ireland*	13	D4
Dungeness, *U.K.*	11	G8
Dungo, L. do, *Angola*	48	B2
Dungog, *Australia*	55	E5
Dungu, *Zaïre*	46	D5
Dunhuang, *China*	30	B4
Dunk I., *Australia*	54	B4
Dunkeld, *U.K.*	12	E5
Dunkerque, *France*	18	A5
Dunkery Beacon, *U.K.*	11	F4
Dunkirk = Dunkerque, *France*	18	A5
Dunkirk, *U.S.A.*	68	D6
Dunkwa, *Ghana*	44	G4
Dunlap, *U.S.A.*	70	E7
Dúnleary = Dun Laoghaire, *Ireland*	13	C5
Dunmanus B., *Ireland*	13	E2
Dunmara, *Australia*	54	B1
Dunmore, *U.S.A.*	68	E8
Dunmore Hd., *Ireland*	13	D1
Dunn, *U.S.A.*	69	H6
Dunnellon, *U.S.A.*	69	L4
Dunning, *U.S.A.*	70	E4
Dunolly, *Australia*	55	F3
Dunoon, *U.K.*	12	F4
Dunqul, *Egypt*	45	D11
Duns, *U.K.*	12	F6
Dunseith, *U.S.A.*	70	A4
Dunsmuir, *U.S.A.*	72	F2
Dunstable, *U.K.*	11	F7
Dunstan Mts., *N.Z.*	51	L2
Dunster, *Canada*	64	C5
Dunvegan L., *Canada*	65	A7
Dupree, *U.S.A.*	70	C4
Dupuyer, *U.S.A.*	72	B7
Durack →, *Australia*	52	C4
Durack Ra., *Australia*	52	C4
Durance →, *France*	18	E6
Durand, *U.S.A.*	68	D4
Durango = Victoria de Durango, *Mexico*	74	C4
Durango, *Spain*	19	A4
Durango, *U.S.A.*	73	H10
Duranillin, *Australia*	53	F2
Durant, *U.S.A.*	71	J6
Durazno, *Uruguay*	80	C5
Durazzo = Durrësi, *Albania*	21	D8
Durban, *S. Africa*	49	D5
Düren, *Germany*	16	C4
Durg, *India*	37	J12
Durgapur, *India*	37	H15
Durham, *Canada*	62	D3
Durham, *U.K.*	10	C6
Durham, *U.S.A.*	69	G6
Durham □, *U.K.*	10	C6
Durham Downs, *Australia*	55	D4
Durmitor, *Montenegro, Yug.*	21	C8
Durness, *U.K.*	12	C4
Durrësi, *Albania*	21	D8
Durrie, *Australia*	54	D3
Dursunbey, *Turkey*	21	E13
D'Urville, Tanjung, *Indonesia*	33	E9
D'Urville I., *N.Z.*	51	J4
Dusa Mareb, *Somali Rep.*	40	F4
Dushak, *Turkmenistan*	24	F7
Dushanbe, *Tajikistan*	24	F7
Dusky Sd., *N.Z.*	51	L1
Dussejour, C., *Australia*	52	B4
Düsseldorf, *Germany*	16	C4
Dutch Harbor, *U.S.A.*	60	C3
Dutlwe, *Botswana*	48	C3
Dutton, *Australia*	54	C3
Duyun, *China*	30	D5
Duzdab = Zāhedān, *Iran*	39	D9
Dvina, Severnaya →, *Russia*	22	B7
Dvinsk = Daugavpils, *Latvia*	9	J22
Dvinskaya Guba, *Russia*	22	B6
Dwarka, *India*	36	H6
Dwellingup, *Australia*	53	F2
Dwight, *U.S.A.*	68	E1
Dyatlovo = Dzyatlava, *Belarus*	17	B13
Dyer, C., *Canada*	61	B13
Dyer Plateau, *Antarctica*	5	D17
Dyersburg, *U.S.A.*	71	G10
Dyfed □, *U.K.*	11	E3
Dyfi →, *U.K.*	11	E4
Dymer, *Ukraine*	17	C16
Dynevor Downs, *Australia*	55	D3
Dysart, *U.S.A.*	70	E8
Dzamin Üüd, *Mongolia*	31	B6
Dzerzhinsk, *Russia*	22	C7
Dzhalinda, *Russia*	25	D13
Dzhambul = Zhambyl, *Kazakhstan*	24	E8
Dzhankoy, *Ukraine*	23	E5
Dzhardzhan, *Russia*	25	C13
Dzhetygara = Zhetiqara, *Kazakhstan*	24	D7

Dzhezkazgan = Zhezqazghan, *Kazakhstan*	24	E7
Dzhizak = Jizzakh, *Uzbekistan*	24	E7
Dzhugdzur, Khrebet, *Russia*	25	D14
Dzhungarskiye Vorota, *Kazakhstan*	30	B3
Działdowa, *Poland*	17	B11
Dzierzoniów, *Poland*	17	C9
Dzungaria = Junggar Pendi, *China*	30	B3
Dzungarian Gates = Dzhungarskiye Vorota, *Kazakhstan*	30	B3
Dzuumod, *Mongolia*	30	B5
Dzyarzhynsk, *Belarus*	17	B14
Dzyatlava, *Belarus*	17	B13

E

Eabamet, L., *Canada*	62	B2
Eads, *U.S.A.*	70	F3
Eagle, *U.S.A.*	72	G10
Eagle →, *Canada*	63	B8
Eagle Butte, *U.S.A.*	70	C4
Eagle Grove, *U.S.A.*	70	D8
Eagle L., *Calif., U.S.A.*	72	F3
Eagle L., *Maine, U.S.A.*	63	C6
Eagle Lake, *U.S.A.*	71	L6
Eagle Nest, *U.S.A.*	73	H11
Eagle Pass, *U.S.A.*	71	L4
Eagle Pt., *Australia*	52	C3
Eagle River, *U.S.A.*	70	C10
Ealing, *U.K.*	11	F7
Earaheedy, *Australia*	53	E3
Earl Grey, *Canada*	65	C8
Earle, *U.S.A.*	71	H9
Earlimart, *U.S.A.*	73	J4
Earn →, *U.K.*	12	E5
Earn, L., *U.K.*	12	E4
Earnslaw, Mt., *N.Z.*	51	L2
Earth, *U.S.A.*	71	H3
Easley, *U.S.A.*	69	H4
East Angus, *Canada*	63	C5
East B., *U.S.A.*	71	L10
East Bengal, *Bangla.*	37	G17
East Beskids = Vychodné Beskydy, *Europe*	17	D11
East, C., *N.Z.*	51	G7
East Chicago, *U.S.A.*	68	E2
East China Sea, *Asia*	31	C7
East Coulee, *Canada*	64	C6
East Falkland, *Falk. Is.*	80	G5
East Grand Forks, *U.S.A.*	70	B6
East Helena, *U.S.A.*	72	C8
East Indies, *Asia*	33	E6
East Jordan, *U.S.A.*	68	C3
East Lansing, *U.S.A.*	68	D3
East Liverpool, *U.S.A.*	68	E5
East London, *S. Africa*	49	E4
East Main = Eastmain, *Canada*	62	B4
East Orange, *U.S.A.*	68	E8
East Pacific Ridge, *Pac. Oc.*	57	J17
East Pakistan = Bangladesh ■, *Asia*	37	H17
East Pine, *Canada*	64	B4
East Point, *U.S.A.*	69	J3
East Pt., *Canada*	63	C7
East Retford = Retford, *U.K.*	10	D7
East St. Louis, *U.S.A.*	70	F9
East Schelde = Oosterschelde, *Neths.*	15	C4
East Siberian Sea, *Russia*	25	B17
East Sussex □, *U.K.*	11	G8
East Tawas, *U.S.A.*	68	C4
East Toorale, *Australia*	55	E4
Eastbourne, *N.Z.*	51	J5
Eastbourne, *U.K.*	11	G8
Eastend, *Canada*	65	D7
Easter Islands = Pascua, I. de, *Pac. Oc.*	57	K17
Eastern Cape □, *S. Africa*	48	E4
Eastern Cr. →, *Australia*	54	C3
Eastern Ghats, *India*	36	N11
Eastern Group = Lau Group, *Fiji*	51	C9
Eastern Group, *Australia*	53	E3
Eastern Transvaal □, *S. Africa*	49	B5
Easterville, *Canada*	65	C9
Eastland, *U.S.A.*	71	J5
Eastleigh, *U.K.*	11	G6
Eastmain, *Canada*	62	B4
Eastmain →, *Canada*	62	B4
Eastman, *U.S.A.*	69	J4
Easton, *Md., U.S.A.*	68	F7
Easton, *Pa., U.S.A.*	68	E8
Easton, *Wash., U.S.A.*	72	C3
Eastport, *U.S.A.*	63	D6
Eatonia, *Canada*	65	C7
Eatonton, *U.S.A.*	69	J4
Eau Claire, *U.S.A.*	70	C9
Ebagoola, *Australia*	54	A3
Ebbw Vale, *U.K.*	11	F4
Ebeltoft, *Denmark*	9	H14
Eberswalde-Finow, *Germany*	16	B7
Ebetsu, *Japan*	28	C10
Ebolowa, *Cameroon*	46	D2

Ebro ➤, Spain 19 B6
Eceabat, Turkey 21 D12
Ech Cheliff, Algeria . . 44 A5
Echigo-Sammyaku,
Japan 29 F9
Echizen-Misaki, Japan 29 G7
Echo Bay, N.W.T.,
Canada 60 B8
Echo Day, Ont., Canada 62 C3
Echoing ➤, Canada . . 65 B10
Echternach, Lux. 15 E6
Echuca, Australia . . . 55 F3
Ecija, Spain 19 D3
Eclipse Is., Australia . 52 B4
Ecuador ■, S. Amer. . 78 D3
Ed Dâmer, Sudan . . . 45 E11
Ed Debba, Sudan . . . 45 E11
Ed Dueim, Sudan . . . 45 F11
Edah, Australia 53 E2
Edam, Canada 65 C7
Edam, Neths. 15 B5
Eday, U.K. 12 B6
Edd, Eritrea 40 E3
Eddrachillis B., U.K. . 12 C3
Eddystone, U.K. 11 G3
Eddystone Pt., Australia 54 G4
Ede, Neths. 15 B5
Édea, Cameroon 44 H7
Edehon L., Canada . . 65 A9
Eden, Australia 55 F4
Eden, N.C., U.S.A. . . . 69 G6
Eden, Tex., U.S.A. . . . 71 K5
Eden, Wyo., U.S.A. . . 72 E9
Eden ➤, U.K. 10 C4
Eden L., Canada 65 B8
Edenburg, S. Africa . . 48 D4
Edendale, S. Africa . . 49 D5
Edenderry, Ireland . . 13 C4
Edenton, U.S.A. 69 G7
Edenville, S. Africa . . 49 D4
Eder ➤, Germany . . . 16 C5
Edgar, U.S.A. 70 E5
Edge Hill, U.K. 11 E6
Edgefield, U.S.A. 69 J5
Edgeley, U.S.A. 70 B5
Edgemont, U.S.A. . . . 70 D3
Edgeøya, Svalbard . . 4 B9
Édhessa, Greece 21 D10
Edievale, N.Z. 51 L2
Edina, U.S.A. 70 E8
Edinburg, U.S.A. 71 M5
Edinburgh, U.K. 12 F5
Ediniţa, Moldova . . . 17 D14
Edirne, Turkey 21 D12
Edithburgh, Australia . 55 F2
Edjudina, Australia . . 53 E3
Edmond, U.S.A. 71 H6
Edmonds, U.S.A. 72 C2
Edmonton, Australia . . 54 B4
Edmonton, Canada . . 64 C6
Edmund L., Canada . . 65 C10
Edmundston, Canada . 63 C6
Edna, U.S.A. 71 L6
Edna Bay, U.S.A. 64 B2
Edremit, Turkey 21 E12
Edremit Körfezi, Turkey 21 E12
Edson, Canada 64 C5
Edward ➤, Australia . 55 F3
Edward, L., Africa . . . 46 E5
Edward I., Canada . . . 62 C2
Edward River, Australia 54 A3
Edward VII Land,
Antarctica 5 E13
Edwards Plateau,
U.S.A. 71 K4
Edzo, Canada 64 A5
Eekloo, Belgium 15 C3
Effingham, U.S.A. . . . 68 F1
Égadi, Ísole, Italy . . . 20 F5
Eganville, Canada . . . 62 C4
Egeland, U.S.A. 70 A5
Egenolf L., Canada . . 65 B9
Eger = Cheb, Czech. . 16 C7
Eger, Hungary 17 E11
Egersund, Norway . . . 9 G12
Egg L., Canada 65 B7
Eginbah, Australia . . . 52 D2
Egmont, C., N.Z. 51 H4
Egmont, Mt., N.Z. . . . 51 H5
Eğridir, Turkey 23 G5
Eğridir Gölü, Turkey . 23 G5
Egvekinot, Russia . . . 25 C19
Egypt ■, Africa 45 C11
Ehime □, Japan 29 H6
Eibar, Spain 19 A4
Eidsvold, Australia . . 55 D5
Eidsvoll, Norway 9 F14
Eifel, Germany 16 C4
Eigg, U.K. 12 E2
Eighty Mile Beach,
Australia 52 C3
Eil, Somali Rep. 40 F4
Eil, L., U.K. 12 E3
Eildon, L., Australia . . 55 F4
Eileen L., Canada . . . 65 A7
Einasleigh, Australia . 54 B3
Einasleigh ➤,
Australia 54 B3
Eindhoven, Neths. . . . 15 C5
Eire = Ireland ■,
Europe 13 D4
Eiríksjökull, Iceland . . 8 D3
Eirunepé, Brazil 78 E5
Eisenach, Germany . . 16 C6
Eisenerz, Austria . . . 16 E8
Eivissa = Ibiza, Spain 19 C6
Ekalaka, U.S.A. 70 C2
Eketahuna, N.Z. 51 J5
Ekibastuz, Kazakhstan 24 D8
Ekimchan, Russia . . . 25 D14
Eksjö, Sweden 9 H16
Ekwan ➤, Canada . . 62 B3
Ekwan Pt., Canada . . 62 B3

El Aaiún, W. Sahara . . 44 C2
El 'Agrûd, Egypt 41 E3
El Alamein, Egypt . . . 45 B10
El 'Aqaba, W. ➤,
Egypt 41 E2
El Aricha, Algeria . . . 44 B4
El Arîhâ, West Bank . . 41 D4
El Arish, Australia . . . 54 B4
El 'Arîsh, Egypt 41 D2
El 'Arîsh, W. ➤, Egypt 41 D2
El Asnam = Ech Cheliff,
Algeria 44 A5
El Bawiti, Egypt 45 C10
El Bayadh, Algeria . . 44 B5
El Brûk, W. ➤, Egypt 41 E2
El Cajon, U.S.A. 73 K5
El Callao, Venezuela . 78 B6
El Campo, U.S.A. . . . 71 L6
El Centro, U.S.A. 73 K6
El Cerro, Bolivia 78 G6
El Cuy, Argentina . . . 80 D3
El Cuyo, Mexico 74 C7
El Daheir, Egypt 41 D3
El Dere, Somali Rep. . 40 G4
El Diviso, Colombia . . 78 C3
El Djouf, Mauritania . . 44 E3
El Dorado, Ark., U.S.A. 71 J8
El Dorado, Kans.,
U.S.A. 71 G6
El Dorado, Venezuela . 78 B6
El Escorial, Spain . . . 19 B3
El Faiyûm, Egypt . . . 45 C11
El Fâsher, Sudan 45 F10
El Ferrol, Spain 19 A1
El Fuerte, Mexico . . . 74 B3
El Gal, Somali Rep. . . 40 E5
El Geteina, Sudan . . . 45 F11
El Gîza, Egypt 45 C11
El Iskandarîya, Egypt . 45 B10
El Jadida, Morocco . . 44 B3
El Jebelein, Sudan . . . 45 F11
El Kab, Sudan 45 E11
El Kabrît, G., Egypt . . 41 F2
El Kala, Algeria 44 A6
El Kamlin, Sudan 45 E11
El Kef, Tunisia 44 A6
El Khandaq, Sudan . . 45 E11
El Khârga, Egypt 45 C11
El Khartûm, Sudan . . 45 E11
El Khartûm Bahrî,
Sudan 45 E11
El Kuntilla, Egypt . . . 41 E3
El Laqâwa, Sudan . . . 45 F10
El Mafâza, Sudan . . . 45 F11
El Mahalla el Kubra,
Egypt 45 B11
El Mansûra, Egypt . . . 45 B11
El Minyâ, Egypt 45 C11
El Obeid, Sudan 45 F11
El Odaiya, Sudan . . . 45 F10
El Oued, Algeria 44 B6
El Paso, U.S.A. 73 L10
El Portal, U.S.A. 73 H4
El Prat de Llobregat,
Spain 19 B7
El Puerto de Santa
María, Spain 19 D2
El Qâhira, Egypt 45 B11
El Qantara, Egypt . . . 41 E1
El Qasr, Egypt 45 C10
El Quseima, Egypt . . . 41 E3
El Reno, U.S.A. 71 H6
El Saheira, W. ➤,
Egypt 41 E2
El Salvador ■,
Cent. Amer. 74 E7
El Shallal, Egypt 45 D11
El Suweis, Egypt 45 C11
El Tamarâni, W. ➤,
Egypt 41 E3
El Thamad, Egypt . . . 41 F3
El Tigre, Venezuela . . 78 B6
El Tîh, G., Egypt 41 F2
El Tina, Khalîg, Egypt 41 D1
El Tocuyo, Venezuela . 78 B5
El Turbio, Argentina . . 80 G2
El Uqsur, Egypt 45 C11
El Vigía, Venezuela . . 78 B4
El Wabeira, Egypt . . . 41 F2
El Wak, Kenya 46 D8
El Wuz, Sudan 45 E11
Elat, Israel 41 F3
Elâzığ, Turkey 23 G6
Elba, Italy 20 C4
Elba, U.S.A. 69 K2
Elbasani, Albania . . . 21 D9
Elbe ➤, Europe 16 B5
Elbert, Mt., U.S.A. . . . 73 G10
Elberta, U.S.A. 68 C2
Elberton, U.S.A. 69 H4
Elbeuf, France 18 B4
Elbing = Elbląg, Poland 17 A10
Elbląg, Poland 17 A10
Elbow, Canada 65 C7
Elbrus, Asia 23 F7
Elburg, Neths. 15 B5
Elburz Mts. = Alborz,
Reshteh-ye Kūhhā-ye,
Iran 39 C7
Elche, Spain 19 C5
Elcho I., Australia . . . 54 A2
Elda, Spain 19 C5
Elde ➤, Germany . . . 16 B6
Eldon, U.S.A. 70 F8
Eldora, U.S.A. 70 D8
Eldorado, Canada . . . 65 B7
Eldorado, Ill., U.S.A. . 68 G1
Eldorado, Tex., U.S.A. 71 K4
Eldorado Springs,
U.S.A. 71 G8
Eldoret, Kenya 46 D7
Electra, U.S.A. 71 H5
Elefantes ➤, Mozam. 49 C5

Elektrostal, Russia . . . 22 C6
Elephant Butte
Reservoir, U.S.A. . . . 73 K10
Elephant I., Antarctica 5 C18
Eleuthera, Bahamas . 75 C9
Elgin, Canada 63 C6
Elgin, U.K. 12 D5
Elgin, Ill., U.S.A. 68 D1
Elgin, N. Dak., U.S.A. . 70 B4
Elgin, Nebr., U.S.A. . . 70 E5
Elgin, Nev., U.S.A. . . . 73 H6
Elgin, Oreg., U.S.A. . . 72 D5
Elgin, Tex., U.S.A. . . . 71 K6
Elgon, Mt., Africa . . . 46 D6
Eliase, Indonesia . . . 33 F8
Elida, U.S.A. 71 J3
Elim, S. Africa 48 E2
Elisabethville =
Lubumbashi, Zaïre . 47 G5
Elista, Russia 23 E7
Elizabeth, Australia . . 55 E2
Elizabeth, U.S.A. 68 E8
Elizabeth City, U.S.A. . 69 G7
Elizabethton, U.S.A. . 69 G4
Elizabethtown, U.S.A. . 68 G3
Elk, Poland 17 B12
Elk City, U.S.A. 71 H5
Elk Island Nat. Park,
Canada 64 C6
Elk Lake, Canada . . . 62 C3
Elk Point, Canada . . . 65 C6
Elk River, Idaho, U.S.A. 72 C5
Elk River, Minn., U.S.A. 70 C8
Elkedra, Australia . . . 54 C2
Elkedra ➤, Australia . 54 C2
Elkhart, Ind., U.S.A. . . 68 E3
Elkhart, Kans., U.S.A. 71 G4
Elkhorn, Canada 65 D8
Elkhorn ➤, U.S.A. . . 70 E6
Elkhovo, Bulgaria . . . 21 C12
Elkin, U.S.A. 69 G5
Elkins, U.S.A. 68 F6
Elko, Canada 64 D5
Elko, U.S.A. 72 F6
Ell, L., Australia 53 E4
Ellef Ringnes I., Canada 4 B2
Ellendale, Australia . . 52 C3
Ellendale, U.S.A. 70 B5
Ellensburg, U.S.A. . . . 72 C3
Ellenville, U.S.A. 68 E8
Ellery, Mt., Australia . 55 F4
Ellesmere, L., N.Z. . . . 51 M4
Ellesmere I., Canada . 4 B4
Ellesmere Port, U.K. . 10 D5
Ellice Is. = Tuvalu ■,
Pac. Oc. 56 H9
Ellinwood, U.S.A. . . . 70 F5
Elliot, Australia 54 B1
Elliot, S. Africa 49 E4
Elliot Lake, Canada . . 62 C3
Elliotdale = Xhora,
S. Africa 49 E4
Ellis, U.S.A. 70 F5
Elliston, Australia . . . 55 E1
Ellisville, U.S.A. 71 K10
Ellon, U.K. 12 D6
Ellore = Eluru, India . 37 L12
Ells ➤, Canada 64 B6
Ellsworth, U.S.A. 70 F5
Ellsworth Land,
Antarctica 5 D16
Ellsworth Mts.,
Antarctica 5 D16
Ellwood City, U.S.A. . 68 E5
Elma, Canada 65 D9
Elma, U.S.A. 72 C2
Elmalı, Turkey 23 G4
Elmhurst, U.S.A. 68 E2
Elmira, U.S.A. 68 D7
Elmore, Australia . . . 55 F3
Elmshorn, Germany . . 16 B5
Eloy, U.S.A. 73 K8
Elrose, Canada 65 C7
Elsas, Canada 62 C3
Elsinore = Helsingør,
Denmark 9 H15
Elsinore, U.S.A. 73 G7
Eltham, N.Z. 51 H5
Eluru, India 37 L12
Elvas, Portugal 19 C2
Elverum, Norway . . . 9 F14
Elvire ➤, Australia . . 52 C4
Elwood, Ind., U.S.A. . 68 E3
Elwood, Nebr., U.S.A. 70 E5
Elx = Elche, Spain . . 19 C5
Ely, U.K. 11 E8
Ely, Minn., U.S.A. . . . 70 B9
Ely, Nev., U.S.A. 72 G6
Elyria, U.S.A. 68 E4
Emämrüd, Iran 39 B7
Emba = Embi,
Kazakhstan 24 E6
Emba = Embi ➤,
Kazakhstan 24 E6
Embarcación, Argentina 80 A4
Embarras Portage,
Canada 65 B6
Embetsu, Japan 28 B10
Embi, Kazakhstan . . . 24 E6
Embi ➤, Kazakhstan . 23 E9
Embrun, France 18 D7
Embu, Kenya 46 E7
Emden, Germany . . . 16 B4
Emerald, Australia . . . 54 C4
Emerson, Canada . . . 65 D9
Emery, U.S.A. 73 G8
Emet, Turkey 21 E13
Emi Koussi, Chad . . . 45 E8
Emine, Nos, Bulgaria . 21 C12
Emmeloord, Neths. . . 15 B5
Emmen, Neths. 15 B6
Emmet, Australia . . . 54 C3
Emmetsburg, U.S.A. . 70 D7

Emmett, U.S.A. 72 E5
Empalme, Mexico . . . 74 B2
Empangeni, S. Africa . 49 D5
Empedrado, Argentina 80 B5
Emperor Seamount
Chain, Pac. Oc. 56 D9
Emporia, Kans., U.S.A. 70 F6
Emporia, Va., U.S.A. . 69 G7
Emporium, U.S.A. . . . 68 E6
Empress, Canada . . . 65 C6
Empty Quarter = Rub'
al Khali, Si. Arabia . 40 D4
Ems ➤, Germany . . . 16 B4
Emu Park, Australia . . 54 C5
Ena, Japan 29 G8
Enana, Namibia 48 B2
Enaratoli, Indonesia . 33 E9
Enard B., U.K. 12 C3
Enare = Inarijärvi,
Finland 8 B22
Encanto, C., Phil. . . . 33 A6
Encarnación, Paraguay 80 B5
Encinal, U.S.A. 71 L5
Encino, U.S.A. 73 J11
Encounter B., Australia 55 F2
Endau ➤, Malaysia . . 34 S16
Ende, Indonesia 33 F6
Endeavour, Canada . . 65 C8
Endeavour Str.,
Australia 54 A3
Enderbury I., Kiribati . 56 H10
Enderby, Canada . . . 64 C5
Enderby I., Australia . 52 D2
Enderby Land,
Antarctica 5 C5
Enderlin, U.S.A. 70 B6
Endicott, N.Y., U.S.A. . 68 D7
Endicott, Wash., U.S.A. 72 C5
Endyalgout I., Australia 52 B5
Enewetak Atoll,
Pac. Oc. 56 F8
Enez, Turkey 21 D12
Enfield, U.K. 11 F7
Engadin, Switz. 16 E6
Engaño, C., Phil. 33 A6
Engcobo, S. Africa . . 49 E4
Engels, Russia 22 D8
Engemann L., Canada 65 B7
Enggano, Indonesia . . 32 F2
Enghien, Belgium . . . 15 D4
Engkilili, Malaysia . . . 32 D4
England ➤, U.S.A. . . 71 H9
England □, U.K. 7 E5
Englee, Canada 63 B8
Englehart, Canada . . . 62 C4
Engler L., Canada . . . 65 B7
Englewood, Colo.,
U.S.A. 70 F2
Englewood, Kans.,
U.S.A. 71 G5
English ➤, Canada . . 65 C10
English Bazar = Ingraj
Bazar, India 37 G16
English Channel,
Europe 18 A3
English River, Canada 62 C1
Enid, U.S.A. 71 G6
Enkhuizen, Neths. . . . 15 B5
Enna, Italy 20 F6
Ennadai, Canada . . . 65 A8
Ennadai L., Canada . . 65 A8
Ennedi, Chad 45 E9
Ennis, Ireland 13 D3
Ennis, Mont., U.S.A. . 72 D8
Ennis, Tex., U.S.A. . . 71 J6
Enniscorthy, Ireland . 13 D5
Enniskillen, U.K. 13 B4
Ennistimon, Ireland . . 13 D2
Enns ➤, Austria 16 D8
Enontekiö, Finland . . 8 B20
Enschede, Neths. . . . 15 B6
Ensenada, Mexico . . . 74 A1
Entebbe, Uganda . . . 46 D6
Enterprise, Canada . . 64 A5
Enterprise, Oreg.,
U.S.A. 72 D5
Enterprise, Utah, U.S.A. 73 H7
Entroncamento,
Portugal 19 C1
Enugu, Nigeria 44 G6
Enugu Ezike, Nigeria . 44 G6
Enumclaw, U.S.A. . . . 72 C3
Éolie, Ís., Italy 20 E6
Epe, Neths. 15 B5
Épernay, France 18 B5
Ephesus, Turkey 21 F12
Ephraim, U.S.A. 72 G8
Ephrata, U.S.A. 72 C4
Épinal, France 18 B7
Epping, U.K. 11 F8
Epukiro, Namibia . . . 48 C2
Equatorial Guinea ■,
Africa 46 D1
Er Rahad, Sudan 45 F11
Er Rif, Morocco 44 A4
Er Roseires, Sudan . . 45 F11
Erāwadī Myit ➤,
Burma 37 M19
Er = Arbīl, Iraq 38 B5
Erciyaş Dağı, Turkey . 23 G6
Érd, Hungary 17 E10
Erdek, Turkey 21 D12
Erebus, Mt., Antarctica 5 D11
Erechim, Brazil 80 B6
Ereğli, Konya, Turkey . 23 G5
Ereğli, Zonguldak,
Turkey 23 F5
Eresma ➤, Spain . . . 19 B3

Erewadi Myitwanya,
Burma 37 M19
Erfenisdam, S. Africa . 48 D4
Erfurt, Germany 16 C6
Ergeni Vozvyshennost,
Russia 23 E7
Ērgli, Latvia 9 H21
Eriboll, L., U.K. 12 C4
Érice, Italy 20 E5
Erie, U.S.A. 68 D5
Erie, L., N. Amer. . . . 68 D5
Erigavo, Somali Rep. . 40 E4
Eriksdale, Canada . . . 65 C9
Erimanthos, Greece . . 21 F9
Erimo-misaki, Japan . 28 D11
Eritrea ■, Africa 45 F12
Erlangen, Germany . . 16 D6
Erldunda, Australia . . 54 D1
Ermelo, Neths. 15 B5
Ermelo, S. Africa 49 D4
Ermoúpolis = Síros,
Greece 21 F11
Ernakulam = Cochin,
India 36 Q10
Erne ➤, Ireland 13 B3
Erne, Lower L., U.K. . . 13 B4
Erne, Upper L., U.K. . 13 B4
Ernest Giles Ra.,
Australia 53 E3
Erode, India 36 P10
Eromanga, Australia . 55 D3
Erongo, Namibia 48 C2
Errabiddy, Australia . . 53 E2
Erramala Hills, India . 36 M11
Errigal, Ireland 13 A3
Erris Hd., Ireland . . . 13 B1
Erskine, U.S.A. 70 B7
Ertis = Irtysh ➤,
Russia 24 C7
Erwin, U.S.A. 69 G4
Erzgebirge, Germany . 16 C7
Erzin, Russia 25 D10
Erzincan, Turkey 23 G6
Erzurum, Turkey 23 G7
Es Sahrâ' Esh Sharqîya,
Egypt 45 C11
Es Sînâ', Egypt 45 C11
Esan-Misaki, Japan . . 28 D10
Esashi, Hokkaidō,
Japan 28 B11
Esashi, Hokkaidō,
Japan 28 D10
Esbjerg, Denmark . . . 9 J13
Escalante, U.S.A. . . . 73 H8
Escalante ➤, U.S.A. . 73 H8
Escambia ➤, U.S.A. . 69 K2
Escanaba, U.S.A. . . . 68 C2
Esch-sur-Alzette, Lux. . 18 B6
Escobal, Panama . . . 74 H14
Escondido, U.S.A. . . . 73 K5
Escuinapa, Mexico . . 74 C3
Eşfahān, Iran 39 C6
Esfideh, Iran 39 C8
Esh Sham = Dimashq,
Syria 41 B5
Eshowe, S. Africa . . . 49 D5
Esil = Ishim ➤,
Russia 24 D8
Esk ➤, Cumb., U.K. . 12 G5
Esk ➤, N. Yorks., U.K. 10 C7
Eskifjörður, Iceland . . 8 D7
Eskilstuna, Sweden . . 9 G17
Eskimo Pt., Canada . . 65 A10
Eskişehir, Turkey 23 G5
Esla ➤, Spain 19 B2
Eslāmābād-e Gharb,
Iran 38 C5
Eşme, Turkey 21 E13
Esmeraldas, Ecuador . 78 C3
Espanola, Canada . . . 62 C3
Esperance, Australia . 53 F3
Esperance B., Australia 53 F3
Esperanza, Argentina . 80 C4
Espichel, C., Portugal . 19 C1
Espinal, Colombia . . . 78 C4
Espinazo, Sierra del =
Espinhaço, Serra do,
Brazil 79 G10
Espinhaço, Serra do,
Brazil 79 G10
Espírito Santo □, Brazil 79 G10
Espoo, Finland 9 F21
Espungabera, Mozam. 49 C5
Esquel, Argentina . . . 80 E2
Esquina, Argentina . . 80 C5
Essaouira, Morocco . . 44 B3
Essen, Belgium 15 C4
Essen, Germany 16 C4
Essendon, Mt.,
Australia 53 E3
Essequibo ➤, Guyana 78 B7
Essex □, U.K. 11 F8
Esslingen, Germany . . 16 D5
Estados, I. de Los,
Argentina 80 G4
Eşţahbānāt, Iran 39 D7
Estância, Brazil 79 F11
Estancia, U.S.A. 73 J10
Estārm, Iran 39 D8
Estcourt, S. Africa . . . 49 D4
Estelline, S. Dak.,
U.S.A. 70 C6
Estelline, Tex., U.S.A. 71 H4
Esterhazy, Canada . . 65 C8
Estevan, Canada 65 D8
Estevan Group, Canada 64 C3
Estherville, U.S.A. . . . 70 D7
Eston, Canada 65 C7
Estonia ■, Europe . . . 9 G21
Estrêla, Serra da,
Portugal 19 B2
Estremoz, Portugal . . 19 C2

Estrondo, Serra do,
Brazil 79 E9
Esztergom, Hungary . . 17 E10
Etadunna, Australia . . 55 D2
Etamamu, Canada . . . 63 B8
Étampes, France 18 B5
Etanga, Namibia 48 B1
Etawah, India 36 F11
Etawah ➤, U.S.A. . . . 69 H3
Etawney L., Canada . . 65 B9
Ethel Creek, Australia . 52 D3
Ethelbert, Canada . . . 65 C8
Ethiopia ■, Africa . . . 40 F3
Ethiopian Highlands,
Ethiopia 42 E7
Etive, L., U.K. 12 E3
Etna, Italy 20 F6
Etolin I., U.S.A. 64 B2
Etosha Pan, Namibia . 48 B2
Etowah, U.S.A. 69 H3
Ettrick Water ➤, U.K. 12 F6
Euboea = Évvoia,
Greece 21 E11
Eucla Motel, Australia 53 F4
Euclid, U.S.A. 68 E5
Eucumbene, L.,
Australia 55 F4
Eudora, U.S.A. 71 J9
Eufaula, Ala., U.S.A. . 69 K3
Eufaula, Okla., U.S.A. . 71 H7
Eufaula L., U.S.A. . . . 71 H7
Eugene, U.S.A. 72 E2
Eugowra, Australia . . 55 E4
Eulo, Australia 55 D4
Eunice, La., U.S.A. . . 71 K8
Eunice, N. Mex., U.S.A. 71 J3
Eupen, Belgium 15 D6
Euphrates = Furât,
Nahr al ➤, Asia . . . 38 D5
Eureka, Canada 4 B3
Eureka, Calif., U.S.A. . 72 F1
Eureka, Kans., U.S.A. 71 G6
Eureka, Mont., U.S.A. 72 B6
Eureka, Nev., U.S.A. . 72 G5
Eureka, S. Dak., U.S.A. 70 C5
Eureka, Utah, U.S.A. . 72 G7
Eureka, Mt., Australia 53 E3
Euroa, Australia 55 F4
Europa, I., Ind. Oc. . . 47 J8
Europa, Picos de, Spain 19 A3
Europa, Pta. de, Gib. . 19 D3
Europa Pt. = Europa,
Pta. de, Gib. 19 D3
Europoort, Neths. . . . 15 C4
Eustis, U.S.A. 69 L5
Eutsuk L., Canada . . . 64 C3
Eva Downs, Australia . 54 B1
Evale, Angola 48 B2
Evans, U.S.A. 70 E2
Evans Head, Australia 55 D5
Evans L., Canada . . . 62 B4
Evanston, Ill., U.S.A. . 68 D2
Evanston, Wyo., U.S.A. 72 F8
Evansville, Ind., U.S.A. 68 G2
Evansville, Wis., U.S.A. 70 D10
Evaz, Iran 39 E7
Eveleth, U.S.A. 70 B8
Evensk, Russia 25 C16
Everard, L., Australia . 55 E1
Everard Park, Australia 53 E5
Everard Ras., Australia 53 E5
Everest, Mt., Nepal . . 37 E15
Everett, U.S.A. 72 C2
Everglades, The, U.S.A. 69 N5
Everglades City, U.S.A. 69 N5
Everglades National
Park, U.S.A. 69 N5
Evergreen, U.S.A. . . . 69 K2
Everson, U.S.A. 72 B2
Evesham, U.K. 11 E6
Evinayong, Eq. Guin. . 46 D2
Evje, Norway 9 G12
Évora, Portugal 19 C2
Evowghlī, Iran 38 B5
Évreux, France 18 B4
Évros ➤, Bulgaria . . 21 D12
Evry, France 18 B5
Évvoia, Greece 21 E11
Ewe, L., U.K. 12 D3
Ewing, U.S.A. 70 D5
Ewo, Congo 46 E2
Exaltación, Bolivia . . . 78 F5
Excelsior Springs,
U.S.A. 70 F7
Exe ➤, U.K. 11 G4
Exeter, U.K. 11 G4
Exeter, Calif., U.S.A. . 73 H4
Exeter, Nebr., U.S.A. . 70 E6
Exmoor, U.K. 11 F4
Exmouth, Australia . . 52 D1
Exmouth, U.K. 11 G4
Exmouth G., Australia 52 D1
Expedition Ra.,
Australia 54 C4
Extremadura □, Spain 19 C2
Eyasi, L., Tanzania . . 46 E6
Eyeberry L., Canada . 65 A8
Eyemouth, U.K. 12 F6
Eyjafjörður, Iceland . . 8 C4
Eyre, Australia 53 F4
Eyre (North), L.,
Australia 55 D2
Eyre (South), L.,
Australia 55 D2
Eyre Cr. ➤, Australia 55 D2
Eyre Mts., N.Z. 51 L2
Eyre Pen., Australia . . 55 E2
Eysturoy, Færoe Is. . . 8 E9
Eyvānkī, Iran 39 C6
Ezine, Turkey 21 E12

F

F.Y.R.O.M. =
  Macedonia ■, Europe 21 D9
Fabens, U.S.A. 73 L10
Fabriano, Italy 20 C5
Facatativá, Colombia . 78 C4
Fachi, Niger 44 E7
Fada, Chad 45 E9
Fada-n-Gourma,
  Burkina Faso 44 F5
Faddeyevskiy, Ostrov,
  Russia 25 B15
Fadghāmī, Syria 38 C4
Faenza, Italy 20 B4
Færoe Is. = Føroyar,
  Atl. Oc. 8 F9
Fágáras, Romania ... 17 F13
Fagersta, Sweden 9 F16
Fagnano, L., Argentina 80 G3
Fahliān, Iran 39 D6
Fahraj, Kermān, Iran . 39 D8
Fahraj, Yazd, Iran ... 39 D7
Fair Hd., U.K. 13 A5
Fairbank, U.S.A. 73 L8
Fairbanks, U.S.A. ... 60 B5
Fairbury, U.S.A. 70 E6
Fairfax, U.S.A. 71 G6
Fairfield, Ala., U.S.A. 69 J2
Fairfield, Calif., U.S.A. 72 G2
Fairfield, Idaho, U.S.A. 72 E6
Fairfield, Ill., U.S.A. . 68 F1
Fairfield, Iowa, U.S.A. 70 E9
Fairfield, Mont., U.S.A. 72 C8
Fairfield, Tex., U.S.A. . 71 K7
Fairford, Canada 65 C9
Fairhope, U.S.A. 69 K2
Fairlie, N.Z. 51 L3
Fairmont, Minn., U.S.A. 70 D7
Fairmont, W. Va.,
  U.S.A. 68 F5
Fairplay, U.S.A. 73 G11
Fairport, U.S.A. 68 D7
Fairview, Australia ... 54 B3
Fairview, Canada 64 B5
Fairview, Mont., U.S.A. 70 B2
Fairview, Okla., U.S.A. 71 G5
Fairview, Utah, U.S.A. 72 G8
Fairweather, Mt., U.S.A. 60 C6
Faisalabad, Pakistan . 36 D8
Faith, U.S.A. 70 C3
Faizabad, India 37 F13
Fakfak, Indonesia ... 33 E8
Falaise, France 18 B3
Falam, Burma 37 H18
Falcon Dam, U.S.A. . 71 M5
Falconara Marittima,
  Italy 20 C5
Falcone, C., Italy 20 D3
Faleshty = Fălești,
  Moldova 17 E14
Fălești, Moldova 17 E14
Falfurrias, U.S.A. 71 M5
Falher, Canada 64 B5
Falkenberg, Sweden . 9 H15
Falkirk, U.K. 12 F5
Falkland Is. □, Atl. Oc. 80 G5
Falkland Sd., Falk. Is. . 80 G5
Falköping, Sweden .. 9 G15
Fall River, U.S.A. ... 68 E10
Fall River Mills, U.S.A. 72 F3
Fallbrook, U.S.A. 73 K5
Fallon, Mont., U.S.A. . 70 B2
Fallon, Nev., U.S.A. . 72 G4
Falls City, Nebr., U.S.A. 70 E7
Falls City, Oreg., U.S.A. 72 D2
Falmouth, Jamaica .. 74 J16
Falmouth, U.K. 11 G2
Falmouth, U.S.A. 68 F3
False B., S. Africa ... 48 E2
Falster, Denmark ... 9 J14
Falsterbo, Sweden .. 9 J15
Fălticeni, Romania .. 17 E14
Falun, Sweden 9 F16
Famagusta, Cyprus .. 38 C2
Family L., Canada ... 65 C9
Fandriana, Madag. .. 49 C8
Fannich, L., U.K. 12 D4
Fannūj, Iran 39 E8
Fanny Bay, Canada .. 64 D4
Fanø, Denmark 9 J13
Fano, Italy 20 C5
Fanshaw, U.S.A. 64 B2
Fao = Al Fāw, Iraq .. 39 D6
Faradje, Zaïre 46 D5
Farafangana, Madag. . 49 C8
Farāh, Afghan. 36 C3
Farāh □, Afghan. 36 C3
Farahalana, Madag. .. 49 A9
Faranah, Guinea 44 F2
Farasān, Jazā'ir,
  Si. Arabia 40 D3
Farasan Is. = Farasān,
  Jazā'ir, Si. Arabia . 40 D3
Faratsiho, Madag. ... 49 B8
Fareham, U.K. 11 G6
Farewell, C., N.Z. ... 51 J4
Farewell C. = Farvel,
  Kap, Greenland ... 4 D5
Farghona, Uzbekistan 24 E8
Fargo, U.S.A. 70 B6
Fār'iah, W. al →,
  West Bank 41 C4
Faribault, U.S.A. 70 C8
Farim, Guinea-Biss. .. 44 F1
Farīmān, Iran 39 C8
Farina, Australia 55 E2
Farmerville, U.S.A. .. 71 J8
Farmington, N. Mex.,
  U.S.A. 73 H9
Farmington, Utah,
  U.S.A. 72 F8

Farmville, U.S.A. 68 G6
Farnborough, U.K. ... 11 F7
Farne Is., U.K. 10 B6
Faro, Brazil 79 D7
Faro, Portugal 19 D2
Fårö, Sweden 9 H18
Farquhar, C., Australia 53 D1
Farquhar Is., Seychelles 35 F4
Farrars Cr. →,
  Australia 54 D3
Farrāshband, Iran ... 39 D7
Farrell, U.S.A. 68 E5
Farrell Flat, Australia . 55 E2
Farrokhī, Iran 39 C8
Farrukhabad-cum-
  Fatehgarh, India ... 36 F11
Fārs □, Iran 39 D7
Fársala, Greece 21 E10
Farsund, Norway ... 9 G12
Fartak, Rãs, Si. Arabia 38 D2
Fārūj, Iran 39 B8
Farvel, Kap, Greenland 4 D5
Farwell, U.S.A. 71 H3
Fasā, Iran 39 D7
Fasano, Italy 20 D7
Fastiv, Ukraine 17 C15
Fastnet Rock, Ireland . 13 E2
Fastov = Fastiv,
  Ukraine 17 C15
Fatagar, Tanjung,
  Indonesia 33 E8
Fatehgarh, India 36 F11
Fatehpur, Raj., India . 36 F9
Fatehpur, Ut. P., India 37 G12
Fatima, Canada 63 C7
Faulkton, U.S.A. 70 C5
Faure I., Australia ... 53 E1
Fauresmith, S. Africa . 48 D4
Fauske, Norway 8 C16
Favara, Italy 20 F5
Favignana, Italy 20 F5
Favourable Lake,
  Canada 62 B1
Fawn →, Canada ... 62 A2
Faxaflói, Iceland 8 D2
Faya-Largeau, Chad . 45 E8
Fayd, Si. Arabia 38 E4
Fayette, Ala., U.S.A. . 69 J2
Fayette, Mo., U.S.A. . 70 F8
Fayetteville, Ark.,
  U.S.A. 71 G7
Fayetteville, N.C.,
  U.S.A. 69 H6
Fayetteville, Tenn.,
  U.S.A. 69 H2
Fazilka, India 36 D9
Fdérik, Mauritania .. 44 D2
Feale →, Ireland ... 13 D2
Fear, C., U.S.A. 69 J7
Feather →, U.S.A. .. 72 G3
Featherston, N.Z. ... 51 J5
Fécamp, France 18 B4
Fedeshkūh, Iran 39 D7
Fehmarn, Germany .. 16 A6
Fehmarn Bælt,
  Denmark 9 J14
Feilding, N.Z. 51 J5
Feira de Santana, Brazil 79 F11
Feldkirch, Austria ... 16 E5
Felipe Carrillo Puerto,
  Mexico 74 D7
Felixstowe, U.K. 11 F9
Felton, U.K. 10 B6
Femunden, Norway . 9 E14
Fengjie, China 31 C5
Fenit, Ireland 13 D2
Fennimore, U.S.A. .. 70 D9
Fenoarivo Afovoany,
  Madag. 49 B8
Fenoarivo Atsinanana,
  Madag. 49 B8
Fens, The, U.K. 10 E8
Fenton, U.S.A. 68 D4
Fenyang, China 31 C6
Feodosiya, Ukraine .. 23 E6
Ferdows, Iran 39 C8
Ferfer, Somali Rep. .. 40 F4
Fergana = Farghona,
  Uzbekistan 24 E8
Fergus, Canada 62 D3
Fergus Falls, U.S.A. . 70 B6
Ferland, Canada 62 B2
Fermanagh □, U.K. .. 13 B4
Fermo, Italy 20 C5
Fermoy, Ireland 13 D3
Fernandina Beach,
  U.S.A. 69 K5
Fernando de Noronha,
  Brazil 79 D12
Fernando Póo = Bioko,
  Eq. Guin. 44 H6
Ferndale, Calif., U.S.A. 72 F1
Ferndale, Wash., U.S.A. 72 B2
Fernie, Canada 64 D5
Fernlees, Australia .. 54 C4
Fernley, U.S.A. 72 G4
Ferozepore = Firozpur,
  India 36 D9
Ferrara, Italy 20 B4
Ferreñafe, Peru 78 E3
Ferret, C., France ... 18 D3
Ferriday, U.S.A. 71 K9
Ferrol = El Ferrol,
  Spain 19 A1
Ferron, U.S.A. 73 G8
Ferryland, Canada .. 63 C9
Fertile, U.S.A. 70 B6
Fès, Morocco 44 B4
Feshi, Zaïre 46 F3
Fessenden, U.S.A. .. 70 B5
Feteşti, Romania ... 17 F14
Fetlar, U.K. 12 A8
Feuilles →, Canada . 61 C12

Fezzan, Libya 45 C8
Ffestiniog, U.K. 10 E4
Fianarantsoa, Madag. 49 C8
Fianarantsoa □, Madag. 49 B8
Fianga, Cameroon ... 45 G8
Ficksburg, S. Africa .. 49 D4
Field, Canada 62 C3
Field →, Australia .. 54 C2
Field I., Australia ... 52 B5
Fieri, Albania 21 D8
Fife □, U.K. 12 E5
Fife Ness, U.K. 12 E6
Figeac, France 18 D5
Figueira da Foz,
  Portugal 19 B1
Figueras, Spain 19 A7
Figuig, Morocco 44 B4
Fihaonana, Madag. .. 49 B8
Fiherenana, Madag. . 49 B8
Fiherenana →,
  Madag. 49 C7
Fiji ■, Pac. Oc. 51 C8
Filer, U.S.A. 72 E6
Filey, U.K. 10 C7
Filiatrá, Greece 21 F9
Filipstad, Sweden ... 9 G16
Fillmore, Canada ... 65 D8
Fillmore, Calif., U.S.A. 73 J4
Fillmore, Utah, U.S.A. 73 G7
Findhorn →, U.K. .. 12 D5
Findlay, U.S.A. 68 E4
Finger L., Canada ... 65 C10
Fingöe, Mozam. 47 G6
Finisterre, C., Spain . 19 A1
Finke, Australia 54 D1
Finke →, Australia . 54 D2
Finland ■, Europe .. 8 E22
Finland, G. of, Europe 9 G21
Finlay →, Canada .. 64 B3
Finley, Australia 55 F4
Finley, U.S.A. 70 B6
Finn →, Ireland ... 13 B4
Finnigan, Mt., Australia 54 B4
Finniss, C., Australia . 55 E1
Finnmark, Norway .. 8 B20
Finnsnes, Norway ... 8 B18
Finspång, Sweden .. 9 G16
Fiora →, Italy 20 C4
Fiq, Syria 41 C4
Firat = Furāt, Nahr
  al →, Asia 38 D5
Fire River, Canada .. 62 C3
Firebag →, Canada . 65 B6
Firedrake L., Canada . 65 A8
Firenze, Italy 20 C4
Firk →, Iraq 38 D5
Firozabad, India 36 F11
Firozpur, India 36 D9
Firūzābād, Iran 39 D7
Firūzkūh, Iran 39 C7
Firvale, Canada 64 C3
Fish →, Namibia ... 48 D2
Fish →, S. Africa .. 48 E3
Fisher, Australia 53 F5
Fisher B., Canada ... 65 C9
Fishguard, U.K. 11 F3
Fishing L., Canada .. 65 C9
Fitchburg, U.S.A. ... 68 D10
Fitri, L., Chad 45 F8
Fitz Roy, Argentina .. 80 F3
Fitzgerald, Canada .. 64 B6
Fitzgerald, U.S.A. ... 69 K4
Fitzmaurice →,
  Australia 52 B5
Fitzroy →, Queens.,
  Australia 54 C5
Fitzroy →, W. Austral.,
  Australia 52 C3
Fitzroy Crossing,
  Australia 52 C4
Fiume = Rijeka, Croatia 16 F8
Fizi, Zaïre 46 E5
Flagler, U.S.A. 70 F3
Flagstaff, U.S.A. 73 J8
Flaherty I., Canada .. 62 A4
Flåm, Norway 9 F12
Flambeau →, U.S.A. 70 C9
Flamborough Hd., U.K. 10 C7
Flaming Gorge Dam,
  U.S.A. 72 F9
Flaming Gorge
  Reservoir, U.S.A. .. 72 F9
Flamingo, Teluk,
  Indonesia 33 F9
Flanders = West-
  Vlaanderen □,
  Belgium 15 D3
Flandre, Europe 16 C2
Flandre Occidentale =
  West-Vlaanderen □,
  Belgium 15 D3
Flandre Orientale =
  Oost-Vlaanderen □,
  Belgium 15 C3
Flandreau, U.S.A. ... 70 C6
Flannan Is., U.K. 12 C1
Flåsjön, Sweden 8 D16
Flat →, Canada 64 A3
Flat River, U.S.A. ... 71 G9
Flathead L., U.S.A. .. 72 C6
Flattery, C., Australia 54 A4
Flattery, C., U.S.A. .. 72 B1
Flaxton, U.S.A. 70 A3
Flekkefjord, Norway . 9 G12
Flensburg, Germany . 16 A5
Flers, France 18 B3
Flesko, Tanjung,
  Indonesia 33 D6
Flevoland □, Neths. . 15 B5
Flin Flon, Canada ... 65 C8
Flinders →, Australia 54 B3
Flinders B., Australia . 53 F2

Flinders Group,
  Australia 54 A3
Flinders I., Australia . 54 F4
Flinders Ras., Australia 55 E2
Flinders Reefs,
  Australia 54 B4
Flint, U.K. 10 D4
Flint, U.S.A. 68 D4
Flint →, U.S.A. 69 K3
Flint I., Kiribati 57 J12
Flinton, Australia ... 55 D4
Flodden, U.K. 10 B5
Floodwood, U.S.A. .. 70 B8
Flora, U.S.A. 68 F1
Florala, U.S.A. 69 K2
Florence = Firenze,
  Italy 20 C4
Florence, Ala., U.S.A. 69 H2
Florence, Ariz., U.S.A. 73 K8
Florence, Colo., U.S.A. 70 F2
Florence, Oreg., U.S.A. 72 E1
Florence, S.C., U.S.A. 69 H6
Florence, L., Australia 55 D2
Florennes, Belgium .. 15 D4
Florenville, Belgium . 15 E5
Flores, Indonesia ... 33 F6
Flores I., Canada ... 64 D3
Flores Sea, Indonesia 33 F6
Floreşti, Moldova ... 17 E15
Floresville, U.S.A. ... 71 L5
Floriano, Brazil 79 E10
Florianópolis, Brazil . 80 B7
Florida, Uruguay 80 C5
Florida □, U.S.A. ... 69 L5
Florida, Straits of,
  U.S.A. 75 C9
Florida Keys, U.S.A. . 67 F10
Flórina, Greece 21 D9
Florø, Norway 9 F11
Flower's Cove, Canada 63 B8
Floydada, U.S.A. 71 J4
Fluk, Indonesia 33 E7
Flushing = Vlissingen,
  Neths. 15 C3
Flying Fish, C.,
  Antarctica 5 D15
Foam Lake, Canada . 65 C8
Foça, Turkey 21 E12
Focşani, Romania ... 17 F14
Fóggia, Italy 20 D6
Fogo, Canada 63 C9
Fogo I., Canada 63 C9
Föhr, Germany 16 A5
Foix, France 18 E4
Folda, Nord-Trøndelag,
  Norway 8 D14
Folda, Nordland,
  Norway 8 C16
Foleyet, Canada 62 C3
Folgefonni, Norway . 9 F12
Foligno, Italy 20 C5
Folkestone, U.K. 11 F9
Folkston, U.S.A. 69 K5
Follett, U.S.A. 71 G4
Fond-du-Lac, Canada 65 B7
Fond du Lac, U.S.A. . 70 D10
Fond-du-Lac →,
  Canada 65 B7
Fondi, Italy 20 D5
Fonsagrada, Spain .. 19 A2
Fonseca, G. de,
  Cent. Amer. 74 E7
Fontainebleau, France 18 B5
Fontas →, Canada . 64 B4
Fonte Boa, Brazil ... 78 D5
Fontenay-le-Comte,
  France 18 C3
Fontur, Iceland 8 C6
Foochow = Fuzhou,
  China 31 D6
Forbes, Australia 55 E4
Førde, Norway 9 F11
Ford's Bridge, Australia 55 D4
Fordyce, U.S.A. 71 J8
Forécariah, Guinea .. 44 G2
Forel, Mt., Greenland 4 C6
Foremost, Canada .. 64 D6
Forest, U.S.A. 71 J10
Forest City, Iowa,
  U.S.A. 70 D8
Forest City, N.C., U.S.A. 69 H5
Forest Grove, U.S.A. 72 D2
Forestburg, Canada . 64 C6
Forestier Pen., Australia 54 G4
Forestville, Canada .. 63 C6
Forestville, U.S.A. .. 68 C2
Forfar, U.K. 12 E6
Forks, U.S.A. 72 C1
Forlì, Italy 20 B5
Forman, U.S.A. 70 B6
Formby Pt., U.K. 10 D4
Formentera, Spain .. 19 C6
Formentor, C. de, Spain 19 C7
Former Yugoslav
  Republic of
  Macedonia =
  Macedonia ■, Europe 21 D9
Fórmia, Italy 20 D5
Formosa = Taiwan ■,
  Asia 31 D7
Formosa, Argentina . 80 B5
Formosa, Serra, Brazil 79 F8
Formosa Bay, Kenya . 46 E8
Føroyar, Atl. Oc. 8 F9
Forres, U.K. 12 D5
Forrest, Vic., Australia 55 F3
Forrest, W. Austral.,
  Australia 53 F4
Forrest, Mt., Australia 53 D4
Forrest City, U.S.A. . 71 H9
Forsayth, Australia .. 54 B3
Forssa, Finland 9 F20
Forst, Germany 16 C8

Forster, Australia ... 55 E5
Forsyth, Ga., U.S.A. . 69 J4
Forsyth, Mont., U.S.A. 72 C10
Fort Albany, Canada . 62 B3
Fort Apache, U.S.A. . 73 K9
Fort Assiniboine,
  Canada 64 C6
Fort Augustus, U.K. . 12 D4
Fort Beaufort, S. Africa 48 E4
Fort Benton, U.S.A. . 72 C8
Fort Bragg, U.S.A. .. 72 G2
Fort Bridger, U.S.A. . 72 F8
Fort Chipewyan,
  Canada 65 B6
Fort Clayton, Panama 74 H14
Fort Collins, U.S.A. . 70 E2
Fort-Coulonge, Canada 62 C4
Fort Davis, Panama . 74 H14
Fort Davis, U.S.A. .. 71 K3
Fort Defiance, U.S.A. 73 J9
Fort Dodge, U.S.A. . 70 D7
Fort Frances, Canada 65 D10
Fort Franklin, Canada 60 B7
Fort Garland, U.S.A. 73 H11
Fort George =
  Chisasibi, Canada . 62 B4
Fort Good-Hope,
  Canada 60 B7
Fort Hancock, U.S.A. 73 L11
Fort Hertz = Putao,
  Burma 37 F20
Fort Hope, Canada .. 62 B2
Fort Jameson =
  Chipata, Zambia .. 47 G6
Fort Kent, U.S.A. ... 63 C6
Fort Klamath, U.S.A. 72 E3
Fort-Lamy =
  Ndjamena, Chad .. 45 F7
Fort Laramie, U.S.A. 70 D2
Fort Lauderdale, U.S.A. 69 M5
Fort Liard, Canada .. 64 A4
Fort Lupton, U.S.A. . 70 E2
Fort Mackay, Canada 64 B6
Fort McKenzie, Canada 63 A6
Fort Macleod, Canada 64 D6
Fort McMahon,
  Algeria 44 C5
Fort McMurray, Canada 64 B6
Fort McPherson,
  Canada 60 B6
Fort Madison, U.S.A. 70 E9
Fort Meade, U.S.A. . 69 M5
Fort Miribel, Algeria . 44 C5
Fort Morgan, U.S.A. 70 E3
Fort Myers, U.S.A. .. 69 M5
Fort Nelson, Canada 64 B4
Fort Nelson →,
  Canada 64 B4
Fort Norman, Canada 60 B7
Fort Payne, U.S.A. .. 69 H3
Fort Peck, U.S.A. ... 72 B10
Fort Peck Dam, U.S.A. 72 C10
Fort Peck L., U.S.A. . 72 C10
Fort Pierce, U.S.A. .. 69 M5
Fort Pierre, U.S.A. .. 70 C4
Fort Portal, Uganda . 46 D6
Fort Providence,
  Canada 64 A5
Fort Qu'Appelle,
  Canada 65 C8
Fort Randolph, Panama 74 H14
Fort Resolution, Canada 64 A6
Fort Rosebery =
  Mansa, Zambia ... 46 G5
Fort Rupert =
  Waskaganish, Canada 62 B4
Fort St. James, Canada 64 C4
Fort St. John, Canada 64 B4
Fort Sandeman,
  Pakistan 36 D6
Fort Saskatchewan,
  Canada 64 C6
Fort Scott, U.S.A. ... 71 G7
Fort Severn, Canada . 62 A2
Fort Sherman, Panama 74 H14
Fort Shevchenko,
  Kazakhstan 23 F9
Fort Simpson, Canada 64 A4
Fort Smith, Canada . 64 B6
Fort Smith, U.S.A. .. 71 H7
Fort Stanton, U.S.A. 73 K11
Fort Stockton, U.S.A. 71 K3
Fort Sumner, U.S.A. 71 H2
Fort Trinquet = Bir
  Mogrein, Mauritania 44 C2
Fort Valley, U.S.A. .. 69 J4
Fort Vermilion, Canada 64 B5
Fort Walton Beach,
  U.S.A. 69 K2
Fort Wayne, U.S.A. . 68 E3
Fort William, U.K. ... 12 E3
Fort Worth, U.S.A. .. 71 J6
Fort Yates, U.S.A. ... 70 B4
Fort Yukon, U.S.A. .. 60 B5
Fortaleza, Brazil 79 D11
Forteau, Canada 63 B8
Forth →, U.K. 12 E5
Forth, Firth of, U.K. . 12 E6
Fortrose, U.K. 12 D4
Fortuna, Calif., U.S.A. 72 F1
Fortuna, N. Dak., U.S.A. 70 A3
Fortune B., Canada .. 63 C8
Foshan, China 31 D6
Fosna, Norway 8 E14
Fosnavåg, Norway .. 9 E11
Fossano, Italy 20 B2
Fossil, U.S.A. 72 D3
Fossilbrook, Australia 54 B3
Fosston, U.S.A. 70 B7

Foster →, Canada ... 65 B7
Fosters Ra., Australia . 54 C1
Fostoria, U.S.A. 68 E4
Fougamou, Gabon .. 46 E2
Fougères, France 18 B3
Foul Pt., Sri Lanka .. 36 Q12
Foula, U.K. 12 A6
Foulness I., U.K. 11 F8
Foulpointe, Madag. . 49 B8
Fouman, Cameroon . 44 G7
Fountain, Colo., U.S.A. 70 F2
Fountain, Utah, U.S.A. 72 G8
Fourchu, Canada ... 63 C7
Fouriesburg, S. Africa 48 D4
Foúrnoi, Greece 21 F12
Fouta Djalon, Guinea 44 F2
Foveaux Str., N.Z. .. 51 M2
Fowey, U.K. 11 G3
Fowler, Calif., U.S.A. 73 H4
Fowler, Colo., U.S.A. 70 F2
Fowler, Kans., U.S.A. 71 G4
Fowlers B., Australia . 53 F5
Fowlerton, U.S.A. ... 71 L5
Fox →, Canada 65 B10
Fox Valley, Canada .. 65 C7
Foxe Basin, Canada . 61 B12
Foxe Chan., Canada . 61 B11
Foxe Pen., Canada .. 61 B12
Foxpark, U.S.A. 72 F10
Foxton, N.Z. 51 J5
Foyle, Lough, U.K. .. 13 A4
Foynes, Ireland 13 D2
Fóz do Cunene, Angola 48 B1
Foz do Gregório, Brazil 78 E4
Foz do Iguaçu, Brazil 80 B6
Franca, Brazil 79 H9
Francavilla Fontana,
  Italy 21 D7
France ■, Europe ... 18 C5
Frances, Australia ... 55 F3
Frances →, Canada 64 A3
Frances L., Canada .. 64 A3
Franceville, Gabon .. 46 E2
Franche-Comté, France 18 C6
Francistown, Botswana 49 C4
François, Canada ... 63 C8
François L., Canada . 64 C3
Franeker, Neths. 15 A5
Frankford, S. Africa . 49 D4
Frankfort, Ind., U.S.A. 68 E2
Frankfort, Kans., U.S.A. 70 F6
Frankfort, Ky., U.S.A. 68 F3
Frankfort, Mich., U.S.A. 68 C2
Frankfurt, Brandenburg,
  Germany 16 B8
Frankfurt, Hessen,
  Germany 16 C5
Fränkische Alb,
  Germany 16 D6
Frankland →,
  Australia 53 G2
Franklin, Ky., U.S.A. 69 G2
Franklin, La., U.S.A. 71 L9
Franklin, N.H., U.S.A. 68 D10
Franklin, Nebr., U.S.A. 70 E5
Franklin, Pa., U.S.A. 68 E6
Franklin, Tenn., U.S.A. 69 H2
Franklin, Va., U.S.A. 68 G7
Franklin, W. Va., U.S.A. 68 F6
Franklin B., Canada . 60 B7
Franklin D. Roosevelt
  L., U.S.A. 72 B4
Franklin I., Antarctica . 5 D11
Franklin L., U.S.A. .. 72 F6
Franklin Mts., Canada 60 B7
Franklin Str., Canada 60 A10
Franklinton, U.S.A. . 71 K9
Franks Pk., U.S.A. .. 72 E9
Frankston, Australia . 55 F4
Frantsa Iosifa, Zemlya,
  Russia 24 A6
Franz, Canada 62 C3
Franz Josef Land =
  Frantsa Iosifa,
  Zemlya, Russia 24 A6
Fraser →, B.C.,
  Canada 64 D4
Fraser →, Nfld.,
  Canada 63 A7
Fraser, Mt., Australia . 53 E2
Fraser I., Australia .. 55 D5
Fraser Lake, Canada 64 C4
Fraserburg, S. Africa . 48 E3
Fraserburgh, U.K. ... 12 D6
Fraserdale, Canada .. 62 C3
Fray Bentos, Uruguay 80 C5
Frazier Downs,
  Australia 52 C3
Fredericia, Denmark . 9 J13
Frederick, Md., U.S.A. 68 F7
Frederick, Okla., U.S.A. 71 H5
Frederick, S. Dak.,
  U.S.A. 70 C5
Frederick Sd., U.S.A. 64 B2
Fredericksburg, Tex.,
  U.S.A. 71 K5
Fredericksburg, Va.,
  U.S.A. 68 F7
Fredericktown, U.S.A. 71 G9
Fredericton, Canada . 63 C6
Fredericton Junc.,
  Canada 63 C6
Frederikshåb,
  Greenland 4 C5
Frederikshavn,
  Denmark 9 H14
Fredonia, Ariz., U.S.A. 73 H7
Fredonia, Kans., U.S.A. 71 G7
Fredonia, N.Y., U.S.A. 68 D6
Fredrikstad, Norway . 9 G14
Freels, C., Canada .. 63 C9
Freeman, U.S.A. 70 D6
Freeport, Bahamas .. 75 B9

Freeport, *Canada* 63 D6
Freeport, *Ill., U.S.A.* . 70 D10
Freeport, *N.Y., U.S.A.* 68 E9
Freeport, *Tex., U.S.A.* 71 L7
Freetown, *S. Leone* ... 44 G2
Frégate, L., *Canada* .. 62 B5
Fregenal de la Sierra,
  Spain 19 C2
Freibourg = Fribourg,
  Switz. 16 E4
Freiburg, *Germany* ... 16 E4
Freire, *Chile* 80 D2
Freising, *Germany* ... 16 D6
Freistadt, *Austria* ... 16 D8
Fréjus, *France* 18 E7
Fremantle, *Australia* . 53 F2
Fremont, *Calif., U.S.A.* 73 H2
Fremont, *Mich., U.S.A.* 68 D3
Fremont, *Nebr., U.S.A.* 70 E6
Fremont, *Ohio, U.S.A.* 68 E4
Fremont →, *U.S.A.* .. 73 G8
Fremont L., *U.S.A.* ... 72 E9
French Creek →,
  U.S.A. 68 E6
French Guiana ■,
  S. Amer. 79 C8
French Pass, *N.Z.* ... 51 J4
French Polynesia ■,
  Pac. Oc. 57 J13
French Terr. of Afars &
  Issas = Djibouti ■,
  Africa 40 E3
Frenchglen, *U.S.A.* ... 72 E4
Frenchman Butte,
  Canada 65 C7
Frenchman Cr. →,
  Mont., U.S.A. 72 B10
Frenchman Cr. →,
  Nebr., U.S.A. 70 E4
Fresco →, *Brazil* ... 79 E8
Freshfield, C.,
  Antarctica 5 C10
Fresnillo, *Mexico* ... 74 C4
Fresno, *U.S.A.* 73 H4
Fresno Reservoir,
  U.S.A. 72 B9
Frew →, *Australia* .. 54 C2
Frewena, *Australia* .. 54 B2
Freycinet Pen.,
  Australia 54 G4
Fria, C., *Namibia* ... 48 B1
Frías, *Argentina* 80 B3
Fribourg, *Switz.* 16 E4
Friedrichshafen,
  Germany 16 E5
Friendly Is. = Tonga ■,
  Pac. Oc. 51 D11
Friesland □, *Neths.* .. 15 A5
Frijoles, *Panama* 74 H14
Frio →, *U.S.A.* 71 L5
Friona, *U.S.A.* 71 H3
Fritch, *U.S.A.* 71 H4
Frobisher B., *Canada* . 61 B13
Frobisher Bay = Iqaluit,
  Canada 61 B13
Frobisher L., *Canada* . 65 B7
Frohavet, *Norway* ... 8 E13
Froid, *U.S.A.* 70 A2
Fromberg, *U.S.A.* ... 72 D9
Frome, *U.K.* 11 F5
Frome, L., *Australia* .. 55 E2
Frome Downs,
  Australia 55 E2
Front Range, *U.S.A.* . 72 G11
Front Royal, *U.S.A.* .. 68 F6
Frosinone, *Italy* 20 D5
Frostburg, *U.S.A.* ... 68 F6
Frostisen, *Norway* .. 8 B17
Frøya, *Norway* 8 E13
Frunze = Bishkek,
  Kyrgyzstan 24 E8
Frutal, *Brazil* 79 G9
Frýdek-Mistek, *Czech.* 17 D10
Fuchou = Fuzhou,
  China 31 D6
Fuchū, *Japan* 29 G6
Fuengirola, *Spain* ... 19 D3
Fuentes de Oñoro,
  Spain 19 B2
Fuerte →, *Mexico* .. 74 B3
Fuerte Olimpo,
  Paraguay 78 H7
Fuerteventura,
  Canary Is. 44 C2
Fuhai, *China* 30 B3
Fuḥaymī, *Iraq* 38 C4
Fuji, *Japan* 29 G9
Fuji-San, *Japan* 29 G9
Fuji-yoshida, *Japan* .. 29 G9
Fujian □, *China* 31 D6
Fujinomiya, *Japan* ... 29 G9
Fujisawa, *Japan* 29 G9
Fukien = Fujian □,
  China 31 D6
Fukuchiyama, *Japan* . 29 G7
Fukue-Shima, *Japan* . 29 H4
Fukui, *Japan* 29 F8
Fukui □, *Japan* 29 G8
Fukuoka, *Japan* 29 H5
Fukuoka □, *Japan* ... 29 H5
Fukushima, *Japan* ... 28 F10
Fukushima □, *Japan* . 29 F10
Fukuyama, *Japan* ... 29 G6
Fulda, *Germany* 16 C5
Fulda →, *Germany* . 16 C5
Fullerton, *Calif., U.S.A.* 73 K5
Fullerton, *Nebr., U.S.A.* 70 E6
Fulton, *Mo., U.S.A.* . 70 F9
Fulton, *N.Y., U.S.A.* . 68 D7
Fulton, *Tenn., U.S.A.* 69 G1
Funabashi, *Japan* ... 29 G10
Funchal, *Madeira* ... 44 B1
Fundación, *Colombia* . 78 A4

Fundão, *Portugal* 19 B2
Fundy, B. of, *Canada* . 63 D6
Funtua, *Nigeria* 44 F6
Furano, *Japan* 28 C11
Furāt, Nahr al →, *Asia* 38 D5
Fürg, *Iran* 39 D7
Furneaux Group,
  Australia 54 G4
Furnooo, *U.K.* 10 C4
Furqlus, *Syria* 41 A6
Fürstenwalde, *Germany* 16 B8
Fürth, *Germany* 16 D6
Furukawa, *Japan* ... 28 E10
Fury and Hecla Str.,
  Canada 61 B11
Fusagasuga, *Colombia* 78 C4
Fushun, *China* 31 B7
Futuna, *Wall. & F. Is.* . 51 B8
Fuxin, *China* 31 B7
Fuzhou, *China* 31 D6
Fylde, *U.K.* 10 D5
Fyn, *Denmark* 9 J14
Fyne, L., *U.K.* 12 F3

G

Gabela, *Angola* 46 G2
Gabès, *Tunisia* 44 B7
Gabès, G. de, *Tunisia* . 44 B7
Gabon ■, *Africa* 46 E2
Gaborone, *Botswana* . 48 C4
Gābrīk, *Iran* 39 E8
Gāch Sār, *Iran* 39 B6
Gachsārān, *Iran* 39 D6
Gadag, *India* 36 M9
Gadarwara, *India* ... 36 H11
Gadhada, *India* 36 J7
Gadsden, *Ala., U.S.A.* 69 H2
Gadsden, *Ariz., U.S.A.* 73 K6
Gadwal, *India* 36 L10
Gaffney, *U.S.A.* 69 H5
Gafsa, *Tunisia* 44 B6
Gagetown, *Canada* .. 63 C6
Gagnoa, *Ivory C.* ... 44 G3
Gagnon, *Canada* 63 B6
Gagnon, L., *Canada* . 65 A6
Gail →, *U.S.A.* 71 J4
Gaillimh = Galway,
  Ireland 13 C2
Gainesville, *Fla., U.S.A.* 69 L4
Gainesville, *Ga., U.S.A.* 69 H4
Gainesville, *Mo., U.S.A.* 71 G8
Gainesville, *Tex., U.S.A.* 71 J6
Gainsborough, *U.K.* .. 10 D7
Gairdner, L., *Australia* 55 E2
Gairloch, *U.K.* 12 D3
Galangue, *Angola* ... 47 G3
Galápagos, *Pac. Oc.* . 57 H18
Galas →, *Malaysia* .. 34 Q14
Galashiels, *U.K.* 12 F6
Galaţi, *Romania* 17 F15
Galatina, *Italy* 21 D8
Galax, *U.S.A.* 69 G5
Galbraith, *Australia* . 54 B3
Galcaio, *Somali Rep.* . 40 F4
Galdhøpiggen, *Norway* 9 F12
Galela, *Indonesia* ... 33 D7
Galesburg, *U.S.A.* ... 70 E9
Galich, *Russia* 22 C7
Galicia □, *Spain* 19 A2
Galilee = Hagalil, *Israel* 41 C4
Galilee, L., *Australia* . 54 C4
Galilee, Sea of = Yam
  Kinneret, *Israel* ... 41 C4
Galiuro Mts., *U.S.A.* . 73 K8
Gallabat, *Sudan* 45 F12
Gallatin, *U.S.A.* 69 G2
Galle, *Sri Lanka* 36 R12
Gállego →, *Spain* ... 19 B5
Gallegos →,
  Argentina 80 G3
Galley Hd., *Ireland* .. 13 E3
Gallinas, Pta., *Colombia* 78 A4
Gallipoli = Gelibolu,
  Turkey 21 D12
Gallípoli, *Italy* 21 D8
Gallipolis, *U.S.A.* ... 68 F4
Gällivare, *Sweden* ... 8 C19
Galloway, *U.K.* 12 G4
Galloway, Mull of, *U.K.* 12 G4
Galong, *Australia* ... 55 E4
Galoya, *Sri Lanka* ... 36 Q12
Galty Mts., *Ireland* .. 13 D3
Galtymore, *Ireland* .. 13 D3
Galva, *U.S.A.* 70 E9
Galveston, *U.S.A.* ... 71 L7
Galveston B., *U.S.A.* . 71 L7
Gálvez, *Argentina* ... 80 C4
Galway, *Ireland* 13 C2
Galway □, *Ireland* .. 13 C2
Galway B., *Ireland* .. 13 C2
Gamagōri, *Japan* ... 29 G8
Gambaga, *Ghana* ... 44 F4
Gambia ■, *W. Afr.* .. 44 F1
Gambia →, *W. Afr.* . 44 F1
Gambier, C., *Australia* 52 B5
Gambier Is., *Australia* 55 F2
Gamboma, *Congo* ... 46 E3
Gamerco, *U.S.A.* ... 73 J9
Gamlakarleby =
  Kokkola, *Finland* .. 8 E20
Gammon →, *Canada* 65 C9
Gan Jiang →, *China* . 31 D6
Ganado, *Ariz., U.S.A.* 73 J9
Ganado, *Tex., U.S.A.* 71 L6
Gananoque, *Canada* . 62 D4
Ganāveh, *Iran* 39 D6

Gäncä, *Azerbaijan* ... 23 F8
Gand = Gent, *Belgium* 15 C3
Ganda, *Angola* 47 G2
Gandak →, *India* ... 37 G14
Gandava, *Pakistan* .. 36 E5
Gander, *Canada* 63 C9
Gander L., *Canada* .. 63 C9
Gandhi Sagar, *India* . 36 G9
Gandi, *Nigeria* 44 F6
Gandía, *Spain* 19 C5
Ganedidalem = Gani,
  Indonesia 33 E7
Ganga →, *India* 37 H17
Ganganagar, *India* .. 36 E8
Gangara, *Niger* 44 F6
Gangaw, *Burma* 37 H19
Gangdisê Shan, *China* 37 D12
Ganges = Ganga →,
  India 37 H17
Gangtok, *India* 37 F16
Gani, *Indonesia* 33 E7
Gannett Peak, *U.S.A.* 72 E9
Gannvalley, *U.S.A.* .. 70 C5
Gansu □, *China* 30 C5
Ganta, *Liberia* 44 G3
Gantheaume, C.,
  Australia 55 F2
Gantheaume B.,
  Australia 53 E1
Gantsevichi =
  Hantsavichy, *Belarus* 17 B14
Ganyem, *Indonesia* . 33 E10
Ganzhou, *China* 31 D6
Gao Bang, *Vietnam* . 34 A9
Gaoua, *Burkina Faso* 44 F4
Gaoual, *Guinea* 44 F2
Gaoxiong, *Taiwan* .. 31 D7
Gap, *France* 18 D7
Gar, *China* 30 C2
Garabogazköl Aylagy,
  Turkmenistan 23 F9
Garanhuns, *Brazil* .. 79 E11
Garawe, *Liberia* 44 H3
Garber, *U.S.A.* 71 G6
Garberville, *U.S.A.* .. 72 F2
Gard →, *France* 18 D6
Gard, *Somali Rep.* .. 40 F4
Garda, L. di, *Italy* ... 20 B4
Garde L., *Canada* ... 65 A7
Garden City, *Kans.,*
  U.S.A. 71 G4
Garden City, *Tex.,*
  U.S.A. 71 K4
Garden Grove, *U.S.A.* 73 K5
Gardez, *Afghan.* 36 C6
Gardiner, *U.S.A.* 72 D8
Gardner, *U.S.A.* 68 D10
Gardner Canal, *Canada* 64 C3
Gardnerville, *U.S.A.* . 72 G4
Garfield, *U.S.A.* 72 C5
Gargano, Mte., *Italy* . 20 D6
Garibaldi Prov. Park,
  Canada 64 D4
Garies, *S. Africa* 48 E2
Garigliano →, *Italy* . 20 D5
Garland, *U.S.A.* 72 F7
Garm, *Tajikistan* ... 24 F8
Garmāb, *Iran* 39 C8
Garmisch-
  Partenkirchen,
  Germany 16 E6
Garmsār, *Iran* 39 C7
Garner, *U.S.A.* 70 D8
Garnett, *U.S.A.* 70 F7
Garoe, *Somali Rep.* . 40 F4
Garonne →, *France* . 18 D3
Garoua, *Cameroon* .. 45 G7
Garrison, *Mont., U.S.A.* 72 C7
Garrison, *N. Dak.,*
  U.S.A. 70 B4
Garrison, *Tex., U.S.A.* 71 K7
Garrison Res. =
  Sakakawea, L., *U.S.A.* 70 B3
Garry →, *U.K.* 12 E5
Garry, L., *Canada* ... 60 B9
Garsen, *Kenya* 46 E8
Garson L., *Canada* .. 65 B6
Garut, *Indonesia* ... 33 G12
Garvie Mts., *N.Z.* ... 51 L2
Garwa = Garoua,
  Cameroon 45 G7
Gary, *U.S.A.* 68 E2
Garzê, *China* 30 C5
Garzón, *Colombia* .. 78 C3
Gas-San, *Japan* 28 E10
Gasan Kuli = Hasan
  Kuli, *Turkmenistan* . 24 F6
Gascogne, *France* ... 18 E4
Gascogne, G. de,
  Europe 18 D2
Gascony = Gascogne,
  France 18 E4
Gascoyne →,
  Australia 53 D1
Gascoyne Junc. T.O.,
  Australia 53 E2
Gashaka, *Nigeria* ... 44 G7
Gaspé, *Canada* 63 C7
Gaspé, C. de, *Canada* 63 C7
Gaspé, Pén. de, *Canada* 63 C6
Gaspésie, Parc Prov. de
  la, *Canada* 63 C6
Gasteiz = Vitoria, *Spain* 19 A4
Gastonia, *U.S.A.* 69 H5
Gastre, *Argentina* ... 80 E3
Gata, C. de, *Spain* .. 19 D4
Gata, Sierra de, *Spain* 19 B2
Gataga →, *Canada* . 64 B3
Gateshead, *U.K.* 10 C6
Gatesville, *U.S.A.* ... 71 K6
Gaticau →, *Canada* . 62 C4
Gatineau →, *Canada* 62 C4

Gatineau, Parc de la,
  Canada 62 C4
Gatun, *Panama* 74 H14
Gatun, L., *Panama* .. 74 H14
Gatun Dam, *Panama* . 74 H14
Gatun Locks, *Panama* 74 H14
Gatyana, *S. Africa* .. 49 E4
Gau, *Fiji* 51 D8
Gauer L., *Canada* ... 65 B9
Gauhati, *India* 37 F17
Gauja →, *Latvia* ... 9 H21
Gaula →, *Norway* .. 8 E14
Gausta, *Norway* 9 G13
Gauteng = P.W.V. □,
  S. Africa 49 D4
Gāv Koshī, *Iran* 39 D8
Gāvakān, *Iran* 39 D7
Gavāter, *Iran* 39 E9
Gāvbandī, *Iran* 39 E7
Gávdhos, *Greece* ... 21 G11
Gävle, *Sweden* 9 F17
Gawachab, *Namibia* . 48 D2
Gawilgarh Hills, *India* 36 J10
Gawler, *Australia* ... 55 E2
Gaxun Nur, *China* .. 30 B5
Gaya, *India* 37 G14
Gaya, *Niger* 44 F5
Gaylord, *U.S.A.* 68 C3
Gayndah, *Australia* . 55 D5
Gaysin = Haysyn,
  Ukraine 17 D15
Gayvoron = Hayvoron,
  Ukraine 17 D15
Gaza, *Gaza Strip* ... 41 D3
Gaza □, *Mozam.* ... 49 C5
Gaza Strip □, *Asia* .. 41 D3
Gāzbor, *Iran* 39 D8
Gaziantep, *Turkey* .. 23 G6
Gazli, *Uzbekistan* ... 24 E7
Gcuwa, *S. Africa* ... 49 E4
Gdańsk, *Poland* 17 A10
Gdańsk, Zatoka,
  Poland 17 A10
Gdov, *Russia* 9 G22
Gdynia, *Poland* 17 A10
Gebe, *Indonesia* 33 D7
Gebeit Mine, *Sudan* . 45 D12
Gebze, *Turkey* 21 D13
Gedaref, *Sudan* 45 F12
Gede, Tanjung,
  Indonesia 32 F3
Gediz →, *Turkey* ... 21 E12
Gedser, *Denmark* ... 9 J14
Geelong, *Australia* .. 55 F3
Geelvink Chan.,
  Australia 53 E1
Geesthacht, *Germany* 16 B6
Geidam, *Nigeria* 45 F7
Geikie →, *Canada* .. 65 B8
Geili, *Sudan* 45 E11
Geita, *Tanzania* 46 E6
Gejiu, *China* 30 D5
Gela, *Italy* 20 F6
Geladi, *Ethiopia* 40 F4
Gelderland □, *Neths.* 15 B6
Geldermalsen, *Neths.* 15 C5
Geldrop, *Neths.* 15 C5
Geleen, *Neths.* 15 D5
Gelehun, *S. Leone* .. 44 G2
Gelibolu, *Turkey* ... 21 D12
Gelsenkirchen,
  Germany 16 C4
Gemas, *Malaysia* ... 34 S15
Gembloux, *Belgium* . 15 D4
Gemena, *Zaïre* 46 D3
Gemlik, *Turkey* 21 D13
Gendringen, *Neths.* . 15 C6
General Acha,
  Argentina 80 D4
General Alvear,
  Buenos Aires,
  Argentina 80 D5
General Alvear,
  Mendoza, Argentina 80 D3
General Artigas,
  Paraguay 80 B5
General Belgrano,
  Argentina 80 D5
General Guido,
  Argentina 80 D5
General Juan
  Madariaga, *Argentina* 80 D5
General La Madrid,
  Argentina 80 D4
General MacArthur,
  Phil. 33 B7
General Martin Miguel
  de Güemes,
  Argentina 80 A4
General Paz, *Argentina* 80 B5
General Pico, *Argentina* 80 D4
General Pinedo,
  Argentina 80 B4
General Santos, *Phil.* 33 C7
General Villegas,
  Argentina 80 D4
Genesee, *U.S.A.* 72 C5
Genesee →, *U.S.A.* . 68 D7
Geneseo, *Ill., U.S.A.* . 70 E9
Geneseo, *Kans., U.S.A.* 70 F5
Geneva = Genève,
  Switz. 16 E4
Geneva, *Ala., U.S.A.* 69 K3
Geneva, *N.Y., U.S.A.* 68 D7
Geneva, *Nebr., U.S.A.* 70 E6
Geneva, *Ohio, U.S.A.* 68 E5
Geneva, L. = Léman,
  L., *Europe* 16 E4
Geneva, L., *U.S.A.* .. 68 D1
Genève, *Switz.* 16 E4

Genil →, *Spain* 19 D3
Genk, *Belgium* 15 D5
Gennargentu, Mti. del,
  Italy 20 D3
Gennep, *Neths.* 15 C5
Genoa = Génova, *Italy* 20 B3
Genoa, *Australia* ... 55 F4
Genoa, *U.S.A.* 70 E6
Génova, *Italy* 20 B3
Génova, G. di, *Italy* . 20 C3
Gent, *Belgium* 15 C3
Geographe B., *Australia* 53 F2
Geographe Chan.,
  Australia 53 D1
Georga, Zemlya, *Russia* 22 A5
George, *S. Africa* ... 48 E3
George →, *Canada* . 63 A6
George, L., *N.S.W.,*
  Australia 55 F4
George, L., *S. Austral.,*
  Australia 55 F3
George, L., *W. Austral.,*
  Australia 52 D3
George, L., *Uganda* .. 46 D6
George, L., *U.S.A.* .. 69 L5
George Gill Ra.,
  Australia 52 D5
George River =
  Kangiqsualujjuaq,
  Canada 61 C13
George Sound, *N.Z.* . 51 L1
George Town, *Malaysia* 34 P13
George V Land,
  Antarctica 5 C10
George VI Sound,
  Antarctica 5 D17
George West, *U.S.A.* . 71 L5
Georgetown, *Australia* 54 B3
Georgetown, *Ont.,*
  Canada 62 D4
Georgetown, *P.E.I.,*
  Canada 63 C7
Georgetown, *Gambia* . 44 F2
Georgetown, *Guyana* . 78 B7
Georgetown, *Colo.,*
  U.S.A. 72 G11
Georgetown, *Ky.,*
  U.S.A. 68 F3
Georgetown, *S.C.,*
  U.S.A. 69 J6
Georgetown, *Tex.,*
  U.S.A. 71 K6
Georgia ■, *U.S.A.* .. 69 J4
Georgia ■, *Asia* 23 F7
Georgia, Str. of,
  Canada 64 D4
Georgian B., *Canada* . 62 C3
Georgina →, *Australia* 54 C2
Georgina Downs,
  Australia 54 C2
Georgiu-Dezh = Liski,
  Russia 23 D6
Georgiyevsk, *Russia* . 23 F7
Gera, *Germany* 16 C7
Geraardsbergen,
  Belgium 15 D3
Geral, Serra, *Brazil* .. 80 B7
Geral de Goiás, Serra,
  Brazil 79 F9
Geraldine, *U.S.A.* ... 72 C8
Geraldton, *Australia* . 53 E1
Geraldton, *Canada* .. 62 C2
Gereshk, *Afghan.* ... 36 D4
Gerik, *Malaysia* 34 P14
Gering, *U.S.A.* 70 E3
Gerlach, *U.S.A.* 72 F4
Gerlogubi, *Ethiopia* . 40 F4
Germansen Landing,
  Canada 64 B4
Germany ■, *Europe* . 16 C6
Germiston, *S. Africa* . 49 D4
Gero, *Japan* 29 G8
Gerona, *Spain* 19 B7
Gerrard, *Canada* ... 64 C5
Geser, *Indonesia* ... 33 E8
Getafe, *Spain* 19 B4
Gethsémani, *Canada* . 63 B7
Gettysburg, *Pa.,*
  U.S.A. 68 F7
Gettysburg, *S. Dak.,*
  U.S.A. 70 C5
Getz Ice Shelf,
  Antarctica 5 D14
Geyser, *U.S.A.* 72 C8
Ghaghara →, *India* . 37 G14
Ghana ■, *W. Afr.* ... 44 G4
Ghanzi, *Botswana* .. 48 C3
Ghanzi □, *Botswana* . 48 C3
Ghardaïa, *Algeria* ... 44 B5
Gharyān, *Libya* 45 B7
Ghat, *Libya* 44 D7
Ghatti, *Si. Arabia* ... 38 D3
Ghawdex = Gozo,
  Malta 20 F6
Ghazal, Bahr el →,
  Chad 45 F8
Ghazâl, Bahr el →,
  Sudan 45 G11
Ghazaouet, *Algeria* .. 44 A4
Ghaziabad, *India* ... 36 E10
Ghazipur, *India* 37 G13
Ghaznī, *Afghan.* 36 C6
Ghaznī □, *Afghan.* .. 36 C6
Ghêlinsor, *Somali Rep.* 40 F4
Ghent = Gent, *Belgium* 15 C3
Ghizao, *Afghan.* 36 C4
Ghowr □, *Afghan.* .. 36 C4
Ghudaf, W. al →, *Iraq* 38 C4
Ghugus, *India* 36 K11
Ghūrīān, *Afghan.* ... 36 B2
Gia Lai = Pleiku,
  Vietnam 34 F10
Gia Nghia, *Vietnam* . 34 G9
Gian, *Phil.* 33 C7

Giants Causeway, *U.K.* 13 A5
Giarabub = Al
  Jaghbūb, *Libya* 45 C9
Giarre, *Italy* 20 F6
Gibb River, *Australia* . 52 C4
Gibbon, *U.S.A.* 70 E5
Gibraltar ■, *Europe* . 19 D3
Gibraltar, Str. of,
  Medit. S. 19 E3
Gibson Desert,
  Australia 52 D4
Gibsons, *Canada* ... 64 D4
Giddings, *U.S.A.* ... 71 K6
Gidole, *Ethiopia* 45 G12
Giessen, *Germany* .. 16 C5
Gīfān, *Iran* 39 B8
Gifford Creek, *Australia* 52 D2
Gifu, *Japan* 29 G8
Gifu □, *Japan* 29 G8
Gigha, *U.K.* 12 F3
Giglio, *Italy* 20 C4
Gijón, *Spain* 19 A3
Gil I., *Canada* 64 C3
Gila →, *U.S.A.* 73 K6
Gila Bend, *U.S.A.* ... 73 K7
Gila Bend Mts., *U.S.A.* 73 K7
Gīlān □, *Iran* 39 B6
Gilbert →, *Australia* 54 B3
Gilbert Is., *Kiribati* .. 56 G9
Gilbert Plains, *Canada* 65 C8
Gilbert River, *Australia* 54 B3
Gilberton, *Australia* . 54 B3
Gilford I., *Canada* ... 64 C3
Gilgandra, *Australia* . 55 E4
Gilgit, *India* 36 B9
Gillam, *Canada* 65 B10
Gillen, L., *Australia* . 53 E3
Gilles, L., *Australia* . 55 E2
Gillette, *U.S.A.* 70 C2
Gilliat, *Australia* ... 54 C3
Gillingham, *U.K.* ... 11 F8
Gilmer, *U.S.A.* 71 J7
Gilmore, *Australia* .. 55 F4
Gilmore, L., *Australia* 53 F3
Gilmour, *Canada* ... 62 D4
Gilroy, *U.S.A.* 73 H3
Gimbi, *Ethiopia* 45 G12
Gimli, *Canada* 65 C9
Gin Gin, *Australia* .. 55 D5
Gindie, *Australia* ... 54 C4
Gingin, *Australia* ... 53 F2
Ginir, *Ethiopia* 40 F3
Giohar, *Somali Rep.* . 40 G4
Gióna, Óros, *Greece* . 21 E10
Girâfi, W. →, *Egypt* . 41 F3
Girard, *U.S.A.* 71 G7
Girardot, *Colombia* . 78 C4
Girdle Ness, *U.K.* ... 12 D6
Giresun, *Turkey* 23 F6
Girga, *Egypt* 45 C11
Giridih, *India* 37 G15
Girilambone, *Australia* 55 E4
Girne = Kyrenia,
  Cyprus 38 C2
Girona = Gerona,
  Spain 19 B7
Gironde →, *France* . 18 D3
Giru, *Australia* 54 B4
Girvan, *U.K.* 12 F4
Gisborne, *N.Z.* 51 H7
Gisenyi, *Rwanda* ... 46 E5
Gislaved, *Sweden* .. 9 H15
Gitega, *Burundi* 46 E5
Giuba →, *Somali Rep.* 40 G4
Giurgiu, *Romania* .. 17 G13
Giza = El Gîza, *Egypt* 45 C11
Gizhiga, *Russia* 25 C17
Gizhiginskaya Guba,
  Russia 25 C16
Giżycko, *Poland* 17 A11
Gjirokastra, *Albania* . 21 D9
Gjoa Haven, *Canada* . 60 B10
Gjøvik, *Norway* 9 F14
Glace Bay, *Canada* .. 63 C8
Glacier Bay, *U.S.A.* . 64 B1
Glacier Nat. Park,
  Canada 64 C5
Glacier Peak, *U.S.A.* . 72 B3
Gladewater, *U.S.A.* . 71 J7
Gladstone, *Queens.,*
  Australia 54 C5
Gladstone, *S. Austral.,*
  Australia 55 E2
Gladstone, *W. Austral.,*
  Australia 53 E1
Gladstone, *Canada* .. 65 C9
Gladstone, *U.S.A.* .. 68 C2
Gladwin, *U.S.A.* 68 D3
Gladys L., *Canada* .. 64 B2
Glåma = Glomma →,
  Norway 9 G14
Gláma, *Iceland* 8 D2
Glasco, *U.S.A.* 70 F6
Glasgow, *U.K.* 12 F4
Glasgow, *Ky., U.S.A.* 68 G3
Glasgow, *Mont., U.S.A.* 70 A2
Glastonbury, *U.K.* .. 11 F5
Glazov, *Russia* 22 C9
Gleiwitz = Gliwice,
  Poland 17 C10
Glen Affric, *U.K.* 12 D4
Glen Canyon Dam,
  U.S.A. 73 H8
Glen Canyon National
  Recreation Area,
  U.S.A. 73 H8
Glen Coe, *U.K.* 12 E4
Glen Garry, *U.K.* ... 12 D4
Glen Innes, *Australia* 55 D5
Glen Mor, *U.K.* 12 D4
Glen Moriston, *U.K.* . 12 D4
Glen Orchy, *U.K.* ... 12 E4

Glen Spean, *U.K.* 12 E4
Glen Ullin, *U.S.A.* 70 B4
Glenburgh, *Australia* . 53 E2
Glencoe, *S. Africa* . . . 49 D5
Glencoe, *U.S.A.* 70 C7
Glendale, *Ariz., U.S.A.* 73 K7
Glendale, *Calif., U.S.A.* 73 J4
Glendale, *Oreg., U.S.A.* 72 E2
Glendive, *U.S.A.* 70 B2
Glendo, *U.S.A.* 70 D2
Glenelg, *Australia* . . . 55 E2
Glenelg →, *Australia* 55 F3
Glenflorrie, *Australia* . 52 D2
Glengarriff, *Ireland* . . 13 E2
Glengyle, *Australia* . . 54 C2
Glenmora, *U.S.A.* . . . 71 K8
Glenmorgan, *Australia* 55 D4
Glenns Ferry, *U.S.A.* . 72 E6
Glenorchy, *Australia* . . 54 G4
Glenore, *Australia* . . . 54 B3
Glenormiston, *Australia* 54 C2
Glenreagh, *Australia* . 55 E5
Glenrock, *U.S.A.* 72 E11
Glenrothes, *U.K.* 12 E5
Glens Falls, *U.S.A.* . . 68 D9
Glenties, *Ireland* 13 B3
Glenville, *U.S.A.* 68 F5
Glenwood, *Alta.,*
Canada 64 D6
Glenwood, *Nfld.,*
Canada 63 C9
Glenwood, *Ark., U.S.A.* 71 H8
Glenwood, *Hawaii,*
U.S.A. 66 J17
Glenwood, *Iowa, U.S.A.* 70 E7
Glenwood, *Minn.,*
U.S.A. 70 C7
Glenwood Springs,
U.S.A. 72 G10
Glettinganes, *Iceland* . 8 D7
Gliwice, *Poland* 17 C10
Globe, *U.S.A.* 73 K8
Głogów, *Poland* 16 C9
Glomma →, *Norway* . 9 G14
Glorieuses, Is., *Ind. Oc.* 49 A8
Glossop, *U.K.* 10 D6
Gloucester, *Australia* . 55 E5
Gloucester, *U.K.* 11 F5
Gloucester I., *Australia* 54 B4
Gloucestershire □, *U.K.* 11 F5
Gloversville, *U.S.A.* . . 68 D8
Glovertown, *Canada* . 63 C9
Glusk, *Belarus* 17 B15
Gmünd, *Austria* 16 D8
Gmunden, *Austria* . . . 16 E7
Gniezno, *Poland* 17 B9
Gnowangerup,
Australia 53 F2
Go Cong, *Vietnam* . . 34 G9
Gō-no-ura, *Japan* . . . 29 H4
Goa, *India* 36 M8
Goa □, *India* 36 M8
Goalen Hd., *Australia* . 55 F5
Goalpara, *India* 37 F17
Goat Fell, *U.K.* 12 F3
Goba, *Ethiopia* 40 F2
Goba, *Mozam.* 49 D5
Gobabis, *Namibia* . . . 48 C2
Gobi, *Asia* 31 B6
Gobō, *Japan* 29 H7
Gochas, *Namibia* 48 C2
Godavari →, *India* . . . 37 L13
Godavari Point, *India* . 37 L13
Godbout, *Canada* . . . 63 C6
Goderich, *Canada* . . . 62 D3
Godhavn, *Greenland* . 4 C5
Godhra, *India* 36 H8
Gods →, *Canada* . . . 65 B10
Gods L., *Canada* 65 C10
Godthåb, *Greenland* . 61 B14
Godwin Austen = K2,
Mt., Pakistan . . . 36 B10
Goeie Hoop, Kaap die
= Good Hope, C. of,
S. Africa 48 E2
Goéland, L. au, *Canada* 62 C4
Goeree, *Neths.* 15 C3
Goes, *Neths.* 15 C3
Gogama, *Canada* . . . 62 C3
Gogango, *Australia* . . 54 C5
Gogebic, L., *U.S.A.* . . 70 B10
Gogland, Ostrov,
Russia 9 F22
Gogra = Ghaghara →,
India 37 G14
Goiânia, *Brazil* 79 G9
Goiás, *Brazil* 79 G8
Goiás □, *Brazil* 79 F9
Goio-Ere, *Brazil* 80 A6
Gojō, *Japan* 29 G7
Gojra, *Pakistan* 36 D8
Gökçeada, *Turkey* . . . 21 D11
Gökteik, *Burma* 37 H20
Golan Heights =
Hagolan, *Syria* . . . 41 B4
Goläshkerd, *Iran* 39 E8
Golchikha, *Russia* . . . 4 B12
Golconda, *U.S.A.* . . . 72 F5
Gold Beach, *U.S.A.* . . 72 E1
Gold Coast, *Australia* . 55 D5
Gold Coast, *W. Afr.* . . 42 F3
Gold Hill, *U.S.A.* 72 E2
Golden, *Canada* 64 C5
Golden, *U.S.A.* 70 F2
Golden B., *N.Z.* 51 J4
Golden Gate, *U.S.A.* . 72 H2
Golden Hinde, *Canada* 64 D3
Golden Prairie, *Canada* 65 C7
Golden Vale, *Ireland* . 13 D3
Goldendale, *U.S.A.* . . 72 D3
Goldfield, *U.S.A.* 73 H5
Goldfields, *Canada* . . 65 B7
Goldsand L., *Canada* . 65 B8

Goldsboro, *U.S.A.* 69 H7
Goldsmith, *U.S.A.* 71 K3
Goldsworthy, *Australia* 52 D2
Goldthwaite, *U.S.A.* . . 71 K5
Golęniów, *Poland* 16 B8
Golfo Aranci, *Italy* . . . 20 D3
Goliad, *U.S.A.* 71 L6
Golpāyegān, *Iran* 39 C6
Golspie, *U.K.* 12 D5
Goma, *Rwanda* 46 E5
Gomel = Homyel,
Belarus 17 B16
Gomera, *Canary Is.* . . 44 C1
Gómez Palacio, *Mexico* 74 B4
Gomīshān, *Iran* 39 B7
Gomogomo, *Indonesia* 33 F8
Gomoh, *India* 37 H15
Gompa = Ganta,
Liberia 44 G3
Gonābād, *Iran* 39 C8
Gonaïves, *Haiti* 75 D10
Gonbad-e Kāvūs, *Iran* . 39 B7
Gonda, *India* 37 F12
Gonder, *Ethiopia* 45 F12
Gondia, *India* 36 J12
Gönen, *Turkey* 21 D12
Gonghe, *China* 30 C5
Gongolgon, *Australia* . 55 E4
Goniri, *Nigeria* 45 F7
Gonzales, *Calif., U.S.A.* 73 H3
Gonzales, *Tex., U.S.A.* 71 L6
Good Hope, C. of,
S. Africa 48 E2
Gooderham, *Canada* . 62 D4
Goodeve, *Canada* . . . 65 C8
Gooding, *U.S.A.* 72 E6
Goodland, *U.S.A.* 70 F4
Goodnight, *U.S.A.* . . . 71 H4
Goodooga, *Australia* . 55 D4
Goodsoil, *Canada* . . . 65 C7
Goodsprings, *U.S.A.* . . 73 J6
Goole, *U.K.* 10 D7
Goolgowi, *Australia* . . 55 E4
Goomalling, *Australia* . 53 F2
Goombalie, *Australia* . 55 D4
Goondiwindi, *Australia* 55 D5
Goongarrie, L.,
Australia 53 F3
Goonyella, *Australia* . . 54 C4
Goor, *Neths.* 15 B6
Gooray, *Australia* 55 D5
Goose →, *Canada* . . . 63 B7
Goose L., *U.S.A.* 72 F3
Gop, *India* 36 H6
Göppingen, *Germany* . 16 D5
Gorakhpur, *India* 37 F13
Goražde, *Bos.-H.* 21 C8
Gordan B., *Australia* . . 52 B5
Gordon, *U.S.A.* 70 D3
Gordon →, *Australia* . 54 G4
Gordon Downs,
Australia 52 C4
Gordon L., *Alta.,*
Canada 65 B6
Gordon L., *N.W.T.,*
Canada 64 A6
Gordonvale, *Australia* 54 B4
Gore, *Australia* 55 D5
Goré, *Chad* 45 G8
Gore, *Ethiopia* 45 G12
Gore, *N.Z.* 51 M2
Gore Bay, *Canada* . . . 62 C3
Gorey, *Ireland* 13 D5
Gorg, *Iran* 39 D8
Gorgān, *Iran* 39 B7
Gorgona, I., *Colombia* 78 C3
Gorinchem, *Neths.* . . 15 C4
Gorizia, *Italy* 20 B5
Gorki = Nizhniy
Novgorod, *Russia* . . 22 C7
Gorkiy = Nizhniy
Novgorod, *Russia* . . 22 C7
Gorkovskoye Vdkhr.,
Russia 22 C7
Görlitz, *Germany* 16 C8
Gorlovka = Horlivka,
Ukraine 23 E6
Gorman, *U.S.A.* 71 J5
Gorna Dzhumayo =
Blagoevgrad,
Bulgaria 21 C10
Gorna Oryakhovitsa,
Bulgaria 21 C11
Gorno-Altay □, *Russia* 24 D9
Gorno-Altaysk, *Russia* 24 D9
Gorno Slinkino =
Gornopravdinsk,
Russia 24 C8
Gornopravdinsk, *Russia* 24 C8
Gornyatski, *Russia* . . 22 A11
Gornyi, *Russia* 28 B6
Gorodenka =
Horodenka, *Ukraine* 17 D13
Gorodok = Horodok,
Ukraine 17 D12
Gorokhov = Horokhiv,
Ukraine 17 C13
Gorongose →,
Mozam. 49 C5
Gorontalo, *Indonesia* . 33 D6
Gort, *Ireland* 13 C3
Gorzów Wielkopolski,
Poland 16 B8
Gosford, *Australia* . . . 55 E5
Goshen, *U.S.A.* 68 E3
Goshogawara, *Japan* . 28 D10
Goslar, *Germany* 16 C6
Gospić, *Croatia* 16 F8
Gosport, *U.K.* 11 G6
Gosse →, *Australia* . . 54 B1
Göta älv →, *Sweden* . 9 H14
Göta kanal, *Sweden* . 9 G16

Götaland, *Sweden* . . . 9 G15
Göteborg, *Sweden* . . . 9 H14
Gotha, *Germany* 16 C6
Gothenburg =
Göteborg, *Sweden* . 9 H14
Gothenburg, *U.S.A.* . . 70 E4
Gotland, *Sweden* 9 H18
Gotska Sandön,
Sweden 9 G18
Gōtsu, *Japan* 29 G6
Göttingen, *Germany* . 16 C5
Gottwaldov = Zlín,
Czech. 17 D9
Gouda, *Neths.* 15 B4
Gough I., *Atl. Oc.* 2 G9
Gouin, Rés., *Canada* . 62 C5
Goulburn, *Australia* . . 55 E4
Goulburn Is., *Australia* 54 A1
Gounou-Gaya, *Chad* . 45 G8
Gouri, *Chad* 45 E8
Gourits →, *S. Africa* . 48 E3
Gourma Rharous, *Mali* 44 E4
Gourock Ra., *Australia* 55 F4
Govan, *Canada* 65 C8
Governador Valadares,
Brazil 79 G10
Gowan Ra., *Australia* . 54 C4
Gowanda, *U.S.A.* 68 D6
Gowd-e Zirreh, *Afghan.* 36 E3
Gower, *U.K.* 11 F3
Gowna, L., *Ireland* . . . 13 C4
Goya, *Argentina* 80 B5
Goyder Lagoon,
Australia 55 D2
Goyllarisquisga, *Peru* . 78 F3
Goz Beïda, *Chad* 45 F9
Gozo, *Malta* 20 F6
Graaff-Reinet, *S. Africa* 48 E3
Gračac, *Croatia* 16 F8
Grace, *U.S.A.* 72 E8
Graceville, *U.S.A.* . . . 70 C6
Gracias a Dios, C.,
Honduras 75 E8
Grado, *Spain* 19 A2
Gradule, *Australia* . . . 55 D4
Grady, *U.S.A.* 71 H3
Grafton, *Australia* . . . 55 D5
Grafton, *U.S.A.* 70 A6
Graham, *Canada* 62 C1
Graham, *N.C., U.S.A.* . 69 G6
Graham, *Tex., U.S.A.* . 71 J5
Graham →, *Canada* . 64 B4
Graham, Mt., *U.S.A.* . . 73 K9
Graham Bell, Os.,
Russia 24 A7
Graham I., *Canada* . . 64 C2
Graham Land,
Antarctica 5 C17
Grahamdale, *Canada* . 65 C9
Grahamstown, *S. Africa* 48 E4
Grain Coast, *W. Afr.* . . 42 F2
Grajaú, *Brazil* 79 E9
Grajaú →, *Brazil* 79 D10
Grampian □, *U.K.* 12 D6
Grampian Highlands =
Grampian Mts., *U.K.* 12 E5
Grampian Mts., *U.K.* . 12 E5
Gran Canaria,
Canary Is. 44 C1
Gran Chaco, *S. Amer.* 80 B3
Gran Paradiso, *Italy* . . 20 B2
Gran Sasso d'Italia,
Italy 20 C5
Granada, *Nic.* 74 E7
Granada, *Spain* 19 D4
Granada, *U.S.A.* 71 F3
Granard, *Ireland* 13 C4
Granbury, *U.S.A.* 71 J6
Granby, *Canada* 62 C5
Grand →, *Mo., U.S.A.* 70 F8
Grand →, *S. Dak.,*
U.S.A. 70 C4
Grand Bahama,
Bahamas 75 B9
Grand Bank, *Canada* . 63 C8
Grand Bassam, *Ivory C.* 44 G4
Grand-Bourg,
Guadeloupe 74 M20
Grand Canyon, *U.S.A.* 73 H7
Grand Canyon National
Park, *U.S.A.* 73 H7
Grand Cayman,
Cayman Is. 75 D8
Grand Coulee, *U.S.A.* 72 C4
Grand Coulee Dam,
U.S.A. 72 C4
Grand Falls, *Canada* . 63 C8
Grand Forks, *Canada* . 64 D5
Grand Forks, *U.S.A.* . . 70 B6
Grand Haven, *U.S.A.* . 68 D2
Grand I., *U.S.A.* 68 B2
Grand Island, *U.S.A.* . 70 E5
Grand Isle, *U.S.A.* . . . 71 L10
Grand Junction, *U.S.A.* 73 G9
Grand L., *N.B., Canada* 63 C6
Grand L., *Nfld., Canada* 63 C8
Grand L., *Nfld., Canada* 63 B7
Grand L., *U.S.A.* 71 L8
Grand Lac Victoria,
Canada 62 C4
Grand Lahou, *Ivory C.* 44 G3
Grand Lake, *U.S.A.* . . 72 F11
Grand Manan I.,
Canada 63 D6
Grand Marais, *Canada* 62 C2
Grand Marais, *U.S.A.* . 68 B3
Grand-Mère, *Canada* . 62 C5
Grand Portage, *U.S.A.* 62 C2
Grand Rapids, *Canada* 65 C9
Grand Rapids, *Mich.,*
U.S.A. 68 D2
Grand Rapids, *Minn.,*
U.S.A. 70 B8

Grand St.-Bernard, Col
du, *Europe* 16 F4
Grand Teton, *U.S.A.* . . 72 E8
Grand Valley, *U.S.A.* . . 72 G9
Grand View, *Canada* . 65 C8
Grande →, *Argentina* 80 A3
Grande →, *Bolivia* . . 78 G6
Grande →, *Bahia,*
Brazil 79 F10
Grande →,
Minas Gerais, Brazil 79 H8
Grande, B., *Argentina* . 80 G3
Grande, Rio →, *U.S.A.* 71 N6
Grande Baie, *Canada* . 63 C5
Grande Baleine, R. de
la →, *Canada* 62 A4
Grande Cache, *Canada* 64 C5
Grande de
Santiago →, *Mexico* 74 C3
Grande-Entrée, *Canada* 63 C7
Grande Prairie, *Canada* 64 B5
Grande-Rivière, *Canada* 63 C7
Grande-Vallée, *Canada* 63 C6
Grandes-Bergeronnes,
Canada 63 C6
Grandfalls, *U.S.A.* . . . 71 K3
Grandoe Mines,
Canada 64 B3
Grandview, *U.S.A.* . . . 72 C4
Grangemouth, *U.K.* . . 12 E5
Granger, *Wash., U.S.A.* 72 C3
Granger, *Wyo., U.S.A.* 72 F9
Grangeville, *U.S.A.* . . 72 D5
Granite City, *U.S.A.* . . 70 F9
Granite Falls, *U.S.A.* . . 70 C7
Granite Peak, *Australia* 53 E3
Granite Peak, *U.S.A.* . 72 D9
Granity, *N.Z.* 51 J3
Granja, *Brazil* 79 D10
Granollers, *Spain* 19 B7
Grant, *U.S.A.* 70 E4
Grant, Mt., *U.S.A.* 72 G4
Grant City, *U.S.A.* 70 E7
Grant I., *Australia* 52 B5
Grant Range, *U.S.A.* . . 73 G6
Grantown-on-Spey,
U.K. 12 D5
Grants, *U.S.A.* 73 J10
Grants Pass, *U.S.A.* . . 72 E2
Grantsburg, *U.S.A.* . . 70 C8
Grantsville, *U.S.A.* . . . 72 F7
Granville, *France* 18 B3
Granville, *N. Dak.,*
U.S.A. 70 A4
Granville, *N.Y., U.S.A.* 68 D9
Granville L., *Canada* . 65 B8
Grapeland, *U.S.A.* . . . 71 K7
Gras, L. de, *Canada* . . 60 B8
Graskop, *S. Africa* . . . 49 C5
Grass →, *Canada* . . . 65 B9
Grass Range, *U.S.A.* . 72 C9
Grass River Prov. Park,
Canada 65 C8
Grass Valley, *Calif.,*
U.S.A. 72 G3
Grass Valley, *Oreg.,*
U.S.A. 72 D3
Grasse, *France* 18 E7
Grassmere, *Australia* . 55 E3
Graulhet, *France* 18 E4
Gravelbourg, *Canada* . 65 D7
's-Gravenhage, *Neths.* 15 B4
Gravesend, *Australia* . 55 D5
Gravesend, *U.K.* 11 F8
Grayling, *U.S.A.* 68 C3
Grayling →, *Canada* . 64 B3
Grays Harbor, *U.S.A.* . 72 C1
Grays L., *U.S.A.* 72 E8
Grayson, *Canada* . . . 65 C8
Graz, *Austria* 16 E8
Greasy L., *Canada* . . . 64 A4
Great Abaco I.,
Bahamas 75 B9
Great Artesian Basin,
Australia 54 C3
Great Australian Bight,
Australia 53 F5
Great Barrier I., *N.Z.* . . 51 G5
Great Barrier Reef,
Australia 54 B4
Great Basin, *U.S.A.* . . 72 G5
Great Bear →, *Canada* 60 B7
Great Bear L., *Canada* 60 B7
Great Belt = Store
Bælt, *Denmark* 9 J14
Great Bend, *U.S.A.* . . . 70 F5
Great Blasket I., *Ireland* 13 D1
Great Britain, *Europe* . 6 E5
Great Central, *Canada* 64 D3
Great Dividing Ra.,
Australia 54 C4
Great Driffield =
Driffield, *U.K.* 10 C7
Great Falls, *Canada* . . 65 C9
Great Falls, *U.S.A.* . . . 72 C8
Great Fish = Groot
Vis →, *S. Africa* . . . 48 E4
Great Harbour Deep,
Canada 63 B8
Great I., *Canada* 65 B9
Great Inagua I.,
Bahamas 75 C10
Great Indian Desert =
Thar Desert, *India* . . 36 F7
Great Karoo, *S. Africa* 48 E3
Great Lake, *Australia* . 54 G4
Great Malvern, *U.K.* . . 11 E5
Great Ormes Head,
U.K. 10 D4
Great Ouse →, *U.K.* . . 10 E8
Great Palm I., *Australia* 54 B4
Great Plains, *N. Amer.* 66 A6

Great Ruaha →,
Tanzania 46 F7
Great Saint Bernard P.
= Grand St.-Bernard,
Col du, *Europe* 16 F4
Great Salt L., *U.S.A.* . . 72 F7
Great Salt Lake Desert,
U.S.A. 72 F7
Great Salt Plains L.,
U.S.A. 71 G5
Great Sandy Desert,
Australia 52 D3
Great Sangi = Sangihe,
P., *Indonesia* 33 D7
Great Slave L., *Canada* 64 A5
Great Smoky Mts. Nat.
Pk., *U.S.A.* 69 H4
Great Stour =
Stour →, *U.K.* 11 F9
Great Victoria Desert,
Australia 53 E4
Great Wall, *China* 31 C5
Great Whernside, *U.K.* 10 C6
Great Yarmouth, *U.K.* . 10 E9
Greater Antilles,
W. Indies 75 D10
Greater London □, *U.K.* 11 F7
Greater Manchester □,
U.K. 10 D5
Greater Sunda Is.,
Indonesia 32 F4
Gredos, Sierra de,
Spain 19 B3
Greece ■, *Europe* . . . 21 E9
Greeley, *Colo., U.S.A.* 70 E2
Greeley, *Nebr., U.S.A.* 70 E5
Green →, *Ky., U.S.A.* 68 G2
Green →, *Utah, U.S.A.* 73 G9
Green B., *U.S.A.* 68 C2
Green Bay, *U.S.A.* . . . 68 C2
Green C., *Australia* . . . 55 F5
Green Cove Springs,
U.S.A. 69 L5
Green River, *U.S.A.* . . 73 G8
Greenbush, *U.S.A.* . . . 70 A6
Greencastle, *U.S.A.* . . 68 F2
Greenfield, *Ind., U.S.A.* 68 F3
Greenfield, *Iowa, U.S.A.* 70 E7
Greenfield, *Mass.,*
U.S.A. 68 D9
Greenfield, *Mo., U.S.A.* 71 G8
Greenland ■, *N. Amer.* 4 C5
Greenland Sea, *Arctic* 4 B7
Greenock, *U.K.* 12 F4
Greenore, *Ireland* . . . 13 B5
Greenore Pt., *Ireland* . 13 D5
Greenough →,
Australia 53 E1
Greensboro, *Ga., U.S.A.* 69 J4
Greensboro, *N.C.,*
U.S.A. 69 G6
Greensburg, *Ind.,*
U.S.A. 68 F3
Greensburg, *Kans.,*
U.S.A. 71 G5
Greensburg, *Pa., U.S.A.* 68 E6
Greenville, *Liberia* . . . 44 G3
Greenville, *Ala., U.S.A.* 69 K2
Greenville, *Calif., U.S.A.* 72 F3
Greenville, *Ill., U.S.A.* . 70 F10
Greenville, *Maine,*
U.S.A. 63 C6
Greenville, *Mich.,*
U.S.A. 68 D3
Greenville, *Miss.,*
U.S.A. 71 J9
Greenville, *N.C., U.S.A.* 69 H7
Greenville, *Ohio, U.S.A.* 68 E3
Greenville, *Pa., U.S.A.* 68 E5
Greenville, *S.C., U.S.A.* 69 H4
Greenville, *Tenn.,*
U.S.A. 69 G4
Greenville, *Tex., U.S.A.* 71 J6
Greenwater Lake Prov.
Park, *Canada* 65 C8
Greenwich, *U.K.* 11 F8
Greenwood, *Canada* . 64 D5
Greenwood, *Miss.,*
U.S.A. 71 J9
Greenwood, *S.C.,*
U.S.A. 69 H4
Greenwood, *Mt.,*
Australia 52 B5
Gregory, *U.S.A.* 70 D5
Gregory →, *Australia* 54 B2
Gregory, L., *S. Austral.,*
Australia 55 D2
Gregory, L.,
W. Austral., Australia 53 E2
Gregory Downs,
Australia 54 B2
Gregory L., *Australia* . 52 D4
Gregory Ra., *Queens.,*
Australia 54 B3
Gregory Ra.,
W. Austral., Australia 52 D3
Greifswald, *Germany* . 16 A7
Greiz, *Germany* 16 C7
Gremikha, *Russia* . . . 22 A6
Grená, *Denmark* 9 H14
Grenada, *U.S.A.* 71 J10
Grenada ■, *W. Indies* 74 Q20
Grenadines, *W. Indies* 74 Q20
Grenen, *Denmark* . . . 9 H14
Grenfell, *Australia* . . . 55 E4
Grenfell, *Canada* 65 C8
Grenoble, *France* . . . 18 D6
Grenora, *U.S.A.* 70 A3
Grenville, C., *Australia* 54 A3
Grenville Chan.,
Canada 64 C3
Gresham, *U.S.A.* 72 D2
Gresik, *Indonesia* 33 G15

Gretna Green, *U.K.* . . . 12 F5
Grevenmacher, *Lux.* . . 15 E6
Grey →, *N.Z.* 51 K3
Grey, C., *Australia* . . . 54 A2
Grey Ra., *Australia* . . . 55 D3
Grey Res., *Canada* . . 63 C8
Greybull, *U.S.A.* 72 D9
Greymouth, *N.Z.* 51 K3
Greytown, *N.Z.* 51 J5
Greytown, *S. Africa* . . 49 D5
Gribbell I., *Canada* . . . 64 C3
Gridley, *U.S.A.* 72 G3
Griekwastad, *S. Africa* 48 D3
Griffin, *U.S.A.* 69 J3
Griffith, *Australia* 55 E4
Grimari, *C.A.R.* 45 G9
Grimaylov =
Hrymayliv, *Ukraine* . 17 D14
Grimsby, *U.K.* 10 D7
Grimsey, *Iceland* 8 C5
Grimshaw, *Canada* . . 64 B5
Grimstad, *Norway* . . . 9 G13
Grinnell, *U.S.A.* 70 E8
Gris-Nez, C., *France* . . 18 A4
Groais I., *Canada* . . . 63 B8
Groblersdal, *S. Africa* . 49 D4
Grodno = Hrodna,
Belarus 17 B12
Grodzyanka =
Hrodzyanka, *Belarus* 17 B15
Groesbeck, *U.S.A.* . . . 71 K6
Grójec, *Poland* 17 C11
Grong, *Norway* 8 D15
Groningen, *Neths.* . . . 15 A6
Groningen □, *Neths.* . 15 A6
Groom, *U.S.A.* 71 H4
Groot →, *S. Africa* . . 48 E3
Groot Berg →,
S. Africa 48 E2
Groot-Brakrivier,
S. Africa 48 E3
Groot-Kei →, *S. Africa* 49 E4
Groot Vis →, *S. Africa* 48 E4
Groote Eylandt,
Australia 54 A2
Grootfontein, *Namibia* 48 B2
Grootlaagte →, *Africa* 48 C3
Grootvloer, *S. Africa* . 48 E3
Gros C., *Canada* 64 A6
Gross Glockner, *Austria* 16 E7
Grosser Arber,
Germany 16 D7
Grosseto, *Italy* 20 C4
Groswater B., *Canada* 63 B8
Groton, *U.S.A.* 70 C5
Grouard Mission,
Canada 64 B5
Groundhog →,
Canada 62 C3
Grouse Creek, *U.S.A.* . 72 F7
Groveton, *N.H., U.S.A.* 68 C10
Groveton, *Tex., U.S.A.* 71 K7
Groznyy, *Russia* 23 F8
Grudziądz, *Poland* . . . 17 B10
Grundy Center, *U.S.A.* 70 D8
Gruver, *U.S.A.* 71 G4
Gryazi, *Russia* 22 D6
Gryazovets, *Russia* . . 24 C7
Gua, *India* 37 H14
Guadalajara, *Mexico* . 74 C4
Guadalajara, *Spain* . . 19 B4
Guadalcanal,
Solomon Is. 56 H8
Guadalete →, *Spain* . 19 D2
Guadalquivir →,
Spain 19 D2
Guadalupe =
Guadeloupe ■,
W. Indies 74 L20
Guadalupe, *U.S.A.* . . . 73 J3
Guadalupe →, *U.S.A.* 71 L6
Guadalupe, Sierra de,
Spain 19 C3
Guadalupe Peak, *U.S.A.* 73 L11
Guadarrama, Sierra de,
Spain 19 B4
Guadeloupe ■,
W. Indies 74 L20
Guadeloupe Passage,
W. Indies 74 L19
Guadiana →, *Portugal* 19 D2
Guadix, *Spain* 19 D4
Guafo, Boca del, *Chile* 80 E2
Guaíra, *Brazil* 80 A6
Guaitecas, Is., *Chile* . . 80 E2
Guajará-Mirim, *Brazil* . 78 F5
Guajira, Pen. de la,
Colombia 78 A4
Gualeguay, *Argentina* 80 C5
Gualeguaychú,
Argentina 80 C5
Guam ■, *Pac. Oc.* . . . 56 F6
Guamúchil, *Mexico* . . 74 B3
Guanahani = San
Salvador, *Bahamas* . 75 C10
Guanajuato, *Mexico* . 74 C4
Guandacol, *Argentina* 80 B3
Guane, *Cuba* 75 C8
Guangdong □, *China* . 31 D6
Guangxi Zhuangzu
Zizhiqu □, *China* . . 31 D5
Guangzhou, *China* . . . 31 D6
Guanipa →,
Venezuela 78 B6
Guantánamo, *Cuba* . . 75 C9
Guaporé →, *Brazil* . . 78 F5
Guaqui, *Bolivia* 78 G5
Guarapuava, *Brazil* . . 80 B6
Guarda, *Portugal* 19 B2
Guardafui, C. = Asir,
Ras, *Somali Rep.* . . 40 E5
Guasdualito, *Venezuela* 78 B4
Guasipati, *Venezuela* . 78 B6

Guatemala

Guatemala, *Guatemala* 74 E6
Guatemala ■,
  Cent. Amer. 74 D6
Guatire, *Venezuela* . . . 78 A5
Guaviare □, *Colombia* 78 C4
Guaviare →,
  Colombia 78 C5
Guaxupé, *Brazil* 79 H9
Guayama, *Puerto Rico* 75 D11
Guayaquil, *Ecuador* . . . 78 D3
Guayaquil, G. de,
  Ecuador 78 D2
Guaymas, *Mexico* 74 B2
Guchil, *Malaysia* 34 P15
Gudbrandsdalen,
  Norway 9 F14
Guddu Barrage,
  Pakistan 36 E6
Gudivada, *India* 37 L12
Gudur, *India* 36 M11
Guecho, *Spain* 19 A4
Guékédou, *Guinea* . . . 44 G2
Guelma, *Algeria* 44 A6
Guelph, *Canada* 62 D3
Guéréda, *Chad* 45 F9
Guéret, *France* 18 C4
Guernica, *Spain* 19 A4
Guernsey, *U.K.* 11 H5
Guernsey, *U.S.A.* 70 D2
Gueydan, *U.S.A.* 71 K8
Gügher, *Iran* 39 D8
Guidónia-Montecélio,
  Italy 20 C5
Guiglo, *Ivory C.* 44 G3
Guijá, *Mozam.* 49 C5
Guildford, *U.K.* 11 F7
Guilford, *U.S.A.* 63 C6
Guilin, *China* 31 D6
Guimarães, *Brazil* . . . 79 D10
Guimarães, *Portugal* . . 19 B1
Guimaras, *Phil.* 33 B6
Guinea ■, *W. Afr.* . . . 44 F2
Guinea, Gulf of, *Atl. Oc.* 42 F3
Guinea-Bissau ■, *Africa* 44 F2
Guingamp, *France* . . . 18 B2
Güiria, *Venezuela* . . . 78 A6
Guiuan, *Phil.* 33 B7
Guiyang, *China* 30 D5
Guizhou □, *China* . . . 30 D5
Gujarat □, *India* 36 H7
Gujranwala, *Pakistan* . 36 C9
Gujrat, *Pakistan* 36 C9
Gulbarga, *India* 36 L10
Gulbene, *Latvia* 9 H22
Gulf, The, *Asia* 39 E6
Gulfport, *U.S.A.* 71 K10
Gulgong, *Australia* . . . 55 E4
Gull Lake, *Canada* . . . 65 C7
Güllük, *Turkey* 21 F12
Gulshad, *Kazakhstan* . 24 E8
Gulu, *Uganda* 46 D6
Gum Lake, *Australia* . . 55 E3
Gumlu, *Australia* 54 B4
Gumma □, *Japan* . . . 29 F9
Gummi, *Nigeria* 44 F6
Gumzai, *Indonesia* . . . 33 F8
Guna, *India* 36 G10
Gundih, *Indonesia* . . 33 G14
Gungu, *Zaïre* 46 F3
Gunisao →, *Canada* . . 65 C9
Gunisao L., *Canada* . . 65 C9
Gunnbjørn Fjeld,
  Greenland 4 C6
Gunnedah, *Australia* . . 55 E5
Gunningbar Cr. →,
  Australia 55 E4
Gunnison, *Colo., U.S.A.* 73 G10
Gunnison, *Utah, U.S.A.* 72 G8
Gunnison →, *U.S.A.* . . 73 G9
Gunpowder, *Australia* . 54 B2
Guntakal, *India* 36 M10
Guntersville, *U.S.A.* . . 69 H2
Guntur, *India* 37 L12
Gunungapi, *Indonesia* . 33 F7
Gunungsitoli, *Indonesia* 32 D1
Gunza, *Angola* 46 G2
Gupis, *Pakistan* 36 A8
Gurdaspur, *India* 36 C9
Gurdon, *U.S.A.* 71 J8
Gurgaon, *India* 36 E10
Gurkha, *Nepal* 37 E14
Gurley, *Australia* 55 D4
Gurun, *Malaysia* 34 P13
Gurupá, *Brazil* 79 D8
Gurupá, I. Grande de,
  Brazil 79 D8
Gurupi →, *Brazil* 79 D9
Guryev = Atyraŭ,
  Kazakhstan 23 E9
Gusau, *Nigeria* 44 F6
Gusev, *Russia* 9 J20
Gushgy, *Turkmenistan* 24 F7
Gusinoozersk, *Russia* . 25 D11
Gustine, *U.S.A.* 73 H3
Güstrow, *Germany* . . . 16 B7
Gütersloh, *Germany* . . 16 C5
Gutha, *Australia* 53 E2
Guthalongra, *Australia* 54 B4
Guthrie, *U.S.A.* 71 H6
Guttenberg, *U.S.A.* . . 70 D9
Guyana ■, *S. Amer.* . . 78 C7
Guyane française =
  French Guiana ■,
  S. Amer. 79 C8
Guyenne, *France* 18 D4
Guymon, *U.S.A.* 71 G4
Guyra, *Australia* 55 E5
Gvardeysk, *Russia* . . . 9 J19
Gwa, *Burma* 37 L19
Gwaai, *Zimbabwe* . . . 47 H5
Gwabegar, *Australia* . . 55 E4
Gwādar, *Pakistan* . . . 36 G3

Gwalia, *Australia* 53 E3
Gwalior, *India* 36 F11
Gwanda, *Zimbabwe* . . 47 J5
Gweebarra B., *Ireland* . 13 B3
Gweedore, *Ireland* . . . 13 A3
Gwent □, *U.K.* 11 F5
Gweru, *Zimbabwe* . . . 47 H5
Gwinn, *U.S.A.* 68 B2
Gwydir →, *Australia* . . 55 D4
Gwynedd □, *U.K.* . . . 10 E4
Gyandzha = Gäncä,
  Azerbaijan 23 F8
Gyaring Hu, *China* . . . 30 C4
Gydanskiy P-ov., *Russia* 24 C8
Gympie, *Australia* . . . 55 D5
Gyöngyös, *Hungary* . . 17 E10
Győr, *Hungary* 17 E9
Gypsum Pt., *Canada* . . 64 A6
Gypsumville, *Canada* . 65 C9
Gyula, *Hungary* 17 E11
Gyumri, *Armenia* . . . 23 F7
Gyzylarbat,
  Turkmenistan 24 F6

H

Ha 'Arava →, *Israel* . . 41 E4
Haapsalu, *Estonia* 9 G20
Haarlem, *Neths.* 15 B4
Haast →, *N.Z.* 51 K2
Haast Bluff, *Australia* . 52 D5
Hab Nadi Chauki,
  Pakistan 36 G5
Habaswein, *Kenya* . . . 46 D7
Habay, *Canada* 64 B5
Ḥabbānīyah, *Iraq* . . . 38 C4
Haboro, *Japan* 28 B10
Hachijō-Jima, *Japan* . . 29 H9
Hachinohe, *Japan* . . . 28 D10
Hachiōji, *Japan* 29 G9
Hadarba, Ras, *Sudan* . 45 D12
Hadarom □, *Israel* . . . 41 E3
Haddington, *U.K.* . . . 12 F6
Hadejia, *Nigeria* 44 F7
Haden, *Australia* 55 D5
Hadera, *Israel* 41 C3
Hadera, N. →, *Israel* . 41 C3
Haderslev, *Denmark* . . 9 J13
Hadhramaut =
  Ḥaḑramawt, *Yemen* . 40 D4
Ḥaḑramawt, *Yemen* . . 40 D4
Ḥaḑrānīya, *Iraq* 38 C4
Hadrian's Wall, *U.K.* . . 10 C5
Haeju, *N. Korea* 31 C7
Haerhpin = Harbin,
  China 31 B7
Hafar al Bāṭin,
  Si. Arabia 38 D5
Ḥafirat al 'Aydā,
  Si. Arabia 38 E3
Hafizabad, *Pakistan* . . 36 C8
Haflong, *India* 37 G18
Hafnarfjörður, *Iceland* . 8 D3
Hafun, Ras,
  Somali Rep. 40 E5
Hagalil, *Israel* 41 C4
Hagen, *Germany* 16 C4
Hagerman, *U.S.A.* . . . 71 J2
Hagerstown, *U.S.A.* . . 68 F7
Hagfors, *Sweden* 9 F15
Hagi, *Japan* 29 G5
Hagolan, *Syria* 41 B4
Hagondange-Briey,
  France 18 B7
Hags Hd., *Ireland* . . . 13 D2
Hague, C. de la, *France* 18 B3
Hague, The = 's-
  Gravenhage, *Neths.* . 15 B4
Haguenau, *France* . . . 18 B7
Haifa = Ḥefa, *Israel* . 41 C3
Haig, *Australia* 53 F4
Haikou, *China* 31 D6
Ḥā'il, *Si. Arabia* 38 E4
Hailar, *China* 31 B6
Hailey, *U.S.A.* 72 E6
Haileybury, *Canada* . . 62 C4
Hailuoto, *Finland* 8 D21
Hainan □, *China* 31 E5
Hainaut □, *Belgium* . . 15 D4
Haines City, *U.S.A.* . . 69 L5
Haines Junction,
  Canada 64 A1
Haiphong, *Vietnam* . . 30 D5
Haiti ■, *W. Indies* . . . 75 D10
Haiya Junction, *Sudan* 45 E12
Hajar Bangar, *Sudan* . 45 F9
Hajdúböszörmény,
  Hungary 17 E11
Hājjī Muḥsin, *Iraq* . . . 38 C5
Ḥājjīābād, *Eṣfahan, Iran* 39 C7
Ḥājjīābād, *Hormozgān,*
  Iran 39 D7
Hajnówka, *Poland* . . . 17 B12
Hakken-Zan, *Japan* . . 29 G7
Hakodate, *Japan* 28 D10
Haku-San, *Japan* 29 F8
Hakui, *Pakistan* 36 G6
Halab, *Syria* 38 B3
Ḥalabja, *Iraq* 38 C5
Halaib, *Sudan* 45 D12
Ḥalat 'Ammār,
  Si. Arabia 38 D3
Halbā, *Lebanon* 41 A5
Halberstadt, *Germany* . 16 C6
Halcombe, *N.Z.* 51 J5
Halcon, Mt., *Phil.* . . . 33 B6
Halden, *Norway* 9 G14
Haldia, *India* 37 H16

Haldwani, *India* 36 E11
Hale →, *Australia* . . . 54 C2
Haleakala Crater, *U.S.A.* 66 H16
Haleyville, *U.S.A.* . . . 69 H2
Halfway →, *Canada* . . 64 B4
Haliburton, *Canada* . . 62 C4
Halifax, *Australia* . . . 54 B4
Halifax, *Canada* 63 D7
Halifax, *U.K.* 10 D6
Halifax B., *Australia* . . 54 B4
Halifax I., *Namibia* . . 48 D2
Ḥalīl →, *Iran* 39 E8
Hall Beach, *Canada* . . 61 B11
Hall Pt., *Australia* . . . 52 C3
Halland, *Sweden* 9 H15
Halle, *Belgium* 15 D4
Halle, *Germany* 16 C6
Hällefors, *Sweden* . . . 9 G16
Hallett, *Australia* 55 E2
Hallettsville, *U.S.A.* . . 71 L6
Halliday, *U.S.A.* 70 B3
Halliday L., *Canada* . . 65 A7
Hallingdalselva →,
  Norway 9 F13
Hallock, *U.S.A.* 65 D9
Halls Creek, *Australia* . 52 C4
Hallsberg, *Sweden* . . . 9 G16
Halmahera, *Indonesia* . 33 D7
Halmstad, *Sweden* . . . 9 H15
Halq el Oued, *Tunisia* . 45 A7
Hälsingborg =
  Helsingborg, *Sweden* 9 H15
Hälsingland, *Sweden* . . 9 F16
Halstad, *U.S.A.* 70 B6
Halti, *Finland* 8 B19
Halul, *Qatar* 39 E7
Ḥalvān, *Iran* 39 C8
Hamab, *Namibia* 48 D2
Hamada, *Japan* 29 G6
Hamadān, *Iran* 39 C6
Hamadān □, *Iran* . . . 39 C6
Ḥamāh, *Syria* 38 C3
Hamamatsu, *Japan* . . 29 G8
Hamar, *Norway* 9 F14
Hambantota, *Sri Lanka* 36 R12
Hamber Prov. Park,
  Canada 64 C5
Hamburg, *Germany* . . 16 B5
Hamburg, *Ark., U.S.A.* 71 J9
Hamburg, *Iowa, U.S.A.* 70 E7
Häme, *Finland* 9 F20
Hämeenlinna, *Finland* . 9 F21
Hamelin Pool, *Australia* 53 E1
Hameln, *Germany* . . . 16 B5
Hamerkaz □, *Israel* . . 41 C3
Hamersley Ra.,
  Australia 52 D2
Hami, *China* 30 B4
Hamilton, *Australia* . . 55 F3
Hamilton, *Bermuda* . . 75 A12
Hamilton, *Canada* . . . 62 D4
Hamilton, *N.Z.* 51 G5
Hamilton, *U.K.* 12 F4
Hamilton, *Mo., U.S.A.* 70 F8
Hamilton, *Mont., U.S.A.* 72 C6
Hamilton, *N.Y., U.S.A.* 68 D8
Hamilton, *Ohio, U.S.A.* 68 F3
Hamilton, *Tex., U.S.A.* 71 K5
Hamilton →, *Australia* 54 C2
Hamilton Hotel,
  Australia 54 C3
Hamilton Inlet, *Canada* 63 B8
Hamina, *Finland* 9 F22
Hamiota, *Canada* . . . 65 C8
Hamlet, *U.S.A.* 69 H6
Hamley Bridge,
  Australia 55 E2
Hamlin = Hameln,
  Germany 16 B5
Hamlin, *U.S.A.* 71 J4
Hamm, *Germany* 16 C4
Hammerfest, *Norway* . 8 A20
Hammond, *Ind., U.S.A.* 68 E2
Hammond, *La., U.S.A.* 71 K9
Hammonton, *U.S.A.* . . 68 F8
Hampden, *N.Z.* 51 L3
Hampshire □, *U.K.* . . . 11 F6
Hampshire Downs, *U.K.* 11 F6
Hampton, *Ark., U.S.A.* 71 J8
Hampton, *Iowa, U.S.A.* 70 D8
Hampton, *S.C., U.S.A.* 69 J5
Hampton, *Va., U.S.A.* . 68 G7
Hampton Tableland,
  Australia 53 F4
Hamrat esh Sheykh,
  Sudan 45 F10
Han Pijesak, *Bos.-H.* . 21 B8
Hanak, *Si. Arabia* . . . 38 E3
Hanamaki, *Japan* . . . 28 E10
Hanau, *Germany* 16 C5
Hancock, *Mich., U.S.A.* 70 B10
Hancock, *Minn., U.S.A.* 70 C7
Handa, *Japan* 29 G8
Handa, *Somali Rep.* . . 40 E5
Handan, *China* 31 C6
Handeni, *Tanzania* . . . 46 F7
Hanegev, *Israel* 41 E3
Hanford, *U.S.A.* 73 H4
Hangayn Nuruu,
  Mongolia 30 B4
Hangchou = Hangzhou,
  China 31 C7
Hangzhou, *China* . . . 31 C7
Hangzhou Wan, *China* 31 C7
Ḥanīdh, *Si. Arabia* . . . 39 E6
Ḥanīsh, *Yemen* 40 E3
Hankinson, *U.S.A.* . . . 70 B6
Hanko, *Finland* 9 G20
Hanksville, *U.S.A.* . . . 73 G8

Hanle, *India* 36 C11
Hanmer Springs, *N.Z.* . 51 K4
Hann →, *Australia* . . . 52 C4
Hann, Mt., *Australia* . . 52 C4
Hanna, *Canada* 64 C6
Hannaford, *U.S.A.* . . . 70 B5
Hannah, *U.S.A.* 70 A5
Hannah B., *Canada* . . 62 B4
Hannibal, *U.S.A.* 70 F9
Hannover, *Germany* . . 16 B5
Hanoi, *Vietnam* 30 D5
Hanover = Hannover,
  Germany 16 B5
Hanover, *S. Africa* . . . 48 E3
Hanover, *N.H., U.S.A.* . 68 D9
Hanover, *Pa., U.S.A.* . 68 F7
Hanover, I., *Chile* . . . 80 G2
Hansi, *India* 36 E9
Hanson, L., *Australia* . 55 E2
Hantsavichy, *Belarus* . 17 B14
Hanzhong, *China* . . . 30 C5
Haora, *India* 37 H16
Haparanda, *Sweden* . . 8 D21
Happy, *U.S.A.* 71 H4
Happy Camp, *U.S.A.* . 72 F2
Happy Valley-Goose
  Bay, *Canada* 63 B7
Hapur, *India* 36 E10
Ḥaql, *Si. Arabia* 41 F3
Har, *Indonesia* 33 F8
Har Hu, *China* 30 C4
Har Us Nuur, *Mongolia* 30 B4
Har Yehuda, *Israel* . . 41 D3
Ḥaraḑ, *Si. Arabia* . . . 40 C4
Haranomachi, *Japan* . 28 F10
Harardera, *Somali Rep.* 40 G4
Harare, *Zimbabwe* . . . 47 H6
Harazé, *Chad* 45 F8
Harbin, *China* 31 B7
Harbor Beach, *U.S.A.* . 68 D4
Harbor Springs, *U.S.A.* 68 C3
Harbour Breton,
  Canada 63 C8
Harbour Grace, *Canada* 63 C9
Hardangerfjorden,
  Norway 9 F12
Hardangervidda,
  Norway 9 F12
Hardap Dam, *Namibia* 48 C2
Hardenberg, *Neths.* . . 15 B6
Harderwijk, *Neths.* . . 15 B5
Hardey →, *Australia* . . 52 D2
Hardin, *U.S.A.* 72 D10
Harding, *S. Africa* . . . 49 E4
Harding Ra., *Australia* 52 C3
Hardisty, *Canada* . . . 64 C6
Hardman, *U.S.A.* 72 D4
Hardoi, *India* 36 F12
Hardwar = Haridwar,
  India 36 E11
Hardy, *U.S.A.* 71 G9
Hardy, Pen., *Chile* . . . 80 H3
Hare B., *Canada* 63 B8
Hareid, *Norway* 9 E12
Harer, *Ethiopia* 40 F3
Hargeisa, *Somali Rep.* 40 F3
Hari →, *Indonesia* . . . 32 E2
Haridwar, *India* 36 E11
Haringhata →, *Bangla.* 37 J16
Harīrūd →, *Asia* 36 A2
Härjedalen, *Sweden* . . 9 E15
Harlan, *Iowa, U.S.A.* . 70 E7
Harlan, *Ky., U.S.A.* . . 69 G4
Harlech, *U.K.* 10 E3
Harlem, *U.S.A.* 72 B9
Harlingen, *Neths.* . . . 15 A5
Harlingen, *U.S.A.* . . . 71 M6
Harlowton, *U.S.A.* . . . 72 C9
Harney Basin, *U.S.A.* . 72 E4
Harney L., *U.S.A.* . . . 72 E4
Harney Peak, *U.S.A.* . 70 D3
Härnösand, *Sweden* . . 9 E17
Harp L., *Canada* 63 A7
Harriman, *U.S.A.* 69 H3
Harrington Harbour,
  Canada 63 B8
Harris, *U.K.* 12 D2
Harris, Sd. of, *U.K.* . . 12 D1
Harris L., *Australia* . . 55 E2
Harrisburg, *Ill., U.S.A.* 71 G10
Harrisburg, *Nebr.,*
  U.S.A. 70 E3
Harrisburg, *Oreg.,*
  U.S.A. 72 D2
Harrisburg, *Pa., U.S.A.* 68 E7
Harrismith, *S. Africa* . 49 D4
Harrison, *Ark., U.S.A.* 71 G8
Harrison, *Nebr., U.S.A.* 70 D3
Harrison, C., *Canada* . 63 B8
Harrison Bay, *U.S.A.* . 60 A4
Harrison L., *Canada* . . 64 D4
Harrisonburg, *U.S.A.* . 68 F6
Harrisonville, *U.S.A.* . . 70 F7
Harriston, *Canada* . . . 62 D3
Harrisville, *U.S.A.* . . . 68 C4
Harrogate, *U.K.* 10 D6
Harrow, *U.K.* 11 F7
Harsīn, *Iran* 38 C5
Harstad, *Norway* 8 B17
Hart, *U.S.A.* 68 D2
Hart, L., *Australia* . . . 55 E2
Hartbees →, *S. Africa* . 48 D3
Hartford, *Conn., U.S.A.* 68 E9
Hartford, *Ky., U.S.A.* . 68 G2
Hartford, *S. Dak.,*
  U.S.A. 70 D6
Hartford, *Wis., U.S.A.* 70 D10
Hartford City, *U.S.A.* . 68 E3
Hartland, *Canada* . . . 63 C6
Hartland Pt., *U.K.* . . . 11 F3
Hartlepool, *U.K.* 10 C6
Hartley Bay, *Canada* . 64 C3

Hartmannberge,
  Namibia 48 B1
Hartney, *Canada* 65 D8
Harts →, *S. Africa* . . . 48 D3
Hartselle, *U.S.A.* 69 H2
Hartshorne, *U.S.A.* . . 71 H7
Hartsville, *U.S.A.* . . . 69 H5
Hartwell, *U.S.A.* 69 H4
Harvand, *Iran* 39 D7
Harvey, *Australia* . . . 53 F2
Harvey, *Ill., U.S.A.* . . 68 E2
Harvey, *N. Dak., U.S.A.* 70 B5
Harwich, *U.K.* 11 F9
Haryana □, *India* . . . 36 E10
Haryn →, *Belarus* . . . 17 B14
Harz, *Germany* 16 C6
Hasan Kīādeh, *Iran* . . 39 B6
Hasan Kuli,
  Turkmenistan 24 F6
Hasanābād, *Iran* 39 C7
Hashimoto, *Japan* . . . 29 G7
Hashtjerd, *Iran* 39 C6
Haskell, *Okla., U.S.A.* . 71 H7
Haskell, *Tex., U.S.A.* . 71 J5
Hasselt, *Belgium* 15 D5
Hassi Inifel, *Algeria* . . 44 C5
Hassi Messaoud,
  Algeria 44 B6
Hässleholm, *Sweden* . . 9 H15
Hastings, *N.Z.* 51 H6
Hastings, *U.K.* 11 G8
Hastings, *Mich., U.S.A.* 68 D3
Hastings, *Minn., U.S.A.* 70 C8
Hastings, *Nebr., U.S.A.* 70 E5
Hastings Ra., *Australia* 55 E5
Hat Nhao, *Laos* 34 E9
Hatay = Antalya,
  Turkey 23 G5
Hatch, *U.S.A.* 73 K10
Hatches Creek,
  Australia 54 C2
Hatchet L., *Canada* . . 65 B8
Hateruma-Shima,
  Japan 29 M1
Hatfield P.O., *Australia* 55 E3
Hatgal, *Mongolia* . . . 30 A5
Hathras, *India* 36 F11
Hatia, *Bangla.* 37 H17
Hattah, *Australia* . . . 55 E3
Hatteras, C., *U.S.A.* . . 69 H8
Hattiesburg, *U.S.A.* . . 71 K10
Hatvan, *Hungary* . . . 17 E10
Hau Bon = Cheo Reo,
  Vietnam 34 F10
Haugesund, *Norway* . . 9 G11
Haukipudas, *Finland* . 8 D21
Haultain →, *Canada* . . 65 B7
Hauraki G., *N.Z.* 51 G5
Haut Atlas, *Morocco* . 44 B3
Hauterive, *Canada* . . . 63 C6
Hautes Fagnes = Hohe
  Venn, *Belgium* 15 D6
Hauts Plateaux, *Algeria* 44 A5
Havana = La Habana,
  Cuba 75 C8
Havana, *U.S.A.* 70 E9
Havant, *U.K.* 11 G7
Havasu, L., *U.S.A.* . . . 73 J6
Havel →, *Germany* . . . 16 B7
Havelange, *Belgium* . . 15 D5
Havelock, *N.B., Canada* 63 C6
Havelock, *Ont., Canada* 62 D4
Havelock, *N.Z.* 51 J4
Havelock I., *India* . . . 34 G2
Haverfordwest, *U.K.* . . 11 F3
Haverhill, *U.S.A.* 68 D10
Havering, *U.K.* 11 F8
Havířov, *Czech Rep.* . . 17 D10
Havlíčkův Brod, *Czech.* 16 D8
Havre, *U.S.A.* 72 B9
Havre-Aubert, *Canada* 63 C7
Havre-St.-Pierre,
  Canada 63 B7
Haw →, *U.S.A.* 69 H6
Hawaii □, *U.S.A.* . . . 66 H16
Hawaii I., *Pac. Oc.* . . 66 J17
Hawaiian Is., *Pac. Oc.* 66 H17
Hawaiian Ridge,
  Pac. Oc. 57 E11
Hawarden, *Canada* . . 65 C7
Hawarden, *U.S.A.* . . . 70 D6
Hawea, L., *N.Z.* 51 L2
Hawera, *N.Z.* 51 H5
Hawick, *U.K.* 12 F6
Hawk Junction, *Canada* 62 C3
Hawke B., *N.Z.* 51 H6
Hawker, *Australia* . . . 55 E2
Hawkesbury, *Canada* . 62 C5
Hawkesbury I., *Canada* 64 C3
Hawkesbury Pt.,
  Australia 54 A1
Hawkinsville, *U.S.A.* . . 69 J4
Hawkwood, *Australia* . 55 D5
Hawley, *U.S.A.* 70 B6
Hawrān, *Syria* 41 C5
Hawsh Mūssá, *Lebanon* 41 B4
Hawthorne, *U.S.A.* . . 72 G4
Haxtun, *U.S.A.* 70 E3
Hay, *Australia* 55 E3
Hay →, *Australia* 54 C2
Hay →, *Canada* 64 A5
Hay, C., *Australia* . . . 52 B4
Hay, L., *Canada* 64 B5
Hay Lakes, *Canada* . . 64 C6
Hay River, *Canada* . . . 64 A5
Hay Springs, *U.S.A.* . . 70 D3
Haya, *Indonesia* 33 E7
Hayachine-San, *Japan* 28 E10
Hayden, *Ariz., U.S.A.* . 73 K8
Hayden, *Colo., U.S.A.* 72 F10
Haydon, *Australia* . . . 54 B3
Hayes, *U.S.A.* 70 C4

Hayes →, *Canada* . . . 65 B10
Haynesville, *U.S.A.* . . 71 J8
Hayrabolu, *Turkey* . . 21 D12
Hays, *Canada* 64 C6
Hays, *U.S.A.* 70 F5
Haysyn, *Ukraine* 17 D15
Hayward, *U.S.A.* 70 B9
Haywards Heath, *U.K.* 11 F7
Hazafon □, *Israel* . . . 41 C4
Hazarām, Kūh-e, *Iran* . 39 D8
Hazard, *U.S.A.* 68 G4
Hazaribag, *India* . . . 37 H14
Hazelton, *Canada* . . . 64 B3
Hazelton, *U.S.A.* 70 B4
Hazen, *N. Dak., U.S.A.* 70 B4
Hazen, *Nev., U.S.A.* . . 72 G4
Hazlehurst, *Ga., U.S.A.* 69 K4
Hazlehurst, *Miss.,*
  U.S.A. 71 K9
Hazleton, *U.S.A.* 68 E8
Hazlett, L., *Australia* . 52 D4
Hazor, *Israel* 41 B4
Head of Bight, *Australia* 53 F5
Healdsburg, *U.S.A.* . . 72 G2
Healdton, *U.S.A.* 71 H6
Healesville, *Australia* . 55 F4
Heanor, *U.K.* 10 D6
Heard I., *Ind. Oc.* . . . 35 K6
Hearne, *U.S.A.* 71 K6
Hearne B., *Canada* . . 65 A9
Hearne L., *Canada* . . 64 A6
Hearst, *Canada* 62 C3
Heart →, *U.S.A.* 70 B4
Heart's Content,
  Canada 63 C9
Heath Pt., *Canada* . . . 63 C7
Heath Steele, *Canada* . 63 C6
Heavener, *U.S.A.* . . . 71 H7
Hebbronville, *U.S.A.* . 71 M5
Hebei □, *China* 31 C6
Hebel, *Australia* 55 D4
Heber, *U.S.A.* 72 F8
Heber Springs, *U.S.A.* 71 H9
Hebert, *Canada* 65 C7
Hebgen L., *U.S.A.* . . . 72 D8
Hebrides, *U.K.* 12 D1
Hebron = Al Khalīl,
  West Bank 41 D4
Hebron, *Canada* 61 C13
Hebron, *N. Dak., U.S.A.* 70 B3
Hebron, *Nebr., U.S.A.* 70 E6
Hecate Str., *Canada* . . 64 C2
Hechi, *China* 30 D5
Hechuan, *China* 30 C5
Hecla, *U.S.A.* 70 C5
Hecla I., *Canada* 65 C9
Hede, *Sweden* 9 E15
Hedemora, *Sweden* . . 9 F16
Hedley, *U.S.A.* 71 H4
Heemstede, *Neths.* . . 15 B4
Heerde, *Neths.* 15 B6
Heerenveen, *Neths.* . . 15 B5
Heerlen, *Neths.* 18 A6
Ḥefa, *Israel* 41 C3
Ḥefa □, *Israel* 41 C4
Hefei, *China* 31 C6
Hegang, *China* 31 B8
Heidelberg, *Germany* . 16 D5
Heidelberg, *S. Africa* . 48 E3
Heilbron, *S. Africa* . . . 49 D4
Heilbronn, *Germany* . . 16 D5
Heilongjiang □, *China* 31 B7
Heilunkiang =
  Heilongjiang □,
  China 31 B7
Heimaey, *Iceland* 8 E3
Heinola, *Finland* 9 F22
Heinze Is., *Burma* . . . 34 E4
Hejaz = Al Ḥijāz,
  Si. Arabia 40 B2
Hekla, *Iceland* 8 E4
Hekou, *China* 30 D5
Helena, *Ark., U.S.A.* . . 71 H9
Helena, *Mont., U.S.A.* . 72 C7
Helensburgh, *U.K.* . . . 12 E4
Helensville, *N.Z.* 51 G5
Helgeland, *Norway* . . 8 C15
Helgoland, *Germany* . 16 A4
Heligoland =
  Helgoland, *Germany* . 16 A4
Heligoland B. =
  Deutsche Bucht,
  Germany 16 A5
Hella, *Iceland* 8 E3
Hellendoorn, *Neths.* . . 15 B6
Hellevoetsluis, *Neths.* . 15 C4
Hellín, *Spain* 19 C5
Helmand □, *Afghan.* . 36 D4
Helmand →, *Afghan.* . 36 D2
Helmond, *Neths.* 15 C5
Helmsdale, *U.K.* 12 C5
Helper, *U.S.A.* 72 G8
Helsingborg, *Sweden* . 9 H15
Helsingfors = Helsinki,
  Finland 9 F21
Helsingør, *Denmark* . . 9 H15
Helsinki, *Finland* 9 F21
Helston, *U.K.* 11 G2
Helvellyn, *U.K.* 10 C4
Helwân, *Egypt* 45 C11
Hemet, *U.S.A.* 73 K5
Hemingford, *U.S.A.* . . 70 D3
Hemphill, *U.S.A.* 71 K8
Hempstead, *U.S.A.* . . 71 K6
Hemse, *Sweden* 9 H18
Henan □, *China* 31 C6
Henares →, *Spain* . . . 19 B4
Henashi-Misaki, *Japan* 28 D9
Henderson, *Ky., U.S.A.* 68 G2
Henderson, *N.C., U.S.A.* 69 G6
Henderson, *Nev.,*
  U.S.A. 73 H6

Henderson, Tenn., U.S.A. 69 H1
Henderson, Tex., U.S.A. 71 J7
Hendersonville, U.S.A. 69 H4
Hendijān, Iran 39 D6
Hendon, Australia 55 D5
Hengelo, Neths. 15 B6
Hengyang, China 31 D6
Henley, Australia 55 F4
Henlopen, C., U.S.A. 68 F8
Hennenman, S. Africa 48 D4
Hennessey, U.S.A. 71 G6
Henrietta, U.S.A. 71 J5
Henrietta, Ostrov, Russia 25 B16
Henrietta Maria, C., Canada 62 A3
Henry, U.S.A. 70 E10
Henryetta, U.S.A. 71 H6
Hentiyn Nuruu, Mongolia 31 B5
Henty, Australia 55 F4
Henzada, Burma 37 L19
Heppner, U.S.A. 72 D4
Héraðsflói, Iceland 8 D6
Héraðsvötn →, Iceland 8 D4
Herald Cays, Australia 54 B4
Herāt, Afghan. 36 B3
Herāt □, Afghan. 36 B3
Herbert →, Australia 54 B4
Herbert Downs, Australia 54 C2
Herberton, Australia 54 B4
Hercegnovi, Montenegro, Yug. 21 C8
Herðubreið, Iceland 8 D5
Hereford, U.K. 11 E5
Hereford, U.S.A. 71 H3
Hereford and Worcester □, U.K. 11 E5
Herentals, Belgium 15 C4
Herford, Germany 16 B5
Herington, U.S.A. 70 F6
Herkimer, U.S.A. 68 D8
Herman, U.S.A. 70 C6
Hermann, U.S.A. 70 F9
Hermannsburg Mission, Australia 52 D5
Hermanus, S. Africa 48 E2
Hermidale, Australia 55 E4
Hermiston, U.S.A. 72 D4
Hermitage, N.Z. 51 K3
Hermite, I., Chile 80 H3
Hermon, Mt. = Ash Shaykh, J., Lebanon 41 B4
Hermosillo, Mexico 74 B2
Hernád →, Hungary 17 D11
Hernandarias, Paraguay 80 B6
Hernando, U.S.A. 71 H10
Herne, Germany 15 C7
Herne Bay, U.K. 11 F9
Herning, Denmark 9 H13
Heroica Nogales = Nogales, Mexico 74 A2
Heron Bay, Canada 62 C2
Herreid, U.S.A. 70 C4
Herrick, Australia 54 G4
Herrin, U.S.A. 71 G10
Herstal, Belgium 15 D5
Hertford, U.K. 11 F7
Hertfordshire □, U.K. 11 F7
's-Hertogenbosch, Neths. 15 C5
Hertzogville, S. Africa 48 D4
Herzliyya, Israel 41 C3
Ḥeṣār, Fārs, Iran 39 D6
Ḥeṣār, Markazī, Iran 39 C6
Hesse = Hessen □, Germany 16 C5
Hessen □, Germany 16 C5
Hettinger, U.S.A. 70 C3
Hewett, C., Canada 61 A13
Hexham, U.K. 10 C5
Ḥeydarābād, Iran 39 D7
Heyfield, Australia 55 F4
Heysham, U.K. 10 C5
Heywood, Australia 55 F3
Hialeah, U.S.A. 69 N5
Hiawatha, Kans., U.S.A. 70 F7
Hiawatha, Utah, U.S.A. 72 G8
Hibbing, U.S.A. 70 B8
Hibbs B., Australia 54 G4
Hibernia Reef, Australia 52 B3
Hickory, U.S.A. 69 H5
Hicks, Pt., Australia 55 F4
Hida-Gawa →, Japan 29 G8
Hida-Sammyaku, Japan 29 F8
Hidaka-Sammyaku, Japan 28 C11
Hidalgo del Parral, Mexico 74 B3
Higashiajima-San, Japan 28 F10
Higashiōsaka, Japan 29 G7
Higgins, U.S.A. 71 G4
Higginsville, Australia 53 F3
High Atlas = Haut Atlas, Morocco 44 B3
High I., Canada 63 A7
High Island, U.S.A. 71 L7
High Level, Canada 64 B5
High Point, U.S.A. 69 H6
High Prairie, Canada 64 B5
High River, Canada 64 C6
High Springs, U.S.A. 69 L4
High Tatra = Tatry, Slovak Rep. 17 D11
High Wycombe, U.K. 11 F7
Highbury, Australia 54 B3
Highland □, U.K. 12 D4
Highland Park, U.S.A. 68 D2
Highmore, U.S.A. 70 C5
Highrock L., Canada 65 B7

Hiiumaa, Estonia 9 G20
Ḥijāz □, Si. Arabia 40 C2
Hijo = Tagum, Phil. 33 C7
Hikari, Japan 29 H5
Hikone, Japan 29 G8
Hiko, U.S.A. 73 H6
Hikurangi, N.Z. 51 F5
Hikurangi, Mt., N.Z. 51 H6
Hildesheim, Germany 16 B5
Hill →, Australia 53 F2
Hill City, Idaho, U.S.A. 72 E6
Hill City, Kans., U.S.A. 70 F5
Hill City, Minn., U.S.A. 70 B8
Hill City, S. Dak., U.S.A. 70 D3
Hill Island L., Canada 65 A7
Hillegom, Neths. 15 B4
Hillerød, Denmark 9 J15
Hillingdon, U.K. 11 F7
Hillman, U.S.A. 68 C4
Hillmond, Canada 65 C7
Hillsboro, Kans., U.S.A. 70 F6
Hillsboro, N. Dak., U.S.A. 70 B6
Hillsboro, N.H., U.S.A. 68 D10
Hillsboro, N. Mex., U.S.A. 73 K10
Hillsboro, Oreg., U.S.A. 72 D2
Hillsboro, Tex., U.S.A. 71 J6
Hillsdale, U.S.A. 68 E3
Hillside, Australia 52 D2
Hillsport, Canada 62 C2
Hillston, Australia 55 E4
Hilo, U.S.A. 66 J17
Hilversum, Neths. 15 B5
Himachal Pradesh □, India 36 D10
Himalaya, Asia 37 E14
Himatnagar, India 36 H8
Himeji, Japan 29 G7
Himi, Japan 29 F8
Ḥimṣ, Syria 41 A5
Ḥimṣ □, Syria 41 A5
Hinchinbrook I., Australia 54 B4
Hinckley, U.K. 11 E6
Hinckley, U.S.A. 72 G7
Hindmarsh, L., Australia 55 F3
Hindu Kush, Asia 36 B7
Hindubagh, Pakistan 36 D5
Hindupur, India 36 N10
Hines Creek, Canada 64 B5
Hinganghat, India 36 J11
Hingham, U.S.A. 72 B8
Hingoli, India 36 K10
Hinna = Imi, Ethiopia 40 F3
Hinnøya, Norway 8 B16
Hinojosa del Duque, Spain 19 C3
Hinsdale, U.S.A. 72 B10
Hinton, Canada 64 C5
Hinton, U.S.A. 68 G5
Hippolytushoef, Neths. 15 B4
Hirado, Japan 29 H4
Hirakud Dam, India 37 J13
Hiratsuka, Japan 29 G9
Hiroo, Japan 28 C11
Hirosaki, Japan 28 D10
Hiroshima, Japan 29 G6
Hiroshima □, Japan 29 G6
Hisar, India 36 E9
Hisb →, Iraq 38 D5
Ḥismá, Si. Arabia 38 D3
Hispaniola, W. Indies 75 D10
Hīt, Iraq 38 C4
Hita, Japan 29 H5
Hitachi, Japan 29 F10
Hitchin, U.K. 11 F7
Hitoyoshi, Japan 29 H5
Hitra, Norway 8 E13
Hjalmar L., Canada 65 A7
Hjälmaren, Sweden 9 G16
Hjørring, Denmark 9 H13
Hluhluwe, S. Africa 49 D5
Hlyboka, Ukraine 17 D13
Ho, Ghana 44 G5
Ho Chi Minh City = Phanh Bho Ho Chi Minh, Vietnam 34 G9
Hoa Binh, Vietnam 34 B8
Hoai Nhon, Vietnam 34 E10
Hoare B., Canada 61 B13
Hobart, Australia 54 G4
Hobart, U.S.A. 71 H5
Hobbs, U.S.A. 71 J3
Hobbs Coast, Antarctica 5 D14
Hoboken, Belgium 15 C4
Hobro, Denmark 9 H13
Hoburgen, Sweden 9 H18
Hodaka-Dake, Japan 29 F8
Hodgson, Canada 65 C9
Hódmezővásárhely, Hungary 17 E11
Hodna, Chott el, Algeria 44 A5
Hodonín, Czech. 17 D9
Hoek van Holland, Neths. 15 C4
Hof, Germany 16 C6
Hofðhakaupstaður, Iceland 8 D3
Hofmeyr, S. Africa 48 E4
Höfn, Iceland 8 D6
Hofors, Sweden 9 F17
Hofsjökull, Iceland 8 D4
Hōfu, Japan 29 G5
Hogan Group, Australia 54 F4
Hogansville, U.S.A. 69 J3
Hogeland, U.S.A. 72 B9
Hoggar = Ahaggar, Algeria 44 D6
Hohe Rhön, Germany 16 C5
Hohe Venn, Belgium 15 D6

Hohenwald, U.S.A. 69 H2
Hohhot, China 31 B6
Hoi An, Vietnam 34 E10
Hoi Xuan, Vietnam 34 B8
Hoisington, U.S.A. 70 F5
Hōjō, Japan 29 H6
Hokianga Harbour, N.Z. 51 F4
Hokitika, N.Z. 51 K3
Hokkaidō □, Japan 28 C11
Holbrook, Australia 55 F4
Holbrook, U.S.A. 73 J8
Holden, Canada 64 C6
Holden, U.S.A. 72 G7
Holdenville, U.S.A. 71 H6
Holderness, U.K. 10 D7
Holdfast, Canada 65 C7
Holdrege, U.S.A. 70 E5
Hollams Bird I., Namibia 48 C1
Holland, U.S.A. 68 D2
Hollandia = Jayapura, Indonesia 33 E10
Hollidaysburg, U.S.A. 68 E6
Hollis, U.S.A. 71 H5
Hollister, Calif., U.S.A. 73 H3
Hollister, Idaho, U.S.A. 72 E6
Holly, U.S.A. 70 F3
Holly Hill, U.S.A. 69 L5
Holly Springs, U.S.A. 71 H10
Hollywood, Calif., U.S.A. 73 J4
Hollywood, Fla., U.S.A. 69 N5
Holman Island, Canada 60 A8
Hólmavík, Iceland 8 D3
Holmes Reefs, Australia 54 B4
Holmsund, Sweden 8 E19
Holroyd →, Australia 54 A3
Holstebro, Denmark 9 H13
Holsworthy, U.K. 11 G3
Holton, Canada 63 B8
Holton, U.S.A. 70 F7
Holtville, U.S.A. 73 K6
Holwerd, Neths. 15 A5
Holy Cross, U.S.A. 60 B4
Holy I., Gwynedd, U.K. 10 D3
Holy I., Northumb., U.K. 10 B6
Holyhead, U.K. 10 D3
Holyoke, Colo., U.S.A. 70 E3
Holyoke, Mass., U.S.A. 68 D9
Holyrood, Canada 63 C9
Homalin, Burma 37 G19
Homand, Iran 39 C8
Hombori, Mali 44 E4
Home B., Canada 61 B13
Home Hill, Australia 54 B4
Homedale, U.S.A. 72 E5
Homer, Alaska, U.S.A. 60 C4
Homer, La., U.S.A. 71 J8
Homestead, Australia 54 C4
Homestead, Fla., U.S.A. 69 N5
Homestead, Oreg., U.S.A. 72 D5
Hominy, U.S.A. 71 G6
Homoine, Mozam. 49 C6
Homs = Ḥimṣ, Syria 41 A5
Homyel, Belarus 17 B16
Hon Chong, Vietnam 34 G8
Honan = Henan □, China 31 C6
Honbetsu, Japan 28 C11
Honda, Colombia 78 B4
Hondeklipbaai, S. Africa 48 E2
Hondo, Japan 29 H5
Hondo, U.S.A. 71 L5
Honduras ■, Cent. Amer. 74 E7
Honduras, G. de, Caribbean 74 D7
Hønefoss, Norway 9 F14
Honey L., U.S.A. 72 F3
Honfleur, France 18 B4
Hong Kong ■, Asia 31 D6
Hongha →, Vietnam 30 D5
Hongjiang, China 31 D5
Hongshui He →, China 31 D5
Honguedo, Détroit d', Canada 63 C7
Hongze Hu, China 31 C6
Honiara, Solomon Is. 56 H7
Honiton, U.K. 11 G4
Honjō, Japan 28 E10
Honningsvåg, Norway 8 A21
Honolulu, U.S.A. 66 H16
Honshū, Japan 29 G9
Hood, Mt., U.S.A. 72 D3
Hood, Pt., Australia 53 F2
Hood River, U.S.A. 72 D3
Hoodsport, U.S.A. 72 C2
Hoogeveen, Neths. 15 B6
Hoogezand, Neths. 15 A6
Hooghly = Hughli →, India 37 J16
Hook Hd., Ireland 13 D5
Hook I., Australia 54 C4
Hook of Holland = Hoek van Holland, Neths. 15 C4
Hooker, U.S.A. 71 G4
Hooker Creek, Australia 52 C5
Hoopeston, U.S.A. 68 E2
Hoopstad, S. Africa 48 D4
Hoorn, Neths. 15 B5
Hoover Dam, U.S.A. 73 J6
Hope, Canada 64 D4
Hope, Ark., U.S.A. 71 J8
Hope, N. Dak., U.S.A. 70 B6
Hope, Pt., Australia 55 D2
Hope, Pt., U.S.A. 60 B3
Hopedale, Canada 63 A7
Hopefield, S. Africa 48 E2

Hopei = Hebei □, China 31 C6
Hopetoun, Vic., Australia 55 F3
Hopetoun, W. Austral., Australia 53 F3
Hopetown, S. Africa 48 D3
Hopkins, U.S.A. 70 E7
Hopkins, L., Australia 52 D4
Hopkinsville, U.S.A. 69 G2
Hopland, U.S.A. 72 G2
Hoquiam, U.S.A. 72 C2
Horden Hills, Australia 52 D5
Horlick Mts., Antarctica 5 E15
Horlivka, Ukraine 23 E6
Hormoz, Iran 39 E7
Hormoz, Jaz. ye, Iran 39 E8
Hormuz, Str. of, The Gulf 39 E8
Horn, Austria 16 D8
Horn, Iceland 8 C2
Horn →, Canada 64 A5
Horn, Cape = Hornos, C. de, Chile 80 H3
Horn Head, Ireland 13 A3
Horn I., Australia 54 A3
Horn I., U.S.A. 69 K1
Horn Mts., Canada 64 A5
Hornavan, Sweden 8 C17
Hornbeck, U.S.A. 71 K8
Hornbrook, U.S.A. 72 F2
Horncastle, U.K. 10 D7
Hornell, U.S.A. 68 D7
Hornell L., Canada 64 A5
Hornepayne, Canada 62 C3
Hornos, C. de, Chile 80 H3
Hornsby, Australia 55 E5
Hornsea, U.K. 10 D7
Horobetsu, Japan 28 C10
Horodenka, Ukraine 17 D13
Horodok, Khmelnytskyy, Ukraine 17 D14
Horodok, Lviv, Ukraine 17 D12
Horokhiv, Ukraine 17 C13
Horqin Youyi Qianqi, China 31 B7
Horqueta, Paraguay 80 A5
Horse Creek, U.S.A. 70 E3
Horse Is., Canada 63 B8
Horsefly L., Canada 64 C4
Horsens, Denmark 9 J13
Horsham, Australia 55 F3
Horsham, U.K. 11 F7
Horten, Norway 9 G14
Horton, U.S.A. 70 F7
Horton →, Canada 60 B7
Horwood, L., Canada 62 C3
Hose, Gunung-Gunung, Malaysia 32 D4
Hoshangabad, India 36 H10
Hoshiarpur, India 36 D9
Hosmer, U.S.A. 70 C5
Hospet, India 36 M10
Hospitalet de Llobregat, Spain 19 B7
Hoste, I., Chile 80 H3
Hot, Thailand 34 C5
Hot Creek Range, U.S.A. 72 G5
Hot Springs, Ark., U.S.A. 71 H8
Hot Springs, S. Dak., U.S.A. 70 D3
Hotagen, Sweden 8 E16
Hotan, China 30 C2
Hotazel, S. Africa 48 D3
Hotchkiss, U.S.A. 73 G10
Hotham, C., Australia 52 B5
Hoting, Sweden 8 D17
Houck, U.S.A. 73 J9
Houffalize, Belgium 15 D5
Houghton, U.S.A. 70 B10
Houghton L., U.S.A. 68 C3
Houghton-le-Spring, U.K. 10 C6
Houhora Heads, N.Z. 51 F4
Houlton, U.S.A. 63 C6
Houma, U.S.A. 71 L9
Houston, Canada 64 C3
Houston, Mo., U.S.A. 71 G9
Houston, Tex., U.S.A. 71 L7
Houtman Abrolhos, Australia 53 E1
Hovd, Mongolia 30 B4
Hove, U.K. 11 G7
Hoveyzeh, Iran 39 D6
Hövsgöl Nuur, Mongolia 30 A5
Howard, Australia 55 D5
Howard, Kans., U.S.A. 71 G6
Howard, S. Dak., U.S.A. 70 C6
Howard I., Australia 54 A2
Howard L., Canada 65 A7
Howe, U.S.A. 72 E7
Howe, C., Australia 55 F5
Howell, U.S.A. 68 D4
Howick, S. Africa 49 D5
Howick Group, Australia 54 A4
Howitt, L., Australia 55 D2
Howland I., Pac. Oc. 56 G10
Howley, U.S.A. 72 E6
Howrah = Haora, India 37 H16
Howth Hd., Ireland 13 C5
Hoy, U.K. 12 C5

Høyanger, Norway 9 F12
Hoyerswerda, Germany 16 C8
Hpungan Pass, Burma 37 F20
Hradec Králové, Czech. 16 C8
Hrodna, Belarus 17 B12
Hrodzyanka, Belarus 17 B15
Hron →, Slovak Rep. 17 E10
Hrvatska = Croatia ■, Europe 16 F9
Hrymayliv, Ukraine 17 D14
Hsenwi, Burma 37 H20
Hsiamen = Xiamen, China 31 D6
Hsian = Xi'an, China 31 C5
Hsinhailien = Lianyungang, China 31 C6
Hsüchou = Xuzhou, China 31 C6
Hua Hin, Thailand 34 F5
Huacho, Peru 78 F3
Huachón, Peru 78 F3
Huai He →, China 31 C6
Huainan, China 31 C6
Huairou, China 31 B6
Hualapai Peak, U.S.A. 73 J7
Huallaga →, Peru 78 E3
Huambo, Angola 47 G3
Huancabamba, Peru 78 E3
Huancane, Peru 78 G5
Huancapi, Peru 78 F4
Huancavelica, Peru 78 F3
Huancayo, Peru 78 F3
Huang Hai = Yellow Sea, China 31 C7
Huang He →, China 31 C6
Huangshi, China 31 C6
Huánuco, Peru 78 E3
Huaraz, Peru 78 E3
Huarmey, Peru 78 F3
Huascarán, Peru 78 E3
Huasco, Chile 80 B2
Huatabampo, Mexico 74 B3
Huayllay, Peru 78 F3
Hubbard, U.S.A. 71 K6
Hubbart Pt., Canada 65 B10
Hubei □, China 31 C6
Hubli-Dharwad = Dharwad, India 36 M9
Huddersfield, U.K. 10 D6
Hudiksvall, Sweden 9 F17
Hudson, Canada 65 C10
Hudson, Mich., U.S.A. 68 E3
Hudson, N.Y., U.S.A. 68 D9
Hudson, Wis., U.S.A. 70 C8
Hudson, Wyo., U.S.A. 72 E9
Hudson →, U.S.A. 68 E8
Hudson Bay, N.W.T., Canada 61 C11
Hudson Bay, Sask., Canada 65 C8
Hudson Falls, U.S.A. 68 D9
Hudson Mts., Antarctica 5 D16
Hudson Str., Canada 61 B13
Hudson's Hope, Canada 64 B4
Hue, Vietnam 34 D9
Huelva, Spain 19 D2
Huesca, Spain 19 A5
Hugh →, Australia 54 D1
Hughenden, Australia 54 C3
Hughes, Australia 53 F4
Hughli →, India 37 J16
Hugo, U.S.A. 71 H7
Hugoton, U.S.A. 71 G4
Huila, Nevado del, Colombia 78 C3
Huinca Renancó, Argentina 80 C4
Huize, China 30 D5
Hukawng Valley, Burma 37 F20
Hukuntsi, Botswana 48 C3
Hulayfā', Si. Arabia 38 E4
Huld, Mongolia 30 B5
Hull = Kingston upon Hull, U.K. 10 D7
Hull, Canada 62 C4
Hull →, U.K. 10 D7
Hulst, Neths. 15 C4
Hulun Nur, China 31 B6
Humahuaca, Argentina 80 A3
Humaitá, Brazil 78 E6
Humaitá, Paraguay 80 B5
Humansdorp, S. Africa 48 E3
Humbe, Angola 48 B1
Humber →, U.K. 10 D7
Humberside □, U.K. 10 D7
Humble, U.S.A. 71 L8
Humboldt, Canada 65 C7
Humboldt, Iowa, U.S.A. 70 D7
Humboldt, Tenn., U.S.A. 71 H10
Humboldt →, U.S.A. 72 F4
Humboldt Gletscher, Greenland 4 B4
Hume, L., Australia 55 F4
Humenné, Slovak Rep. 17 D11
Humphreys Peak, U.S.A. 73 J8
Hūn, Libya 45 C8
Húnaflói, Iceland 8 D3
Hunan □, China 31 D6
Hundred Mile House, Canada 64 C4
Hunedoara, Romania 17 F12
Hungary ■, Europe 17 E10
Hungary, Plain of, Europe 6 F9
Hungerford, Australia 55 D3
Hŭngnam, N. Korea 31 C7
Hunsberge, Namibia 48 D2
Hunsrück, Germany 16 D4

Hunstanton, U.K. 10 E8
Hunter, U.S.A. 70 B6
Hunter I., Australia 54 G3
Hunter I., Canada 64 C3
Hunter Ra., Australia 55 E5
Hunterville, N.Z. 51 H5
Huntingburg, U.S.A. 68 F2
Huntingdon, Canada 62 C5
Huntingdon, U.K. 11 E7
Huntingdon, U.S.A. 68 E6
Huntington, Ind., U.S.A. 68 E3
Huntington, Oreg., U.S.A. 72 D5
Huntington, Utah, U.S.A. 72 G8
Huntington, W. Va., U.S.A. 68 F4
Huntington Beach, U.S.A. 73 K5
Huntington Park, U.S.A. 73 K4
Huntly, N.Z. 51 G5
Huntly, U.K. 12 D6
Huntsville, Canada 62 C4
Huntsville, Ala., U.S.A. 69 H2
Huntsville, Tex., U.S.A. 71 K7
Huonville, Australia 54 G4
Hupeh = Hubei □, China 31 C6
Ḥūr, Iran 39 D8
Hurley, N. Mex., U.S.A. 73 K9
Hurley, Wis., U.S.A. 70 B9
Huron, U.S.A. 70 C5
Huron, L., U.S.A. 68 C4
Hurricane, U.S.A. 73 H7
Hurunui →, N.Z. 51 K4
Húsavík, Iceland 8 C5
Huşi, Romania 17 E15
Huskvarna, Sweden 9 H16
Hussar, Canada 64 C6
Hustadvika, Norway 8 E12
Hutchinson, Kans., U.S.A. 71 F6
Hutchinson, Minn., U.S.A. 70 C7
Huttig, U.S.A. 71 J8
Hutton, Mt., Australia 55 D4
Huy, Belgium 15 D5
Hvammstangi, Iceland 8 D3
Hvar, Croatia 20 C7
Hvítá →, Iceland 8 D3
Hwachon, Zimbabwe 47 H5
Hwang Ho = Huang He →, China 31 C6
Hwange, Zimbabwe 47 H5
Hwange Nat. Park, Zimbabwe 48 B4
Hyannis, U.S.A. 70 E4
Hyargas Nuur, Mongolia 30 B4
Hyden, Australia 53 F2
Hyderabad, India 36 L11
Hyderabad, Pakistan 36 G6
Hyères, France 18 E7
Hyères, Is. d', France 18 E7
Hyland →, Canada 64 B3
Hyndman Peak, U.S.A. 72 E6
Hyōgo □, Japan 29 G7
Hyrum, U.S.A. 72 F8
Hysham, U.S.A. 72 C10
Hythe, U.K. 11 F9
Hyūga, Japan 29 H5
Hyvinge = Hyvinkää, Finland 9 F21
Hyvinkää, Finland 9 F21

I

I-n-Gall, Niger 44 E6
Iaco →, Brazil 78 E5
Iakora, Madag. 49 C8
Ialomița →, Romania 17 F14
Iași, Romania 17 E14
Iba, Phil. 33 A6
Ibadan, Nigeria 44 G5
Ibagué, Colombia 78 C3
Ibar →, Serbia, Yug. 21 C9
Ibaraki □, Japan 29 F10
Ibarra, Ecuador 78 C3
Iberian Peninsula, Europe 6 G5
Iberville, Canada 62 C5
Iberville, Lac d', Canada 62 A5
Ibi, Nigeria 44 G6
Ibiá, Brazil 79 G9
Ibicuy, Argentina 80 C5
Ibioapaba, Sa. da, Brazil 79 D10
Ibiza, Spain 19 C6
Ibonma, Indonesia 33 E8
Ibotirama, Brazil 79 F10
Ibrāhīm →, Lebanon 41 A4
Ibu, Indonesia 33 D7
Ibusuki, Japan 29 J5
Icá, Peru 78 F3
Içá →, Brazil 78 D5
Içana, Brazil 78 C5
İçel = Mersin, Turkey 23 G5
Iceland ■, Europe 8 D4
Icha, Russia 25 D16
Ich'ang = Yichang, China 31 C6
Ichchapuram, India 37 K14
Ichihara, Japan 29 G10
Ichikawa, Japan 29 G9
Ichilo →, Bolivia 78 G6
Ichinohe, Japan 28 D10
Ichinomiya, Japan 29 G8
Ichinoseki, Japan 28 E10
Icy Str., U.S.A. 64 C6
Ida Grove, U.S.A. 70 D7
Ida Valley, Australia 53 E3

Idabel, U.S.A. 71 J7
Idaho □, U.S.A. 72 D6
Idaho City, U.S.A. 72 E6
Idaho Falls, U.S.A. 72 E7
Idaho Springs, U.S.A. . 72 G11
Idar-Oberstein, Germany 16 D4
Idd el Ghanam, Sudan ... 45 F9
Iddan, Somali Rep. 40 F4
Idehan, Libya 45 C7
Idehan Marzūq, Libya . 45 D7
Idelès, Algeria 44 D6
Idfû, Egypt 45 D11
Ídhi Óros, Greece ... 21 G11
Ídhra, Greece 21 F10
Idi, Indonesia 32 C1
Idiofa, Zaïre 46 E3
Idlib, Syria 38 C3
Idutywa, S. Africa ... 49 E4
Ieper, Belgium 15 D2
Ierápetra, Greece ... 21 G11
Iesi, Italy 20 C5
'Ifal, W. al →, Si. Arabia 38 D2
Ifanadiana, Madag. ... 49 C8
Ife, Nigeria 44 G5
Iffley, Australia 54 B3
Ifni, Morocco 44 C2
Iforas, Adrar des, Mali 44 E5
Ifould, L., Australia .. 53 F5
Igarapava, Brazil 79 H9
Igarapé Açu, Brazil .. 79 D9
Igarka, Russia 24 C9
Igbetti, Nigeria 44 G5
Iggesund, Sweden ... 9 F17
Iglésias, Italy 20 E3
Igli, Algeria 44 B4
Igloolik, Canada 61 B11
Ignace, Canada 62 C1
İğneada Burnu, Turkey 21 D13
Igoumenítsa, Greece . 21 E9
Iguaçu →, Brazil 80 B6
Iguaçu, Cat. del, Brazil 80 B6
Iguaçu Falls = Iguaçu Cat. del, Brazil 80 B6
Iguala, Mexico 74 D5
Igualada, Spain 19 B6
Iguassu = Iguaçu →, Brazil 80 B6
Iguatu, Brazil 79 E11
Iguéla, Gabon 46 E1
Iheya-Shima, Japan .. 29 L3
Ihosy, Madag. 49 C8
Ihotry, L., Madag. ... 49 C7
Ii, Finland 8 D21
Ii-Shima, Japan 29 L3
Iida, Japan 29 G8
Iijoki →, Finland 8 D21
Iisalmi, Finland 8 E22
Iiyama, Japan 29 F9
Iizuka, Japan 29 H5
Ijebu-Ode, Nigeria ... 44 G5
IJmuiden, Neths. 15 B4
IJssel →, Neths. 15 B5
IJsselmeer, Neths. ... 15 B5
Ikaría, Greece 21 F12
Ikeda, Japan 29 G6
Ikela, Zaïre 46 E4
Iki, Japan 29 H4
Ikopa →, Madag. ... 49 B8
Ilagan, Phil. 33 A6
Īlām, Iran 38 C5
Ilanskiy, Russia 25 D10
Iława, Poland 17 B10
Ilbilbie, Australia 54 C4
Ile-à-la-Crosse, Canada 65 B7
Ile-à-la-Crosse, Lac, Canada 65 B7
Île-de-France, France . 18 B5
Ilebo, Zaïre 46 E4
Ilek, Russia 24 D6
Ilek →, Russia 22 D9
Ilford, Canada 65 B9
Ilfracombe, Australia .. 54 C3
Ilfracombe, U.K. 11 F3
Ilhéus, Brazil 79 F11
Ili →, Kazakhstan ... 24 E8
Ilich, Kazakhstan 24 E7
Iliff, U.S.A. 70 E3
Iligan, Phil. 33 C6
Ilion, U.S.A. 68 D8
Ilkeston, U.K. 10 E6
Illampu = Ancohuma, Nevada, Bolivia ... 78 G5
Illana B., Phil. 33 C6
Illapel, Chile 80 C2
Iller →, Germany ... 16 D6
Illimani, Bolivia 78 G5
Illinois □, U.S.A. ... 67 C9
Illinois →, U.S.A. ... 67 C8
Illium = Troy, Turkey . 21 E12
Ilmajoki, Finland 9 E20
Ilmen, Ozero, Russia . 22 C5
Ilo, Peru 78 G4
Iloilo, Phil. 33 B6
Ilorin, Nigeria 44 G5
Ilwaki, Indonesia 33 F7
Imabari, Japan 29 G6
Imaloto →, Madag. . 49 C8
Imandra, Ozero, Russia 22 A5
Imari, Japan 29 H4
Imbler, U.S.A. 72 D5
imeni 26 Bakinskikh Komissarov = Neftçala, Azerbaijan 23 G8
imeni 26 Bakinskikh Komissarov, Turkmenistan ... 23 G9
Imeni Poliny Osipenko, Russia 25 D14
Imeri, Serra, Brazil ... 78 C5
Imerimandroso, Madag. 49 B8
Imi, Ethiopia 40 F3

Imlay, U.S.A. 72 F4
Immingham, U.K. 10 D7
Immokalee, U.S.A. ... 69 M5
Imola, Italy 20 B4
Imperatriz, Brazil 79 E9
Impéria, Italy 20 C3
Imperial, Canada 65 C7
Imperial, Calif., U.S.A. 73 K6
Imperial, Nebr., U.S.A. 70 E4
Imperial Dam, U.S.A. . 73 K6
Imperieuse Reef, Australia 52 C2
Impfondo, Congo 46 D3
Imphal, India 37 G18
İmroz = Gökçeada, Turkey 21 D11
Imuruan B., Phil. 33 B5
In Belbel, Algeria 44 C5
In Salah, Algeria 44 C5
Ina, Japan 29 G8
Inangahua Junction, N.Z. 51 J3
Inanwatan, Indonesia . 33 E8
Iñapari, Peru 78 F5
Inari, Finland 8 B22
Inarijärvi, Finland ... 8 B22
Inawashiro-Ko, Japan . 28 F10
Inca, Spain 19 C7
İnce-Burnu, Turkey .. 23 F5
Inchon, S. Korea 31 C7
İncirliova, Turkey 21 F12
Incomáti →, Mozam. 49 D5
Indalsälven →, Sweden 9 E17
Indaw, Burma 37 G20
Independence, Calif., U.S.A. 73 H4
Independence, Iowa, U.S.A. 70 D9
Independence, Kans., U.S.A. 71 G7
Independence, Mo., U.S.A. 70 F7
Independence, Oreg., U.S.A. 72 D2
Independence Fjord, Greenland 4 A6
Independence Mts., U.S.A. 72 F5
India ■, Asia 36 K11
Indian →, U.S.A. ... 69 M5
Indian Cabins, Canada 64 B5
Indian Harbour, Canada 63 B8
Indian Head, Canada . 65 C8
Indian Ocean 26 J10
Indiana, U.S.A. 68 E6
Indiana □, U.S.A. ... 68 E3
Indianapolis, U.S.A. .. 68 F2
Indianola, Iowa, U.S.A. 70 E8
Indianola, Miss., U.S.A. 71 J9
Indiga, Russia 22 A8
Indigirka →, Russia . 25 B15
Indio, U.S.A. 73 K5
Indonesia ■, Asia ... 32 F5
Indore, India 36 H9
Indramayu, Indonesia . 33 G13
Indravati →, India .. 37 K12
Indre →, France 18 C4
Indus →, Pakistan .. 36 G5
İnebolu, Turkey 23 F5
Ingende, Zaïre 46 E3
Ingham, Australia 54 B4
Ingleborough, U.K. .. 10 C5
Inglewood, Queens., Australia 55 D5
Inglewood, Vic., Australia 55 F3
Inglewood, N.Z. 51 H5
Inglewood, U.S.A. ... 73 K4
Ingólfshöfði, Iceland . 8 E5
Ingolstadt, Germany . 16 D6
Ingomar, U.S.A. 72 C10
Ingonish, Canada 63 C7
Ingraj Bazar, India ... 37 G16
Ingrid Christensen Coast, Antarctica .. 5 C6
Ingulec = Inhulec, Ukraine 23 E5
Ingwavuma, S. Africa . 49 D5
Inhaca, I., Mozam. .. 49 D5
Inhafenga, Mozam. .. 49 C5
Inhambane, Mozam. .. 49 C6
Inhambane □, Mozam. 49 C5
Inhaminga, Mozam. .. 47 H7
Inharrime, Mozam. ... 49 C6
Inharrime →, Mozam. 49 C6
Inhulec, Ukraine 23 E5
Ining = Yining, China . 24 E9
Inírida →, Colombia . 78 C5
Inishbofin, Ireland ... 13 C1
Inishmore, Ireland ... 13 C2
Inishowen Pen., Ireland 13 A4
Injune, Australia 55 D4
Inklin, Canada 64 B2
Inklin →, Canada ... 64 B2
Inkom, U.S.A. 72 E7
Inle L., Burma 37 J20
Inn →, Austria 16 D7
Innamincka, Australia . 55 D3
Inner Hebrides, U.K. . 12 E3
Inner Mongolia = Nei Monggol Zizhiqu □, China 31 B6
Inner Sound, U.K. ... 12 D3
Innetalling I., Canada . 62 A4
Innisfail, Australia 54 B4
Innisfail, Canada 64 C6
In'no-shima, Japan ... 29 G6
Innsbruck, Austria ... 16 E6
Inny →, Ireland 13 C4
Inongo, Zaïre 46 E3
Inoucdjouac = Inukjuak, Canada .. 61 C12
Inowrocław, Poland .. 17 B10

Inquisivi, Bolivia 78 G5
Inscription, C., Australia 53 E1
Insein, Burma 37 L20
Inta, Russia 22 A11
Interior, U.S.A. 70 D4
Interlaken, Switz. 16 E4
International Falls, U.S.A. 70 A8
Interview I., India 34 F2
Inthanon, Doi, Thailand 34 C5
Intiyaco, Argentina ... 80 B4
Inukjuak, Canada 61 C12
Inútil, B., Chile 80 G2
Inuvik, Canada 60 B6
Inveraray, U.K. 12 E3
Inverbervie, U.K. 12 E6
Invercargill, N.Z. 51 M2
Inverell, Australia 55 D5
Invergordon, U.K. ... 12 D4
Invermere, Canada ... 64 C5
Inverness, Canada ... 63 C7
Inverness, U.K. 12 D4
Inverness, U.S.A. 69 L4
Inverurie, U.K. 12 D6
Inverway, Australia ... 52 C4
Investigator Group, Australia 55 E1
Investigator Str., Australia 55 F2
Inya, Russia 24 D9
Inyo Mts., U.S.A. ... 73 H5
Inyokern, U.S.A. 73 J5
Inza, Russia 22 D8
Iô-Jima, Japan 29 J5
Ioánnina, Greece 21 E9
Iola, U.S.A. 71 G7
Iona, U.K. 12 E2
Ione, Calif., U.S.A. .. 72 G3
Ione, Wash., U.S.A. . 72 B5
Ionia, U.S.A. 68 D3
Ionian Is. = Iónioi Nísoi, Greece 21 E9
Ionian Sea, Medit. S. . 21 E7
Iónioi Nísoi, Greece . 21 E9
Íos, Greece 21 F11
Iowa □, U.S.A. 70 D8
Iowa City, U.S.A. 70 E9
Iowa Falls, U.S.A. ... 70 D8
Ipameri, Brazil 79 G9
Ipatinga, Brazil 79 G10
Ipiales, Colombia 78 C3
Ipin = Yibin, China .. 30 D5
Ipixuna, Brazil 78 E4
Ipoh, Malaysia 34 Q14
Ippy, C.A.R. 45 G9
Ipsala, Turkey 21 D12
Ipswich, Australia 55 D5
Ipswich, U.K. 11 E9
Ipswich, U.S.A. 70 C5
Ipu, Brazil 79 D10
Iqaluit, Canada 61 B13
Iquique, Chile 78 H4
Iquitos, Peru 78 D4
Irabu-Jima, Japan 29 M2
Iracoubo, Fr. Guiana . 79 B8
Irafshān, Iran 39 E9
Iráklion, Greece 21 G11
Iran ■, Asia 39 C7
Iran, Gunung-Gunung, Malaysia 32 D4
Iran Ra. = Iran, Gunung-Gunung, Malaysia 32 D4
Īränshahr, Iran 39 E9
Irapuato, Mexico 74 C4
Iraq ■, Asia 38 C5
Irbid, Jordan 41 C4
Irbid □, Jordan 41 C5
Irebu, Zaïre 46 E3
Ireland ■, Europe ... 13 D4
Ireland's Eye, Ireland 13 C5
Iret, Russia 25 C16
Irian Jaya □, Indonesia 33 E9
Iringa, Tanzania 46 D4
Iriomote-Jima, Japan . 29 M1
Iriri →, Brazil 79 D8
Irish Republic ■, Europe 13 D4
Irish Sea, U.K. 10 D3
Irkineyeva, Russia ... 25 D10
Irkutsk, Russia 25 D11
Irma, Canada 65 C6
Iró-Zaki, Japan 29 G9
Iron Baron, Australia . 55 E2
Iron Gate = Portile de Fier, Europe 17 F12
Iron Knob, Australia .. 55 E2
Iron Mountain, U.S.A. 68 C1
Iron Ra., Australia ... 54 A3
Iron River, U.S.A. ... 70 B10
Ironbridge, U.K. 11 E5
Ironstone Kopje, Botswana 48 D3
Ironton, Mo., U.S.A. . 71 G9
Ironton, Ohio, U.S.A. . 68 F4
Ironwood, U.S.A. 70 B9
Iroquois Falls, Canada 62 C3
Irpin, Ukraine 17 C16
Irrara Cr. →, Australia 55 D4
Irrawaddy □, Burma . 37 L19
Irrawaddy →, Burma 37 M19
Irtysh →, Russia 24 C7
Irumu, Zaïre 46 D5
Irún, Spain 19 A5
Irunea = Pamplona, Spain 19 A5
Irvine, Canada 65 D6
Irvine, U.K. 12 F4
Irvine, U.S.A. 68 G4
Irvinestown, U.K. 13 B4
Irving, U.S.A. 71 J6
Irwin →, Australia ... 53 E1
Irymple, Australia 55 E3

Isaac →, Australia ... 54 C4
Isabel, U.S.A. 70 C4
Isabella, Phil. 33 C6
Isabella Ra., Australia 52 D3
Isafjarðardjúp, Iceland 8 C2
Ísafjörður, Iceland ... 8 C2
Isahaya, Japan 29 H5
Isangi, Zaïre 46 D4
Isar →, Germany ... 16 D7
Íschia, Italy 20 D5
Isdell →, Australia .. 52 C3
Ise, Japan 29 G8
Ise-Wan, Japan 29 G8
Isère □, France 18 D6
Isère →, France 18 D6
Isérnia, Italy 20 D6
Ishikari-Gawa →, Japan 28 C10
Ishikari-Sammyaku, Japan 28 C11
Ishikari-Wan, Japan .. 28 C10
Ishikawa □, Japan .. 29 F8
Ishim, Russia 24 D7
Ishim →, Russia 24 D8
Ishinomaki, Japan ... 28 E10
Ishioka, Japan 29 F10
Ishkuman, Pakistan .. 36 A8
Ishpeming, U.S.A. ... 68 B2
Isil Kul, Russia 24 D8
Isiolo, Kenya 46 D7
Isiro, Zaïre 46 D5
Isisford, Australia 54 C3
İskenderun, Turkey .. 23 G6
İskenderun Körfezi, Turkey 23 G6
İskür →, Bulgaria .. 21 C11
Iskut →, Canada ... 64 B2
Isla →, U.K. 12 E5
Islamabad, Pakistan .. 36 C8
Island →, Canada .. 64 A4
Island Falls, Canada . 62 C3
Island Falls, U.S.A. .. 63 C6
Island L., Canada 65 C10
Island Lagoon, Australia 55 E2
Island Pond, U.S.A. . 68 C10
Islands, B. of, Canada 63 C8
Islay, U.K. 12 F2
Isle →, France 18 D3
Isle aux Morts, Canada 63 C8
Isle of Wight □, U.K. 11 G6
Isle Royale, U.S.A. .. 70 A10
Isleta, U.S.A. 73 J10
Ismail = Izmayil, Ukraine 17 F15
Ismâ'ilîya, Egypt 45 B11
Ismay, U.S.A. 70 B2
Isna, Egypt 45 C11
Isparta, Turkey 23 G5
İspica, Italy 20 F6
Israel ■, Asia 41 D3
Issoire, France 18 D5
Issyk-Kul, Ozero = Ysyk-Köl, Ozero, Kyrgyzstan 24 E8
Istaihah, U.A.E. 39 F7
İstanbul, Turkey 21 D13
İstiaia, Greece 21 E10
Istokpoga, L., U.S.A. . 69 M5
Istra, Croatia 16 F7
İstranca Dağları, Turkey 21 D12
Istres, France 18 E6
Istria = Istra, Croatia . 16 F7
Itabaiana, Brazil 79 E11
Itaberaba, Brazil 79 F10
Itabira, Brazil 79 G10
Itabuna, Brazil 79 F11
Itaipú, Reprêsa de, Brazil 80 B6
Itaituba, Brazil 79 D7
Itajaí, Brazil 80 B7
Italy ■, Europe 20 C5
Itampolo, Madag. 49 C7
Itapecuru-Mirim, Brazil 79 D10
Itaperuna, Brazil 79 H10
Itapicuru →, Bahia, Brazil 79 F11
Itapicuru →, Maranhão, Brazil .. 79 D10
Itapipoca, Brazil 79 D11
Itaquatiara, Brazil 78 D7
Itaquí, Brazil 80 B5
Itatuba, Brazil 78 E6
Itchen →, U.K. 11 G6
Ithaca = Itháki, Greece 21 E9
Ithaca, U.S.A. 68 D7
Itháki, Greece 21 E9
Ito, Japan 29 G9
Itoigawa, Japan 29 F8
Itonamas →, Bolivia . 78 F6
Ittoqqortoormiit = Scoresbysund, Greenland 4 B6
Ituaçu, Brazil 79 F10
Ituiutaba, Brazil 79 G9
Itumbiara, Brazil 79 G9
Ituna, Canada 65 C8
Iturbe, Argentina 80 A3
Iturup, Ostrov, Russia 25 E15
Ituyuro →, Brazil ... 79 G10
Itzehoe, Germany ... 16 B5
Ivalo, Finland 8 B22
Ivalojoki →, Finland . 8 B22
Ivanava, Belarus 17 B13
Ivanhoe, N.S.W., Australia 55 E3
Ivanhoe, W. Austral., Australia 52 C4
Ivanhoe L., Canada .. 65 A7
Ivano-Frankivsk, Ukraine 17 D13
Ivano-Frankovsk = Ivano-Frankivsk, Ukraine 17 D13

Ivanovo = Ivanava, Belarus 17 B13
Ivanovo, Russia 22 C7
Ivato, Madag. 49 C8
Ivatsevichy, Belarus . 17 B13
Ivdel, Russia 22 B11
Ivory Coast ■, Africa 44 G3
Ivrea, Italy 20 B2
Ivujivik, Canada 61 B12
Iwahig, Phil. 32 C5
Iwaizumi, Japan 28 E10
Iwaki, Japan 29 F10
Iwakuni, Japan 29 G6
Iwamizawa, Japan ... 28 C10
Iwanai, Japan 28 C10
Iwata, Japan 29 G8
Iwate □, Japan 28 E10
Iwate-San, Japan 28 E10
Iwo, Nigeria 44 G5
Ixiamas, Bolivia 78 F5
Ixopo, S. Africa 49 E5
Iyo, Japan 29 H6
Izegem, Belgium 15 D3
Izena-Shima, Japan .. 29 L3
Izhevsk, Russia 22 C9
Izmayil, Ukraine 17 F15
İzmir, Turkey 21 E12
İzmit, Turkey 23 F4
İznik Gölü, Turkey ... 21 D13
Izra, Syria 41 C5
Izu-Shotō, Japan 29 G10
Izumi-sano, Japan ... 29 G7
Izumo, Japan 29 G6
Izyaslav, Ukraine 17 C14

J

Jabal Lubnān, Lebanon 41 B4
Jabalpur, India 36 H11
Jabbūl, Syria 38 B3
Jablah, Syria 38 C3
Jablanica, Macedonia . 21 D9
Jablonec, Czech. 16 C8
Jaboatão, Brazil 79 E11
Jaburu, Brazil 78 E6
Jaca, Spain 19 A5
Jacarei, Brazil 80 A7
Jacarèzinho, Brazil ... 80 A7
Jackman, U.S.A. 63 C5
Jacksboro, U.S.A. ... 71 J5
Jackson, Australia ... 55 D4
Jackson, Ala., U.S.A. . 69 K2
Jackson, Calif., U.S.A. 72 G3
Jackson, Ky., U.S.A. . 68 G4
Jackson, Mich., U.S.A. 68 D3
Jackson, Minn., U.S.A. 70 D7
Jackson, Miss., U.S.A. 71 J9
Jackson, Mo., U.S.A. . 71 G10
Jackson, Ohio, U.S.A. 68 F4
Jackson, Tenn., U.S.A. 69 H1
Jackson, Wyo., U.S.A. 72 E8
Jackson B., N.Z. 51 K2
Jackson L., U.S.A. ... 72 E8
Jacksons, N.Z. 51 K3
Jacksonville, Ala., U.S.A. 69 J3
Jacksonville, Fla., U.S.A. 69 K5
Jacksonville, Ill., U.S.A. 70 F9
Jacksonville, N.C., U.S.A. 69 H7
Jacksonville, Oreg., U.S.A. 72 E2
Jacksonville, Tex., U.S.A. 71 K7
Jacksonville Beach, U.S.A. 69 K5
Jacmel, Haiti 75 D10
Jacob Lake, U.S.A. .. 73 H7
Jacobabad, Pakistan . 36 E6
Jacobina, Brazil 79 F10
Jacques-Cartier, Mt., Canada 63 C6
Jacundá →, Brazil .. 79 D8
Jadotville = Likasi, Zaïre 46 G5
Jādū, Libya 45 B7
Jaén, Peru 78 E3
Jaén, Spain 19 D4
Jaffa = Tel Aviv-Yafo, Israel 41 C3
Jaffa, C., Australia ... 55 F2
Jaffna, Sri Lanka 36 Q12
Jagadhri, India 36 D10
Jagdalpur, India 37 K12
Jagersfontein, S. Africa 48 D4
Jagraon, India 36 D9
Jagtial, India 36 K11
Jaguariaíva, Brazil ... 80 A7
Jaguaribe →, Brazil . 79 D11
Jahrom, Iran 39 D7
Jailolo, Indonesia 33 D7
Jailolo, Selat, Indonesia 33 D7
Jaipur, India 36 F9
Jājarm, Iran 39 B8
Jakarta, Indonesia ... 33 G12
Jakobstad = Pietarsaari, Finland . 8 E20
Jal, U.S.A. 71 J3
Jalalabad, Afghan. ... 36 B7
Jalapa Enríquez, Mexico 74 D5
Jalasjärvi, Finland ... 9 E20
Jalgaon, Maharashtra, India 36 J10
Jalgaon, Maharashtra, India 36 J9
Jalībah, Iraq 38 D5

Jalna, India 36 K9
Jalón →, Spain 19 B5
Jalpaiguri, India 37 F16
Jaluit I., Pac. Oc. 56 G8
Jalūlā, Iraq 38 C5
Jamaica ■, W. Indies 74 J16
Jamalpur, Bangla. ... 37 G16
Jamalpur, India 37 G15
Jamanxim →, Brazil . 79 D7
Jambe, Indonesia 33 E8
Jambi, Indonesia 32 E2
Jambi □, Indonesia .. 32 E2
James →, U.S.A. ... 70 D6
James B., Canada ... 61 C11
James Ras., Australia 52 D5
James Ross I., Antarctica 5 C18
Jamestown, Australia 55 E2
Jamestown, S. Africa 48 E4
Jamestown, Ky., U.S.A. 68 G3
Jamestown, N. Dak., U.S.A. 70 B5
Jamestown, N.Y., U.S.A. 68 D6
Jamestown, Tenn., U.S.A. 69 G3
Jamilābād, Iran 39 C6
Jamkhandi, India 36 L9
Jammu, India 36 C9
Jammu & Kashmir □, India 36 B10
Jamnagar, India 36 H7
Jamrud, Pakistan 36 C7
Jämsä, Finland 9 F21
Jamshedpur, India ... 37 H15
Jämtland, Sweden ... 8 E15
Jan L., Canada 65 C8
Jan Mayen, Arctic ... 4 B7
Janakkala, Finland ... 9 F21
Jand, Pakistan 36 C8
Jandowae, Australia . 55 D5
Janesville, U.S.A. 70 D10
Janin, West Bank 41 C4
Januária, Brazil 79 G10
Jaora, India 36 H9
Japan ■, Asia 29 G8
Japan, Sea of, Asia .. 28 E7
Japan Trench, Pac. Oc. 56 D6
Japen = Yapen, Indonesia 33 E9
Japurá →, Brazil ... 78 D5
Jaque, Panama 78 B3
Jarābulus, Syria 38 B3
Jarama →, Spain ... 19 B4
Jarash, Jordan 41 C4
Jargalant = Hovd, Mongolia 30 B4
Jarīr, W. al →, Si. Arabia 38 E4
Jarosław, Poland 17 C12
Jarrahdale, Australia . 53 F2
Jarso, Ethiopia 45 G12
Järvenpää, Finland .. 9 F21
Jarvis I., Pac. Oc. ... 57 H12
Jarwa, India 37 F13
Jāsimīyah, Iraq 38 C5
Jasin, Malaysia 34 S15
Jāsk, Iran 39 E8
Jasło, Poland 17 D11
Jasper, Canada 64 C5
Jasper, Ala., U.S.A. .. 69 J2
Jasper, Fla., U.S.A. .. 69 K4
Jasper, Minn., U.S.A. 70 D6
Jasper, Tex., U.S.A. .. 71 K8
Jasper Nat. Park, Canada 64 C5
Jassy = Iaşi, Romania 17 E14
Jászberény, Hungary . 17 E10
Jataí, Brazil 79 G8
Jatibarang, Indonesia . 33 G13
Jatinegara, Indonesia . 33 G12
Játiva, Spain 19 C5
Jaú, Brazil 79 H9
Jauja, Peru 78 F3
Jaunpur, India 37 G13
Java = Jawa, Indonesia 33 G14
Java Sea, Indonesia .. 32 E3
Java Trench, Ind. Oc. . 56 H2
Javhlant = Ulyasutay, Mongolia 30 B4
Jawa, Indonesia 33 G14
Jay, U.S.A. 71 G7
Jaya, Puncak, Indonesia 33 F16
Jayanti, India 37 F16
Jayapura, Indonesia . 33 E10
Jayawijaya, Pegunungan, Indonesia 33 E9
Jaynagar, India 37 F15
Jayrūd, Syria 38 C3
Jayton, U.S.A. 71 J4
Jazīreh-ye Shīf, Iran . 39 D6
Jazzin, Lebanon 41 B4
Jean, U.S.A. 73 J6
Jean Marie River, Canada 64 A4
Jeanerette, U.S.A. ... 71 L9
Jeanette, Ostrov, Russia 25 B16
Jebba, Nigeria 44 G5
Jebel, Bahr el →, Sudan 45 G11
Jedburgh, U.K. 12 F6
Jedda = Jiddah, Si. Arabia 40 C2
Jędrzejów, Poland ... 17 C11
Jedway, Canada 64 C2
Jefferson, Iowa, U.S.A. 70 D7
Jefferson, Tex., U.S.A. 71 J7
Jefferson, Wis., U.S.A. 70 D10
Jefferson, Mt., Nev., U.S.A. 72 G5

Karatau

Jefferson, Mt., Oreg., U.S.A. 72 D3
Jefferson City, Mo., U.S.A. 70 F8
Jefferson City, Tenn., U.S.A. 69 G4
Jeffersonville, U.S.A. 68 F3
Jega, Nigeria 44 F5
Jēkabpils, Latvia 9 H21
Jelenia Góra, Poland 16 C8
Jelgava, Latvia 9 H20
Jellicoe, Canada 62 C2
Jemaja, Indonesia 32 D3
Jember, Indonesia 33 H15
Jembongan, Malaysia 32 C5
Jemeppe, Belgium 15 D5
Jena, Germany 16 C6
Jena, U.S.A. 71 K8
Jenkins, U.S.A. 68 G4
Jennings, U.S.A. 71 K8
Jennings →, Canada 64 B2
Jeparit, Australia 55 F3
Jequié, Brazil 79 F10
Jequitinhonha, Brazil 79 G10
Jequitinhonha →, Brazil 79 G11
Jerada, Morocco 44 B4
Jerantut, Malaysia 34 R15
Jérémie, Haiti 75 D10
Jerez de la Frontera, Spain 19 D2
Jerez de los Caballeros, Spain 19 C2
Jericho = Arīḥā, Syria 38 C3
Jericho = El Arīḥā, West Bank 41 D4
Jericho, Australia 54 C4
Jerilderie, Australia 55 F4
Jerome, U.S.A. 73 J8
Jersey, U.K. 11 H5
Jersey City, U.S.A. 68 E8
Jersey Shore, U.S.A. 68 E7
Jerseyville, U.S.A. 70 F9
Jerusalem, Israel 41 D4
Jervis B., Australia 55 F5
Jesselton = Kota Kinabalu, Malaysia 32 C5
Jessore, Bangla. 37 H16
Jesup, U.S.A. 69 K5
Jetmore, U.S.A. 71 F5
Jevnaker, Norway 9 F14
Jewett, U.S.A. 71 K6
Jeyḥūnābād, Iran 39 C6
Jeypore, India 37 K13
Jhal Jhao, Pakistan 36 F4
Jhalawar, India 36 G10
Jhang Maghiana, Pakistan 36 D8
Jhansi, India 36 G11
Jharsaguda, India 37 J14
Jhelum, Pakistan 36 C8
Jhelum →, Pakistan 36 D8
Jhunjhunu, India 36 E9
Jiamusi, China 31 B8
Ji'an, China 31 D6
Jiangcheng, China 30 D5
Jiangmen, China 31 D6
Jiangsu □, China 31 C7
Jiangxi □, China 31 D6
Jiaxing, China 31 C7
Jiayi, Taiwan 31 D7
Jibuti = Djibouti ■, Africa 40 E3
Jiddah, Si. Arabia 40 C2
Jido, India 37 E19
Jiggalong, Australia 52 D3
Jihlava, Czech. 16 D8
Jihlava →, Czech. 17 D9
Jijel, Algeria 44 A6
Jijiga, Ethiopia 40 F3
Jilin, China 31 B7
Jilin □, China 31 B7
Jilong, Taiwan 31 D7
Jima, Ethiopia 45 G12
Jiménez, Mexico 74 B4
Jinan, China 31 C6
Jindabyne, Australia 55 F4
Jindrichuv Hradeç, Czech. 16 D8
Jingdezhen, China 31 D6
Jinggu, China 30 D5
Jinhua, China 31 D6
Jining, Nei Mongol Zizhiqu, China 31 B6
Jining, Shandong, China 31 C6
Jinja, Uganda 46 D6
Jinnah Barrage, Pakistan 36 C7
Jinotega, Nic. 74 E7
Jinsha Jiang →, China 30 D5
Jinzhou, China 31 B7
Jiparaná →, Brazil 78 E6
Jipijapa, Ecuador 78 D2
Jisr ash Shughūr, Syria 38 C3
Jitarning, Australia 53 F2
Jitra, Malaysia 34 N13
Jiu →, Romania 17 F12
Jiujiang, China 31 D6
Jixi, China 31 B8
Jizān, Si. Arabia 40 D3
Jizō-Zaki, Japan 29 G6
Jizzakh, Uzbekistan 24 E7
Joaçaba, Brazil 80 B6
João Pessoa, Brazil 79 E12
Joaquín V. González, Argentina 80 B4
Jodhpur, India 36 F8
Joensuu, Finland 22 B4
Jofane, Mozam. 49 C5
Jõgeva, Estonia 9 G22
Joggins, Canada 63 C7
Jogjakarta = Yogyakarta, Indonesia 33 G14
Johannesburg, S. Africa 49 D4
John Day, U.S.A. 72 D4
John Day →, U.S.A. 72 D3
John H. Kerr Reservoir, U.S.A. 69 G6
John o' Groats, U.K. 12 C5
John's Ra., Australia 54 C1
Johnson, U.S.A. 71 G4
Johnson City, N.Y., U.S.A. 68 D8
Johnson City, Tenn., U.S.A. 69 G4
Johnson City, Tex., U.S.A. 71 K5
Johnson's Crossing, Canada 64 A2
Johnston, L., Australia 53 F3
Johnston Falls = Mambilima Falls, Zambia 46 G5
Johnston I., Pac. Oc. 57 F11
Johnstone Str., Canada 64 C3
Johnstown, N.Y., U.S.A. 68 D8
Johnstown, Pa., U.S.A. 68 E6
Johor □, Malaysia 34 S16
Johor Baharu, Malaysia 34 T16
Jõhvi, Estonia 9 G22
Joinvile, Brazil 80 B7
Joinville I., Antarctica 5 C18
Jokkmokk, Sweden 8 C18
Jökulsá á Bru →, Iceland 8 D6
Jökulsá á Fjöllum →, Iceland 8 C5
Jolfā, Āzarbājān-e Sharqī, Iran 38 B5
Jolfā, Eşfahan, Iran 39 C6
Joliet, U.S.A. 68 E1
Joliette, Canada 62 C5
Jolo, Phil. 33 C6
Jombang, Indonesia 33 G15
Jome, Indonesia 33 E7
Jonava, Lithuania 9 J21
Jones Sound, Canada 4 B3
Jonesboro, Ark., U.S.A. 71 H9
Jonesboro, Ill., U.S.A. 71 G10
Jonesboro, La., U.S.A. 71 J8
Jonesport, U.S.A. 63 D6
Joniškis, Lithuania 9 H20
Jönköping, Sweden 9 H16
Jonquière, Canada 63 C5
Joplin, U.S.A. 71 G7
Jordan, U.S.A. 72 C10
Jordan ■, Asia 41 E5
Jordan →, Asia 41 D4
Jordan Valley, U.S.A. 72 E5
Jorhat, India 37 F19
Jörn, Sweden 8 D19
Jorong, Indonesia 32 E4
Jørpeland, Norway 9 G11
Jos, Nigeria 44 G6
Joseph, U.S.A. 72 D5
Joseph, L., Canada 63 B6
Joseph Bonaparte G., Australia 52 B4
Joseph City, U.S.A. 73 J8
Jostedalsbreen, Norway 9 F12
Jotunheimen, Norway 9 F13
Jourdanton, U.S.A. 71 L5
Joussard, Canada 64 B5
Juan de Fuca Str., Canada 72 B2
Juan de Nova, Ind. Oc. 49 B7
Juan Fernández, Arch. de, Pac. Oc. 57 L20
Juankoski, Finland 8 E23
Juárez, Argentina 80 D5
Juàzeiro, Brazil 79 E10
Juàzeiro do Norte, Brazil 79 E11
Jubayl, Lebanon 41 A4
Jubbah, Si. Arabia 38 D4
Jubbulpore = Jabalpur, India 36 H11
Jubilee L., Australia 53 E4
Juby, C., Morocco 44 C2
Júcar →, Spain 19 C5
Juchitán, Mexico 74 D5
Judaea = Har Yehuda, Israel 41 D3
Judith →, U.S.A. 72 C9
Judith Gap, U.S.A. 72 C9
Jugoslavia = Yugoslavia ■, Europe 21 B9
Juiz de Fora, Brazil 79 H10
Julesburg, U.S.A. 70 E3
Juli, Peru 78 G5
Julia Cr. →, Australia 54 C3
Julia Creek, Australia 54 C3
Juliaca, Peru 78 G4
Julian, U.S.A. 73 K5
Julianehåb, Greenland 4 C5
Jullundur, India 36 D9
Jumet, Belgium 15 D4
Jumilla, Spain 19 C5
Jumla, Nepal 37 E13
Jumna = Yamuna →, India 37 G12
Junagadh, India 36 J7
Junction, Tex., U.S.A. 71 K5
Junction, Utah, U.S.A. 73 G7
Junction B., Australia 54 A1
Junction City, Kans., U.S.A. 70 F6
Junction City, Oreg., U.S.A. 72 D2
Junction Pt., Australia 54 A1
Jundah, Australia 54 C3
Jundiaí, Brazil 80 A7
Juneau, U.S.A. 60 C6
Junee, Australia 55 E4
Jungfrau, Switz. 16 E4
Junggar Pendi, China 30 B3
Junín, Argentina 80 C4
Junín de los Andes, Argentina 80 D2
Jūniyah, Lebanon 41 B4
Juntura, U.S.A. 72 E4
Jupiter →, Canada 63 C7
Jur, Nahr el →, Sudan 45 G10
Jura = Schwäbische Alb, Germany 16 D5
Jura, Europe 16 E4
Jura, U.K. 12 F3
Jura, Sd. of, U.K. 12 F3
Jurado, Colombia 78 B3
Jurbarkas, Lithuania 9 J20
Jūrmala, Latvia 9 H20
Juruá →, Brazil 78 D5
Juruena →, Brazil 78 E7
Juruti, Brazil 79 D7
Justo Daract, Argentina 80 C3
Jutland = Jylland, Denmark 9 H13
Juventud, I. de la, Cuba 75 C8
Juwain, Afghan. 36 D2
Jūy Zar, Iran 38 C5
Jylland, Denmark 9 H13
Jyväskylä, Finland 9 E21

K

K2, Mt., Pakistan 36 B10
Kaap Plateau, S. Africa 48 D3
Kaapkruis, Namibia 48 C1
Kaapstad = Cape Town, S. Africa 48 E2
Kabaena, Indonesia 33 F6
Kabala, S. Leone 44 G2
Kabale, Uganda 46 E6
Kabalo, Zaïre 46 F5
Kabambare, Zaïre 46 E5
Kabanjahe, Indonesia 32 D1
Kabara, Mali 44 E4
Kabardino-Balkar Republic = Kabardino Balkaria □, Russia 23 F7
Kabardino Balkaria □, Russia 23 F7
Kabare, Indonesia 33 E8
Kabarega Falls, Uganda 46 D6
Kabasalan, Phil. 33 C6
Kabba, Nigeria 44 G6
Kabinakagami L., Canada 62 C3
Kabīr, Zab al →, Iraq 38 C4
Kabkabīyah, Sudan 45 F9
Kabompo →, Zambia 47 G4
Kabongo, Zaïre 46 F5
Kabra, Australia 54 C5
Kabūd Gonbad, Iran 39 B8
Kābul, Afghan. 36 B6
Kābul □, Afghan. 36 B6
Kabul →, Pakistan 36 C8
Kaburuang, Indonesia 33 D7
Kabwe, Zambia 47 G5
Kachchh, Gulf of, India 36 H6
Kachchh, Rann of, India 36 H7
Kachin □, Burma 37 F20
Kachiry, Kazakhstan 24 D8
Kaçkar, Turkey 23 F7
Kadan Kyun, Burma 34 F5
Kadina, Australia 55 E2
Kadiyevka = Stakhanov, Ukraine 23 E6
Kadoka, U.S.A. 70 D4
Kadoma, Zimbabwe 47 H5
Kâdugli, Sudan 45 F10
Kaduna, Nigeria 44 F6
Kaédi, Mauritania 44 E2
Kaelé, Cameroon 45 F7
Kaesŏng, N. Korea 31 C7
Kāf, Si. Arabia 38 D3
Kafakumba, Zaïre 46 F4
Kafan = Kapan, Armenia 23 G8
Kafanchan, Nigeria 44 G6
Kaffrine, Senegal 44 F1
Kafia Kingi, Sudan 45 G9
Kafirévs, Ákra, Greece 21 E11
Kafue →, Zambia 47 H5
Kafulwe, Zambia 46 F5
Kaga Bandoro, C.A.R. 45 G8
Kagan, Uzbekistan 24 F7
Kagawa □, Japan 29 G6
Kagoshima, Japan 29 J5
Kagoshima □, Japan 29 J5
Kagul = Cahul, Moldova 17 F15
Kahak, Iran 39 B6
Kahama, Tanzania 46 E6
Kahayan →, Indonesia 32 E4
Kahemba, Zaïre 46 F3
Kahniah →, Canada 64 B4
Kahnūj, Iran 39 E8
Kahoka, U.S.A. 70 E9
Kahoolawe, U.S.A. 66 H16
Kahramanmaraş, Turkey 23 G6
Kai, Kepulauan, Indonesia 33 F8
Kai Besar, Indonesia 33 F8
Kai Is. = Kai, Kepulauan, Indonesia 33 F8
Kai Kecil, Indonesia 33 F8
Kaiama, Nigeria 44 G5
Kaiapoi, N.Z. 51 K4
Kaieteur Falls, Guyana 78 B7
Kaifeng, China 31 C6
Kaikohe, N.Z. 51 F4
Kaikoura, N.Z. 51 K4
Kaikoura Ra., N.Z. 51 J4
Kailua Kona, U.S.A. 66 J17
Kaimana, Indonesia 33 E8
Kaimanawa Mts., N.Z. 51 H5
Kaingaroa Forest, N.Z. 51 H6
Kainji Res., Nigeria 44 F5
Kainuu, Finland 8 D23
Kaipara Harbour, N.Z. 51 G5
Kaipokok B., Canada 63 B8
Kaironi, Indonesia 33 E8
Kairouan, Tunisia 44 A7
Kaiserslautern, Germany 16 D4
Kaitaia, N.Z. 51 F4
Kaitangata, N.Z. 51 M2
Kaiwi Channel, U.S.A. 66 H16
Kajaani, Finland 8 D22
Kajabbi, Australia 54 B3
Kajana = Kajaani, Finland 8 D22
Kajang, Malaysia 34 S14
Kajo Kaji, Sudan 45 H11
Kaka, Sudan 45 F11
Kakabeka Falls, Canada 62 C2
Kakamas, S. Africa 48 D3
Kakamega, Kenya 46 D6
Kakanui Mts., N.Z. 51 L3
Kake, Japan 29 G6
Kakegawa, Japan 29 G9
Kakeroma-Jima, Japan 29 K4
Kakhovka, Ukraine 23 E5
Kakhovske Vdskh., Ukraine 23 E5
Kakinada, India 37 L13
Kakisa →, Canada 64 A5
Kakisa L., Canada 64 A5
Kakogawa, Japan 29 G7
Kakwa →, Canada 64 C5
Kāl Gūsheh, Iran 39 D8
Kal Safīd, Iran 38 C5
Kalabagh, Pakistan 36 C7
Kalabahi, Indonesia 33 F6
Kalabo, Zambia 47 G4
Kalach, Russia 23 D7
Kaladan →, Burma 37 J18
Kalahari, Africa 48 C3
Kalahari Gemsbok Nat. Park, S. Africa 48 D3
Kalajoki, Finland 8 D20
Kālak, Iran 39 E8
Kalakamati, Botswana 49 C4
Kalakan, Russia 25 D12
Kalakh, Syria 38 C3
Kalama, U.S.A. 72 D2
Kalámai, Greece 21 F10
Kalamata = Kalámai, Greece 21 F10
Kalamazoo, U.S.A. 68 D3
Kalamazoo →, U.S.A. 68 D2
Kalannie, Australia 53 F2
Kalāntarī, Iran 39 C7
Kalao, Indonesia 33 F6
Kalaotoa, Indonesia 33 F6
Kalasin, Thailand 34 D7
Kalat, Pakistan 36 E5
Kalāteh, Iran 39 B7
Kalāteh-ye-Ganj, Iran 39 E8
Kalbarri, Australia 53 E1
Kalce, Slovenia 16 F8
Kale, Turkey 21 F13
Kalegauk Kyun, Burma 37 M20
Kalemie, Zaïre 46 F5
Kalewa, Burma 37 H19
Kalgan = Zhangjiakou, China 31 B6
Kalgoorlie-Boulder, Australia 53 F3
Kaliakra, Nos, Bulgaria 21 C13
Kalianda, Indonesia 32 F3
Kalibo, Phil. 33 B6
Kalima, Zaïre 46 E5
Kalimantan, Indonesia 32 E4
Kalimantan Barat □, Indonesia 32 E4
Kalimantan Selatan □, Indonesia 32 E5
Kalimantan Tengah □, Indonesia 32 E4
Kalimantan Timur □, Indonesia 32 D5
Kálimnos, Greece 21 F12
Kalinin = Tver, Russia 22 C6
Kaliningrad, Kaliningd., Russia 9 J19
Kaliningrad, Moskva, Russia 22 C6
Kalinkavichy, Belarus 17 B15
Kalinkovichi = Kalinkavichy, Belarus 17 B15
Kalispell, U.S.A. 72 B6
Kalisz, Poland 17 C10
Kaliua, Tanzania 46 F6
Kalix, Sweden 8 D20
Kalix →, Sweden 8 D20
Kalkaska, U.S.A. 68 C3
Kalkfeld, Namibia 48 C2
Kalkfontein, Botswana 48 C3
Kalkrand, Namibia 48 C2
Kallavesi, Finland 8 E22
Kallsjön, Sweden 8 E15
Kalmar, Sweden 9 H17
Kalmyk Republic = Kalmykia □, Russia 23 E8
Kalmykia □, Russia 23 E8
Kalmykovo, Kazakhstan 23 E9
Kalocsa, Hungary 17 E10
Kalomo, Zambia 47 H5
Kaluga, Russia 22 D6
Kalundborg, Denmark 9 J14
Kalush, Ukraine 17 D13
Kalutara, Sri Lanka 36 R11
Kalya, Russia 22 B10
Kama →, Russia 22 C9
Kamaishi, Japan 28 E10
Kamaran, Yemen 40 D3
Kambalda, Australia 53 F3
Kambarka, Russia 22 C9
Kamchatka, P-ov., Russia 25 D16
Kamchatka Pen. = Kamchatka, P-ov., Russia 25 D16
Kamchiya →, Bulgaria 21 C12
Kamen, Russia 24 D9
Kamen-Rybolov, Russia 28 B6
Kamenjak, Rt., Croatia 16 F7
Kamenka, Russia 22 A7
Kamenka Bugskaya = Kamyanka-Buzka, Ukraine 17 C13
Kamensk Uralskiy, Russia 24 D7
Kamenskoye, Russia 25 C17
Kameoka, Japan 29 G7
Kamiah, U.S.A. 72 C5
Kamieskroon, S. Africa 48 E2
Kamilukuak, L., Canada 65 A8
Kamin-Kashyrskyy, Ukraine 17 C13
Kamina, Zaïre 46 F5
Kaminak L., Canada 65 A9
Kaminoyama, Japan 28 E10
Kamloops, Canada 64 C4
Kamo, Japan 28 F9
Kampala, Uganda 46 D6
Kampar, Malaysia 34 Q14
Kampar →, Indonesia 32 D2
Kampen, Neths. 15 B5
Kampot, Cambodia 34 G8
Kampuchea = Cambodia ■, Asia 34 F8
Kampung →, Indonesia 33 F9
Kampungbaru = Tolitoli, Indonesia 33 D6
Kamrau, Teluk, Indonesia 33 E8
Kamsack, Canada 65 C8
Kamskoye Vdkhr., Russia 22 C10
Kamuchawie L., Canada 65 B8
Kamui-Misaki, Japan 28 C10
Kamyanets-Podilskyy, Ukraine 17 D14
Kamyanka-Buzka, Ukraine 17 C13
Kāmyārān, Iran 38 C5
Kamyshin, Russia 23 D8
Kanaaupscow, Canada 62 B4
Kanab, U.S.A. 73 H7
Kanab →, U.S.A. 73 H7
Kanagi, Japan 28 D10
Kanairiktok →, Canada 63 A7
Kananga, Zaïre 46 F4
Kanarraville, U.S.A. 73 H7
Kanash, Russia 22 C8
Kanastraíon, Ákra = Palioúrion, Ákra, Greece 21 E10
Kanawha →, U.S.A. 68 F4
Kanazawa, Japan 29 F8
Kanchanaburi, Thailand 34 E5
Kanchenjunga, Nepal 37 F16
Kanchipuram, India 36 N11
Kanda Kanda, Zaïre 46 F4
Kandahar = Qandahār, Afghan. 36 D4
Kandalaksha, Russia 22 A5
Kandalakshkiy Zaliv, Russia 22 A5
Kandalu, Afghan. 36 E3
Kandangan, Indonesia 32 E5
Kandi, Benin 44 F5
Kandla, India 36 H7
Kandos, Australia 55 E4
Kandy, Sri Lanka 36 R12
Kane, U.S.A. 68 E6
Kane Basin, Greenland 4 B4
Kangān, Fārs, Iran 39 E7
Kangān, Hormozgān, Iran 39 E8
Kangar, Malaysia 34 N13
Kangaroo I., Australia 55 F2
Kangasala, Finland 9 F21
Kangāvar, Iran 39 C6
Kangean, Kepulauan, Indonesia 32 F5
Kangean Is. = Kangean, Kepulauan, Indonesia 32 F5
Kangiqsualujjuaq, Canada 61 C13
Kangiqsujuaq, Canada 61 B12
Kangirsuk, Canada 61 B13
Kango, Gabon 46 D2
Kangto, India 37 F18
Kaniapiskau →, Canada 63 A6
Kaniapiskau L., Canada 63 B6
Kanin, Poluostrov, Russia 22 A8
Kanin Nos, Mys, Russia 22 A7
Kanin Pen. = Kanin, Poluostrov, Russia 22 A8
Kaniva, Australia 55 F3
Kankaanpää, Finland 9 F20
Kankakee, U.S.A. 68 E2
Kankakee →, U.S.A. 68 E1
Kankan, Guinea 44 F3
Kankendy = Xankändi, Azerbaijan 23 G8
Kanker, India 37 J12
Kankunskiy, Russia 25 D13
Kannapolis, U.S.A. 69 H5
Kannauj, India 36 F11
Kannod, India 36 H10
Kano, Nigeria 44 F6
Kan'onji, Japan 29 G6
Kanowit, Malaysia 32 D4
Kanowna, Australia 53 F3
Kanoya, Japan 29 J5
Kanpetlet, Burma 37 J18
Kanpur, India 36 F12
Kansas □, U.S.A. 70 F6
Kansas →, U.S.A. 70 F7
Kansas City, Kans., U.S.A. 70 F7
Kansas City, Mo., U.S.A. 70 F7
Kansk, Russia 25 D10
Kansu = Gansu □, China 30 C5
Kantang, Thailand 34 J5
Kantō □, Japan 29 F9
Kantō-Sanchi, Japan 29 G9
Kanturk, Ireland 13 D3
Kanuma, Japan 29 F9
Kanus, Namibia 48 D2
Kanye, Botswana 48 C4
Kaohsiung = Gaoxiong, Taiwan 31 D7
Kaohsiung, Taiwan 31 D7
Kaokoveld, Namibia 48 B1
Kaolack, Senegal 44 F1
Kapan, Armenia 23 G8
Kapanga, Zaïre 46 F4
Kapchagai = Qapshaghay, Kazakhstan 24 E8
Kapfenberg, Austria 16 E8
Kapiri Mposhi, Zambia 47 G5
Kapiskau →, Canada 62 B3
Kapit, Malaysia 32 D4
Kapiti I., N.Z. 51 J5
Kapoeta, Sudan 45 H11
Kaposvár, Hungary 17 E9
Kapps, Namibia 48 C2
Kapsukas = Marijampolė, Lithuania 9 J20
Kapuas →, Indonesia 32 E3
Kapuas Hulu, Pegunungan, Malaysia 32 D4
Kapuas Hulu Ra. = Kapuas Hulu, Pegunungan, Malaysia 32 D4
Kapunda, Australia 55 E2
Kapuni, N.Z. 51 H5
Kapuskasing, Canada 62 C3
Kapuskasing →, Canada 62 C3
Kaputar, Australia 55 E5
Kara, Russia 24 C7
Kara Bogaz Gol, Zaliv = Garabogazköl Aylagy, Turkmenistan 23 F9
Kara Kalpak Republic = Karakalpakstan □, Uzbekistan 24 E6
Kara Kum, Turkmenistan 24 F6
Kara Sea, Russia 24 B7
Karabiğa, Turkey 21 D12
Karaburun, Turkey 21 E12
Karabutak = Qarabutaq, Kazakhstan 24 E7
Karacabey, Turkey 21 D13
Karacasu, Turkey 21 F13
Karachi, Pakistan 36 G5
Karad, India 36 L9
Karadeniz Boğazı, Turkey 21 D13
Karaganda = Qaraghandy, Kazakhstan 24 E8
Karagayly, Kazakhstan 24 E8
Karaginskiy, Ostrov, Russia 25 D17
Karagiye, Vpadina, Kazakhstan 23 F9
Karagiye Depression = Karagiye, Vpadina, Kazakhstan 23 F9
Karaikal, India 36 P11
Karaikkudi, India 36 P11
Karaj, Iran 39 C6
Karakalpakstan □, Uzbekistan 24 E6
Karakas, Kazakhstan 24 E9
Karakitang, Indonesia 33 D7
Karaklis = Vanadzor, Armenia 23 F7
Karakoram Pass, Pakistan 36 B10
Karakoram Ra., Pakistan 36 B10
Karalon, Russia 25 D12
Karaman, Turkey 23 G5
Karamay, China 30 B3
Karambu, Indonesia 32 E5
Karamea Bight, N.Z. 51 J3
Karand, Iran 38 C5
Karanganyar, Indonesia 33 G13
Karasburg, Namibia 48 D2
Karasino, Russia 24 C9
Karasjok, Norway 8 B21
Karasuk, Russia 24 D8
Karasuyama, Japan 29 F10
Karatau = Qarataū, Kazakhstan 24 E8

Karatau, Khrebet,
  Kazakhstan 24 E7
Karawang, Indonesia . 33 G12
Karawanken, Europe .. 16 E8
Karazhal, Kazakhstan . 24 E8
Karbalā, Iraq 38 C5
Karcag, Hungary 17 E11
Karda, Russia 25 D11
Kardhítsa, Greece 21 E9
Kärdla, Estonia 9 G20
Kareeberge, S. Africa . 48 E3
Karelia □, Russia 22 A5
Karelian Republic =
  Karelia □, Russia .. 22 A5
Karen, India 34 F2
Kārevāndar, Iran 39 E9
Kargasok, Russia 24 D9
Kargat, Russia 24 D9
Kargil, India 36 B10
Kargopol, Russia 22 B6
Kariān, Iran 39 E8
Kariba, L., Zimbabwe . 47 H5
Kariba Dam, Zimbabwe 47 H5
Kariba Gorge, Zambia . 47 H5
Karibib, Namibia 48 C2
Karimata, Kepulauan,
  Indonesia 32 E3
Karimata, Selat,
  Indonesia 32 E3
Karimata Is. =
  Karimata, Kepulauan,
  Indonesia 32 E3
Karimnagar, India ... 36 K11
Karimunjawa,
  Kepulauan, Indonesia 32 F4
Karin, Somali Rep. .. 40 E4
Karīt, Iran 39 C8
Kariya, Japan 29 G8
Karkaralinsk =
  Qarqaraly,
  Kazakhstan 24 E8
Karkinitska Zatoka,
  Ukraine 23 E5
Karkinitskiy Zaliv =
  Karkinitska Zatoka,
  Ukraine 23 E5
Karl-Marx-Stadt =
  Chemnitz, Germany 16 C7
Karlovac, Croatia 16 F8
Karlovo, Bulgaria 21 C11
Karlovy Vary, Czech. .. 16 C7
Karlsbad = Karlovy
  Vary, Czech. 16 C7
Karlsborg, Sweden ... 9 G16
Karlshamn, Sweden .. 9 H16
Karlskoga, Sweden .. 9 G16
Karlskrona, Sweden .. 9 H16
Karlsruhe, Germany .. 16 D5
Karlstad, Sweden ... 9 G15
Karlstad, U.S.A. 70 A6
Karnal, India 36 E10
Karnali →, Nepal ... 37 E12
Karnaphuli Res.,
  Bangla. 37 H18
Karnataka □, India .. 36 N10
Karnes City, U.S.A. .. 71 L6
Karnische Alpen,
  Europe 16 E7
Kärnten □, Austria .. 16 E8
Karonga, Malawi 46 F6
Karoonda, Australia . 55 F2
Karora, Sudan 45 E12
Kárpathos, Greece ... 21 G12
Karpinsk, Russia 22 C11
Karpogory, Russia .. 22 B7
Karpuz Burnu =
  Apostolos Andreas,
  C., Cyprus 38 C2
Kars, Turkey 23 F7
Karsakpay, Kazakhstan 24 E7
Karshi = Qarshi,
  Uzbekistan 24 F7
Karsun, Russia 22 D8
Kartaly, Russia 24 D7
Karufa, Indonesia ... 33 E8
Karumba, Australia . 54 B3
Karungu, Kenya 46 E6
Karviná, Czech. 17 D10
Karwar, India 36 M9
Kas Kong, Cambodia . 34 G7
Kasai →, Zaïre 46 E3
Kasama, Zambia 46 G6
Kasane, Namibia 48 B3
Kasanga, Tanzania .. 46 F6
Kasangulu, Zaïre 46 E3
Kasaragod, India 36 N9
Kasba L., Canada 65 A8
Kāseh Garān, Iran .. 38 C5
Kasempa, Zambia ... 47 G5
Kasenga, Zaïre 46 G5
Kashabowie, Canada . 62 C1
Kāshān, Iran 39 C6
Kashi, China 30 C2
Kashiwazaki, Japan . 29 F9
Kashk-e Kohneh,
  Afghan. 36 B3
Kāshmar, Iran 39 C8
Kashmir, Asia 36 B10
Kashun Noerh = Gaxun
  Nur, China 30 B5
Kasimov, Russia 22 D7
Kasirutā, Indonesia .. 33 E7
Kaskaskia →, U.S.A. 70 G10
Kaskattama →,
  Canada 65 B10
Kaskinen, Finland ... 9 E19
Kaslo, Canada 64 D5
Kasmere L., Canada . 65 B8
Kasongo, Zaïre 46 E5
Kasongo Lunda, Zaïre 46 F3
Kásos, Greece 21 G12
Kassalā, Sudan 45 E12
Kassel, Germany 16 C5

Kassue, Indonesia 33 F9
Kastamonu, Turkey .. 23 F5
Kastoría, Greece 21 D9
Kasulu, Tanzania 46 E6
Kasumi, Japan 29 G7
Kasur, Pakistan 36 D9
Kata, Russia 25 D11
Katako Kombe, Zaïre 46 E4
Katamatite, Australia . 55 F4
Katanga = Shaba □,
  Zaïre 46 F4
Katangi, India 36 J11
Katangli, Russia 25 D15
Kateríni, Greece 21 D10
Katha, Burma 37 G20
Katherine, Australia . 52 B5
Kathiawar, India 36 H7
Kathikar, India 37 G15
Katima Mulilo, Zambia 48 B3
Katingan =
  Mendawai →,
  Indonesia 32 E4
Katiola, Ivory C. 44 G3
Katmandu, Nepal ... 37 F14
Katoomba, Australia . 55 E5
Katowice, Poland ... 17 C10
Katrine, L., U.K. 12 E4
Katrineholm, Sweden . 9 G17
Katsepe, Madag. 49 B8
Katsina, Nigeria 44 F6
Katsumoto, Japan ... 29 H4
Katsuura, Japan 29 G10
Katsuyama, Japan ... 29 F8
Kattegat, Denmark .. 9 H14
Katwijk-aan-Zee, Neths. 15 B4
Kauai, U.S.A. 66 H15
Kauai Channel, U.S.A. 66 H15
Kaufman, U.S.A. 71 J6
Kauhajoki, Finland .. 9 E20
Kaukauna, U.S.A. .. 68 C1
Kaukauveld, Namibia . 48 B3
Kaunas, Lithuania .. 9 J20
Kaura Namoda, Nigeria 44 F6
Kautokeino, Norway . 8 B20
Kavacha, Russia 25 C17
Kavalerovo, Russia .. 28 B7
Kavali, India 36 M12
Kaválla, Greece 21 D11
Kavār, Iran 39 D7
Kaw, Fr. Guiana 79 C8
Kawagoe, Japan 29 G9
Kawaguchi, Japan ... 29 G9
Kawaihae, U.S.A. ... 66 H17
Kawambwa, Zambia . 46 F5
Kawanoe, Japan 29 G6
Kawardha, India 37 J12
Kawasaki, Japan 29 G9
Kawene, Canada 62 C1
Kawerau, N.Z. 51 H6
Kawhia Harbour, N.Z. 51 H5
Kawio, Kepulauan,
  Indonesia 33 D7
Kawnro, Burma 37 H21
Kawthaung, Burma .. 34 G5
Kawthoolei =
  Kawthule □, Burma 37 L20
Kawthule □, Burma . 37 L20
Kaya, Burkina Faso .. 44 F4
Kayah □, Burma 37 K20
Kayan →, Indonesia . 32 D5
Kaycee, U.S.A. 72 E10
Kayeli, Indonesia 33 E7
Kayenta, U.S.A. 73 H8
Kayes, Mali 44 F2
Kayoa, Indonesia 33 D7
Kayrunnera, Australia . 55 E3
Kayseri, Turkey 23 G6
Kaysville, U.S.A. 72 F8
Kayuagung, Indonesia 32 E2
Kazachye, Russia 25 B14
Kazakhstan ■, Asia .. 24 E7
Kazan, Russia 22 C8
Kazan-Rettō, Pac. Oc. 56 E6
Kazanlŭk, Bulgaria .. 21 C11
Kazatin = Kozyatyn,
  Ukraine 17 D15
Kāzerūn, Iran 39 D6
Kazumba, Zaïre 46 F4
Kazuno, Japan 28 D10
Kazym →, Russia ... 24 C7
Ké-Macina, Mali 44 F3
Kéa, Greece 21 F11
Keams Canyon, U.S.A. 73 J8
Kearney, U.S.A. 70 E5
Keban, Turkey 23 G6
Kebnekaise, Sweden . 8 C18
Kebri Dehar, Ethiopia 40 F3
Kebumen, Indonesia . 33 G13
Kechika →, Canada . 64 B3
Kecskemét, Hungary . 17 E10
Kedah □, Malaysia .. 34 P13
Kedgwick, Canada .. 63 C6
Kedia Hill, Botswana . 48 C3
Kediniai, Lithuania .. 9 J21
Kediri, Indonesia 33 G15
Kédougou, Senegal .. 44 F2
Keeley L., Canada ... 65 C7
Keeling Is. = Cocos Is.,
  Ind. Oc. 35 F8
Keelung = Chilung,
  Taiwan 31 D7
Keene, U.S.A. 68 D9
Keeper Hill, Ireland .. 13 D3
Keer-Weer, C., Australia 54 A3
Keetmanshoop,
  Namibia 48 D2
Keewatin, U.S.A. ... 70 B8
Keewatin □, Canada . 65 A9
Keewatin →, Canada 65 B8
Kefallinía, Greece ... 21 E9
Kefamenanu, Indonesia 33 F6
Keffi, Nigeria 44 G6
Keflavík, Iceland 8 D2

Keg River, Canada .. 64 B5
Kegaska, Canada ... 63 B7
Keighley, U.K. 10 D6
Keila, Estonia 9 G21
Keimoes, S. Africa .. 48 D3
Keitele, Finland 8 E22
Keith, Australia 55 F3
Keith, U.K. 12 D6
Keith Arm, Canada .. 60 B7
Kejser Franz Joseph
  Fjord = Kong Franz
  Joseph Fd.,
  Greenland 4 B6
Kekri, India 36 G9
Kël, Russia 25 C13
Kelang, Malaysia ... 34 R14
Kelantan □, Malaysia 34 P15
Kelantan →, Malaysia 34 N15
Kelibia, Tunisia 45 A7
Kellé, Congo 46 E2
Keller, U.S.A. 72 B4
Kellerberrin, Australia 53 F2
Kellett, C., Canada .. 4 B1
Kellogg, U.S.A. 72 C5
Kells = Ceanannus
  Mor, Ireland 13 C5
Kélo, Chad 45 G8
Kelowna, Canada ... 64 D5
Kelsey Bay, Canada . 64 C3
Kelso, N.Z. 51 L2
Kelso, U.K. 12 F6
Kelso, U.S.A. 72 C2
Keluang, Malaysia ... 34 S16
Kelvington, Canada . 65 C8
Kem, Russia 22 B5
Kem →, Russia 22 B5
Kema, Indonesia 33 D7
Kemano, Canada ... 64 C3
Kemerovo, Russia .. 24 D9
Kemi, Finland 8 D21
Kemijärvi, Finland ... 8 C22
Kemijoki →, Finland 8 D21
Kemmerer, U.S.A. ... 72 F8
Kemp, L., U.S.A. ... 71 J5
Kemp Land, Antarctica 5 C5
Kempsey, Australia .. 55 E5
Kempt, L., Canada .. 62 C5
Kempten, Germany .. 16 E6
Kemptville, Canada . 62 C4
Kendal, Indonesia ... 32 F4
Kendal, U.K. 10 C5
Kendall, Australia ... 55 E5
Kendall →, Australia 54 A3
Kendallville, U.S.A. .. 68 E3
Kendari, Indonesia .. 33 E6
Kendawangan,
  Indonesia 32 E4
Kende, Nigeria 44 F5
Kendenup, Australia . 53 F2
Kendrapara, India ... 37 J15
Kendrew, S. Africa .. 48 E3
Kendrick, U.S.A. 72 C5
Kenedy, U.S.A. 71 L6
Kenema, S. Leone .. 44 G2
Keng Tawng, Burma . 37 J21
Keng Tung, Burma .. 37 J21
Kenge, Zaïre 46 E3
Kenhardt, S. Africa .. 48 D3
Kenitra, Morocco ... 44 B3
Kenmare, Ireland ... 13 E2
Kenmare, U.S.A. 70 A3
Kenmare →, Ireland 13 E2
Kennebec, U.S.A. ... 70 D5
Kennedy Ra., Australia 53 D2
Kennedy Taungdeik,
  Burma 37 H18
Kennet →, U.K. 11 F7
Kenneth Ra., Australia 52 D2
Kennett, U.S.A. 71 G9
Kennewick, U.S.A. .. 72 C4
Kénogami, Canada .. 63 C5
Kenogami →, Canada 62 B3
Kenora, Canada 65 D10
Kenosha, U.S.A. 68 D2
Kensington, Canada . 63 C7
Kensington, U.S.A. .. 70 F5
Kensington Downs,
  Australia 54 C3
Kent, Ohio, U.S.A. .. 68 E5
Kent, Oreg., U.S.A. .. 72 D3
Kent, Tex., U.S.A. ... 71 K2
Kent □, U.K. 11 F8
Kent Group, Australia 54 F4
Kent Pen., Canada .. 60 B9
Kentau, Kazakhstan . 24 E7
Kentland, U.S.A. 68 E2
Kenton, U.S.A. 68 E4
Kentucky □, U.S.A. . 68 G3
Kentucky →, U.S.A. 68 F3
Kentucky L., U.S.A. . 69 G2
Kentville, Canada ... 63 C7
Kentwood, U.S.A. ... 71 K9
Kenya ■, Africa 46 B4
Kenya, Mt., Kenya .. 46 E4
Keokuk, U.S.A. 70 E9
Kepi, Indonesia 33 F9
Kerala □, India 36 P10
Kerama-Rettō, Japan . 29 L3
Kerang, Australia ... 55 F3
Kerava, Finland 9 F21
Kerch, Ukraine 23 E6
Kerchoual, Mali 44 E5
Kerema, Papua N. G. 56 H6
Keren, Eritrea 45 E12
Kerguelen, Ind. Oc. . 35 J5
Kericho, Kenya 46 E7
Kerinci, Indonesia ... 32 E2
Kerki, Turkmenistan . 24 F7
Kérkira, Greece 21 E8
Kerkrade, Neths. ... 15 D6
Kermadec Is., Pac. Oc. 56 K10

Kermadec Trench,
  Pac. Oc. 56 L10
Kermān, Iran 39 D8
Kermān □, Iran 39 D8
Kermānshāh =
  Bākhtarān, Iran ... 38 C5
Kerme Körfezi, Turkey 21 F12
Kermit, U.S.A. 71 K3
Kern →, U.S.A. 73 J4
Kerrobert, Canada .. 65 C7
Kerry □, Ireland 13 D2
Kerry Hd., Ireland .. 13 D2
Kertosono, Indonesia 33 G15
Kerulen →, Asia ... 31 B6
Kerzaz, Algeria 44 C4
Kesagami →, Canada 62 B4
Kesagami L., Canada . 62 B3
Keşan, Turkey 21 D12
Kesennuma, Japan .. 28 E10
Keshit, Iran 39 D8
Kestell, S. Africa 49 D4
Kestenga, Russia .. 22 A5
Keswick, U.K. 10 C4
Ket →, Russia 24 D9
Keta, Ghana 44 G5
Ketapang, Indonesia . 32 E4
Ketchikan, U.S.A. ... 60 C6
Ketchum, U.S.A. ... 72 E6
Kętrzyn, Poland 17 A11
Kettering, U.K. 11 E7
Kettle →, Canada .. 65 B11
Khóra Sfakíon, Greece 21 G11
Khorāsān □, Iran ... 39 C8
Khorat = Nakhon
  Ratchasima, Thailand 34 E7
Khorat, Cao Nguyen,
  Thailand 34 E7
Khorixas, Namibia .. 48 C1
Khorramābād,
  Khorāsān, Iran ... 39 C8
Khorramābād,
  Lorestān, Iran 39 C6
Khorramshahr, Iran . 39 D6
Khorugh, Tajikistan . 24 F8
Khosravī, Iran 39 D6
Khosrowābād,
  Khuzestān, Iran ... 39 D6
Khosrowābād,
  Kordestān, Iran ... 38 C5
Khosūyeh, Iran 39 D7
Khotyn, Ukraine 17 D14
Khouribga, Morocco . 44 B3
Khowai, Bangla. 37 G17
Khoyniki, Belarus ... 17 C15
Khu Khan, Thailand . 34 E8
Khudzhand, Tajikistan 24 E7
Khuff, Si. Arabia 38 E5
Khūgīānī, Afghan. .. 36 D4
Khulna, Bangla. 37 H16
Khulna □, Bangla. .. 37 H16
Khumago, Botswana . 48 C3
Khūr, Iran 39 C8
Khurayş, Si. Arabia . 39 E6
Khūrīyā Mūrīyā, Jazā
  'ir, Oman 40 D6
Khūsf, Iran 39 C8
Khush, Afghan. 36 C3
Khushab, Pakistan .. 36 C5
Khust, Ukraine 17 D12
Khuzdar, Pakistan .. 36 F5
Khūzestān □, Iran .. 39 D6
Khvājeh, Iran 38 B5
Khvānsār, Iran 39 D7
Khvor, Iran 39 C7
Khvorgū, Iran 39 E8
Khvormūj, Iran 39 D6
Khvoy, Iran 38 B5
Khyber Pass, Afghan. 36 B7
Kiama, Australia 55 E5
Kiamba, Phil. 33 C6
Kiangsi = Jiangxi □,
  China 31 D6
Kiangsu = Jiangsu □,
  China 31 C7
Kibangou, Congo ... 46 E2
Kibombo, Congo ... 46 E5
Kibondo, Tanzania .. 46 E6
Kibwesa, Tanzania .. 46 F5
Kibwezi, Kenya 46 E7
Kichiga, Russia 25 D17
Kicking Horse Pass,
  Canada 64 C5
Kidal, Mali 44 E5
Kidderminster, U.K. . 11 E5
Kidnappers, C., N.Z. . 51 H6
Kidston, Australia .. 54 B3
Kidstone, U.S.A.
Kiel, Germany 16 A6
Kiel Kanal = Nord-
  Ostsee-Kanal →,
  Germany 16 A5
Kielce, Poland 17 C11
Kieler Bucht, Germany 16 A6
Kiev = Kyyiv, Ukraine 17 C16
Kiffa, Mauritania ... 44 E2
Kifrī, Iraq 38 C5
Kigali, Rwanda 46 E6
Kigoma-Ujiji, Tanzania 46 E5
Kihee, Australia 55 D3
Kii-Sanchi, Japan ... 29 G7
Kii-Suidō, Japan 29 H7
Kikaiga-Shima, Japan 29 K4
Kikinda, Serbia, Yug. . 21 B9
Kikládhes, Greece ... 21 F11
Kikwit, Zaïre 46 E3
Kilauea Crater, U.S.A. 66 J17
Kilcoy, Australia 55 D5
Kildare, Ireland 13 C5
Kildare □, Ireland ... 13 C5
Kilgore, U.S.A. 71 J7
Kilimanjaro, Tanzania 46 E7
Kilindini, Kenya 46 E7

Kiliya, Ukraine 17 F15
Kilkee, Ireland 13 D2
Kilkenny, Ireland 13 D4
Kilkenny □, Ireland .. 13 D4
Kilkieran B., Ireland . 13 C2
Kilkis, Greece 21 D10
Killala, Ireland 13 B2
Killala B., Ireland ... 13 B2
Killaloe, Ireland 13 D3
Killam, Canada 64 C6
Killarney, Australia .. 55 D5
Killarney, Canada ... 62 C3
Killarney, Ireland ... 13 D2
Killarney, Lakes of,
  Ireland 13 E2
Killary Harbour, Ireland 13 C2
Killdeer, Canada 65 D7
Killdeer, U.S.A. 70 B3
Killeen, U.S.A. 71 K6
Killiecrankie, Pass of,
  U.K. 12 E5
Killin, U.K. 12 E4
Killíni, Greece 21 F10
Killybegs, Ireland ... 13 B3
Kilmarnock, U.K. ... 12 F4
Kilmore, Australia .. 55 F3
Kilosa, Tanzania 46 F7
Kilrush, Ireland 13 D2
Kilwa Kivinje, Tanzania 46 F7
Kim, U.S.A. 71 G3
Kimaam, Indonesia .. 33 F9
Kimba, Australia 55 E2
Kimball, Nebr., U.S.A. 70 E3
Kimball, S. Dak., U.S.A. 70 D5
Kimberley, Canada .. 64 D5
Kimberley, S. Africa . 48 D3
Kimberley Downs,
  Australia 52 C3
Kimberly, U.S.A. 72 E6
Kimry, Russia 22 C6
Kimsquit, Canada ... 64 C3
Kinabalu, Gunong,
  Malaysia 32 C5
Kinaskan L., Canada . 64 B2
Kinbasket L., Canada . 64 C5
Kincaid, Canada 65 D7
Kincardine, Canada . 62 D3
Kinder Scout, U.K. .. 10 D6
Kindersley, Canada . 65 C7
Kindia, Guinea 44 G2
Kindu, Zaïre 46 E5
Kineshma, Russia .. 22 C7
King, L., Australia .. 53 F2
King, Mt., Australia . 54 D4
King City, U.S.A. ... 73 H3
King Cr. →, Australia 54 C2
King Edward →,
  Australia 52 B4
King Frederick VI Land
  = Kong Frederik VI.s
  Kyst, Greenland ... 4 C5
King George B., Falk. Is. 80 G4
King George I.,
  Antarctica 5 C18
King George Is.,
  Canada 61 C11
King I. = Kadan Kyun,
  Burma 34 F5
King I., Australia 54 F3
King I., Canada 64 C3
King Leopold Ras.,
  Australia 52 C4
King Sd., Australia .. 52 C3
King William I., Canada 60 B10
King William's Town,
  S. Africa 48 E4
Kingaroy, Australia . 55 D5
Kingfisher, U.S.A. ... 71 H6
Kingirbān, Iraq 38 C5
Kingisepp =
  Kuressaare, Estonia 9 G20
Kingman, Ariz., U.S.A. 73 J6
Kingman, Kans., U.S.A. 71 G5
Kingoonya, Australia 55 E2
Kings →, U.S.A. 73 H4
Kings Canyon National
  Park, U.S.A. 73 H4
King's Lynn, U.K. ... 10 E8
Kings Mountain, U.S.A. 69 H5
King's Peak, U.S.A. . 72 F8
Kingsbridge, U.K. ... 11 G4
Kingsburg, U.S.A. ... 73 H4
Kingscote, Australia . 55 F2
Kingscourt, Ireland .. 13 C5
Kingsley, U.S.A. 70 D7
Kingsport, U.S.A. ... 69 G4
Kingston, Canada ... 62 D4
Kingston, Jamaica .. 74 K17
Kingston, N.Z. 51 L2
Kingston, N.Y., U.S.A. 68 E8
Kingston, Pa., U.S.A. 68 E8
Kingston South East,
  Australia 55 F2
Kingston upon Hull,
  U.K. 10 D7
Kingston-upon-Thames,
  U.K. 11 F7
Kingstown, St. Vincent 74 P20
Kingstree, U.S.A. ... 69 J6
Kingsville, Canada .. 62 D3
Kingsville, U.S.A. ... 71 M6
Kingussie, U.K. 12 D4
Kınık, Turkey 21 E12
Kinistino, Canada ... 65 C7
Kinkala, Congo 46 E2
Kinki □, Japan 29 H8
Kinleith, N.Z. 51 H5
Kinna, Sweden 9 H15
Kinnaird, Canada ... 64 D5
Kinnairds Hd., U.K. . 12 D7
Kinnarodden, Norway 6 A11
Kinoje →, Canada .. 62 B3
Kinomoto, Japan ... 29 G8

Kinross, *U.K.*	12	E5
Kinsale, *Ireland*	13	E3
Kinsale, Old Hd. of, *Ireland*	13	E3
Kinsha = Chang Jiang →, *China*	31	C7
Kinshasa, *Zaïre*	46	E3
Kinsley, *U.S.A.*	71	G5
Kinston, *U.S.A.*	69	H7
Kintampo, *Ghana*	44	G4
Kintap, *Indonesia*	32	E5
Kintore Ra., *Australia*	52	D4
Kintyre, *U.K.*	12	F3
Kintyre, Mull of, *U.K.*	12	F3
Kinushseo →, *Canada*	62	A3
Kinuso, *Canada*	64	B5
Kiosk, *Canada*	62	C4
Kiowa, *Kans., U.S.A.*	71	G5
Kiowa, *Okla., U.S.A.*	71	H7
Kipahigan L., *Canada*	65	B8
Kiparissía, *Greece*	21	F9
Kiparissiakós Kólpos, *Greece*	21	F9
Kipembawe, *Tanzania*	46	F6
Kipili, *Tanzania*	46	F6
Kipling, *Canada*	65	C8
Kippure, *Ireland*	13	C5
Kipushi, *Zaïre*	47	G5
Kirensk, *Russia*	25	D11
Kirgella Rocks, *Australia*	53	F3
Kirghizia = Kyrgyzstan ■, *Asia*	24	E8
Kirghizstan = Kyrgyzstan ■, *Asia*	24	E8
Kirgiziya Steppe, *Eurasia*	23	D10
Kiri, *Zaïre*	46	E3
Kiribati ■, *Pac. Oc.*	56	H10
Kırıkkale, *Turkey*	23	G5
Kirillov, *Russia*	22	C6
Kirin = Jilin, *China*	31	B7
Kirin = Jilin □, *China*	31	B7
Kiritimati, *Kiribati*	57	G12
Kirkcaldy, *U.K.*	12	E5
Kirkcudbright, *U.K.*	12	G4
Kirkee, *India*	36	K8
Kirkenes, *Norway*	8	B23
Kirkintilloch, *U.K.*	12	F4
Kirkjubæjarklaustr, *Iceland*	8	E4
Kirkkonummi, *Finland*	9	F21
Kirkland, *U.S.A.*	73	J7
Kirkland Lake, *Canada*	62	C3
Kırklareli, *Turkey*	21	D12
Kirksville, *U.S.A.*	70	E8
Kirkük, *Iraq*	38	C5
Kirkwall, *U.K.*	12	C6
Kirkwood, *S. Africa*	48	E4
Kirov, *Russia*	24	D5
Kirovabad = Gäncä, *Azerbaijan*	23	F8
Kirovakan = Vanadzor, *Armenia*	23	F7
Kirovograd = Kirovohrad, *Ukraine*	23	E5
Kirovohrad, *Ukraine*	23	E5
Kirovsk = Babadayhan, *Turkmenistan*	24	F7
Kirovsk, *Russia*	22	A5
Kirovskiy, *Kamchatka, Russia*	25	D16
Kirovskiy, *Sib., Russia*	28	B6
Kirriemuir, *U.K.*	12	E5
Kirsanov, *Russia*	22	D7
Kirthar Range, *Pakistan*	36	F5
Kiruna, *Sweden*	8	C19
Kirundu, *Zaïre*	46	E5
Kirup, *Australia*	53	F2
Kiryū, *Japan*	29	F9
Kisangani, *Zaïre*	46	D5
Kisar, *Indonesia*	33	F7
Kisaran, *Indonesia*	32	D1
Kiselevsk, *Russia*	24	D9
Kishanganj, *India*	37	F16
Kishangarh, *India*	36	F7
Kishinev = Chişinău, *Moldova*	17	E15
Kishiwada, *Japan*	29	G7
Kishtwar, *India*	36	C9
Kisii, *Kenya*	46	E6
Kisiju, *Tanzania*	46	F7
Kiska I., *U.S.A.*	60	C1
Kiskatinaw →, *Canada*	64	B4
Kiskittogisu L., *Canada*	65	C9
Kiskörös, *Hungary*	17	E10
Kiskunfélegyháza, *Hungary*	17	E10
Kiskunhalas, *Hungary*	17	E10
Kislovodsk, *Russia*	23	F7
Kiso-Gawa →, *Japan*	29	G8
Kiso-Sammyaku, *Japan*	29	G8
Kisofukushima, *Japan*	29	G8
Kissidougou, *Guinea*	44	G2
Kissimmee, *U.S.A.*	69	L5
Kissimmee →, *U.S.A.*	69	M5
Kississing L., *Canada*	65	B8
Kisumu, *Kenya*	46	E6
Kit Carson, *U.S.A.*	70	F3
Kita, *Mali*	44	F3
Kitab, *Uzbekistan*	24	F7
Kitaibaraki, *Japan*	29	F10
Kitakami, *Japan*	28	E10
Kitakami-Gawa →, *Japan*	28	E10
Kitakami-Sammyaku, *Japan*	28	E10
Kitakata, *Japan*	28	F9
Kitakyūshū, *Japan*	29	H5
Kitale, *Kenya*	46	D7
Kitami, *Japan*	28	C11

Kitami-Sammyaku, *Japan*	28	B11
Kitchener, *Australia*	53	F3
Kitchener, *Canada*	62	D3
Kitega = Gitega, *Burundi*	46	E5
Kitgum, *Uganda*	46	D6
Kíthira, *Greece*	21	F10
Kíthnos, *Greece*	21	F11
Kitikmeot □, *Canada*	60	A9
Kitimat, *Canada*	64	C3
Kitinen →, *Finland*	8	C22
Kitsuki, *Japan*	29	H5
Kittakittaooloo, L., *Australia*	55	D2
Kittanning, *U.S.A.*	68	E6
Kittery, *U.S.A.*	68	D10
Kittilä, *Finland*	8	C21
Kitui, *Kenya*	46	E7
Kitwe, *Zambia*	47	G5
Kivertsi, *Ukraine*	17	C13
Kivu, L., *Zaïre*	46	E5
Kiyev = Kyyiv, *Ukraine*	17	C16
Kiyevskoye Vdkhr. = Kyyivske Vdskh., *Ukraine*	17	C16
Kizel, *Russia*	22	C10
Kızıl Irmak →, *Turkey*	23	F6
Kizlyar, *Russia*	23	F8
Kizyl-Arvat = Gyzylarbat, *Turkmenistan*	24	F6
Kjölur, *Iceland*	8	D4
Kladno, *Czech.*	16	C8
Klagenfurt, *Austria*	16	E8
Klaipeda, *Lithuania*	9	J19
Klaksvík, *Færoe Is.*	8	E9
Klamath →, *U.S.A.*	72	F1
Klamath Falls, *U.S.A.*	72	E3
Klamath Mts., *U.S.A.*	72	F2
Klappan →, *Canada*	64	B3
Klarälven →, *Sweden*	9	G15
Klaten, *Indonesia*	33	G14
Klatovy, *Czech.*	16	D7
Klawer, *S. Africa*	48	E2
Klawock, *U.S.A.*	64	B2
Kleena Kleene, *Canada*	64	C4
Klein, *U.S.A.*	72	C9
Klein-Karas, *Namibia*	48	D2
Klerksdorp, *S. Africa*	48	D4
Kletsk = Klyetsk, *Belarus*	17	B14
Kletskiy, *Russia*	24	E5
Klickitat, *U.S.A.*	72	D3
Klin, *Russia*	24	D4
Klinaklini →, *Canada*	64	C3
Klipdale, *S. Africa*	48	E2
Klipplaat, *S. Africa*	48	E3
Kłodzko, *Poland*	17	C9
Klondike, *Canada*	60	B6
Klouto, *Togo*	44	G5
Kluane L., *Canada*	60	B6
Kluczbork, *Poland*	17	C10
Klyetsk, *Belarus*	17	B14
Klyuchevskaya, Gora, *Russia*	25	D17
Knaresborough, *U.K.*	10	C6
Knee L., *Man., Canada*	65	B10
Knee L., *Sask., Canada*	65	B7
Knight Inlet, *Canada*	64	C3
Knighton, *U.K.*	11	E4
Knights Landing, *U.S.A.*	72	G3
Knob, C., *Australia*	53	F2
Knockmealdown Mts., *Ireland*	13	D4
Knokke, *Belgium*	15	C3
Knossós, *Greece*	21	G11
Knox, *U.S.A.*	68	E2
Knox, *U.S.A.*	64	C2
Knox City, *U.S.A.*	71	J5
Knox Coast, *Antarctica*	5	C8
Knoxville, *Iowa, U.S.A.*	70	E8
Knoxville, *Tenn., U.S.A.*	69	H4
Knysna, *S. Africa*	48	E3
Ko Chang, *Thailand*	34	F7
Ko Kut, *Thailand*	34	G7
Ko Phra Thong, *Thailand*	34	H5
Ko Tao, *Thailand*	34	G5
Koartac = Quaqtaq, *Canada*	61	B13
Koba, Aru, *Indonesia*	33	F8
Koba, Bangka, *Indonesia*	32	E3
Kobarid, *Slovenia*	16	E7
Kobayashi, *Japan*	29	J5
Kobdo = Hovd, *Mongolia*	30	B4
Kōbe, *Japan*	29	G7
København, *Denmark*	9	J15
Kōbi-Sho, *Japan*	29	M1
Koblenz, *Germany*	16	C4
Kobroor, Kepulauan, *Indonesia*	33	F8
Kobryn, *Belarus*	17	B13
Kocaeli = İzmit, *Turkey*	23	F4
Kočani, *Macedonia*	21	D10
Koch Bihar, *India*	37	F16
Kocheya, *Russia*	25	D13
Kōchi, *Japan*	29	H6
Kōchi □, *Japan*	29	H6
Kochiu = Gejiu, *China*	30	D5
Kodiak, *U.S.A.*	60	C4
Kodiak I., *U.S.A.*	60	C4
Kodiang, *Malaysia*	34	N13
Koes, *Namibia*	48	D2
Koffiefontein, *S. Africa*	48	D4
Kofiau, *Indonesia*	33	E7
Koforidua, *Ghana*	44	G4
Kōfu, *Japan*	29	G9
Koga, *Japan*	29	F9
Kogaluk →, *Canada*	63	A7
Kogan, *Australia*	55	D5

Køge, *Denmark*	9	J15
Koh-i-Bābā, *Afghan.*	36	B5
Kohat, *Pakistan*	36	C7
Kohima, *India*	37	G19
Kohkīlūyeh va Būyer Aḥmadī □, *Iran*	39	D6
Kohler Ra., *Antarctica*	5	D15
Kohtla-Järve, *Estonia*	9	G22
Koillismaa, *Finland*	8	D23
Kojonup, *Australia*	53	F2
Kojūr, *Iran*	39	B6
Kokand = Qŭqon, *Uzbekistan*	24	E8
Kokanee Glacier Prov. Park, *Canada*	64	D5
Kokas, *Indonesia*	33	E8
Kokchetav = Kökshetaū, *Kazakhstan*	24	D7
Kokemäenjoki →, *Finland*	9	F19
Kokkola, *Finland*	8	E20
Koko Kyunzu, *Burma*	34	E2
Kokomo, *U.S.A.*	68	E2
Kokonau, *Indonesia*	33	E9
Kökshetaū, *Kazakhstan*	24	D7
Koksoak →, *Canada*	61	C13
Kokstad, *S. Africa*	49	E4
Kokubu, *Japan*	29	J5
Kokuora, *Russia*	25	B15
Kola, *Indonesia*	33	F8
Kola, *Russia*	22	A5
Kola Pen. = Kolskiy Poluostrov, *Russia*	22	A6
Kolaka, *Indonesia*	33	E6
Kolar, *India*	36	N11
Kolar Gold Fields, *India*	36	N11
Kolari, *Finland*	8	C20
Kolayat, *India*	36	F8
Kolchugino = Leninsk-Kuznetskiy, *Russia*	24	D9
Kolda, *Senegal*	44	F2
Kolding, *Denmark*	9	J13
Kole, *Zaïre*	46	E4
Kolepom = Yos Sudarso, Pulau, *Indonesia*	33	F9
Kolguyev, Ostrov, *Russia*	22	A8
Kolhapur, *India*	36	L9
Kolín, *Czech.*	16	C8
Kolkas Rags, *Latvia*	9	H20
Kolmanskop, *Namibia*	48	D2
Köln, *Germany*	16	C4
Koło, *Poland*	17	B10
Kołobrzeg, *Poland*	16	A8
Kolokani, *Mali*	44	F3
Kolomna, *Russia*	22	C6
Kolomyya, *Ukraine*	17	D13
Kolonodale, *Indonesia*	33	E6
Kolosib, *India*	37	G18
Kolpashevo, *Russia*	24	D9
Kolpino, *Russia*	22	C5
Kolskiy Poluostrov, *Russia*	22	A6
Kolskiy Zaliv, *Russia*	22	A5
Kolwezi, *Zaïre*	46	G5
Kolyma →, *Russia*	25	C17
Kolymskoye, Okhotsko-, *Russia*	25	C16
Kolymskoye Nagorye, *Russia*	25	C16
Komandorskiye Is. = Komandorskiye Ostrova, *Russia*	25	D17
Komandorskiye Ostrova, *Russia*	25	D17
Komárno, *Slovak Rep.*	17	E10
Komatipoort, *S. Africa*	49	D5
Komatsu, *Japan*	29	F8
Komatsujima, *Japan*	29	H7
Komi □, *Russia*	22	B10
Kommunarsk = Alchevsk, *Ukraine*	23	E6
Kommunizma, Pik, *Tajikistan*	24	F8
Komodo, *Indonesia*	33	F5
Komono, *Congo*	46	E2
Komoran, Pulau, *Indonesia*	33	F9
Komoro, *Japan*	29	F9
Komotini, *Greece*	21	D11
Kompasberg, *S. Africa*	48	E3
Kompong Cham, *Cambodia*	34	F8
Kompong Chhnang, *Cambodia*	34	F8
Kompong Som, *Cambodia*	34	G7
Kompong Speu, *Cambodia*	34	G8
Kompong Thom, *Cambodia*	34	F8
Komrat = Comrat, *Moldova*	17	E15
Komsberg, *S. Africa*	48	E3
Komsomolets, Ostrov, *Russia*	25	A10
Komsomolsk, *Russia*	25	D14
Konarhá □, *Afghan.*	36	B7
Konārī, *Iran*	39	D6
Konawa, *U.S.A.*	71	H6
Konch, *India*	36	G11
Kondakovo, *Russia*	25	C16
Kondinin, *Australia*	53	F2
Kondoa, *Tanzania*	46	E7
Kondopaga, *Russia*	22	B5
Konduga, *Nigeria*	45	F7

Kong, Koh, *Cambodia*	34	G7
Kong Christian IX.s Land, *Greenland*	4	C6
Kong Christian X.s Land, *Greenland*	4	B6
Kong Franz Joseph Fd., *Greenland*	4	B6
Kong Frederik IX.s Land, *Greenland*	4	C5
Kong Frederik VI.s Kyst, *Greenland*	4	C5
Kong Frederik VIII.s Land, *Greenland*	4	B6
Kong Oscar Fjord, *Greenland*	4	B6
Konglu, *Burma*	37	F20
Kongolo, *Zaïre*	46	F5
Kongor, *Sudan*	45	G11
Kongsberg, *Norway*	9	G13
Kongsvinger, *Norway*	9	F15
Königsberg = Kaliningrad, *Russia*	9	J19
Konin, *Poland*	17	B10
Konjic, *Bos.-H.*	21	C7
Konkiep, *Namibia*	48	D2
Konosha, *Russia*	22	B7
Konosu, *Japan*	29	F9
Konotop, *Ukraine*	23	D5
Końskie, *Poland*	17	C11
Konstanz, *Germany*	16	E5
Kont, *Iran*	39	E9
Kontagora, *Nigeria*	44	F6
Kontum, *Vietnam*	34	E10
Konya, *Turkey*	23	G5
Konza, *Kenya*	46	E7
Kookynie, *Australia*	53	E3
Kooline, *Australia*	52	D2
Kooloonong, *Australia*	55	E3
Koolyanobbing, *Australia*	53	F2
Koondrook, *Australia*	55	F3
Koonibba, *Australia*	55	E1
Koorawatha, *Australia*	55	E4
Koorda, *Australia*	53	F2
Kooskia, *U.S.A.*	72	C6
Kootenai →, *Canada*	72	B5
Kootenay L., *Canada*	64	D5
Kootenay Nat. Park, *Canada*	64	C5
Kootjieskolk, *S. Africa*	48	E3
Kopaonik, *Serbia, Yug.*	21	C9
Kópavogur, *Iceland*	8	D3
Koper, *Slovenia*	16	F7
Kopervik, *Norway*	9	G11
Kopeysk, *Russia*	24	D7
Kopi, *Australia*	55	E2
Köping, *Sweden*	9	G17
Koppies, *S. Africa*	49	D4
Koprivnica, *Croatia*	20	A7
Kopychyntsi, *Ukraine*	17	D13
Korab, *Macedonia*	21	D9
Korça, *Albania*	21	D9
Korce = Korça, *Albania*	21	D9
Korčula, *Croatia*	20	C7
Kord Kūy, *Iran*	39	B7
Kord Sheykh, *Iran*	39	D7
Kordestān □, *Iran*	38	C5
Kordofân, *Sudan*	45	F10
Korea, North ■, *Asia*	31	C7
Korea, South ■, *Asia*	31	C7
Korea Bay, *Korea*	31	C7
Korea Strait, *Asia*	31	C7
Korets, *Ukraine*	17	C14
Korhogo, *Ivory C.*	44	G3
Korim, *Indonesia*	33	E9
Korinthiakós Kólpos, *Greece*	21	E10
Kórinthos, *Greece*	21	F10
Kōriyama, *Japan*	28	F10
Korla, *China*	30	B3
Kornešty = Corneşti, *Moldova*	17	E15
Koro, *Fiji*	51	C8
Koro, *Ivory C.*	44	G3
Koro, *Mali*	44	F4
Koro Sea, *Fiji*	51	C9
Korogwe, *Tanzania*	46	F7
Koroit, *Australia*	55	F3
Koror, *Pac. Oc.*	33	C8
Körös →, *Hungary*	17	E11
Korosten, *Ukraine*	17	C15
Korostyshev, *Ukraine*	17	C15
Korraraika, Helodranon' i, *Madag.*	49	B7
Korsakov, *Russia*	25	E15
Korshunovo, *Russia*	25	D12
Korsør, *Denmark*	9	J14
Korti, *Sudan*	45	E11
Kortrijk, *Belgium*	15	D3
Koryakskoye Nagorye, *Russia*	25	C18
Kos, *Greece*	21	F12
Koschagyl, *Kazakhstan*	23	E9
Kościan, *Poland*	17	B9
Kosciusko, *U.S.A.*	71	J10
Kosciusko, Mt., *Australia*	55	F4
Kosciusko I., *U.S.A.*	64	B2
Kosha, *Sudan*	45	D11
K'oshih = Kashi, *China*	30	C2
Koshiki-Rettō, *Japan*	29	J4
Košice, *Slovak Rep.*	17	D11
Koslan, *Russia*	22	B8
Kosŏng, *S. Korea*	31	E7
Kosovo □, *Serbia, Yug.*	21	C9
Kosovska-Mitrovica = Titova-Mitrovica, *Serbia, Yug.*	21	C9
Kostamuksa, *Russia*	22	B5
Koster, *S. Africa*	48	D4
Kôstî, *Sudan*	45	F11
Kostopil, *Ukraine*	17	C14
Kostroma, *Russia*	22	C7
Kostrzyn, *Poland*	16	B8

Koszalin, *Poland*	16	A9
Kota, *India*	36	G9
Kota Baharu, *Malaysia*	34	N15
Kota Belud, *Malaysia*	32	C5
Kota Kinabalu, *Malaysia*	32	C5
Kota Tinggi, *Malaysia*	34	T16
Kotaagung, *Indonesia*	32	F2
Kotabaru, *Indonesia*	32	E5
Kotabumi, *Indonesia*	32	E2
Kotagede, *Indonesia*	33	G14
Kotamobagu, *Indonesia*	33	D6
Kotaneelee →, *Canada*	64	A4
Kotawaringin, *Indonesia*	32	E4
Kotcho L., *Canada*	64	B4
Kotelnich, *Russia*	22	C8
Kotelnikovo, *Russia*	24	E5
Kotelnyy, Ostrov, *Russia*	25	B14
Kotka, *Finland*	9	F22
Kotlas, *Russia*	22	B8
Kotli, *Pakistan*	36	C8
Kotor, *Montenegro, Yug.*	21	C8
Kotovsk, *Ukraine*	17	E15
Kotri, *Pakistan*	36	G6
Kottayam, *India*	36	Q10
Kotturu, *India*	36	M10
Kotuy →, *Russia*	25	B11
Kotzebue, *U.S.A.*	60	B3
Kouango, *C.A.R.*	46	C4
Koudougou, *Burkina Faso*	44	F4
Kougaberge, *S. Africa*	48	E3
Kouilou →, *Congo*	46	E2
Kouki, *C.A.R.*	46	C3
Koula Moutou, *Gabon*	46	E2
Koulen, *Cambodia*	34	F8
Koulikoro, *Mali*	44	F3
Koumala, *Australia*	54	C4
Koumra, *Chad*	45	G8
Kounradskiy, *Kazakhstan*	24	E8
Kountze, *U.S.A.*	71	K7
Kouroussa, *Guinea*	44	F3
Kousséri, *Cameroon*	45	F7
Koutiala, *Mali*	44	F3
Kouvola, *Finland*	9	F22
Kovdor, *Russia*	22	A5
Kovel, *Ukraine*	17	C13
Kovrov, *Russia*	22	C7
Kowanyama, *Australia*	54	B3
Kowkash, *Canada*	62	B2
Köyceğiz, *Turkey*	21	F13
Koyuk, *U.S.A.*	60	B3
Koyukuk →, *U.S.A.*	60	B4
Koza, *Japan*	29	L3
Kozáni, *Greece*	21	D9
Kozhikode = Calicut, *India*	36	P9
Kozhva, *Russia*	22	A10
Kozyatyn, *Ukraine*	17	D15
Kpalimé, *Togo*	44	G5
Kra, Isthmus of = Kra, Kho Khot, *Thailand*	34	G5
Kra, Kho Khot, *Thailand*	34	G5
Kra Buri, *Thailand*	34	G5
Kragan, *Indonesia*	33	G14
Kragerø, *Norway*	9	G13
Kragujevac, *Serbia, Yug.*	21	B9
Krajina, *Bos.-H.*	20	B7
Krakatau = Rakata, Pulau, *Indonesia*	32	F3
Kraków, *Poland*	17	C10
Kraksaan, *Indonesia*	33	G15
Kraljevo, *Serbia, Yug.*	21	C9
Kramatorsk, *Ukraine*	23	E6
Kramfors, *Sweden*	9	E17
Kranj, *Slovenia*	16	E8
Krankskop, *S. Africa*	49	D5
Krasavino, *Russia*	22	B8
Kraskino, *Russia*	25	E14
Kraśnik, *Poland*	17	C12
Krasnoarmeysk, *Russia*	24	D5
Krasnodar, *Russia*	23	E6
Krasnokamsk, *Russia*	22	C10
Krasnoperekopsk, *Ukraine*	23	E5
Krasnorechenskiy, *Russia*	28	B7
Krasnoselkupsk, *Russia*	24	C9
Krasnoturinsk, *Russia*	22	C11
Krasnoufimsk, *Russia*	22	C10
Krasnouralsk, *Russia*	22	C11
Krasnovishersk, *Russia*	22	B10
Krasnovodsk = Krasnowodsk, *Turkmenistan*	23	F9
Krasnovodsk = Krasnowodsk, *Turkmenistan*	23	F9
Krasnoyarsk, *Russia*	25	D10
Krasnyy Luch, *Ukraine*	23	E6
Krasnyy Yar, *Russia*	24	E5
Kratie, *Cambodia*	34	F9
Krau, *Indonesia*	33	E10
Kravanh, Chuor Phnom, *Cambodia*	34	F9
Krefeld, *Germany*	16	C4
Kremen, *Croatia*	16	F8
Kremenchug = Kremenchuk, *Ukraine*	23	E5
Kremenchuk, *Ukraine*	23	E5
Kremenchuksk Vdskh., *Ukraine*	23	E5
Kremenets, *Ukraine*	17	C13
Kremmling, *U.S.A.*	72	F10
Krems, *Austria*	16	D8
Kretinga, *Lithuania*	9	J19
Krichev = Krychaw, *Belarus*	17	B16

Krishna →, *India*	37	M12
Krishnanagar, *India*	37	H16
Kristiansand, *Norway*	9	G13
Kristianstad, *Sweden*	9	H16
Kristiansund, *Norway*	8	E12
Kristiinankaupunki, *Finland*	9	E19
Kristinehamn, *Sweden*	9	G16
Kristinestad = Kristiinankaupunki, *Finland*	9	E19
Kríti, *Greece*	21	G11
Krivoy Rog = Kryvyy Rih, *Ukraine*	23	E5
Krk, *Croatia*	16	F8
Krokodil →, *Mozam.*	49	D5
Kronprins Olav Kyst, *Antarctica*	5	C5
Kronshtadt, *Russia*	22	B4
Kroonstad, *S. Africa*	48	D4
Kropotkin, *Irkutsk, Russia*	25	D12
Kropotkin, *Krasnodar, Russia*	23	E7
Krosno, *Poland*	17	D11
Krotoszyn, *Poland*	17	C9
Kruger Nat. Park, *S. Africa*	49	C5
Krugersdorp, *S. Africa*	49	D4
Kruisfontein, *S. Africa*	48	E3
Krung Thep = Bangkok, *Thailand*	34	F6
Krupki, *Belarus*	17	A15
Kruševac, *Serbia, Yug.*	21	C9
Kruzof I., *U.S.A.*	64	B1
Krychaw, *Belarus*	17	B16
Krymskiy Poluostrov = Krymskyy Pivostriv, *Ukraine*	23	E5
Krymskyy Pivostriv, *Ukraine*	23	E5
Kryvyy Rih, *Ukraine*	23	E5
Ksar el Boukhari, *Algeria*	44	A5
Ksar el Kebir, *Morocco*	44	B3
Ksar es Souk = Ar Rachidiya, *Morocco*	44	B4
Kuala, *Indonesia*	32	D3
Kuala Kangsar, *Malaysia*	34	Q13
Kuala Kerai, *Malaysia*	34	P15
Kuala Kubu Baharu, *Malaysia*	34	R14
Kuala Lipis, *Malaysia*	34	Q15
Kuala Lumpur, *Malaysia*	34	R14
Kuala Sedili Besar, *Malaysia*	34	T17
Kuala Terengganu, *Malaysia*	32	C2
Kualajelai, *Indonesia*	32	E4
Kualakapuas, *Indonesia*	32	E4
Kualakurun, *Indonesia*	32	E4
Kualapembuang, *Indonesia*	32	E4
Kualasimpang, *Indonesia*	32	D1
Kuandang, *Indonesia*	33	D6
Kuangchou = Guangzhou, *China*	31	D6
Kuantan, *Malaysia*	34	R16
Kuba = Quba, *Azerbaijan*	23	F8
Kuban →, *Russia*	23	E6
Kubokawa, *Japan*	29	H6
Kuchino-eruba-Jima, *Japan*	29	J5
Kuchino-Shima, *Japan*	29	K4
Kuchinotsu, *Japan*	29	H5
Kucing, *Malaysia*	32	D4
Kuda, *India*	36	H7
Kudat, *Malaysia*	32	C5
Kudus, *Indonesia*	33	G14
Kudymkar, *Russia*	24	D6
Kueiyang = Guiyang, *China*	30	D5
Kufstein, *Austria*	16	E7
Kugong I., *Canada*	62	A4
Küh-e-Hazārām, *Iran*	39	D8
Kūhak, *Iran*	36	F3
Kūhbonān, *Iran*	39	D8
Kühestak, *Iran*	39	E8
Kūhīn, *Iran*	39	C6
Kūhīrī, *Iran*	39	E9
Kūhpāyeh, *Eşfahan, Iran*	39	C7
Kūhpāyeh, *Kermān, Iran*	39	D8
Kuito, *Angola*	47	G3
Kuji, *Japan*	28	D10
Kujū-San, *Japan*	29	H5
Kukawa, *Nigeria*	45	F7
Kukerin, *Australia*	53	F2
Kukësi, *Albania*	21	C9
Kula, *Turkey*	21	E13
Kulai, *Malaysia*	34	T16
Kulasekarappattinam, *India*	36	Q11
Kuldiga, *Latvia*	9	H19
Kuldja = Yining, *China*	24	E9
Kulin, *Australia*	53	F2
Kulja, *Australia*	53	F2
Kulm, *U.S.A.*	70	B5
Kŭlob, *Tajikistan*	24	F7
Kulsary, *Kazakhstan*	23	E9
Kulumbura, *Australia*	52	B4
Kulunda, *Russia*	24	D8
Kulwin, *Australia*	55	F3
Kulyab = Kŭlob, *Tajikistan*	24	F7
Kum Tekei, *Kazakhstan*	24	E8
Kuma →, *Russia*	23	F8

Kumagaya, *Japan* . . . 29 F9
Kumai, *Indonesia* 32 E4
Kumamba, Kepulauan,
  Indonesia 33 E9
Kumamoto, *Japan* 29 H5
Kumamoto □, *Japan* . . 29 H5
Kumanovo, *Macedonia* 21 C9
Kumara, *N.Z.* 51 K3
Kumarl, *Australia* . . . 53 F3
Kumasi, *Ghana* 44 G4
Kumayri = Gyumri,
  Armenia 23 F7
Kumba, *Cameroon* . . . 44 H6
Kumbakonam, *India* . 36 P11
Kumbarilla, *Australia* . 55 D5
Kume-Shima, *Japan* . . 29 L3
Kumertau, *Russia* . . . 22 D10
Kumla, *Sweden* 9 G16
Kumo, *Nigeria* 44 F7
Kumon Bum, *Burma* . 37 F20
Kunama, *Australia* . . . 55 F4
Kunashir, Ostrov,
  Russia 25 E15
Kunda, *Estonia* 9 G22
Kungala, *Australia* . . . 55 D5
Kunghit I., *Canada* . . 64 C2
Kungrad = Qünghirot,
  Uzbekistan 24 E6
Kungsbacka, *Sweden* . 9 H15
Kungur, *Russia* 22 C10
Kungurri, *Australia* . . 54 C4
Kuningan, *Indonesia* . 33 G13
Kunlong, *Burma* . . . 37 H21
Kunlun Shan, *Asia* . . 30 C3
Kunming, *China* 30 D5
Kununurra, *Australia* . 52 C4
Kunwarara, *Australia* . 54 C5
Kunya-Urgench =
  Köneürgench,
  Turkmenistan 24 E6
Kuopio, *Finland* 8 E22
Kupa →, *Croatia* . . . 16 F9
Kupang, *Indonesia* . . 33 F6
Kupyansk, *Ukraine* . . 24 E4
Kuqa, *China* 30 B3
Kür = Azərbaijan . . 23 G8
Kura = Kür →,
  Azerbaijan 23 G8
Kuranda, *Australia* . . 54 B4
Kurashiki, *Japan* 29 G6
Kurayoshi, *Japan* . . . 29 G6
Kürdzhali, *Bulgaria* . . 21 D11
Kure, *Japan* 29 G6
Kuressaare, *Estonia* . . 9 G20
Kurgaldzhinskiy,
  Kazakhstan 24 D8
Kurgan, *Russia* 24 D7
Kuria Maria Is. =
  Khūrīyā Mūrīyā, Jazā
  'ir, *Oman* 40 D6
Kuridala, *Australia* . . 54 C3
Kurigram, *Bangla.* . . 37 G16
Kurikka, *Finland* 9 E20
Kuril Is. = Kurilskiye
  Ostrova, *Russia* . . . 25 E15
Kuril Trench, *Pac. Oc.* 56 C7
Kurilsk, *Russia* 25 E15
Kurilskiye Ostrova,
  Russia 25 E15
Kurino, *Japan* 29 J5
Kurmuk, *Sudan* 45 F11
Kurnool, *India* 36 M10
Kuro-Shima,
  Kagoshima, Japan . 29 J4
Kuro-Shima, *Okinawa,
  Japan* 29 M2
Kurow, *N.Z.* 51 L3
Kurrajong, *Australia* . 55 E5
Kurri Kurri, *Australia* . 55 E5
Kurshskiy Zaliv, *Russia* 9 J19
Kursk, *Russia* 22 D6
Kuruktag, *China* 30 B3
Kuruman, *S. Africa* . . 48 D3
Kuruman →, *S. Africa* 48 D3
Kurume, *Japan* 29 H5
Kurunegala, *Sri Lanka* 36 R12
Kurya, *Russia* 25 C11
Kus Gölü, *Turkey* . . . 21 D12
Kuşadası, *Turkey* . . . 21 F12
Kusatsu, *Japan* 29 F9
Kusawa L., *Canada* . . 64 A1
Kushikino, *Japan* . . . 29 J5
Kushima, *Japan* 29 J5
Kushimoto, *Japan* . . . 29 H7
Kushiro, *Japan* 28 C12
Kushiro →, *Japan* . . 28 C12
Küshk, *Iran* 39 D8
Kushka = Gushgy,
  Turkmenistan 24 F7
Küshkī, *Īlām, Iran* . . 38 C5
Küshkī, *Khorāsān, Iran* 39 B8
Küshkü, *Iran* 39 E7
Kushtia, *Bangla.* . . . 37 H16
Kushva, *Russia* 22 C10
Kuskokwim →, *U.S.A.* 60 B3
Kuskokwim B., *U.S.A.* 60 C3
Kussharo-Ko, *Japan* . 28 C12
Kustanay = Qostanay,
  Kazakhstan 24 D7
Kütahya, *Turkey* 23 G5
Kutaisi, *Georgia* 23 F7
Kutaraja = Banda Aceh,
  Indonesia 32 C1
Kutch, Gulf of =
  Kachchh, Gulf of,
  India 36 H6
Kutch, Rann of =
  Kachchh, Rann of,
  India 36 H7
Kutno, *Poland* 17 B10
Kuttabul, *Australia* . . 54 C4
Kutu, *Zaïre* 46 E3
Kutum, *Sudan* 45 F9

Kuujjuaq, *Canada* . . . 61 C13
Kuusamo, *Finland* . . . 8 D23
Kuusankoski, *Finland* . 9 F22
Kuwait = Al Kuwayt,
  Kuwait 38 D5
Kuwait ■, *Asia* 38 D5
Kuwana, *Japan* 29 G8
Kuybyshev = Samara,
  Russia 22 D9
Kuybyshev, *Russia* . . 24 D8
Kuybyshevskoye
  Vdkhr., *Russia* 22 C8
Küyeh, *Iran* 38 B5
Küysanjaq, *Iraq* 38 B5
Kuyto, Ozero, *Russia* . 22 B5
Kuyumba, *Russia* . . . 25 C10
Kuzey Anadolu Dağları,
  Turkey 23 F6
Kuznetsk, *Russia* . . . 22 D8
Kuzomen, *Russia* . . . 22 A6
Kvænangen, *Norway* . 8 A19
Kvaløy, *Norway* 8 B18
Kvarner, *Croatia* 16 F8
Kvarnerič, *Croatia* . . . 16 F8
Kwabhaca, *S. Africa* . 49 E4
Kwadacha →, *Canada* 64 B3
Kwakhanai, *Botswana* 48 C3
Kwakoegron, *Surinam* 79 B7
KwaMashu, *S. Africa* . 49 D5
Kwamouth, *Zaïre* . . . 46 E3
Kwando →, *Africa* . . 48 B3
Kwangju, *S. Korea* . . 31 C7
Kwangsi-Chuang =
  Guangxi Zhuangzu
  Zizhiqu □, *China* . . 31 D5
Kwangtung =
  Guangdong □, *China* 31 D6
Kwataboahegan →,
  Canada 62 B3
Kwatisore, *Indonesia* . 33 E8
KwaZulu Natal □,
  S. Africa 49 D5
Kweichow =
  Guizhou □, *China* . . 30 D5
Kwekwe, *Zimbabwe* . . 47 H5
Kwidzyn, *Poland* . . . 17 B10
Kwinana New Town,
  Australia 53 F2
Kwoka, *Indonesia* . . . 33 E8
Kyabé, *Chad* 45 G8
Kyabra Cr. →,
  Australia 55 D3
Kyabram, *Australia* . . 55 F4
Kyaikto, *Burma* 34 D4
Kyakhta, *Russia* 25 D11
Kyancutta, *Australia* . 55 E2
Kyangin, *Burma* . . . 37 K19
Kyaukpadaung, *Burma* 37 J19
Kyaukpyu, *Burma* . . 37 K18
Kyaukse, *Burma* 37 J20
Kyle Dam, *Zimbabwe* . 47 J6
Kyle of Lochalsh, *U.K.* 12 D3
Kymijoki →, *Finland* . 9 F22
Kyneton, *Australia* . . 55 F3
Kynuna, *Australia* . . . 54 C3
Kyō-ga-Saki, *Japan* . . 29 G7
Kyoga, L., *Uganda* . . 46 D6
Kyogle, *Australia* . . . 55 D5
Kyongpyaw, *Burma* . 37 L19
Kyōto, *Japan* 29 G7
Kyōto □, *Japan* 29 G7
Kyren, *Russia* 25 D11
Kyrenia, *Cyprus* 38 C2
Kyrgyzstan ■, *Asia* . . 24 E8
Kyrönjoki →, *Finland* . 8 E19
Kystatyam, *Russia* . . 25 C13
Kytal Ktakh, *Russia* . 25 C13
Kyulyunken, *Russia* . 25 C14
Kyunhla, *Burma* . . . 37 H19
Kyuquot, *Canada* . . . 64 C3
Kyūshū, *Japan* 29 H5
Kyūshū □, *Japan* . . . 29 H5
Kyūshū-Sanchi, *Japan* 29 H5
Kyustendil, *Bulgaria* . 21 C10
Kyusyur, *Russia* 25 B13
Kywong, *Australia* . . 55 E4
Kyyiv, *Ukraine* 17 C16
Kyyivske Vdskh.,
  Ukraine 17 C16
Kyzyl, *Russia* 25 D10
Kyzyl Kum, *Uzbekistan* 24 E7
Kyzyl-Kyya, *Kyrgyzstan* 24 E8
Kzyl-Orda = Qyzylorda,
  Kazakhstan 24 E7

L

La Albufera, *Spain* . . 19 C5
La Alcarria, *Spain* . . . 19 B4
La Asunción, *Venezuela* 78 A6
La Banda, *Argentina* . 80 B4
La Barge, *U.S.A.* . . . 72 E8
La Belle, *U.S.A.* 69 M5
La Biche →, *Canada* . 64 B4
La Boca, *Panama* . . . 74 H14
La Calera, *Chile* 80 C2
La Carlota, *Argentina* . 80 C4
La Ceiba, *Honduras* . . 74 D7
La Chaux de Fonds,
  Switz. 16 E4
La Chorrera, *Panama* . 74 H14
La Cocha, *Argentina* . 80 B3
La Conner, *U.S.A.* . . 72 B2
La Coruña, *Spain* . . . 19 A1
La Crete, *Canada* . . . 64 B5
La Crosse, *Kans.,
  U.S.A.* 70 F5
La Crosse, *Wis., U.S.A.* 70 D9
La Dorada, *Colombia* . 78 B4
La Estrada, *Spain* . . . 19 A1

La Fayette, *U.S.A.* . . . 69 H3
La Follette, *U.S.A.* . . 69 G3
La Grande, *U.S.A.* . . 72 D4
La Grande, *Ga., U.S.A.* 69 J3
La Grange, *Ky., U.S.A.* 68 F3
La Grange, *Tex., U.S.A.* 71 L6
La Guaira, *Venezuela* . 78 A5
La Güera, *Mauritania* . 44 D1
La Habana, *Cuba* . . . 75 C8
La Harpe, *U.S.A.* . . . 70 E9
La Jara, *U.S.A.* 73 H11
La Junta, *U.S.A.* . . . 71 F3
La Línea de la
  Concepción, *Spain* . 19 D3
La Loche, *Canada* . . . 65 B7
La Louvière, *Belgium* . 15 D4
La Malbaie, *Canada* . . 63 C5
La Mancha, *Spain* . . . 19 C4
La Mesa, *Calif., U.S.A.* 73 K5
La Mesa, *N. Mex.,
  U.S.A.* 73 K10
La Moure, *U.S.A.* . . . 70 B5
La Palma, *Canary Is.* . 44 C1
La Palma, *Panama* . . 75 F9
La Palma del Condado,
  Spain 19 D2
La Paragua, *Venezuela* 78 B6
La Paz, *Entre Ríos,
  Argentina* 80 C5
La Paz, *San Luis,
  Argentina* 80 C3
La Paz, *Bolivia* 78 G5
La Paz, *Mexico* 74 C2
La Pedrera, *Colombia* . 78 D5
La Perouse Str., *Asia* . 28 B11
La Pine, *U.S.A.* 72 E3
La Plant, *U.S.A.* 70 C4
La Plata, *Argentina* . . 80 D5
La Porte, *U.S.A.* 68 E2
La Push, *U.S.A.* 72 C1
La Quiaca, *Argentina* . 80 A3
La Reine, *Canada* . . . 62 C4
La Rioja, *Argentina* . . 80 B3
La Rioja □, *Spain* . . . 19 A4
La Robla, *Spain* 19 A3
La Roche-sur-Yon,
  France 18 C3
La Rochelle, *France* . . 18 C3
La Roda, *Spain* 19 C4
La Romana, *Dom. Rep.* 75 D11
La Ronge, *Canada* . . 65 B7
La Salle, *U.S.A.* 70 E10
La Sarre, *Canada* . . . 62 C4
La Scie, *Canada* 63 C8
La Serena, *Chile* 80 B2
La Seyne-sur-Mer,
  France 18 E6
La Spézia, *Italy* 20 B3
La Tortuga, *Venezuela* 75 E11
La Tuque, *Canada* . . 62 C5
La Unión, *Chile* 80 E2
La Urbana, *Venezuela* 78 B5
La Vega, *Dom. Rep.* . 75 D10
Labe = Elbe →,
  Europe 16 B5
Labé, *Guinea* 44 F2
Laberge, L., *Canada* . 64 A1
Labis, *Malaysia* 34 S16
Laboulaye, *Argentina* . 80 C4
Labrador, Coast of □,
  Canada 63 B7
Labrador City, *Canada* 63 B6
Lábrea, *Brazil* 78 E6
Labuan, Pulau,
  Malaysia 32 C5
Labuha, *Indonesia* . . 33 E7
Labuhan, *Indonesia* . . 33 G11
Labuhanbajo, *Indonesia* 33 F6
Labuk, Telok, *Malaysia* 32 C5
Labyrinth L., *Australia* 55 E2
Labytnangi, *Russia* . . 22 A12
Lac Allard, *Canada* . . 63 B7
Lac Bouchette, *Canada* 63 C5
Lac du Flambeau,
  U.S.A. 70 B10
Lac Édouard, *Canada* . 62 C5
Lac La Biche, *Canada* . 64 C6
Lac la Martre, *Canada* 60 B8
Lac-Mégantic, *Canada* 63 C5
Lac Seul, Res., *Canada* 62 B1
Lacanau, *France* 18 D3
Laccadive Is. =
  Lakshadweep Is.,
  Ind. Oc. 26 H11
Lacepede B., *Australia* 55 F2
Lacepede Is., *Australia* 52 C3
Lachine, *Canada* 62 C5
Lachlan →, *Australia* . 55 E3
Lachute, *Canada* 62 C5
Lackawanna, *U.S.A.* . 68 D6
Lacombe, *Canada* . . . 64 C6
Laconia, *U.S.A.* 68 D10
Lacrosse, *U.S.A.* . . . 72 C5
Ladakh Ra., *India* . . 36 C11
Ladismith, *S. Africa* . 48 E3
Lādīz, *Iran* 39 D9
Ladoga, L. =
  Ladozhskoye Ozero,
  Russia 22 B5
Ladozhskoye Ozero,
  Russia 22 B5
Lady Grey, *S. Africa* . 48 E4
Ladybrand, *S. Africa* . 48 D4
Ladysmith, *Canada* . . 64 D4
Ladysmith, *S. Africa* . 49 D4
Ladysmith, *U.S.A.* . . 70 C9
Lae, *Papua N. G.* . . . 56 H6
Læsø, *Denmark* 9 H14
Lafayette, *Colo., U.S.A.* 70 F2
Lafayette, *Ind., U.S.A.* 68 E2
Lafayette, *La., U.S.A.* 71 K9
Lafayette, *Tenn., U.S.A.* 69 G3
Laferte →, *Canada* . 64 A5

Lafia, *Nigeria* 44 G6
Lafleche, *Canada* . . . 65 D7
Lagan →, *U.K.* 13 B6
Lagarfljót →, *Iceland* . 8 D6
Lågen →, *Oppland,
  Norway* 9 F14
Lågen →, *Vestfold,
  Norway* 9 G14
Laghouat, *Algeria* . . . 44 B5
Lagonoy Gulf, *Phil.* . . 33 B6
Lagos, *Nigeria* 44 G5
Lagos, *Portugal* 19 D1
Lagrange, *Australia* . . 52 C3
Lagrange B., *Australia* 52 C3
Laguna, *Brazil* 80 B7
Laguna, *U.S.A.* 73 J10
Laguna Beach, *U.S.A.* 73 K5
Lagunas, *Chile* 78 H5
Lagunas, *Peru* 78 E3
Lahad Datu, *Malaysia* . 33 C5
Lahat, *Indonesia* 32 E2
Lahewa, *Indonesia* . . 32 D1
Lāhījān, *Iran* 39 B6
Lahn →, *Germany* . . 16 C4
Laholm, *Sweden* 9 H15
Lahontan Reservoir,
  U.S.A. 72 G4
Lahore, *Pakistan* . . . 36 D9
Lahti, *Finland* 9 F21
Lahtis = Lahti, *Finland* 9 F21
Laï, *Chad* 45 G8
Lai Chau, *Vietnam* . . 34 A7
Laidley, *Australia* . . . 55 D5
Laingsburg, *S. Africa* . 48 E3
Lainio älv →, *Sweden* 8 C20
Lairg, *U.K.* 12 C4
Lajere, *Nigeria* 44 F7
Lajes, *Brazil* 80 B6
Lake Andes, *U.S.A.* . 70 D5
Lake Anse, *U.S.A.* . . 68 B1
Lake Arthur, *U.S.A.* . 71 K8
Lake Cargelligo,
  Australia 55 E4
Lake Charles, *U.S.A.* . 71 K8
Lake City, *Colo., U.S.A.* 73 G10
Lake City, *Fla., U.S.A.* 69 K4
Lake City, *Iowa, U.S.A.* 70 D7
Lake City, *Mich., U.S.A.* 68 C3
Lake City, *Minn., U.S.A.* 70 C8
Lake City, *S.C., U.S.A.* 69 J6
Lake Grace, *Australia* . 53 F2
Lake Harbour, *Canada* 61 B13
Lake Havasu City,
  U.S.A. 73 J6
Lake King, *Australia* . 53 F2
Lake Lenore, *Canada* . 65 C8
Lake Louise, *Canada* . 64 C5
Lake Mead National
  Recreation Area,
  U.S.A. 73 J6
Lake Mills, *U.S.A.* . . 70 D8
Lake Nash, *Australia* . 54 C2
Lake Providence, *U.S.A.* 71 J9
Lake River, *Canada* . . 62 B3
Lake Superior Prov.
  Park, *Canada* 62 C3
Lake Village, *U.S.A.* . 71 J9
Lake Wales, *U.S.A.* . . 69 M5
Lake Worth, *U.S.A.* . . 69 M5
Lakefield, *Canada* . . . 62 D4
Lakeland, *Australia* . . 54 B3
Lakeland, *U.S.A.* . . . 69 L5
Lakemba, *Fiji* 51 D9
Lakes Entrance,
  Australia 55 F4
Lakeside, *Ariz., U.S.A.* 73 J9
Lakeside, *Nebr., U.S.A.* 70 D3
Lakeview, *U.S.A.* . . . 72 E3
Lakewood, *Colo.,
  U.S.A.* 70 F2
Lakewood, *N.J., U.S.A.* 68 E8
Lakewood, *Ohio, U.S.A.* 68 E5
Lakin, *U.S.A.* 71 G4
Lakitusaki →, *Canada* 62 B3
Lakonikós Kólpos,
  Greece 21 F10
Lakor, *Indonesia* 33 F7
Lakota, *Ivory C.* 44 G3
Lakota, *U.S.A.* 70 A5
Laksefjorden, *Norway* . 8 A22
Lakselv, *Norway* 8 A21
Lakshadweep Is.,
  Ind. Oc. 26 H11
Lala Ghat, *India* . . . 37 G18
Lalibela, *Ethiopia* . . . 45 F12
Lalín, *Spain* 19 A1
Lalitapur = Patan,
  Nepal 37 F14
Lamaing, *Burma* . . . 37 M20
Lamar, *Colo., U.S.A.* . 70 F3
Lamar, *Mo., U.S.A.* . 71 G7
Lamas, *Peru* 78 E3
Lambaréné, *Gabon* . . 46 E2
Lambasa, *Fiji* 51 C8
Lambay I., *Ireland* . . . 13 C5
Lambert, *U.S.A.* 70 B2
Lambert Glacier,
  Antarctica 5 D6
Lamberts Bay, *S. Africa* 48 E2
Lambi Kyun, *Burma* . 34 G5
Lame, *Nigeria* 44 F6
Lame Deer, *U.S.A.* . . 72 D10
Lamego, *Portugal* . . . 19 B2
Lamon Bay, *Phil.* . . . 33 B6
Lamont, *Canada* 64 C6
Lampa, *Peru* 78 G4
Lampang, *Thailand* . . 34 C5
Lampasas, *U.S.A.* . . . 71 K5

Lampedusa, *Medit. S.* 20 G5
Las Anod, *Somali Rep.* 40 F4
Lampione, *Medit. S.* . 20 G5
Lampman, *Canada* . . 65 D8
Lamprey, *Canada* . . . 65 B10
Lampung □, *Indonesia* 32 F2
Lamu, *Kenya* 46 E8
Lamy, *U.S.A.* 73 J11
Lanai I., *U.S.A.* 66 H16
Lanak La, *India* 36 B11
Lanak'o Shank'ou =
  Lanak La, *India* . . . 36 B11
Lanao, L., *Phil.* 33 C6
Lanark, *U.K.* 12 F5
Lancang Jiang →,
  China 30 D5
Lancashire □, *U.K.* . . 10 D5
Lancaster, *U.K.* 10 C5
Lancaster, *Calif., U.S.A.* 73 J4
Lancaster, *Ky., U.S.A.* 68 G3
Lancaster, *N.H., U.S.A.* 68 C10
Lancaster, *Pa., U.S.A.* 68 E7
Lancaster, *S.C., U.S.A.* 69 H5
Lancaster, *Wis., U.S.A.* 70 D9
Lancaster Sd., *Canada* 61 A11
Lancer, *Canada* 65 C7
Lanchow = Lanzhou,
  China 30 C5
Lanciano, *Italy* 20 C6
Landeck, *Austria* . . . 16 E6
Landen, *Belgium* . . . 15 D5
Lander, *U.S.A.* 72 E9
Landes, *France* 18 D3
Landi Kotal, *Pakistan* . 36 B7
Landor, *Australia* . . . 53 E2
Land's End, *U.K.* . . . 11 G2
Landsborough Cr. →,
  Australia 54 C3
Landshut, *Germany* . . 16 D7
Landskrona, *Sweden* . 9 J15
Lanett, *U.S.A.* 69 J3
Lang Bay, *Canada* . . 64 D4
Lang Son, *Vietnam* . . 34 B9
La'nga Co, *China* . . . 37 D12
Langar, *Iran* 39 C9
Langara I., *Canada* . . 64 C2
Langdon, *U.S.A.* 70 A5
Langeberg, *S. Africa* . 48 E3
Langeberge, *S. Africa* . 48 D3
Langeland, *Denmark* . 9 J14
Langenburg, *Canada* . 65 C8
Langholm, *U.K.* 12 F6
Langjökull, *Iceland* . . 8 D3
Langkawi, P., *Malaysia* 34 J5
Langklip, *S. Africa* . . 48 D3
Langkon, *Malaysia* . . 32 C5
Langlade, St- P. & M. . 63 C8
Langlois, *U.S.A.* 72 E1
Langøya, *Norway* . . . 8 B16
Langres, *France* 18 C6
Langres, Plateau de,
  France 18 C6
Langsa, *Indonesia* . . . 32 D1
Langtry, *U.S.A.* 71 L4
Languedoc, *France* . . 18 E5
Lanigan, *Canada* . . . 65 C7
Länkäran, *Azerbaijan* . 23 G8
Lannion, *France* 18 B2
L'Annonciation, *Canada* 62 C5
Lansdowne, *Australia* . 55 E5
Lansdowne House,
  Canada 62 B2
L'Anse, *U.S.A.* 62 C2
L'Anse au Loup,
  Canada 63 B8
Lansing, *U.S.A.* 68 D3
Lanusei, *Italy* 20 E3
Lanzarote, *Canary Is.* . 44 C2
Lanzhou, *China* 30 C5
Lao Cai, *Vietnam* . . . 34 A7
Laoag, *Phil.* 33 A6
Laoang, *Phil.* 33 B7
Laois □, *Ireland* 13 C4
Laon, *France* 18 B5
Laona, *U.S.A.* 68 C1
Laos ■, *Asia* 34 D8
Lapa, *Brazil* 80 B7
Laparan, *Phil.* 33 C6
Lapeer, *U.S.A.* 68 D4
Lapland = Lappland,
  Europe 8 B21
Lappeenranta, *Finland* 9 F23
Lappland, *Europe* . . . 8 B21
Lapseki, *Turkey* 21 D12
Laptev Sea, *Russia* . . 25 B13
Lapua, *Finland* 8 E20
L'Áquila, *Italy* 20 C5
Lār, *Āzarbāyjān-e Sharqī,
  Iran* 38 B5
Lār, *Fārs, Iran* 39 E7
Larache, *Morocco* . . . 44 A3
Laramie, *U.S.A.* 70 E2
Laramie Mts., *U.S.A.* . 70 E2
Larantuka, *Indonesia* . 33 F6
Larap, *Phil.* 33 B6
Larat, *Indonesia* 33 F8
Larder Lake, *Canada* . 62 C4
Laredo, *U.S.A.* 71 M5
Laredo Sd., *Canada* . . 64 C3
Largs, *U.K.* 12 F4
Lariang, *Indonesia* . . 33 E5
Larimore, *U.S.A.* . . . 70 B6
Lārīn, *Iran* 39 C7
Lárisa, *Greece* 21 E10
Larnaca, *Cyprus* 38 C2
Larned, *U.S.A.* 70 F5
Larrimah, *Australia* . . 52 C5
Larsen Ice Shelf,
  Antarctica 5 C17
Larvik, *Norway* 9 G14
Laryak, *Russia* 24 C8

Las Animas, *U.S.A.* . . 70 F3
Las Cascadas, *Panama* 74 H14
Las Cruces, *U.S.A.* . . 73 K10
Las Flores, *Argentina* . 80 D5
Las Khoreh,
  Somali Rep. 40 E4
Las Lajas, *Argentina* . 80 D2
Las Lomitas, *Argentina* 80 A4
Las Palmas, *Canary Is.* 44 C1
Las Pipinas, *Argentina* 80 D5
Las Plumas, *Argentina* 80 E3
Las Rosas, *Argentina* . 80 C4
Las Varillas, *Argentina* 80 C4
Las Vegas, *N. Mex.,
  U.S.A.* 73 J11
Las Vegas, *Nev., U.S.A.* 73 J6
Lashburn, *Canada* . . . 65 C7
Lashio, *Burma* 37 H20
Lassen Pk., *U.S.A.* . . 72 F3
Last Mountain L.,
  Canada 65 C7
Lastoursville, *Gabon* . 46 E2
Lastovo, *Croatia* 20 C7
Latacunga, *Ecuador* . . 78 D3
Latakia = Al
  Lādhiqīyah, *Syria* . . 38 C2
Latchford, *Canada* . . 62 C4
Latham, *Australia* . . . 53 E2
Latina, *Italy* 20 D5
Latium = Lazio □, *Italy* 20 C5
Latouche Treville, C.,
  Australia 52 C3
Latrobe, *Australia* . . . 54 G4
Latvia ■, *Europe* . . . 9 H20
Lau Group, *Fiji* 51 C9
Lauchhammer,
  Germany 16 C7
Laukaa, *Finland* 9 E21
Launceston, *Australia* . 54 G4
Launceston, *U.K.* . . . 11 G3
Laune →, *Ireland* . . . 13 D2
Launglon Bok, *Burma* . 34 G5
Laura, *Australia* 54 B3
Laurel, *Miss., U.S.A.* . 71 K10
Laurel, *Mont., U.S.A.* . 72 D9
Laurencekirk, *U.K.* . . 12 E6
Laurens, *U.S.A.* 69 H4
Laurentian Plateau,
  Canada 63 B6
Laurentides, Parc Prov.
  des, *Canada* 63 C5
Lauria, *Italy* 20 E6
Laurie L., *Canada* . . . 65 B8
Laurinburg, *U.S.A.* . . 69 H6
Laurium, *U.S.A.* 62 B1
Lausanne, *Switz.* 16 E4
Laut, *Indonesia* 32 D3
Laut Kecil, Kepulauan,
  Indonesia 32 E5
Lautoka, *Fiji* 51 C7
Lauzon, *Canada* 63 C5
Lava Hot Springs,
  U.S.A. 72 E7
Laval, *France* 18 B3
Laverne, *U.S.A.* 71 G5
Laverton, *Australia* . . 53 E3
Lavrentiya, *Russia* . . 25 C19
Lávrion, *Greece* 21 F11
Lavumisa, *Swaziland* . 49 D5
Lawas, *Malaysia* 32 C5
Lawele, *Indonesia* . . . 33 F6
Lawn Hill, *Australia* . . 54 B2
Lawng Pit, *Burma* . . 37 G20
Lawqah, *Si. Arabia* . . 38 D4
Lawrence, *N.Z.* 51 L2
Lawrence, *Kans., U.S.A.* 70 F7
Lawrence, *Mass.,
  U.S.A.* 68 D10
Lawrenceburg, *Ind.,
  U.S.A.* 68 F3
Lawrenceburg, *Tenn.,
  U.S.A.* 69 H2
Lawrenceville, *U.S.A.* . 69 J4
Lawton, *U.S.A.* 71 H5
Lawu, *Indonesia* 33 G14
Laxford, L., *U.K.* . . . 12 C3
Laylān, *Iraq* 38 C5
Laysan I., *Pac. Oc.* . . 57 F11
Laytonville, *U.S.A.* . . 72 G2
Lazio □, *Italy* 20 C5
Lazo, *Russia* 28 C6
Le François, *Martinique* 74 N21
Le Havre, *France* . . . 18 B4
Le Mans, *France* 18 C4
Le Mars, *U.S.A.* 70 D6
Le Mont-St.-Michel,
  France 18 B3
Le Moule, *Guadeloupe* 75 D12
Le Puy-en-Velay, *France* 18 D5
Le Roy, *U.S.A.* 71 F7
Le Sueur, *U.S.A.* . . . 70 C8
Le Touquet-Paris-Plage,
  France 18 A4
Le Tréport, *France* . . 18 A4
Le Verdon-sur-Mer,
  France 18 D3
Lea →, *U.K.* 11 F7
Lead, *U.S.A.* 70 C3
Leader, *Canada* 65 C7
Leadhills, *U.K.* 12 F5
Leadville, *U.S.A.* . . . 73 G10
Leaf →, *U.S.A.* 71 K10
Leakey, *U.S.A.* 71 L5
Leamington, *Canada* . 62 D3
Leamington, *U.S.A.* . . 72 G7
Leamington Spa =
  Royal Leamington
  Spa, *U.K.* 11 E6
Leandro Norte Alem,
  Argentina 80 B5
Learmonth, *Australia* . 52 D1

Leask, Canada 65 C7
Leavenworth, Kans.,
  U.S.A. 70 F7
Leavenworth, Wash.,
  U.S.A. 72 C3
Lebak, Phil. 33 C6
Lebanon, Ind., U.S.A. . 68 E2
Lebanon, Kans., U.S.A. 70 F5
Lebanon, Ky., U.S.A. . . 68 G3
Lebanon, Mo., U.S.A. . 71 G8
Lebanon, Oreg., U.S.A. 72 D2
Lebanon, Pa., U.S.A. . . 68 E7
Lebanon, Tenn., U.S.A. 69 G2
Lebanon ■, Asia 41 B4
Lebec, U.S.A. 73 J4
Lebomboberge,
  S. Africa 49 C5
Lębork, Poland 17 A9
Lebrija, Spain 19 D2
Lebu, Chile 80 D2
Lecce, Italy 21 D8
Lecco, Italy 20 B3
Lech →, Germany 16 D6
Łęczyca, Poland 17 B10
Ledbury, U.K. 11 E5
Leduc, Canada 64 C6
Lee →, Ireland 13 E3
Leech L., U.S.A. 70 B7
Leedey, U.S.A. 71 H5
Leeds, U.K. 10 D6
Leeds, U.S.A. 69 J2
Leek, U.K. 10 D5
Leer, Germany 16 B4
Leesburg, U.S.A. 69 L5
Leesville, U.S.A. 71 K8
Leeton, Australia 55 E4
Leeu Gamka, S. Africa 48 E3
Leeuwarden, Neths. . . 15 A5
Leeuwin, C., Australia 53 F2
Leeward Is., Atl. Oc. . 74 L18
Lefors, U.S.A. 71 H4
Lefroy, L., Australia . . 53 F3
Legal, Canada 64 C6
Leganés, Spain 19 B4
Legazpi, Phil. 33 B6
Legendre I., Australia . 52 D2
Leghorn = Livorno,
  Italy 20 C4
Legionowo, Poland . . . 17 B11
Legnago, Italy 20 B4
Legnica, Poland 16 C9
Legume, Australia . . . 55 D5
Leh, India 36 B10
Lehi, U.S.A. 72 F8
Lehututu, Botswana . . 48 C3
Leicester, U.K. 11 E6
Leicestershire □, U.K. . 11 E6
Leichhardt →,
  Australia 54 B2
Leichhardt Ra.,
  Australia 54 C4
Leiden, Neths. 15 B4
Leie →, Belgium 15 C3
Leine →, Germany . . . 16 B5
Leinster, Australia . . . 53 E3
Leinster □, Ireland . . . 13 C4
Leinster, Mt., Ireland . 13 D5
Leipzig, Germany 16 C7
Leiria, Portugal 19 C1
Leirvik, Norway 9 G11
Leisler, Mt., Australia . 52 D4
Leith, U.K. 12 F5
Leith Hill, U.K. 11 F7
Leitrim, Ireland 13 B3
Leitrim □, Ireland 13 B3
Leizhou Bandao, China 31 D6
Lek →, Neths. 15 C4
Leka, Norway 8 D14
Leksula, Indonesia . . . 33 E7
Lékva Ori, Greece . . . 21 G11
Leland, U.S.A. 71 J9
Leland Lakes, Canada . 65 A6
Lelystad, Neths. 15 B5
Léman, L., Europe . . . 16 E4
Lemhi Ra., U.S.A. 72 D7
Lemmer, Neths. 15 B5
Lemmon, U.S.A. 70 C3
Lemoore, U.S.A. 73 H4
Lemvig, Denmark 9 H13
Lena →, Russia 25 B13
Lendeh, Iran 39 D6
Lenggong, Malaysia . . 34 P13
Leninabad =
  Khudzhand, Tajikistan 24 E7
Leninakan = Gyumri,
  Armenia 23 F7
Leningrad = Sankt-
  Peterburg, Russia . . 22 C5
Leninogorsk = Ridder,
  Kazakhstan 24 D9
Leninsk, Russia 23 E8
Leninsk-Kuznetskiy,
  Russia 24 D9
Leninskoye, Russia . . . 25 E14
Lenkoran = Länkäran,
  Azerbaijan 23 G8
Lenmalu, Indonesia . . 33 E8
Lenoir, U.S.A. 69 H5
Lenoir City, U.S.A. . . . 69 H3
Lenora, U.S.A. 70 F4
Lenore L., Canada . . . 65 C8
Lens, France 18 A5
Lensk, Russia 25 C12
Lentini, Italy 20 F6
Leoben, Austria 16 E8
Leodhas = Lewis, U.K. 12 C2
Leola, U.S.A. 70 C5
Leominster, U.K. 11 E5
Leominster, U.S.A. . . . 68 D10
León, Mexico 74 C4
León, Nic. 74 E7
León, Spain 19 A3

Leon, U.S.A. 70 E8
León, Montañas de,
  Spain 19 A2
Leonardtown, U.S.A. . . 68 F7
Leongatha, Australia . . 55 F4
Leonora, Australia . . . 53 E3
Léopold II, Lac = Mai-
  Ndombe, L., Zaïre . . 46 E3
Leopoldsburg, Belgium 15 C5
Léopoldville =
  Kinshasa, Zaïre . . . 46 E3
Leoti, U.S.A. 70 F4
Leova, Moldova 17 E15
Leoville, Canada 65 C7
Lépa, L. do, Angola . . 48 B2
Lepel = Lyepyel,
  Belarus 22 D4
Lepikha, Russia 25 C13
Léré, Chad 45 G7
Leribe, Lesotho 49 D4
Lérida, Spain 19 B6
Lerwick, U.K. 12 A7
Les Cayes, Haiti 75 D10
Les Étroits, Canada . . 63 C6
Les Sables-d'Olonne,
  France 18 C3
Lesbos = Lésvos,
  Greece 21 E12
Leshan, China 30 D5
Leshukonskoye, Russia 22 B8
Leskov I., Antarctica . . 5 B1
Leskovac, Serbia, Yug. 21 C9
Leslie, U.S.A. 71 H8
Lesopilnoye, Russia . . 28 A7
Lesotho ■, Africa 49 D4
Lesozavodsk, Russia . . 25 E14
Lesse →, Belgium . . . 15 D4
Lesser Antilles,
  W. Indies 75 E12
Lesser Slave L., Canada 64 B5
Lesser Sunda Is.,
  Indonesia 33 F6
Lessines, Belgium 15 D3
Lestock, Canada 65 C8
Lesuer I., Australia . . . 52 B4
Lésvos, Greece 21 E12
Leszno, Poland 17 C9
Letchworth, U.K. 11 F7
Lethbridge, Canada . . 64 D6
Leti, Kepulauan,
  Indonesia 33 F7
Leti Is. = Leti,
  Kepulauan, Indonesia 33 F7
Letiahau →, Botswana 48 C3
Leticia, Colombia 78 D4
Letjiesbos, S. Africa . . 48 E3
Letlhakane, Botswana . 48 C4
Letpadan, Burma 37 L19
Letpan, Burma 37 K19
Letsôk-aw Kyun, Burma 34 G5
Letterkenny, Ireland . . 13 B4
Leuser, G., Indonesia . 32 D1
Leuven, Belgium 15 D4
Leuze, Hainaut,
  Belgium 15 D3
Leuze, Namur, Belgium 15 D4
Levádhia, Greece 21 E10
Levan, U.S.A. 72 G8
Levanger, Norway 8 E14
Levelland, U.S.A. 71 J3
Leven, U.K. 12 E6
Leven, L., U.K. 12 E5
Leven, Toraka, Madag. 49 A8
Leveque, C., Australia . 52 C3
Levice, Slovak Rep. . . . 17 D10
Levin, N.Z. 51 J5
Lévis, Canada 63 C5
Levis, L., Canada 64 A5
Levkás, Greece 21 E9
Levkôsia = Nicosia,
  Cyprus 38 C2
Levskigrad = Karlovo,
  Bulgaria 21 C11
Lewellen, U.S.A. 70 E3
Lewes, U.K. 11 G8
Lewes, U.S.A. 68 F8
Lewis, U.S.A. 12 C2
Lewis, Butt of, U.K. . . 12 C2
Lewis Ra., Australia . . 52 D4
Lewis Range, U.S.A. . . 72 C7
Lewisburg, U.S.A. 69 H2
Lewisporte, Canada . . 63 C8
Lewiston, Idaho, U.S.A. 72 C5
Lewiston, Maine, U.S.A. 69 C11
Lewistown, Mont.,
  U.S.A. 72 C9
Lewistown, Pa., U.S.A. 68 E7
Lexington, Ill., U.S.A. . 70 E10
Lexington, Ky., U.S.A. . 68 F3
Lexington, Miss., U.S.A. 71 J9
Lexington, Mo., U.S.A. 70 F8
Lexington, N.C., U.S.A. 69 H5
Lexington, Nebr.,
  U.S.A. 70 E5
Lexington, Oreg.,
  U.S.A. 72 D4
Lexington, Tenn.,
  U.S.A. 69 H1
Lexington Park, U.S.A. 68 F7
Leyte, Phil. 33 B6
Lezha, Albania 21 D8
Lhasa, China 30 D4
Lhazê, China 30 D3
Lhokkruet, Indonesia . . 32 D1
Lhokseumawe,
  Indonesia 32 C1
Lhuntsi Dzong, India . . 37 F17
Lianga, Phil. 33 C7
Lianyungang, China . . 31 C6
Liaoning □, China . . . 31 B7
Liaoyang, China 31 B7
Liaoyuan, China 31 B7

Liard →, Canada 64 A4
Libau = Liepāja, Latvia 9 H19
Libby, U.S.A. 72 B6
Libenge, Zaïre 46 D3
Liberal, Kans., U.S.A. . 71 G4
Liberal, Mo., U.S.A. . . 71 G7
Liberec, Czech. 16 C8
Liberia, Costa Rica . . . 75 F13
Liberia ■, W. Afr. 44 G3
Liberty, Mo., U.S.A. . . 70 F7
Liberty, Tex., U.S.A. . . 71 K7
Lîbîya, Sahrâ', Africa . 45 C9
Libobo, Tanjung,
  Indonesia 33 E7
Libode, S. Africa 49 E4
Libonda, Zambia 47 G4
Libourne, France 18 D3
Libramont, Belgium . . 15 E5
Libreville, Gabon 46 D1
Libya ■, N. Afr. 45 C8
Libyan Desert = Lîbîya,
  Sahrâ', Africa 45 C9
Licantén, Chile 80 D2
Licata, Italy 20 F5
Lichfield, U.K. 10 E6
Lichinga, Mozam. 47 G7
Lichtenburg, S. Africa . 48 D4
Lida, Belarus 9 K21
Lida, U.S.A. 73 H5
Lidköping, Sweden . . . 9 G15
Liebig, Mt., Australia . 52 D5
Liechtenstein ■, Europe 16 E5
Liège, Belgium 15 D5
Liège □, Belgium 15 D5
Liegnitz = Legnica,
  Poland 16 C9
Lienyünchiangshih =
  Lianyungang, China . 31 C6
Lienz, Austria 16 E7
Liepāja, Latvia 9 H19
Lier, Belgium 15 C4
Lièvre →, Canada . . . 62 C4
Liffey →, Ireland 13 C5
Lifford, Ireland 13 B4
Lifudzin, Russia 28 B7
Lightning Ridge,
  Australia 55 D4
Liguria □, Italy 20 B3
Ligurian Sea, Medit. S. 20 C3
Lihou Reefs and Cays,
  Australia 54 B5
Lihue, U.S.A. 66 H15
Lijiang, China 30 D5
Likasi, Zaïre 46 G5
Likati, Zaïre 46 D4
Lille, France 18 A5
Lille Bælt, Denmark . . 9 J13
Lillehammer, Norway . 9 F14
Lillesand, Norway 9 G13
Lilleshall, U.K. 11 E5
Lillian Point, Mt.,
  Australia 53 E4
Lillooet →, Canada . . 64 D4
Lilongwe, Malawi 47 G6
Liloy, Phil. 33 C6
Lim →, Bos.-H. 21 C8
Lima, Indonesia 33 E7
Lima, Peru 78 F3
Lima, Mont., U.S.A. . . 72 D7
Lima, Ohio, U.S.A. . . . 68 E3
Lima →, Portugal . . . 19 B1
Limassol, Cyprus 38 C2
Limavady, U.K. 13 A5
Limavady □, U.K. 13 B5
Limay →, Argentina . . 80 D3
Limay Mahuida,
  Argentina 80 D3
Limbang, Brunei 32 D5
Limbaži, Latvia 9 H21
Limbe, Cameroon 44 H6
Limbri, Australia 55 E5
Limbunya, Australia . . 52 C4
Limburg, Germany . . . 16 C5
Limburg □, Belgium . . 15 C5
Limburg □, Neths. . . . 15 C5
Limeira, Brazil 80 A7
Limerick, Ireland 13 D3
Limerick □, Ireland . . . 13 D3
Limestone →, Canada 65 B10
Limfjorden, Denmark . 9 H13
Limia = Lima →,
  Portugal 19 B1
Limingen, Norway 8 D15
Limmen Bight,
  Australia 54 A2
Limmen Bight →,
  Australia 54 B2
Límnos, Greece 21 E11
Limoeiro do Norte,
  Brazil 79 E11
Limoges, France 18 D4
Limón, Costa Rica . . . 75 F8
Limon, Panama 74 H14
Limon, U.S.A. 70 F3
Limon B., Panama . . . 74 H14
Limousin, France 18 D4
Limoux, France 18 E5
Limpopo →, Africa . . 49 D5
Limuru, Kenya 46 E7
Linares, Chile 80 D2
Linares, Mexico 74 C5
Linares, Spain 19 C4
Linaro, Argentina 80 D3
Lincheng, China 31 D6
Lincoln, N.Z. 51 K4
Lincoln, U.K. 10 D7
Lincoln, Ill., U.S.A. . . . 70 E10
Lincoln, Kans., U.S.A. . 70 F5
Lincoln, Maine, U.S.A. 63 C6
Lincoln, N. Mex., U.S.A. 73 K11
Lincoln, Nebr., U.S.A. . 70 E6
Lincoln Hav = Lincoln
  Sea, Arctic 4 A5
Lincoln Sea, Arctic . . . 4 A5
Lincolnshire □, U.K. . . 10 D7

Lincolnshire Wolds,
  U.K. 10 D7
Lincolnton, U.S.A. 69 H5
Lind, U.S.A. 72 C4
Linden, Guyana 78 B7
Linden, U.S.A. 71 J7
Lindesnes, Norway . . . 9 H12
Lindhos, Greece 21 F13
Lindi, Tanzania 46 F7
Lindsay, Canada 62 D4
Lindsay, Calif., U.S.A. . 73 H4
Lindsay, Okla., U.S.A. . 71 H6
Lindsborg, U.S.A. 70 F6
Lingayen, Phil. 33 A6
Lingayen G., Phil. 33 A6
Lingen, Germany 16 B4
Lingga, Indonesia 32 E2
Lingga, Kepulauan,
  Indonesia 32 E2
Lingga Arch. = Lingga,
  Kepulauan, Indonesia 32 E2
Lingle, U.S.A. 70 D2
Linguère, Senegal . . . 44 E1
Linh Cam, Vietnam . . . 34 C8
Linhai, China 31 D7
Linhares, Brazil 79 G10
Linköping, Sweden . . . 9 G16
Linlithgow, U.K. 12 F5
Linnhe, L., U.K. 12 E3
Linosa, I., Medit. S. . . 20 G5
Lins, Brazil 80 A7
Lintlaw, Canada 65 C8
Linton, Canada 63 C5
Linton, Ind., U.S.A. . . . 68 F2
Linton, N. Dak., U.S.A. 70 B4
Linville, Australia 55 D5
Linxia, China 30 C5
Linyanti →, Africa . . . 48 B4
Linz, Austria 16 D8
Lion, G. du, France . . 18 E6
Lions, G. of = Lion, G.
  du, France 18 E6
Lion's Head, Canada . 62 D3
Lipa, Phil. 33 B6
Lipari, Italy 20 E6
Lipari, Is. = Éolie, Ís.,
  Italy 20 E6
Lipcani, Moldova 17 D14
Lipetsk, Russia 22 D6
Lipkany = Lipcani,
  Moldova 17 D14
Lipovcy Manzovka,
  Russia 28 B6
Lipovets, Ukraine 17 D15
Lippe →, Germany . . . 16 C4
Lipscomb, U.S.A. 71 G4
Liptrap C., Australia . . 55 F4
Lira, Uganda 46 D6
Liria, Spain 19 C5
Lisala, Zaïre 46 D4
Lisboa, Portugal 19 C1
Lisbon = Lisboa,
  Portugal 19 C1
Lisbon, U.S.A. 70 B6
Lisburn, U.K. 13 B5
Lisburne, C., U.S.A. . . 60 B3
Liscannor, B., Ireland . 13 D2
Lisianski I., Pac. Oc. . . 56 E10
Lisichansk =
  Lysychansk, Ukraine 23 E6
Lisieux, France 18 B4
Liski, Russia 23 D6
Lismore, Australia . . . 55 D5
Lismore, Ireland 13 D4
Lisse, Neths. 15 B4
Lista, Norway 9 G12
Lister, Mt., Antarctica . 5 D11
Liston, Australia 55 D5
Listowel, Canada 62 D3
Listowel, Ireland 13 D2
Litang, Malaysia 33 C5
Litani →, Lebanon . . . 41 B4
Litchfield, Ill., U.S.A. . . 70 F10
Litchfield, Minn., U.S.A. 70 C7
Lithgow, Australia 55 E5
Líthinon, Ákra, Greece 21 G11
Lithuania ■, Europe . . 9 J20
Litoměřice, Czech. . . . 16 C8
Little Andaman I., India 34 G2
Little Barrier I., N.Z. . . 51 G5
Little Belt Mts., U.S.A. 72 C8
Little Blue →, U.S.A. . 70 F6
Little Cadotte →,
  Canada 64 B5
Little Churchill →,
  Canada 65 B9
Little Colorado →,
  U.S.A. 73 H8
Little Current, Canada 62 C3
Little Current →,
  Canada 62 B3
Little Falls, Minn.,
  U.S.A. 70 C7
Little Falls, N.Y., U.S.A. 68 D8
Little Fork →, U.S.A. . 70 A8
Little Grand Rapids,
  Canada 65 C9
Little Humboldt →,
  U.S.A. 72 F5
Little Karoo, S. Africa . 48 E3
Little Lake, U.S.A. . . . 73 J5
Little Laut = Laut
  Kecil, Kepulauan,
  Indonesia 32 E5
Little Missouri →,
  U.S.A. 70 B3
Little Ouse →, U.K. . . 11 E8
Little Red →, U.S.A. . 71 H9
Little River, N.Z. 51 K4
Little Rock, U.S.A. . . . 71 H8
Little Sable Pt., U.S.A. 68 D2
Little Sioux →, U.S.A. 70 E6

Little Smoky →,
  Canada 64 C5
Little Snake →, U.S.A. 72 F9
Little Wabash →,
  U.S.A. 68 G1
Littlefield, U.S.A. 71 J3
Littlefork, U.S.A. 70 A8
Littlehampton, U.K. . . 11 G7
Littleton, U.S.A. 68 C10
Liukang Tenggaja,
  Indonesia 33 F5
Liuwa Plain, Zambia . . 47 G4
Liuzhou, China 31 D5
Live Oak, U.S.A. 69 K4
Liveringa, Australia . . 52 C3
Livermore, Mt., U.S.A. 71 K2
Liverpool, Australia . . 55 E5
Liverpool, Canada . . . 63 D7
Liverpool, U.K. 10 D5
Liverpool Plains,
  Australia 55 E5
Liverpool Ra., Australia 55 E5
Livingston, Mont.,
  U.S.A. 72 D8
Livingston, Tex., U.S.A. 71 K7
Livingstone, Zambia . . 47 H5
Livingstonia, Malawi . 46 G6
Livny, Russia 22 D6
Livonia, U.S.A. 68 D4
Livorno, Italy 20 C4
Livramento, Brazil . . . 80 C5
Liwale, Tanzania 46 F7
Lizard I., Australia . . . 54 A4
Lizard Pt., U.K. 11 H2
Ljubljana, Slovenia . . . 16 E8
Ljungan →, Sweden . . 9 E17
Ljungby, Sweden 9 H15
Ljusdal, Sweden 9 F17
Ljusnan →, Sweden . . 9 F17
Ljusne, Sweden 9 F17
Llancanelo, Salina,
  Argentina 80 D3
Llandeilo, U.K. 11 F3
Llandovery, U.K. 11 F4
Llandrindod Wells, U.K. 11 E4
Llandudno, U.K. 10 D4
Llanelli, U.K. 11 F3
Llanes, Spain 19 A3
Llangollen, U.K. 10 E4
Llanidloes, U.K. 11 E4
Llano, U.S.A. 71 K5
Llano →, U.S.A. 71 K5
Llano Estacado, U.S.A. 71 J3
Llanos, S. Amer. 78 B4
Lleida = Lérida, Spain 19 B6
Llobregat →, Spain . . 19 B7
Lloyd B., Australia . . . 54 A3
Lloyd L., Canada 65 B7
Lloydminster, Canada . 65 C6
Lluchmayor, Spain . . . 19 C7
Llullaillaco, Volcán,
  S. Amer. 80 A3
Loa, U.S.A. 73 G8
Loa →, Chile 80 A2
Lobatse, Botswana . . . 48 D4
Loberia, Argentina . . . 80 D5
Lobito, Angola 47 G2
Loc Binh, Vietnam . . . 34 B9
Loc Ninh, Vietnam . . . 34 G9
Locarno, Switz. 16 E5
Loch Garman =
  Wexford, Ireland . . 13 D5
Lochaber, U.K. 12 E4
Locharron, U.K. 12 D3
Lochem, Neths. 15 B6
Loches, France 18 C4
Lochgelly, U.K. 12 E5
Lochgilphead, U.K. . . . 12 E3
Lochinver, U.K. 12 C3
Lochnagar, Australia . . 54 C4
Lochnagar, U.K. 12 E5
Lochy →, U.K. 12 E3
Lock, Australia 55 E2
Lock Haven, U.S.A. . . 68 E7
Lockeport, Canada . . . 63 D6
Lockerbie, U.K. 12 F5
Lockhart, U.S.A. 71 L6
Lockhart, L., Australia . 53 F2
Lockney, U.S.A. 71 H4
Lockport, U.S.A. 68 D6
Lod, Israel 41 D3
Lodeinoye Pole, Russia 22 B5
Lodge Grass, U.S.A. . . 72 D10
Lodgepole, U.S.A. . . . 70 E3
Lodgepole Cr. →,
  U.S.A. 70 E2
Lodhran, Pakistan . . . 36 E7
Lodi, Italy 20 B3
Lodi, U.S.A. 72 G3
Lodja, Zaïre 46 E4
Lodwar, Kenya 46 D7
Łódź, Poland 17 C10
Loeriesfontein, S. Africa 48 E2
Lofoten, Norway 8 B15
Logan, Kans., U.S.A. . . 70 F5
Logan, Ohio, U.S.A. . . 68 F4
Logan, Utah, U.S.A. . . 72 F8
Logan, W. Va., U.S.A. . 68 G5
Logan, Mt., Canada . . 60 B5
Logan Pass, U.S.A. . . 64 D6
Logansport, Ind., U.S.A. 68 E2
Logansport, La., U.S.A. 71 K8
Logone →, Chad 45 F8
Logroño, Spain 19 A4
Lohardaga, India 37 H14
Lohja, Finland 9 F21
Loi-kaw, Burma 37 K20
Loimaa, Finland 9 F20
Loir →, France 18 C3
Loire →, France 18 C2
Loja, Ecuador 78 D3
Loja, Spain 19 D3

Loji, Indonesia 33 E7
Lokandu, Zaïre 46 E5
Lokeren, Belgium 15 C3
Lokitaung, Kenya 46 D7
Lokkan tekojärvi,
  Finland 8 C22
Lokoja, Nigeria 44 G6
Lokolama, Zaïre 46 E3
Loliondo, Tanzania . . . 46 E7
Lolland, Denmark 9 J14
Lolo, U.S.A. 72 C6
Lom, Bulgaria 21 C10
Loma, U.S.A. 72 C8
Lomami →, Zaïre 46 D4
Lombadina, Australia . 52 C3
Lombárdia □, Italy . . . 20 B3
Lombardy =
  Lombárdia □, Italy . 20 B3
Lomblen, Indonesia . . 33 F6
Lombok, Indonesia . . . 32 F5
Lomé, Togo 44 G5
Lomela, Zaïre 46 E4
Lomela →, Zaïre 46 E4
Lometa, U.S.A. 71 K5
Lomié, Cameroon 46 D2
Lomond, Canada 64 C6
Lomond, L., U.K. 12 E4
Lompobatang,
  Indonesia 33 F5
Lompoc, U.S.A. 73 J3
Łomża, Poland 17 B12
Loncoche, Chile 80 D2
Londa, India 36 M9
London, Canada 62 D3
London, U.K. 11 F7
London, Ky., U.S.A. . . 68 G3
London, Ohio, U.S.A. . 68 F4
London, Greater □,
  U.K. 11 F7
Londonderry, U.K. . . . 13 B4
Londonderry □, U.K. . 13 B4
Londonderry, C.,
  Australia 52 B4
Londonderry, I., Chile . 80 H2
Londrina, Brazil 80 A6
Lone Pine, U.S.A. 73 H4
Long Beach, Calif.,
  U.S.A. 73 K4
Long Beach, Wash.,
  U.S.A. 72 C1
Long Branch, U.S.A. . . 68 E9
Long Creek, U.S.A. . . . 72 D4
Long Eaton, U.K. 10 E6
Long I., Australia 54 C4
Long I., Bahamas 75 C9
Long I., U.S.A. 68 E9
Long L., Canada 62 C2
Long Pine, U.S.A. 70 D5
Long Pt., Canada 63 C8
Long Range Mts.,
  Canada 63 C8
Long Reef, Australia . . 52 B4
Long Str. = Longa,
  Proliv, Russia 4 C16
Long Xuyen, Vietnam . 34 G8
Longa, Proliv, Russia . 4 C16
Longford, Australia . . . 54 G4
Longford, Ireland 13 C4
Longford □, Ireland . . 13 C4
Longiram, Indonesia . . 32 E5
Longlac, Canada 62 C2
Longmont, U.S.A. 70 E2
Longnawan, Indonesia 32 D4
Longreach, Australia . . 54 C3
Longton, Australia . . . 54 C4
Longtown, U.K. 11 F5
Longview, Canada . . . 64 C6
Longview, Tex., U.S.A. 71 J7
Longview, Wash.,
  U.S.A. 72 C2
Lonoke, U.S.A. 71 H9
Lons-le-Saunier, France 18 C6
Lookout, C., Canada . . 62 A3
Lookout, C., U.S.A. . . 69 H7
Loon →, Alta., Canada 64 B5
Loon →, Man.,
  Canada 65 B8
Loon Lake, Canada . . 65 C7
Loongana, Australia . . 53 F4
Loop Hd., Ireland 13 D2
Lop Nor = Lop Nur,
  China 30 B4
Lop Nur, China 30 B4
Lopatina, G., Russia . . 25 D15
Lopez, C., Gabon 46 E1
Lopphavet, Norway . . 8 A19
Lora →, Afghan. 36 D4
Lora, Hamun-i-,
  Pakistan 36 E4
Lora Cr. →, Australia . 55 D2
Lora del Rio, Spain . . 19 D3
Lorain, U.S.A. 68 E4
Loralai, Pakistan 36 D6
Lorca, Spain 19 D5
Lord Howe I., Pac. Oc. 56 L7
Lord Howe Ridge,
  Pac. Oc. 56 L8
Lordsburg, U.S.A. 73 K9
Loreto, Brazil 79 E9
Lorient, France 18 C2
Lorn, U.K. 12 E3
Lorn, Firth of, U.K. . . . 12 E3
Lorne, Australia 55 F3
Lorraine, France 18 B7
Lorrainville, Canada . . 62 C4
Los Alamos, U.S.A. . . 73 J10
Los Andes, Chile 80 C2
Los Angeles, Chile . . . 80 D2
Los Angeles, U.S.A. . . 73 K4
Los Angeles Aqueduct,
  U.S.A. 73 J5
Los Banos, U.S.A. . . . 73 H3
Los Blancos, Argentina 80 A4

Los Hermanos

Los Hermanos, Venezuela 78 A6
Los Lunas, U.S.A. 73 J10
Los Mochis, Mexico 74 B3
Los Olivos, U.S.A. 73 J3
Los Roques, Venezuela 78 A5
Los Testigos, Venezuela 78 A6
Los Vilos, Chile 80 C2
Loshkalakh, Russia 25 C15
Lošinj, Croatia 16 F8
Lossiemouth, U.K. 12 D5
Lot →, France 18 D4
Lota, Chile 80 D2
Loṭfābād, Iran 39 B8
Lothair, S. Africa 49 D5
Lothian □, U.K. 12 F5
Loubomo, Congo 46 E2
Loudon, U.S.A. 69 H3
Louga, Senegal 44 E1
Loughborough, U.K. 10 E6
Loughrea, Ireland 13 C3
Loughros More B., Ireland 13 B3
Louis Trichardt, S. Africa 49 C4
Louis XIV, Pte., Canada 62 B4
Louisa, U.S.A. 68 F4
Louisbourg, Canada 63 C8
Louise I., Canada 64 C2
Louiseville, Canada 62 C5
Louisiade Arch., Papua N. G. 56 J7
Louisiana, U.S.A. 70 F9
Louisiana □, U.S.A. 71 K9
Louisville, Ky., U.S.A. 68 F3
Louisville, Miss., U.S.A. 71 J10
Loulé, Portugal 19 D1
Loup City, U.S.A. 70 E5
Lourdes, France 18 E3
Lourdes-du-Blanc-Sablon, Canada 63 B8
Lourenço-Marques = Maputo, Mozam. 49 D5
Louth, Australia 55 E4
Louth, Ireland 13 C5
Louth, U.K. 10 D7
Louth □, Ireland 13 C5
Louvain = Leuven, Belgium 15 D4
Louwsburg, S. Africa 49 D5
Love, Canada 65 C8
Lovech, Bulgaria 21 C11
Loveland, U.S.A. 70 E2
Lovell, U.S.A. 72 D9
Lovelock, U.S.A. 72 F4
Loviisa, Finland 9 F22
Loving, U.S.A. 71 J2
Lovington, U.S.A. 71 J3
Lovisa = Loviisa, Finland 9 F22
Low Pt., Australia 53 F4
Low Tatra = Nízké Tatry, Slovak Rep. 17 D10
Lowell, U.S.A. 68 D10
Lower Arrow L., Canada 64 D5
Lower California = Baja California, Mexico 74 B2
Lower Hutt, N.Z. 51 J5
Lower L., U.S.A. 72 F3
Lower Lake, U.S.A. 72 G2
Lower Post, Canada 64 B3
Lower Red L., U.S.A. 70 B7
Lower Saxony = Niedersachsen □, Germany 16 B5
Lower Tunguska = Tunguska, Nizhnyaya →, Russia 25 C9
Lowestoft, U.K. 11 E9
Łowicz, Poland 17 B10
Lowville, U.S.A. 68 D8
Loxton, Australia 55 E3
Loxton, S. Africa 48 E3
Loyalty Is. = Loyauté, Is., N. Cal. 56 K8
Loyang = Luoyang, China 31 C6
Loyauté, Is., N. Cal. 56 K8
Loyev = Loyew, Belarus 17 C16
Loyew, Belarus 17 C16
Luachimo, Angola 46 F4
Luacono, Angola 46 G4
Lualaba →, Zaïre 46 D5
Luan Chau, Vietnam 34 B7
Luanda, Angola 46 F2
Luang Prabang, Laos 34 C7
Luangwa, Zambia 47 H6
Luangwa →, Zambia 47 G6
Luanshya, Zambia 47 G5
Luapula →, Africa 46 F5
Luarca, Spain 19 A2
Luashi, Zaïre 46 G4
Luau, Angola 46 G4
Lubalo, Angola 46 F3
Lubana, Ozero = Lubānas Ezers, Latvia 9 H22
Lubānas Ezers, Latvia 9 H22
Lubang Is., Phil. 33 B6
Lubbock, U.S.A. 71 J4
Lübeck, Germany 16 B6
Lubefu, Zaïre 46 E4
Lubero = Luofu, Zaïre 46 E5
Lubicon L., Canada 64 B5
Lubin, Poland 16 C9
Lublin, Poland 17 C12
Lubnān, J., Lebanon 41 B4
Lubny, Ukraine 24 D4
Lubuagan, Phil. 33 A6
Lubuk Antu, Malaysia 32 D4
Lubuklinggau, Indonesia 32 E2
Lubuksikaping, Indonesia 32 D2
Lubumbashi, Zaïre 47 G5
Lubutu, Zaïre 46 E5
Lucca, Italy 20 C4
Luce Bay, U.K. 12 G4
Lucea, Jamaica 74 J15
Lucedale, U.S.A. 69 K1
Lucena, Phil. 33 B6
Lucena, Spain 19 D3
Lučenec, Slovak Rep. 17 D10
Lucerne = Luzern, Switz. 16 E5
Lucira, Angola 47 G2
Luckenwalde, Germany 16 B7
Lucknow, India 37 F12
Lüda = Dalian, China 31 C7
Lüderitz, Namibia 48 D2
Ludhiana, India 36 D9
Ludington, U.S.A. 68 D2
Ludlow, U.K. 11 E5
Ludlow, U.S.A. 73 J5
Ludvika, Sweden 9 F16
Ludwigsburg, Germany 16 D5
Ludwigshafen, Germany 16 D5
Luebo, Zaïre 46 F4
Lufira →, Zaïre 46 F5
Lufkin, U.S.A. 71 K7
Luga, Russia 22 C4
Lugano, Switz. 16 E5
Lugansk = Luhansk, Ukraine 23 E6
Lugh Ganana, Somali Rep. 40 G3
Lugnaquilla, Ireland 13 D5
Lugo, Italy 20 B4
Lugo, Spain 19 A2
Lugoj, Romania 17 F11
Lugovoy, Kazakhstan 24 E8
Luhansk, Ukraine 23 E6
Luiana, Angola 48 B3
Luimneach = Limerick, Ireland 13 D3
Luís Correia, Brazil 79 D10
Luitpold Coast, Antarctica 5 D1
Luiza, Zaïre 46 F4
Luján, Argentina 80 C5
Lukanga Swamp, Zambia 47 G5
Lukenie →, Zaïre 46 E3
Lukolela, Zaïre 46 E3
Łuków, Poland 17 C12
Lule älv →, Sweden 8 D19
Luleå, Sweden 8 D20
Lüleburgaz, Turkey 21 D12
Luling, U.S.A. 71 L6
Lulonga →, Zaïre 46 D3
Lulua →, Zaïre 46 E4
Luluabourg = Kananga, Zaïre 46 F4
Lumai, Angola 47 G4
Lumajang, Indonesia 33 H15
Lumbala N'guimbo, Angola 47 G4
Lumberton, Miss., U.S.A. 71 K10
Lumberton, N.C., U.S.A. 69 H6
Lumberton, N. Mex., U.S.A. 73 H10
Lumsden, N.Z. 51 L2
Lumut, Malaysia 34 Q13
Lumut, Tg., Indonesia 32 E3
Lund, Sweden 9 J15
Lund, U.S.A. 72 G6
Lundazi, Zambia 47 G6
Lundu, Malaysia 32 D3
Lundy, U.K. 11 F3
Lune →, U.K. 10 C5
Lüneburg, Germany 16 B6
Lüneburg Heath = Lüneburger Heide, Germany 16 B6
Lüneburger Heide, Germany 16 B6
Lunenburg, Canada 63 D7
Lunéville, France 18 B7
Lunglei, India 37 H18
Luni, India 36 G8
Luni →, India 36 G7
Luninets = Luninyets, Belarus 17 B14
Luning, U.S.A. 72 G4
Luninyets, Belarus 17 B14
Luofu, Zaïre 46 E5
Luoyang, China 31 C6
Luozi, Zaïre 46 E2
Lupanshui, China 30 D5
Luray, U.S.A. 68 F6
Luremo, Angola 46 F3
Lurgan, U.K. 13 B5
Lusaka, Zambia 47 H5
Lusambo, Zaïre 46 E4
Luseland, Canada 65 C7
Lushnja, Albania 21 D8
Lushoto, Tanzania 46 E7
Lusk, U.S.A. 70 D2
Luta = Dalian, China 31 C7
Luton, U.K. 11 F7
Lutong, Malaysia 32 D4
Lutsk, Ukraine 17 C13
Lützow Holmbukta, Antarctica 5 C4
Lutzputs, S. Africa 48 D3
Luverne, U.S.A. 70 D6
Luwuk, Indonesia 33 E6
Luxembourg, Lux. 18 B7
Luxembourg □, Belgium 15 E5
Luxembourg ■, Europe 18 B7
Luxi, China 30 D4
Luxor = El Uqsur, Egypt 45 C11
Luza, Russia 22 B8
Luzern, Switz. 16 E5
Luzhou, China 30 D5
Luziânia, Brazil 79 G9
Luzon, Phil. 33 A6
Lviv, Ukraine 17 D13
Lvov = Lviv, Ukraine 17 D13
Lyakhavichy, Belarus 17 B14
Lyakhovskiye, Ostrova, Russia 25 B15
Lyallpur = Faisalabad, Pakistan 36 D8
Lycksele, Sweden 8 D18
Lydda = Lod, Israel 41 D3
Lydenburg, S. Africa 49 D5
Lydia, Turkey 21 E13
Lyell, N.Z. 51 J4
Lyell I., Canada 64 C2
Lyepyel, Belarus 22 D4
Lyman, U.S.A. 72 F8
Lyme Regis, U.K. 11 G5
Lymington, U.K. 11 G6
Łyna →, Poland 9 J19
Lynchburg, U.S.A. 68 G6
Lynd →, Australia 54 B3
Lynd Ra., Australia 55 D4
Lynden, U.S.A. 72 B2
Lyndhurst, Queens., Australia 54 B3
Lyndhurst, S. Austral., Australia 55 E2
Lyndon →, Australia 53 D1
Lyngen, Norway 8 B19
Lynher Reef, Australia 52 C3
Lynn, U.S.A. 68 D10
Lynn Canal, U.S.A. 64 B1
Lynn Lake, Canada 65 B8
Lynton, U.K. 11 F4
Lyntupy, Belarus 9 J22
Lynx L., Canada 65 A7
Lyon, France 18 D6
Lyonnais, France 18 D6
Lyons = Lyon, France 18 D6
Lyons, Colo., U.S.A. 70 E2
Lyons, Ga., U.S.A. 69 J4
Lyons, Kans., U.S.A. 70 F5
Lyons, N.Y., U.S.A. 68 D7
Lys = Leie →, Belgium 15 C3
Lysva, Russia 22 C10
Lysychansk, Ukraine 23 E6
Lytle, U.S.A. 71 L5
Lyttelton, N.Z. 51 K4
Lytton, Canada 64 C4
Lyubertsy, Russia 22 C6
Lyuboml, Ukraine 17 C13

M

Ma'adaba, Jordan 41 E4
Maamba, Zambia 48 B4
Ma'ān, Jordan 41 E4
Ma'ān □, Jordan 41 F5
Maanselkä, Finland 8 C23
Ma'anshan, China 31 C6
Maarianhamina, Finland 9 F18
Ma'arrat an Nu'mān, Syria 38 C3
Maas →, Neths. 15 C4
Maaseik, Belgium 15 C5
Maassluis, Neths. 15 C4
Maastricht, Neths. 18 A6
Maave, Mozam. 49 C5
Mabel L., Canada 64 C5
Mablethorpe, U.K. 10 D8
Mabrouk, Mali 44 E4
Mabton, U.S.A. 72 C3
Macaé, Brazil 79 H10
McAlester, U.S.A. 71 H7
McAllen, U.S.A. 71 M5
Macamic, Canada 62 C4
Macao = Macau ■, China 31 D6
Macapá, Brazil 79 C8
McArthur →, Australia 54 B2
McArthur, Port, Australia 54 B2
McArthur River, Australia 54 B2
Macau, Brazil 79 E11
Macau ■, China 31 D6
McBride, Canada 64 C4
McCall, U.S.A. 72 D5
McCamey, U.S.A. 71 K3
McCammon, U.S.A. 72 E7
McCauley I., Canada 64 C2
Macclesfield, U.K. 10 D5
McClintock, Canada 65 B10
M'Clintock Chan., Canada 60 A9
McClintock Ra., Australia 52 C4
McCloud, U.S.A. 72 F2
McCluer I., Australia 52 B5
M'Clure Str., Canada 4 B2
McClusky, U.S.A. 70 B4
McComb, U.S.A. 71 K9
McConaughy, L., U.S.A. 70 E4
McCook, U.S.A. 70 E4
McCusker →, Canada 65 B7
McDame, Canada 64 B3
McDermitt, U.S.A. 72 F5
Macdonald, L., Australia 52 D4
McDonald Is., Ind. Oc. 35 K6
Macdonnell Ras., Australia 52 D5
McDouall Peak, Australia 55 D1
Macdougall L., Canada 60 B10
MacDowell L., Canada 62 B1
Macduff, U.K. 12 D6
Macedonia = Makedhonía □, Greece 21 D10
Macedonia ■, Europe 21 D9
Maceió, Brazil 79 E11
Macenta, Guinea 44 G3
Macerata, Italy 20 C5
McFarlane →, Canada 65 B7
Macfarlane, L., Australia 55 E2
McGehee, U.S.A. 71 J9
McGill, U.S.A. 72 G6
Macgillycuddy's Reeks, Ireland 13 D2
MacGregor, Canada 65 D9
McGregor, U.S.A. 70 D9
McGregor →, Canada 64 B4
McGregor Ra., Australia 55 D3
Mach, Pakistan 36 E5
Māch Kowr, Iran 39 E9
Machado = Jiparaná →, Brazil 78 E6
Machakos, Kenya 46 E7
Machala, Ecuador 78 D3
Machanga, Mozam. 49 C6
Machattie, L., Australia 54 C2
Machava, Mozam. 49 D5
Machevna, Russia 25 C18
Machias, U.S.A. 63 D6
Machichi →, Canada 65 B10
Machilipatnam, India 37 L12
Machiques, Venezuela 78 A4
Machupicchu, Peru 78 F4
Machynlleth, U.K. 11 E4
McIlwraith Ra., Australia 54 A3
McIntosh, U.S.A. 70 C4
McIntosh L., Canada 65 B8
Macintosh Ra., Australia 53 E4
Macintyre →, Australia 55 D5
Mackay, Australia 54 C4
Mackay, U.S.A. 72 E7
MacKay →, Canada 64 B6
Mackay, L., Australia 52 D4
McKay Ra., Australia 52 D3
McKeesport, U.S.A. 68 E6
Mackenzie, Canada 64 B4
McKenzie, U.S.A. 69 G1
Mackenzie →, Australia 54 C4
Mackenzie →, Canada 60 B6
McKenzie →, U.S.A. 72 D2
Mackenzie Bay, Canada 4 B1
Mackenzie City = Linden, Guyana 78 B7
Mackenzie Highway, Canada 64 B5
Mackenzie Mts., Canada 60 B6
Mackinaw City, U.S.A. 68 C3
McKinlay, Australia 54 C3
McKinlay →, Australia 54 C3
McKinley, Mt., U.S.A. 60 B4
McKinley Sea, Arctic 4 A7
McKinney, U.S.A. 71 J6
Macksville, Australia 55 E5
McLaughlin, U.S.A. 70 C4
Maclean, Australia 55 D5
McLean, U.S.A. 71 H4
McLeansboro, U.S.A. 70 F10
Maclear, S. Africa 49 E4
Macleay →, Australia 55 E5
McLennan, Canada 64 B5
MacLeod, B., Canada 65 A7
McLeod, L., Australia 53 D1
MacLeod Lake, Canada 64 C4
McLoughlin, Mt., U.S.A. 72 E2
McLure, Canada 64 C4
McMillan, L., U.S.A. 71 J2
McMinnville, Oreg., U.S.A. 72 D2
McMinnville, Tenn., U.S.A. 69 H3
McMorran, Canada 65 C7
McMurdo Sd., Antarctica 5 D11
McMurray = Fort McMurray, Canada 64 B6
McNary, U.S.A. 73 J9
MacNutt, Canada 65 C8
Macodoene, Mozam. 49 C6
Macomb, U.S.A. 70 E9
Mâcon, France 18 C6
Macon, Ga., U.S.A. 69 J4
Macon, Miss., U.S.A. 69 J1
Macon, Mo., U.S.A. 70 F8
Macondo, Angola 47 G4
Macoun L., Canada 65 B8
Macovane, Mozam. 49 C6
McPherson, U.S.A. 70 F6
McPherson Ra., Australia 55 D5
Macquarie Harbour, Australia 54 G4
Macquarie Is., Pac. Oc. 56 N7
MacRobertson Land, Antarctica 5 D6
Macroom, Ireland 13 E3
Macroy, Australia 52 D2
Macusse, Angola 48 B3
McVille, U.S.A. 70 B5
Madadeni, S. Africa 49 D5
Madagali, Nigeria 45 F7
Madagascar ■, Africa 49 C8
Madā'in Sālih, Si. Arabia 38 E3
Madama, Niger 45 D7
Madame I., Canada 63 C7
Madaoua, Niger 44 F6
Madaripur, Bangla. 37 H17
Madauk, Burma 37 L20
Madawaska →, Canada 62 C4
Madaya, Burma 37 H20
Maddalena, Italy 20 D3
Madden Dam, Panama 74 H14
Madden L., Panama 74 H14
Madeira, Atl. Oc. 44 B1
Madeira →, Brazil 78 D7
Madeleine, Is. de la, Canada 63 C7
Madera, U.S.A. 73 H3
Madha, India 36 L9
Madhya Pradesh □, India 36 H11
Madikeri, India 36 N9
Madill, U.S.A. 71 H6
Madimba, Zaïre 46 E3
Ma'din, Syria 38 C3
Madīnat ash Sha'b, Yemen 40 E3
Madingou, Congo 46 E2
Madirovalo, Madag. 49 B8
Madison, Fla., U.S.A. 69 K4
Madison, Ind., U.S.A. 68 F3
Madison, Nebr., U.S.A. 70 E6
Madison, S. Dak., U.S.A. 70 D6
Madison, Wis., U.S.A. 70 D10
Madison →, U.S.A. 72 D8
Madisonville, Ky., U.S.A. 68 G2
Madisonville, Tex., U.S.A. 71 K7
Madista, Botswana 48 C4
Madiun, Indonesia 33 G14
Madley, U.K. 11 E5
Madona, Latvia 9 H22
Madras = Tamil Nadu □, India 36 P10
Madras, India 36 N12
Madras, U.S.A. 72 D3
Madre, Laguna, U.S.A. 71 M6
Madre, Sierra, Phil. 33 A6
Madre de Dios →, Bolivia 78 F5
Madre de Dios, I., Chile 80 G1
Madre Occidental, Sierra, Mexico 74 B3
Madre Oriental, Sierra, Mexico 74 C5
Madrid, Spain 19 B4
Madura, Selat, Indonesia 33 G15
Madura Motel, Australia 53 F4
Madurai, India 36 Q11
Madurantakam, India 36 N11
Mae Hong Son, Thailand 34 C5
Mae Sot, Thailand 34 D5
Maebashi, Japan 29 F9
Maesteg, U.K. 11 F4
Maestrazgo, Mts. del, Spain 19 B5
Maevatanana, Madag. 49 B8
Mafeking = Mafikeng, S. Africa 48 D4
Mafeking, Canada 65 C8
Mafeteng, Lesotho 48 D4
Maffra, Australia 55 F4
Mafia I., Tanzania 46 F7
Mafikeng, S. Africa 48 D4
Mafra, Brazil 80 B7
Mafra, Portugal 19 C1
Magadan, Russia 25 D16
Magadi, Kenya 46 E7
Magaliesburg, S. Africa 49 D4
Magallanes, Estrecho de, Chile 80 G2
Magangué, Colombia 78 B4
Magburaka, S. Leone 44 G2
Magdalen Is. = Madeleine, Is. de la, Canada 63 C7
Magdalena, Argentina 80 D5
Magdalena, Bolivia 78 F6
Magdalena, Malaysia 32 D5
Magdalena, U.S.A. 73 J10
Magdalena →, Colombia 78 A4
Magdeburg, Germany 16 B6
Magdelaine Cays, Australia 54 B5
Magee, U.S.A. 71 K10
Magee, I., U.K. 13 B6
Magelang, Indonesia 33 G14
Magellan's Str. = Magallanes, Estrecho de, Chile 80 G2
Magenta, L., Australia 53 F2
Magerøya, Norway 8 A21
Maggiore, L., Italy 20 B3
Magherafelt, U.K. 13 B5
Magistralnyy, Russia 25 D11
Magnetic Pole (North) = North Magnetic Pole, Canada 4 B2
Magnetic Pole (South) = South Magnetic Pole, Antarctica 5 C9
Magnitogorsk, Russia 22 D10
Magnolia, Ark., U.S.A. 71 J8
Magnolia, Miss., U.S.A. 71 K9
Magog, Canada 63 C5
Magosa = Famagusta, Cyprus 38 C2
Magpie L., Canada 63 B7
Magrath, Canada 64 D6
Maguarinho, C., Brazil 79 D9
Mağusa = Famagusta, Cyprus 38 C2
Maguse L., Canada 65 A9
Maguse Pt., Canada 65 A10
Magwe, Burma 37 J19
Mahābād, Iran 38 B5
Mahabo, Madag. 49 C7
Mahagi, Zaïre 46 D6
Mahajamba →, Madag. 49 B8
Mahajamba, Helodranon' i, Madag. 49 B8
Mahajanga, Madag. 49 B8
Mahajanga □, Madag. 49 B8
Mahajilo →, Madag. 49 B8
Mahakam →, Indonesia 32 E5
Mahalapye, Botswana 48 C4
Maḥallāt, Iran 39 C6
Māhān, Iran 39 D8
Mahanadi →, India 37 J15
Mahanoro, Madag. 49 B8
Maharashtra □, India 36 J9
Mahasham, W. →, Egypt 41 E3
Mahasolo, Madag. 49 B8
Mahattat ash Shīdīyah, Jordan 41 F4
Mahattat 'Unayzah, Jordan 41 E4
Mahbubnagar, India 36 L10
Maḥḍah, Oman 39 E7
Mahdia, Tunisia 45 A7
Mahé, Seychelles 35 E4
Mahenge, Tanzania 46 F7
Maheno, N.Z. 51 L3
Mahesana, India 36 H8
Mahia Pen., N.Z. 51 H6
Mahilyow, Belarus 17 B16
Mahnomen, U.S.A. 70 B7
Mahón, Spain 19 C8
Mahone Bay, Canada 63 D7
Mai-Ndombe, L., Zaïre 46 E3
Maicurú →, Brazil 79 D8
Maidenhead, U.K. 11 F7
Maidstone, Canada 65 C7
Maidstone, U.K. 11 F8
Maiduguri, Nigeria 45 F7
Maijdi, Bangla. 37 H17
Maikala Ra., India 37 J12
Main →, Germany 16 C5
Main →, U.K. 13 B5
Main Centre, Canada 65 C7
Maine, France 18 C3
Maine □, U.S.A. 63 C6
Maine →, Ireland 13 D2
Maingkwan, Burma 37 F20
Mainit, L., Phil. 33 C7
Mainland, Orkney, U.K. 12 C5
Mainland, Shet., U.K. 12 A7
Maintirano, Madag. 49 B7
Mainz, Germany 16 C5
Maipú, Argentina 80 D5
Maiquetía, Venezuela 78 A5
Mairabari, India 37 F18
Maitland, N.S.W., Australia 55 E5
Maitland, S. Austral., Australia 55 E2
Maizuru, Japan 29 G7
Majalengka, Indonesia 33 G13
Majene, Indonesia 33 E5
Maji, Ethiopia 45 G12
Major, Canada 65 C7
Majorca = Mallorca, Spain 19 C7
Maka, Senegal 44 F2
Makale, Indonesia 33 E5
Makari, Cameroon 46 B2
Makarikari = Makgadikgadi Salt Pans, Botswana 48 C4
Makarovo, Russia 25 D11
Makasar = Ujung Pandang, Indonesia 33 F5
Makasar, Selat, Indonesia 33 E5
Makasar, Str. of = Makasar, Selat, Indonesia 33 E5
Makat, Kazakhstan 23 E9
Makedhonía □, Greece 21 D10
Makedonija = Macedonia ■, Europe 21 D9
Makena, U.S.A. 66 H16
Makeni, S. Leone 44 G2
Makeyevka = Makiyivka, Ukraine 23 E6
Makgadikgadi Salt Pans, Botswana 48 C4
Makhachkala, Russia 23 F8
Makhmūr, Iraq 38 C4
Makian, Indonesia 33 D7
Makindu, Kenya 46 E7
Makinsk, Kazakhstan 24 D8
Makiyivka, Ukraine 23 E6
Makkah, Si. Arabia 40 C2
Makkovik, Canada 63 A8
Makó, Hungary 17 E11
Makokou, Gabon 46 D2
Makoua, Congo 46 E3
Makrai, India 36 H10
Makran Coast Range, Pakistan 36 G4
Maksimkin Yar, Russia 24 D9
Mākū, Iran 38 B5
Makumbi, Zaïre 46 F4
Makunda, Botswana 48 C3
Makurazaki, Japan 29 J5
Makurdi, Nigeria 44 G6
Makūyeh, Iran 39 D7
Makwassie, S. Africa 48 D4
Mal B., Ireland 13 D2
Malabang, Phil. 33 C6

Malabar Coast, *India* . 36 P9
Malabo = Rey Malabo,
Eq. Guin. 44 H6
Malacca, Str. of,
Indonesia 34 S14
Malad City, U.S.A. . . 72 E7
Maladzyechna, Belarus 17 A14
Málaga, Spain 19 D3
Malaga, U.S.A. 71 J2
Malaimbandy, Madag. 49 C8
Malakâl, Sudan 45 G11
Malakoff, U.S.A. . . . 71 J7
Malamyzh, Russia . . 25 E14
Malang, Indonesia . . 33 G15
Malangen, Norway . . 8 B18
Malanje, Angola . . . 46 F3
Mälaren, Sweden . . . 9 G17
Malargüe, Argentina . 80 D3
Malartic, Canada . . . 62 C4
Malaryta, Belarus . . 17 C13
Malatya, Turkey . . . 23 G6
Malawi ■, Africa . . . 47 G6
Malawi, L., Africa . . . 47 G6
Malay Pen., Asia . . . 34 J4
Malaybalay, Phil. . . . 33 C7
Malâyer, Iran 39 C6
Malaysia ■, Asia . . . 32 D4
Malazgirt, Turkey . . . 23 G7
Malbon, Australia . . . 54 C3
Malbooma, Australia . 55 E1
Malbork, Poland . . . 17 B10
Malcolm, Australia . . 53 E3
Malcolm, Pt., Australia 53 F3
Maldegem, Belgium . 15 C3
Malden, U.S.A. 71 G10
Malden I., Kiribati . . 57 H12
Maldives ■, Ind. Oc. . 27 J11
Maldonado, Uruguay . 80 C6
Malé Karpaty,
Slovak Rep. 17 D9
Maléa, Ákra, Greece . 21 F10
Malegaon, India . . . 36 J9
Malek Kandī, Iran . . 38 B5
Malema, Mozam. . . . 47 G7
Malgomaj, Sweden . . 8 D17
Malha, Sudan 45 E10
Malheur →, U.S.A. . . 72 D5
Malheur L., U.S.A. . . 72 E4
Mali ■, Africa 44 E4
Mali →, Burma 37 G20
Mali Kyun, Burma . . 34 F5
Malik, Indonesia . . . 33 E6
Malili, Indonesia . . . 33 E6
Malin Hd., Ireland . . 13 A4
Malindi, Kenya 46 E8
Malines = Mechelen,
Belgium 15 C4
Malino, Indonesia . . 33 D6
Malita, Phil. 33 C7
Malkara, Turkey . . . 21 D12
Mallacoota, Australia . 55 F4
Mallacoota Inlet,
Australia 55 F4
Mallaig, U.K. 12 E3
Mallawi, Egypt 45 C11
Mallorca, Spain . . . 19 C7
Mallow, Ireland 13 D3
Malmberget, Sweden . 8 C19
Malmédy, Belgium . . 15 D6
Malmesbury, S. Africa 48 E2
Malmö, Sweden . . . 9 J15
Malolos, Phil. 33 B6
Malone, U.S.A. 68 C8
Måløy, Norway 9 F11
Malozemelskaya
Tundra, Russia . . . 22 A9
Malpelo, Colombia . . 78 C2
Malta, Idaho, U.S.A. . 72 E7
Malta, Mont., U.S.A. . 72 B10
Malta ■, Europe . . . 20 G6
Maltahöhe, Namibia . 48 C2
Malton, U.K. 10 C7
Maluku, Indonesia . . 33 E7
Maluku □, Indonesia . 33 E7
Maluku Sea = Molucca
Sea, Indonesia . . . 33 E6
Malvan, India 36 L8
Malvern, U.S.A. . . . 71 H8
Malvern Hills, U.K. . . 11 E5
Malvinas, Is. = Falkland
Is. □, Atl. Oc. . . . 80 G5
Malyn, Ukraine 17 C15
Malyy Lyakhovskiy,
Ostrov, Russia . . . 25 B15
Malyy Nimnyr, Russia . 25 D12
Mama, Russia 25 D12
Mamanguape, Brazil . 79 E11
Mamasa, Indonesia . . 33 E5
Mamberamo →,
Indonesia 33 E9
Mambilima Falls,
Zambia 46 G5
Mamburao, Phil. . . . 33 B6
Mameigwess L.,
Canada 62 B2
Mamfe, Cameroon . . 44 G6
Mammoth, U.S.A. . . 73 K8
Mamoré →, Bolivia . . 78 F5
Mamou, Guinea . . . 44 F2
Mamuju, Indonesia . . 33 E5
Man, Ivory C. 44 G3
Man, I. of, U.K. 10 C3
Man Na, Burma . . . 37 H20
Mana, Fr. Guiana . . . 79 B8
Manaar, G. of =
Mannar, G. of, Asia . 36 Q11
Manacapuru, Brazil . . 78 D6
Manacor, Spain . . . 19 C7
Manado, Indonesia . . 33 D6
Managua, Nic. 74 E7
Managua, L., Nic. . . 74 E7
Manakara, Madag. . . 49 C8
Manama = Al
Manāmah, Bahrain . 39 E6

Manambao →,
Madag. 49 B7
Manambato, Madag. . 49 A8
Manambolo →,
Madag. 49 B7
Manambolosy, Madag. 49 B8
Mananara, Madag. . . 49 B8
Mananara →, Madag. . 49 C8
Mananjary, Madag. . . 49 C8
Manantenina, Madag. 49 C8
Manaos = Manaus,
Brazil 78 D7
Manapouri, N.Z. . . . 51 L1
Manapouri, L., N.Z. . . 51 L1
Manas, China 30 B3
Manas →, India 37 F17
Manassa, U.S.A. . . . 73 H11
Manaung, Burma . . . 37 K18
Manawan L., Canada . 65 B8
Manay, Phil. 33 C7
Manbij, Syria 38 B3
Mancelona, U.S.A. . . 68 C3
Manchester, U.K. . . . 10 D5
Manchester, Conn.,
U.S.A. 68 E9
Manchester, Ga., U.S.A. 69 J3
Manchester, Iowa,
U.S.A. 70 D9
Manchester, Ky., U.S.A. 68 G4
Manchester, N.H.,
U.S.A. 68 D10
Manchester L., Canada 65 A7
Manchuria = Dongbei,
China 31 B7
Mand →, Iran 39 D7
Manda, Tanzania . . . 46 G6
Mandabé, Madag. . . 49 C7
Mandal, Norway . . . 9 G12
Mandalay, Burma . . 37 J20
Mandale = Mandalay,
Burma 37 J20
Mandalī, Iraq 38 C5
Mandan, U.S.A. . . . 70 B4
Mandar, Teluk,
Indonesia 33 E5
Mandasor = Mandsaur,
India 36 G9
Mandimba, Mozam. . . 47 G7
Mandioli, Indonesia . . 33 E7
Mandla, India 37 H12
Mandoto, Madag. . . . 49 B8
Mandrare →, Madag. . 49 D8
Mandritsara, Madag. . 49 B8
Mandsaur, India . . . 36 G9
Mandurah, Australia . 53 F2
Mandvi, India 36 H6
Mandya, India 36 N10
Maneh, Iran 39 B8
Maneroo, Australia . . 54 C3
Maneroo Cr. →,
Australia 54 C3
Manfalût, Egypt . . . 45 C11
Manfred, Australia . . 55 E3
Manfredónia, Italy . . 20 D6
Mangalia, Romania . . 17 G15
Mangalore, India . . . 36 N9
Mangaweka, N.Z. . . 51 H5
Manggar, Indonesia . . 32 E3
Manggawitu, Indonesia 33 E8
Mangkalihat, Tanjung,
Indonesia 33 D5
Mangla Dam, Pakistan 36 C8
Mangnai, China 30 C4
Mango, Togo 44 F5
Mangoche, Malawi . . 47 G7
Mangoky →, Madag. . 49 C7
Mangole, Indonesia . . 33 E7
Mangonui, N.Z. 51 F4
Mangueigne, Chad . . 45 F9
Mangueira, L. da, Brazil 80 C6
Mangum, U.S.A. . . . 71 H5
Mangyshlak Poluostrov,
Kazakhstan 24 E6
Manhattan, U.S.A. . . 70 F6
Manhiça, Mozam. . . . 49 D5
Manhuaçu, Brazil . . . 79 H10
Mania →, Madag. . . . 49 B8
Manica, Mozam. . . . 49 B5
Manica e Sofala □,
Mozam. 49 B5
Manicoré, Brazil . . . 78 E6
Manicouagan →,
Canada 63 C6
Manīfah, Si. Arabia . . 39 E6
Manifold, Australia . . 54 C5
Manifold, C., Australia 54 C5
Manigotagan, Canada 65 C9
Manihiki, Cook Is. . . 57 J11
Manila, Phil. 33 B6
Manila, U.S.A. 72 F9
Manila B., Phil. 33 B6
Manilla, Australia . . . 55 E5
Maningrida, Australia . 54 A1
Manipur □, India . . . 37 G18
Manipur →, Burma . . 37 H19
Manisa, Turkey 21 E12
Manistee, U.S.A. . . . 68 C2
Manistee →, U.S.A. . . 68 C2
Manistique, U.S.A. . . 68 C2
Manito L., Canada . . 65 C7
Manitoba □, Canada . 65 B9
Manitoba, L., Canada . 65 C9
Manitou, Canada . . . 65 D9
Manitou I., U.S.A. . . . 62 C2
Manitou Is., U.S.A. . . 68 C2
Manitou L., Canada . . 63 B6
Manitou Springs,
U.S.A. 70 F2
Manitoulin I., Canada . 62 C3
Manitowaning, Canada 62 C3

Manitowoc, U.S.A. . . 68 C2
Manizales, Colombia . 78 B3
Manja, Madag. 49 C7
Manjacaze, Mozam. . . 49 C5
Manjakandriana,
Madag. 49 B8
Manjhand, Pakistan . . 36 G6
Manjil, Iran 39 B6
Manjimup, Australia . 53 F2
Manjra →, India . . . 36 K10
Mankato, Kans., U.S.A. 70 F5
Mankato, Minn., U.S.A. 70 C8
Mankayane, Swaziland 49 D5
Mankono, Ivory C. . . 44 G3
Mankota, Canada . . . 65 D7
Manly, Australia . . . 55 E5
Manmad, India 36 J9
Mann Ras., Australia . 53 E5
Manna, Indonesia . . 32 E2
Mannahill, Australia . 55 E3
Mannar, Sri Lanka . . 36 Q11
Mannar, G. of, Asia . . 36 Q11
Mannar I., Sri Lanka . 36 Q11
Mannheim, Germany . 16 D5
Manning, Canada . . . 64 B5
Manning, U.S.A. . . . 69 J5
Mannington, U.S.A. . . 68 F5
Mannum, Australia . . 55 E2
Mano, S. Leone . . . 44 G2
Manokwari, Indonesia 33 E8
Manombo, Madag. . . 49 C7
Manono, Zaïre 46 F5
Manosque, France . . 18 E6
Manouane, L., Canada 63 B5
Manresa, Spain . . . 19 B6
Mansa, Zambia 46 G5
Mansel I., Canada . . 61 B11
Mansfield, Australia . 55 F4
Mansfield, U.K. 10 D6
Mansfield, La., U.S.A. . 71 J8
Mansfield, Ohio, U.S.A. 68 E4
Mansfield, Wash.,
U.S.A. 72 C4
Manson Creek, Canada 64 B4
Manta, Ecuador . . . 78 D2
Mantalingajan, Mt.,
Phil. 32 C5
Manteca, U.S.A. . . . 73 H3
Manteo, U.S.A. 69 H8
Mantes-la-Jolie, France 18 B4
Manthani, India 36 K11
Manti, U.S.A. 72 G8
Mantiqueira, Serra da,
Brazil 79 H10
Manton, U.S.A. 68 C3
Mántova, Italy 20 B4
Mantua = Mántova,
Italy 20 B4
Manu, Peru 78 F4
Manua Is.,
Amer. Samoa 51 B14
Manuae, Cook Is. . . . 57 J12
Manuel Alves →,
Brazil 79 F9
Manui, Indonesia . . . 33 E6
Manville, U.S.A. . . . 70 D2
Many, U.S.A. 71 K8
Manyara, L., Tanzania 46 E7
Manych-Gudilo, Ozero,
Russia 23 E7
Manyoni, Tanzania . . 46 F6
Manzai, Pakistan . . . 36 C7
Manzanares, Spain . . 19 C4
Manzanillo, Cuba . . . 75 C9
Manzanillo, Mexico . . 74 D4
Manzano Mts., U.S.A. 73 J10
Manzariyeh, Iran . . . 39 C6
Manzhouli, China . . . 31 B6
Manzini, Swaziland . . 49 D5
Mao, Chad 45 F8
Maoke, Pegunungan,
Indonesia 33 E9
Maoming, China . . . 31 D6
Mapam Yumco, China 30 C3
Mapia, Kepulauan,
Indonesia 33 D8
Mapinhane, Mozam. . . 49 C6
Maple Creek, Canada . 65 D7
Mapleton, U.S.A. . . . 72 D2
Mapuera →, Brazil . . 78 D7
Maputo, Mozam. . . . 49 D5
Maputo, B. de, Mozam. 49 D5
Maqnā, Si. Arabia . . 38 D2
Maquela do Zombo,
Angola 46 F3
Maquinchao, Argentina 80 E3
Maquoketa, U.S.A. . . 70 D9
Mar, Serra do, Brazil . 80 B7
Mar Chiquita, L.,
Argentina 80 C4
Mar del Plata,
Argentina 80 D5
Mar Menor, Spain . . 19 D5
Maraä, Brazil 78 D5
Marabá, Brazil 79 E9
Maracá, I. de, Brazil . 79 C8
Maracaibo, Venezuela 78 A4
Maracaibo, L. de,
Venezuela 78 B4
Maracay, Venezuela . 78 A5
Marādah, Libya 45 C8
Maradi, Niger 44 F6
Marāgheh, Iran 38 B5
Marāh, Si. Arabia . . . 38 E5
Marajó, I. de, Brazil . 79 D9
Marākand, Iran 38 B5
Maralal, Kenya 46 D7
Maralinga, Australia . 53 F5
Marama, Australia . . 55 F3
Marampa, S. Leone . . 44 G2

Marana, U.S.A. 73 K8
Maranboy, Australia . 52 B5
Marand, Iran 38 B5
Maranguape, Brazil . . 79 D11
Maranhão = São Luís,
Brazil 79 D10
Maranhão □, Brazil . . 79 E9
Maranoa →, Australia 55 D4
Marañón →, Peru . . 78 D4
Marão, Mozam. 49 C5
Maraş =
Kahramanmaraş,
Turkey 23 G6
Marathon, Australia . 54 C3
Marathon, Canada . . 62 C2
Marathon, U.S.A. . . . 71 K3
Maratua, Indonesia . . 33 D5
Marāwih, U.A.E. . . . 39 E7
Marbella, Spain . . . 19 D3
Marble Bar, Australia . 52 D2
Marble Falls, U.S.A. . 71 K5
Marburg, Germany . . 16 C5
March, U.K. 11 E8
Marche, France 18 C4
Marche-en-Famenne,
Belgium 15 D5
Marchena, Spain . . . 19 D3
Marcus I. = Minami-
Tori-Shima, Pac. Oc. 56 E7
Marcus Necker Ridge,
Pac. Oc. 56 F9
Mardan, Pakistan . . . 36 B8
Mardie, Australia . . . 52 D2
Mardin, Turkey 23 G7
Maree, L., U.K. 12 D3
Mareeba, Australia . . 54 B4
Marek = Stanke
Dimitrov, Bulgaria . 21 C10
Marek, Indonesia . . . 33 E6
Marengo, U.S.A. . . . 70 E8
Marerano, Madag. . . 49 C7
Marfa, U.S.A. 71 K2
Margaret →, Australia 52 C4
Margaret Bay, Canada 64 C3
Margaret L., Canada . 64 B5
Margaret River,
Australia 52 C4
Margarita, Panama . . 74 H14
Margarita, I. de,
Venezuela 78 A6
Margaritovo, Russia . 28 C7
Margate, S. Africa . . 49 E5
Margate, U.K. 11 F9
Margelan = Marghilon,
Uzbekistan 24 E8
Marghilon, Uzbekistan 24 E8
Marguerite, Canada . 64 C4
Mari El □, Russia . . 22 C8
Mari Republic = Mari
El □, Russia 22 C8
Maria I., N. Terr.,
Australia 54 A2
Maria I., Tas., Australia 54 G4
Maria van Diemen, C.,
N.Z. 51 F4
Marian L., Canada . . 64 A5
Mariana Trench,
Pac. Oc. 56 F6
Marianao, Cuba 75 C8
Marianna, Ark., U.S.A. 71 H9
Marianna, Fla., U.S.A. 69 K3
Marias →, U.S.A. . . . 72 C8
Ma'rib, Yemen 40 D4
Maribor, Slovenia . . 16 E8
Marico →, Africa . . . 48 C4
Maricopa, Ariz., U.S.A. 73 K7
Maricopa, Calif., U.S.A. 73 J4
Maricourt, Canada . . 61 C12
Marīdī, Sudan 45 H10
Marie Byrd Land,
Antarctica 5 D14
Marie-Galante,
Guadeloupe 75 D12
Mariecourt =
Kangiqsujuaq,
Canada 61 B12
Marienberg, Neths. . . 15 B6
Marienbourg, Belgium 15 D4
Mariental, Namibia . . 48 C2
Mariestad, Sweden . . 9 G15
Marietta, Ga., U.S.A. . 69 J3
Marietta, Ohio, U.S.A. 68 F5
Mariinsk, Russia . . . 24 D9
Marijampolė, Lithuania 9 J20
Marília, Brazil 79 H8
Marillana, Australia . 52 D2
Marín, Spain 19 A1
Marina Plains, Australia 54 A3
Marinduque, Phil. . . 33 B6
Marine City, U.S.A. . . 68 D4
Marinette, U.S.A. . . . 68 C2
Maringá, Brazil 80 A6
Marion, Ala., U.S.A. . 69 J2
Marion, Ill., U.S.A. . . 71 G10
Marion, Ind., U.S.A. . 68 E3
Marion, Iowa, U.S.A. . 70 D9
Marion, Kans., U.S.A. 70 F6
Marion, Mich., U.S.A. 68 C3
Marion, N.C., U.S.A. . 69 H4
Marion, Ohio, U.S.A. . 68 E4
Marion, S.C., U.S.A. . 69 H6
Marion, Va., U.S.A. . . 69 G5
Marion, I., Ind. Oc. . . 35 J2
Marion I., Ind. Oc. . . 35 J2
Mariposa, U.S.A. . . . 73 H4
Mariscal Estigarribia,
Paraguay 78 H6
Maritime Alps =
Maritimes, Alpes,
Europe 16 F4
Mary, Turkmenistan . 24 F7
Mary Frances L.,
Canada 65 A7
Mary Kathleen,
Australia 54 C2

Mariupol, Ukraine . . . 23 E6
Marīvān, Iran 38 C5
Markazī □, Iran 39 C6
Marked Tree, U.S.A. . 71 H9
Market Drayton, U.K. . 10 E5
Market Harborough,
U.K. 11 E7
Markham, Mt.,
Antarctica 5 E11
Markham L., Canada . 65 A8
Markovo, Russia . . . 25 C17
Marks, Russia 22 D8
Marksville, U.S.A. . . 71 K8
Marla, Australia . . . 55 D1
Marlborough, Australia 54 C4
Marlborough Downs,
U.K. 11 F6
Marlin, U.S.A. 71 K6
Marlow, U.S.A. 71 H6
Marmagao, India . . . 36 M8
Marmara, Turkey . . . 21 D12
Marmara, Sea of =
Marmara Denizi,
Turkey 21 D13
Marmara Denizi, Turkey 21 D13
Marmaris, Turkey . . 21 F13
Marmarth, U.S.A. . . 70 B3
Marmion, Mt., Australia 53 E2
Marmion L., Canada . 62 C1
Marmolada, Mte., Italy 20 A4
Marmora, Canada . . 62 D4
Marne →, France . . . 18 B5
Maroala, Madag. . . . 49 B8
Maroantsetra, Madag. 49 B8
Maromandia, Madag. . 49 A8
Maromokotro, Madag. 49 A8
Maroochydore,
Australia 55 D5
Maroona, Australia . . 55 F3
Marosakoa, Madag. . 49 B8
Marotandrano, Madag. 49 B8
Marovoay, Madag. . . 49 B8
Marquard, S. Africa . 48 D4
Marquesas Is. =
Marquises, Is.,
Pac. Oc. 57 H14
Marquette, U.S.A. . . 68 B2
Marquises, Is., Pac. Oc. 57 H14
Marracuene, Mozam. . 49 D5
Marrakech, Morocco . 44 B3
Marrawah, Australia . 54 G3
Marree, Australia . . . 55 D2
Marrilla, Australia . . 52 D1
Marrimane, Mozam. . 49 C5
Marromeu, Mozam. . . 49 B6
Marrowie Cr. →,
Australia 55 E4
Marrupa, Mozam. . . . 47 G7
Marsá Matrûh, Egypt . 45 B10
Marsá Susah, Libya . 45 B9
Marsabit, Kenya . . . 46 D7
Marsala, Italy 20 F5
Marsden, Australia . . 55 E4
Marseille, France . . . 18 E6
Marseilles = Marseille,
France 18 E6
Marsh I., U.S.A. . . . 71 L9
Marsh L., U.S.A. . . . 70 C6
Marshall, Liberia . . . 44 G2
Marshall, Ark., U.S.A. 71 H8
Marshall, Mich., U.S.A. 68 D3
Marshall, Minn., U.S.A. 70 C7
Marshall, Mo., U.S.A. 70 F8
Marshall, Tex., U.S.A. 71 J7
Marshall →, Australia 54 C2
Marshall Is. ■, Pac. Oc. 56 G9
Marshalltown, U.S.A. . 70 D8
Marshfield, Mo., U.S.A. 71 G8
Marshfield, Wis., U.S.A. 70 C9
Marshûn, Iran 39 B6
Märsta, Sweden . . . 9 G17
Mart, U.S.A. 71 K6
Martaban, Burma . . 37 L20
Martaban, G. of, Burma 37 L20
Martapura, Kalimantan,
Indonesia 32 E4
Martapura, Sumatera,
Indonesia 32 E2
Marte, Nigeria 45 F8
Martelange, Belgium . 15 E5
Martha's Vineyard,
U.S.A. 68 E10
Martigny, Switz. . . . 16 E4
Martigues, France . . 18 E6
Martin, Slovak Rep. . 17 D10
Martin, S. Dak., U.S.A. 70 D4
Martin, Tenn., U.S.A. 71 G10
Martin L., U.S.A. . . . 69 J3
Martina Franca, Italy . 20 D7
Martinborough, N.Z. . 51 J5
Martinique ■, W. Indies 75 E12
Martinique Passage,
W. Indies 75 D12
Martinsburg, U.S.A. . 68 F7
Martinsville, Ind.,
U.S.A. 68 F2
Martinsville, Va., U.S.A. 69 G6
Marton, N.Z. 51 J5
Martos, Spain 19 D4
Marudi, Malaysia . . . 32 D4
Ma'ruf, Afghan. . . . 36 D5
Marugame, Japan . . 29 G6
Marulan, Australia . . 55 E5
Marunga, Angola . . . 48 B3
Marvast, India 39 D7
Marwar, India 36 G8
Mary, Turkmenistan . 24 F7
Mary Frances L.,
Canada 65 A7
Mary Kathleen,
Australia 54 C2

Maryborough = Port
Laoise, Ireland . . . 13 C4
Maryborough, Queens.,
Australia 55 D5
Maryborough, Vic.,
Australia 55 F3
Maryfield, Canada . . 65 D8
Maryland □, U.S.A. . 68 F7
Maryport, U.K. 10 C4
Mary's Harbour,
Canada 63 B8
Marystown, Canada . 63 C8
Marysvale, U.S.A. . . 73 G7
Marysville, Canada . . 64 D5
Marysville, Calif.,
U.S.A. 72 G3
Marysville, Kans.,
U.S.A. 70 F6
Marysville, Ohio, U.S.A. 68 E4
Maryvale, Australia . . 55 D5
Maryville, U.S.A. . . . 69 H4
Marzūq, Libya 45 C7
Masaka, Uganda . . . 46 E6
Masalembo,
Kepulauan, Indonesia 32 F4
Masalima, Kepulauan,
Indonesia 32 F5
Masamba, Indonesia . 33 E6
Masan, S. Korea . . . 31 C7
Masasi, Tanzania . . . 46 G7
Masaya, Nic. 74 E7
Masbate, Phil. 33 B6
Mascara, Algeria . . . 44 A5
Mascarene Is., Ind. Oc. 35 G4
Masela, Indonesia . . 33 F7
Maseru, Lesotho . . . 48 D4
Mashābih, Si. Arabia . 38 E3
Mashhad, Iran 39 B8
Mashīz, Iran 39 D8
Mashkel, Hamun-i-,
Pakistan 36 E3
Mashki Chāh, Pakistan 36 E3
Mashonaland
Central □, Zimbabwe 49 B5
Mashonaland East □,
Zimbabwe 49 B5
Mashonaland West □,
Zimbabwe 49 B5
Masi Manimba, Zaïre . 46 E3
Masindi, Uganda . . . 46 D6
Masisea, Peru 78 E4
Masjed Soleyman, Iran 39 D6
Mask, L., Ireland . . . 13 C2
Masoala, Tanjon' i,
Madag. 49 B9
Masoarivo, Madag. . . 49 B7
Masohi, Indonesia . . 33 E7
Masomeloka, Madag. . 49 C8
Mason, U.S.A. 71 K5
Mason City, U.S.A. . . 70 D8
Masqat, Oman 40 C6
Massa, Italy 20 B4
Massachusetts □,
U.S.A. 68 D10
Massaguet, Chad . . . 45 F8
Massakory, Chad . . . 45 F8
Massangena, Mozam. 49 C5
Massawa = Mitsiwa,
Eritrea 45 E12
Massena, U.S.A. . . . 68 C8
Massénya, Chad . . . 45 F8
Masset, Canada . . . 64 C2
Massif Central, France 18 D5
Massillon, U.S.A. . . . 68 E5
Massinga, Mozam. . . 49 C6
Masson I., Antarctica . 5 C7
Mastanli =
Momchilgrad,
Bulgaria 21 D11
Masterton, N.Z. 51 J5
Mastuj, Pakistan . . . 36 A8
Mastung, Pakistan . . 36 E5
Masty, Belarus 17 B13
Masuda, Japan 29 G5
Masvingo, Zimbabwe . 47 J6
Maşyaf, Syria 38 C3
Mataboor, Indonesia . 33 E9
Matachewan, Canada . 62 C3
Matadi, Zaïre 46 F2
Matagalpa, Nic. . . . 74 E7
Matagami, Canada . . 62 C4
Matagami, L., Canada 62 C4
Matagorda, U.S.A. . . 71 L7
Matagorda B., U.S.A. . 71 L6
Matagorda I., U.S.A. . 71 L6
Matak, P., Indonesia . 32 D3
Matakana, Australia . 55 E4
Matam, Senegal . . . 44 E2
Matamoros, Coahuila,
Mexico 74 B4
Matamoros,
Tamaulipas, Mexico 74 B5
Ma'tan as Sarra, Libya 45 D9
Matane, Canada . . . 63 C6
Matanzas, Cuba . . . 75 C8
Matapan, C. =
Taínaron, Ákra,
Greece 21 F10
Matapédia, Canada . . 63 C6
Matara, Sri Lanka . . 36 S12
Mataram, Indonesia . 32 F5
Matarani, Peru 78 G4
Mataranka, Australia . 52 B5
Matarma, Râs, Egypt . 41 E1
Mataró, Spain 19 B7
Matatiele, S. Africa . . 49 E4
Mataura, N.Z. 51 M2
Matehuala, Mexico . . 74 C4
Matera, Italy 20 D7
Matheson Island,
Canada 65 C9
Mathis, U.S.A. 71 L6
Mathura, India 36 F10

Mati, Phil. ... 33 C7
Matima, Botswana ... 48 C3
Matiri Ra., N.Z. ... 51 J4
Matlock, U.K. ... 10 D6
Matmata, Tunisia ... 44 B6
Mato Grosso □, Brazil 79 F8
Mato Grosso, Planalto do, Brazil ... 79 G8
Mato Grosso do Sul □, Brazil ... 79 G8
Matochkin Shar, Russia 24 B6
Matosinhos, Portugal . 19 B1
Matsue, Japan ... 29 G6
Matsumae, Japan ... 28 D10
Matsumoto, Japan ... 29 F9
Matsusaka, Japan ... 29 G8
Matsuura, Japan ... 29 H4
Matsuyama, Japan ... 29 H6
Mattagami →, Canada 62 B3
Mattancheri, India ... 36 Q10
Mattawa, Canada ... 62 C4
Mattawamkeag, U.S.A. 63 C6
Matterhorn, Switz. ... 16 F4
Matthew's Ridge, Guyana ... 78 B6
Mattice, Canada ... 62 C3
Matuba, Mozam. ... 49 C5
Matucana, Peru ... 78 F3
Matun, Afghan. ... 36 C6
Maturín, Venezuela ... 78 B6
Mau Ranipur, India ... 36 G11
Maubeuge, France ... 18 A6
Maud, Pt., Australia ... 52 D1
Maude, Australia ... 55 E3
Maudin Sun, Burma ... 37 M19
Maués, Brazil ... 78 D7
Mauganj, India ... 37 G12
Maui, U.S.A. ... 66 H16
Maulamyaing = Moulmein, Burma ... 37 L20
Maumee, U.S.A. ... 68 E4
Maumee →, U.S.A. ... 68 E4
Maumere, Indonesia ... 33 F6
Maun, Botswana ... 48 B3
Mauna Kea, U.S.A. ... 66 J17
Mauna Loa, U.S.A. ... 66 J17
Maungmagan Kyunzu, Burma ... 34 E4
Maupin, U.S.A. ... 72 D3
Maurepas, L., U.S.A. ... 71 K9
Maurice, L., Australia . 53 E5
Mauritania ■, Africa ... 44 D3
Mauritius ■, Ind. Oc. ... 43 J9
Mauston, U.S.A. ... 70 D9
Mavinga, Angola ... 47 H4
Mawk Mai, Burma ... 37 J20
Mawlaik, Burma ... 37 H19
Mawquq, Si. Arabia ... 38 E4
Mawson Coast, Antarctica ... 5 C6
Max, U.S.A. ... 70 B4
Maxesibeni, S. Africa ... 49 E4
Maxhamish L., Canada 64 B4
Maxixe, Mozam. ... 49 C6
Maxwelton, Australia ... 54 C3
May Downs, Australia ... 54 C4
May Pen, Jamaica ... 74 K16
Maya →, Russia ... 25 D14
Mayaguana, Bahamas . 75 C10
Mayagüez, Puerto Rico 75 D11
Mayāmey, Iran ... 39 B7
Maybell, U.S.A. ... 72 F9
Maydan, Iraq ... 38 C5
Maydena, Australia ... 54 G4
Mayenne →, France ... 18 C3
Mayer, U.S.A. ... 73 J7
Mayerthorpe, Canada . 64 C5
Mayfield, U.S.A. ... 69 G1
Mayhill, U.S.A. ... 73 K11
Maykop, Russia ... 23 F7
Maymyo, Burma ... 34 A4
Maynard Hills, Australia 53 E2
Mayne →, Australia . 54 C3
Maynooth, Ireland ... 13 C5
Mayo, Canada ... 60 B6
Mayo □, Ireland ... 13 C2
Mayo L., Canada ... 60 B6
Mayon Volcano, Phil. . 33 B6
Mayor I., N.Z. ... 51 G6
Mayotte, I., Mayotte ... 35 F3
Mayson L., Canada ... 65 B7
Maysville, U.S.A. ... 68 F4
Mayu, Indonesia ... 33 D7
Mayville, U.S.A. ... 70 B6
Mayya, Russia ... 25 C14
Mazabuka, Zambia ... 47 H5
Mazagán = El Jadida, Morocco ... 44 B3
Mazagão, Brazil ... 79 D8
Mazán, Peru ... 78 D4
Māzandarān □, Iran ... 39 B7
Mazara del Vallo, Italy 20 F5
Mazarredo, Argentina . 80 F3
Mazarrón, Spain ... 19 D5
Mazaruni →, Guyana 78 B7
Mazatlán, Mexico ... 74 C3
Mažeikiai, Lithuania ... 9 H20
Māzhān, Iran ... 39 C8
Mazīnān, Iran ... 39 B8
Mazoe →, Mozam. ... 47 H6
Mazurian Lakes = Mazurski, Pojezierze, Poland ... 17 B11
Mazurski, Pojezierze, Poland ... 17 B11
Mazyr, Belarus ... 17 B15
Mbabane, Swaziland ... 49 D5
Mbaïki, C.A.R. ... 46 D3
Mbala, Zambia ... 46 F6
Mbale, Uganda ... 46 D6
Mbalmayo, Cameroon ... 46 D2
Mbamba Bay, Tanzania 46 F6
Mbandaka, Zaïre ... 46 D3

Mbanza Congo, Angola 46 F2
Mbanza Ngungu, Zaïre 46 F2
Mbarara, Uganda ... 46 E6
Mbashe →, S. Africa 49 E4
Mbeya, Tanzania ... 46 F6
Mbini □, Eq. Guin. ... 46 D2
Mbour, Senegal ... 44 F1
Mbout, Mauritania ... 44 E2
Mbuji-Mayi, Zaïre ... 46 F4
Mbulu, Tanzania ... 46 E7
Mchinji, Malawi ... 47 G6
Mead, L., U.S.A. ... 73 H6
Meade, U.S.A. ... 71 G4
Meadow, Australia ... 53 E1
Meadow Lake, Canada 65 C7
Meadow Lake Prov. Park, Canada ... 65 C7
Meadow Valley Wash →, U.S.A. ... 73 H6
Meadville, U.S.A. ... 68 E5
Meaford, Canada ... 62 D3
Mealy Mts., Canada ... 63 B8
Meander River, Canada 64 B5
Meares, C., U.S.A. ... 72 D2
Mearim →, Brazil ... 79 D10
Meath □, Ireland ... 13 C5
Meath Park, Canada ... 65 C7
Meaux, France ... 18 B5
Mebechi-Gawa →, Japan ... 28 D10
Mecca = Makkah, Si. Arabia ... 40 C2
Mecca, U.S.A. ... 73 K5
Mechelen, Belgium ... 15 C4
Mecheria, Algeria ... 44 B4
Mecklenburg, Germany 16 B6
Mecklenburger Bucht, Germany ... 16 A6
Meconta, Mozam. ... 47 G7
Meda, Australia ... 52 C3
Medan, Indonesia ... 32 D1
Medanosa, Pta., Argentina ... 80 F3
Médéa, Algeria ... 44 A5
Medellín, Colombia ... 78 B3
Medelpad, Sweden ... 9 E17
Medemblik, Neths. ... 15 B5
Mederdra, Mauritania . 44 E1
Medford, Oreg., U.S.A. 72 E2
Medford, Wis., U.S.A. 70 C9
Medgidia, Romania ... 17 F15
Mediaş, Romania ... 17 E13
Medical Lake, U.S.A. ... 72 C5
Medicine Bow, U.S.A. 72 F10
Medicine Bow Pk., U.S.A. ... 72 F10
Medicine Bow Ra., U.S.A. ... 72 F10
Medicine Hat, Canada 65 D6
Medicine Lake, U.S.A. 70 A2
Medicine Lodge, U.S.A. 71 G5
Medina = Al Madīnah, Si. Arabia ... 40 C2
Medina, N. Dak., U.S.A. 70 B5
Medina, N.Y., U.S.A. ... 68 D6
Medina, Ohio, U.S.A. ... 68 E5
Medina →, U.S.A. ... 71 L5
Medina del Campo, Spain ... 19 B3
Medina L., U.S.A. ... 71 L5
Medina-Sidonia, Spain 19 D3
Medinipur, India ... 37 H15
Mediterranean Sea, Europe ... 42 C5
Medley, Canada ... 65 C6
Médoc, France ... 18 D3
Medstead, Canada ... 65 C7
Medveditsa →, Russia 23 E7
Medvezhi, Ostrava, Russia ... 25 B17
Medvezhyegorsk, Russia ... 22 B5
Medway →, U.K. ... 11 F8
Meeberrie, Australia ... 53 E2
Meekatharra, Australia 53 E2
Meeker, U.S.A. ... 72 F10
Meerut, India ... 36 E10
Meeteetse, U.S.A. ... 72 D9
Mega, Ethiopia ... 45 H12
Mégara, Greece ... 21 F10
Megasini □, India ... 37 G17
Mehr Jān, Iran ... 39 C7
Mehrābād, Iran ... 38 B5
Mehrān, Iran ... 38 C5
Mehrīz, Iran ... 39 D7
Mei Xian, China ... 31 D6
Meiganga, Cameroon ... 46 C2
Meiktila, Burma ... 37 J19
Meissen, Germany ... 16 C7
Mejillones, Chile ... 80 A2
Meka, Australia ... 53 E2
Mékambo, Gabon ... 46 D2
Mekdela, Ethiopia ... 45 F12
Mekhtar, Pakistan ... 36 D6
Meknès, Morocco ... 44 B3
Mekong →, Asia ... 34 H9
Mekongga, Indonesia . 33 E6
Mekvari = Kür →, Azerbaijan ... 23 G8
Melagiri Hills, India ... 36 N10
Melaka, Malaysia ... 34 S15
Melaka □, Malaysia ... 34 S15
Melalap, Malaysia ... 32 C5
Melanesia, Pac. Oc. ... 56 H7
Melbourne, Australia . 55 F3
Melbourne, U.S.A. ... 69 L5
Mélèzes →, Canada ... 61 C12
Melfi, Chad ... 45 F8
Melfort, Canada ... 65 C8
Melhus, Norway ... 8 E14
Melilla, N. Afr. ... 19 E4
Melita, Canada ... 65 D8

Melitopol, Ukraine ... 23 E6
Melk, Austria ... 16 D8
Mellansel, Sweden ... 8 E18
Mellen, U.S.A. ... 70 B9
Mellerud, Sweden ... 9 G15
Mellette, U.S.A. ... 70 C5
Melo, Uruguay ... 80 C6
Melolo, Indonesia ... 33 F6
Melrose, N.S.W., Australia ... 55 E4
Melrose, W. Austral., Australia ... 53 E3
Melrose, U.K. ... 12 F6
Melrose, U.S.A. ... 71 H3
Melstone, U.S.A. ... 72 C10
Melton Mowbray, U.K. 10 E7
Melun, France ... 18 B5
Melut, Sudan ... 45 F11
Melville, Canada ... 65 C8
Melville, C., Australia . 54 A3
Melville, L., Canada ... 63 B8
Melville B., Australia ... 54 A2
Melville I., Australia ... 52 B5
Melville I., Canada ... 4 B2
Melville Pen., Canada . 61 B11
Melvin →, Canada ... 64 B5
Memba, Mozam. ... 47 G8
Memboro, Indonesia ... 33 F5
Memel = Klaipeda, Lithuania ... 9 J19
Memel, S. Africa ... 49 D4
Memmingen, Germany 16 E6
Mempawah, Indonesia 32 D3
Memphis, Tenn., U.S.A. 71 H10
Memphis, Tex., U.S.A. 71 H4
Mena, U.S.A. ... 71 H7
Menai Strait, U.K. ... 10 D3
Ménaka, Mali ... 44 E5
Menan = Chao Phraya →, Thailand 34 F6
Menarandra →, Madag. ... 49 D7
Menard, U.S.A. ... 71 K5
Menasha, U.S.A. ... 68 C1
Menate, Indonesia ... 32 E4
Mendawai →, Indonesia ... 32 E4
Mende, France ... 18 D5
Mendip Hills, U.K. ... 11 F5
Mendocino, U.S.A. ... 72 G2
Mendocino, C., U.S.A. 72 F1
Mendota, Calif., U.S.A. 73 H3
Mendota, Ill., U.S.A. ... 70 E10
Mendoza, Argentina ... 80 C3
Mene Grande, Venezuela ... 78 B4
Menemen, Turkey ... 21 E12
Menen, Belgium ... 15 D3
Menggala, Indonesia . 32 E3
Mengzi, China ... 30 D5
Menihek L., Canada ... 63 B6
Menin = Menen, Belgium ... 15 D3
Menindee, Australia ... 55 E3
Menindee L., Australia 55 E3
Meningie, Australia ... 55 F2
Menominee, U.S.A. ... 68 C2
Menominee →, U.S.A. 68 C2
Menomonie, U.S.A. ... 70 C9
Menongue, Angola ... 47 G3
Menorca, Spain ... 19 C8
Mentawai, Kepulauan, Indonesia ... 32 E1
Menton, France ... 18 E7
Menzelinsk, Russia ... 22 C9
Menzies, Australia ... 53 E3
Me'ona, Israel ... 41 B4
Meppel, Neths. ... 15 B6
Mer Rouge, U.S.A. ... 71 J9
Merabéllou, Kólpos, Greece ... 21 G11
Meramangye, L., Australia ... 53 E5
Meran = Merano, Italy 20 A4
Merano, Italy ... 20 A4
Merauke, Indonesia ... 33 F10
Merbabu, Indonesia ... 33 G14
Merbein, Australia ... 55 E3
Merca, Somali Rep. ... 40 G3
Merced, U.S.A. ... 73 H3
Mercedes, Buenos Aires, Argentina ... 80 C5
Mercedes, Corrientes, Argentina ... 80 B5
Mercedes, San Luis, Argentina ... 80 C3
Mercedes, Uruguay ... 80 C5
Merceditas, Chile ... 80 B2
Mercer, N.Z. ... 51 G5
Mercy C., Canada ... 61 B13
Meredith, C., Falk. Is. 80 G4
Meredith, L., U.S.A. ... 71 H4
Merga = Nukheila, Sudan ... 45 E10
Mergui Arch. = Myeik Kyunzu, Burma ... 34 G4
Mérida, Mexico ... 74 C7
Mérida, Spain ... 19 C2
Mérida, Venezuela ... 78 B4
Mérida, Cord. de, Venezuela ... 76 C3
Meriden, U.S.A. ... 68 E9
Meridian, Idaho, U.S.A. 72 E5
Meridian, Miss., U.S.A. 69 J1
Meridian, Tex., U.S.A. 71 K6
Meriruma, Brazil ... 79 C8
Merkel, U.S.A. ... 71 J4
Merksem, Belgium ... 15 C4
Mermaid Reef, Australia ... 52 C2
Merowe, Sudan ... 45 E11
Merredin, Australia ... 53 F2

Merrick, U.K. ... 12 F4
Merrill, Oreg., U.S.A. . 72 E3
Merrill, Wis., U.S.A. ... 70 C10
Merriman, U.S.A. ... 70 D4
Merritt, Canada ... 64 C4
Merriwa, Australia ... 55 E5
Merriwagga, Australia 55 E4
Merry I., Canada ... 62 A4
Merrygoen, Australia . 55 E4
Merryville, U.S.A. ... 71 K8
Mersa Fatma, Eritrea . 40 E3
Mersch, Lux. ... 15 E6
Merseburg, Germany . 16 C6
Mersey →, U.K. ... 10 D5
Merseyside □, U.K. ... 10 D5
Mersin, Turkey ... 23 G5
Mersing, Malaysia ... 34 S16
Merthyr Tydfil, U.K. ... 11 F4
Mértola, Portugal ... 19 D2
Mertzon, U.S.A. ... 71 K4
Meru, Kenya ... 46 D7
Mesa, U.S.A. ... 73 K8
Mesgouez, L., Canada 62 B4
Meshed = Mashhad, Iran ... 39 B8
Meshra er Req, Sudan 45 G10
Mesick, U.S.A. ... 68 C3
Mesilinka →, Canada 64 B4
Mesilla, U.S.A. ... 73 K10
Mesolóngion, Greece . 21 E9
Mesopotamia = Al Jazirah, Iraq ... 38 C5
Mesquite, U.S.A. ... 73 H6
Mess Cr. →, Canada 64 B2
Messina, Italy ... 20 E6
Messina, S. Africa ... 49 C5
Messina, Str. di, Italy . 20 F6
Messíni, Greece ... 21 F10
Messiniakós Kólpos, Greece ... 21 F10
Mesta →, Bulgaria ... 21 D11
Meta →, S. Amer. ... 78 B5
Metairie, U.S.A. ... 71 L9
Metaline Falls, U.S.A. . 72 B5
Metán, Argentina ... 80 B4
Metangula, Mozam. ... 47 G6
Metema, Ethiopia ... 45 F12
Methven, N.Z. ... 51 K3
Methy L., Canada ... 65 B7
Metil, Mozam. ... 47 H7
Metlakatla, U.S.A. ... 64 B2
Metropolis, U.S.A. ... 71 G10
Mettur Dam, India ... 36 P10
Metz, France ... 18 B7
Meulaboh, Indonesia . 32 D1
Meureudu, Indonesia . 32 C1
Meuse →, Europe ... 18 A6
Mexborough, U.K. ... 10 D6
Mexia, U.S.A. ... 71 K6
Mexiana, I., Brazil ... 79 C9
Mexicali, Mexico ... 74 A1
México, Mexico ... 74 D5
Mexico, U.S.A. ... 70 F9
México □, Mexico ... 74 D5
Mexico ■, Cent. Amer. 74 C4
Mexico, G. of, Cent. Amer. ... 74 B7
Meymaneh, Afghan. ... 36 B4
Mezen, Russia ... 22 A7
Mezen →, Russia ... 22 A7
Mézenc, France ... 18 D6
Mezökövesd, Hungary 17 E11
Mezötúr, Hungary ... 17 E11
Mhow, India ... 36 H9
Miallo, Australia ... 54 B4
Miami, Ariz., U.S.A. ... 73 K8
Miami, Fla., U.S.A. ... 69 N5
Miami, Tex., U.S.A. ... 71 H4
Miami →, U.S.A. ... 68 F3
Miami Beach, U.S.A. ... 69 N5
Miamisburg, U.S.A. ... 68 F3
Miāndowāb, Iran ... 38 B5
Miandrivazo, Madag. . 49 B8
Miāneh, Iran ... 38 B5
Mianwali, Pakistan ... 36 C7
Miarinarivo, Madag. ... 49 B8
Miass, Russia ... 22 D11
Michalovce, Slovak Rep. ... 17 D11
Michigan □, U.S.A. ... 68 C3
Michigan, L., U.S.A. ... 68 C2
Michigan City, U.S.A. 68 E2
Michikamau L., Canada 63 B7
Michipicoten, Canada . 62 C3
Michipicoten I., Canada 62 C2
Michurin, Bulgaria ... 21 C12
Michurinsk, Russia ... 22 D7
Miclere, Australia ... 54 C4
Micronesia, Pac. Oc. . 56 G7
Micronesia, Federated States of ■, Pac. Oc. 56 G7
Mid Glamorgan □, U.K. 11 F4
Mid-Indian Ridge, Ind. Oc. ... 35 H6
Midai, P., Indonesia ... 32 D3
Midale, Canada ... 65 D8
Middelburg, Eastern Cape, S. Africa ... 48 E3
Middelburg, Eastern Trans., S. Africa ... 49 D4
Middelburg, Neths. ... 15 C3
Middelwit, S. Africa ... 48 C4
Middle Alkali L., U.S.A. 72 F3
Middle Andaman I., India ... 34 F2
Middle I., Australia ... 53 F3
Middle Loup →, U.S.A. ... 70 E5
Middleboro, Ky., U.S.A. ... 67 C10
Middlesboro, Ky., U.S.A. ... 69 G4

Middlesbrough, U.K. . 10 C6
Middleton, Australia ... 54 C3
Middleton, Canada ... 63 D6
Middletown, Conn., U.S.A. ... 68 E9
Middletown, N.Y., U.S.A. ... 68 E8
Middletown, Ohio, U.S.A. ... 68 F3
Midi, Canal du →, France ... 18 E4
Midland, Canada ... 62 D4
Midland, Mich., U.S.A. 68 D3
Midland, Tex., U.S.A. . 71 K3
Midleton, Ireland ... 13 E3
Midlothian, U.S.A. ... 71 J6
Midongy, Tangorombohitr' i, Madag. ... 49 C8
Midongy Atsimo, Madag. ... 49 C8
Midway Is., Pac. Oc. . 56 E10
Midwest, U.S.A. ... 67 B9
Midwest, Wyo., U.S.A. 72 E10
Midžor, Bulgaria ... 21 C10
Mie □, Japan ... 29 G8
Międzychód, Poland . 16 B8
Międzyrzec Podlaski, Poland ... 17 C12
Mielec, Poland ... 17 C11
Mienga, Angola ... 48 B2
Miercurea Ciuc, Romania ... 17 E13
Mieres, Spain ... 19 A3
Mifraz Hefa, Israel ... 41 C4
Migdāl, Israel ... 41 C4
Miguel Alves, Brazil ... 79 D10
Mihara, Japan ... 29 G6
Mikhaylovgrad, Bulgaria ... 21 C10
Mikkeli, Finland ... 9 F22
Mikkwa →, Canada ... 64 B6
Míkonos, Greece ... 21 F11
Mikun, Russia ... 22 B9
Milaca, U.S.A. ... 70 C8
Milagro, Ecuador ... 78 D3
Milan = Milano, Italy . 20 B3
Milan, Mo., U.S.A. ... 70 E8
Milan, Tenn., U.S.A. ... 69 H1
Milano, Italy ... 20 B3
Milâs, Turkey ... 21 F12
Milazzo, Italy ... 20 E6
Milbank, U.S.A. ... 70 C6
Milden, Canada ... 65 C7
Mildura, Australia ... 55 E3
Miles, Australia ... 55 D5
Miles, U.S.A. ... 71 K4
Miles City, U.S.A. ... 70 B2
Milestone, Canada ... 65 D8
Miletus, Turkey ... 21 F12
Mileura, Australia ... 53 E2
Milford, Del., U.S.A. ... 68 F8
Milford, Utah, U.S.A. ... 73 G7
Milford Haven, U.K. ... 11 F2
Milford Sd., N.Z. ... 51 L1
Milgun, Australia ... 53 D2
Milh, Bahr al, Iraq ... 38 C4
Miling, Australia ... 53 F2
Milk →, U.S.A. ... 72 B10
Milk River, Canada ... 64 D6
Mill City, U.S.A. ... 72 D2
Mill I., Antarctica ... 5 C8
Millau, France ... 18 D5
Mille Lacs, L. des, Canada ... 62 C1
Mille Lacs L., U.S.A. ... 70 B8
Milledgeville, U.S.A. ... 69 J4
Millen, U.S.A. ... 69 J5
Miller, U.S.A. ... 70 C5
Millicent, Australia ... 55 F3
Millinocket, U.S.A. ... 63 C6
Millmerran, Australia . 55 D5
Mills L., Canada ... 64 A5
Milltown Malbay, Ireland ... 13 D2
Millville, U.S.A. ... 68 F8
Millwood L., U.S.A. ... 71 J8
Milne →, Australia ... 54 C2
Milne Inlet, Canada ... 61 A11
Milnor, U.S.A. ... 70 B6
Milo, Canada ... 64 C6
Milos, Greece ... 21 F11
Milparinka P.O., Australia ... 55 D3
Milton, N.Z. ... 51 M2
Milton, U.K. ... 12 D4
Milton, Fla., U.S.A. ... 69 K2
Milton, Pa., U.S.A. ... 68 E7
Milton-Freewater, U.S.A. ... 72 D4
Milton Keynes, U.K. ... 11 E7
Miltou, Chad ... 45 F8
Milwaukee, U.S.A. ... 68 D2
Milwaukie, U.S.A. ... 72 D2
Min Chiang →, China 31 D6
Min Jiang →, China ... 30 D5
Mina, U.S.A. ... 73 G4
Mina Pirquitas, Argentina ... 80 A3
Mīnā Su'ud, Si. Arabia 39 D6
Mīnā'al Aḥmadī, Kuwait 39 D6
Mīnāb, Iran ... 39 E8
Minago →, Canada ... 65 C9
Minaki, Canada ... 65 D10
Minamata, Japan ... 29 H5
Minami-Tori-Shima, Pac. Oc. ... 56 E7
Minas, Uruguay ... 80 C5
Minas Basin, Canada . 63 C7
Minas Gerais □, Brazil 79 G9
Minatitlán, Mexico ... 74 D6

Minbu, Burma ... 37 J19
Mindanao, Phil. ... 33 C6
Mindanao Sea = Bohol Sea, Phil. ... 33 C6
Mindanao Trench, Pac. Oc. ... 33 B7
Minden, Germany ... 16 B5
Minden, U.S.A. ... 71 J8
Mindiptana, Indonesia 33 F10
Mindoro, Phil. ... 33 B6
Mindoro Str., Phil. ... 33 B6
Mindouli, Congo ... 46 E2
Mine, Japan ... 29 G5
Minehead, U.K. ... 11 F4
Mineola, U.S.A. ... 71 J7
Mineral Wells, U.S.A. . 71 J5
Minersville, U.S.A. ... 73 G7
Mingäçevir Su Anban, Azerbaijan ... 23 F8
Mingan, Canada ... 63 B7
Mingechaurskoye Vdkhr. = Mingäçevir Su Anban, Azerbaijan 23 F8
Mingela, Australia ... 54 B4
Mingenew, Australia . 53 E2
Mingera Cr. →, Australia ... 54 C2
Mingin, Burma ... 37 H19
Mingt'iehkaitafan = Mintaka Pass, Pakistan ... 36 A9
Minho = Miño →, Spain ... 19 A2
Minho, Portugal ... 19 B1
Minidoka, U.S.A. ... 72 E7
Minigwal, L., Australia 53 E3
Minilya, Australia ... 53 D1
Minilya →, Australia ... 53 D1
Minipi, L., Canada ... 63 B7
Mink L., Canada ... 64 A5
Minna, Nigeria ... 44 G6
Minneapolis, Kans., U.S.A. ... 70 F6
Minneapolis, Minn., U.S.A. ... 70 C8
Minnedosa, Canada ... 65 C9
Minnesota □, U.S.A. . 70 B7
Minnie Creek, Australia 53 D2
Minnipa, Australia ... 55 E2
Minnitaki L., Canada . 62 C1
Mino, Japan ... 29 G8
Miño →, Spain ... 19 A2
Minorca = Menorca, Spain ... 19 C8
Minore, Australia ... 55 E4
Minot, U.S.A. ... 70 A4
Minsk, Belarus ... 17 B14
Mińsk Mazowiecki, Poland ... 17 B11
Mintaka Pass, Pakistan 36 A9
Minto, Canada ... 65 D8
Minturn, U.S.A. ... 72 G10
Minusinsk, Russia ... 25 D10
Minutang, India ... 37 E20
Minvoul, Gabon ... 46 D2
Mir, Niger ... 45 F7
Mīr Kūh, Iran ... 39 E8
Mīr Shahdād, Iran ... 39 E8
Mira, Italy ... 20 B5
Miraflores Locks, Panama ... 74 H14
Miraj, India ... 36 L9
Miram Shah, Pakistan 36 C7
Miramar, Mozam. ... 49 C6
Miramichi B., Canada . 63 C7
Miranda, Brazil ... 79 H8
Miranda de Ebro, Spain 19 A4
Miranda do Douro, Portugal ... 19 B2
Mirando City, U.S.A. ... 71 M5
Mirani, Australia ... 54 C4
Mirbāţ, Oman ... 40 D5
Miri, Malaysia ... 32 D4
Miriam Vale, Australia 54 C5
Mirim, L., S. Amer. ... 80 C6
Mirnyy, Russia ... 25 C12
Mirond L., Canada ... 65 B8
Mirpur Khas, Pakistan 36 G6
Mirror, Canada ... 64 C6
Mirzapur, India ... 37 G13
Mirzapur-cum-Vindhyachal = Mirzapur, India ... 37 G13
Misawa, Japan ... 28 D10
Miscou I., Canada ... 63 C7
Mish'āb, Ra's al, Si. Arabia ... 39 D6
Mishan, China ... 31 B8
Mishawaka, U.S.A. ... 68 E2
Mishima, Japan ... 29 G9
Miskah, Si. Arabia ... 38 E4
Miskolc, Hungary ... 17 D11
Misool, Indonesia ... 33 E8
Miṣrātah, Libya ... 45 B8
Missanabie, Canada ... 62 C3
Missinaibi →, Canada 62 B3
Missinaibi L., Canada . 62 C3
Mission, S. Dak., U.S.A. 70 D4
Mission, Tex., U.S.A. . 71 M5
Mission City, Canada . 64 D4
Missisa L., Canada ... 62 B2
Mississagi →, Canada 62 C3
Mississippi □, U.S.A. . 71 J10
Mississippi →, U.S.A. 71 L10
Mississippi River Delta, U.S.A. ... 71 L9
Mississippi Sd., U.S.A. 71 K10
Missoula, U.S.A. ... 72 C6
Missouri □, U.S.A. ... 70 F8
Missouri →, U.S.A. ... 70 F9
Missouri Valley, U.S.A. 70 E7
Mistake B., Canada ... 65 A10

Mistassini →, Canada 63 C5
Mistassini L., Canada . 62 B5
Mistastin L., Canada . . 63 A7
Mistatim, Canada 65 C8
Misty L., Canada 65 B8
Misurata = Misrātah,
  Libya 45 B8
Mitchell, Australia 55 D4
Mitchell, Ind., U.S.A. . . 68 F2
Mitchell, Nebr., U.S.A. . 70 E3
Mitchell, Oreg., U.S.A. . 72 D3
Mitchell, S. Dak., U.S.A. 70 D5
Mitchell →, Australia . . 54 B3
Mitchell, Mt., U.S.A. . . 69 H4
Mitchell Ras., Australia . 54 A2
Mitchelstown, Ireland . 13 D3
Mitilíni, Greece 21 E12
Mito, Japan 29 F10
Mitrovica = Titova-
  Mitrovica,
  Serbia, Yug. 21 C9
Mitsinjo, Madag. 49 B8
Mitsiwa, Eritrea 45 E12
Mitsukaidō, Japan . . . 29 F9
Mittagong, Australia . . 55 E5
Mitú, Colombia 78 C4
Mitumba, Chaîne des,
  Zaïre 46 F5
Mitumba Mts. =
  Mitumba, Chaîne des,
  Zaïre 46 F5
Mitwaba, Zaïre 46 F5
Mitzic, Gabon 46 D2
Miyagi □, Japan 28 E10
Miyah, W. el →, Syria . 38 C3
Miyake, Japan 28 E10
Miyako, Japan 28 E10
Miyako-Jima, Japan . . 29 M2
Miyako-Rettō, Japan . . 29 M2
Miyakonojō, Japan . . . 29 J5
Miyazaki, Japan 29 J5
Miyazaki □, Japan . . . 29 H5
Miyazu, Japan 29 G7
Miyet, Bahr el = Dead
  Sea, Asia 41 D4
Miyoshi, Japan 29 G6
Mizamis = Ozamiz,
  Phil. 33 C6
Mizdah, Libya 45 B7
Mizen Hd., Cork, Ireland 13 E2
Mizen Hd., Wick.,
  Ireland 13 D5
Mizoram □, India 37 H18
Mizpe Ramon, Israel . . 41 E3
Mizusawa, Japan 28 E10
Mjölby, Sweden 9 G16
Mjøsa, Norway 9 F14
Mkomazi →, S. Africa 49 E5
Mkuze, S. Africa 49 D5
Mladá Boleslav, Czech. 16 C8
Mława, Poland 17 B11
Mljet, Croatia 20 C7
Mmabatho, S. Africa . 48 D4
Mo i Rana, Norway . . 8 C16
Moa, Indonesia 33 F7
Moab, U.S.A. 73 G9
Moabi, Gabon 46 E2
Moala, Fiji 51 D8
Moalie Park, Australia 55 D3
Moba, Zaïre 46 F5
Mobārakābād, Iran . . 39 D7
Mobārakīyeh, Iran . . . 39 C6
Mobaye, C.A.R. 46 D4
Mobayi, Zaïre 46 D4
Moberly, U.S.A. 70 F8
Moberly →, Canada . 64 B4
Mobile, U.S.A. 69 K1
Mobile B., U.S.A. 69 K2
Mobridge, U.S.A. 70 C4
Mobutu Sese Seko, L.
  = Albert L., Africa . 46 D6
Moçambique, Mozam. 47 H8
Moçâmedes = Namibe,
  Angola 47 H2
Mochudi, Botswana . . 48 C4
Mocimboa da Praia,
  Mozam. 46 G8
Moclips, U.S.A. 72 C1
Mocoa, Colombia 78 C3
Mocuba, Mozam. 47 H7
Modane, France 18 D7
Modder →, S. Africa . 48 D3
Modderrivier, S. Africa 48 D3
Módena, Italy 20 B4
Modena, U.S.A. 73 H7
Modesto, U.S.A. 73 H3
Módica, Italy 20 F6
Moe, Australia 55 F4
Moei →, Thailand . . . 34 D5
Moengo, Surinam . . . 79 B8
Moffat, U.K. 12 F5
Mogadishu =
  Muqdisho,
  Somali Rep. 40 G4
Mogador = Essaouira,
  Morocco 44 B3
Mogalakwena →,
  S. Africa 49 C4
Mogami →, Japan . . 28 E10
Mogaung, Burma 37 G20
Mogi das Cruzes, Brazil 80 A7
Mogi-Mirim, Brazil . . 80 A7
Mogilev = Mahilyow,
  Belarus 17 B16
Mogilev-Podolskiy =
  Mohyliv-Podilskyy,
  Ukraine 17 D14
Mogocha, Russia 25 D12
Mogoi, Indonesia 33 E8
Mogok, Burma 37 H20
Mogumber, Australia . 53 F2
Mohács, Hungary . . . 17 F10

Mohales Hoek, Lesotho 48 E4
Mohall, U.S.A. 70 A4
Moḥammadābād, Iran . 39 B8
Mohoro, Tanzania 46 F7
Mohyliv-Podilskyy,
  Ukraine 17 D14
Moidart, L., U.K. 12 E3
Mointy, Kazakhstan . . 24 E8
Moisaküla, Estonia . . 9 G21
Moisie, Canada 63 B6
Moisie →, Canada . . 63 B6
Moissala, Chad 45 G8
Mojave, U.S.A. 73 J4
Mojave Desert, U.S.A. 73 J5
Mojokerto, Indonesia . 33 G15
Mokai, N.Z. 51 H5
Mokhotlong, Lesotho . 49 D4
Mokokchung, India . . 37 F19
Mokra Gora,
  Serbia, Yug. 21 C9
Mol, Belgium 15 C5
Molchanovo, Russia . . 24 D9
Mold, U.K. 10 D4
Moldavia =
  Moldova ■, Europe . 17 E15
Molde, Norway 8 E12
Moldova ■, Europe . . 17 E15
Moldoveanu, Romania 17 F13
Molepolole, Botswana 48 C4
Molfetta, Italy 20 D7
Moline, U.S.A. 70 E9
Moliro, Zaïre 46 F6
Mollendo, Peru 78 G4
Mollerin, L., Australia . 53 F2
Mölndal, Sweden 9 H15
Molodechno =
  Maladzyechna,
  Belarus 17 A14
Molokai, U.S.A. 66 H16
Molong, Australia 55 E4
Molopo →, Africa . . . 48 D3
Molotov = Perm,
  Russia 22 C10
Moloundou, Cameroon 46 D3
Molson L., Canada . . . 65 C9
Molteno, S. Africa . . . 48 E4
Molu, Indonesia 33 F8
Molucca Sea, Indonesia 33 E6
Moluccas = Maluku,
  Indonesia 33 E7
Moma, Mozam. 47 H7
Mombasa, Kenya 46 E7
Mombetsu, Japan 28 B11
Momchilgrad, Bulgaria 21 D11
Mompós, Colombia . . 78 B4
Møn, Denmark 9 J15
Mon →, Burma 37 J19
Mona, Canal de la,
  W. Indies 75 D11
Monach Is., U.K. 12 D1
Monaco ■, Europe . . . 18 E7
Monadhliath Mts., U.K. 12 D4
Monaghan, Ireland . . . 13 B5
Monaghan □, Ireland . 13 B5
Monahans, U.S.A. . . . 71 K3
Monarch Mt., Canada . 64 C3
Monastir = Bitola,
  Macedonia 21 D9
Monastir, Tunisia 45 A7
Moncayo, Sierra del,
  Spain 19 B5
Monchegorsk, Russia . 22 A5
Mönchengladbach,
  Germany 16 C4
Monchique, Portugal . 19 D1
Monclova, Mexico . . . 74 B4
Moncton, Canada 63 C7
Mondego →, Portugal 19 B1
Mondeodo, Indonesia . 33 E6
Mondovì, Italy 20 D7
Mondovi, U.S.A. 70 C9
Mondrain I., Australia . 53 F3
Monessen, U.S.A. 68 E6
Monett, U.S.A. 71 G8
Monforte de Lemos,
  Spain 19 A2
Mong Cai, Vietnam . . 34 B9
Mong Hsu, Burma . . . 37 J21
Mong Kung, Burma . . 37 J21
Mong Lang, Burma . . 34 B4
Mong Nai, Burma . . . 37 J20
Mong Pawk, Burma . . 34 B5
Mong Ton, Burma . . . 37 J21
Mong Wa, Burma . . . 37 J22
Mong Yai, Burma . . . 37 H21
Mongalla, Sudan 45 G11
Mongers, L., Australia 53 E2
Monghyr = Munger,
  India 37 G15
Mongibello = Etna,
  Italy 20 F6
Mongo, Chad 45 F8
Mongolia ■, Asia . . . 25 E10
Mongororo, Chad . . . 45 F9
Mongu, Zambia 47 H4
Môngua, Angola 48 B2
Monkira, Australia . . . 54 C3
Monkoto, Zaïre 46 E4
Monmouth, U.K. 11 F5
Monmouth, U.S.A. . . . 70 E9
Mono L., U.S.A. 73 H4
Monópoli, Italy 20 D7
Monqoumba, C.A.R. . 46 D3
Monroe, Ga., U.S.A. . . 69 J4
Monroe, La., U.S.A. . . 71 J8
Monroe, Mich., U.S.A. 68 E4
Monroe, N.C., U.S.A. . 69 H5
Monroe, Utah, U.S.A. . 73 G7
Monroe, Wis., U.S.A. . 70 D10
Monroe City, U.S.A. . . 70 F9
Monroeville, U.S.A. . . 69 K2
Monrovia, Liberia . . . 44 G2
Monrovia, U.S.A. 73 J4

Mons, Belgium 15 D3
Monse, Indonesia 33 E6
Mont-de-Marsan,
  France 18 E3
Mont-Joli, Canada . . . 63 C6
Mont-Laurier, Canada . 62 C4
Mont-St.-Michel, Le =
  Le Mont-St.-Michel,
  France 18 B3
Mont Tremblant Prov.
  Park, Canada 62 C5
Montagu, S. Africa . . 48 E3
Montagu I., Antarctica 5 B1
Montague, Canada . . 63 C7
Montague, U.S.A. . . . 72 F2
Montague Ra.,
  Australia 53 E2
Montague Sd.,
  Australia 52 B4
Montalbán, Spain 19 B5
Montaña, Peru 78 E4
Montana □, U.S.A. . . . 72 C9
Montargis, France . . . 18 C5
Montauban, France . . 18 D4
Montauk, U.S.A. 68 E10
Montbéliard, France . . 18 C7
Montceau-les-Mines,
  France 18 C6
Monte Alegre, Brazil . 79 D8
Monte Azul, Brazil . . . 79 G10
Monte Bello Is.,
  Australia 52 D2
Monte-Carlo, Monaco . 16 G4
Monte Caseros,
  Argentina 80 C5
Monte Comán,
  Argentina 80 C3
Monte Santu, C. di,
  Italy 20 D3
Monte Vista, U.S.A. . . 73 H10
Montebello, Canada . . 62 C5
Montecristi, Ecuador . 78 D2
Montecristo, Italy 20 C4
Montego Bay, Jamaica 74 J16
Montejinnie, Australia 52 C5
Montélimar, France . . 18 D6
Montemorelos, Mexico 74 B5
Montenegro □,
  Yugoslavia 21 C8
Montepuez, Mozam. . 47 G7
Monteria, Colombia . . 78 B3
Monterey, U.S.A. 73 H3
Monterrey, Mexico . . . 74 B4
Montes Claros, Brazil . 79 G10
Montesano, U.S.A. . . . 72 C2
Montesilvano Marina,
  Italy 20 C6
Montevideo, Uruguay . 80 C5
Montevideo, U.S.A. . . 70 C7
Montezuma, U.S.A. . . 70 E8
Montgomery =
  Sahiwal, Pakistan . . 36 D8
Montgomery, U.K. . . . 11 E4
Montgomery, Ala.,
  U.S.A. 69 J2
Montgomery, W. Va.,
  U.S.A. 68 F5
Monticello, Ark., U.S.A. 71 J9
Monticello, Fla., U.S.A. 69 K4
Monticello, Ind., U.S.A. 68 E2
Monticello, Iowa,
  U.S.A. 70 D9
Monticello, Ky., U.S.A. 69 G3
Monticello, Minn.,
  U.S.A. 70 C8
Monticello, Miss.,
  U.S.A. 71 K9
Monticello, Utah,
  U.S.A. 73 H9
Montijo, Spain 19 C1
Montilla, Spain 19 D3
Montluçon, France . . . 18 C5
Montmagny, Canada . 63 C5
Montmartre, Canada . 65 C8
Montmorency, Canada 63 C5
Montmorillon, France . 18 C4
Monto, Australia 54 C5
Montoro, Spain 19 C3
Montpelier, Idaho,
  U.S.A. 72 E8
Montpelier, Ohio,
  U.S.A. 68 E3
Montpelier, Vt., U.S.A. 68 C9
Montpellier, France . . 18 E5
Montréal, Canada . . . 62 C5
Montreal L., Canada . . 65 C7
Montreal Lake, Canada 65 C7
Montreux, Switz. 16 E4
Montrose, U.K. 12 E6
Montrose, U.S.A. 73 G10
Monts, Pte. des,
  Canada 63 C6
Montserrat ■, W. Indies 74 L19
Monveda, Zaïre 46 D4
Monywa, Burma 37 H19
Monza, Italy 20 B3
Monze, Zambia 47 H5
Monze, C., Pakistan . . 36 G5
Monzón, Spain 19 B6
Mooi River, S. Africa . 49 D4
Moolawatana, Australia 55 D2
Mooloogool, Australia 53 E2
Moomin Cr. →,
  Australia 55 D4
Moonah →, Australia 54 C2
Moonbeam, Canada . . 62 C3
Moonda, L., Australia . 54 D3
Moonie, Australia . . . 55 D5
Moonie →, Australia . 55 D4
Moonta, Australia . . . 55 E2

Moora, Australia 53 F2
Mooraberree, Australia 54 D3
Moorarie, Australia . . 53 E2
Moorcroft, U.S.A. . . . 70 C2
Moore →, Australia . . 53 F2
Moore, L., Australia . . 53 E2
Moore Reefs, Australia 54 B4
Moorefield, U.S.A. . . . 68 F6
Mooresville, U.S.A. . . 69 H5
Moorfoot Hills, U.K. . . 12 F5
Moorhead, U.S.A. . . . 70 B6
Mooroopna, Australia 55 F4
Moorreesburg, S. Africa 48 E2
Moose →, Canada . . 62 B3
Moose Factory, Canada 62 B3
Moose Jaw, Canada . . 65 C7
Moose Jaw →,
  Canada 65 C7
Moose Lake, Canada . 65 C8
Moose Lake, U.S.A. . . 70 B8
Moose Mountain
  Cr. →, Canada . . . 65 D8
Moose Mountain Prov.
  Park, Canada 65 D8
Moose River, Canada . 62 B3
Moosehead L., U.S.A. . 63 C6
Moosomin, Canada . . 65 C8
Moosonee, Canada . . 62 B3
Mopeia Velha, Mozam. 47 H7
Mopipi, Botswana . . . 48 C3
Mopti, Mali 44 F4
Moquegua, Peru 78 G4
Mora, Sweden 9 F16
Mora, Minn., U.S.A. . . 70 C8
Mora, N. Mex., U.S.A. 73 J11
Moradabad, India . . . 36 E11
Morafenobe, Madag. . 49 B7
Moramanga, Madag. . 49 B8
Moran, Kans., U.S.A. . 71 G7
Moran, Wyo., U.S.A. . 72 E8
Moranbah, Australia . 54 C4
Morant Pt., Jamaica . . 74 K17
Morar, L., U.K. 12 E3
Moratuwa, Sri Lanka . 36 R11
Morava →,
  Serbia, Yug. 21 B9
Morava →,
  Slovak Rep. 17 D9
Moravia, U.S.A. 70 E8
Moravian Hts. =
  Českomoravská
  Vrchovina, Czech. . 16 D8
Morawa, Australia . . . 53 E2
Morawhanna, Guyana 78 B7
Moray Firth, U.K. 12 D5
Morden, Canada 65 D9
Mordovian Republic =
  Mordvinia □, Russia 22 D7
Mordvinia □, Russia . 22 D7
Morea, Australia 55 F3
Morea, Greece 6 H10
Moreau →, U.S.A. . . 70 C4
Morecambe, U.K. 10 C5
Morecambe B., U.K. . . 10 C5
Moree, Australia 55 D4
Morehead, U.S.A. . . . 68 F4
Morehead City, U.S.A. 69 H7
Morelia, Mexico 74 D4
Morella, Australia . . . 54 C3
Morella, Spain 19 B5
Morena, Sierra, Spain 19 C3
Morenci, U.S.A. 73 K9
Moresby I., Canada . . 64 C2
Moreton, Australia . . . 54 A3
Moreton I., Australia . 55 D5
Morgan, Australia . . . 55 E2
Morgan, U.S.A. 72 F8
Morgan City, U.S.A. . . 71 L9
Morganfield, U.S.A. . . 68 G2
Morganton, U.S.A. . . . 69 H5
Morgantown, U.S.A. . 68 F6
Morgenzon, S. Africa . 49 D4
Morghak, Iran 39 D8
Morice L., Canada . . . 64 C3
Morinville, Canada . . 64 C6
Morioka, Japan 28 E10
Morlaix, France 18 B2
Mornington, Vic.,
  Australia 55 F4
Mornington,
  W. Austral., Australia 52 C4
Mornington, I., Chile . 80 F1
Mornington I., Australia 54 B2
Moro G., Phil. 33 C6
Morocco ■, N. Afr. . . 44 B3
Morococha, Peru 78 F3
Morogoro, Tanzania . . 46 F7
Morombe, Madag. . . . 49 C7
Morón, Cuba 75 C9
Morón de la Frontera,
  Spain 19 D3
Morondava, Madag. . . 49 C7
Morotai, Indonesia . . 33 D7
Moroto, Uganda 46 D6
Morpeth, U.K. 10 B6
Morphou, Cyprus . . . 38 C2
Morrilton, U.S.A. 71 H8
Morrinhos, Brazil . . . 79 G9
Morrinsville, N.Z. . . . 51 G5
Morris, Canada 65 D9
Morris, Ill., U.S.A. . . . 68 E1
Morris, Minn., U.S.A. . 70 C7
Morris, Mt., Australia . 53 E5
Morrisburg, Canada . . 62 D4
Morrison, U.S.A. 70 E10
Morristown, Ariz.,
  U.S.A. 73 K7
Morristown, S. Dak.,
  U.S.A. 70 C4
Morristown, Tenn.,
  U.S.A. 69 G4
Morro Bay, U.S.A. . . . 73 J3

Morrumbene, Mozam. 49 C6
Mors Nykøbing,
  Denmark 9 H13
Morshansk, Russia . . 22 D7
Morteros, Argentina . 80 C4
Mortes, R. das →,
  Brazil 79 F8
Mortlake, Australia . . 55 F3
Morton, Tex., U.S.A. . . 71 J3
Morton, Wash., U.S.A. 72 C2
Morundah, Australia . 55 E4
Moruya, Australia . . . 55 F5
Morvan, France 18 C6
Morven, Australia . . . 55 D4
Morvern, U.K. 12 E3
Morwell, Australia . . . 55 F4
Morzhovets, Ostrov,
  Russia 22 A7
Moscos Is., Burma . . . 34 F4
Moscow = Moskva,
  Russia 22 C6
Moscow, U.S.A. 72 C5
Mosel →, Europe . . . 18 A7
Moselle = Mosel →,
  Europe 18 A7
Moses Lake, U.S.A. . . 72 C4
Mosgiel, N.Z. 51 L3
Moshi, Tanzania 46 E7
Moshupa, Botswana . 48 C4
Mosjøen, Norway . . . 8 D15
Moskenesøya, Norway 8 C15
Moskenstraumen,
  Norway 8 C15
Moskva, Russia 22 C6
Moskva →, Russia . . 22 C6
Mosomane, Botswana 48 C4
Moson-magyaróvar,
  Hungary 17 E9
Mosquera, Colombia . 78 C3
Mosquero, U.S.A. . . . 71 H3
Moss, Norway 9 G14
Moss Vale, Australia . 55 E5
Mossaka, Congo 46 E3
Mossbank, Canada . . 65 D7
Mossburn, N.Z. 51 L2
Mosselbaai, S. Africa . 48 E3
Mossendjo, Congo . . 46 E2
Mossgiel, Australia . . 55 E3
Mossman, Australia . . 54 B4
Mossoró, Brazil 79 E11
Mossuril, Mozam. . . . 47 G8
Mossy →, Canada . . 65 C8
Most, Czech. 16 C7
Moştafáābād, Iran . . . 39 C7
Mostaganem, Algeria . 44 A5
Mostar, Bos.-H. 21 C7
Mostardas, Brazil . . . 80 C6
Mostiska = Mostyska,
  Ukraine 17 D12
Mosty = Masty,
  Belarus 17 B13
Mostyska, Ukraine . . 17 D12
Mosul = Al Mawşil,
  Iraq 38 B4
Motala, Sweden 9 G16
Motherwell, U.K. 12 F5
Motihari, India 37 F14
Motril, Spain 19 D4
Mott, U.S.A. 70 B3
Motueka, N.Z. 51 J4
Motueka →, N.Z. . . . 51 J4
Mouanda, Gabon . . . 46 E2
Mouchalagane →,
  Canada 63 B6
Moúdhros, Greece . . . 21 E11
Moudjeria, Mauritania 44 E2
Mouila, Gabon 46 E2
Moulamein, Australia . 55 F3
Moulins, France 18 C5
Moulmein, Burma . . . 37 L20
Moulton, U.S.A. 71 L6
Moultrie, U.S.A. 69 K4
Moultrie, L., U.S.A. . . 69 J5
Mound City, Mo.,
  U.S.A. 70 E7
Mound City, S. Dak.,
  U.S.A. 70 C4
Moundou, Chad 45 G8
Moundsville, U.S.A. . . 68 F5
Mount Airy, U.S.A. . . . 69 G5
Mount Amherst,
  Australia 52 C4
Mount Angel, U.S.A. . 72 D2
Mount Augustus,
  Australia 52 D2
Mount Barker,
  S. Austral., Australia 55 F2
Mount Barker,
  W. Austral., Australia 53 F2
Mount Carmel, U.S.A. 68 F2
Mount Clemens, U.S.A. 62 D3
Mount Coolon,
  Australia 54 C4
Mount Darwin,
  Zimbabwe 47 H6
Mount Desert I., U.S.A. 63 D6
Mount Dora, U.S.A. . . 69 L5
Mount Douglas,
  Australia 54 C4
Mount Eba, Australia . 55 E2
Mount Edgecumbe,
  U.S.A. 64 B1
Mount Elizabeth,
  Australia 52 C4
Mount Fletcher,
  S. Africa 49 E4
Mount Forest, Canada 62 D3
Mount Gambier,
  Australia 55 F3
Mount Garnet,
  Australia 54 B4
Mount Hope, N.S.W.,
  Australia 55 E4

Mount Hope,
  S. Austral., Australia 55 E2
Mount Hope, U.S.A. . . 68 G5
Mount Horeb, U.S.A. . 70 D10
Mount Howitt, Australia 55 D3
Mount Isa, Australia . . 54 C2
Mount Keith, Australia 53 E3
Mount Larcom,
  Australia 54 C5
Mount Lofty Ra.,
  Australia 55 E2
Mount McKinley
  National Park, U.S.A. 60 B5
Mount Magnet,
  Australia 53 E2
Mount Margaret,
  Australia 55 D3
Mount Maunganui, N.Z. 51 G6
Mount Molloy,
  Australia 54 B4
Mount Monger,
  Australia 53 F3
Mount Morgan,
  Australia 54 C5
Mount Morris, U.S.A. . 68 D7
Mount Mulligan,
  Australia 54 B3
Mount Narryer,
  Australia 53 E2
Mount Olympus =
  Uludağ, Turkey . . . 21 D13
Mount Oxide Mine,
  Australia 54 B2
Mount Pearl, Canada . 63 C9
Mount Perry, Australia 55 D5
Mount Phillips,
  Australia 52 D2
Mount Pleasant, Iowa,
  U.S.A. 70 E9
Mount Pleasant, Mich.,
  U.S.A. 68 D3
Mount Pleasant, S.C.,
  U.S.A. 69 J6
Mount Pleasant, Tenn.,
  U.S.A. 69 H2
Mount Pleasant, Tex.,
  U.S.A. 71 J7
Mount Pleasant, Utah,
  U.S.A. 72 G8
Mount Rainier National
  Park, U.S.A. 72 C3
Mount Revelstoke Nat.
  Park, Canada 64 C5
Mount Robson Prov.
  Park, Canada 64 C5
Mount Sandiman,
  Australia 53 D2
Mount Shasta, U.S.A. . 72 F2
Mount Sterling, Ill.,
  U.S.A. 70 F9
Mount Sterling, Ky.,
  U.S.A. 68 F4
Mount Surprise,
  Australia 54 B3
Mount Vernon,
  Australia 52 D2
Mount Vernon, Ind.,
  U.S.A. 70 F10
Mount Vernon, N.Y.,
  U.S.A. 68 E9
Mount Vernon, Ohio,
  U.S.A. 68 E4
Mount Vernon, Wash.,
  U.S.A. 72 B2
Mountain City, Nev.,
  U.S.A. 72 F6
Mountain City, Tenn.,
  U.S.A. 69 G5
Mountain Grove, U.S.A. 71 G8
Mountain Home, Ark.,
  U.S.A. 71 G8
Mountain Home, Idaho,
  U.S.A. 72 E6
Mountain Iron, U.S.A. 70 B8
Mountain Park, Canada 64 C5
Mountain View, Ark.,
  U.S.A. 71 H8
Mountain View, Calif.,
  U.S.A. 73 H2
Mountainair, U.S.A. . . 73 J10
Mountmellick, Ireland 13 C4
Moura, Australia 54 C4
Moura, Brazil 78 D6
Moura, Portugal 19 C2
Mourdi, Dépression du,
  Chad 45 E9
Mourdiah, Mali 44 F3
Mourilyan, Australia . 54 B4
Mourne →, U.K. 13 B4
Mourne Mts., U.K. . . . 13 B5
Mouscron, Belgium . . 15 D3
Moussoro, Chad 45 F8
Moutohara, N.Z. 51 H6
Moutong, Indonesia . 33 D6
Moville, Ireland 13 A4
Moy →, Ireland 13 B3
Moyale, Kenya 40 G2
Moyamba, S. Leone . . 44 G2
Moyen Atlas, Morocco 44 B3
Moyle □, U.K. 13 A5
Moyo, Indonesia 32 F5
Moyobamba, Peru . . . 78 E3
Moyyero →, Russia . 25 C11
Mozambique =
  Moçambique,
  Mozam. 47 H8
Mozambique ■, Africa 47 H7
Mozambique Chan.,
  Africa 49 B7
Mozdok, Russia 23 F7
Mozdūrān, Iran 39 B9
Mozhnābād, Iran 39 C9
Mozyr = Mazyr,
  Belarus 17 B15

Mpanda

Mpanda, *Tanzania* 46 F6
Mpika, *Zambia* 47 G6
Mpumalanga, *S. Africa* 49 D5
Mpwapwa, *Tanzania* 46 F7
Msaken, *Tunisia* 45 A7
Msoro, *Zambia* 47 G6
Mstislavl = Mstsislaw, *Belarus* 17 A16
Mstsislaw, *Belarus* 17 A16
Mtubatuba, *S. Africa* 49 D5
Mu Us Shamo, *China* 31 C5
Muaná, *Brazil* 79 D9
Muang Chiang Rai, *Thailand* 34 C5
Muang Lamphun, *Thailand* 34 C5
Muar, *Malaysia* 34 S15
Muar →, *Malaysia* 34 S15
Muarabungo, *Indonesia* 32 E2
Muaraenim, *Indonesia* 32 E2
Muarajuloi, *Indonesia* 32 E4
Muarakaman, *Indonesia* 32 E5
Muaratebo, *Indonesia* 32 E2
Muaratembesi, *Indonesia* 32 E2
Muaratewe, *Indonesia* 32 E4
Mubarraz = Al Mubarraz, *Si. Arabia* 39 E6
Mubende, *Uganda* 46 D6
Mubi, *Nigeria* 45 F7
Muck, *U.K.* 12 E2
Muckadilla, *Australia* 55 D4
Muconda, *Angola* 46 G4
Mucuri, *Brazil* 79 G11
Mucusso, *Angola* 48 B3
Mudanjiang, *China* 31 B7
Mudanya, *Turkey* 21 D13
Muddy Cr. →, *U.S.A.* 73 H8
Mudgee, *Australia* 55 E4
Mudjatik →, *Canada* 65 B7
Mueller Ra., *Australia* 52 C4
Mufulira, *Zambia* 47 G5
Mughayrā', *Si. Arabia* 38 D3
Mugi, *Japan* 29 H7
Muğla, *Turkey* 21 F13
Mugu, *Nepal* 37 E13
Muhammad Qol, *Sudan* 45 D12
Mühlhausen, *Germany* 16 C6
Mühlig Hofmann fjella, *Antarctica* 5 D3
Muhos, *Finland* 8 D22
Muhu, *Estonia* 9 G20
Mui Bai Bung, *Vietnam* 34 H8
Mui Ron, *Vietnam* 34 C9
Muikamachi, *Japan* 29 F9
Muine Bheag, *Ireland* 13 D5
Muir, L., *Australia* 53 F2
Mukacheve, *Ukraine* 17 D12
Mukachevo = Mukacheve, *Ukraine* 17 D12
Mukah, *Malaysia* 32 D4
Mukden = Shenyang, *China* 31 B7
Mukhtuya = Lensk, *Russia* 25 C12
Mukinbudin, *Australia* 53 F2
Mukomuko, *Indonesia* 32 E2
Muktsar, *India* 36 D9
Mukur, *Afghan.* 36 C5
Mukutawa →, *Canada* 65 C9
Mula, *Spain* 19 C5
Mulchén, *Chile* 80 D2
Mulde →, *Germany* 16 C7
Mule Creek, *U.S.A.* 70 D2
Muleshoe, *U.S.A.* 71 H3
Mulgathing, *Australia* 55 E1
Mulgrave, *Canada* 63 C7
Mulhacén, *Spain* 19 D4
Mulhouse, *France* 18 C7
Mull, *U.K.* 12 E3
Mullaittvu, *Sri Lanka* 36 Q12
Mullen, *U.S.A.* 70 D4
Mullengudgery, *Australia* 55 E4
Mullens, *U.S.A.* 68 G5
Muller, Pegunungan, *Indonesia* 32 D4
Mullet Pen., *Ireland* 13 B1
Mullewa, *Australia* 53 E2
Mulligan →, *Australia* 54 C2
Mullin, *U.S.A.* 71 K5
Mullingar, *Ireland* 13 C4
Mullins, *U.S.A.* 69 H6
Mullumbimby, *Australia* 55 D5
Multan, *Pakistan* 36 D7
Mulvane, *U.S.A.* 71 G6
Mulwala, *Australia* 55 F4
Mumbaī = Bombay, *India* 36 K8
Mumbwa, *Zambia* 47 H5
Mun →, *Thailand* 34 E7
Muna, *Indonesia* 33 F6
Munamagi, *Estonia* 9 H22
München, *Germany* 16 D6
Munchen-Gladbach = Mönchengladbach, *Germany* 16 C4
Muncho Lake, *Canada* 64 B3
Muncie, *U.S.A.* 68 E3
Muncoonie, L., *Australia* 54 D2
Mundala, *Indonesia* 33 E10
Mundare, *Canada* 64 C6
Munday, *U.S.A.* 71 J5
Münden, *Germany* 16 C5
Mundiwindi, *Australia* 52 D3
Mundo Novo, *Brazil* 79 F10
Mundrabilla, *Australia* 53 F4
Mungallala, *Australia* 55 D4
Mungallala Cr. →, *Australia* 55 D4
Mungana, *Australia* 54 B3
Mungbere, *Zaïre* 46 D5
Munger, *India* 37 G15
Mungindi, *Australia* 55 D4
Munhango, *Angola* 47 G3
Munich = München, *Germany* 16 D6
Munising, *U.S.A.* 68 B2
Munku-Sardyk, *Russia* 25 D11
Muñoz Gamero, Pen., *Chile* 80 G2
Munroe L., *Canada* 65 B9
Münster, *Germany* 16 C4
Munster □, *Ireland* 13 D3
Muntadgin, *Australia* 53 F2
Muntok, *Indonesia* 32 E3
Muon Pak Beng, *Laos* 34 C6
Muonio, *Finland* 8 C20
Muonionjoki →, *Finland* 8 C20
Mupa, *Angola* 47 H3
Muqdisho, *Somali Rep.* 40 G4
Mur →, *Austria* 17 E9
Murakami, *Japan* 28 E9
Murallón, Cuerro, *Chile* 80 F2
Murang'a, *Kenya* 46 E7
Murashi, *Russia* 22 C8
Muratlı, *Turkey* 21 D12
Murayama, *Japan* 28 E10
Murban, *U.A.E.* 39 F7
Murchison →, *Australia* 53 E1
Murchison, Mt., *Antarctica* 5 D11
Murchison Falls = Kabarega Falls, *Uganda* 46 D6
Murchison House, *Australia* 53 E1
Murchison Ra., *Australia* 54 C1
Murcia, *Spain* 19 D5
Murcia □, *Spain* 19 D5
Murdo, *U.S.A.* 70 D4
Murdoch Pt., *Australia* 54 A3
Mureş →, *Romania* 17 E11
Mureşul = Mureş →, *Romania* 17 E11
Murfreesboro, *U.S.A.* 69 H2
Murgab = Murghob, *Tajikistan* 24 F8
Murghob, *Tajikistan* 24 F8
Murgon, *Australia* 55 D5
Murgoo, *Australia* 53 E2
Muria, *Indonesia* 33 G14
Müritz-see, *Germany* 16 B7
Murmansk, *Russia* 22 A5
Murom, *Russia* 22 C7
Muroran, *Japan* 28 C10
Muroto, *Japan* 29 H7
Muroto-Misaki, *Japan* 29 H7
Murphy, *U.S.A.* 72 E5
Murphysboro, *U.S.A.* 71 G10
Murray, *Ky., U.S.A.* 69 G1
Murray, *Utah, U.S.A.* 72 F8
Murray →, *Australia* 55 F2
Murray →, *Canada* 64 B4
Murray, L., *U.S.A.* 69 H5
Murray Bridge, *Australia* 55 F2
Murray Downs, *Australia* 54 C1
Murray Harbour, *Canada* 63 C7
Murraysburg, *S. Africa* 48 E3
Murree, *Pakistan* 36 C8
Murrin Murrin, *Australia* 53 E3
Murrumbidgee →, *Australia* 55 E3
Murrumburrah, *Australia* 55 E4
Murrurundi, *Australia* 55 E5
Murtle L., *Canada* 64 C5
Murtoa, *Australia* 55 F3
Murwara, *India* 37 H12
Murwillumbah, *Australia* 55 D5
Mürzzuschlag, *Austria* 16 E8
Muş, *Turkey* 23 G7
Mûsa, G., *Egypt* 45 C11
Musa Khel, *Pakistan* 36 D6
Mūsá Qal'eh, *Afghan.* 36 C4
Musaffargarh, *Pakistan* 36 D7
Musala, *Bulgaria* 21 C10
Musala, *Indonesia* 32 D1
Musay'īd, *Qatar* 39 E6
Muscat = Masqat, *Oman* 40 C6
Muscat & Oman = Oman ■, *Asia* 40 C6
Muscatine, *U.S.A.* 70 E9
Musgrave, *Australia* 54 A3
Musgrave Ras., *Australia* 53 E5
Mushie, *Zaïre* 46 E3
Musi →, *Indonesia* 32 E2
Muskeg →, *Canada* 64 A4
Muskegon, *U.S.A.* 68 D2
Muskegon →, *U.S.A.* 68 D2
Muskegon Heights, *U.S.A.* 68 D2
Muskogee, *U.S.A.* 71 H7
Muskwa →, *Canada* 64 B4
Muslīmiyah, *Syria* 38 B3
Musmar, *Sudan* 45 E12
Musoma, *Tanzania* 46 E6
Musquaro, L., *Canada* 63 B7
Musquodoboit Harbour, *Canada* 63 D7
Musselburgh, *U.K.* 12 F5
Musselshell →, *U.S.A.* 72 C10
Mussoorie, *India* 36 D11
Mussuco, *Angola* 48 B2
Mustafakemalpaşa, *Turkey* 21 D13
Mustang, *Nepal* 37 E13
Musters, L., *Argentina* 80 F3
Muswellbrook, *Australia* 55 E5
Mût, *Egypt* 45 C10
Mutanda, *Mozam.* 49 C5
Mutare, *Zimbabwe* 47 H6
Muting, *Indonesia* 33 F10
Mutoray, *Russia* 25 C11
Mutsu, *Japan* 28 D10
Mutsu-Wan, *Japan* 28 D10
Muttaburra, *Australia* 54 C3
Muweilih, *Egypt* 41 E3
Muxima, *Angola* 46 F2
Muynak, *Uzbekistan* 24 E6
Muzaffarabad, *Pakistan* 36 B8
Muzaffarnagar, *India* 36 E10
Muzaffarpur, *India* 37 F14
Muzhi, *Russia* 24 C7
Muzon, C., *U.S.A.* 64 C2
Mvuma, *Zimbabwe* 47 H6
Mwanza, *Tanzania* 46 E6
Mwanza, *Zaïre* 46 F5
Mweelrea, *Ireland* 13 C2
Mweka, *Zaïre* 46 E4
Mwenezi, *Zimbabwe* 47 J6
Mwenga, *Zaïre* 46 E5
Mweru, L., *Zambia* 46 F5
Mwinilunga, *Zambia* 47 G4
My Tho, *Vietnam* 34 G9
Myanaung, *Burma* 37 K19
Myanmar = Burma ■, *Asia* 37 J20
Myaungmya, *Burma* 37 L19
Mycenæ, *Greece* 21 F10
Myeik Kyunzu, *Burma* 34 G4
Myingyan, *Burma* 37 J19
Myitkyina, *Burma* 37 G20
Mykines, *Færoe Is.* 8 E9
Mykolayiv, *Ukraine* 23 E5
Mymensingh, *Bangla.* 37 G17
Mynydd Du, *U.K.* 11 F4
Mýrdalsjökull, *Iceland* 8 E4
Myroodah, *Australia* 52 C3
Myrtle Beach, *U.S.A.* 69 J6
Myrtle Creek, *U.S.A.* 72 E2
Myrtle Point, *U.S.A.* 72 E1
Mysia, *Turkey* 21 E12
Mysore = Karnataka □, *India* 36 N10
Mysore, *India* 36 N10
Myszków, *Poland* 17 C10
Mytishchi, *Russia* 22 C6
Myton, *U.S.A.* 72 F8
Mývatn, *Iceland* 8 D5
Mzimkulu →, *S. Africa* 49 E5
Mzimvubu →, *S. Africa* 49 E4

N

Na Hearadh = Harris, *U.K.* 12 D2
Naab →, *Germany* 16 D6
Naantali, *Finland* 9 F19
Naas, *Ireland* 13 C5
Nababiep, *S. Africa* 48 D2
Nabari, *Japan* 29 G8
Nabawa, *Australia* 53 E1
Nabberu, L., *Australia* 53 E3
Naberezhnyye Chelny, *Russia* 22 C9
Nabeul, *Tunisia* 45 A7
Nabīd, *Iran* 39 D8
Nabire, *Indonesia* 33 E9
Nabisipi →, *Canada* 63 B7
Nablus = Nābulus, *West Bank* 41 C4
Naboomspruit, *S. Africa* 49 C4
Nābulus, *West Bank* 41 C4
Naches, *U.S.A.* 72 C3
Nachingwea, *Tanzania* 46 G7
Nackara, *Australia* 55 E2
Naco, *U.S.A.* 73 L9
Nacogdoches, *U.S.A.* 71 K7
Nacozari, *Mexico* 74 A3
Nadiad, *India* 36 H8
Nadūshan, *Iran* 39 C7
Nadvirna, *Ukraine* 17 D13
Nadvoitsy, *Russia* 22 B5
Nadvornaya = Nadvirna, *Ukraine* 17 D13
Nadym, *Russia* 24 C8
Nadym →, *Russia* 24 C8
Nærbø, *Norway* 9 G11
Næstved, *Denmark* 9 J14
Nafada, *Nigeria* 44 F7
Naftshahr, *Iran* 38 C5
Nafud Desert = An Nafūd, *Si. Arabia* 38 D4
Naga, *Phil.* 33 B6
Nagagami →, *Canada* 62 C3
Nagahama, *Japan* 29 G8
Nagai, *Japan* 28 E10
Nagaland □, *India* 37 F19
Nagano, *Japan* 29 F9
Nagano □, *Japan* 29 F9
Nagaoka, *Japan* 29 F9
Nagappattinam, *India* 36 P11
Nagar Parkar, *Pakistan* 36 G7
Nagasaki, *Japan* 29 H4
Nagasaki □, *Japan* 29 H4
Nagato, *Japan* 29 G5
Nagaur, *India* 36 F8
Nagercoil, *India* 36 Q10
Nagīneh, *Iran* 39 C8
Nagoorin, *Australia* 54 C5
Nagornyy, *Russia* 25 D13
Nagoya, *Japan* 29 G8
Nagpur, *India* 36 J11
Nagykanizsa, *Hungary* 17 E9
Nagykörös, *Hungary* 17 E10
Naha, *Japan* 29 L3
Nahanni Butte, *Canada* 64 A4
Nahanni Nat. Park, *Canada* 64 A3
Nahariyya, *Israel* 38 C2
Nahāvand, *Iran* 39 C6
Nahlin, *Canada* 64 B2
Naicam, *Canada* 65 C8
Nā'ifah, *Si. Arabia* 40 D5
Nain, *Canada* 63 A7
Nā'īn, *Iran* 39 C7
Nainpur, *India* 36 H12
Naira, *Indonesia* 33 E7
Nairn, *U.K.* 12 D5
Nairobi, *Kenya* 46 E7
Naissaar, *Estonia* 9 G21
Naivasha, *Kenya* 46 E7
Najafābād, *Iran* 39 C6
Najibabad, *India* 36 E11
Najmah, *Si. Arabia* 39 E6
Nakadōri-Shima, *Japan* 29 H4
Nakaminato, *Japan* 29 F10
Nakamura, *Japan* 29 H6
Nakano, *Japan* 29 F9
Nakano-Shima, *Japan* 29 K4
Nakashibetsu, *Japan* 28 C12
Nakfa, *Eritrea* 45 E12
Nakhichevan = Naxçıvan, *Azerbaijan* 23 G8
Nakhichevan Republic = Naxçıvan □, *Azerbaijan* 23 G8
Nakhl, *Egypt* 41 F2
Nakhl-e Taqī, *Iran* 39 E7
Nakhodka, *Russia* 25 E14
Nakhon Phanom, *Thailand* 34 D8
Nakhon Ratchasima, *Thailand* 34 E7
Nakhon Sawan, *Thailand* 34 E6
Nakhon Si Thammarat, *Thailand* 34 H6
Nakina, *B.C., Canada* 64 B2
Nakina, *Ont., Canada* 62 B2
Nakskov, *Denmark* 9 J14
Nakuru, *Kenya* 46 E7
Nakusp, *Canada* 64 C5
Nal →, *Pakistan* 36 G4
Nalchik, *Russia* 23 F7
Nalgonda, *India* 36 L11
Nallamalai Hills, *India* 36 M11
Nālūt, *Libya* 45 B7
Nam Co, *China* 30 C4
Nam Dinh, *Vietnam* 34 B9
Nam-Phan, *Vietnam* 34 G9
Nam Phong, *Thailand* 34 D7
Nam Tha, *Laos* 34 B6
Namacunde, *Angola* 48 B2
Namacurra, *Mozam.* 49 B6
Namak, Daryācheh-ye, *Iran* 39 C7
Namak, Kavir-e, *Iran* 39 C8
Namaland, *Namibia* 48 C2
Namangan, *Uzbekistan* 24 E8
Namapa, *Mozam.* 47 G7
Namaqualand, *S. Africa* 48 D2
Namber, *Indonesia* 33 E8
Nambour, *Australia* 55 D5
Nambucca Heads, *Australia* 55 E5
Namcha Barwa, *China* 30 D4
Nameh, *Indonesia* 32 D5
Namew L., *Canada* 65 C8
Namib Desert = Namibwoestyn, *Namibia* 48 C2
Namibe, *Angola* 47 H2
Namibe □, *Angola* 48 B1
Namibia ■, *Africa* 48 C2
Namibwoestyn, *Namibia* 48 C2
Namlea, *Indonesia* 33 E7
Namoi →, *Australia* 55 E4
Nampa, *U.S.A.* 72 E5
Nampō-Shotō, *Japan* 29 J10
Nampula, *Mozam.* 47 H7
Namrole, *Indonesia* 33 E7
Namse Shankou, *China* 37 E13
Namsen →, *Norway* 8 D14
Namsos, *Norway* 8 D14
Namtsy, *Russia* 25 C13
Namtu, *Burma* 37 H20
Namu, *Canada* 64 C3
Namur, *Belgium* 15 D4
Namur □, *Belgium* 15 D4
Namutoni, *Namibia* 48 B2
Namwala, *Zambia* 47 H5
Nan, *Thailand* 34 C6
Nanaimo, *Canada* 64 D4
Nanango, *Australia* 55 D5
Nanao, *Japan* 29 F8
Nanchang, *China* 31 D6
Nanching = Nanjing, *China* 31 C6
Nanchong, *China* 30 C5
Nancy, *France* 18 B7
Nanda Devi, *India* 36 D11
Nandan, *Japan* 29 G7
Nanded, *India* 36 K10
Nandewar Ra., *Australia* 55 E5
Nandi, *Fiji* 51 C7
Nandurbar, *India* 36 J9
Nandyal, *India* 36 M11
Nanga, *Australia* 53 E1
Nanga-Eboko, *Cameroon* 46 D2
Nanga Parbat, *Pakistan* 36 B9
Nangapinoh, *Indonesia* 32 E4
Nangarhár □, *Afghan.* 36 B7
Nangatayap, *Indonesia* 32 E4
Nanjing, *China* 31 C6
Nanking = Nanjing, *China* 31 C6
Nankoku, *Japan* 29 H6
Nanning, *China* 30 D5
Nannup, *Australia* 53 F2
Nanping, *China* 31 D6
Nansei-Shotō = Ryūkyū-rettō, *Japan* 29 M2
Nansen Sd., *Canada* 4 A3
Nantes, *France* 18 C3
Nanticoke, *U.S.A.* 68 E7
Nanton, *Canada* 64 C6
Nantong, *China* 31 C7
Nantucket I., *U.S.A.* 58 E12
Nanuque, *Brazil* 79 G10
Nanutarra, *Australia* 52 D2
Nanyang, *China* 31 C6
Nanyuki, *Kenya* 46 D7
Nao, C. de la, *Spain* 19 C6
Naococane L., *Canada* 63 B5
Naoetsu, *Japan* 29 F9
Napa, *U.S.A.* 72 G2
Napanee, *Canada* 62 D4
Napier, *N.Z.* 51 H6
Napier Broome B., *Australia* 52 B4
Napier Downs, *Australia* 52 C3
Napier Pen., *Australia* 54 A2
Naples = Nápoli, *Italy* 20 D6
Naples, *U.S.A.* 69 M5
Napo →, *Peru* 78 D4
Napoleon, *N. Dak., U.S.A.* 70 B5
Napoleon, *Ohio, U.S.A.* 68 E3
Nápoli, *Italy* 20 D6
Nappa Merrie, *Australia* 55 D3
Naqqāsh, *Iran* 39 C6
Nara, *Japan* 29 G7
Nara, *Mali* 44 E3
Nara □, *Japan* 29 G8
Nara Visa, *U.S.A.* 71 H3
Naracoorte, *Australia* 55 F3
Naradhan, *Australia* 55 E4
Narasapur, *India* 37 L12
Narathiwat, *Thailand* 34 N14
Narayanganj, *Bangla.* 37 H17
Narayanpet, *India* 36 L10
Narbonne, *France* 18 E5
Nardīn, *Iran* 39 B7
Nardò, *Italy* 21 D8
Narembeen, *Australia* 53 F2
Nares Str., *Arctic* 58 B13
Naretha, *Australia* 53 F3
Narew →, *Poland* 17 B11
Narin, *Afghan.* 36 A6
Narindra, Helodranon' i, *Madag.* 49 A8
Narita, *Japan* 29 G10
Narmada →, *India* 36 J8
Narmland, *Sweden* 9 F15
Narodnaya, *Russia* 22 A10
Narooma, *Australia* 55 F5
Narrabri, *Australia* 55 E4
Narran →, *Australia* 55 D4
Narrandera, *Australia* 55 E4
Narraway →, *Canada* 64 B5
Narrogin, *Australia* 53 F2
Narromine, *Australia* 55 E4
Narsimhapur, *India* 36 H11
Naruto, *Japan* 29 G7
Narva, *Estonia* 22 C4
Narva →, *Russia* 9 G22
Narvik, *Norway* 8 B17
Naryan-Mar, *Russia* 22 A9
Naryilco, *Australia* 55 D3
Narym, *Russia* 24 D9
Narymskoye, *Kazakhstan* 24 E9
Naryn, *Kyrgyzstan* 24 E8
Nasa, *Norway* 8 C16
Nasarawa, *Nigeria* 44 G6
Naseby, *N.Z.* 51 L3
Naser, Buheirat en, *Egypt* 45 D11
Nashua, *Iowa, U.S.A.* 70 D8
Nashua, *Mont., U.S.A.* 72 B10
Nashua, *N.H., U.S.A.* 68 D10
Nashville, *Ark., U.S.A.* 71 J8
Nashville, *Ga., U.S.A.* 69 K4
Nashville, *Tenn., U.S.A.* 69 G2
Nasik, *India* 36 K8
Nasirabad, *India* 36 F9
Naskaupi →, *Canada* 63 B7
Naṣrīān-e Pā'īn, *Iran* 38 C5
Nass →, *Canada* 64 B3
Nassau, *Bahamas* 75 B9
Nassau, B., *Chile* 80 H3
Nasser, L. = Naser, Buheirat en, *Egypt* 45 D11
Nässjö, *Sweden* 9 H16
Nat Kyizin, *Burma* 34 E4
Nata, *Botswana* 48 C4
Natagaima, *Colombia* 78 C3
Natal, *Brazil* 79 E11
Natal, *Canada* 64 D6
Natal, *Indonesia* 32 D1
Naṭanz, *Iran* 39 C6
Natashquan, *Canada* 63 B7
Natashquan →, *Canada* 63 B7
Natchez, *U.S.A.* 71 K9
Natchitoches, *U.S.A.* 71 K8
Nathalia, *Australia* 55 F4
Nathdwara, *India* 36 G8
Natimuk, *Australia* 55 F3
Nation →, *Canada* 64 B4
National City, *U.S.A.* 73 K5
Natitingou, *Benin* 44 F5
Natoma, *U.S.A.* 70 F5
Natron, L., *Tanzania* 46 E7
Natuna Besar, Kepulauan, *Indonesia* 32 D3
Natuna Is. = Natuna Besar, Kepulauan, *Indonesia* 32 D3
Natuna Selatan, Kepulauan, *Indonesia* 32 D3
Naturaliste, C., *Australia* 54 G4
Naubinway, *U.S.A.* 62 C2
Naumburg, *Germany* 16 C6
Nā'ūr at Tunayb, *Jordan* 41 D4
Nauru ■, *Pac. Oc.* 56 H8
Naushahra = Nowshera, *Pakistan* 36 B8
Nauta, *Peru* 78 D4
Nautanwa, *India* 37 F13
Navahrudak, *Belarus* 17 B13
Navajo Reservoir, *U.S.A.* 73 H10
Navalmoral de la Mata, *Spain* 19 C3
Navan = An Uaimh, *Ireland* 13 C5
Navarino, I., *Chile* 80 H3
Navarra □, *Spain* 19 A5
Navasota, *U.S.A.* 71 K6
Naver →, *U.K.* 12 C4
Nǎvodari, *Romania* 17 F15
Navoi = Nawoiy, *Uzbekistan* 24 E7
Navojoa, *Mexico* 74 B3
Návpaktos, *Greece* 21 E9
Návplion, *Greece* 21 F10
Navsari, *India* 36 J8
Nawabshah, *Pakistan* 36 F6
Nawakot, *Nepal* 37 F14
Nawalgarh, *India* 36 F9
Nawoiy, *Uzbekistan* 24 E7
Naxçıvan, *Azerbaijan* 23 G8
Naxçıvan □, *Azerbaijan* 23 G8
Náxos, *Greece* 21 F11
Nāy Band, *Iran* 39 E7
Nayakhan, *Russia* 25 C16
Nayoro, *Japan* 28 B11
Nayyāl, W. →, *Si. Arabia* 38 D3
Nazareth = Naẓerat, *Israel* 41 C4
Nazas →, *Mexico* 74 B4
Naze, The, *U.K.* 11 F9
Naẓerat, *Israel* 41 C4
Nāzīk, *Iran* 38 B5
Nazilli, *Turkey* 21 F13
Nazir Hat, *Bangla.* 37 H17
Nazko, *Canada* 64 C4
Nazko →, *Canada* 64 C4
Ncheu, *Malawi* 47 G6
Ndalatando, *Angola* 46 F2
Ndélé, *C.A.R.* 45 G9
Ndendé, *Gabon* 46 E2
Ndjamena, *Chad* 45 F7
Ndjolé, *Gabon* 46 E2
Ndola, *Zambia* 47 G5
Neagh, Lough, *U.K.* 13 B5
Neah Bay, *U.S.A.* 72 B1
Neale, L., *Australia* 52 D5
Near Is., *U.S.A.* 60 C1
Neath, *U.K.* 11 F4
Nebine Cr. →, *Australia* 55 D4
Nebitdag, *Turkmenistan* 23 G9
Nebraska □, *U.S.A.* 70 E5
Nebraska City, *U.S.A.* 70 E7
Nébrodi, Monti, *Italy* 20 F6
Necedah, *U.S.A.* 70 C9
Nechako →, *Canada* 64 C4
Neches →, *U.S.A.* 71 L8
Neckar →, *Germany* 16 D5
Necochea, *Argentina* 80 D5
Needles, *U.S.A.* 73 J6
Needles, The, *U.K.* 11 G6
Neemuch = Nimach, *India* 36 G9
Neenah, *U.S.A.* 68 C1
Neepawa, *Canada* 65 C9
Nefta, *Tunisia* 44 B6
Neftçala, *Azerbaijan* 23 G8
Neftyannyye Kamni, *Azerbaijan* 23 F9
Negapatam = Nagappattinam, *India* 36 P11
Negaunee, *U.S.A.* 68 B2
Negele, *Ethiopia* 40 F2
Negeri Sembilan □, *Malaysia* 34 S15
Negev Desert = Hanegev, *Israel* 41 E3
Negombo, *Sri Lanka* 36 R11
Negotin, *Serbia, Yug.* 21 B10
Negra Pt., *Phil.* 33 A6
Negrais, C. = Maudin Sun, *Burma* 37 M19
Negro →, *Argentina* 80 E4
Negro →, *Brazil* 78 D6
Negro →, *Uruguay* 80 C5
Negros, *Phil.* 33 C6
Nehāvand, *Iran* 39 C6
Nehbandān, *Iran* 39 D9
Nei Monggol Zizhiqu □, *China* 31 B6
Neidpath, *Canada* 65 C7
Neihart, *U.S.A.* 72 C8
Neijiang, *China* 30 D5
Neilton, *U.S.A.* 72 C2
Neiva, *Colombia* 78 C3
Nejanilini L., *Canada* 65 B9
Nekā, *Iran* 39 B7
Nekemte, *Ethiopia* 45 G12

Neksø, *Denmark* 9 J16
Nelia, *Australia* 54 C3
Neligh, *U.S.A.* 70 D5
Nelkan, *Russia* 25 D14
Nellore, *India* 36 M11
Nelma, *Russia* 25 E14
Nelson, *Canada* 64 D5
Nelson, *N.Z.* 51 J4
Nelson, *U.K.* 10 D5
Nelson, *U.S.A.* 73 J7
Nelson →, *Canada* ... 65 C9
Nelson, C., *Australia* .. 55 F3
Nelson, Estrecho, *Chile* 80 G2
Nelson Forks, *Canada* 64 B4
Nelson House, *Canada* 65 B9
Nelson L., *Canada* 65 B8
Nelspoort, *S. Africa* .. 48 E3
Nelspruit, *S. Africa* ... 49 D5
Néma, *Mauritania* 44 E3
Neman →, *Lithuania* . 9 J19
Nemeiben L., *Canada* . 65 B7
Nemunas =
   Neman →,
   Lithuania 9 J19
Nemuro, *Japan* 28 C12
Nemuro-Kaikyō, *Japan* 28 C12
Nemuy, *Russia* 25 D14
Nen Jiang →, *China* . 31 B7
Nenagh, *Ireland* 13 D3
Nenana, *U.S.A.* 60 B5
Nene →, *U.K.* 10 E8
Nenjiang, *China* 31 B7
Nenusa, Kepulauan,
   Indonesia 33 D7
Neodesha, *U.S.A.* ... 71 G7
Neosho, *U.S.A.* 71 G7
Neosho →, *U.S.A.* .. 71 H7
Nepal ■, *Asia* 37 F14
Nepalganj, *Nepal* ... 37 E12
Nephi, *U.S.A.* 72 G8
Nephin, *Ireland* 13 B2
Nerchinsk, *Russia* .. 25 D12
Nerchinskiy Zavod,
   Russia 25 D12
Néret L., *Canada* ... 63 B5
Neretva →, *Croatia* . 21 C7
Neringa, *Lithuania* .. 9 J19
Ness, *U.K.* 12 D4
Nesterov, *Ukraine* .. 17 C12
Nesvizh = Nyasvizh,
   Belarus 17 B14
Netanya, *Israel* 41 C3
Nète →, *Belgium* ... 15 C4
Netherdale, *Australia* 54 C4
Netherlands ■, *Europe* 15 C5
Netherlands Antilles ■,
   W. Indies 75 E11
Nettilling L., *Canada* . 61 B12
Neubrandenburg,
   Germany 16 B7
Neuchâtel, *Switz.* ... 16 E4
Neuchâtel, Lac de,
   Switz. 16 E4
Neufchâteau, *Belgium* 15 E5
Neumünster, *Germany* 16 A5
Neunkirchen, *Germany* 16 D4
Neuquén, *Argentina* . 80 D3
Neuruppin, *Germany* . 16 B7
Neuse →, *U.S.A.* ... 69 H7
Neusiedler See, *Austria* 17 E9
Neuss, *Germany* 15 C6
Neustrelitz, *Germany* . 16 B7
Neva →, *Russia* 22 C5
Nevada, *U.S.A.* 71 G7
Nevada □, *U.S.A.* ... 72 G5
Nevada, Sierra, *Spain* 19 D4
Nevada, Sierra, *U.S.A.* 72 G3
Nevada City, *U.S.A.* . 72 G3
Nevanka, *Russia* ... 25 D10
Nevers, *France* 18 C5
Nevertire, *Australia* .. 55 E4
Neville, *Canada* 65 D7
Nevinnomyssk, *Russia* 23 F7
Nevis, *W. Indies* 75 D12
Nevyansk, *Russia* ... 22 C11
New Albany, *Ind.,*
   U.S.A. 68 F3
New Albany, *Miss.,*
   U.S.A. 71 H10
New Amsterdam,
   Guyana 78 B7
New Angledool,
   Australia 55 D4
New Bedford, *U.S.A.* . 68 E10
New Bern, *U.S.A.* ... 69 H7
New Boston, *U.S.A.* . 71 J7
New Braunfels, *U.S.A.* 71 L5
New Brighton, *N.Z.* .. 51 K4
New Britain,
   Papua N. G. 56 H7
New Britain, *U.S.A.* .. 68 E9
New Brunswick, *U.S.A.* 68 E8
New Brunswick □,
   Canada 63 C6
New Caledonia ■,
   Pac. Oc. 56 K8
New Castle, *Ind., U.S.A.* 68 F3
New Castle, *Pa., U.S.A.* 68 E5
New Cristóbal, *Panama* 74 H14
New Delhi, *India* 36 E10
New Denver, *Canada* . 64 D5
New England, *U.S.A.* . 70 B3
New England Ra.,
   Australia 55 E5
New Forest, *U.K.* 11 G6
New Glasgow, *Canada* 63 C7
New Guinea, *Oceania* . 56 H5
New Hampshire □,
   U.S.A. 68 D10
New Hampton, *U.S.A.* 70 D8
New Hanover, *S. Africa* 49 D5
New Haven, *U.S.A.* .. 68 E9
New Hazelton, *Canada* 64 B3

New Hebrides =
   Vanuatu ■, *Pac. Oc.* 56 J8
New Iberia, *U.S.A.* ... 71 K9
New Ireland,
   Papua N. G. 56 H7
New Jersey □, *U.S.A.* 68 E8
New Kensington,
   U.S.A. 68 E6
New Lexington, *U.S.A.* 68 F4
New Liskeard, *Canada* 62 C4
New London, *Conn.,*
   U.S.A. 68 E9
New London, *Minn.,*
   U.S.A. 70 C7
New London, *Wis.,*
   U.S.A. 70 C10
New Madrid, *U.S.A.* .. 71 G10
New Meadows, *U.S.A.* 72 D5
New Mexico □, *U.S.A.* 73 J10
New Norcia, *Australia* 53 F2
New Norfolk, *Australia* 54 G4
New Orleans, *U.S.A.* . 71 K9
New Philadelphia,
   U.S.A. 68 E5
New Plymouth, *N.Z.* .. 51 H5
New Plymouth, *U.S.A.* 72 E5
New Providence,
   Bahamas 75 B9
New Radnor, *U.K.* ... 11 E4
New Richmond, *U.S.A.* 70 C8
New Roads, *U.S.A.* .. 71 K9
New Rockford, *U.S.A.* 70 B5
New Ross, *Ireland* ... 13 D5
New Salem, *U.S.A.* .. 70 B4
New Scone, *U.K.* 12 E5
New Siberian Is. =
   Novosibirskiye
   Ostrova, *Russia* .. 25 B15
New Smyrna Beach,
   U.S.A. 69 L5
New South Wales □,
   Australia 55 E4
New Springs, *Australia* 53 E3
New Town, *U.S.A.* ... 70 A3
New Ulm, *U.S.A.* 70 C7
New Waterford, *Canada* 63 C7
New Westminster,
   Canada 64 D4
New York □, *U.S.A.* . 68 D8
New York City, *U.S.A.* 68 E9
New Zealand ■,
   Oceania 51 J5
Newala, *Tanzania* ... 46 G7
Newark, *Del., U.S.A.* . 68 F8
Newark, *N.J., U.S.A.* . 68 E8
Newark, *N.Y., U.S.A.* . 68 D7
Newark, *Ohio, U.S.A.* 68 E4
Newark-on-Trent, *U.K.* 10 D7
Newaygo, *U.S.A.* 68 D3
Newberg, *U.S.A.* 72 D2
Newberry, *Mich.,*
   U.S.A. 68 B3
Newberry, *S.C., U.S.A.* 69 H5
Newbridge =
   Droichead Nua,
   Ireland 13 C5
Newbrook, *Canada* .. 64 C6
Newburgh, *U.S.A.* ... 68 E8
Newbury, *U.K.* 11 F6
Newburyport, *U.S.A.* . 68 D10
Newcastle, *Australia* . 55 E5
Newcastle, *Canada* .. 63 C6
Newcastle, *S. Africa* . 49 D4
Newcastle, *U.K.* 13 B6
Newcastle, *U.S.A.* ... 70 D2
Newcastle Emlyn, *U.K.* 11 E3
Newcastle Ra.,
   Australia 52 C5
Newcastle-under-Lyme,
   U.K. 10 D5
Newcastle-upon-Tyne,
   U.K. 10 C6
Newcastle Waters,
   Australia 54 B1
Newdegate, *Australia* 53 F2
Newell, *U.S.A.* 70 C3
Newfoundland □,
   Canada 63 B8
Newhalem, *U.S.A.* ... 64 D4
Newham, *U.K.* 11 F8
Newhaven, *U.K.* 11 G8
Newkirk, *U.S.A.* 71 G6
Newman, *Australia* .. 52 D2
Newmarket, *Ireland* .. 13 D3
Newmarket, *U.K.* 11 E8
Newnan, *U.S.A.* 69 J3
Newport, *Gwent, U.K.* 11 F5
Newport, *I. of W., U.K.* 11 G6
Newport, *Ark., U.S.A.* 71 H9
Newport, *Ky., U.S.A.* . 68 F3
Newport, *N.H., U.S.A.* 68 D9
Newport, *Oreg., U.S.A.* 72 D1
Newport, *R.I., U.S.A.* . 68 E10
Newport, *Tenn., U.S.A.* 69 H4
Newport, *Vt., U.S.A.* . 68 D9
Newport, *Wash., U.S.A.* 72 B5
Newport Beach, *U.S.A.* 73 K5
Newport News, *U.S.A.* 68 G7
Newquay, *U.K.* 11 G2
Newry, *U.K.* 13 B5
Newry & Mourne □,
   U.K. 13 B5
Newton, *Iowa, U.S.A.* 70 E8
Newton, *Mass., U.S.A.* 68 D10
Newton, *Miss., U.S.A.* 71 J10
Newton, *N.C., U.S.A.* 69 H5
Newton, *N.J., U.S.A.* . 68 E8
Newton, *Tex., U.S.A.* 71 K8
Newton Abbot, *U.K.* . 11 G4
Newton Boyd, *Australia* 55 D5
Newton Stewart, *U.K.* 12 G4
Newtonmore, *U.K.* .. 12 D4
Newtown, *U.K.* 11 E4

Newtownabbey □, *U.K.* 13 B6
Newtownards, *U.K.* .. 13 B6
Neya, *Russia* 22 C7
Neyriz, *Iran* 39 D7
Neyshābūr, *Iran* 39 B8
Nezhin = Nizhyn,
   Ukraine 23 D5
Nezperce, *U.S.A.* ... 72 C5
Ngabang, *Indonesia* . 32 D3
Ngabordamlu, Tanjung,
   Indonesia 33 F8
Ngami Depression,
   Botswana 48 C3
Nganglong Kangri,
   China 37 C12
Nganjuk, *Indonesia* .. 33 G14
Ngaoundéré, *Cameroon* 46 C2
Ngapara, *N.Z.* 51 L3
Ngawi, *Indonesia* ... 33 G14
Ngha Lo, *Vietnam* ... 34 B8
Ngoring Hu, *China* .. 30 C4
Ngudu, *Tanzania* ... 46 E6
Nguigmi, *Niger* 45 F7
Ngukurr, *Australia* .. 54 A1
Nguru, *Nigeria* 45 F7
Nha Trang, *Vietnam* . 34 F10
Nhacoongo, *Mozam.* . 49 C6
Nhangutazi, L., *Mozam.* 49 C5
Nhill, *Australia* 55 F3
Nhulunbuy, *Australia* . 54 A2
Niafounké, *Mali* 44 E4
Niagara, *U.S.A.* 68 C1
Niagara Falls, *Canada* 62 D4
Niagara Falls, *U.S.A.* 68 D6
Niah, *Malaysia* 32 D4
Niamey, *Niger* 44 F5
Niangara, *Zaïre* 46 D5
Nias, *Indonesia* 32 D1
Nicaragua ■,
   Cent. Amer. 74 E7
Nicaragua, L. de, *Nic.* 74 E7
Nicastro, *Italy* 20 E7
Nice, *France* 18 E7
Niceville, *U.S.A.* 69 K2
Nichinan, *Japan* 29 J5
Nicholasville, *U.S.A.* . 68 G3
Nicholson →,
   Australia 54 B2
Nicholson Ra., *Australia* 53 E2
Nicobar Is., *Ind. Oc.* . 26 J13
Nicola, *Canada* 64 C4
Nicolet, *Canada* 62 C5
Nicosia, *Cyprus* 38 C2
Nicoya, Pen. de,
   Costa Rica 74 F7
Nidd →, *U.K.* 10 C6
Nidderdale, *U.K.* 10 C6
Niederbronn □,
   Germany 16 B5
Niekerkshoop, *S. Africa* 48 D3
Niemen = Neman →,
   Lithuania 9 J19
Nienburg, *Germany* . 16 B5
Nieu Bethesda,
   S. Africa 48 E3
Nieuw Amsterdam,
   Surinam 79 B7
Nieuw Nickerie,
   Surinam 79 B7
Nieuwoudtville,
   S. Africa 48 E2
Nieuwpoort, *Belgium* . 15 C2
Niğde, *Turkey* 23 G5
Nigel, *S. Africa* 49 D4
Niger ■, *W. Afr.* 44 E6
Niger →, *W. Afr.* 44 G6
Nigeria ■, *W. Afr.* .. 44 G6
Nightcaps, *N.Z.* 51 L2
Nii-Jima, *Japan* 29 G9
Niigata, *Japan* 28 F9
Niigata □, *Japan* 29 F9
Niihama, *Japan* 29 H6
Niihau, *U.S.A.* 66 H14
Niimi, *Japan* 29 G6
Niitsu, *Japan* 28 F9
Nijil, *Jordan* 41 E4
Nijkerk, *Neths.* 15 B5
Nijmegen, *Neths.* ... 15 C5
Nijverdal, *Neths.* 15 B6
Nīk Pey, *Iran* 39 B6
Nikiniki, *Indonesia* .. 33 F6
Nikki, *Benin* 44 G5
Nikkō, *Japan* 29 F9
Nikolayev = Mykolayiv,
   Ukraine 23 E5
Nikolayevsk, *Russia* . 23 D8
Nikolayevsk-na-Amur,
   Russia 25 D15
Nikolskoye, *Russia* .. 25 D17
Nikopol, *Ukraine* 23 E5
Nīkshahr, *Iran* 39 E9
Nikšić,
   Montenegro, Yug. 21 C8
Nîl, Nahr en →, *Africa* 45 B11
Nîl el Abyad →,
   Sudan 45 E11
Nîl el Azraq →, *Sudan* 45 E11
Niland, *U.S.A.* 73 K6
Nile = Nîl, Nahr
   en →, *Africa* 45 B11
Niles, *U.S.A.* 68 E5
Nimach, *India* 36 G9
Nîmes, *France* 18 E6
Nimfaíon, Ákra =
   Pínnes, Ákra, *Greece* 21 D11
Nimmitabel, *Australia* 55 F4
Nimule, *Sudan* 46 D6
Ninawá, *Iraq* 38 B4
Nindigully, *Australia* . 55 D4
Ninemile, *U.S.A.* 64 D2
Nineveh = Nīnawá,
   Iraq 38 B4

Ningaloo, *Australia* .. 52 D1
Ningbo, *China* 31 D7
Ningjing Shan, *China* 30 C4
Ningpo = Ningbo,
   China 31 D7
Ningsia Hui A.R. =
   Ningxia Huizu
   Zizhiqu □, *China* . 30 C5
Ningxia Huizu
   Zizhiqu □, *China* . 30 C5
Ninh Binh, *Vietnam* .. 34 B8
Ninove, *Belgium* 15 D4
Niobrara, *U.S.A.* 70 D6
Niobrara →, *U.S.A.* . 70 D6
Nioro du Sahel, *Mali* . 44 E3
Niort, *France* 18 C3
Nipawin, *Canada* 65 C8
Nipawin Prov. Park,
   Canada 65 C8
Nipigon, *Canada* 62 C2
Nipigon, L., *Canada* . 62 C2
Nipin →, *Canada* ... 65 B7
Nipishish L., *Canada* 63 B7
Nipissing L., *Canada* 62 C4
Nipomo, *U.S.A.* 73 J3
Niquelândia, *Brazil* .. 79 F9
Nīr, *Iran* 38 B5
Nirasaki, *Japan* 29 G9
Nirmal, *India* 36 K11
Nirmali, *India* 37 F15
Niš, *Serbia, Yug.* ... 21 C9
Nişāb, *Si. Arabia* ... 38 D5
Nişāb, *Yemen* 40 E4
Nishinomiya, *Japan* . 29 G7
Nishin'omote, *Japan* . 29 J5
Nishiwaki, *Japan* 29 G7
Niskibi →, *Canada* .. 62 A2
Nissum Bredning,
   Denmark 9 H13
Nistru = Dnister →,
   Europe 17 E16
Nisutlin →, *Canada* . 64 A2
Nitchequon, *Canada* . 63 B5
Niterói, *Brazil* 79 H10
Nith →, *U.K.* 12 F5
Nitra, *Slovak Rep.* .. 17 D10
Nitra →, *Slovak Rep.* 17 E10
Niuafo'ou, *Tonga* 51 B11
Niue, *Cook Is.* 57 J11
Niut, *Indonesia* 32 D4
Nivala, *Finland* 8 E21
Nivelles, *Belgium* ... 15 D4
Nivernais, *France* ... 18 C5
Nixon, *U.S.A.* 71 L6
Nizamabad, *India* ... 36 K11
Nizamghat, *India* 37 E19
Nizhne Kolymsk, *Russia* 25 C17
Nizhne-Vartovsk, *Russia* 24 C8
Nizhneangarsk, *Russia* 25 D11
Nizhnekamsk, *Russia* 22 C9
Nizhneudinsk, *Russia* 25 D10
Nizhnevartovsk, *Russia* 25 B14
Nizhniy Novgorod,
   Russia 22 C7
Nizhniy Tagil, *Russia* 22 C10
Nizhyn, *Ukraine* 23 D5
Nízké Tatry,
   Slovak Rep. 17 D10
North Adams, *U.S.A.* 68 D9
North Andaman I.,
   India 34 F2
North Battleford,
   Canada 65 C7
North Bay, *Canada* .. 62 C4
North Belcher Is.,
   Canada 62 A4
North Bend, *Canada* . 64 D4
North Bend, *U.S.A.* .. 72 E1
North Berwick, *U.K.* . 12 E6
North C., *Canada* ... 63 C7
North C., *N.Z.* 51 F4
North Canadian →,
   U.S.A. 71 H7
North Cape =
   Nordkapp, *Norway* . 8 A21
North Cape =
   Nordkapp, *Svalbard* 4 A9
North Caribou L.,
   Canada 62 B1
North Carolina □,
   U.S.A. 69 H5
North Channel, *Canada* 62 C3
North Channel, *U.K.* . 12 G3
North Chicago, *U.S.A.* 68 D2
North Dakota □, *U.S.A.* 70 B5
North Dandalup,
   Australia 53 F2
North Down □, *U.K.* . 13 B6
North Downs, *U.K.* .. 11 F8
North East Frontier
   Agency = Arunachal
   Pradesh □, *India* . 37 E19
North Esk →, *U.K.* .. 12 E6
North European Plain,
   Europe 6 D11
North Foreland, *U.K.* 11 F9
North Frisian Is. =
   Nordfriesische Inseln,
   Germany 16 A5
North Henik L., *Canada* 65 A9
North I., *N.Z.* 51 H5
North Knife →,
   Canada 65 B10
North Korea ■, *Asia* . 31 D7
North Lakhimpur, *India* 37 F19
North Las Vegas,
   U.S.A. 73 H6
North Loup →, *U.S.A.* 70 E5
North Magnetic Pole,
   Canada 4 B2
North Minch, *U.K.* ... 12 C3
North Nahanni →,
   Canada 64 A4
North Ossetia □, *Russia* 23 F7
North Pagai, I. = Pagai
   Utara, *Indonesia* . 32 E2
North Palisade, *U.S.A.* 73 H4
North Platte, *U.S.A.* . 70 E4

North Platte →, *U.S.A.* 70 E4
North Pole, *Arctic* ... 4 A
North Portal, *Canada* . 65 D8
North Powder, *U.S.A.* 72 D5
North Pt., *Canada* ... 63 C7
North Rhine Westphalia
   = Nordrhein-
   Westfalen □,
   Germany 16 C4
North Ronaldsay, *U.K.* 12 B6
North
   Saskatchewan →,
   Canada 65 C7
North Sea, *Europe* ... 6 D6
North Sentinel I., *India* 34 G2
North Sporades =
   Voríai Sporádhes,
   Greece 21 E10
North Sydney, *Canada* 63 C7
North Taranaki Bight,
   N.Z. 51 H5
North Thompson →,
   Canada 64 C4
North Tonawanda,
   U.S.A. 68 D6
North Truchas Pk.,
   U.S.A. 73 J11
North Twin I., *Canada* 62 B3
North Tyne →, *U.K.* . 10 C5
North Uist, *U.K.* 12 D1
North Vancouver,
   Canada 64 D4
North Vernon, *U.S.A.* 68 F3
North Wabasca L.,
   Canada 64 B6
North Walsham, *U.K.* 10 E9
North-West □, *S. Africa* 48 D4
North West C.,
   Australia 52 D1
North West Christmas I.
   Ridge, *Pac. Oc.* .. 57 G11
North West Frontier □,
   Pakistan 36 B8
North West Highlands,
   U.K. 12 D3
North West River,
   Canada 63 B7
North West
   Territories □, *Canada* 60 B9
North York Moors, *U.K.* 10 C7
North Yorkshire □, *U.K.* 10 C6
Northallerton, *U.K.* .. 10 C6
Northam, *S. Africa* .. 48 C4
Northam, *Australia* .. 53 F2
Northampton, *Australia* 53 E1
Northampton, *U.K.* .. 11 E7
Northampton, *U.S.A.* 68 D9
Northampton Downs,
   Australia 54 C4
Northamptonshire □,
   U.K. 11 E7
Northcliffe, *Australia* . 53 F2
Northern Cape □,
   S. Africa 48 D3
Northern Circars, *India* 37 L13
Northern Indian L.,
   Canada 65 B9
Northern Ireland □,
   U.K. 13 B5
Northern Light, L.,
   Canada 62 C1
Northern Marianas ■,
   Pac. Oc. 56 F6
Northern Territory □,
   Australia 52 D5
Northern Transvaal □,
   S. Africa 49 C4
Northfield, *U.S.A.* ... 70 C8
Northland □, *N.Z.* ... 51 F4
Northome, *U.S.A.* ... 70 B7
Northport, *Ala., U.S.A.* 69 J2
Northport, *Mich.,*
   U.S.A. 68 C3
Northport, *Wash.,*
   U.S.A. 72 B5
Northumberland □,
   U.K. 10 B5
Northumberland, C.,
   Australia 55 F3
Northumberland Is.,
   Australia 54 C4
Northumberland Str.,
   Canada 63 C7
Northwich, *U.K.* 10 D5
Northwood, *Iowa,*
   U.S.A. 70 D8
Northwood, *N. Dak.,*
   U.S.A. 70 B6
Norton, *U.S.A.* 70 F5
Norton Sd., *U.S.A.* .. 60 B3
Norwalk, *Conn., U.S.A.* 68 E9
Norwalk, *Ohio, U.S.A.* 68 E4
Norway, *U.S.A.* 68 C2
Norway ■, *Europe* .. 8 E14
Norway House, *Canada* 65 C9
Norwegian Sea, *Atl. Oc.* 4 C8
Norwich, *U.K.* 10 E9
Norwich, *U.S.A.* 68 D8
Noshiro, *Japan* 28 D10
Nosok, *Russia* 24 B9
Noss Hd., *U.K.* 12 C5
Nossob →, *S. Africa* 48 D3
Nosy Bé, *Madag.* ... 49 G9
Nosy Boraha, *Madag.* 49 B8
Nosy Mitsio, *Madag.* 47 G9
Nosy Varika, *Madag.* 49 C8
Noteć →, *Poland* ... 16 B8
Notikewin →, *Canada* 64 B5
Notodden, *Norway* .. 9 G13
Notre-Dame, *Canada* 63 C7
Notre Dame B., *Canada* 63 C9
Notre Dame de Koartac
   = Quaqtaq, *Canada* 61 B13

Notre Dame d'Ivugivic

Notre Dame d'Ivugivic = Ivujivik, Canada 61 B12
Nottaway →, Canada 62 B4
Nottingham, U.K. 10 E6
Nottinghamshire □, U.K. 10 D7
Nottoway →, U.S.A. 68 G7
Notwane →, Botswana 48 C4
Nouâdhibou, Mauritania 44 D1
Nouâdhibou, Ras, Mauritania 44 D1
Nouakchott, Mauritania 44 E1
Nouméa, N. Cal. 56 K8
Noupoort, S. Africa 48 E3
Nouveau Comptoir = Wemindji, Canada 62 B4
Nouvelle-Calédonie = New Caledonia ■, Pac. Oc. 56 K8
Nova Casa Nova, Brazil 79 E10
Nova Cruz, Brazil 79 E11
Nova Friburgo, Brazil 79 H10
Nova Gaia = Cambundi-Catembo, Angola 46 G3
Nova Iguaçu, Brazil 79 H10
Nova Iorque, Brazil 79 E10
Nova Lima, Brazil 79 G10
Nova Lisboa = Huambo, Angola 47 G3
Nova Mambone, Mozam. 49 C6
Nova Scotia □, Canada 63 C7
Nova Sofala, Mozam. 49 C5
Nova Venécia, Brazil 79 G10
Nova Zagora, Bulgaria 21 C11
Novara, Italy 20 B3
Novaya Ladoga, Russia 22 B5
Novaya Lyalya, Russia 24 D7
Novaya Zemlya, Russia 24 B6
Nové Zámky, Slovak Rep. 17 D10
Novgorod, Russia 22 C5
Novgorod-Severskiy = Novhorod-Siverskyy, Ukraine 22 D5
Novhorod-Siverskyy, Ukraine 22 D5
Novi Ligure, Italy 20 B3
Novi Pazar, Serbia, Yug. 21 C9
Novi Sad, Serbia, Yug. 21 B8
Novo Mesto, Slovenia 16 F8
Novo Remanso, Brazil 79 E10
Novoataysk, Russia 24 D9
Novocherkassk, Russia 23 E7
Novogrudok = Navahrudak, Belarus 17 B13
Novohrad-Volynskyy, Ukraine 17 C14
Novokachalinsk, Russia 28 B6
Novokazalinsk = Zhangaqazaly, Kazakhstan 24 E7
Novokuybyshevsk, Russia 22 D8
Novokuznetsk, Russia 24 D9
Novomoskovsk, Russia 22 D6
Novorossiysk, Russia 23 F6
Novorybnoye, Russia 25 B11
Novoselytsya, Ukraine 17 D14
Novoshakhtinsk, Russia 23 E6
Novosibirsk, Russia 24 D9
Novosibirskiye Ostrova, Russia 25 B15
Novotroitsk, Russia 24 D6
Novouzensk, Russia 23 D8
Novovolynsk, Ukraine 17 C13
Novska, Croatia 20 B7
Novyy Port, Russia 24 C8
Now Shahr, Iran 39 B6
Nowa Sól, Poland 16 C8
Nowbarān, Iran 39 C6
Nowghāb, Iran 39 C8
Nowgong, India 37 F18
Nowra, Australia 55 E5
Nowshera, Pakistan 36 B8
Nowy Sącz, Poland 17 D11
Nowy Targ, Poland 17 D11
Nowy Tomyśl, Poland 16 B9
Noxon, U.S.A. 72 C6
Noyes I., U.S.A. 64 B2
Noyon, France 18 B5
Nsanje, Malawi 47 H7
Nsawam, Ghana 44 G4
Nsukka, Nigeria 44 G6
Nu Jiang →, China 30 D4
Nu Shan, China 30 D4
Nubian Desert = Nûbîya, Es Sahrâ En, Sudan 45 D11
Nûbîya, Es Sahrâ En, Sudan 45 D11
Nuboai, Indonesia 33 E9
Nueces →, U.S.A. 71 M6
Nueltin L., Canada 65 A9
Nueva Imperial, Chile 80 D2
Nueva Rosita, Mexico 74 B4
Nuéve de Julio, Argentina 80 D4
Nuevitas, Cuba 75 C9
Nuevo, G., Argentina 80 E4
Nuevo Laredo, Mexico 74 B5
Nugget Pt., N.Z. 51 M2
Nuhaka, N.Z. 51 H6
Nukey Bluff, Australia 55 E2
Nukheila, Sudan 45 E10
Nuku'alofa, Tonga 51 E11
Nukus, Uzbekistan 24 E6
Nulato, U.S.A. 60 B4
Nullagine →, Australia 52 D3
Nullarbor, Australia 53 F5
Nullarbor Plain, Australia 53 F4
Numalla, L., Australia 55 D3
Numan, Nigeria 45 G7
Numata, Japan 29 F9
Numazu, Japan 29 G9
Numbulwar, Australia 54 A2
Numfoor, Indonesia 33 E8
Numurkah, Australia 55 F4
Nunaksaluk I., Canada 63 A7
Nuneaton, U.K. 11 E6
Nunivak I., U.S.A. 60 B3
Nunkun, India 36 C10
Nunspeet, Neths. 15 B5
Nùoro, Italy 20 D3
Nūrābād, Iran 39 E8
Nuremburg = Nürnberg, Germany 16 D6
Nurina, Australia 53 F4
Nuriootpa, Australia 55 E2
Nurmes, Finland 8 E23
Nürnberg, Germany 16 D6
Nurran, L. = Terewah, L., Australia 55 D4
Nurrari Lakes, Australia 53 E5
Nusa Barung, Indonesia 33 H15
Nusa Kambangan, Indonesia 33 G13
Nusa Tenggara Barat □, Indonesia 32 F5
Nusa Tenggara Timur □, Indonesia 33 F6
Nusaybin, Turkey 23 G7
Nushki, Pakistan 36 E5
Nutak, Canada 61 C13
Nutwood Downs, Australia 54 B1
Nuuk = Godthåb, Greenland 61 B14
Nuwakot, Nepal 37 E13
Nuweveldberge, S. Africa 48 E3
Nuyts, C., Australia 53 F5
Nuyts Arch., Australia 55 E1
Nxau-Nxau, Botswana 48 B3
Nyah West, Australia 55 F3
Nyahanga, Tanzania 46 E6
Nyahururu, Kenya 46 D7
Nyainqentanglha Shan, China 30 D3
Nyâlâ, Sudan 45 F9
Nyandoma, Russia 22 B7
Nyangana, Namibia 48 B3
Nyarling →, Canada 64 A6
Nyasa, L. = Malawi, L., Africa 47 G6
Nyasvizh, Belarus 17 B14
Nyazepetrovsk, Russia 22 C10
Nybro, Sweden 9 H16
Nyda, Russia 24 C8
Nyeri, Kenya 46 E7
Nyíregyháza, Hungary 17 E11
Nykøbing, Sjælland, Denmark 9 J14
Nykøbing, Storstrøm, Denmark 9 J14
Nyköping, Sweden 9 G17
Nylstroom, S. Africa 49 C4
Nymagee, Australia 55 E4
Nynäshamn, Sweden 9 G17
Nyngan, Australia 55 E4
Nyoman = Neman →, Lithuania 9 J19
Nysa, Poland 17 C9
Nysa →, Europe 16 B8
Nyssa, U.S.A. 72 E5
Nyurbe, Russia 25 C12
Nzega, Tanzania 46 E6
N'Zérékoré, Guinea 44 G3
Nzeto, Angola 46 F2

O

Ō-Shima, Nagasaki, Japan 29 G4
Ō-Shima, Shizuoka, Japan 29 G9
Oacoma, U.S.A. 70 D5
Oahe, L., U.S.A. 70 C4
Oahe Dam, U.S.A. 70 C4
Oahu, U.S.A. 66 H16
Oak Creek, U.S.A. 72 F10
Oak Harbor, U.S.A. 72 B2
Oak Hill, U.S.A. 68 G5
Oak Park, U.S.A. 68 E2
Oak Ridge, U.S.A. 69 G3
Oakan-Dake, Japan 28 C12
Oakbank, Australia 55 E3
Oakdale, Calif., U.S.A. 73 H3
Oakdale, La., U.S.A. 71 K8
Oakengates, U.K. 10 E5
Oakes, U.S.A. 70 B5
Oakesdale, U.S.A. 72 C5
Oakey, Australia 55 D5
Oakham, U.K. 10 E7
Oakland, Calif., U.S.A. 73 H2
Oakland, Oreg., U.S.A. 72 E2
Oakland City, U.S.A. 68 F2
Oakley, Idaho, U.S.A. 72 E7
Oakley, Kans., U.S.A. 70 F4
Oakover →, Australia 52 D3
Oakridge, U.S.A. 72 E2
Oamaru, N.Z. 51 L3
Oates Land, Antarctica 5 C11
Oatman, U.S.A. 73 J6
Oaxaca, Mexico 74 D5
Ob →, Russia 24 C7
Oba, Canada 62 C3
Obama, Japan 29 G7
Oban, U.K. 12 E3
Obbia, Somali Rep. 40 F4
Obed, Canada 64 C5
Oberhausen, Germany 16 C4
Oberlin, Kans., U.S.A. 70 F4
Oberlin, La., U.S.A. 71 K8
Oberon, Australia 55 E4
Obi, Kepulauan, Indonesia 33 E7
Obi Is. = Obi, Kepulauan, Indonesia 33 E7
Óbidos, Brazil 79 D7
Obihiro, Japan 28 C11
Obilatu, Indonesia 33 E7
Obluchye, Russia 25 E14
Obo, C.A.R. 46 C5
Oboyan, Russia 24 D4
Obozerskaya = Obozerskiy, Russia 24 C5
Obozerskiy, Russia 24 C5
Observatory Inlet, Canada 64 B3
Obshchi Syrt, Russia 6 D16
Obskaya Guba, Russia 24 C8
Obuasi, Ghana 44 G4
Ocala, U.S.A. 69 L4
Ocaña, Spain 19 C4
Ocanomowoc, U.S.A. 70 D10
Ocate, U.S.A. 71 G2
Occidental, Cordillera, Colombia 78 C3
Ocean City, U.S.A. 68 F8
Ocean I. = Banaba, Kiribati 56 H8
Ocean Park, U.S.A. 72 C1
Oceanside, U.S.A. 73 K5
Ochil Hills, U.K. 12 E5
Ochre River, Canada 65 C9
Ocilla, U.S.A. 69 K4
Ocmulgee →, U.S.A. 69 K4
Ocniţa, Moldova 17 D14
Oconee →, U.S.A. 69 K4
Oconto, U.S.A. 68 C2
Oconto Falls, U.S.A. 68 C1
Octave, U.S.A. 73 J7
Ocumare del Tuy, Venezuela 78 A5
Ōda, Japan 29 G6
Ódáðahraun, Iceland 8 D5
Odate, Japan 28 D10
Odawara, Japan 29 G9
Odda, Norway 9 F12
Oddur, Somali Rep. 40 G3
Odei →, Canada 65 B9
Ödemiş, Turkey 21 E13
Odendaalsrus, S. Africa 48 D4
Odense, Denmark 9 J14
Oder →, Germany 16 B8
Odesa, Ukraine 23 E5
Odessa = Odesa, Ukraine 23 E5
Odessa, Tex., U.S.A. 71 K3
Odessa, Wash., U.S.A. 72 C4
Odiakwe, Botswana 48 C4
Odienné, Ivory C. 44 G3
Odintsovo, Russia 22 C6
O'Donnell, U.S.A. 71 J4
Odorheiu Secuiesc, Romania 17 E13
Odra = Oder →, Germany 16 B8
Odzi, Zimbabwe 49 B5
Oeiras, Brazil 79 E10
Oelrichs, U.S.A. 70 D3
Oelwein, U.S.A. 70 D9
Oenpelli, Australia 52 B5
Ofanto →, Italy 20 D7
Offa, Nigeria 44 G5
Offaly □, Ireland 13 C4
Offenbach, Germany 16 C5
Offenburg, Germany 16 D4
Ofotfjorden, Norway 8 B17
Ōfunato, Japan 28 E10
Oga, Japan 28 E9
Oga-Hantō, Japan 28 E9
Ogahalla, Canada 62 B2
Ōgaki, Japan 29 G8
Ogallala, U.S.A. 70 E4
Ogasawara Gunto, Pac. Oc. 56 E6
Ogbomosho, Nigeria 44 G5
Ogden, Iowa, U.S.A. 70 D8
Ogden, Utah, U.S.A. 72 F7
Ogdensburg, U.S.A. 68 C8
Ogeechee →, U.S.A. 69 K5
Oglio →, Italy 20 B4
Ogmore, Australia 54 C4
Ogoki →, Canada 62 B2
Ogoki L., Canada 62 B2
Ogoki Res., Canada 62 B2
Ogooué →, Gabon 46 E1
Ogowe = Ogooué →, Gabon 46 E1
Ogre, Latvia 9 H21
Ohai, N.Z. 51 L2
Ohakune, N.Z. 51 H5
Ohanet, Algeria 44 C6
Ohata, Japan 28 D10
Ohau, L., N.Z. 51 L2
Ohey, Belgium 15 D5
Ohio □, U.S.A. 68 E3
Ohio →, U.S.A. 68 G1
Ohre →, Czech. 16 C8
Ohrid, Macedonia 21 D9
Ohridsko Jezero, Macedonia 21 D9
Ohrigstad, S. Africa 49 C5
Oil City, U.S.A. 68 E6
Oise →, France 18 B5
Ōita, Japan 29 H5
Ōita □, Japan 29 H5
Oiticica, Brazil 79 E10
Ojai, U.S.A. 73 J4
Ojiya, Japan 29 F9
Ojos del Salado, Cerro, Argentina 80 B3
Oka →, Russia 24 D5
Okaba, Indonesia 33 F9
Okahandja, Namibia 48 C2
Okahukura, N.Z. 51 H5
Okanagan L., Canada 64 C5
Okandja, Gabon 46 E2
Okanogan, U.S.A. 72 B4
Okanogan →, U.S.A. 72 B4
Okaputa, Namibia 48 C2
Okara, Pakistan 36 D8
Okarito, N.Z. 51 K3
Okaukuejo, Namibia 48 B2
Okavango Swamps, Botswana 48 B3
Okaya, Japan 29 F9
Okayama, Japan 29 G6
Okayama □, Japan 29 G6
Okazaki, Japan 29 G8
Okeechobee, U.S.A. 69 M5
Okeechobee, L., U.S.A. 69 M5
Okefenokee Swamp, U.S.A. 69 K4
Okehampton, U.K. 11 G3
Okha, Russia 25 D15
Okhotsk, Russia 25 D15
Okhotsk, Sea of, Asia 25 D15
Okhotskiy Perevoz, Russia 25 C14
Oki-Shotō, Japan 29 F6
Okiep, S. Africa 48 D2
Okinawa □, Japan 29 L3
Okinawa-Guntō, Japan 29 L3
Okinawa-Jima, Japan 29 L4
Okino-erabu-Shima, Japan 29 L4
Oklahoma □, U.S.A. 71 H6
Oklahoma City, U.S.A. 71 H6
Okmulgee, U.S.A. 71 H7
Oknitsa = Ocniţa, Moldova 17 D14
Okolona, U.S.A. 71 H10
Okrika, Nigeria 44 H6
Oksovskiy, Russia 22 B6
Oktabrsk = Oktyabrsk, Kazakhstan 23 E10
Oktyabrsk, Kazakhstan 23 E10
Oktyabrskiy = Aktsyabrski, Belarus 17 B15
Oktyabrskiy, Russia 22 D9
Oktyabrskoy Revolyutsii, Os., Russia 25 B10
Oktyabrskoye, Russia 24 C7
Okuru, N.Z. 51 K2
Okushiri-Tō, Japan 28 C9
Okwa →, Botswana 48 C3
Ola, U.S.A. 71 H8
Ólafsfjörður, Iceland 8 C4
Ólafsvík, Iceland 8 D2
Olancha, U.S.A. 73 H4
Öland, Sweden 9 H17
Olary, Australia 55 E3
Olathe, U.S.A. 70 F7
Olavarría, Argentina 80 D4
Oława, Poland 17 C9
Ólbia, Italy 20 D3
Old Cork, Australia 54 C3
Old Crow, Canada 60 B6
Old Fletton, U.K. 11 E7
Old Fort →, Canada 65 B6
Old Town, U.S.A. 63 D6
Old Wives L., Canada 65 C7
Oldbury, U.K. 11 F5
Oldcastle, Ireland 13 C4
Oldenburg, Germany 16 B5
Oldenzaal, Neths. 15 B6
Oldham, U.K. 10 D5
Oldman →, Canada 64 D6
Olds, Canada 64 C6
Olean, U.S.A. 68 D6
Olekma →, Russia 25 C13
Olekminsk, Russia 25 C13
Oleksandriya, Ukraine 17 C14
Olenegorsk, Russia 22 A5
Olenek, Russia 25 C12
Olenek →, Russia 25 B13
Oléron, I. d', France 18 D3
Oleśnica, Poland 17 C9
Olevsk, Ukraine 17 C14
Olga, Russia 25 E14
Olga, L., Canada 62 C4
Olga, Mt., Australia 53 E5
Olhão, Portugal 19 D2
Olifants →, Africa 49 C5
Olifantshoek, S. Africa 48 D3
Ólimbos, Óros, Greece 21 D10
Olinda, Brazil 79 E12
Oliveira, Brazil 79 H10
Olivenza, Spain 19 C2
Oliver, Canada 64 D5
Oliver L., Canada 65 B8
Ollagüe, Chile 78 H5
Olney, Ill., U.S.A. 68 F1
Olney, Tex., U.S.A. 71 J5
Olomane →, Canada 63 B7
Olomouc, Czech. 17 D9
Olonets, Russia 22 B5
Olongapo, Phil. 33 B6
Olot, Spain 19 A7
Olovyannaya, Russia 25 D12
Oloy →, Russia 25 C16
Olsztyn, Poland 17 B11
Olt →, Romania 17 G13
Olteniţa, Romania 17 F14
Olton, U.S.A. 71 H3
Olympia, Greece 21 F9
Olympia, U.S.A. 72 C2
Olympic Mts., U.S.A. 72 C2
Olympic Nat. Park, U.S.A. 72 C2
Olympus, Mt. = Ólimbos, Óros, Greece 21 D10
Olympus, Mt., U.S.A. 72 C2
Om →, Russia 24 D8
Ōma, Japan 28 D10
Ōmachi, Japan 29 F8
Omae-Zaki, Japan 29 G9
Ōmagari, Japan 28 E10
Omagh, U.K. 13 B4
Omagh □, U.K. 13 B4
Omaha, U.S.A. 70 E7
Omak, U.S.A. 72 B4
Oman ■, Asia 40 C6
Oman, G. of, Asia 39 E8
Omaruru, Namibia 48 C2
Omaruru →, Namibia 48 C1
Omate, Peru 78 G4
Ombai, Selat, Indonesia 33 F6
Omboué, Gabon 46 E1
Ombrone →, Italy 20 C4
Omdurmân, Sudan 45 E11
Ometepec, Mexico 74 D5
Ominato, Japan 28 D10
Omineca →, Canada 64 B4
Omitara, Namibia 48 C2
Ōmiya, Japan 29 G9
Ommen, Neths. 15 B6
Omo →, Ethiopia 45 G12
Omolon →, Russia 25 C16
Omono-Gawa →, Japan 28 E10
Omsk, Russia 24 D8
Omsukchan, Russia 25 C16
Omul, Vf., Romania 17 F13
Ōmura, Japan 29 H4
Omuramba Omatako →, Namibia 47 H4
Ōmuta, Japan 29 H5
Onaga, U.S.A. 70 F6
Onalaska, U.S.A. 70 D9
Onamia, U.S.A. 70 B8
Onancock, U.S.A. 68 G8
Onang, Indonesia 33 E5
Onaping L., Canada 62 C3
Onawa, U.S.A. 70 D6
Onaway, U.S.A. 68 C3
Oncócua, Angola 48 B1
Onda, Spain 19 C5
Ondangua, Namibia 48 B2
Ondjiva, Angola 48 B2
Ondo, Nigeria 44 G5
Öndverðarnes, Iceland 8 D1
Onega, Russia 22 B6
Onega →, Russia 22 B6
Onega, G. of = Onezhskaya Guba, Russia 22 B6
Onega, L. = Onezhskoye Ozero, Russia 22 B6
Onehunga, N.Z. 51 G5
Oneida, U.S.A. 68 D8
Oneida L., U.S.A. 68 D8
O'Neill, U.S.A. 70 D5
Onekotan, Ostrov, Russia 25 E16
Oneonta, Ala., U.S.A. 69 J2
Oneonta, N.Y., U.S.A. 68 D8
Oneşti, Romania 17 E14
Onezhskaya Guba, Russia 22 B6
Onezhskoye Ozero, Russia 22 B6
Ongarue, N.Z. 51 H5
Ongerup, Australia 53 F2
Ongole, India 36 M12
Onguren, Russia 25 D11
Onida, U.S.A. 70 C4
Onilahy →, Madag. 49 C7
Onitsha, Nigeria 44 G6
Onoda, Japan 29 G5
Onslow, Australia 52 D2
Onslow B., U.S.A. 69 H7
Onstwedde, Neths. 15 A7
Ontake-San, Japan 29 G8
Ontario, Calif., U.S.A. 73 J5
Ontario, Oreg., U.S.A. 72 D5
Ontario □, Canada 62 B2
Ontario, L., U.S.A. 62 D4
Ontonagon, U.S.A. 70 B10
Oodnadatta, Australia 55 D2
Ooldea, Australia 53 F5
Oombulgurri, Australia 52 C4
Oona River, Canada 64 C2
Oorindi, Australia 54 C3
Oost-Vlaanderen □, Belgium 15 C3
Oostende, Belgium 15 C2
Oosterhout, Neths. 15 C4
Oosterschelde, Neths. 15 C4
Ootacamund, India 36 P10
Ootsa L., Canada 64 C3
Opala, Russia 25 D16
Opala, Zaïre 46 E4
Opanake, Sri Lanka 36 R12
Opasatika, Canada 62 C3
Opasquia, Canada 65 C10
Opava, Czech. 17 D9
Opelousas, U.S.A. 71 K8
Opémisca, L., Canada 62 C5
Opheim, U.S.A. 72 B10
Ophthalmia Ra., Australia 52 D2
Opinaca →, Canada 62 B4
Opinaca L., Canada 62 B4
Opiskotish, L., Canada 63 B6
Opole, Poland 17 C9
Oporto = Porto, Portugal 19 B1
Opotiki, N.Z. 51 H6
Opp, U.S.A. 69 K2
Oppdal, Norway 9 E13
Opua, N.Z. 51 F5
Opunake, N.Z. 51 H4
Ora Banda, Australia 53 F3
Oracle, U.S.A. 73 K8
Oradea, Romania 17 E11
Öræfajökull, Iceland 8 D5
Orai, India 36 G11
Oral = Zhayyq →, Kazakhstan 23 E9
Oral, Kazakhstan 22 D9
Oran, Algeria 44 A4
Oran, Argentina 80 A4
Orange = Oranje →, S. Africa 48 D2
Orange, Australia 55 E4
Orange, France 18 D6
Orange, Tex., U.S.A. 71 K8
Orange, Va., U.S.A. 68 F6
Orange, C., Brazil 79 C8
Orange Free State □, S. Africa 48 D4
Orange Grove, U.S.A. 71 M6
Orangeburg, U.S.A. 69 J5
Orangeville, Canada 62 D3
Oranienburg, Germany 16 B7
Oranje →, S. Africa 48 D2
Oranje Vrystaat = Orange Free State □, S. Africa 48 D4
Oranjemund, Namibia 48 D2
Oranjerivier, S. Africa 48 D3
Oras, Phil. 33 B7
Oraşul Stalin = Braşov, Romania 17 F13
Orbetello, Italy 20 C4
Orbost, Australia 55 F4
Orchila, I., Venezuela 78 A5
Ord →, Australia 52 C4
Ord, Mt., Australia 52 C4
Orderville, U.S.A. 73 H7
Ordos = Mu Us Shamo, China 31 C5
Ordway, U.S.A. 70 F3
Ordzhonikidze = Vladikavkaz, Russia 23 F7
Ore Mts. = Erzgebirge, Germany 16 C7
Örebro, Sweden 9 G16
Oregon, U.S.A. 70 D10
Oregon □, U.S.A. 72 E3
Oregon City, U.S.A. 72 D2
Orekhovo-Zuyevo, Russia 22 C6
Orel, Russia 22 D6
Orem, U.S.A. 72 F8
Ören, Turkey 21 F12
Orenburg, Russia 22 D10
Orense, Spain 19 A2
Orepuki, N.Z. 51 M1
Orestiás, Greece 21 D12
Orford Ness, U.K. 11 E9
Orgaz, Spain 19 C4
Orgeyev = Orhei, Moldova 17 E15
Orhaneli, Turkey 21 E13
Orhangazi, Turkey 21 D13
Orhei, Moldova 17 E15
Orhon Gol →, Mongolia 30 A5
Orient, Australia 55 D3
Oriental, Cordillera, Colombia 78 B4
Orihuela, Spain 19 C5
Orinoco →, Venezuela 78 B6
Orissa □, India 37 K14
Orissaare, Estonia 9 G20
Oristano, Italy 20 E3
Oristano, G. di, Italy 20 E3
Orizaba, Mexico 74 D5
Orkanger, Norway 8 E13
Orkla →, Norway 8 E13
Orkney, S. Africa 48 D4
Orkney □, U.K. 12 C6
Orkney Is., U.K. 12 C6
Orland, U.S.A. 72 G2
Orlando, U.S.A. 69 L5
Orléanais, France 18 C5
Orléans, France 18 C4
Orléans, I. d', Canada 63 C5
Ormara, Pakistan 36 G4
Ormoc, Phil. 33 B6
Ormond, N.Z. 51 H6
Ormond Beach, U.S.A. 69 L5
Örnsköldsvik, Sweden 8 E18
Orocué, Colombia 78 C4
Orogrande, U.S.A. 73 K10
Orol Dengizi = Aral Sea, Asia 24 E7
Oromocto, Canada 63 C6
Oroqen Zizhiqi, China 31 A7
Oroquieta, Phil. 33 C6
Orós, Brazil 79 E11
Orosháza, Hungary 17 E11
Orotukan, Russia 25 C16
Oroville, Calif., U.S.A. 72 G3
Oroville, Wash., U.S.A. 72 B4
Orroroo, Australia 55 E2
Orsha, Belarus 22 D5
Orsk, Russia 22 D10
Orşova, Romania 17 F12
Ortaca, Turkey 21 F13
Ortegal, C., Spain 19 A2
Orthez, France 18 E3
Ortigueira, Spain 19 A2
Ortles, Italy 20 A4
Ortón →, Bolivia 78 F5
Orūmīyeh, Iran 38 B5
Orūmīyeh, Daryācheh-ye, Iran 38 B5
Oruro, Bolivia 78 G5
Orust, Sweden 9 G14

Oruzgān □, Afghan. . . 36 C5
Orvieto, Italy 20 C5
Orwell →, U.K. 11 E9
Oryakhovo, Bulgaria . . 21 C10
Osa, Russia 22 C10
Osage, Iowa, U.S.A. . . 70 D8
Osage, Wyo., U.S.A. . . 70 D2
Osage →, U.S.A. 70 F9
Osage City, U.S.A. . . . 70 F7
Ōsaka, Japan 29 G7
Osawatomie, U.S.A. . . 70 F7
Osborne, U.S.A. 70 F5
Osceola, Ark., U.S.A. . 71 H10
Osceola, Iowa, U.S.A. . 70 E8
Oscoda, U.S.A. 68 C4
Ösel = Saaremaa,
Estonia 9 G20
Osh, Kyrgyzstan 24 E8
Oshawa, Canada 62 D4
Oshkosh, Nebr., U.S.A. 70 E3
Oshkosh, Wis., U.S.A. 70 C10
Oshmyany =
Ashmyany, Belarus . 9 J21
Oshnoviyeh, Iran 38 B5
Oshogbo, Nigeria 44 G5
Oshtorīnān, Iran 39 C6
Oshwe, Zaïre 46 E3
Osijek, Croatia 21 B8
Osipenko = Berdyansk,
Ukraine 23 E6
Osipovichi =
Asipovichy, Belarus 17 B15
Osizweni, S. Africa . . . 49 D5
Oskaloosa, U.S.A. . . . 70 E8
Oskarshamn, Sweden . 9 H17
Öskelané̇o, Canada . . 62 C4
Öskemen, Kazakhstan . 24 E9
Oslo, Norway 9 G14
Oslob, Phil. 33 C6
Oslofjorden, Norway . . 9 G14
Osmanabad, India . . . 36 K10
Osmaniye, Turkey . . . 23 G6
Osnabrück, Germany . 16 B5
Osorio, Brazil 80 B6
Osorno, Chile 80 E2
Osoyoos, Canada 64 D5
Osøyri, Norway 9 F11
Ospika →, Canada . . . 64 B4
Osprey Reef, Australia 54 A4
Oss, Neths. 15 C5
Ossa, Mt., Australia . . 54 G4
Óssa, Oros, Greece . . 21 E10
Ossabaw I., U.S.A. . . . 69 K5
Ossining, U.S.A. 68 E9
Ossokmanuan L.,
Canada 63 B7
Ossora, Russia 25 D17
Ostend = Oostende,
Belgium 15 C2
Oster, Ukraine 17 C16
Österdalälven, Sweden 9 F16
Østerdalen, Norway . . 9 F14
Östersund, Sweden . . 8 E16
Ostfriesische Inseln,
Germany 16 B4
Ostrava, Czech. 17 D10
Ostróda, Poland 17 B10
Ostroh, Ukraine 17 C14
Ostrołęka, Poland 17 B11
Ostrów Mazowiecka,
Poland 17 B11
Ostrów Wielkopolski,
Poland 17 C9
Ostrowiec-
Świętokrzyski, Poland 17 C11
Ostuni, Italy 21 D7
Ōsumi-Kaikyō, Japan . 29 J5
Ōsumi-Shotō, Japan . . 29 J5
Osuna, Spain 19 D3
Oswego, U.S.A. 68 D7
Oswestry, U.K. 10 E4
Oświęcim, Poland 17 C10
Otago □, N.Z. 51 L2
Otago Harbour, N.Z. . . 51 L3
Ōtake, Japan 29 G6
Otaki, N.Z. 51 J5
Otaru, Japan 28 C10
Otaru-Wan = Ishikari-
Wan, Japan 28 C10
Otavalo, Ecuador 78 C3
Otavi, Namibia 48 B2
Otchinjau, Angola 48 B1
Othello, U.S.A. 72 C4
Otira Gorge, N.Z. 51 K3
Otis, U.S.A. 70 E3
Otjiwarongo, Namibia . 48 C2
Otoineppu, Japan 28 B11
Otorohanga, N.Z. 51 H5
Otoskwin →, Canada . 62 B2
Otosquen, Canada . . . 65 C8
Otra →, Norway 9 G13
Otranto, Italy 21 D8
Otranto, C. d', Italy . . 21 D8
Otranto, Str. of, Italy . 21 D8
Otse, S. Africa 48 D4
Ōtsu, Japan 29 G7
Ōtsuki, Japan 29 G9
Ottawa =
Outaouais →,
Canada 62 C5
Ottawa, Canada 62 C4
Ottawa, Ill., U.S.A. . . . 70 E10
Ottawa, Kans., U.S.A. . 70 F7
Ottawa →, Canada . . . 61 C11
Otter L., Canada 65 B8
Otter Rapids, Ont.,
Canada 62 B3
Otter Rapids, Sask.,
Canada 65 B8
Ottosdal, S. Africa . . . 48 D4
Ottumwa, U.S.A. 70 E8
Oturkpo, Nigeria 44 G6
Otway, B., Chile 80 G2

Otway, C., Australia . . 55 F3
Otwock, Poland 17 B11
Ou →, Laos 34 B7
Ou-Sammyaku, Japan . 28 E10
Ouachita →, U.S.A. . . 71 K9
Ouachita, L., U.S.A. . . 71 H8
Ouachita Mts., U.S.A. . 71 H7
Ouâdâne, Mauritania . 44 D2
Ouadda, C.A.R. 45 G9
Ouagadougou,
Burkina Faso 44 F4
Ouahran = Oran,
Algeria 44 A4
Ouallene, Algeria 44 D5
Ouanda Djallé, C.A.R. . 45 G9
Ouango, C.A.R. 46 D4
Ouargla, Algeria 44 B6
Ouarzazate, Morocco . 44 B3
Oubangi →, Zaïre . . . 46 E3
Ouddorp, Neths. 15 C3
Oude Rijn →, Neths. . 15 B4
Oudenaarde, Belgium . 15 D3
Oudtshoorn, S. Africa . 48 E3
Ouessant, I. d', France 18 B1
Ouesso, Congo 46 D3
Ouest, Pte., Canada . . 63 C7
Ouezzane, Morocco . . 44 B3
Ouidah, Benin 44 G5
Oujda, Morocco 44 B4
Oujeft, Mauritania . . . 44 D2
Oulainen, Finland 8 D21
Ouled Djellal, Algeria . 44 B6
Oulu, Finland 8 D21
Oulujärvi, Finland 8 D22
Oulujoki →, Finland . . 8 D21
Oum Chalouba, Chad . 45 E9
Ounasjoki →, Finland . 8 C21
Ounguati, Namibia . . . 48 C2
Ounianga-Kébir, Chad . 45 E9
Ounianga Sérir, Chad . 45 E9
Our →, Lux. 15 E6
Ouray, U.S.A. 73 G10
Ourense = Orense,
Spain 19 A2
Ouricuri, Brazil 79 E10
Ouro Prêto, Brazil . . . 79 H10
Ourthe →, Belgium . . 15 D5
Ouse, Australia 54 G4
Ouse →, E. Susx.,
U.K. 11 G8
Ouse →, N. Yorks.,
U.K. 10 C8
Outaouais →, Canada 62 C5
Outardes →, Canada . 63 C6
Outer Hebrides, U.K. . 12 D1
Outer I., Canada 63 B8
Outjo, Namibia 48 C2
Outlook, Canada 65 C7
Outlook, U.S.A. 70 A2
Outokumpu, Finland . . 8 E23
Ouyen, Australia 55 F3
Ovalau, Fiji 51 C8
Ovalle, Chile 80 C2
Ovamboland, Namibia . 48 B2
Overflakkee, Neths. . . 15 C4
Overijssel □, Neths. . . 15 B6
Overpelt, Belgium . . . 15 C5
Overton, U.S.A. 73 H6
Övertorneå, Sweden . . 8 C20
Ovid, U.S.A. 70 E3
Oviedo, Spain 19 A3
Oviši, Latvia 9 H19
Øvre Årdal, Norway . . 9 F12
Ovruch, Ukraine 17 C15
Owaka, N.Z. 51 M2
Owambo =
Ovamboland,
Namibia 48 B2
Owase, Japan 29 G8
Owatonna, U.S.A. 70 C8
Owbeh, Afghan. 36 B3
Owego, U.S.A. 68 D7
Owen Sound, Canada . 62 D3
Owendo, Gabon 46 D1
Owens →, U.S.A. 73 H5
Owens L., U.S.A. 73 J5
Owensboro, U.S.A. . . . 68 G2
Owensville, U.S.A. . . . 70 F9
Owl →, Canada 65 B10
Owo, Nigeria 44 G6
Owosso, U.S.A. 68 D3
Owyhee, U.S.A. 72 F5
Owyhee →, U.S.A. . . . 72 E5
Owyhee, L., U.S.A. . . . 72 E5
Oxelösund, Sweden . . 9 G17
Oxford, N.Z. 51 K4
Oxford, U.K. 11 F6
Oxford, Miss., U.S.A. . 71 H10
Oxford, N.C., U.S.A. . . 69 G6
Oxford, Ohio, U.S.A. . . 68 F3
Oxford L., Canada . . . 65 C9
Oxfordshire □, U.K. . . 11 F6
Oxley, Australia 55 E3
Oxnard, U.S.A. 73 J4
Oxus = Amudarya →,
Uzbekistan 24 E6
Oya, Malaysia 32 D4
Oyama, Japan 29 F9
Oyem, Gabon 46 D2
Oyen, Canada 65 C6
Oykel →, U.K. 12 D4
Oymyakon, Russia . . . 25 C15
Oyo, Nigeria 44 G5
Öyübari, Japan 28 C11
Ozamiz, Phil. 33 C6
Ozark, Ala., U.S.A. . . . 69 K3
Ozark, Ark., U.S.A. . . . 71 H8
Ozark, Mo., U.S.A. . . . 71 G8
Ozark Plateau, U.S.A. . 71 G9
Ozarks, L. of the, U.S.A. 70 F8
Ózd, Hungary 17 D11
Ozona, U.S.A. 71 K4

P

P.W.V. □, S. Africa . . . 49 D4
Pa-an, Burma 37 L20
Pa Sak →, Thailand . . 34 E6
Paamiut =
Frederikshåb,
Greenland 4 C5
Paarl, S. Africa 48 E2
Paauilo, U.S.A. 66 H17
Pab Hills, Pakistan . . . 36 F5
Pabianice, Poland 17 C10
Pabna, Bangla. 37 G16
Pacaja →, Brazil 79 D8
Pacaraima, Sierra,
Venezuela 78 C6
Pacasmayo, Peru 78 E3
Pachpadra, India 36 G8
Pachuca, Mexico 74 C5
Pacific, Canada 64 C3
Pacific-Antarctic Ridge,
Pac. Oc. 57 M16
Pacific Grove, U.S.A. . 73 H3
Pacific Ocean, Pac. Oc. 57 G14
Pacitan, Indonesia . . . 33 H14
Padaido, Kepulauan,
Indonesia 33 E9
Padang, Indonesia . . . 32 E2
Padang Endau,
Malaysia 34 S16
Padangpanjang,
Indonesia 32 E2
Padangsidempuan,
Indonesia 32 D1
Paddockwood, Canada 65 C7
Paderborn, Germany . . 16 C5
Padloping Island,
Canada 61 B13
Pádova, Italy 20 B4
Padre I., U.S.A. 71 M6
Padstow, U.K. 11 G3
Padua = Pádova, Italy 20 B4
Paducah, Ky., U.S.A. . 68 G1
Paducah, Tex., U.S.A. . 71 H4
Paeroa, N.Z. 51 G5
Pafúri, Mozam. 49 C5
Pag, Croatia 16 F8
Pagadian, Phil. 33 C6
Pagai Selatan, P.,
Indonesia 32 E2
Pagai Utara, Indonesia 32 E2
Pagalu = Annobón,
Atl. Oc. 43 G4
Pagastikós Kólpos,
Greece 21 E10
Pagatan, Indonesia . . 32 E5
Page, Ariz., U.S.A. . . . 73 H8
Page, N. Dak., U.S.A. . 70 B6
Pago Pago,
Amer. Samoa 51 B13
Pagosa Springs, U.S.A. 73 H10
Pagwa River, Canada . 62 B2
Pahala, U.S.A. 66 J17
Pahang □, Malaysia . . 34 R16
Pahang →, Malaysia . 34 R16
Pahiatua, N.Z. 51 J5
Pahokee, U.S.A. 69 M5
Pahrump, U.S.A. 73 H6
Paia, U.S.A. 66 H16
Paide, Estonia 9 G21
Paignton, U.K. 11 G4
Päijänne, Finland 9 F21
Pailin, Cambodia 34 F7
Painan, Indonesia . . . 32 E2
Painesville, U.S.A. . . . 68 E5
Paint Hills = Wemindji,
Canada 62 B4
Paint L., Canada 65 B9
Paint Rock, U.S.A. . . . 71 K5
Painted Desert, U.S.A. 73 J8
Paintsville, U.S.A. . . . 68 G4
Pais Vasco □, Spain . . 19 A4
Paisley, Canada 62 D3
Paisley, U.K. 12 F4
Paisley, U.S.A. 72 E3
Paita, Peru 78 E2
Pajares, Puerto de,
Spain 19 A3
Pak Lay, Laos 34 C6
Pakaraima Mts.,
Guyana 78 B6
Pakistan ■, Asia 36 E6
Pakistan, East =
Bangladesh ■, Asia 37 H17
Pakokku, Burma 37 J19
Pakse, Laos 34 E8
Paktiā □, Afghan. 36 C6
Pala, Chad 45 G9
Palacios, U.S.A. 71 L6
Palagruža, Croatia . . . 20 C7
Palam, India 36 K10
Palampur, India 36 C10
Palana, Australia 54 F4
Palana, Russia 25 D16
Palanan, Phil. 33 A6
Palanan Pt., Phil. 33 A6
Palanga, Lithuania . . . 9 J19
Palangkaraya,
Indonesia 32 E4
Palani Hills, India 36 P10
Palanpur, India 36 G8
Palanro, Indonesia . . . 33 E5
Palapye, Botswana . . . 48 C4
Palatka, Russia 25 C16
Palatka, U.S.A. 69 L5
Palau = Belau ■,
Pac. Oc. 56 G5
Palauk, Burma 34 F5
Palawan, Phil. 32 C5
Palayankottai, India . . 36 Q10
Paldiski, Estonia 9 G21
Paleleh, Indonesia . . . 33 D6
Palembang, Indonesia 32 E2

Palencia, Spain 19 A3
Palermo, Italy 20 E5
Palermo, U.S.A. 72 G3
Palestine, Asia 41 D4
Palestine, U.S.A. 71 K7
Paletwa, Burma 37 J18
Palghat, India 36 P10
Palgrave, Mt., Australia 52 D2
Pali, India 36 G8
Palioúrion, Ákra,
Greece 21 E10
Palisade, U.S.A. 70 E4
Palitana, India 36 J7
Palk Bay, Asia 36 Q11
Palk Strait, Asia 36 Q11
Palkānah, Iraq 38 C5
Palla Road = Dinokwe,
Botswana 48 C4
Pallanza = Verbánia,
Italy 20 B3
Palm Beach, U.S.A. . . 69 M6
Palm Is., Australia . . . 54 B4
Palm Springs, U.S.A. . 73 K5
Palma, Mozam. 46 G8
Palma →, Brazil 79 F9
Palma, B. de, Spain . . 19 C7
Palma de Mallorca,
Spain 19 C7
Palmares, Brazil 79 E11
Palmas, C., Liberia . . . 44 H3
Pálmas, G. di, Italy . . 20 E3
Palmdale, U.S.A. 73 J4
Palmeira dos Índios,
Brazil 79 E11
Palmeirinhas, Pta. das,
Angola 46 F2
Palmer, U.S.A. 60 B5
Palmer →, Australia . . 54 B3
Palmer Arch.,
Antarctica 5 C17
Palmer Lake, U.S.A. . . 70 F2
Palmer Land, Antarctica 5 D18
Palmerston, N.Z. 51 L3
Palmerston North, N.Z. 51 J5
Palmetto, U.S.A. 69 M4
Palmi, Italy 20 E6
Palmira, Colombia . . . 78 C3
Palmyra = Tudmur,
Syria 38 C3
Palmyra, U.S.A. 70 F9
Palmyra Is., Pac. Oc. . 57 G11
Palo Alto, U.S.A. 73 H2
Palopo, Indonesia . . . 33 E6
Palos, C. de, Spain . . 19 D5
Palouse, U.S.A. 72 C5
Palparara, Australia . . 54 C3
Palu, Indonesia 33 E5
Palu, Turkey 23 G7
Pama, Burkina Faso . . 44 F5
Pamanukan, Indonesia 33 G12
Pamekasan, Indonesia 33 G15
Pamiers, France 18 E4
Pamirs, Tajikistan . . . 24 F8
Pamlico →, U.S.A. . . . 69 H7
Pamlico Sd., U.S.A. . . 69 H8
Pampa, U.S.A. 71 H4
Pampa de las Salinas,
Argentina 80 C3
Pampanua, Indonesia . 33 E6
Pampas, Argentina . . . 80 D4
Pampas, Peru 78 F4
Pamplona, Colombia . . 78 B4
Pamplona, Spain 19 A5
Pampoenpoort,
S. Africa 48 E3
Pana, U.S.A. 70 F10
Panaca, U.S.A. 73 H6
Panaitan, Indonesia . . 33 G11
Panaji, India 36 M8
Panamá ■, Cent. Amer. 75 F9
Panamá, G. de, Panama 75 F9
Panama Canal, Panama 74 H14
Panama City, U.S.A. . . 69 K3
Panamint Range, U.S.A. 73 H5
Panão, Peru 78 E3
Panarukan, Indonesia . 33 G15
Panay, Phil. 33 B6
Panay, G., Phil. 33 B6
Pancake Range, U.S.A. 73 G6
Pančevo, Serbia, Yug. 21 B9
Pandan, Phil. 33 B6
Pandegelang, Indonesia 33 G12
Pandharpur, India . . . 36 L9
Pando, Uruguay 80 C5
Pando, L. = Hope, L.,
Australia 55 D2
Panevežys, Lithuania . 9 J21
Panfilov, Kazakhstan . 24 E8
Pang-Long, Burma . . . 37 H21
Pang-Yang, Burma . . . 37 H21
Pangalanes, Canal des,
Madag. 49 C8
Pangani, Tanzania . . . 46 F7
Pangfou = Bengbu,
China 31 C6
Pangkah, Tanjung,
Indonesia 33 G15
Pangkajene, Indonesia 33 E5
Pangkalanbrandan,
Indonesia 32 D1
Pangkalanbuun,
Indonesia 32 E4
Pangkalansusu,
Indonesia 32 D1
Pangkalpinang,
Indonesia 32 E3
Pangkoh, Indonesia . . 32 E4
Pangnirtung, Canada . 61 B13
Pangrango, Indonesia 33 G12
Panguitch, U.S.A. 73 H7
Pangutaran Group, Phil. 33 C6

Panhandle, U.S.A. . . . 71 H4
Park Rynie, S. Africa . . 49 E5
Parkā Bandar, Iran . . . 39 E8
Parkano, Finland 9 E20
Parker, Ariz., U.S.A. . . 73 J6
Parker, S. Dak., U.S.A. 70 D6
Parker Dam, U.S.A. . . 73 J6
Parkersburg, U.S.A. . . 68 F5
Parkerview, Canada . . 65 C8
Parkes, Australia 55 E4
Parkside, Canada 65 C7
Parkston, U.S.A. 70 D5
Parksville, Canada . . . 64 D4
Parla, Spain 19 B4
Parma, Italy 20 B4
Parma, U.S.A. 72 E5
Parnaguá, Brazil 79 F10
Parnaíba, Piauí, Brazil 79 D10
Parnaíba, São Paulo,
Brazil 79 G8
Parnaíba →, Brazil . . 79 D10
Parnassós, Greece . . 21 E10
Pärnu, Estonia 9 G21
Paroo →, Australia . . . 55 E3
Páros, Greece 21 F11
Parowan, U.S.A. 73 H7
Parral, Chile 80 D2
Parramatta, Australia . 55 E5
Parrett →, U.K. 11 F5
Parris I., U.S.A. 69 J5
Parrsboro, Canada . . . 63 C7
Parry Is., Canada 4 B2
Parry Sound, Canada . 62 C3
Parshall, U.S.A. 70 B3
Parsnip →, Canada . . 64 B4
Parsons, U.S.A. 71 G7
Parsons Ra., Australia . 54 A2
Partinico, Italy 20 E5
Paru →, Brazil 79 D8
Paruro, Peru 78 F4
Parvān □, Afghan. . . . 36 B6
Parvatipuram, India . . 37 K13
Parys, S. Africa 48 D4
Pasadena, Calif., U.S.A. 73 J4
Pasadena, Tex., U.S.A. 71 L7
Pasaje, Ecuador 78 D3
Pascagoula, U.S.A. . . . 71 K10
Pascagoula →, U.S.A. 71 K10
Paşcani, Romania . . . 17 E14
Pasco, U.S.A. 72 C4
Pasco, Cerro de, Peru 78 F3
Pascua, I. de, Pac. Oc. 57 K17
Pasfield L., Canada . . 65 B7
Pashmakli = Smolyan,
Bulgaria 21 D11
Pasir Mas, Malaysia . . 34 N15
Pasir Putih, Malaysia . 34 P15
Pasirian, Indonesia . . 33 H15
Paskūh, Iran 39 E9
Pasley, C., Australia . . 53 F3
Pašman, Croatia 16 G8
Pasni, Pakistan 36 G3
Paso de Indios,
Argentina 80 E3
Paso Robles, U.S.A. . . 73 J3
Paspébiac, Canada . . . 63 C6
Passage West, Ireland 13 E3
Passau, Germany 16 D7
Passero, C., Italy 20 F6
Passo Fundo, Brazil . . 80 B6
Passos, Brazil 79 H9
Pastavy, Belarus 9 J22
Pastaza →, Peru 78 D3
Pasto, Colombia 78 C3
Pasuruan, Indonesia . 33 G15
Patagonia, Argentina . 80 F3
Patagonia, U.S.A. 73 L8
Patambar, Iran 39 D9
Patan, India 36 H8
Patan, Nepal 37 F14
Patani, Indonesia 33 D7
Patchewollock,
Australia 55 F3
Patchogue, U.S.A. . . . 68 E9
Patea, N.Z. 51 H5
Pategi, Nigeria 44 G6
Patensie, S. Africa . . . 48 E3
Paternò, Italy 20 F6
Paterson, U.S.A. 68 E8
Paterson Ra., Australia 52 D3
Pathankot, India 36 C9
Pathfinder Reservoir,
U.S.A. 72 E10
Pati, Indonesia 33 G14
Patiala, India 36 D10
Patkai Bum, India 37 F19
Pátmos, Greece 21 F12
Patna, India 37 G14
Patos, I. dos, Brazil . . 80 C6
Patos de Minas, Brazil 79 G9
Patquia, Argentina . . . 80 C3
Pátrai, Greece 21 E9
Pátraïkós Kólpos,
Greece 21 E9
Patras = Pátrai, Greece 21 E9
Patrocínio, Brazil 79 G9
Pattani, Thailand 34 N14
Patten, U.S.A. 63 C6
Patterson, Calif., U.S.A. 73 H3
Patterson, La., U.S.A. . 71 L9
Patuakhali, Bangla. . . 37 H17
Pau, France 18 E3
Pauini →, Brazil 78 D6
Pauk, Burma 37 J19
Paul I., Canada 63 A7
Paulis = Isiro, Zaïre . . 46 D5
Paulistana, Brazil 79 E10
Paullina, U.S.A. 70 D7
Paulo Afonso, Brazil . . 79 E11
Paulpietersburg,
S. Africa 49 D5
Pauls Valley, U.S.A. . . 71 H6

Pāveh, *Iran* 38 C5
Pavia, *Italy* 20 B3
Pāvilosta, *Latvia* 9 H19
Pavlodar, *Kazakhstan* . 24 D8
Pavlograd = Pavlohrad,
 Ukraine 23 E6
Pavlohrad, *Ukraine* . . . 23 E6
Pavlovo, *Russia* 22 C7
Pavlovo, *Russia* 25 C12
Pavlovsk, *Russia* 23 D7
Pawhuska, *U.S.A.* 71 G6
Pawnee, *U.S.A.* 71 G6
Pawnee City, *U.S.A.* . . 70 E6
Pawtucket, *U.S.A.* 68 E10
Paxoí, *Greece* 21 E9
Paxton, *Ill., U.S.A.* . . . 68 E1
Paxton, *Nebr., U.S.A.* . 70 E4
Paya Bakri, *Malaysia* . 34 S15
Payakumbuh, *Indonesia* 32 E2
Payette, *U.S.A.* 72 D5
Payne Bay =
 Kangirsuk, *Canada* . 61 B13
Paynes Find, *Australia* 53 E2
Paynesville, *U.S.A.* . . . 70 C7
Paysandú, *Uruguay* . . . 80 C5
Payson, *Ariz., U.S.A.* . 73 J8
Payson, *Utah, U.S.A.* . 72 F8
Paz, B. la, *Mexico* 74 C2
Pāzanān, *Iran* 39 D6
Pazardzhik, *Bulgaria* . 21 C11
Pe Ell, *U.S.A.* 72 C2
Peace →, *Canada* 64 B6
Peace Point, *Canada* . . 64 B6
Peace River, *Canada* . . 64 B5
Peach Springs, *U.S.A.* . 73 J7
Peak, The = Kinder
 Scout, *U.K.* 10 D6
Peak Downs, *Australia* 54 C4
Peak Downs Mine,
 Australia 54 C4
Peak Hill, *N.S.W.,*
 Australia 55 E4
Peak Hill, *W. Austral.,*
 Australia 53 E2
Peak Ra., *Australia* . . . 54 C4
Peake, *Australia* 55 F2
Peake Cr. →, *Australia* 55 D2
Peale, Mt., *U.S.A.* 73 G9
Pearl →, *U.S.A.* 71 K10
Pearl City, *U.S.A.* 66 H16
Pearsall, *U.S.A.* 71 L5
Pearse I., *Canada* 64 C2
Peary Land, *Greenland* . 4 A6
Pease →, *U.S.A.* 71 H5
Pebane, *Mozam.* 47 H7
Pebas, *Peru* 78 D4
Peć, *Serbia, Yug.* 21 C9
Pechenga, *Russia* 22 A5
Pechenizhyn, *Ukraine* . 17 D13
Pechora →, *Russia* . . . 22 A9
Pechorskaya Guba,
 Russia 22 A9
Pečory, *Russia* 9 H22
Pecos, *U.S.A.* 71 K3
Pecos →, *U.S.A.* 71 L3
Pécs, *Hungary* 17 E10
Pedder, L., *Australia* . . 54 G4
Peddie, *S. Africa* 49 E4
Pedirka, *Australia* 55 D2
Pedra Azul, *Brazil* 79 G10
Pedreiras, *Brazil* 79 D10
Pedro Afonso, *Brazil* . . 79 E9
Pedro Juan Caballero,
 Paraguay 80 A5
Pedro Miguel Locks,
 Panama 74 H14
Peebinga, *Australia* . . . 55 E3
Peebles, *U.K.* 12 F5
Peekskill, *U.S.A.* 68 E9
Peel, *U.K.* 10 C3
Peel →, *Australia* 55 E5
Peel →, *Canada* 60 B6
Peera Peera Poolanna
 L., *Australia* 55 D2
Peers, *Canada* 64 C5
Pegasus Bay, *N.Z.* 51 K4
Pegu, *Burma* 37 L20
Pegu Yoma, *Burma* . . . 37 K19
Pehuajó, *Argentina* . . . 80 D4
Peine, *Germany* 16 B6
Peip'ing = Beijing,
 China 31 C6
Peipus, L. =
 Chudskoye, Oz.,
 Russia 9 G22
Peixe, *Brazil* 79 F9
Pekalongan, *Indonesia* 33 G13
Pekan, *Malaysia* 34 R16
Pekanbaru, *Indonesia* . 32 D2
Pekin, *U.S.A.* 70 E10
Peking = Beijing, *China* 31 C6
Pelabuhan Kelang,
 Malaysia 34 S14
Pelabuhan Ratu, Teluk,
 Indonesia 33 G12
Pelabuhanratu,
 Indonesia 33 G12
Pelagie, Is., *Italy* 20 G5
Pelaihari, *Indonesia* . . 32 E4
Peleaga, Vf., *Romania* 17 F12
Pelée, Mt., *Martinique* 74 N20
Pelee, Pt., *Canada* . . . 62 D3
Pelee I., *Canada* 62 D3
Peleng, *Indonesia* 33 E6
Pelham, *U.S.A.* 69 K3
Pelican L., *Canada* . . . 65 C8
Pelican Narrows,
 Canada 65 B8
Pelican Rapids, *Canada* 65 C8
Pelješac, *Croatia* 20 C7
Pelkosenniemi, *Finland* 8 C22
Pella, *S. Africa* 48 D2
Pella, *U.S.A.* 70 E8

Pello, *Finland* 8 C21
Pelly →, *Canada* 60 B6
Pelly Bay, *Canada* . . . 61 B11
Pelly L., *Canada* 60 B9
Peloponnese =
 Pelopónnisos □,
 Greece 21 F10
Pelopónnisos □,
 Greece 21 F10
Peloro, C., *Italy* 20 E6
Pelorus Sd., *N.Z.* 51 J4
Pelotas, *Brazil* 80 C6
Pelvoux, Massif du,
 France 18 D7
Pemalang, *Indonesia* . 33 G13
Pematangsiantar,
 Indonesia 32 D1
Pemba I., *Tanzania* . . . 46 F7
Pemberton, *Australia* . 53 F2
Pemberton, *Canada* . . 64 C4
Pembina, *U.S.A.* 70 A6
Pembina →, *U.S.A.* . . . 65 D9
Pembine, *U.S.A.* 68 C2
Pembroke, *Canada* . . . 62 C4
Pembroke, *U.K.* 11 F3
Pembroke, *U.S.A.* 69 J5
Pen-y-Ghent, *U.K.* 10 C5
Penang = Pinang,
 Malaysia 34 P13
Penápolis, *Brazil* 80 A6
Peñarroya-
 Pueblonuevo, *Spain* 19 C3
Peñas, C. de, *Spain* . . 19 A3
Penas, G. de, *Chile* . . . 80 F2
Pench'i = Benxi, *China* 31 B7
Pend Oreille →,
 U.S.A. 72 B5
Pend Oreille L., *U.S.A.* 72 C5
Pendembu, *S. Leone* . . 44 G2
Pender B., *Australia* . . 52 C3
Pendleton, *U.S.A.* 72 D4
Penedo, *Brazil* 79 F11
Penetanguishene,
 Canada 62 D4
Pengalengan, *Indonesia* 33 G12
Penguin, *Australia* . . . 54 G4
Peniche, *Portugal* 19 C1
Penicuik, *U.K.* 12 F5
Penida, *Indonesia* 32 F5
Peninsular Malaysia □,
 Malaysia 34 Q15
Penmarch, Pte. de,
 France 18 C1
Penn Yan, *U.S.A.* 68 D7
Pennant, *Canada* 65 C7
Penner →, *India* 36 M12
Pennines, *U.K.* 10 C5
Pennsylvania □, *U.S.A.* 68 E6
Penny, *Canada* 64 C4
Penola, *Australia* 55 F3
Penong, *Australia* 53 F5
Penrith, *Australia* 55 E5
Penrith, *U.K.* 10 C5
Pensacola, *U.S.A.* 69 K2
Pensacola Mts.,
 Antarctica 5 E1
Pense, *Canada* 65 C8
Penshurst, *Australia* . . 55 F3
Penticton, *Canada* . . . 64 D5
Pentland, *Australia* . . . 54 C4
Pentland Firth, *U.K.* . . 12 C5
Pentland Hills, *U.K.* . . 12 F5
Penylan L., *Canada* . . . 65 A7
Penza, *Russia* 22 D8
Penzance, *U.K.* 11 G2
Penzhino, *Russia* 25 C17
Penzhinskaya Guba,
 Russia 25 C17
Peoria, *Ariz., U.S.A.* . . 73 K7
Peoria, *Ill., U.S.A.* . . . 70 E10
Pera Hd., *Australia* . . . 54 A3
Perabumilih, *Indonesia* 32 E2
Perak →, *Malaysia* . . . 34 P14
Perämeri, *Finland* 8 C22
Percé, *Canada* 63 C7
Perche, Collines du,
 France 18 B4
Percival Lakes,
 Australia 52 D4
Percy Is., *Australia* . . . 54 C5
Perdido, Mte., *Spain* . . 19 A6
Perdu, Mt. = Perdido,
 Mte., *Spain* 19 A6
Pereira, *Colombia* 78 C3
Perekerten, *Australia* . 55 E3
Perenjori, *Australia* . . . 53 E2
Pereyaslav-
 Khmelnytskyy,
 Ukraine 23 D5
Pergamino, *Argentina* 80 C4
Perham, *U.S.A.* 70 B7
Perhentian, Kepulauan,
 Malaysia 34 P15
Péribonca →, *Canada* . 63 C5
Péribonca, L., *Canada* . 63 B5
Perico, *Argentina* 80 A3
Périgueux, *France* 18 D4
Perijá, Sierra de,
 Colombia 78 B4
Perlas, Arch. de las,
 Panama 75 F9
Perlis □, *Malaysia* . . . 34 N13
Perm, *Russia* 22 C10
Pernambuco = Recife,
 Brazil 79 E12
Pernambuco □, *Brazil* . 79 E11
Pernatty Lagoon,
 Australia 55 E2
Pernik, *Bulgaria* 21 C10
Peron, C., *Australia* . . 53 E1
Peron Is., *Australia* . . . 52 B5
Peron Pen., *Australia* . 53 E1
Perow, *Canada* 64 C3

Perpendicular Pt.,
 Australia 55 E5
Perpignan, *France* . . . 18 E5
Perry, *Fla., U.S.A.* . . . 69 K4
Perry, *Ga., U.S.A.* 69 J4
Perry, *Iowa, U.S.A.* . . . 70 E7
Perry, *Maine, U.S.A.* . . 69 C12
Perry, *Okla., U.S.A.* . . 71 G6
Perryton, *U.S.A.* 71 G4
Perryville, *U.S.A.* 71 G10
Pershotravensk,
 Ukraine 17 C14
Persia = Iran ■, *Asia* . 39 C7
Persian Gulf = Gulf,
 The, *Asia* 39 E6
Perth, *Australia* 53 F2
Perth, *Canada* 62 D4
Perth, *U.K.* 12 E5
Perth Amboy, *U.S.A.* . 68 E8
Peru, *Ill., U.S.A.* 70 E10
Peru, *Ind., U.S.A.* 68 E2
Peru ■, *S. Amer.* 78 E3
Peru-Chile Trench,
 Pac. Oc. 57 K20
Perúgia, *Italy* 20 C5
Pervomaysk, *Ukraine* . 23 E5
Pervouralsk, *Russia* . . 22 C10
Pésaro, *Italy* 20 C5
Pescara, *Italy* 20 C6
Peshawar, *Pakistan* . . 36 B7
Peshkopi, *Albania* . . . 21 D9
Peshtigo, *U.S.A.* 68 C2
Pesqueira, *Brazil* 79 E11
Petah Tiqwa, *Israel* . . 41 C3
Petaling Jaya, *Malaysia* 34 R14
Petaluma, *U.S.A.* 72 G2
Petange, *Lux.* 15 E5
Petauke, *Zambia* 47 G6
Petawawa, *Canada* . . . 62 C4
Peter I.s Øy, *Antarctica* 5 C16
Peter Pond L., *Canada* 65 B7
Peterbell, *Canada* 62 C3
Peterborough, *Australia* 55 E2
Peterborough, *Canada* 61 D12
Peterborough, *U.K.* . . . 11 E7
Peterhead, *U.K.* 12 D7
Petermann Bjerg,
 Greenland 58 B17
Petersburg, *Alaska,*
 U.S.A. 64 B2
Petersburg, *Ind., U.S.A.* 68 F2
Petersburg, *Va., U.S.A.* 68 G7
Petersburg, *W. Va.,*
 U.S.A. 68 F6
Petford, *Australia* 54 B3
Petit Bois I., *U.S.A.* . . . 69 K1
Petit Cap, *Canada* . . . 63 C7
Petit Lac Manicouagan,
 Canada 63 B6
Petitcodiac, *Canada* . . 63 C6
Petite Baleine →,
 Canada 62 A4
Petite Saguenay,
 Canada 63 C5
Petitsikapau, L., *Canada* 63 B6
Petlad, *India* 36 H8
Peto, *Mexico* 74 C7
Petone, *N.Z.* 51 J5
Petoskey, *U.S.A.* 68 C3
Petra, *Jordan* 41 E4
Petra, Ostrova, *Russia* 4 B13
Petra Velikogo, Zaliv,
 Russia 28 C5
Petrich, *Bulgaria* 21 D10
Petrikov = Pyetrikaw,
 Belarus 17 B15
Petrograd = Sankt-
 Peterburg, *Russia* . . 22 C5
Petrolândia, *Brazil* . . . 79 E11
Petrolia, *Canada* 62 D3
Petrolina, *Brazil* 79 E10
Petropavl, *Kazakhstan* 24 D7
Petropavlovsk =
 Petropavl, *Kazakhstan* 24 D7
Petropavlovsk-
 Kamchatskiy, *Russia* 25 D16
Petrópolis, *Brazil* 79 H10
Petroşani, *Romania* . . 17 F12
Petrovaradin,
 Serbia, Yug. 21 B8
Petrovsk, *Russia* 22 D8
Petrovsk-Zabaykalskiy,
 Russia 25 D11
Petrozavodsk, *Russia* . 22 B5
Petrus Steyn, *S. Africa* 49 D4
Petrusburg, *S. Africa* . 48 D4
Peureulak, *Indonesia* . 32 D1
Pevek, *Russia* 25 C18
Pforzheim, *Germany* . . 16 D5
Phagwara, *India* 36 D9
Phala, *Botswana* 48 C4
Phalodi, *India* 36 F8
Phan Rang, *Vietnam* . . 34 G10
Phan Thiet, *Vietnam* . . 34 G10
Phangan, Ko, *Thailand* 34 H6
Phangnga, *Thailand* . . 34 H5
Phanh Bho Ho Chi
 Minh, *Vietnam* 34 G9
Phatthalung, *Thailand* 34 J6
Phelps, *U.S.A.* 70 B10
Phelps L., *Canada* . . . 65 B8
Phenix City, *U.S.A.* . . . 69 J3
Phet Buri, *Thailand* . . . 34 F5
Phetchabun, *Thailand* . 34 D6
Phetchabun, Thiu Khao,
 Thailand 34 E6
Phetchaburi = Phet
 Buri, *Thailand* 34 F5
Phichai, *Thailand* 34 D6
Phichit, *Thailand* 34 D6

Philip, *U.S.A.* 70 C4
Philippeville, *Belgium* . 15 D4
Philippi L., *Australia* . . 54 C2
Philippines ■, *Asia* . . . 33 B6
Philippolis, *S. Africa* . . 48 E4
Philippopolis = Plovdiv,
 Bulgaria 21 C11
Philipsburg, *U.S.A.* . . . 72 C7
Philipstown =
 Daingean, *Ireland* . . 13 C4
Philipstown, *S. Africa* . 48 E3
Phillip I., *Australia* . . . 55 F4
Phillips, *Tex., U.S.A.* . . 71 H4
Phillips, *Wis., U.S.A.* . . 70 C9
Phillipsburg, *U.S.A.* . . 70 F5
Phillott, *Australia* 55 D4
Philomath, *U.S.A.* 72 D2
Phitsanulok, *Thailand* . 34 D6
Phnom Dangrek,
 Thailand 34 E8
Phnom Penh,
 Cambodia 34 G8
Phnom Thbeng,
 Cambodia 34 F8
Phoenix, *U.S.A.* 73 K7
Phoenix Is., *Kiribati* . . 56 H10
Phong Saly, *Laos* 34 B7
Phosphate Hill,
 Australia 54 C2
Phra Chedi Sam Ong,
 Thailand 34 E5
Phra Nakhon Si
 Ayutthaya, *Thailand* 34 E6
Phrae, *Thailand* 34 C6
Phrao, *Thailand* 34 C5
Phu Doan, *Vietnam* . . 34 B8
Phu Loi, *Laos* 34 B7
Phu Ly, *Vietnam* 34 B8
Phuket, *Thailand* 34 J5
Phumiphon, Khuan,
 Thailand 32 A1
Piacenza, *Italy* 20 B3
Pialba, *Australia* 55 D5
Pian Cr. →, *Australia* . 55 E4
Pianosa, *Italy* 20 C4
Piapot, *Canada* 65 D7
Piatra Neamţ, *Romania* 17 E14
Piauí □, *Brazil* 79 E10
Piave →, *Italy* 20 B5
Pibor Post, *Sudan* . . . 45 G11
Pica, *Chile* 78 H5
Picardie, *France* 18 B5
Picardy = Picardie,
 France 18 B5
Picayune, *U.S.A.* 71 K10
Pichilemu, *Chile* 80 C2
Pickerel L., *Canada* . . . 62 C1
Pickle Lake, *Canada* . . 62 B1
Pico Truncado,
 Argentina 80 F3
Picton, *Australia* 55 E5
Picton, *Canada* 62 D4
Picton, *N.Z.* 51 J5
Pictou, *Canada* 63 C7
Picture Butte, *Canada* . 64 D6
Picún Leufú, *Argentina* 80 D3
Pidurutalagala,
 Sri Lanka 36 R12
Piedmont =
 Piemonte □, *Italy* . . 20 B2
Piedmont, *U.S.A.* 69 J3
Piedmont Plateau,
 U.S.A. 69 J5
Piedras, R. de las →,
 Peru 78 F5
Piedras Negras, *Mexico* 74 B4
Pieksämäki, *Finland* . . 9 E22
Piemonte □, *Italy* 20 B2
Pierce, *U.S.A.* 72 C6
Pierre, *U.S.A.* 70 C4
Piet Retief, *S. Africa* . . 49 D5
Pietarsaari, *Finland* . . 8 E20
Pietermaritzburg,
 S. Africa 49 D5
Pietersburg, *S. Africa* . 49 C4
Pietrosul, *Romania* . . . 17 E13
Pietrosul, *Romania* . . . 17 E13
Pigeon, *U.S.A.* 68 D4
Piggott, *U.S.A.* 71 G9
Pigüe, *Argentina* 80 D4
Pihlajavesi, *Finland* . . 9 F23
Pikes Peak, *U.S.A.* . . . 70 F2
Piketberg, *S. Africa* . . 48 E2
Pikeville, *U.S.A.* 68 G4
Pikwitonei, *Canada* . . . 65 B9
Piła, *Poland* 17 B9
Pilar, *Brazil* 79 E11
Pilar, *Paraguay* 80 B5
Pilas Group, *Phil.* 33 C6
Pilcomayo →,
 Paraguay 80 B5
Pilibhit, *India* 36 E11
Pilica →, *Poland* 17 C11
Pilos, *Greece* 21 F9
Pilot Mound, *Canada* . 65 D9
Pilot Point, *U.S.A.* . . . 71 J6
Pilot Rock, *U.S.A.* 72 D4
Pilsen = Plzeň, *Czech.* 16 D7
Pima, *U.S.A.* 73 K9
Pimba, *Australia* 55 E2
Pimenta Bueno, *Brazil* 78 F6
Pimentel, *Peru* 78 E2
Pinang, *Malaysia* 34 P13
Pinar del Río, *Cuba* . . 75 C8
Pınarhisar, *Turkey* . . . 21 D12
Pincher Creek, *Canada* 64 D6
Pinchi L., *Canada* 64 C4
Pinckneyville, *U.S.A.* . . 70 F10
Pińczów, *Poland* 17 C11
Pindar, *Australia* 53 E2
Pindiga, *Nigeria* 44 G7
Pindos Óros, *Greece* . . 21 E9
Pindus Mts. = Pindos
 Óros, *Greece* 21 E9

Pine, *U.S.A.* 73 J8
Pine →, *Canada* 65 B7
Pine, C., *Canada* 63 C9
Pine Bluff, *U.S.A.* 71 H8
Pine City, *U.S.A.* 70 C8
Pine Falls, *Canada* . . . 65 C9
Pine Pass, *Canada* . . . 64 B4
Pine Point, *Canada* . . . 64 A6
Pine Ridge, *U.S.A.* . . . 70 D3
Pine River, *Canada* . . . 65 C8
Pine River, *U.S.A.* 70 B7
Pinega →, *Russia* 22 B8
Pinehill, *Australia* 54 C4
Pinetop, *U.S.A.* 73 J9
Pinetown, *S. Africa* . . . 49 D5
Pinetree, *U.S.A.* 72 E11
Pineville, *Ky., U.S.A.* . . 69 G4
Pineville, *La., U.S.A.* . . 71 K8
Ping →, *Thailand* 34 E6
Pingaring, *Australia* . . 53 F2
Pingdingshan, *China* . . 31 C6
Pingdong, *Taiwan* 31 D7
Pingelly, *Australia* 53 F2
Pingliang, *China* 30 C5
Pingrup, *Australia* 53 F2
Pingxiang, *China* 30 D5
Pinhel, *Portugal* 19 B2
Pini, *Indonesia* 32 D1
Piniós →, *Greece* 21 E10
Pinjarra, *Australia* 53 F2
Pinnaroo, *Australia* . . . 55 F3
Pinnes, Ákra, *Greece* . 21 D11
Pinos Pt., *U.S.A.* 73 H3
Pinrang, *Indonesia* . . . 33 E5
Pinsk, *Belarus* 17 B14
Pintados, *Chile* 78 H5
Pintumba, *Australia* . . 53 F5
Pinyug, *Russia* 22 B8
Pioche, *U.S.A.* 73 H6
Piombino, *Italy* 20 C4
Pioner, Os., *Russia* . . . 25 B10
Piorini, L., *Brazil* 78 D6
Piotrków Trybunalski,
 Poland 17 C10
Pip, *Iran* 39 E9
Pipestone, *U.S.A.* 70 D6
Pipestone →, *Canada* 62 B2
Pipestone Cr. →,
 Canada 65 D8
Pipmuacan, Rés.,
 Canada 63 C5
Pippingarra, *Australia* . 52 D2
Piqíri →, *Brazil* 80 A6
Piqua, *U.S.A.* 68 E3
Piracicaba, *Brazil* 80 A7
Piracuruca, *Brazil* 79 D10
Piraeus = Piraiévs,
 Greece 21 F10
Piraiévs, *Greece* 21 F10
Pirané, *Argentina* 80 B5
Pirapora, *Brazil* 79 G10
Piripiri, *Brazil* 79 D10
Pirmasens, *Germany* . 16 D4
Pirot, *Serbia, Yug.* . . . 21 C10
Piru, *Indonesia* 33 E7
Pisa, *Italy* 20 C4
Pisagua, *Chile* 78 G4
Pisciotta, *Italy* 20 D6
Pisco, *Peru* 78 F3
Písek, *Czech.* 16 D8
Pishan, *China* 30 C2
Pising, *Indonesia* 33 F6
Pissis, Cerro, *Argentina* 80 B3
Pissouri, *Cyprus* 23 E12
Pistóia, *Italy* 20 C4
Pistol B., *Canada* 65 A10
Pisuerga →, *Spain* . . . 19 B3
Pitarpunga, L., *Australia* 55 E3
Pitcairn I., *Pac. Oc.* . . . 57 K14
Pite älv →, *Sweden* . . 8 D19
Piteå, *Sweden* 8 D19
Piteşti, *Romania* 17 F13
Pithapuram, *India* 37 L13
Pithara, *Australia* 53 F2
Pitlochry, *U.K.* 12 E5
Pitt I., *Canada* 64 C3
Pittsburg, *Kans., U.S.A.* 71 G7
Pittsburg, *Tex., U.S.A.* 71 J7
Pittsburg, *U.S.A.* 68 E6
Pittsfield, *Ill., U.S.A.* . . 70 F9
Pittsfield, *Mass., U.S.A.* 68 D9
Pittston, *U.S.A.* 68 E8
Pittsworth, *Australia* . . 55 D5
Pituri →, *Australia* . . . 54 C2
Piura, *Peru* 78 E2
Placentia, *Canada* . . . 63 C9
Placentia B., *Canada* . 63 C9
Placerville, *U.S.A.* 72 G3
Plain Dealing, *U.S.A.* . 71 J8
Plainfield, *U.S.A.* 68 E8
Plains, *Kans., U.S.A.* . . 71 G4
Plains, *Mont., U.S.A.* . 72 C6
Plains, *Tex., U.S.A.* . . 71 J3
Plainview, *Nebr., U.S.A.* 70 D6
Plainview, *Tex., U.S.A.* 71 H4
Plainville, *U.S.A.* 70 F5
Plainwell, *U.S.A.* 68 D3
Pláka, Ákra, *Greece* . . 21 G12
Plakhino, *Russia* 24 C9
Plankinton, *U.S.A.* . . . 70 D5
Plano, *U.S.A.* 71 J6
Plant City, *U.S.A.* 69 L4
Plaquemine, *U.S.A.* . . . 71 K9
Plasencia, *Spain* 19 B2
Plaster Rock, *Canada* . 63 C6
Plastun, *Russia* 28 B8
Plata, Río de la,
 S. Amer. 80 C5
Platani →, *Italy* 20 F5

Plateau du Coteau du
 Missouri, *U.S.A.* . . . 70 B4
Plato, *Colombia* 78 B4
Platte, *U.S.A.* 70 D5
Platte →, *U.S.A.* 70 F7
Platteville, *U.S.A.* 70 E2
Plattsburgh, *U.S.A.* . . . 68 C9
Plattsmouth, *U.S.A.* . . 70 E7
Plauen, *Germany* 16 C7
Plavinas, *Latvia* 9 H21
Playgreen L., *Canada* . 65 C9
Pleasant Bay, *Canada* . 63 C7
Pleasant Hill, *U.S.A.* . . 70 F7
Pleasanton, *U.S.A.* . . . 71 L5
Pleasantville, *U.S.A.* . . 68 F8
Pleiku, *Vietnam* 34 F10
Plenty →, *Australia* . . . 54 C2
Plenty, B. of, *N.Z.* 51 G6
Plentywood, *U.S.A.* . . . 70 A2
Plesetsk, *Russia* 22 B7
Plessisville, *Canada* . . 63 C5
Pletipi L., *Canada* 63 B5
Pleven, *Bulgaria* 21 C11
Plevlja,
 Montenegro, Yug. . . 21 C8
Płock, *Poland* 17 B10
Plöckenstein, *Germany* 16 D7
Ploieşti, *Romania* 17 F14
Plonge, Lac la, *Canada* 65 B7
Plovdiv, *Bulgaria* 21 C11
Plummer, *U.S.A.* 72 C5
Plumtree, *Zimbabwe* . . 47 J5
Plunge, *Lithuania* 9 J19
Plymouth, *U.K.* 11 G3
Plymouth, *Ind., U.S.A.* 68 E2
Plymouth, *N.C., U.S.A.* 69 H7
Plymouth, *Wis., U.S.A.* 68 D2
Plynlimon =
 Pumlumon Fawr,
 U.K. 11 E4
Plzeň, *Czech.* 16 D7
Po →, *Italy* 20 B5
Po Hai = Bo Hai, *China* 31 C6
Pobeda, *Russia* 25 C15
Pobedino, *Russia* 25 E15
Pobedy Pik, *Kyrgyzstan* 24 E8
Pocahontas, *Ark.,*
 U.S.A. 71 G9
Pocahontas, *Iowa,*
 U.S.A. 70 D7
Pocatello, *U.S.A.* 72 E7
Pocomoke City, *U.S.A.* 68 F8
Poços de Caldas, *Brazil* 79 H9
Podgorica,
 Montenegro, Yug. . . 21 C8
Podilska Vysochyna,
 Ukraine 17 D14
Podkamennaya
 Tunguska →, *Russia* 25 C10
Podolsk, *Russia* 22 C6
Podor, *Senegal* 44 E1
Podporozhy, *Russia* . . 22 B5
Pofadder, *S. Africa* . . . 48 D2
Pogamasing, *Canada* . 62 C3
Pogranitsnyi, *Russia* . . 28 B5
Poh, *Indonesia* 33 E6
Pohjanmaa, *Finland* . . 8 E20
Pohnpei, *Pac. Oc.* . . . 56 G7
Poinsett, C., *Antarctica* 5 C8
Point Edward, *Canada* . 62 D3
Point Pedro, *Sri Lanka* 36 Q12
Point Pleasant, *U.S.A.* . 68 F4
Pointe-à-la Hache,
 U.S.A. 71 L10
Pointe-à-Pitre,
 Guadeloupe 74 L20
Pointe Noire, *Congo* . . 46 E2
Poisonbush Ra.,
 Australia 52 D3
Poitiers, *France* 18 C4
Poitou, *France* 18 C3
Pojoaque Valley, *U.S.A.* 73 J11
Pokaran, *India* 36 F7
Pokataroo, *Australia* . . 55 D4
Pokrovsk = Engels,
 Russia 22 D8
Pokrovsk, *Russia* 25 C13
Pola = Pula, *Croatia* . . 16 F7
Polacca, *U.S.A.* 73 J8
Polan, *Iran* 39 E9
Poland ■, *Europe* 17 C10
Polatsk, *Belarus* 22 C4
Polcura, *Chile* 80 D2
Polden Hills, *U.K.* 11 F5
Polessk, *Russia* 9 J19
Polesye = Pripet
 Marshes, *Europe* . . . 17 B15
Polevskoy, *Russia* . . . 22 C11
Poli, *Cameroon* 46 C2
Police, *Poland* 16 B8
Polillo Is., *Phil.* 33 B6
Políyiros, *Greece* 21 D10
Pollachi, *India* 36 P10
Pollock, *U.S.A.* 70 C4
Polnovat, *Russia* 24 C7
Polo, *U.S.A.* 70 E10
Polonne, *Ukraine* 17 C14
Polonnoye = Polonne,
 Ukraine 17 C14
Polson, *U.S.A.* 72 C6
Poltava, *Ukraine* 23 E5
Põltsamaa, *Estonia* . . . 9 G21
Polunochnoye, *Russia* 22 B11
Põlva, *Estonia* 9 G22
Polyarny, *Russia* 22 A5
Polynesia, *Pac. Oc.* . . 57 H11
Polynésie française =
 French Polynesia ■,
 Pac. Oc. 57 J13
Pombal, *Brazil* 79 E11
Pombal, *Portugal* 19 C1
Pomeroy, *Ohio, U.S.A.* 68 F4
Pomeroy, *Wash., U.S.A.* 72 C5

Pomézia, *Italy* 20 D5
Pomona, *U.S.A.* 73 J5
Pomorski, Pojezierze,
Poland 17 B9
Pompano Beach, *U.S.A.* 69 M5
Pompeys Pillar, *U.S.A.* 72 D10
Ponape = Pohnpei,
Pac. Oc. 56 G7
Ponask, L., *Canada* 62 B1
Ponass L., *Canada* 65 C8
Ponca, *U.S.A.* 70 D6
Ponca City, *U.S.A.* 71 G6
Ponce, *Puerto Rico* ... 75 D11
Ponchatoula, *U.S.A.* ... 71 K9
Poncheville, L., *Canada* 62 B4
Pond Inlet, *Canada* ... 61 A12
Pondicherry, *India* ... 36 P11
Ponds, I. of, *Canada* ... 63 B8
Ponferrada, *Spain* 19 A2
Ponnani, *India* 36 P9
Ponnyadaung, *Burma* . 37 J19
Ponoka, *Canada* 64 C6
Ponorogo, *Indonesia* . 33 G14
Ponoy, *Russia* 22 A7
Ponoy →, *Russia* 22 A7
Ponta Grossa, *Brazil* . 80 B6
Ponta Pora, *Brazil* 80 A5
Pontarlier, *France* 18 C7
Pontchartrain L., *U.S.A.* 71 K9
Ponte Nova, *Brazil* ... 79 H10
Pontefract, *U.K.* 10 D6
Ponteix, *Canada* 65 D7
Pontevedra, *Spain* 19 A1
Pontiac, *Ill., U.S.A.* .. 70 E10
Pontiac, *Mich., U.S.A.* . 68 D4
Pontian Kecil, *Malaysia* 34 T16
Pontianak, *Indonesia* . 32 E3
Pontic Mts. = Kuzey
Anadolu Dağları,
Turkey 23 F6
Pontine Is. = Ponziane,
Ìsole, *Italy* 20 D5
Pontine Mts. = Kuzey
Anadolu Dağları,
Turkey 23 F6
Pontivy, *France* 18 B2
Pontoise, *France* 18 B5
Ponton →, *Canada* .. 64 B5
Pontypool, *U.K.* 11 F4
Pontypridd, *U.K.* 11 F4
Ponziane, Ìsole, *Italy* . 20 D5
Poochera, *Australia* ... 55 E1
Poole, *U.K.* 11 G6
Pooley I., *Canada* 64 C3
Poona = Pune, *India* . 36 K8
Pooncarie, *Australia* .. 55 E3
Poopelloe L., *Australia* 55 E3
Poopó, L. de, *Bolivia* . 78 G5
Popanyinning, *Australia* 53 F2
Popayán, *Colombia* ... 78 C3
Poperinge, *Belgium* ... 15 D2
Popigay, *Russia* 25 B12
Popilta, L., *Australia* .. 55 E3
Popio L., *Australia* 55 E3
Poplar, *U.S.A.* 70 A2
Poplar →, *Man.,*
Canada 65 C9
Poplar →, *N.W.T.,*
Canada 64 A4
Poplar Bluff, *U.S.A.* ... 71 G9
Poplarville, *U.S.A.* 71 K10
Popocatépetl, Volcán,
Mexico 74 D5
Popokabaka, *Zaïre* ... 46 F3
Poprád, *Slovak Rep.* . 17 D11
Porbandar, *India* 36 J6
Porcher I., *Canada* 64 C2
Porcupine →, *Canada* 65 B8
Porcupine →, *U.S.A.* 60 B5
Pordenone, *Italy* 20 B5
Pori, *Finland* 9 F19
Porlamar, *Venezuela* . 78 A6
Poronaysk, *Russia* ... 25 E15
Poroshiri-Dake, *Japan* . 28 C11
Porpoise B., *Antarctica* 5 C9
Porretta, Passo di, *Italy* 20 B4
Porsangen, *Norway* .. 8 A21
Porsgrunn, *Norway* .. 9 G13
Port Adelaide, *Australia* 55 E2
Port Alberni, *Canada* . 64 D4
Port Alfred, *Canada* .. 63 C5
Port Alfred, *S. Africa* . 48 E4
Port Alice, *Canada* 64 C3
Port Allegany, *U.S.A.* . 68 E6
Port Allen, *U.S.A.* 71 K9
Port Alma, *Australia* .. 54 C5
Port Angeles, *U.S.A.* .. 72 B2
Port Antonio, *Jamaica* 74 J17
Port Aransas, *U.S.A.* .. 71 M6
Port Arthur, *Australia* . 54 G4
Port Arthur, *U.S.A.* ... 71 L8
Port au Port B., *Canada* 63 C8
Port-au-Prince, *Haiti* .. 75 D10
Port Augusta, *Australia* 55 E2
Port Augusta West,
Australia 55 E2
Port Austin, *U.S.A.* ... 62 D3
Port Bergé Vaovao,
Madag. 49 B8
Port Blair, *India* 34 G2
Port Blandford, *Canada* 63 C9
Port Bou, *Spain* 19 A7
Port Bradshaw,
Australia 54 A2
Port Broughton,
Australia 55 E2
Port Burwell, *Canada* . 62 D3
Port-Cartier, *Canada* .. 63 B6
Port Chalmers, *N.Z.* .. 51 L3
Port Chester, *U.S.A.* .. 68 E9
Port Clements, *Canada* 64 C2
Port Clinton, *U.S.A.* .. 68 E4

Port Coquitlam, *Canada* 64 D4
Port Curtis, *Australia* . 54 C5
Port Darwin, *Australia* 52 B5
Port Darwin, *Falk. Is.* . 80 G5
Port Davey, *Australia* . 54 G4
Port Dickson, *Malaysia* 34 S14
Port Douglas, *Australia* 54 B4
Port Edward, *Canada* . 64 C2
Port Elgin, *Canada* ... 62 D3
Port Elizabeth, *S. Africa* 48 E4
Port Ellen, *U.K.* 12 F2
Port Erin, *U.K.* 10 C3
Port Essington,
Australia 52 B5
Port Etienne =
Nouâdhibou,
Mauritania 44 D1
Port Fairy, *Australia* .. 55 F3
Port-Gentil, *Gabon* ... 46 E1
Port Gibson, *U.S.A.* ... 71 K9
Port Glasgow, *U.K.* ... 12 F4
Port Harcourt, *Nigeria* 44 H6
Port Hardy, *Canada* .. 64 C3
Port Harrison =
Inukjuak, *Canada* .. 61 C12
Port Hawkesbury,
Canada 63 C7
Port Hedland, *Australia* 52 D2
Port Henry, *U.S.A.* ... 68 C9
Port Hood, *Canada* ... 63 C7
Port Hope, *Canada* ... 62 D4
Port Huron, *U.S.A.* ... 68 D4
Port Isabel, *U.S.A.* ... 71 M6
Port Jefferson, *U.S.A.* . 68 E9
Port Kelang =
Pelabuhan Kelang,
Malaysia 34 S14
Port Kembla, *Australia* 55 E5
Port Kenny, *Australia* . 55 E1
Port Lairge =
Waterford, *Ireland* . 13 D4
Port Laoise, *Ireland* .. 13 C4
Port Lavaca, *U.S.A.* ... 71 L6
Port Lincoln, *Australia* 55 E2
Port Loko, *S. Leone* .. 44 G2
Port Louis, *Mauritius* . 35 G4
Port Lyautey = Kenitra,
Morocco 44 B3
Port MacDonnell,
Australia 55 F3
Port Macquarie,
Australia 55 E5
Port Maria, *Jamaica* .. 74 J17
Port Mellon, *Canada* . 64 D4
Port-Menier, *Canada* . 63 C7
Port Moresby,
Papua N. G. 56 H6
Port Mouton, *Canada* . 63 D7
Port Musgrave,
Australia 54 A3
Port Nelson, *Canada* . 65 B10
Port Nolloth, *S. Africa* 48 D2
Port Nouveau-Québec
= Kangiqsualujjuaq,
Canada 61 C13
Port O'Connor, *U.S.A.* 71 L6
Port of Spain,
Trin. & Tob. 74 S20
Port Orchard, *U.S.A.* .. 72 C2
Port Orford, *U.S.A.* ... 72 E1
Port Pegasus, *N.Z.* ... 51 M1
Port Perry, *Canada* ... 62 D4
Port Phillip B., *Australia* 55 F3
Port Pirie, *Australia* ... 55 E2
Port Radium = Echo
Bay, *Canada* 60 B8
Port Renfrew, *Canada* 64 D4
Port Roper, *Australia* . 54 A2
Port Rowan, *Canada* .. 62 D3
Port Safaga = Bûr
Safâga, *Egypt* 45 C11
Port Said = Bûr Sa'îd,
Egypt 45 B11
Port St. Joe, *U.S.A.* ... 69 L3
Port St. Johns, *S. Africa* 49 E4
Port Sanilac, *U.S.A.* ... 62 D3
Port Saunders, *Canada* 63 B8
Port Shepstone,
S. Africa 49 E5
Port Simpson, *Canada* 64 C2
Port Stanley = Stanley,
Falk. Is. 80 G5
Port Stanley, *Canada* . 62 D3
Port Sudan = Bûr
Sûdân, *Sudan* 45 E12
Port Talbot, *U.K.* 11 F4
Port Townsend, *U.S.A.* 72 B2
Port-Vendres, *France* . 18 E5
Port Vladimir, *Russia* . 22 A5
Port Wakefield,
Australia 55 E2
Port Washington,
U.S.A. 68 D2
Port Weld, *Malaysia* .. 34 Q13
Porta Orientalis,
Romania 17 F12
Portachuelo, *Bolivia* .. 78 G6
Portadown, *U.K.* 13 B5
Portage, *U.S.A.* 70 D10
Portage La Prairie,
Canada 65 D9
Portageville, *U.S.A.* .. 71 G10
Portalegre, *Portugal* .. 19 C2
Portales, *U.S.A.* 71 H3
Portarlington, *Ireland* . 13 C4
Porter L., *N.W.T.,*
Canada 65 A7
Porter L., *Sask., Canada* 65 B7
Porterville, *S. Africa* .. 48 E2
Porterville, *U.S.A.* 73 H4
Porthcawl, *U.K.* 11 F4
Porthill, *U.S.A.* 72 B5
Portile de Fier, *Europe* 17 F12

Portimão, *Portugal* ... 19 D1
Portland, *N.S.W.,*
Australia 55 E4
Portland, *Vic., Australia* 55 F3
Portland, *Maine, U.S.A.* 63 D5
Portland, *Mich., U.S.A.* 68 D3
Portland, *Oreg., U.S.A.* 72 D2
Portland, I. of, *U.K.* ... 11 G5
Portland B., *Australia* . 55 F3
Portland Bill, *U.K.* 11 G5
Portland Prom., *Canada* 61 C12
Portlands Roads,
Australia 54 A3
Portneuf, *Canada* 63 C5
Porto, *Portugal* 19 B1
Pôrto Alegre, *Brazil* .. 80 C6
Porto Amboim =
Gunza, *Angola* 46 G2
Port Fairy, *Australia* .. 55 F3
Pôrto de Móz, *Brazil* . 79 D8
Pôrto Empédocle, *Italy* 20 F5
Pôrto Esperança, *Brazil* 78 G7
Pôrto Franco, *Brazil* .. 79 E9
Porto Mendes, *Brazil* . 80 A6
Pôrto Murtinho, *Brazil* 78 H7
Pôrto Nacional, *Brazil* 79 F9
Porto Novo, *Benin* ... 44 G5
Porto Santo, *Madeira* . 44 B1
Pôrto Seguro, *Brazil* .. 79 G11
Pôrto Tórres, *Italy* ... 20 D3
Pôrto União, *Brazil* ... 80 B6
Pôrto Válter, *Brazil* ... 78 E4
Porto-Vecchio, *France* 18 F8
Pôrto Velho, *Brazil* ... 78 E6
Portoferráio, *Italy* 20 C4
Portola, *U.S.A.* 72 G3
Portoscuso, *Italy* 20 E3
Portoviejo, *Ecuador* .. 78 D2
Portpatrick, *U.K.* 12 G3
Portree, *U.K.* 12 D2
Portrush, *U.K.* 13 A5
Portsmouth, *Domin.* .. 74 M20
Portsmouth, *U.K.* 11 G6
Portsmouth, *N.H.,*
U.S.A. 68 D10
Portsmouth, *Ohio,*
U.S.A. 68 F4
Portsmouth, *Va., U.S.A.* 68 G7
Portsoy, *U.K.* 12 D6
Porttipahtan tekojärvi,
Finland 8 B22
Portugal ■, *Europe* .. 19 C1
Portumna, *Ireland* 13 C3
Porvenir, *Chile* 80 G2
Porvoo, *Finland* 9 F21
Posadas, *Argentina* ... 80 B5
Posht-e-Badam, *Iran* . 39 C7
Poso, *Indonesia* 33 E6
Posse, *Brazil* 79 F9
Possel, *C.A.R.* 46 C3
Possession I.,
Antarctica 5 D11
Post, *U.S.A.* 71 J4
Post Falls, *U.S.A.* 72 C5
Postavy = Pastavy,
Belarus 9 J22
Poste Maurice Cortier,
Algeria 44 D5
Postmasburg, *S. Africa* 48 D3
Postojna, *Slovenia* ... 16 F8
Potchefstroom,
S. Africa 48 D4
Poteau, *U.S.A.* 71 H7
Poteet, *U.S.A.* 71 L5
Potenza, *Italy* 20 D6
Poteriteri, L., *N.Z.* 51 M1
Potgietersrus, *S. Africa* 49 C4
Poti, *Georgia* 23 F7
Potiskum, *Nigeria* 44 F7
Potomac →, *U.S.A.* .. 68 F7
Potosí, *Bolivia* 78 G5
Potrerillos, *Chile* 80 B3
Potsdam, *Germany* ... 16 B7
Potsdam, *U.S.A.* 68 C8
Potter, *U.S.A.* 70 E3
Pottstown, *U.S.A.* 68 E8
Pottsville, *U.S.A.* 68 E8
Pottuvil, *Sri Lanka* ... 36 R12
Pouce Coupé, *Canada* 64 B4
Poughkeepsie, *U.S.A.* . 68 E9
Poulaphouca Res.,
Ireland 13 C5
Poulsbo, *U.S.A.* 72 C2
Pouso Alegre, *Brazil* .. 79 F7
Póvoa de Varzim,
Portugal 19 B1
Powassan, *Canada* ... 62 C4
Powder →, *U.S.A.* ... 70 B2
Powder River, *U.S.A.* . 72 E10
Powell, *U.S.A.* 72 D9
Powell, L., *U.S.A.* 73 H8
Powell River, *Canada* . 64 D4
Powers, *Mich., U.S.A.* 68 C2
Powers, *Oreg., U.S.A.* 72 E1
Powers Lake, *U.S.A.* .. 70 A3
Powys □, *U.K.* 11 E4
Poyang Hu, *China* 31 D6
Poyarkovo, *Russia* ... 25 E13
Požarevac, *Serbia, Yug.* 21 B9
Pozo Almonte, *Chile* . 78 H5
Pozoblanco, *Spain* ... 19 C3
Pozzuoli, *Italy* 20 D6
Prachin Buri, *Thailand* 34 E6
Prachuap Khiri Khan,
Thailand 34 G5
Prado, *Brazil* 79 G11
Prague = Praha, *Czech.* 16 C8
Praha, *Czech.* 16 C8

Prainha, *Amazonas,*
Brazil 78 E6
Prainha, *Pará, Brazil* .. 79 D8
Prairie, *Australia* 54 C3
Prairie →, *U.S.A.* 71 H5
Prairie City, *U.S.A.* ... 72 D4
Prairie du Chien, *U.S.A.* 70 D9
Prairies, *Canada* 60 C9
Prapat, *Indonesia* 32 D1
Prata, *Brazil* 79 G9
Prato, *Italy* 20 C4
Pratt, *U.S.A.* 71 G5
Prattville, *U.S.A.* 69 J2
Pravia, *Spain* 19 A2
Praya, *Indonesia* 32 F5
Preeceville, *Canada* .. 65 C8
Preiļi, *Latvia* 9 H22
Prelate, *Canada* 65 C7
Premier, *Canada* 64 B3
Premont, *U.S.A.* 71 M5
Prentice, *U.S.A.* 70 C9
Preobrazheniye, *Russia* 28 C6
Preparis North Channel,
Ind. Oc. 34 E2
Preparis South
Channel, *Ind. Oc.* .. 34 E2
Přerov, *Czech.* 17 D9
Prescott, *Canada* 62 D4
Prescott, *Ariz., U.S.A.* 73 J7
Prescott, *Ark., U.S.A.* . 71 J8
Preservation Inlet, *N.Z.* 51 M1
Presho, *U.S.A.* 70 D4
Presidencia Roque
Saenz Peña,
Argentina 80 B4
Presidente Epitácio,
Brazil 79 H8
Presidente Hermes,
Brazil 78 F6
Presidente Prudente,
Brazil 79 H8
Presidio, *U.S.A.* 71 L2
Prešov, *Slovak Rep.* . 17 D11
Prespa, L. =
Prespansko Jezero,
Macedonia 21 D9
Prespansko Jezero,
Macedonia 21 D9
Presque Isle, *U.S.A.* .. 63 C6
Prestbury, *U.K.* 11 F5
Presteigne, *U.K.* 11 E5
Preston, *U.K.* 10 D5
Preston, *Idaho, U.S.A.* 72 E8
Preston, *Minn., U.S.A.* 70 D8
Preston, *Nev., U.S.A.* . 72 G6
Preston, C., *Australia* . 52 D2
Prestonpans, *U.K.* 12 F6
Prestwick, *U.K.* 12 F4
Pretoria, *S. Africa* 49 D4
Préveza, *Greece* 21 E9
Prey-Veng, *Cambodia* . 34 G8
Pribilof Is., *Bering S.* . 4 D17
Příbram, *Czech.* 16 D8
Price, *U.S.A.* 72 G8
Price I., *Canada* 64 C3
Prichard, *U.S.A.* 69 K1
Priekule, *Latvia* 9 H19
Prienai, *Lithuania* 9 J20
Prieska, *S. Africa* 48 D3
Priest →, *U.S.A.* 72 B5
Priest L., *U.S.A.* 72 B5
Priestly, *Canada* 64 C3
Prievidza, *Slovak Rep.* 17 D10
Prikaspiyskaya
Nizmennost =
Caspian Depression,
Eurasia 23 E8
Prilep, *Macedonia* 21 D9
Priluki = Pryluky,
Ukraine 23 D5
Prime Seal I., *Australia* 54 G4
Primrose L., *Canada* .. 65 C7
Prince Albert, *Canada* 65 C7
Prince Albert, *S. Africa* 48 E3
Prince Albert Mts.,
Antarctica 5 D11
Prince Albert Nat. Park,
Canada 65 C7
Prince Albert Pen.,
Canada 60 A8
Prince Albert Sd.,
Canada 60 A8
Prince Alfred, C.,
Canada 4 B1
Prince Charles I.,
Canada 61 B12
Prince Charles Mts.,
Antarctica 5 D6
Prince Edward I. □,
Canada 63 C7
Prince Edward Is.,
Ind. Oc. 35 J2
Prince George, *Canada* 64 C4
Prince of Wales, C.,
U.S.A. 58 C3
Prince of Wales I.,
Australia 54 A3
Prince of Wales I.,
Canada 60 A10
Prince of Wales I.,
U.S.A. 64 B2
Prince Patrick I.,
Canada 4 B2
Prince Regent Inlet,
Canada 4 B3
Prince Rupert, *Canada* 64 C2
Princess Charlotte B.,
Australia 54 A3
Princess May Ras.,
Australia 52 C4
Princess Royal I.,
Canada 64 C3
Princeton, *Canada* ... 64 D4

Princeton, *Ill., U.S.A.* . 70 E10
Princeton, *Ind., U.S.A.* 68 F2
Princeton, *Ky., U.S.A.* . 68 G2
Princeton, *Mo., U.S.A.* 70 E8
Princeton, *N.J., U.S.A.* 68 E8
Princeton, *W. Va.,*
U.S.A. 68 G5
Principe, I. de, *Atl. Oc.* 42 F4
Principe Chan., *Canada* 64 C2
Principe da Beira, *Brazil* 78 F6
Prineville, *U.S.A.* 72 D3
Prins Harald Kyst,
Antarctica 5 D4
Prinsesse Astrid Kyst,
Antarctica 5 D3
Prinsesse Ragnhild
Kyst, *Antarctica* ... 5 D4
Priozersk, *Russia* 22 B5
Pripet = Prypyat →,
Europe 17 C16
Pripet Marshes, *Europe* 17 B15
Pripyats =
Pripet Marshes,
Europe 17 B15
Pripyats = Prypyat →,
Europe 17 C16
Priština, *Serbia, Yug.* . 21 C9
Privas, *France* 18 D6
Privolzhskaya
Vozvyshennost,
Russia 23 D8
Prizren, *Serbia, Yug.* . 21 C9
Probolinggo, *Indonesia* 33 G15
Proddatur, *India* 36 M11
Progreso, *Mexico* 74 C7
Prokopyevsk, *Russia* . 24 D9
Prokuplje, *Serbia, Yug.* 21 C9
Prome = Pyè, *Burma* . 37 K19
Prophet →, *Canada* .. 64 B4
Propriá, *Brazil* 79 F11
Proserpine, *Australia* . 54 C4
Prosser, *U.S.A.* 72 C4
Prostějov, *Czech.* 17 D9
Proston, *Australia* 55 D5
Protection, *U.S.A.* 71 G5
Provence, *France* 18 E6
Providence, *Ky., U.S.A.* 68 G2
Providence, *R.I., U.S.A.* 68 E10
Providence Bay,
Canada 62 C3
Providence Mts., *U.S.A.* 73 J6
Providencia, I. de,
Colombia 75 E8
Providenya, *Russia* ... 25 C19
Provins, *France* 18 B5
Provo, *U.S.A.* 72 F8
Provost, *Canada* 65 C6
Prozna →, *Poland* ... 17 B9
Prud'homme, *Canada* 65 C7
Pruszków, *Poland* 17 B11
Prut →, *Romania* 17 F15
Pruzhany, *Belarus* ... 17 B13
Prydz B., *Antarctica* .. 5 C6
Pryluky, *Ukraine* 23 D5
Pryor, *U.S.A.* 71 G7
Prypyat →, *Europe* .. 17 C16
Przemyśl, *Poland* 17 D12
Przhevalsk, *Kyrgyzstan* 24 E8
Psará, *Greece* 21 E11
Pskov, *Russia* 22 C4
Pskovskoye, Ozero,
Russia 9 H22
Ptich = Ptsich →,
Belarus 17 B15
Ptolemaís, *Greece* ... 21 D9
Ptsich →, *Belarus* ... 17 B15
Puán, *Argentina* 80 D4
Pucallpa, *Peru* 78 E4
Pudasjärvi, *Finland* ... 8 D22
Pudozh, *Russia* 22 B6
Pudukkottai, *India* 36 P11
Puebla, *Mexico* 74 D5
Pueblo, *U.S.A.* 70 F2
Pueblo Hundido, *Chile* 80 B2
Puelches, *Argentina* .. 80 D3
Puente Alto, *Chile* 80 C2
Puente-Genil, *Spain* .. 19 D3
Puerco →, *U.S.A.* 73 J10
Puerto Aisén, *Chile* ... 80 F2
Puerto Ayacucho,
Venezuela 78 B5
Puerto Barrios,
Guatemala 74 D7
Puerto Bermejo,
Argentina 80 B5
Puerto Bermúdez, *Peru* 78 F4
Puerto Bolívar, *Ecuador* 78 D3
Puerto Cabello,
Venezuela 78 A5
Puerto Cabezas, *Nic.* . 75 E8
Puerto Carreño,
Colombia 78 B5
Puerto Chicama, *Peru* 78 E3
Puerto Coig, *Argentina* 80 G3
Puerto Cortés,
Honduras 74 D7
Puerto Cumarebo,
Venezuela 78 A5
Puerto del Rosario,
Canary Is. 44 C2
Puerto Deseado,
Argentina 80 F3
Puerto Heath, *Bolivia* . 78 F5
Puerto La Cruz,
Venezuela 78 A6
Puerto Leguízamo,
Colombia 78 D4
Puerto Lobos,
Argentina 80 E3
Puerto Madryn,
Argentina 80 E3
Puerto Maldonado,
Peru 78 F5
Puerto Montt, *Chile* .. 80 E2

Puerto Morelos, *Mexico* 74 C7
Puerto Natales, *Chile* . 80 G2
Puerto Páez, *Venezuela* 78 B5
Puerto Pinasco,
Paraguay 80 A5
Puerto Pirámides,
Argentina 80 E4
Puerto Plata, *Dom. Rep.* 75 D10
Puerto Princesa, *Phil.* . 33 C5
Puerto Quellón, *Chile* . 80 E2
Puerto Rico ■,
W. Indies 75 D11
Puerto Sastre,
Paraguay 78 H7
Puerto Suárez, *Bolivia* 78 G7
Puerto Wilches,
Colombia 78 B4
Puertollano, *Spain* ... 19 C3
Pueyrredón, L.,
Argentina 80 F2
Pugachev, *Russia* 22 D8
Puget Sound, *U.S.A.* . 72 C2
Pūgūnzī, *Iran* 39 E8
Puigcerdá, *Spain* 19 A6
Pukaki, L., *N.Z.* 51 L3
Pukapuka, *Cook Is.* ... 57 J11
Pukatawagan, *Canada* 65 B8
Pukekohe, *N.Z.* 51 G5
Pula, *Croatia* 16 F7
Pulaski, *N.Y., U.S.A.* .. 68 D7
Pulaski, *Tenn., U.S.A.* . 69 H2
Pulaski, *Va., U.S.A.* ... 68 G5
Puławy, *Poland* 17 C11
Pulicat, L., *India* 36 N12
Pullman, *U.S.A.* 72 C5
Pulog, *Phil.* 33 A6
Pułtusk, *Poland* 17 B11
Pumlumon Fawr, *U.K.* 11 E4
Puná, *Bolivia* 78 G5
Puná, I., *Ecuador* 78 D2
Punakha, *Bhutan* 37 F16
Punata, *Bolivia* 78 G5
Punch, *India* 36 C9
Pune, *India* 36 K8
Punjab □, *India* 36 D9
Punjab □, *Pakistan* ... 36 D9
Puno, *Peru* 78 G4
Punta Alta, *Argentina* . 80 D4
Punta Arenas, *Chile* .. 80 G2
Punta de Díaz, *Chile* . 80 B2
Punta Gorda, *U.S.A.* .. 69 M5
Puntabie, *Australia* ... 55 E1
Puntarenas, *Costa Rica* 75 F8
Punto Fijo, *Venezuela* . 78 A4
Punxsatawney, *U.S.A.* 68 E6
Puquio, *Peru* 78 F4
Pur →, *Russia* 24 C8
Purace, Vol., *Colombia* 78 C3
Puralia = Puruliya,
India 37 H15
Purbeck, Isle of, *U.K.* . 11 G5
Purcell, *U.S.A.* 71 H6
Puri, *India* 37 K14
Purmerend, *Neths.* ... 15 B4
Purnia, *India* 37 G15
Pursat, *Cambodia* 34 F7
Purukcahu, *Indonesia* . 32 E4
Puruliya, *India* 37 H15
Purus →, *Brazil* 78 D6
Purwakarta, *Indonesia* 33 G12
Purwodadi, *Jawa,*
Indonesia 33 G14
Purwodadi, *Jawa,*
Indonesia 33 G13
Purwokerto, *Indonesia* 33 G13
Purworejo, *Indonesia* . 33 G14
Pusan, *S. Korea* 31 C7
Pushchino, *Russia* 25 D16
Pushkino, *Russia* 23 D8
Putahow L., *Canada* .. 65 B8
Putao, *Burma* 37 F20
Putaruru, *N.Z.* 51 H5
Puthein Myit →,
Burma 37 M19
Putignano, *Italy* 20 D7
Puting, Tanjung,
Indonesia 32 E4
Putorana, Gory, *Russia* 25 C10
Puttalam, *Sri Lanka* .. 36 Q11
Putten, *Neths.* 15 B5
Puttgarden, *Germany* . 16 A6
Putumayo →,
S. Amer. 78 D5
Putussibau, *Indonesia* 32 D4
Puy-de-Dôme, *France* . 18 D5
Puyallup, *U.S.A.* 72 C2
Pūzeh Rīg, *Iran* 39 E8
Pweto, *Zaïre* 46 F5
Pwllheli, *U.K.* 10 E3
Pya-ozero, *Russia* 22 A5
Pyapon, *Burma* 37 L19
Pyasina →, *Russia* ... 25 B9
Pyatigorsk, *Russia* ... 23 F7
Pyè, *Burma* 37 K19
Pyetrikaw, *Belarus* ... 17 B15
Pyhäjoki, *Finland* 8 D21
Pyinmana, *Burma* 37 K20
P'yŏngyang, *N. Korea* . 31 C7
Pyote, *U.S.A.* 71 K3
Pyramid L., *U.S.A.* ... 72 G4
Pyrénées, *Europe* 19 A6
Pyu, *Burma* 37 K20

Q

Qaanaaq = Thule,
Greenland 4 B4
Qachasnek, *S. Africa* . 49 E4
Qädib, *Yemen* 40 E5
Qa'el Jafr, *Jordan* 41 E5
Qa'emābād, *Iran* 39 D9

Qā'emshahr, *Iran* 39 B7
Qahremānshahr =
  Bākhtarān, *Iran* 38 C5
Qaidam Pendi, *China* .. 30 C4
Qajarīyeh, *Iran* 39 D6
Qal'at al Akhḍar,
  Si. Arabia 38 E3
Qal'at Sukkar, *Iraq* ... 38 D5
Qal'eh Darreh, *Iran* ... 38 B5
Qal'eh Shaharak,
  Afghan. 36 B4
Qamar, Ghubbat al,
  Yemen 40 D5
Qamdo, *China* 30 C4
Qamruddin Karez,
  Pakistan 36 D6
Qandahār, *Afghan.* ... 36 D4
Qandahār □, *Afghan.* . 36 D4
Qapān, *Iran* 39 B7
Qapshaghay,
  Kazakhstan 24 E8
Qaqortoq =
  Julianehåb,
  Greenland 4 C5
Qâra, *Egypt* 45 C10
Qarabutaq, *Kazakhstan* 24 E7
Qaraghandy,
  Kazakhstan 24 E8
Qârah, *Si. Arabia* 38 D4
Qarataū, *Kazakhstan* . 24 E8
Qareh →, *Iran* 38 B5
Qareh Tekān, *Iran* ... 39 B6
Qarqan He →, *China* . 30 C3
Qarqaraly, *Kazakhstan* 24 E8
Qarshi, *Uzbekistan* ... 24 F7
Qartabā, *Lebanon* 41 A4
Qaryat al Gharab, *Iraq* 38 D5
Qaryat al 'Ulyā,
  Si. Arabia 38 E5
Qasr 'Amra, *Jordan* ... 38 D3
Qaşr-e Qand, *Iran* ... 39 E9
Qasr Farâfra, *Egypt* .. 45 C10
Qatanā, *Syria* 41 B5
Qatar ■, *Asia* 39 E6
Qaţlīsh, *Iran* 39 B8
Qattâra, Munkhafed el,
  Egypt 45 C10
Qattâra Depression =
  Qattâra, Munkhafed
  el, *Egypt* 45 C10
Qawām al Ḥamzah, *Iraq* 38 D5
Qāyen, *Iran* 39 C8
Qazaqstan =
  Kazakhstan ■, *Asia* . 24 E7
Qazvin, *Iran* 39 B6
Qena, *Egypt* 45 C11
Qeqertarsuaq = Disko,
  Greenland 4 C5
Qeqertarsuaq =
  Godhavn, *Greenland* 4 C5
Qeshlāq, *Iran* 38 C5
Qeshm, *Iran* 39 E8
Qez'iot, *Israel* 41 E3
Qibā', *Si. Arabia* 38 E5
Qila Safed, *Pakistan* .. 36 E2
Qila Saifullāh, *Pakistan* 36 D6
Qilian Shan, *China* ... 30 C4
Qingdao, *China* 31 C7
Qinghai □, *China* 30 C4
Qinghai Hu, *China* ... 30 C5
Qingjiang, *China* 31 C6
Qinhuangdao, *China* . 31 C6
Qinzhou, *China* 30 D5
Qiqihar, *China* 25 E13
Qiraîya, W. →, *Egypt* 41 E3
Qiryat Ata, *Israel* 41 C4
Qiryat Gat, *Israel* 41 D3
Qiryat Mal'akhi, *Israel* 41 D3
Qiryat Shemona, *Israel* 41 B4
Qiryat Yam, *Israel* ... 41 C4
Qitai, *China* 30 B3
Qojūr, *Iran* 38 B5
Qom, *Iran* 39 C6
Qomsheh, *Iran* 39 D6
Qostanay, *Kazakhstan* 24 D7
Qu Xian, *China* 31 D6
Quairading, *Australia* . 53 F2
Qualeup, *Australia* 53 F2
Quambatook, *Australia* 55 F3
Quambone, *Australia* . 55 E4
Quamby, *Australia* 54 C3
Quan Long, *Vietnam* . 34 H8
Quanah, *U.S.A.* 71 H5
Quandialla, *Australia* . 55 E4
Quang Ngai, *Vietnam* . 34 E10
Quang Yen, *Vietnam* . 34 B9
Quantock Hills, *U.K.* . 11 F4
Quanzhou, *China* 31 D6
Quaqtaq, *Canada* 61 B13
Quarai, *Brazil* 80 C5
Quartu Sant'Elena, *Italy* 20 E3
Quartzsite, *U.S.A.* 73 K6
Quatsino, *Canada* 64 C3
Quatsino Sd., *Canada* . 64 C3
Quba, *Azerbaijan* 23 F8
Qūchān, *Iran* 39 B8
Queanbeyan, *Australia* 55 F4
Québec, *Canada* 63 C5
Québec □, *Canada* ... 63 B6
Queen Alexandra Ra.,
  Antarctica 5 E11
Queen Charlotte,
  Canada 64 C2
Queen Charlotte Is.,
  Canada 64 C2
Queen Charlotte Str.,
  Canada 64 C3
Queen Elizabeth Is.,
  Canada 58 B10
Queen Mary Land,
  Antarctica 5 D7
Queen Maud G.,
  Canada 60 B9

Queen Maud Land,
  Antarctica 5 D3
Queen Maud Mts.,
  Antarctica 5 E13
Queens Chan.,
  Australia 52 C4
Queenscliff, *Australia* . 55 F3
Queensland □,
  Australia 54 C3
Queenstown, *Australia* 54 G4
Queenstown, *N.Z.* ... 51 L2
Queenstown, *S. Africa* 48 E4
Quela, *Angola* 46 F3
Quelimane, *Mozam.* .. 47 H7
Quelpart = Cheju Do,
  S. Korea 31 C7
Quemado, *N. Mex.,*
  U.S.A. 73 J9
Quemado, *Tex., U.S.A.* 71 L4
Quequén, *Argentina* .. 80 D5
Querétaro, *Mexico* ... 74 C4
Quesnel, *Canada* 64 C4
Quesnel →, *Canada* . 64 C4
Quesnel L., *Canada* .. 64 C4
Questa, *U.S.A.* 73 H11
Quetico Prov. Park,
  Canada 62 C1
Quetta, *Pakistan* 36 D5
Quezon City, *Phil.* ... 33 B6
Qufār, *Si. Arabia* 38 E4
Qui Nhon, *Vietnam* .. 34 F10
Quibaxe, *Angola* 46 F2
Quibdo, *Colombia* 78 B3
Quiberon, *France* 18 C2
Quick, *Canada* 64 C3
Quiet L., *Canada* 64 A2
Quilán, C., *Chile* 80 E2
Quilengues, *Angola* ... 47 G2
Quillabamba, *Peru* ... 78 F4
Quillagua, *Chile* 78 H5
Quillota, *Chile* 80 C2
Quilon, *India* 36 Q10
Quilpie, *Australia* 55 D3
Quimili, *Argentina* ... 80 B4
Quimper, *France* 18 B1
Quimperlé, *France* 18 C2
Quincy, *Calif., U.S.A.* 72 G3
Quincy, *Fla., U.S.A.* .. 69 K3
Quincy, *Ill., U.S.A.* ... 70 F9
Quincy, *Mass., U.S.A.* 68 D10
Quincy, *Wash., U.S.A.* 72 C4
Quines, *Argentina* 80 C3
Quinga, *Mozam.* 47 H8
Quintanar de la Orden,
  Spain 19 C4
Quintero, *Chile* 80 C2
Quinyambie, *Australia* 55 E3
Quipungo, *Angola* 47 G2
Quirindi, *Australia* ... 55 E5
Quissanga, *Mozam.* ... 47 G8
Quitilipi, *Argentina* ... 80 B4
Quitman, *Ga., U.S.A.* . 69 K4
Quitman, *Miss., U.S.A.* 69 J1
Quitman, *Tex., U.S.A.* 71 J7
Quito, *Ecuador* 78 D3
Quixadá, *Brazil* 79 D11
Qumbu, *S. Africa* 49 E4
Quneitra, *Syria* 41 B4
Qûnghirot, *Uzbekistan* 24 E6
Quoin I., *Australia* 52 B4
Quoin Pt., *S. Africa* ... 48 E2
Quondong, *Australia* . 55 E3
Quorn, *Australia* 55 E2
Qûqon, *Uzbekistan* ... 24 E8
Qurnat as Sawdā',
  Lebanon 41 A5
Qûs, *Egypt* 45 C11
Qusaybah, *Iraq* 38 C4
Quseir, *Egypt* 45 C11
Qûshchī, *Iran* 38 B5
Quthing, *Lesotho* 49 E4
Qūjiābād, *Iran* 39 C6
Qyzylorda, *Kazakhstan* 24 E7

R

Raahe, *Finland* 8 D21
Raasay, *U.K.* 12 D2
Raasay, Sd. of, *U.K.* . 12 D2
Raba, *Indonesia* 33 F5
Rába →, *Hungary* ... 17 E9
Rabat, *Malta* 20 G6
Rabat, *Morocco* 44 B3
Rabaul, *Papua N. G.* . 56 H7
Rabbit →, *Canada* .. 64 B3
Rabbit Lake, *Canada* . 65 C7
Rabbitskin →, *Canada* 64 A4
Rábor, *Iran* 39 D8
Race, C., *Canada* 63 C9
Rach Gia, *Vietnam* ... 34 G8
Racibórz, *Poland* 17 C10
Racine, *U.S.A.* 68 D2
Radama, Nosy, *Madag.* 49 A8
Radama, Saikanosy,
  Madag. 49 A8
Rădăuţi, *Romania* 17 E13
Radekhiv, *Ukraine* ... 17 C13
Radekhov = Radekhiv,
  Ukraine 17 C13
Radford, *U.S.A.* 68 G5
Radisson, *Canada* 65 C7
Radium Hot Springs,
  Canada 64 C5
Radnor Forest, *U.K.* . 11 E4
Radom, *Poland* 17 C11
Radomsko, *Poland* ... 17 C10
Radomyshl, *Ukraine* . 17 C15
Radstock, *U.K.* 11 F5
Radstock, C., *Australia* 55 E1
Rådviliškis, *Lithuania* . 9 J20
Radville, *Canada* 65 D8
Rae, *Canada* 64 A5
Rae Bareli, *India* 37 F12
Rae Isthmus, *Canada* . 61 B11
Raeren, *Belgium* 15 D6
Raeside, L., *Australia* . 53 E3
Raetihi, *N.Z.* 51 H5
Rafaela, *Argentina* ... 80 C4
Rafah, *Gaza Strip* 41 D3
Rafai, *C.A.R.* 46 D4
Rafḥā, *Si. Arabia* 38 D4
Rafsanjān, *Iran* 39 D8
Raft Pt., *Australia* 52 C3
Ragachow, *Belarus* ... 17 B16
Ragama, *Sri Lanka* ... 36 R11
Ragged, Mt., *Australia* 53 F3
Raglan, *Australia* 54 C5
Raglan, *N.Z.* 51 G5
Ragusa, *Italy* 20 F6
Raha, *Indonesia* 33 E6
Rahad al Bardī, *Sudan* 45 F9
Rahaeng = Tak,
  Thailand 34 D5
Raḥimah, *Si. Arabia* .. 39 E6
Rahimyar Khan,
  Pakistan 36 E7
Rāhjerd, *Iran* 39 C6
Raichur, *India* 36 L10
Raigarh, *India* 37 J13
Raijua, *Indonesia* 33 F6
Railton, *Australia* 54 G4
Rainbow Lake, *Canada* 64 B5
Rainier, *U.S.A.* 72 C2
Rainier, Mt., *U.S.A.* .. 72 C3
Rainy L., *Canada* 65 D10
Rainy River, *Canada* . 65 D10
Rapla, *Estonia* 9 G21
Raipur, *India* 37 J12
Raisio, *Finland* 9 F20
Raj Nandgaon, *India* . 37 J12
Raja, Ujung, *Indonesia* 32 D1
Raja Ampat,
  Kepulauan, *Indonesia* 33 E7
Rajahmundry, *India* .. 37 L12
Rajang →, *Malaysia* . 32 D4
Rajapalaiyam, *India* .. 36 Q10
Rajasthan □, *India* ... 36 F8
Rajasthan Canal, *India* 36 E8
Rajgarh, *India* 36 G10
Rajkot, *India* 36 H7
Rajpipla, *India* 36 J8
Rajshahi, *Bangla.* 37 G16
Rajshahi □, *Bangla.* .. 37 G16
Rakaia, *N.Z.* 51 K4
Rakaia →, *N Z* 51 K4
Rakan, Ra's, *Qatar* ... 39 E6
Rakaposhi, *Pakistan* . 36 A9
Rakata, Pulau,
  Indonesia 32 F3
Rakhiv, *Ukraine* 17 D13
Rakitnoye, *Russia* 28 B7
Rakops, *Botswana* ... 48 C3
Rakvere, *Estonia* 9 G22
Raleigh, *U.S.A.* 69 H6
Raleigh B., *U.S.A.* 69 H7
Ralls, *U.S.A.* 71 J4
Ram →, *Canada* 64 A4
Rām Allāh, *West Bank* 41 D4
Ram Hd., *Australia* ... 55 F4
Ramanathapuram, *India* 36 Q11
Ramanetaka, B. de,
  Madag. 49 A8
Ramat Gan, *Israel* 41 C3
Ramatlhabama,
  S. Africa 48 D4
Rambipuji, *Indonesia* . 33 H15
Ramea, *Canada* 63 C8
Ramechhap, *Nepal* ... 37 F15
Ramelau, *Indonesia* .. 33 F7
Ramgarh, *Bihar, India* 37 H14
Ramgarh, *Raj., India* . 36 F7
Rāmhormoz, *Iran* 39 D6
Ramīān, *Iran* 39 B7
Ramingining, *Australia* 54 A2
Ramla, *Israel* 41 D3
Ramnad =
  Ramanathapuram,
  India 36 Q11
Ramona, *U.S.A.* 73 K5
Ramore, *Canada* 62 C3
Ramotswa, *Botswana* . 48 C4
Rampur, *India* 36 E11
Rampur Hat, *India* ... 37 G15
Ramree I. = Ramree
  Kyun, *Burma* 37 K18
Ramree Kyun, *Burma* 37 K18
Rämsar, *Iran* 39 B6
Ramsey, *Canada* 62 C3
Ramsey, *U.K.* 10 C3
Ramsgate, *U.K.* 11 F9
Ramtek, *India* 36 J11
Ranaghat, *India* 37 H16
Ranau, *Malaysia* 32 C5
Rancagua, *Chile* 80 C2
Rancheria →, *Canada* 64 A3
Ranchester, *U.S.A.* ... 72 D10
Ranchi, *India* 37 H14
Randers, *Denmark* ... 9 H14
Randfontein, *S. Africa* 49 D4
Randolph, *U.S.A.* 72 F8
Råne älv →, *Sweden* 8 D20
Rangaunu B., *N.Z.* ... 51 F4
Rangeley, *U.S.A.* 68 C10
Rangely, *U.S.A.* 72 F9
Ranger, *U.S.A.* 71 J5
Rangia, *India* 37 F17
Rangiora, *N.Z.* 51 K4
Rangitaiki →, *N.Z.* .. 51 G6
Rangitata →, *N.Z.* ... 51 K3
Rangkasbitung,
  Indonesia 33 G12
Rangon →, *Burma* ... 37 L20

Rangoon, *Burma* 37 L20
Rangpur, *Bangla.* 37 G16
Ranibennur, *India* 36 M9
Raniganj, *India* 37 H15
Raniwara, *India* 36 G8
Rānīyah, *Iraq* 38 B5
Ranken →, *Australia* . 54 C2
Rankin, *U.S.A.* 71 K4
Rankin Inlet, *Canada* . 60 B10
Rankins Springs,
  Australia 55 E4
Rannoch, L., *U.K.* 12 E4
Rannoch Moor, *U.K.* . 12 E4
Ranobe, Helodranon' i,
  Madag. 49 C7
Ranohira, *Madag.* 49 C8
Ranomafana,
  Toamasina, Madag. 49 B8
Ranomafana, *Toliara,*
  Madag. 49 C8
Ranong, *Thailand* 34 H5
Ransiki, *Indonesia* ... 33 E8
Rantau, *Indonesia* 32 E5
Rantauprapat,
  Indonesia 32 D1
Rantemario, *Indonesia* 33 E5
Rantoul, *U.S.A.* 68 E1
Rapa, Pac. Oc. 57 K13
Rapallo, *Italy* 20 B3
Rapid →, *Canada* 64 B3
Rapid City, *U.S.A.* ... 70 D3
Rapid River, *U.S.A.* .. 68 C2
Rapides des Joachims,
  Canada 62 C4
Rapla, *Estonia* 9 G21
Rarotonga, *Cook Is.* . 57 K12
Ra's al 'Ayn, *Syria* ... 38 B4
Ra's al Khaymah,
  U.A.E. 39 E8
Ra's al-Unuf, *Libya* ... 45 B8
Ra's an Naqb, *Jordan* 41 F4
Ras Bânâs, *Egypt* 45 D12
Ras Dashen, *Ethiopia* 45 F12
Râs Timirist, *Mauritania* 44 E1
Rasa, Punta, *Argentina* 80 E4
Raseiniai, *Lithuania* .. 9 J20
Rashad, *Sudan* 45 F11
Rashîd, *Egypt* 45 B11
Rasht, *Iran* 39 B6
Rason L., *Australia* ... 53 E3
Rat →, *Canada* 65 C10
Rat Buri, *Thailand* 34 F5
Rat Islands, *U.S.A.* ... 60 C1
Rat River, *Canada* 64 A6
Ratangarh, *India* 36 E9
Raţāwi, *Iraq* 38 D5
Rath Luirc, *Ireland* ... 13 D3
Rathdrum, *Ireland* ... 13 D5
Rathenow, *Germany* . 16 B7
Rathkeale, *Ireland* ... 13 D3
Rathlin, *U.K.* 13 A5
Rathlin O'Birne I.,
  Ireland 13 B3
Ratibor = Racibórz,
  Poland 17 C10
Ratlam, *India* 36 H9
Ratnagiri, *India* 36 L8
Raton, *U.S.A.* 71 G2
Rattray Hd., *U.K.* 12 D7
Ratz, Mt., *Canada* 64 B2
Raub, *Malaysia* 34 R14
Raufarhöfn, *Iceland* .. 8 C6
Raufoss, *Norway* 9 F14
Raukumara Ra., *N.Z.* 51 H6
Rauma, *Finland* 9 F19
Raurkela, *India* 37 H14
Rausu-Dake, *Japan* ... 28 B12
Rava-Ruska, *Ukraine* 17 C12
Rava Russkaya = Rava-
  Ruska, *Ukraine* ... 17 C12
Ravānsar, *Iran* 38 C5
Rāvar, *Iran* 39 D8
Ravena, *U.S.A.* 68 D9
Ravenna, *Italy* 20 B5
Ravenna, *U.S.A.* 70 E5
Ravensburg, *Germany* 16 E5
Ravenshoe, *Australia* . 54 B4
Ravensthorpe, *Australia* 53 F3
Ravenswood, *Australia* 54 C4
Ravenswood, *U.S.A.* . 68 F5
Ravi →, *Pakistan* 36 D7
Rawalpindi, *Pakistan* . 36 C8
Rawāndūz, *Iraq* 38 B5
Rawang, *Malaysia* 34 R14
Rawdon, *Canada* 62 C5
Rawene, *N.Z.* 51 F4
Rawlinna, *Australia* ... 53 F4
Rawlins, *U.S.A.* 72 F10
Rawlinson Ra.,
  Australia 53 D4
Rawson, *Argentina* ... 80 E3
Ray, *U.S.A.* 70 A3
Ray, C., *Canada* 63 C8
Rayadurg, *India* 36 M10
Rayagada, *India* 37 K13
Raychikhinsk, *Russia* . 25 E13
Räyen, *Iran* 39 D8
Raymond, *Canada* ... 64 D6
Raymond, *U.S.A.* 72 C2
Raymondville, *U.S.A.* 71 M6
Raymore, *Canada* 65 C8
Rayne, *U.S.A.* 71 K8
Rayong, *Thailand* 34 F6
Rayville, *U.S.A.* 71 J9
Raz, Pte. du, *France* .. 18 C1
Razan, *Iran* 39 C6
Razdel'naya =
  Rozdilna, *Ukraine* . 17 E16
Razdolnoye, *Russia* .. 28 C5
Razeh, *Iran* 39 C6
Razelm, Lacul, *Romania* 17 F15
Razgrad, *Bulgaria* 21 C12
Ré, I. de, *France* 18 C3

Reading, *U.K.* 11 F7
Reading, *U.S.A.* 68 E8
Realicó, *Argentina* ... 80 D4
Ream, *Cambodia* 34 G7
Rebecca, L., *Australia* 53 F3
Rebi, *Indonesia* 33 F8
Rebiana, *Libya* 45 D9
Rebun-Tō, *Japan* 28 B10
Recherche, Arch. of the,
  Australia 53 F3
Rechytsa, *Belarus* 17 B16
Recife, *Brazil* 79 E12
Recklinghausen,
  Germany 15 C7
Reconquista, *Argentina* 80 B5
Recreo, *Argentina* 80 B3
Red →, *La., U.S.A.* .. 71 K9
Red →, *N. Dak.,*
  U.S.A. 70 A6
Red Bay, *Canada* 63 B8
Red Bluff, *U.S.A.* 72 F2
Red Bluff L., *U.S.A.* .. 71 K3
Red Cliffs, *Australia* . 55 E3
Red Cloud, *U.S.A.* ... 70 E5
Red Deer, *Canada* 64 C6
Red Deer →, *Alta.,*
  Canada 65 C8
Red Deer →, *Man.,*
  Canada 65 C8
Red Deer L., *Canada* . 65 C8
Red Indian L., *Canada* 63 C8
Red Lake, *Canada* 65 C10
Red Lake Falls, *U.S.A.* 70 B6
Red Lodge, *U.S.A.* ... 72 D9
Red Oak, *U.S.A.* 70 E7
Red Rock, *Canada* 62 C2
Red Rock, L., *U.S.A.* . 70 E8
Red Rocks Pt., *Australia* 53 F4
Red Sea, *Asia* 40 C2
Red Sucker L., *Canada* 65 C10
Red Tower Pass =
  Turnu Roşu, P.,
  Romania 17 F13
Red Wing, *U.S.A.* 70 C8
Redbridge, *U.K.* 11 F8
Redcar, *U.K.* 10 C6
Redcliff, *Canada* 65 C6
Redcliffe, *Australia* ... 55 D5
Redcliffe, Mt., *Australia* 53 E3
Reddersburg, *S. Africa* 48 D4
Redding, *U.S.A.* 72 F2
Redditch, *U.K.* 11 E6
Redfield, *U.S.A.* 70 C5
Redknife →, *Canada* . 64 A5
Redlands, *U.S.A.* 73 K5
Redmond, *Australia* .. 53 F2
Redmond, *U.S.A.* 72 D3
Redon, *France* 18 C2
Redonda, *Antigua* 74 L19
Redondela, *Spain* 19 A1
Redrock Pt., *Canada* . 64 A5
Redruth, *U.K.* 11 G2
Redvers, *Canada* 65 D8
Redwater, *Canada* 64 C6
Redwood City, *U.S.A.* 73 H2
Redwood Falls, *U.S.A.* 70 C7
Ree, L., *Ireland* 13 C4
Reed, L., *Canada* 65 C8
Reed City, *U.S.A.* 68 D3
Reeder, *U.S.A.* 70 B3
Reedley, *U.S.A.* 73 H4
Reedsburg, *U.S.A.* ... 70 D9
Reedsport, *U.S.A.* 72 E1
Reefton, *N.Z.* 51 K3
Refugio, *U.S.A.* 71 L6
Regensburg, *Germany* 16 D7
Réggio di Calábria, *Italy* 20 E6
Réggio nell'Emília, *Italy* 20 B4
Reghin, *Romania* 17 E13
Regina, *Canada* 65 C8
Rehoboth, *Namibia* .. 48 C2
Rehovot, *Israel* 41 D3
Rei-Bouba, *Cameroon* 45 G7
Reichenbach, *Germany* 16 C6
Reid, *Australia* 53 F4
Reid River, *Australia* . 54 B4
Reidsville, *U.S.A.* 69 G6
Reigate, *U.K.* 11 F7
Reims, *France* 18 B6
Reina Adelaida, Arch.,
  Chile 80 G2
Reinbeck, *U.S.A.* 70 D8
Reindeer →, *Canada* 65 B8
Reindeer I., *Canada* .. 65 C9
Reindeer L., *Canada* . 65 B8
Reinga, C., *N.Z.* 51 F4
Reinosa, *Spain* 19 A3
Reitz, *S. Africa* 49 D4
Reivilo, *S. Africa* 48 D3
Rekinniki, *Russia* 25 C17
Reliance, *Canada* 65 A7
Remarkable, Mt.,
  Australia 55 E2
Rembang, *Indonesia* . 33 G14
Remeshk, *Iran* 39 E8
Remich, *Lux.* 15 E6
Rendsburg, *Germany* . 16 A5
Rene, *Russia* 25 C19
Renfrew, *Canada* 62 C4
Renfrew, *U.K.* 12 F4
Rengat, *Indonesia* 32 E2
Reni, *Ukraine* 17 F15
Renk, *Sudan* 45 F11
Renkum, *Neths.* 15 C5
Renmark, *Australia* ... 55 E3
Rennell Sd., *Canada* . 64 C2
Renner Springs T.O.,
  Australia 54 B1
Rennes, *France* 18 B3
Reno, *U.S.A.* 72 G4
Reno →, *Italy* 20 B5
Renovo, *U.S.A.* 68 E7
Rensselaer, *U.S.A.* ... 68 E2

Rentería, *Spain* 19 A5
Renton, *U.S.A.* 72 C2
Republic, *Mich., U.S.A.* 68 B2
Republic, *Wash., U.S.A.* 72 B4
Republican →, *U.S.A.* 70 F6
Republican City, *U.S.A.* 70 E5
Repulse Bay, *Canada* . 61 B11
Requena, *Peru* 78 E4
Requena, *Spain* 19 C5
Resadiye = Datça,
  Turkey 21 F12
Reserve, *Canada* 65 C8
Reserve, *U.S.A.* 73 K9
Resht = Rasht, *Iran* .. 39 B6
Resistencia, *Argentina* 80 B5
Resolução, *Romania* .. 17 F11
Resolution I., *Canada* . 61 B13
Resolution I., *N.Z.* ... 51 L1
Ressano Garcia,
  Mozam. 49 D5
Reston, *Canada* 65 D8
Retford, *U.K.* 10 D7
Réthímnon, *Greece* ... 21 G11
Réunion ■, *Ind. Oc.* . 43 J9
Reus, *Spain* 19 B6
Reutlingen, *Germany* . 16 D5
Reval = Tallinn, *Estonia* 9 G21
Revda, *Russia* 22 C10
Revelstoke, *Canada* .. 64 C5
Revilla Gigedo, Is.,
  Pac. Oc. 57 F16
Revillagigedo I., *U.S.A.* 64 B2
Rewa, *India* 37 G12
Rewari, *India* 36 E10
Rexburg, *U.S.A.* 72 E8
Rey, *Iran* 39 C6
Rey Malabo, *Eq. Guin.* 44 H6
Reykjahlið, *Iceland* ... 8 D5
Reykjanes, *Iceland* ... 8 E2
Reykjavík, *Iceland* 8 D3
Reynolds, *Canada* 65 D9
Reynolds Ra., *Australia* 52 D5
Reynosa, *Mexico* 74 B5
Rēzekne, *Latvia* 9 H22
Rezvān, *Iran* 39 E8
Rhayader, *U.K.* 11 E4
Rheden, *Neths.* 15 B6
Rhein, *Canada* 65 C8
Rhein →, *Europe* 15 C6
Rhein-Main-Donau-
  Kanal →, *Germany* 16 D6
Rheine, *Germany* 16 B4
Rheinland-Pfalz □,
  Germany 16 C4
Rhin = Rhein →,
  Europe 15 C6
Rhine = Rhein →,
  Europe 15 C6
Rhineland-Palatinate =
  Rheinland-Pfalz □,
  Germany 16 C4
Rhinelander, *U.S.A.* .. 70 C10
Rhode Island □, *U.S.A.* 68 E10
Rhodes = Ródhos,
  Greece 21 F13
Rhodesia =
  Zimbabwe ■, *Africa* 47 H5
Rhodope Mts. =
  Rhodopi Planina,
  Bulgaria 21 D11
Rhodopi Planina,
  Bulgaria 21 D11
Rhön = Hohe Rhön,
  Germany 16 C5
Rhondda, *U.K.* 11 F4
Rhône →, *France* 18 E6
Rhum, *U.K.* 12 E2
Rhyl, *U.K.* 10 D4
Rhymney, *U.K.* 11 F4
Riachão, *Brazil* 79 E9
Riasi, *India* 36 C9
Riau □, *Indonesia* 32 E2
Riau, Kepulauan,
  Indonesia 32 D2
Riau Arch. = Riau,
  Kepulauan, *Indonesia* 32 D2
Ribadeo, *Spain* 19 A2
Ribble →, *U.K.* 10 C5
Ribe, *Denmark* 9 J13
Ribeirão Prêto, *Brazil* . 79 H9
Riberalta, *Bolivia* 78 F5
Rîbniţa, *Moldova* 17 E15
Riccarton, *N.Z.* 51 K4
Rice Lake, *U.S.A.* 70 C9
Rich Hill, *U.S.A.* 70 F7
Richards Bay, *S. Africa* 49 D5
Richards L., *Canada* .. 65 B7
Richardson →,
  Canada 65 B6
Richardton, *U.S.A.* ... 70 B3
Riche, C., *Australia* ... 53 F2
Richey, *U.S.A.* 70 B2
Richfield, *Idaho, U.S.A.* 72 E6
Richfield, *Utah, U.S.A.* 73 G8
Richibucto, *Canada* ... 63 C7
Richland, *Ga., U.S.A.* . 69 J3
Richland, *Oreg., U.S.A.* 72 D5
Richland, *Wash., U.S.A.* 72 C4
Richland Center, *U.S.A.* 70 D9
Richlands, *U.S.A.* 68 G5
Richmond, *N.S.W.,*
  Australia 55 E5
Richmond, *Queens.,*
  Australia 54 C3
Richmond, *N.Z.* 51 J4
Richmond, *U.K.* 10 C6
Richmond, *Calif., U.S.A.* 72 H2
Richmond, *Ind., U.S.A.* 68 F3
Richmond, *Ky., U.S.A.* 68 G3
Richmond, *Mo., U.S.A.* 70 F8
Richmond, *Tex., U.S.A.* 71 L7
Richmond, *Utah, U.S.A.* 72 F8
Richmond, *Va., U.S.A.* 68 G7

Richmond Ra., Australia 55 D5
Richmond-upon-Thames, U.K. 11 F7
Richton, U.S.A. 69 K1
Richwood, U.S.A. 68 F5
Ridder, Kazakhstan .. 24 D9
Ridgedale, Canada .. 65 C8
Ridgeland, U.S.A. 69 J5
Ridgelands, Australia . 54 C5
Ridgetown, Canada .. 62 D3
Ridgway, U.S.A. 68 E6
Riding Mountain Nat. Park, Canada 65 C8
Ridley, Mt., Australia . 53 F3
Ried, Austria 16 D7
Riesa, Germany 16 C7
Riet →, S. Africa 48 D3
Rieti, Italy 20 C5
Rifle, U.S.A. 72 G10
Rig Rig, Chad 45 F7
Riga, Latvia 9 H21
Riga, G. of, Latvia .. 9 H20
Rīgān, Iran 39 D8
Rīgas Jūras Līcis = Riga, G. of, Latvia .. 9 H20
Rigby, U.S.A. 72 E8
Rigestān □, Afghan. . 36 D4
Riggins, U.S.A. 72 D5
Rigolet, Canada 63 B8
Riihimäki, Finland .. 9 F21
Riiser-Larsen-halvøya, Antarctica 5 C4
Rijeka, Croatia 16 F8
Rijn →, Neths. 15 B4
Rijssen, Neths. 15 B6
Rijswijk, Neths. 15 B4
Rikuzentakada, Japan . 28 E10
Riley, U.S.A. 72 E4
Rimah, Wadi ar →, Si. Arabia 38 E4
Rimbey, Canada 64 C6
Rímini, Italy 20 B5
Rîmnicu Sărat, Romania 17 F14
Rîmnicu Vîlcea, Romania 17 F13
Rimouski, Canada .. 63 C6
Rinca, Indonesia 33 F5
Rinconada, Argentina . 80 A3
Ringkøbing, Denmark . 9 H13
Ringling, U.S.A. 72 C8
Ringvassøy, Norway .. 8 B18
Rinjani, Indonesia .. 32 F5
Rio Branco, Brazil ... 78 E5
Rio Branco, Uruguay . 80 C6
Rio Claro, Trin. & Tob. 74 S20
Rio Colorado, Argentina 80 D4
Rio Cuarto, Argentina . 80 C4
Rio das Pedras, Mozam. 49 C6
Rio de Janeiro, Brazil . 79 H10
Rio de Janeiro □, Brazil 79 H10
Rio do Sul, Brazil 80 B7
Rio Gallegos, Argentina 80 G3
Rio Grande, Argentina . 80 G3
Rio Grande, Brazil ... 80 C6
Rio Grande →, U.S.A. . 71 N6
Rio Grande City, U.S.A. 71 M5
Rio Grande del Norte →, N. Amer. . 67 E7
Rio Grande do Norte □, Brazil 79 E11
Rio Grande do Sul □, Brazil 80 B6
Rio Largo, Brazil 79 E11
Rio Mulatos, Bolivia . 78 G5
Rio Muni = Mbini □, Eq. Guin. 46 D2
Rio Negro, Brazil 80 B7
Rio Verde, Brazil 79 G8
Rio Vista, U.S.A. 72 G3
Riobamba, Ecuador .. 78 D3
Riohacha, Colombia . 78 A4
Riosucio, Caldas, Colombia 78 B3
Riosucio, Choco, Colombia 78 B3
Riou L., Canada 65 B7
Ripley, U.S.A. 71 H10
Ripon, U.K. 10 C6
Ripon, U.S.A. 68 D1
Rishā', W. ar →, Si. Arabia 38 E5
Rishiri-Tō, Japan 28 B10
Rishon le Ziyyon, Israel 41 D3
Rison, U.S.A. 71 J8
Risør, Norway 9 G13
Ritchies Archipelago, India 34 F2
Ritzville, U.S.A. 72 C4
Riva del Garda, Italy . 20 B4
Rivadavia, Chile 80 B2
Rivera, Uruguay 80 C5
Riverhead, U.S.A. 68 E9
Riverhurst, Canada .. 65 C7
Riverina, Australia .. 53 E4
Rivers, Canada 65 C8
Rivers, L. of the, Canada 65 D7
Rivers Inlet, Canada . 64 C3
Riverside, S. Africa .. 48 E3
Riverside, Calif., U.S.A. 73 K5
Riverside, Wyo., U.S.A. 72 F10
Riversleigh, Australia . 54 B2
Riverton, Australia .. 55 E2
Riverton, Canada 65 C9
Riverton, N.Z. 51 M1
Riverton, U.S.A. 72 E9
Riviera di Levante, Italy 20 B3
Riviera di Ponente, Italy 20 B3
Rivière-à-Pierre, Canada 63 C5

Rivière-au-Renard, Canada 63 C7
Rivière-du-Loup, Canada 63 C6
Rivière-Pentecôte, Canada 63 C6
Rivne, Ukraine 17 C14
Rivoli, Italy 20 B2
Rivoli B., Australia .. 55 F3
Riyadh = Ar Riyāḍ, Si. Arabia 40 C4
Rize, Turkey 23 F7
Rizzuto, C., Italy 20 E7
Rjukan, Norway 9 G13
Roag, L., U.K. 12 C2
Roanne, France 18 C6
Roanoke, Ala., U.S.A. . 69 J3
Roanoke, Va., U.S.A. . 68 G7
Roanoke →, U.S.A. .. 69 H7
Roanoke I., U.S.A. .. 69 H8
Roanoke Rapids, U.S.A. 69 G7
Robbins I., Australia . 54 G4
Robe →, Australia .. 52 D2
Robe →, Ireland 13 C2
Robert Lee, U.S.A. .. 71 K4
Roberts, U.S.A. 72 E7
Robertson, S. Africa . 48 E2
Robertson I., Antarctica 5 C18
Robertson Ra., Australia 52 D3
Robertsport, Liberia . 44 G2
Robertstown, Australia 55 E2
Roberval, Canada .. 63 C5
Robeson Chan., Greenland 4 A4
Robinson →, Australia 54 B2
Robinson Ra., Australia 53 E2
Robinson River, Australia 54 B2
Robinvale, Australia . 55 E3
Roblin, Canada 65 C8
Roboré, Bolivia 78 G7
Robson, Mt., Canada . 64 C5
Robstown, U.S.A. .. 71 M6
Roca, C. da, Portugal . 19 C1
Rocas, I., Brazil 79 D12
Rocha, Uruguay 80 C6
Rochdale, U.K. 10 D5
Rochefort, Belgium . 15 D5
Rochefort, France 18 D3
Rochelle, U.S.A. 70 E10
Rocher River, Canada . 64 A6
Rochester, Canada .. 64 C6
Rochester, U.K. 11 F8
Rochester, Ind., U.S.A. 68 E2
Rochester, Minn., U.S.A. 70 C8
Rochester, N.H., U.S.A. 68 D10
Rochester, N.Y., U.S.A. 68 D7
Rock →, Canada 64 A3
Rock Hill, U.S.A. 69 H5
Rock Island, U.S.A. .. 70 E9
Rock Rapids, U.S.A. . 70 D6
Rock River, U.S.A. .. 72 F11
Rock Springs, Mont., U.S.A. 72 C10
Rock Springs, Wyo., U.S.A. 72 F9
Rock Valley, U.S.A. .. 70 D6
Rockall, Atl. Oc. 6 D3
Rockdale, U.S.A. 71 K6
Rockefeller Plateau, Antarctica 5 E14
Rockford, U.S.A. 70 D10
Rockglen, Canada .. 65 D7
Rockhampton, Australia 54 C5
Rockhampton Downs, Australia 54 B2
Rockingham, Australia 53 F2
Rockingham B., Australia 54 B4
Rockingham Forest, U.K. 11 E7
Rocklake, U.S.A. 70 A5
Rockland, Idaho, U.S.A. 72 E7
Rockland, Maine, U.S.A. 63 D6
Rockland, Mich., U.S.A. 70 B10
Rockmart, U.S.A. 69 H3
Rockport, Mo., U.S.A. 70 E7
Rockport, Tex., U.S.A. 71 L6
Rocksprings, U.S.A. . 71 K4
Rockville, U.S.A. 68 F7
Rockwall, U.S.A. 71 J6
Rockwell City, U.S.A. 70 D7
Rockwood, U.S.A. .. 69 H3
Rocky Ford, U.S.A. .. 70 F3
Rocky Gully, Australia 53 F2
Rocky Lane, Canada . 64 B5
Rocky Mount, U.S.A. 69 H7
Rocky Mountain House, Canada 64 C6
Rocky Mts., N. Amer. . 64 C4
Rockyford, Canada .. 64 C6
Rod, Pakistan 36 E3
Rødbyhavn, Denmark . 9 J14
Roddickton, Canada . 63 B8
Roderick I., Canada .. 64 C3
Rodez, France 18 D5
Ródhos, Greece 21 F13
Rodney, C., N.Z. 51 G5
Rodriguez, Ind. Oc. .. 35 F5
Roe →, U.K. 13 A5
Roebourne, Australia . 52 D2
Roebuck B., Australia . 52 C3
Roebuck Plains, Australia 52 C3
Roermond, Neths. .. 15 C5
Roes Welcome Sd., Canada 61 B11
Roeselare, Belgium . 15 D3
Rogachev = Ragachow, Belarus 17 B16

Rogagua, L., Bolivia . 78 F5
Rogatyn, Ukraine 17 D13
Rogers, U.S.A. 71 G7
Rogers City, U.S.A. .. 68 C4
Rogerson, U.S.A. 72 E6
Rogersville, U.S.A. .. 69 G4
Roggan River, Canada 62 B4
Roggeveldberge, S. Africa 48 E3
Rogoaguado, L., Bolivia 78 F5
Rogojampi, Indonesia 33 J17
Rohri, Pakistan 36 F6
Rohtak, India 36 E10
Roi Et, Thailand 34 D7
Roja, Latvia 9 H20
Rojas, Argentina 80 C4
Rojo, C., Mexico 74 C5
Rokan →, Indonesia . 32 D2
Rokeby, Australia .. 54 A3
Rokiškis, Lithuania .. 9 J21
Rolândia, Brazil 80 A6
Rolette, U.S.A. 70 A4
Rolla, Kans., U.S.A. .. 71 G4
Rolla, Mo., U.S.A. .. 71 G9
Rolla, N. Dak., U.S.A. . 70 A5
Rolleston, Australia . 54 C4
Rollingstone, Australia 54 B4
Roma, Australia 55 D4
Roma, Italy 20 D5
Roma, Sweden 9 H18
Roman, Romania 17 E14
Roman, Russia 25 C12
Romang, Indonesia . 33 F7
Români, Egypt 41 E1
Romania ■, Europe . 17 F12
Romanovka = Basarabeasca, Moldova 17 E15
Romans-sur-Isère, France 18 D6
Romblon, Phil. 33 B6
Rome = Roma, Italy . 20 D5
Rome, Ga., U.S.A. 69 H3
Rome, N.Y., U.S.A. .. 68 D8
Romney, U.S.A. 68 F6
Romney Marsh, U.K. . 11 F8
Rømø, Denmark 9 J13
Romorantin-Lanthenay, France 18 C4
Rona, U.K. 12 D3
Ronan, U.S.A. 72 C6
Roncador, Serra do, Brazil 79 F8
Ronceverte, U.S.A. .. 68 G5
Ronda, Spain 19 D3
Rondane, Norway .. 9 F13
Rondônia □, Brazil .. 78 F6
Rondonópolis, Brazil . 79 G8
Rong, Koh, Cambodia 34 G7
Ronge, L. la, Canada . 65 B7
Rønne, Denmark 9 J16
Ronne Ice Shelf, Antarctica 5 D18
Ronsard, C., Australia . 53 D1
Ronse, Belgium 15 D3
Roodepoort, S. Africa . 49 D4
Roof Butte, U.S.A. .. 73 H9
Roorkee, India 36 E10
Roosendaal, Neths. .. 15 C4
Roosevelt, Minn., U.S.A. 70 A7
Roosevelt, Utah, U.S.A. 72 F8
Roosevelt →, Brazil . 78 E6
Roosevelt, Mt., Canada 64 B3
Roosevelt I., Antarctica 5 D12
Roosevelt Res., U.S.A. 73 K8
Roper →, Australia .. 54 A2
Ropesville, U.S.A. .. 71 J3
Roquetas de Mar, Spain 19 D4
Roraima □, Brazil .. 78 C6
Roraima, Mt., Venezuela 78 B6
Rorketon, Canada .. 65 C9
Røros, Norway 9 E14
Rosa, Zambia 46 F6
Rosa, Monte, Europe . 16 F4
Rosalia, U.S.A. 72 C5
Rosario, Argentina .. 80 C4
Rosário, Brazil 79 D10
Rosario, Mexico 74 C3
Rosario, Paraguay .. 80 A5
Rosario de la Frontera, Argentina 80 B4
Rosário do Sul, Brazil . 80 C6
Rosas, G. de, Spain . 19 A7
Roscoe, U.S.A. 70 C5
Roscommon, Ireland . 13 C3
Roscommon, U.S.A. . 68 C3
Roscommon □, Ireland 13 C3
Roscrea, Ireland 13 D4
Rose →, Australia .. 54 A2
Rose Blanche, Canada 63 C8
Rose Harbour, Canada 64 C2
Rose Pt., Canada 64 C2
Rose Valley, Canada . 65 C8
Roseau, Domin. 74 M20
Roseau, U.S.A. 70 A7
Rosebery, Australia . 54 G4
Rosebud, U.S.A. 71 K6
Roseburg, U.S.A. 72 E2
Rosedale, Australia . 54 C5
Rosedale, U.S.A. 71 J9
Rosemary, Canada .. 64 C6
Rosenberg, U.S.A. .. 71 L7
Rosenheim, Germany . 16 E7
Rosetown, Canada .. 65 C7
Rosetta = Rashîd, Egypt 45 B11
Roseville, U.S.A. 72 G3
Rosewood, N. Terr., Australia 52 C4

Rosewood, Queens., Australia 55 D5
Roshkhvār, Iran 39 C8
Rosignano Marittimo, Italy 20 C4
Rosignol, Guyana .. 78 B7
Roşiori-de-Vede, Romania 17 F13
Roskilde, Denmark .. 9 J15
Roslavl, Russia 22 D5
Roslyn, Australia 55 E4
Rosmead, S. Africa .. 48 E4
Ross, Australia 54 G4
Ross, N.Z. 51 K3
Ross I., Antarctica .. 5 D11
Ross Ice Shelf, Antarctica 5 E12
Ross L., U.S.A. 72 B3
Ross-on-Wye, U.K. .. 11 F5
Ross Sea, Antarctica . 5 D11
Rossan Pt., Ireland .. 13 B3
Rossano Cálabro, Italy 20 E7
Rossburn, Canada .. 65 C8
Rossignol, L., Canada . 62 B5
Rossignol Res., Canada 63 D6
Rossland, Canada .. 64 D5
Rosslare, Ireland 13 D5
Rosso, Mauritania .. 44 E1
Rossosh, Russia 23 D6
Rossport, Canada .. 62 C2
Røssvatnet, Norway . 8 D16
Rossville, Australia .. 54 B4
Røst, Norway 8 C15
Rosthern, Canada .. 65 C7
Rostock, Germany .. 16 A7
Rostov, Don, Russia . 23 E6
Rostov, Yarosl, Russia 22 C6
Roswell, U.S.A. 71 J2
Rosyth, U.K. 12 E5
Rotan, U.S.A. 71 J4
Rother →, U.K. 11 G8
Rotherham, U.K. 10 D6
Rothes, U.K. 12 D5
Rothesay, Canada .. 63 C6
Rothesay, U.K. 12 F3
Roti, Indonesia 33 F6
Roto, Australia 55 E4
Rotondo Mte., France . 18 E8
Rotoroa, L., N.Z. 51 J4
Rotorua, N.Z. 51 H6
Rotorua, L., N.Z. 51 H6
Rotterdam, Neths. .. 15 C4
Rottnest I., Australia . 53 F2
Rottumeroog, Neths. . 15 A6
Rottweil, Germany .. 16 D5
Rotuma, Fiji 56 J9
Roubaix, France 18 A5
Rouen, France 18 B4
Rouleau, Canada .. 65 C8
Round Mountain, U.S.A. 72 G5
Round Mt., Australia . 55 E5
Roundup, U.S.A. 72 C9
Rousay, U.K. 12 B5
Roussillon, France .. 18 E5
Rouxville, S. Africa .. 48 E4
Rouyn, Canada 62 C4
Rovaniemi, Finland . 8 C21
Rovereto, Italy 20 B4
Rovigo, Italy 20 B4
Rovinj, Croatia 16 F7
Rovno = Rivne, Ukraine 17 C14
Rovuma →, Tanzania 46 G4
Row'ān, Iran 39 C6
Rowena, Australia .. 55 D4
Rowley Shoals, Australia 52 C2
Roxas, Phil. 33 B6
Roxboro, U.S.A. 69 G6
Roxborough Downs, Australia 54 C2
Roxburgh, N.Z. 51 L2
Roy, Mont., U.S.A. .. 72 C9
Roy, N. Mex., U.S.A. . 71 H2
Roy Hill, Australia .. 52 D2
Royal Leamington Spa, U.K. 11 E6
Royal Tunbridge Wells, U.K. 11 F8
Royan, France 18 D3
Rozdilna, Ukraine .. 17 E16
Rozhyshche, Ukraine . 17 C13
Rtishchevo, Russia .. 22 D7
Ruacaná, Angola .. 48 B1
Ruahine Ra., N.Z. .. 51 H6
Ruapehu, N.Z. 51 H5
Ruapuke I., N.Z. 51 M2
Ruâq, W. →, Egypt . 41 E2
Rub' al Khali, Si. Arabia 40 D4
Rubeho Mts., Tanzania 46 D4
Rubh a' Mhail, U.K. . 12 F2
Rubha Hunish, U.K. . 12 D2
Rubha Robhanais = Lewis, Butt of, U.K. . 12 C2
Rubio, Venezuela .. 78 B4
Rubtsovsk, Russia .. 24 D9
Ruby, U.S.A. 60 B4
Ruby Mts., U.S.A. .. 72 F6
Rūd Sar, Iran 39 B6
Rudall, Australia 55 E2
Rudall →, Australia . 52 D3
Rudnichnyy, Russia . 22 C9
Rudnogorsk, Russia . 25 D11
Rudnyy, Kazakhstan . 24 D7
Rudolf, Ostrov, Russia 24 A6
Rudyard, U.S.A. 68 B3
Rufa'a, Sudan 45 F11
Rufiji →, Tanzania .. 46 D4
Rufino, Argentina .. 80 C4
Rufisque, Senegal .. 44 F1

Ruhnu saar, Estonia . 9 H20
Ruhr →, Germany .. 16 C4
Ruidosa, U.S.A. 71 L2
Ruidoso, U.S.A. 73 K11
Rujm Tal'at al Jamā'ah, Jordan 41 E4
Rukwa L., Tanzania . 46 F6
Rulhieres, C., Australia 52 B4
Rum Jungle, Australia 52 B5
Rumāḥ, Si. Arabia .. 38 E5
Rumania = Romania ■, Europe 17 F12
Rumaylah, Iraq 38 D5
Rumbalara, Australia . 54 D1
Rumbêk, Sudan 45 G10
Rumford, U.S.A. 68 C10
Rumia, Poland 17 A10
Rumoi, Japan 28 C10
Rumsey, Canada .. 64 C6
Rumula, Australia .. 54 B4
Runanga, N.Z. 51 K3
Runaway, C., N.Z. .. 51 G6
Runcorn, U.K. 10 D5
Rungwa, Tanzania .. 46 F6
Runton Ra., Australia . 52 D3
Ruoqiang, China 30 C3
Rupa, India 37 F18
Rupat, Indonesia .. 32 D2
Rupert →, Canada .. 62 B4
Rupert House = Waskaganish, Canada 62 B4
Rurrenabaque, Bolivia 78 F5
Rusape, Zimbabwe .. 47 H6
Ruschuk = Ruse, Bulgaria 21 C12
Ruse, Bulgaria 21 C12
Rushden, U.K. 11 E7
Rushford, U.S.A. 70 D9
Rushville, Ill., U.S.A. . 70 E9
Rushville, Ind., U.S.A. 68 F3
Rushville, Nebr., U.S.A. 70 D3
Rushworth, Australia . 55 F4
Russas, Brazil 79 D11
Russell, Canada 65 C8
Russell, U.S.A. 70 F5
Russell L., Man., Canada 65 B8
Russell L., N.W.T., Canada 64 A5
Russellkonda, India . 37 K14
Russellville, Ala., U.S.A. 69 H2
Russellville, Ark., U.S.A. 71 H8
Russellville, Ky., U.S.A. 69 G2
Russia ■, Eurasia .. 25 C11
Russkaya Polyana, Kazakhstan 24 D8
Russkoye Ustie, Russia 4 B15
Rustavi, Georgia 23 F8
Rustenburg, S. Africa . 48 D4
Ruston, U.S.A. 71 J8
Ruteng, Indonesia .. 33 F6
Ruth, U.S.A. 72 G6
Rutherglen, U.K. 12 F4
Rutland Plains, Australia 54 B3
Rutledge →, Canada 65 A6
Rutledge L., Canada . 65 A6
Rutshuru, Zaïre 46 E5
Ruurlo, Neths. 15 B6
Ruwais, U.A.E. 39 E7
Ruwenzori, Africa .. 46 D5
Ružomberok, Slovak Rep. 17 D10
Rwanda ■, Africa .. 46 E5
Ryan, L., U.K. 12 G3
Ryazan, Russia 22 D6
Ryazhsk, Russia 22 D7
Rybache = Rybachye, Kazakhstan 24 E9
Rybachiy Poluostrov, Russia 22 A5
Rybachye, Kazakhstan 24 E9
Rybinsk, Russia 22 C6
Rybinskoye Vdkhr., Russia 22 C6
Rybnitsa = Rîbniţa, Moldova 17 E15
Ryde, U.K. 11 G6
Rye, U.K. 11 G8
Rye →, U.K. 10 C7
Rye Patch Reservoir, U.S.A. 72 F4
Ryegate, U.S.A. 72 C9
Rylstone, Australia .. 55 E4
Ryōtsu, Japan 28 E9
Rypin, Poland 17 B10
Ryūgasaki, Japan .. 29 G10
Ryūkyū Is. = Ryūkyū-rettō, Japan 29 M2
Ryūkyū-rettō, Japan . 29 M2
Rzeszów, Poland .. 17 C11
Rzhev, Russia 22 C5

S

Sa Dec, Vietnam 34 G8
Sa'ādatābād, Fārs, Iran 39 D7
Sa'ādatābād, Kermān, Iran 39 D7
Saale →, Germany .. 16 C6
Saalfeld, Germany .. 16 C6
Saar →, Europe 16 D4
Saarbrücken, Germany 16 D4
Saaremaa, Estonia .. 9 G20
Saarijärvi, Finland .. 9 E21
Saariselkä, Finland . 8 B23
Saarland □, Germany 15 E7
Saba, W. Indies 74 K18

Šabac, Serbia, Yug. . 21 B8
Sabadell, Spain 19 B7
Sabah □, Malaysia .. 32 C5
Sábanalarga, Colombia 78 A4
Sabang, Indonesia .. 32 C1
Sabará, Brazil 79 G10
Saberania, Indonesia 33 E9
Sabhah, Libya 45 C7
Sabie, S. Africa 49 D5
Sabinal, U.S.A. 71 L5
Sabinas, Mexico 74 B4
Sabinas Hidalgo, Mexico 74 B4
Sabine →, U.S.A. .. 71 L8
Sabine L., U.S.A. 71 L8
Sabine Pass, U.S.A. . 71 L8
Sabkhet el Bardawîl, Egypt 41 D2
Sablayan, Phil. 33 B6
Sable, C., Canada .. 63 D6
Sable, C., U.S.A. 67 E10
Sable I., Canada 63 D8
Sabrina Coast, Antarctica 5 C9
Sabulubek, Indonesia . 32 E1
Sabzevār, Iran 39 B8
Sabzvārān, Iran 39 D8
Sac City, U.S.A. 70 D7
Săcele, Romania .. 17 F13
Sachigo →, Canada . 62 A2
Sachigo, L., Canada . 62 B1
Sachsen □, Germany . 16 C7
Sachsen-Anhalt □, Germany 16 C7
Saco, Maine, U.S.A. . 69 D10
Saco, Mont., U.S.A. . 72 B10
Sacramento, U.S.A. . 72 G3
Sacramento →, U.S.A. 72 G3
Sacramento Mts., U.S.A. 73 K11
Sadani, Tanzania .. 46 F7
Sadao, Thailand 34 N13
Sadd el Aali, Egypt . 45 D11
Sado, Japan 28 E9
Sado →, Portugal .. 19 C1
Sadon, Burma 37 G20
Sæby, Denmark 9 H14
Şafājah, Si. Arabia .. 38 E3
Säffle, Sweden 9 G15
Safford, U.S.A. 73 K9
Saffron Walden, U.K. . 11 E8
Safi, Morocco 44 B3
Şafiābād, Iran 39 B8
Safid Dasht, Iran .. 39 C6
Safid Kūh, Afghan. . 36 B3
Safwān, Iraq 38 D5
Saga, Indonesia .. 33 E8
Saga, Japan 29 H5
Saga □, Japan 29 H5
Sagae, Japan 28 E10
Sagala, Mali 44 F3
Sagar, India 36 M9
Saginaw, U.S.A. 68 D4
Saginaw B., U.S.A. . 68 D4
Şagīr, Zāb as →, Iraq 38 C4
Saglouc = Salluit, Canada 61 B12
Sagua la Grande, Cuba 75 C8
Saguache, U.S.A. .. 73 G10
Saguenay →, Canada 63 C5
Sagunto, Spain 19 C5
Sahagún, Spain 19 A3
Saham al Jawlān, Syria 41 C4
Sahand, Kūh-e, Iran . 38 B5
Sahara, Africa 44 D5
Saharan Atlas = Saharien, Atlas, Algeria 44 B5
Saharanpur, India .. 36 E10
Saharien, Atlas, Algeria 44 B5
Sahasinaka, Madag. . 49 C8
Sāḥiliyah, Iraq 38 C4
Sahiwal, Pakistan .. 36 D8
Şahneh, Iran 38 C5
Sahtaneh →, Canada 64 B4
Sahuarita, U.S.A. .. 73 L8
Sa'id Bundas, Sudan . 45 G9
Saïda, Algeria 44 B5
Sa'īdābād, Kermān, Iran 39 D7
Sa'īdābād, Semnān, Iran 39 B7
Sa'īdīyeh, Iran 39 B6
Saidpur, Bangla. .. 37 G16
Saidu, Pakistan 36 B8
Saigon = Phanh Bho Ho Chi Minh, Vietnam 34 G9
Saijō, Japan 29 H6
Saikhoa Ghat, India . 37 F19
Saiki, Japan 29 H5
Sailolof, Indonesia .. 33 E8
Saimaa, Finland .. 9 F23
Şa'in Dezh, Iran .. 38 B5
St. Abb's Head, U.K. . 12 F6
St. Alban's, Canada . 63 C8
St. Albans, U.K. 11 F7
St. Albans, Vt., U.S.A. 68 C9
St. Albans, W. Va., U.S.A. 68 F5
St. Alban's Head, U.K. 11 G5
St. Albert, Canada .. 64 C6
St. Andrew's, Canada 63 C8
St. Andrews, U.K. .. 12 E6
St. Ann B., Canada . 63 C7
St. Anthony, Canada 63 B8
St. Anthony, U.S.A. . 72 E8
St. Arnaud, Australia . 55 F3
St. Arthur, Canada . 63 C6
St. Asaph, U.K. 10 D4
St-Augustin-Saguenay, Canada 63 B8
St. Augustine, U.S.A. 69 L5
St. Austell, U.K. 11 G3

St.-Barthélemy, I.

St.-Barthélemy, I., *W. Indies* 74 K19
St. Bee's Hd., *U.K.* 10 C4
St. Boniface, *Canada* 65 D9
St. Bride's, *Canada* 63 C9
St. Brides B., *U.K.* 11 F2
St.-Brieuc, *France* 18 B2
St. Catharines, *Canada* 62 D4
St. Catherines I., *U.S.A.* 69 K5
St. Catherine's Pt., *U.K.* 11 G6
St.-Chamond, *France* 18 D6
St. Charles, *Ill., U.S.A.* 68 E1
St. Charles, *Mo., U.S.A.* 70 F9
St. Christopher = St. Kitts, *W. Indies* 74 K19
St. Christopher-Nevis ■, *W. Indies* 74 K19
St. Clair, L., *Canada* 62 D3
St. Claude, *Canada* 65 D9
St. Cloud, *Fla., U.S.A.* 69 L5
St. Cloud, *Minn., U.S.A.* 70 C7
St-Coeur de Marie, *Canada* 63 C5
St. Cricq, C., *Australia* 53 E1
St. Croix, *Virgin Is.* 75 D12
St. Croix →, *U.S.A.* 70 C8
St. Croix Falls, *U.S.A.* 70 C8
St. David's, *Canada* 63 C8
St. David's, *U.K.* 11 F2
St. David's Head, *U.K.* 11 F2
St.-Denis, *France* 18 B5
St.-Denis, *Réunion* 35 G4
St.-Dizier, *France* 18 B6
St. Elias, Mt., *U.S.A.* 60 B5
St. Elias Mts., *Canada* 64 A1
St.-Étienne, *France* 18 D6
St. Eustatius, *W. Indies* 74 K19
St-Félicien, *Canada* 62 C5
St.-Flour, *France* 18 D5
St. Francis, *U.S.A.* 70 F4
St. Francis →, *U.S.A.* 71 H9
St. Francis, C., *S. Africa* 48 E3
St. Francisville, *U.S.A.* 71 K9
St-Gabriel-de-Brandon, *Canada* 62 C5
St. Gallen = Sankt Gallen, *Switz.* 16 E5
St.-Gaudens, *France* 18 E4
St. George, *Australia* 55 D4
St. George, *Canada* 63 C6
St. George, *S.C., U.S.A.* 69 J5
St. George, *Utah, U.S.A.* 73 H7
St. George, C., *Canada* 63 C8
St. George, C., *U.S.A.* 69 L3
St. George Ra., *Australia* 52 C4
St-Georges, *Belgium* 15 D5
St. George's, *Canada* 63 C8
St-Georges, *Canada* 63 C5
St.-Georges, *Fr. Guiana* 79 C8
St. George's, *Grenada* 74 Q20
St. George's B., *Canada* 63 C8
St. Georges Basin, *Australia* 52 C4
St. George's Channel, *Europe* 13 E6
St. Georges Hd., *Australia* 55 F5
St. Gotthard P. = San Gottardo, P. del, *Switz.* 16 E5
St. Helena, *U.S.A.* 72 G2
St. Helena ■, *Atl. Oc.* 2 E9
St. Helena B., *S. Africa* 48 E2
St. Helens, *Australia* 54 G4
St. Helens, *U.K.* 10 D5
St. Helens, *U.S.A.* 72 D2
St. Helier, *U.K.* 11 H5
St-Hubert, *Belgium* 15 D5
St-Hyacinthe, *Canada* 62 C5
St. Ignace, *U.S.A.* 68 C3
St. Ignace I., *Canada* 62 C2
St. Ignatius, *U.S.A.* 72 C6
St. Ives, *Cambs., U.K.* 11 E7
St. Ives, *Corn., U.K.* 11 G2
St. James, *U.S.A.* 70 D7
St-Jean, *Canada* 62 C5
St-Jean →, *Canada* 63 B7
St-Jean, L., *Canada* 63 C5
St. Jean Baptiste, *Canada* 65 D9
St-Jean-Port-Joli, *Canada* 63 C5
St-Jérôme, *Qué., Canada* 62 C5
St-Jérôme, *Qué., Canada* 63 C5
St. John, *Canada* 63 C6
St. John, *Kans., U.S.A.* 71 G5
St. John, *N. Dak., U.S.A.* 70 A5
St. John →, *U.S.A.* 63 C6
St. John, C., *Canada* 63 B8
St. John's, *Antigua* 74 K20
St. John's, *Canada* 63 C9
St. Johns, *Ariz., U.S.A.* 73 J9
St. Johns, *Mich., U.S.A.* 68 D3
St. Johns →, *U.S.A.* 69 K5
St. Johnsbury, *U.S.A.* 68 C9
St. Joseph, *La., U.S.A.* 71 K9
St. Joseph, *Mich., U.S.A.* 68 D2
St. Joseph, *Mo., U.S.A.* 70 F7
St. Joseph →, *U.S.A.* 68 D2
St. Joseph, I., *Canada* 62 C3
St. Joseph, L., *Canada* 62 B1
St-Jovite, *Canada* 62 C5
St. Kilda, *N.Z.* 51 L3
St. Kitts, *W. Indies* 74 K19
St. Kitts-Nevis = St. Christopher-Nevis ■, *W. Indies* 74 K19
St. Laurent, *Canada* 65 C9
St.-Laurent, *Fr. Guiana* 79 B8
St. Lawrence, *Australia* 54 C4
St. Lawrence, *Canada* 63 C8
St. Lawrence →, *Canada* 63 C6
St. Lawrence, Gulf of, *Canada* 63 C7
St. Lawrence I., *U.S.A.* 60 B3
St. Leonard, *Canada* 63 C6
St. Lewis →, *Canada* 63 B8
St.-Lô, *France* 18 B3
St-Louis, *Senegal* 44 E1
St. Louis, *Mich., U.S.A.* 68 D3
St. Louis, *Mo., U.S.A.* 70 F9
St. Louis →, *U.S.A.* 70 B8
St. Lucia ■, *W. Indies* 74 P21
St. Lucia, L., *S. Africa* 49 D5
St. Lucia Channel, *W. Indies* 74 N21
St. Lunaire-Griquet, *Canada* 63 B8
St.-Malo, *France* 18 B2
St-Marc, *Haiti* 75 D10
St. Maries, *U.S.A.* 72 C5
St-Martin, *W. Indies* 74 J18
St. Martin, L., *Canada* 65 C9
St. Martins, *Canada* 63 C6
St. Martinville, *U.S.A.* 71 K9
St. Mary Pk., *Australia* 55 E2
St. Marys, *Australia* 54 G4
St. Mary's, *U.K.* 11 H1
St. Marys, *U.S.A.* 68 E6
St. Mary's, C., *Canada* 63 C9
St. Mary's B., *Canada* 63 C9
St. Marys Bay, *Canada* 63 D6
St.-Mathieu, Pte., *France* 18 B1
St. Matthews, I. = Zadetkyi Kyun, *Burma* 34 H5
St.-Maurice →, *Canada* 62 C5
St. Michael's Mount, *U.K.* 11 G2
St.-Nazaire, *France* 18 C2
St. Neots, *U.K.* 11 E7
St. Niklass = Sint Niklaas, *Belgium* 15 C4
St.-Omer, *France* 18 A5
St-Pacome, *Canada* 63 C6
St-Pamphile, *Canada* 63 C6
St. Pascal, *Canada* 63 C6
St. Paul, *Canada* 64 C6
St. Paul, *Minn., U.S.A.* 70 C8
St. Paul, *Nebr., U.S.A.* 70 E5
St. Paul, I., *Ind. Oc.* 35 H6
St. Paul I., *Canada* 63 C7
St. Peter, *U.S.A.* 70 C8
St. Peter Port, *U.K.* 11 H5
St. Peters, *N.S., Canada* 63 C7
St. Peters, *P.E.I., Canada* 63 C7
St. Petersburg = Sankt-Peterburg, *Russia* 22 C5
St. Petersburg, *U.S.A.* 69 M4
St.-Pierre, *St- P. & M.* 63 C8
St. Pierre, *Seychelles* 35 E3
St-Pierre, L., *Canada* 62 C5
St.-Pierre et Miquelon □, *St- P. & M.* 63 C8
St.-Quentin, *France* 18 B5
St. Regis, *U.S.A.* 72 C6
St. Sebastien, Tanjon' i, *Madag.* 49 A8
St-Siméon, *Canada* 63 C6
St. Stephen, *Canada* 63 C6
St. Thomas, *Canada* 62 D3
St. Thomas I., *Virgin Is.* 75 D12
St-Tite, *Canada* 62 C5
St.-Tropez, *France* 18 E7
St. Troud = Sint Truiden, *Belgium* 15 D5
St. Vincent, G., *Australia* 55 F2
St. Vincent & the Grenadines ■, *W. Indies* 74 Q20
St. Vincent Passage, *W. Indies* 74 P21
St-Vith, *Belgium* 15 D6
Ste-Agathe-des-Monts, *Canada* 62 C5
Ste-Anne de Beaupré, *Canada* 63 C5
Ste-Anne-des-Monts, *Canada* 63 C6
Ste. Genevieve, *U.S.A.* 70 G9
Ste-Marguerite →, *Canada* 63 B6
Ste.-Marie, *Martinique* 74 N20
Ste-Marie de la Madeleine, *Canada* 63 C5
Ste.-Rose, *Guadeloupe* 74 L20
Ste. Rose du Lac, *Canada* 65 C9
Saintes, *France* 18 D3
Saintes, I. des, *Guadeloupe* 74 M20
Saintonge, *France* 18 D3
Saipan, *Pac. Oc.* 56 F6
Sairang, *India* 37 H18
Sairecábur, Cerro, *Bolivia* 80 A3
Saitama □, *Japan* 29 F9
Sajama, *Bolivia* 78 G5
Sajó, *Hungary* 17 D11
Sak →, *S. Africa* 48 E3
Sakai, *Japan* 29 G7
Sakaide, *Japan* 29 G6
Sakaiminato, *Japan* 29 G6
Sakākah, *Si. Arabia* 38 D4
Sakakawea, L., *U.S.A.* 70 B3
Sakami, L., *Canada* 62 B4
Sakarya = Adapazarı, *Turkey* 23 F5
Sakarya →, *Turkey* 23 F5
Sakashima-Guntō, *Japan* 29 M2
Sakata, *Japan* 28 E9
Sakeny →, *Madag.* 49 C8
Sakha □, *Russia* 25 C13
Sakhalin, *Russia* 25 D15
Sakhalinskiy Zaliv, *Russia* 25 D15
Šakiai, *Lithuania* 9 J20
Sakon Nakhon, *Thailand* 34 D8
Sakrivier, *S. Africa* 48 E3
Sakuma, *Japan* 29 G8
Sakurai, *Japan* 29 G7
Sala, *Sweden* 9 G17
Sala Consilina, *Italy* 20 D6
Sala-y-Gómez, *Pac. Oc.* 57 K17
Salaberry-de-Valleyfield, *Canada* 62 C5
Saladillo, *Argentina* 80 D5
Salado →, *Buenos Aires, Argentina* 80 D5
Salado →, *La Pampa, Argentina* 80 D3
Salado →, *Santa Fe, Argentina* 80 C4
Salaga, *Ghana* 44 G4
Sālah, *Syria* 41 C5
Şalālah, *Oman* 40 D5
Salamanca, *Chile* 80 C2
Salamanca, *Spain* 19 B3
Salamanca, *U.S.A.* 68 D6
Salāmatābād, *Iran* 38 C5
Salamís, *Greece* 21 F10
Salar de Atacama, *Chile* 80 A3
Salar de Uyuni, *Bolivia* 78 H5
Salatiga, *Indonesia* 33 G14
Salavat, *Russia* 22 D10
Salaverry, *Peru* 78 E3
Salawati, *Indonesia* 33 E8
Salayar, *Indonesia* 33 F6
Salcombe, *U.K.* 11 G4
Saldanha, *S. Africa* 48 E2
Saldanha B., *S. Africa* 48 E2
Saldus, *Latvia* 9 H20
Sale, *Australia* 55 F4
Salé, *Morocco* 44 B3
Sale, *U.K.* 10 D5
Salekhard, *Russia* 22 A12
Salem, *India* 36 P11
Salem, *Ind., U.S.A.* 68 F2
Salem, *Mass., U.S.A.* 68 D10
Salem, *Mo., U.S.A.* 71 G9
Salem, *N.J., U.S.A.* 68 F8
Salem, *Ohio, U.S.A.* 68 E5
Salem, *Oreg., U.S.A.* 72 D2
Salem, *S. Dak., U.S.A.* 70 D6
Salem, *Va., U.S.A.* 68 G5
Salerno, *Italy* 20 D6
Salford, *U.K.* 10 D5
Salgótarján, *Hungary* 17 D10
Salida, *U.S.A.* 66 C5
Salihli, *Turkey* 21 E13
Salihorsk, *Belarus* 17 B14
Salima, *Malawi* 47 G6
Salina, *Italy* 20 E6
Salina, *U.S.A.* 70 F6
Salina Cruz, *Mexico* 74 D5
Salinas, *Brazil* 79 G10
Salinas, *Ecuador* 78 D2
Salinas, *U.S.A.* 73 H3
Salinas →, *U.S.A.* 73 H3
Salinas Ambargasta, *Argentina* 80 B4
Salinas Grandes, *Argentina* 80 B4
Saline →, *Ark., U.S.A.* 71 J8
Saline →, *Kans., U.S.A.* 70 F6
Salinópolis, *Brazil* 79 D9
Salisbury = Harare, *Zimbabwe* 47 H6
Salisbury, *Australia* 55 E2
Salisbury, *U.K.* 11 F6
Salisbury, *Md., U.S.A.* 68 F8
Salisbury, *N.C., U.S.A.* 69 H5
Salisbury Plain, *U.K.* 11 F6
Şalkhad, *Syria* 41 C5
Salla, *Finland* 8 C23
Sallisaw, *U.S.A.* 71 H7
Salluit, *Canada* 61 B12
Salmās, *Iran* 38 B5
Salmo, *Canada* 64 D5
Salmon, *U.S.A.* 72 D7
Salmon →, *Canada* 64 C4
Salmon →, *U.S.A.* 72 D5
Salmon Arm, *Canada* 64 C5
Salmon Falls, *U.S.A.* 72 E6
Salmon Gums, *Australia* 53 F3
Salmon Res., *Canada* 63 C8
Salmon River Mts., *U.S.A.* 72 D6
Salo, *Finland* 9 F20
Salome, *U.S.A.* 73 K7
Salon-de-Provence, *France* 18 E6
Salonica = Thessaloníki, *Greece* 21 D10
Salonta, *Romania* 17 E11
Salpausselkä, *Finland* 9 F22
Salsk, *Russia* 23 E7
Salso →, *Italy* 20 F5
Salt →, *Canada* 64 B6
Salt →, *U.S.A.* 73 K7
Salt Creek, *Australia* 55 F2
Salt Fork Arkansas →, *U.S.A.* 71 G6
Salt Lake City, *U.S.A.* 72 F8
Salta, *Argentina* 80 A3
Saltcoats, *U.K.* 12 F4
Saltee Is., *Ireland* 13 D5
Saltfjellet, *Norway* 8 C16
Saltfjorden, *Norway* 8 C16
Saltillo, *Mexico* 74 B4
Salto, *Uruguay* 80 C5
Salto →, *Italy* 20 C5
Salton Sea, *U.S.A.* 73 K6
Saltpond, *Ghana* 44 G4
Saltville, *U.S.A.* 68 G5
Saluda →, *U.S.A.* 69 H5
Salûm, *Egypt* 45 B10
Salûm, Khâlig el, *Egypt* 45 B10
Salur, *India* 37 K13
Salvador, *Brazil* 79 F11
Salvador, *Canada* 65 C7
Salvador, L., *U.S.A.* 71 L9
Salween →, *Burma* 37 L20
Salyan, *Azerbaijan* 23 G8
Salyersville, *U.S.A.* 68 G4
Salzach →, *Austria* 16 D7
Salzburg, *Austria* 16 E7
Salzgitter, *Germany* 16 B6
Salzwedel, *Germany* 16 B6
Sam Neua, *Laos* 34 B8
Sam Ngao, *Thailand* 34 D5
Sam Rayburn Reservoir, *U.S.A.* 71 K7
Sama, *Russia* 24 C7
Sama de Langreo, *Spain* 19 A3
Samagaltay, *Russia* 25 D10
Samales Group, *Phil.* 33 C6
Samani, *Japan* 28 C11
Samar, *Phil.* 33 B7
Samara, *Russia* 22 D9
Samaria = Shōmrōn, *West Bank* 41 C4
Samarinda, *Indonesia* 32 E5
Samarkand = Samarqand, *Uzbekistan* 24 F7
Samarqand, *Uzbekistan* 24 F7
Sāmarrā, *Iraq* 38 C4
Sambalpur, *India* 37 J14
Sambar, Tanjung, *Indonesia* 32 E4
Sambas, *Indonesia* 32 D3
Sambava, *Madag.* 49 A9
Sambhal, *India* 36 E11
Sambhar, *India* 36 F9
Sambiase, *Italy* 20 E7
Sambir, *Ukraine* 17 D12
Sambor, *Cambodia* 34 F9
Sambre →, *Europe* 15 D4
Same, *Tanzania* 46 E7
Samnah, *Si. Arabia* 38 E3
Samokov, *Bulgaria* 21 C10
Sámos, *Greece* 21 F12
Samothráki, *Évros, Greece* 21 D11
Samothráki, *Kérkira, Greece* 21 E8
Sampacho, *Argentina* 80 C4
Sampang, *Indonesia* 33 G15
Sampit, *Indonesia* 32 E4
Sampit, Teluk, *Indonesia* 32 E4
Samsø, *Denmark* 9 J14
Samsun, *Turkey* 23 F6
Samui, Ko, *Thailand* 34 H6
Samut Prakan, *Thailand* 34 F6
Samut Sakhon, *Thailand* 34 F6
Samut Songkhram →, *Thailand* 34 F6
San, *Mali* 44 F4
San →, *Poland* 17 C11
San Agustin, C., *Phil.* 33 C7
San Ambrosio, *Pac. Oc.* 57 K20
San Andreas, *U.S.A.* 72 G3
San Andrés, I. de, *Caribbean* 75 E8
San Andres Mts., *U.S.A.* 73 K10
San Andrés Tuxtla, *Mexico* 74 D5
San Angelo, *U.S.A.* 71 K4
San Antonio, *Chile* 80 C2
San Antonio, *Spain* 19 C6
San Antonio, *N. Mex., U.S.A.* 73 K10
San Antonio, *Tex., U.S.A.* 71 L5
San Antonio →, *U.S.A.* 71 L6
San Antonio, C., *Argentina* 80 D5
San Antonio, C., *Cuba* 74 C8
San Antonio Oeste, *Argentina* 80 E4
San Augustine, *U.S.A.* 71 K7
San Benedetto del Tronto, *Italy* 20 C5
San Benito, *U.S.A.* 71 M6
San Bernardino, *U.S.A.* 73 J5
San Bernardino Str., *Phil.* 33 B6
San Bernardo, *Chile* 80 C2
San Bernardo, I. de, *Colombia* 78 B3
San Blas, C., *U.S.A.* 69 L3
San Borja, *Bolivia* 78 F5
San Carlos, *Argentina* 80 C3
San Carlos, *Chile* 80 D2
San Carlos, *Phil.* 33 B6
San Carlos, *U.S.A.* 73 K8
San Carlos, *Amazonas, Venezuela* 78 C5
San Carlos, *Cojedes, Venezuela* 78 B5
San Carlos de Bariloche, *Argentina* 80 E2
San Carlos del Zulia, *Venezuela* 78 B4
San Carlos L., *U.S.A.* 73 K8
San Clemente, *U.S.A.* 73 K5
San Clemente I., *U.S.A.* 73 K4
San Cristóbal, *Argentina* 80 C4
San Cristóbal, *Mexico* 74 D6
San Cristóbal, *Venezuela* 78 B4
San Diego, *Calif., U.S.A.* 73 K5
San Diego, *Tex., U.S.A.* 71 M5
San Diego, C., *Argentina* 80 G3
San Felipe, *Chile* 80 C2
San Felipe, *Venezuela* 78 A5
San Felíu de Guíxols, *Spain* 19 B7
San Félix, *Pac. Oc.* 57 K20
San Fernando, *Chile* 80 C2
San Fernando, *La Union, Phil.* 33 A6
San Fernando, *Pampanga, Phil.* 33 A6
San Fernando, *Spain* 19 D2
San Fernando, *Trin. & Tob.* 74 S20
San Fernando, *U.S.A.* 73 J4
San Fernando de Apure, *Venezuela* 78 B5
San Fernando de Atabapo, *Venezuela* 78 C5
San Francisco, *Argentina* 80 C4
San Francisco, *U.S.A.* 73 H2
San Francisco →, *U.S.A.* 73 K9
San Francisco de Macorîs, *Dom. Rep.* 75 D10
San Francisco del Monte de Oro, *Argentina* 80 C3
San Gil, *Colombia* 78 B4
San Gottardo, P. del, *Switz.* 16 E5
San Ignacio, *Bolivia* 78 G6
San Ignacio, *Paraguay* 80 B5
San Ildefonso, C., *Phil.* 33 A6
San Javier, *Argentina* 80 C5
San Javier, *Bolivia* 78 G6
San Joaquin →, *U.S.A.* 73 G3
San Jorge, B. de, *Mexico* 74 A2
San Jorge, G., *Argentina* 80 F3
San Jorge, G. de, *Spain* 19 B6
San José, *Bolivia* 78 G6
San José, *Costa Rica* 75 F8
San José, *Guatemala* 74 E6
San Jose, *Phil.* 33 A6
San Jose, *U.S.A.* 73 H3
San Jose →, *U.S.A.* 73 J10
San Jose de Buenovista, *Phil.* 33 B6
San José de Jáchal, *Argentina* 80 C3
San José de Mayo, *Uruguay* 80 C5
San José de Ocune, *Colombia* 78 C4
San José del Guaviare, *Colombia* 78 C4
San Juan, *Argentina* 80 C3
San Juan, *Phil.* 33 C7
San Juan, *Puerto Rico* 75 D11
San Juan →, *Nic.* 75 E8
San Juan →, *U.S.A.* 73 H8
San Juan, C., *Eq. Guin.* 46 D1
San Juan Bautista, *U.S.A.* 73 H3
San Juan Capistrano, *U.S.A.* 73 K5
San Juan de los Morros, *Venezuela* 78 B5
San Juan Mts., *U.S.A.* 73 H10
San Julián, *Argentina* 80 F3
San Justo, *Argentina* 80 C4
San Leandro, *U.S.A.* 73 H2
San Lorenzo, *Ecuador* 78 C3
San Lorenzo, I., *Peru* 78 F3
San Lorenzo, Mt., *Argentina* 80 F2
San Lucas, *Bolivia* 78 H5
San Lucas, C., *Mexico* 74 C2
San Luis, *Argentina* 80 C3
San Luis, *U.S.A.* 73 H11
San Luis Obispo, *U.S.A.* 73 J3
San Luis Potosí, *Mexico* 74 C4
San Marcos, *U.S.A.* 71 L6
San Marino, *San Marino* 16 G7
San Marino ■, *Europe* 20 C5
San Martín, L., *Argentina* 80 F2
San Mateo, *U.S.A.* 73 H2
San Matías, *Bolivia* 78 G7
San Matías, G., *Argentina* 80 E4
San Miguel, *El Salv.* 74 E7
San Miguel, *U.S.A.* 73 J3
San Miguel →, *Bolivia* 78 F6
San Miguel de Tucumán, *Argentina* 80 B3
San Narciso, *Phil.* 33 A6
San Nicolás de los Arroyas, *Argentina* 80 C4
San Nicolas I., *U.S.A.* 73 K4
San-Pédro, *Ivory C.* 44 H3
San Pedro →, *U.S.A.* 73 K8
San Pedro de las Colonias, *Mexico* 74 B4
San Pedro de Lloc, *Peru* 78 E3
San Pedro de Macorís, *Dom. Rep.* 75 D11
San Pedro del Paraná, *Paraguay* 80 B5
San Pedro Sula, *Honduras* 74 D7
San Pieto, *Italy* 20 E3
San Rafael, *Argentina* 80 C3
San Rafael, *Calif., U.S.A.* 72 H2
San Rafael, *N. Mex., U.S.A.* 73 J10
San Ramón de la Nueva Orán, *Argentina* 80 A4
San Remo, *Italy* 20 C2
San Roque, *Argentina* 80 B5
San Roque, *Spain* 19 D3
San Rosendo, *Chile* 80 D2
San Saba, *U.S.A.* 71 K5
San Salvador, *Bahamas* 75 C10
San Salvador, *El Salv.* 74 E7
San Salvador de Jujuy, *Argentina* 80 A4
San Sebastián, *Argentina* 80 G3
San Sebastián, *Spain* 19 A5
San Severo, *Italy* 20 D6
San Simon, *U.S.A.* 73 K9
San Valentin, Mte., *Chile* 80 F2
San Vicente de la Barquera, *Spain* 19 A3
San Ygnacio, *U.S.A.* 71 M5
Sana', *Yemen* 40 D3
Sana →, *Bos.-H.* 16 F9
Sanaga →, *Cameroon* 44 H6
Sanana, *Indonesia* 33 E7
Sanandaj, *Iran* 38 C5
Sanco Pt., *Phil.* 33 C7
Sancti-Spíritus, *Cuba* 75 C9
Sancy, Puy de, *France* 18 D5
Sand →, *S. Africa* 49 C5
Sand Springs, *U.S.A.* 71 G6
Sanda, *Japan* 29 G7
Sandakan, *Malaysia* 32 C5
Sandan = Sambor, *Cambodia* 34 F9
Sandanski, *Bulgaria* 21 D10
Sanday, *U.K.* 12 B6
Sandefjord, *Norway* 9 G14
Sanders, *U.S.A.* 73 J9
Sanderson, *U.S.A.* 71 K3
Sandfly L., *Canada* 65 B7
Sandgate, *Australia* 55 D5
Sandía, *Peru* 78 F5
Sandnes, *Norway* 9 G11
Sandness, *U.K.* 12 A7
Sandnessjøen, *Norway* 8 C15
Sandoa, *Zaïre* 46 F4
Sandomierz, *Poland* 17 C11
Sandover →, *Australia* 54 C2
Sandoway, *Burma* 37 K19
Sandoy, *Færoe Is.* 8 F9
Sandpoint, *U.S.A.* 72 B5
Sandringham, *U.K.* 10 E8
Sandspit, *Canada* 64 C2
Sandstone, *Australia* 53 E2
Sandusky, *Mich., U.S.A.* 62 D3
Sandusky, *Ohio, U.S.A.* 68 E4
Sandviken, *Sweden* 9 F17
Sandwich, C., *Australia* 54 B4
Sandwich B., *Canada* 63 B8
Sandwich B., *Namibia* 48 C1
Sandwip Chan., *Bangla.* 37 H17
Sandy Bight, *Australia* 53 F3
Sandy C., *Queens., Australia* 54 C5
Sandy C., *Tas., Australia* 54 G3
Sandy Cr. →, *U.S.A.* 72 F9
Sandy L., *Canada* 62 B1
Sandy Lake, *Canada* 62 B1
Sandy Narrows, *Canada* 65 B8
Sanford, *Fla., U.S.A.* 69 L5
Sanford, *N.C., U.S.A.* 69 H6
Sanford →, *Australia* 53 E2
Sanford, Mt., *U.S.A.* 60 B5
Sanga →, *Congo* 46 E3
Sanga-Tolon, *Russia* 25 C15
Sangamner, *India* 36 K9
Sangar, *Russia* 25 C13
Sangasangadalam, *Indonesia* 32 E5
Sangeang, *Indonesia* 33 F5
Sanger, *U.S.A.* 73 H4
Sangerhausen, *Germany* 16 C6
Sanggau, *Indonesia* 32 D4
Sangihe, Kepulauan, *Indonesia* 33 D7
Sangihe, P., *Indonesia* 33 D7
Sangkapura, *Indonesia* 32 F4
Sangli, *India* 36 L9
Sangmélina, *Cameroon* 46 D2
Sangre de Cristo Mts., *U.S.A.* 71 G2
Sangudo, *Canada* 64 C6
Sanjo, *Japan* 28 F9
Sankt Gallen, *Switz.* 16 E5
Sankt Moritz, *Switz.* 16 E5
Sankt-Peterburg, *Russia* 22 C5
Sankt Pölten, *Austria* 16 D8
Sankuru →, *Zaïre* 46 E4
Sanliurfa, *Turkey* 23 G6
Sanlúcar de Barrameda, *Spain* 19 D2
Sanmenxia, *China* 31 C6

Shafter

Sanming, *China* 31 D6
Sannaspos, *S. Africa* 48 D4
Sannicandro Gargánico, *Italy* 20 D6
Sannieshof, *S. Africa* 48 D4
Sannīn, J., *Lebanon* 41 B4
Sanok, *Poland* 17 D12
Sanquhar, *U.K.* 12 F5
Santa Ana, *Bolivia* 78 F5
Santa Ana, *Ecuador* 78 D2
Santa Ana, *El Salv.* 74 E7
Santa Ana, *U.S.A.* 73 K5
Santa Barbara, *U.S.A.* 73 J4
Santa Catalina, Gulf of, *U.S.A.* 73 K5
Santa Catalina I., *U.S.A.* 73 K4
Santa Catarina □, *Brazil* 80 B7
Santa Clara, *Cuba* 75 C9
Santa Clara, *Calif., U.S.A.* 73 H3
Santa Clara, *Utah, U.S.A.* 73 H7
Santa Clotilde, *Peru* 78 D4
Santa Coloma de Gramanet, *Spain* 19 B7
Santa Cruz, *Argentina* 80 G3
Santa Cruz, *Bolivia* 78 G6
Santa Cruz, *Phil.* 33 B6
Santa Cruz, *U.S.A.* 73 H2
Santa Cruz →, *Argentina* 80 G3
Santa Cruz de Tenerife, *Canary Is.* 44 C1
Santa Cruz do Sul, *Brazil* 80 B6
Santa Cruz I., *Solomon Is.* 56 J8
Santa Cruz I., *U.S.A.* 73 K4
Santa Elena, *Ecuador* 78 D2
Santa Eugenia, Pta., *Mexico* 74 B1
Santa Fe, *Argentina* 80 C4
Santa Fe, *U.S.A.* 73 J11
Santa Filomena, *Brazil* 79 E9
Santa Inés, I., *Chile* 80 G2
Santa Isabel = Rey Malabo, *Eq. Guin.* 44 H6
Santa Isabel, *Argentina* 80 D3
Santa Isabel, *Brazil* 79 F8
Santa Lucia Range, *U.S.A.* 73 J3
Santa Maria, *Brazil* 80 B6
Santa Maria, *U.S.A.* 73 J3
Santa María →, *Mexico* 74 A3
Santa Maria da Vitória, *Brazil* 79 F10
Santa Maria di Leuca, C., *Italy* 21 E8
Santa Marta, *Colombia* 78 A4
Santa Marta, Sierra Nevada de, *Colombia* 78 A4
Santa Maura = Levkás, *Greece* 21 E9
Santa Monica, *U.S.A.* 73 K4
Santa Rita, *U.S.A.* 73 K10
Santa Rosa, *La Pampa, Argentina* 80 D4
Santa Rosa, *San Luis, Argentina* 80 C3
Santa Rosa, *Bolivia* 78 F5
Santa Rosa, *Brazil* 80 B6
Santa Rosa, *Calif., U.S.A.* 72 G2
Santa Rosa, *N. Mex., U.S.A.* 71 H2
Santa Rosa de Copán, *Honduras* 74 E7
Santa Rosa I., *Calif., U.S.A.* 73 K3
Santa Rosa I., *Fla., U.S.A.* 69 K2
Santa Rosa Range, *U.S.A.* 72 F5
Santa Vitória do Palmar, *Brazil* 80 C6
Santai, *China* 30 C5
Santana, Coxilha de, *Brazil* 80 C5
Santana do Livramento, *Brazil* 80 C5
Santander, *Spain* 19 A4
Sant'Antíoco, *Italy* 20 E3
Santaquin, *U.S.A.* 72 G8
Santarém, *Brazil* 79 D8
Santarém, *Portugal* 19 C1
Santiago, *Brazil* 80 B6
Santiago, *Chile* 80 C2
Santiago →, *Peru* 78 D3
Santiago de Compostela, *Spain* 19 A1
Santiago de Cuba, *Cuba* 75 D9
Santiago de los Cabelleros, *Dom. Rep.* 75 D10
Santiago del Estero, *Argentina* 80 B4
Santo Amaro, *Brazil* 79 F11
Santo Ângelo, *Brazil* 80 B6
Santo Antonio, *Brazil* 79 G7
Santo Corazón, *Bolivia* 78 G7
Santo Domingo, *Dom. Rep.* 75 D11
Santo Tomás, *Peru* 78 F4
Santo Tomé, *Argentina* 80 B5
Santo Tomé de Guayana = Ciudad Guayana, *Venezuela* 78 B6
Santoña, *Spain* 19 A4
Santorini = Thíra, *Greece* 21 F11
Santos, *Brazil* 80 A7
Santos Dumont, *Brazil* 80 A8
Sanza Pombo, *Angola* 46 F3
São Anastácio, *Brazil* 80 A6
São Bernado de Campo, *Brazil* 79 H9
São Borja, *Brazil* 80 B5
São Carlos, *Brazil* 80 A7
São Cristóvão, *Brazil* 79 F11
São Domingos, *Brazil* 79 F9
São Francisco, *Brazil* 79 G10
São Francisco →, *Brazil* 79 F11
São Francisco do Sul, *Brazil* 80 B7
São Gabriel, *Brazil* 80 C6
São João da Madeira, *Portugal* 19 B1
São João del Rei, *Brazil* 79 H10
São João do Araguaia, *Brazil* 79 E9
São João do Piauí, *Brazil* 79 E10
São José do Rio Prêto, *Brazil* 80 A7
São Leopoldo, *Brazil* 80 B6
São Lourenço, *Brazil* 79 H9
São Lourenço →, *Brazil* 79 G7
São Luís, *Brazil* 79 D10
São Marcos →, *Brazil* 79 G9
São Marcos, B. de, *Brazil* 79 D10
São Mateus, *Brazil* 79 G11
São Paulo, *Brazil* 80 A7
São Paulo □, *Brazil* 80 A7
São Paulo, I., *Atl. Oc.* 2 D8
São Roque, C. de, *Brazil* 79 E11
São Sebastião, I. de, *Brazil* 80 A7
São Tomé, *Atl. Oc.* 42 F4
São Tomé & Principe ■, *Africa* 43 F4
São Vicente, C. de, *Portugal* 19 D1
Saône →, *France* 18 D6
Saonek, *Indonesia* 33 E8
Saparua, *Indonesia* 33 E7
Sapele, *Nigeria* 44 G6
Sapelo I., *U.S.A.* 69 K5
Saposoa, *Peru* 78 E3
Sapporo, *Japan* 28 C10
Sapudi, *Indonesia* 33 G16
Sapulpa, *U.S.A.* 71 G7
Saqqez, *Iran* 38 B5
Sar Dasht, *Iran* 39 C6
Sar Gachīneh, *Iran* 39 D6
Sar Planina, *Macedonia* 21 C9
Sarāb, *Iran* 38 B5
Sarabadi, *Iraq* 38 C5
Sarada →, *India* 37 F12
Saragossa = Zaragoza, *Spain* 19 B5
Saraguro, *Ecuador* 78 D3
Sarajevo, *Bos.-H.* 21 C8
Saran, G., *Indonesia* 32 E4
Saranac Lake, *U.S.A.* 68 C8
Sarandí del Yi, *Uruguay* 80 C5
Sarangani B., *Phil.* 33 C7
Sarangani Is., *Phil.* 33 C7
Sarangarh, *India* 37 J13
Saransk, *Russia* 22 D8
Sarapul, *Russia* 22 C9
Sarasota, *U.S.A.* 69 M4
Saratoga, *U.S.A.* 72 F10
Saratoga Springs, *U.S.A.* 68 D9
Saratov, *Russia* 22 D8
Saravane, *Laos* 34 E9
Sarawak □, *Malaysia* 32 D4
Saray, *Turkey* 21 D12
Sarayköy, *Turkey* 21 F13
Sarbāz, *Iran* 39 E9
Sarbīsheh, *Iran* 39 C8
Sarda = Sarada →, *India* 37 F12
Sardalas, *Libya* 44 C7
Sardarshahr, *India* 36 E9
Sardegna □, *Italy* 20 D3
Sardinia = Sardegna □, *Italy* 20 D3
Sardis, *Turkey* 21 E12
Sārdūīyeh = Dar Mazār, *Iran* 39 D8
Sargent, *U.S.A.* 70 E5
Sargodha, *Pakistan* 36 C8
Sarh, *Chad* 45 G8
Sārī, *Iran* 39 B7
Sarıgöl, *Turkey* 21 E13
Sarikei, *Malaysia* 32 D4
Sarina, *Australia* 54 C4
Sarita, *U.S.A.* 71 M6
Sark, *U.K.* 11 H5
Şarköy, *Turkey* 21 D12
Sarlat-la-Canéda, *France* 18 D4
Sarles, *U.S.A.* 70 A5
Sarmi, *Indonesia* 33 E9
Sarmiento, *Argentina* 80 F3
Särna, *Sweden* 9 F15
Sarnia, *Canada* 62 D3
Sarny, *Ukraine* 22 D4
Sarolangun, *Indonesia* 32 E2
Saronikós Kólpos, *Greece* 21 F10
Saros Körfezi, *Turkey* 21 D12
Sarpsborg, *Norway* 9 G14
Sarre = Saar →, *Europe* 16 D4
Sarreguemines, *France* 18 B7
Sarro, *Mali* 44 F3
Sarthe →, *France* 18 C3
Sartynya, *Russia* 24 C7
Sarvestān, *Iran* 39 D7
Sary-Tash, *Kyrgyzstan* 24 F8
Saryshagan, *Kazakhstan* 24 E8
Sasabeneh, *Ethiopia* 40 F3
Sasaram, *India* 37 G14
Sasebo, *Japan* 29 H4
Saser, *India* 36 B10
Saskatchewan □, *Canada* 65 C7
Saskatchewan →, *Canada* 65 C8
Saskatoon, *Canada* 65 C7
Saskylakh, *Russia* 25 B12
Sasolburg, *S. Africa* 49 D4
Sasovo, *Russia* 22 D7
Sassandra, *Ivory C.* 44 H3
Sassandra →, *Ivory C.* 44 H3
Sássari, *Italy* 20 D3
Sassnitz, *Germany* 16 A7
Sassuolo, *Italy* 20 B4
Sasyk, Ozero, *Ukraine* 17 F15
Sata-Misaki, *Japan* 29 J5
Satadougou, *Mali* 44 F2
Satakunta, *Finland* 9 F20
Satanta, *U.S.A.* 71 G4
Satara, *India* 36 L8
Satilla →, *U.S.A.* 69 K5
Satka, *Russia* 22 C10
Satmala Hills, *India* 36 J9
Satna, *India* 37 G12
Sátoraljaújhely, *Hungary* 17 D11
Satpura Ra., *India* 36 J10
Satsuna-Shotō, *Japan* 29 K5
Satu Mare, *Romania* 17 E12
Satui, *Indonesia* 32 E5
Satun, *Thailand* 34 N13
Saturnina →, *Brazil* 78 F7
Sauda, *Norway* 9 G12
Sauðarkrókur, *Iceland* 8 D4
Saudi Arabia ■, *Asia* 40 B3
Sauer →, *Germany* 15 E6
Sauerland, *Germany* 16 C4
Saugerties, *U.S.A.* 68 D9
Sauk Centre, *U.S.A.* 70 C7
Sauk Rapids, *U.S.A.* 70 C7
Sault Ste. Marie, *Canada* 62 C3
Sault Ste. Marie, *U.S.A.* 68 B3
Saumlaki, *Indonesia* 33 F8
Saumur, *France* 18 C3
Saunders C., *N.Z.* 51 L3
Saunders I., *Antarctica* 5 B1
Saunders Point, *Australia* 53 E4
Sauri, *Nigeria* 44 F6
Saurimo, *Angola* 46 F4
Sava →, *Serbia, Yug.* 21 B9
Savage, *U.S.A.* 70 B2
Savage I. = Niue, *Cook Is.* 57 J11
Savai'i, *W. Samoa* 51 A12
Savalou, *Benin* 44 G5
Savanna, *U.S.A.* 70 D9
Savanna la Mar, *Jamaica* 74 J15
Savannah, *Ga., U.S.A.* 69 J5
Savannah, *Mo., U.S.A.* 70 F7
Savannah, *Tenn., U.S.A.* 69 H1
Savannah →, *U.S.A.* 69 J5
Savannakhet, *Laos* 34 D8
Savant L., *Canada* 62 B1
Savant Lake, *Canada* 62 B1
Savanur, *India* 36 M9
Savé, *Benin* 44 G5
Save →, *Mozam.* 49 C5
Sāveh, *Iran* 39 C6
Savelugu, *Ghana* 44 G4
Savo, *Finland* 8 E22
Savoie □, *France* 18 D7
Savona, *Italy* 20 B3
Savonlinna, *Finland* 22 B4
Sawahlunto, *Indonesia* 32 E2
Sawai, *Indonesia* 33 E7
Sawai Madhopur, *India* 36 F10
Sawara, *Japan* 29 G10
Sawatch Mts., *U.S.A.* 73 G10
Sawel Mt., *U.K.* 13 B4
Sawmills, *Zimbabwe* 47 H5
Sawu, *Indonesia* 33 F6
Sawu Sea, *Indonesia* 33 F6
Saxby →, *Australia* 54 B3
Saxony, Lower = Niedersachsen □, *Germany* 16 B5
Say, *Niger* 44 F5
Sayabec, *Canada* 63 C6
Sayán, *Peru* 78 F3
Sayan, Vostochnyy, *Russia* 25 D10
Sayan, Zapadnyy, *Russia* 25 D10
Saydā, *Lebanon* 41 B4
Sayḥūt, *Yemen* 40 D5
Saynshand, *Mongolia* 31 B6
Sayre, *Okla., U.S.A.* 71 H5
Sayre, *Pa., U.S.A.* 68 E7
Sazanit, *Albania* 21 D8
Sázava →, *Czech.* 16 D8
Sazin, *Pakistan* 36 B8
Scafell Pike, *U.K.* 10 C4
Scalpay, *U.K.* 12 D2
Scandia, *Canada* 64 C6
Scandicci, *Italy* 20 C4
Scandinavia, *Europe* 6 C8
Scapa Flow, *U.K.* 12 C5
Scarborough, *Trin. & Tob.* 74 R21
Scarborough, *U.K.* 10 C7
Scebeli, Wabi →, *Somali Rep.* 40 G3
Scenic, *U.S.A.* 70 D3
Schaffhausen, *Switz.* 16 E5
Schagen, *Neths.* 15 B4
Schefferville, *Canada* 63 B6
Schelde →, *Belgium* 15 C4
Schell Creek Ra., *U.S.A.* 72 G6
Schenectady, *U.S.A.* 68 D9
Scheveningen, *Neths.* 15 B4
Schiedam, *Neths.* 15 C4
Schiermonnikoog, *Neths.* 15 A6
Schio, *Italy* 20 B4
Schleswig, *Germany* 16 A5
Schleswig-Holstein □, *Germany* 16 A5
Schofield, *U.S.A.* 70 C10
Schouten I., *Australia* 54 G4
Schouten Is. = Supiori, *Indonesia* 33 E9
Schouwen, *Neths.* 15 C3
Schreiber, *Canada* 62 C2
Schuler, *Canada* 65 C6
Schumacher, *Canada* 62 C3
Schurz, *U.S.A.* 72 G4
Schuyler, *U.S.A.* 70 E6
Schwäbische Alb, *Germany* 16 D5
Schwaner, Pegunungan, *Indonesia* 32 E4
Schwarzwald, *Germany* 16 D5
Schwedt, *Germany* 16 B8
Schweinfurt, *Germany* 16 C6
Schweizer-Reneke, *S. Africa* 48 D4
Schwenningen = Villingen-Schwenningen, *Germany* 16 D5
Schwerin, *Germany* 16 B6
Schwyz, *Switz.* 16 E5
Sciacca, *Italy* 20 F5
Scilla, *Italy* 20 E6
Scilly, Isles of, *U.K.* 11 H1
Scioto →, *U.S.A.* 68 F4
Scobey, *U.S.A.* 70 A2
Scone, *Australia* 55 E5
Scoresbysund, *Greenland* 4 B6
Scotia, *U.S.A.* 72 F1
Scotia Sea, *Antarctica* 5 B18
Scotland, *U.S.A.* 70 D6
Scotland □, *U.K.* 12 E5
Scotland Neck, *U.S.A.* 69 G7
Scott, C., *Australia* 52 B4
Scott City, *U.S.A.* 70 F4
Scott Glacier, *Antarctica* 5 C8
Scott I., *Antarctica* 5 C11
Scott Inlet, *Canada* 61 A12
Scott Is., *Canada* 64 C3
Scott L., *Canada* 65 B7
Scott Reef, *Australia* 52 B3
Scottburgh, *S. Africa* 49 E5
Scottsbluff, *U.S.A.* 70 E3
Scottsboro, *U.S.A.* 69 H2
Scottsburg, *U.S.A.* 68 F3
Scottsdale, *Australia* 54 G4
Scottsville, *U.S.A.* 69 G2
Scottville, *U.S.A.* 68 D2
Scranton, *U.S.A.* 68 E8
Scunthorpe, *U.K.* 10 D7
Scusciuban, *Somali Rep.* 40 E5
Scutari = Üsküdar, *Turkey* 23 F4
Seabrook, L., *Australia* 53 F2
Seaford, *U.S.A.* 68 F8
Seaforth, *Canada* 62 D3
Seagraves, *U.S.A.* 71 J3
Seal →, *Canada* 65 B10
Seal Cove, *Canada* 63 C8
Seal L., *Canada* 63 B7
Sealy, *U.S.A.* 71 L6
Searchlight, *U.S.A.* 73 J6
Searcy, *U.S.A.* 71 H9
Searles L., *U.S.A.* 73 J5
Seaside, *U.S.A.* 72 D2
Seaspray, *Australia* 55 F4
Seattle, *U.S.A.* 72 C2
Seaview Ra., *Australia* 54 B4
Sebastopol = Sevastopol, *Ukraine* 23 F5
Sebastopol, *U.S.A.* 72 G2
Sebewaing, *U.S.A.* 68 D4
Sebha = Sabhah, *Libya* 45 C7
Sebring, *U.S.A.* 69 M5
Sebta = Ceuta, *N. Afr.* 19 E3
Sebuku, *Indonesia* 32 E5
Sebuku, Teluk, *Malaysia* 32 D5
Sechelt, *Canada* 64 D4
Sechura, Desierto de, *Peru* 78 E2
Secretary I., *N.Z.* 51 L1
Secunderabad, *India* 36 L11
Sedalia, *U.S.A.* 70 F8
Sedan, *Australia* 55 E2
Sedan, *France* 18 B6
Sedan, *U.S.A.* 71 G6
Seddon, *N.Z.* 51 J5
Seddonville, *N.Z.* 51 J4
Sedeh, *Fārs, Iran* 39 D7
Sedeh, *Khorāsān, Iran* 39 C8
Sederot, *Israel* 41 D3
Sedgewick, *Canada* 64 C6
Sedhiou, *Senegal* 44 F1
Sedley, *Canada* 65 C8
Sedova, Pik, *Russia* 24 B6
Sedro-Woolley, *U.S.A.* 72 B2
Seeheim, *Namibia* 48 D2
Seekoei →, *S. Africa* 48 E4
Seferihisar, *Turkey* 21 E12
Seg-ozero, *Russia* 22 B5
Segamat, *Malaysia* 34 S15
Segesta, *Italy* 20 F5
Seget, *Indonesia* 33 E8
Segezha, *Russia* 22 B5
Ségou, *Mali* 44 F3
Segovia = Coco →, *Cent. Amer.* 75 E8
Segovia, *Spain* 19 B3
Segre →, *Spain* 19 B6
Séguéla, *Ivory C.* 44 G3
Seguin, *U.S.A.* 71 L6
Segura →, *Spain* 19 C5
Seh Qal'eh, *Iran* 39 C8
Sehitwa, *Botswana* 48 C3
Sehore, *India* 36 H10
Seiland, *Norway* 8 A20
Seiling, *U.S.A.* 71 G5
Seinäjoki, *Finland* 9 E20
Seine →, *France* 18 B4
Seistan, *Iran* 39 D9
Sekayu, *Indonesia* 32 E2
Sekondi-Takoradi, *Ghana* 44 H4
Sekuma, *Botswana* 48 C3
Selah, *U.S.A.* 72 C3
Selama, *Malaysia* 34 P13
Selangor □, *Malaysia* 34 R14
Selaru, *Indonesia* 33 F8
Selby, *U.K.* 10 D6
Selby, *U.S.A.* 70 C4
Selçuk, *Turkey* 21 F12
Selden, *U.S.A.* 70 F4
Sele →, *Italy* 20 D6
Selemdzha →, *Russia* 25 D13
Selenga = Selenge Mörön →, *Asia* 30 A5
Selenge Mörön →, *Asia* 30 A5
Seletan, Tg., *Indonesia* 32 E4
Selfridge, *U.S.A.* 70 B4
Sélibabi, *Mauritania* 44 E2
Seligman, *U.S.A.* 73 J7
Selîma, El Wâhât el, *Sudan* 45 D10
Selinda Spillway, *Botswana* 48 B3
Selkirk, *Canada* 65 C9
Selkirk, *U.K.* 12 F6
Selkirk I., *Canada* 65 C9
Selkirk Mts., *Canada* 64 C5
Sells, *U.S.A.* 73 L8
Selma, *Ala., U.S.A.* 69 J2
Selma, *Calif., U.S.A.* 73 H4
Selma, *N.C., U.S.A.* 69 H6
Selmer, *U.S.A.* 69 H1
Selpele, *Indonesia* 33 E8
Selsey Bill, *U.K.* 11 G7
Selu, *Indonesia* 33 F8
Selva, *Argentina* 80 B4
Selvas, *Brazil* 78 E5
Selwyn, *Australia* 54 C3
Selwyn L., *Canada* 65 A8
Selwyn Ra., *Australia* 54 C3
Semani →, *Albania* 21 D8
Semarang, *Indonesia* 33 G14
Semau, *Indonesia* 33 F6
Semeru, *Indonesia* 33 H15
Semey, *Kazakhstan* 24 D9
Seminoe Reservoir, *U.S.A.* 72 E10
Seminole, *Okla., U.S.A.* 71 H6
Seminole, *Tex., U.S.A.* 71 J3
Semiozernoye, *Kazakhstan* 24 D7
Semipalatinsk = Semey, *Kazakhstan* 24 D9
Semirara Is., *Phil.* 33 B6
Semisopochnoi I., *U.S.A.* 60 C2
Semitau, *Indonesia* 32 D4
Semiyarka, *Kazakhstan* 24 D8
Semiyarskoye = Semiyarka, *Kazakhstan* 24 D8
Semmering P., *Austria* 16 E8
Semnān, *Iran* 39 C7
Semnān □, *Iran* 39 C7
Semois →, *Europe* 15 E4
Semporna, *Malaysia* 33 D5
Semuda, *Indonesia* 32 E4
Sen →, *Cambodia* 34 F8
Senā, *Iran* 39 D6
Sena Madureira, *Brazil* 78 E5
Senador Pompeu, *Brazil* 79 E11
Senai, *Malaysia* 34 T16
Senaja, *Malaysia* 32 C5
Senanga, *Zambia* 48 B3
Senatobia, *U.S.A.* 71 H10
Sendai, *Kagoshima, Japan* 29 J5
Sendai, *Miyagi, Japan* 28 E10
Sendai-Wan, *Japan* 28 E10
Seneca, *Oreg., U.S.A.* 72 D4
Seneca, *S.C., U.S.A.* 69 H4
Seneca Falls, *U.S.A.* 68 D7
Seneca L., *U.S.A.* 68 D7
Senegal ■, *W. Afr.* 44 F2
Senegal →, *W. Afr.* 44 E1
Senegambia, *Africa* 42 E2
Senekal, *S. Africa* 49 D4
Senge Khambab = Indus →, *Pakistan* 36 G5
Sengkang, *Indonesia* 33 E6
Senhor-do-Bonfim, *Brazil* 79 F10
Senigállia, *Italy* 20 C5
Senj, *Croatia* 16 F8
Senja, *Norway* 8 B17
Senlis, *France* 18 B5
Senmonorom, *Cambodia* 34 F9
Sennâr, *Sudan* 45 F11
Senneterre, *Canada* 62 C4
Sens, *France* 18 B5
Senta, *Serbia, Yug.* 21 B9
Sentani, *Indonesia* 33 E10
Sentinel, *U.S.A.* 73 K7
Sentolo, *Indonesia* 33 G14
Seo de Urgel, *Spain* 19 A6
Seoul = Sŏul, *S. Korea* 31 C7
Separation Point, *Canada* 63 B8
Sepīdān, *Iran* 39 D7
Sepone, *Laos* 34 D9
Sept-Îles, *Canada* 63 B6
Sequim, *U.S.A.* 72 B2
Sequoia National Park, *U.S.A.* 73 H4
Seraing, *Belgium* 15 D5
Seram, *Indonesia* 33 E7
Seram Laut, Kepulauan, *Indonesia* 33 E8
Seram Sea, *Indonesia* 33 E7
Serang, *Indonesia* 33 G12
Serasan, *Indonesia* 32 D3
Serbia □, *Yugoslavia* 21 C9
Serdobsk, *Russia* 22 D7
Seremban, *Malaysia* 34 S14
Serenje, *Zambia* 47 G6
Sereth = Siret →, *Romania* 17 F14
Sergino, *Russia* 24 C7
Sergipe □, *Brazil* 79 F11
Sergiyev Posad, *Russia* 22 C6
Seria, *Brunei* 32 D4
Serian, *Malaysia* 32 D4
Seribu, Kepulauan, *Indonesia* 32 F3
Sérifos, *Greece* 21 F11
Seringapatam Reef, *Australia* 52 B3
Sermata, *Indonesia* 33 F7
Serny Zavod, *Turkmenistan* 24 F6
Serov, *Russia* 22 C11
Serowe, *Botswana* 48 C4
Serpentine, *Australia* 53 F2
Serpentine Lakes, *Australia* 53 E4
Serpukhov, *Russia* 22 D6
Sérrai, *Greece* 21 D10
Serrezuela, *Argentina* 80 C3
Serrinha, *Brazil* 79 F11
Sertânia, *Brazil* 79 E11
Serua, *Indonesia* 33 F8
Serui, *Indonesia* 33 E9
Serule, *Botswana* 48 C4
Sesepe, *Indonesia* 33 E7
Sesfontein, *Namibia* 48 B1
Sesheke, *Zambia* 48 B3
Setana, *Japan* 28 C9
Sète, *France* 18 E5
Sete Lagôas, *Brazil* 79 G10
Sétif, *Algeria* 44 A6
Seto, *Japan* 29 G8
Setonaikai, *Japan* 29 G6
Settat, *Morocco* 44 B3
Setté-Cama, *Gabon* 46 E1
Setting L., *Canada* 65 B9
Settle, *U.K.* 10 C5
Settlement Pt., *Bahamas* 69 M6
Setúbal, *Portugal* 19 C1
Setúbal, B. de, *Portugal* 19 C1
Seulimeum, *Indonesia* 32 C1
Sevan, Ozero = Sevana Lich, *Armenia* 23 F8
Sevana Lich, *Armenia* 23 F8
Sevastopol, *Ukraine* 23 F5
Seven Emu, *Australia* 54 B2
Seven Sisters, *Canada* 64 C3
Severn →, *Canada* 62 A2
Severn →, *U.K.* 11 F5
Severn L., *Canada* 62 B1
Severnaya Zemlya, *Russia* 25 B10
Severnyye Uvaly, *Russia* 22 C8
Severo-Kurilsk, *Russia* 25 D16
Severo-Yeniseyskiy, *Russia* 25 C10
Severodvinsk, *Russia* 22 B6
Severomorsk, *Russia* 22 A5
Severouralsk, *Russia* 22 B10
Sevier, *U.S.A.* 73 G7
Sevier →, *U.S.A.* 73 G7
Sevier L., *U.S.A.* 72 G7
Sevilla, *Spain* 19 D2
Seville = Sevilla, *Spain* 19 D2
Sevlievo, *Bulgaria* 21 C11
Seward, *Alaska, U.S.A.* 60 B5
Seward, *Nebr., U.S.A.* 70 E6
Seward Pen., *U.S.A.* 60 B3
Sewer, *Indonesia* 33 F8
Sexsmith, *Canada* 64 B5
Seychelles ■, *Ind. Oc.* 27 K9
Seyðisfjörður, *Iceland* 8 D6
Seydvān, *Iran* 38 B5
Seymchan, *Russia* 25 C16
Seymour, *Australia* 55 F4
Seymour, *S. Africa* 49 E4
Seymour, *Ind., U.S.A.* 68 F3
Seymour, *Tex., U.S.A.* 71 J5
Seymour, *Wis., U.S.A.* 68 C1
Sfax, *Tunisia* 45 B7
Sfîntu Gheorghe, *Romania* 17 F13
Shaanxi □, *China* 31 C5
Shaba □, *Zaire* 46 F4
Shabunda, *Zaire* 46 E5
Shache, *China* 30 C2
Shackleton Ice Shelf, *Antarctica* 5 C8
Shackleton Inlet, *Antarctica* 5 E11
Shādegān, *Iran* 39 D6
Shadrinsk, *Russia* 24 D7
Shafter, *Calif., U.S.A.* 73 J4
Shafter, *Tex., U.S.A.* 71 L2

Shaftesbury, *U.K.*	11	F5
Shahba, *Syria*	41	C5
Shahdād, *Iran*	39	D8
Shahdadkot, *Pakistan*	36	F6
Shahgarh, *India*	36	F6
Shaḥḥāt, *Libya*	45	B9
Shahjahanpur, *India*	36	F11
Shahr Kord, *Iran*	39	C6
Shāhrakht, *Iran*	39	C9
Shahrig, *Pakistan*	36	D5
Shaikhabad, *Afghan.*	36	B6
Shajapur, *India*	36	H10
Shakawe, *Botswana*	48	B3
Shakhty, *Russia*	23	E7
Shakhunya, *Russia*	22	C8
Shaki, *Nigeria*	44	G5
Shakopee, *U.S.A.*	70	C8
Shala, L., *Ethiopia*	45	G12
Shalqar, *Kazakhstan*	24	E6
Shaluli Shan, *China*	30	C4
Shām, *Iran*	39	E8
Shamanovo, *Russia*	25	C15
Shamattawa, *Canada*	65	B10
Shamattawa →, *Canada*	62	A2
Shamil, *Iran*	39	E8
Shāmkūh, *Iran*	39	C8
Shamo = Gobi, *Asia*	31	B6
Shamo, L., *Ethiopia*	45	G12
Shamokin, *U.S.A.*	68	E7
Shamrock, *U.S.A.*	71	H4
Shamva, *Zimbabwe*	47	H6
Shan □, *Burma*	37	J21
Shāndak, *Iran*	39	D9
Shandong □, *China*	31	C6
Shanghai, *China*	31	C7
Shangqiu, *China*	31	C6
Shangrao, *China*	31	D6
Shangshui, *China*	31	C6
Shaniko, *U.S.A.*	72	D3
Shannon, *N.Z.*	51	J5
Shannon →, *Ireland*	13	D2
Shansi = Shanxi □, *China*	31	C6
Shantar, Ostrov Bolshoy, *Russia*	25	D14
Shantou, *China*	31	D6
Shantung = Shandong □, *China*	31	C6
Shanxi □, *China*	31	C6
Shaoguan, *China*	31	D6
Shaoxing, *China*	31	C7
Shaoyang, *China*	31	D6
Shapinsay, *U.K.*	12	B6
Shaqra', *Si. Arabia*	38	E5
Shaqrā', *Yemen*	40	E4
Shari, *Japan*	28	C12
Sharjah = Ash Shāriqah, *U.A.E.*	39	E7
Shark B., *Australia*	53	E1
Sharon, *U.S.A.*	68	E5
Sharon Springs, *U.S.A.*	70	F4
Sharp Pt., *Australia*	54	A3
Sharpe L., *Canada*	65	C10
Sharya, *Russia*	22	C8
Shashi, *Botswana*	49	C4
Shashi, *China*	31	C6
Shasta, Mt., *U.S.A.*	72	F2
Shasta L., *U.S.A.*	72	F2
Shatt al'Arab →, *Iraq*	39	D6
Shattuck, *U.S.A.*	71	G5
Shaunavon, *Canada*	65	D7
Shaw →, *Australia*	52	D2
Shaw I., *Australia*	54	C4
Shawano, *U.S.A.*	68	C1
Shawinigan, *Canada*	62	C5
Shawnee, *U.S.A.*	71	H6
Shaybārā, *Si. Arabia*	38	E3
Shaykh Sa'īd, *Iraq*	38	C5
Shcherbakov = Rybinsk, *Russia*	22	C6
Shchuchinsk, *Kazakhstan*	24	D8
Shebele = Scebeli, Wabi →, *Somali Rep.*	40	G3
Sheboygan, *U.S.A.*	68	D2
Shediac, *Canada*	63	C7
Sheelin, L., *Ireland*	13	C4
Sheep Haven, *Ireland*	13	A4
Sheerness, *U.K.*	11	F8
Sheet Harbour, *Canada*	63	D7
Sheffield, *U.K.*	10	D6
Sheffield, *Ala., U.S.A.*	69	H2
Sheffield, *Tex., U.S.A.*	71	K4
Sheho, *Canada*	65	C8
Shekhupura, *Pakistan*	36	D8
Shelburne, *N.S., Canada*	63	D6
Shelburne, *Ont., Canada*	62	D3
Shelburne B., *Australia*	54	A3
Shelby, *Mich., U.S.A.*	68	D2
Shelby, *Mont., U.S.A.*	72	B8
Shelby, *N.C., U.S.A.*	69	H5
Shelbyville, *Ill., U.S.A.*	70	F10
Shelbyville, *Ind., U.S.A.*	68	F3
Shelbyville, *Tenn., U.S.A.*	69	H2
Sheldon, *U.S.A.*	70	D7
Sheldrake, *Canada*	63	B7
Shelikhova, Zaliv, *Russia*	25	D16
Shell Lake, *Canada*	65	C7
Shell Lakes, *Australia*	53	E4
Shellbrook, *Canada*	65	C7
Shellharbour, *Australia*	55	E5
Shelton, *U.S.A.*	72	C2
Shenandoah, *Iowa, U.S.A.*	70	E7
Shenandoah, *Pa., U.S.A.*	68	E7

Shenandoah, *Va., U.S.A.*	68	F6
Shenandoah →, *U.S.A.*	68	F7
Shendam, *Nigeria*	44	G6
Shendî, *Sudan*	45	E11
Shensi = Shaanxi □, *China*	31	C5
Shenyang, *China*	31	B7
Sheopur Kalan, *India*	36	G10
Shepetivka, *Ukraine*	17	C14
Shepetovka = Shepetivka, *Ukraine*	17	C14
Shepparton, *Australia*	55	F4
Sherborne, *U.K.*	11	G5
Sherbro I., *S. Leone*	44	G2
Sherbrooke, *Canada*	63	C5
Sheridan, *Ark., U.S.A.*	71	H8
Sheridan, *Wyo., U.S.A.*	72	D10
Sherman, *U.S.A.*	71	J6
Sherridon, *Canada*	65	B8
Sherwood, *N. Dak., U.S.A.*	70	A4
Sherwood, *Tex., U.S.A.*	71	K4
Sherwood Forest, *U.K.*	10	D6
Sheslay, *Canada*	64	B2
Sheslay →, *Canada*	64	B2
Shethanei L., *Canada*	65	B9
Shetland □, *U.K.*	12	A7
Shetland Is., *U.K.*	12	A7
Sheyenne, *U.S.A.*	70	B5
Sheyenne →, *U.S.A.*	70	B6
Shibām, *Yemen*	40	D4
Shibata, *Japan*	28	F9
Shibecha, *Japan*	28	C12
Shibetsu, *Japan*	28	B11
Shibogama L., *Canada*	62	B2
Shibushi, *Japan*	29	J5
Shickshock Mts. = Chic-Chocs, Mts., *Canada*	63	C6
Shido, *Japan*	29	G7
Shiel, L., *U.K.*	12	E3
Shield, C., *Australia*	54	A2
Shiga □, *Japan*	29	G8
Shihchiachuangi = Shijiazhuang, *China*	31	C6
Shijiazhuang, *China*	31	C6
Shikarpur, *Pakistan*	36	F6
Shikoku □, *Japan*	29	H6
Shikoku-Sanchi, *Japan*	29	H6
Shilabo, *Ethiopia*	40	F3
Shiliguri, *India*	37	F16
Shilka, *Russia*	25	D12
Shilka →, *Russia*	25	D13
Shillelagh, *Ireland*	13	D5
Shillong, *India*	37	G17
Shilo, *West Bank*	41	C4
Shimabara, *Japan*	29	H5
Shimada, *Japan*	29	G9
Shimane □, *Japan*	29	G6
Shimanovsk, *Russia*	25	D13
Shimizu, *Japan*	29	G9
Shimodate, *Japan*	29	F9
Shimoga, *India*	36	N9
Shimonoseki, *Japan*	29	H5
Shimpuru Rapids, *Angola*	48	B2
Shin, L., *U.K.*	12	C4
Shin-Tone →, *Japan*	29	G10
Shinano →, *Japan*	29	F9
Shindand, *Afghan.*	36	C3
Shingleton, *U.S.A.*	62	C2
Shingū, *Japan*	29	H7
Shinjō, *Japan*	28	E10
Shinshār, *Syria*	41	A5
Shinyanga, *Tanzania*	46	E6
Shiogama, *Japan*	28	E10
Shiojiri, *Japan*	29	F8
Ship I., *U.S.A.*	71	K10
Shipehenski Prokhod, *Bulgaria*	21	C11
Shiping, *China*	30	D5
Shipki La, *India*	36	D11
Shippegan, *Canada*	63	C7
Shippensburg, *U.S.A.*	68	E7
Shiprock, *U.S.A.*	73	H9
Shiqma, N. →, *Israel*	41	D3
Shīr Kūh, *Iran*	39	D7
Shiragami-Misaki, *Japan*	28	D10
Shirakawa, *Fukushima, Japan*	29	F10
Shirakawa, *Gifu, Japan*	29	F8
Shirane-San, *Gumma, Japan*	29	F9
Shirane-San, *Yamanashi, Japan*	29	G9
Shiraoi, *Japan*	28	C10
Shīrāz, *Iran*	39	D7
Shire →, *Africa*	47	H7
Shiretoko-Misaki, *Japan*	28	B12
Shiriya-Zaki, *Japan*	28	D10
Shiroishi, *Japan*	28	E10
Shīrvān, *Iran*	39	B8
Shirwa, L. = Chilwa, L., *Malawi*	47	H7
Shivpuri, *India*	36	G10
Shizuoka, *Japan*	29	G9
Shizuoka □, *Japan*	29	G9
Shklov = Shklow, *Belarus*	17	A16
Shklow, *Belarus*	17	A16
Shkoder = Shkodra, *Albania*	21	C8
Shkodra, *Albania*	21	C8
Shkumbini →, *Albania*	21	D8
Shmidta, O., *Russia*	25	A10
Shō-Gawa →, *Japan*	29	F8
Shoal Lake, *Canada*	65	C8
Shōdo-Shima, *Japan*	29	G7
Shoeburyness, *U.K.*	11	F8

Sholapur = Solapur, *India*	36	L9
Shologontsy, *Russia*	25	C12
Shōmrōn, *West Bank*	41	C4
Shoshone, *U.S.A.*	72	E6
Shoshone L., *U.S.A.*	72	D8
Shoshone Mts., *U.S.A.*	72	G5
Shoshong, *Botswana*	48	C4
Shoshoni, *U.S.A.*	72	E9
Show Low, *U.S.A.*	73	J9
Shreveport, *U.S.A.*	71	J8
Shrewsbury, *U.K.*	10	E5
Shrirampur, *India*	37	H16
Shropshire □, *U.K.*	11	E5
Shu, *Kazakhstan*	24	E8
Shuangliao, *China*	31	B7
Shuangyashan, *China*	31	B8
Shule, *China*	30	C2
Shumagin Is., *U.S.A.*	60	C4
Shumikha, *Russia*	24	D7
Shungnak, *U.S.A.*	60	B4
Shūr →, *Iran*	39	D7
Shūr Āb, *Iran*	39	C6
Shūr Gaz, *Iran*	39	D8
Shūrāb, *Iran*	39	C8
Shūrjestān, *Iran*	39	D7
Shurugwi, *Zimbabwe*	47	H6
Shūsf, *Iran*	39	D9
Shūshtar, *Iran*	39	D6
Shuswap L., *Canada*	64	C5
Shūzū, *Iran*	39	D7
Shwebo, *Burma*	37	H19
Shwegu, *Burma*	37	G20
Shweli →, *Burma*	37	H20
Shymkent, *Kazakhstan*	24	E7
Shyok, *India*	36	B11
Shyok →, *Pakistan*	36	B9
Si Kiang = Xi Jiang →, *China*	31	D6
Si-ngan = Xi'an, *China*	31	C5
Si Racha, *Thailand*	34	F6
Siahan Range, *Pakistan*	36	F4
Siaksriindrapura, *Indonesia*	32	D2
Sialkot, *Pakistan*	36	C9
Siam = Thailand ■, *Asia*	34	D6
Siantan, P., *Indonesia*	32	D3
Siāreh, *Iran*	39	D9
Siargao, *Phil.*	33	C7
Siasi, *Phil.*	33	C6
Siau, *Indonesia*	33	D7
Šiauliai, *Lithuania*	9	J20
Sibay, *Russia*	22	D10
Sibayi, L., *S. Africa*	49	D5
Šibenik, *Croatia*	20	C6
Siberia, *Russia*	4	D13
Siberut, *Indonesia*	32	E1
Sibi, *Pakistan*	36	E5
Sibil, *Indonesia*	33	E10
Sibiti, *Congo*	46	E2
Sibiu, *Romania*	17	F13
Sibley, *Iowa, U.S.A.*	70	D7
Sibley, *La., U.S.A.*	71	J8
Sibolga, *Indonesia*	32	D1
Sibsagar, *India*	37	F19
Sibu, *Malaysia*	32	D4
Sibuco, *Phil.*	33	C6
Sibuguey B., *Phil.*	33	C6
Sibut, *C.A.R.*	45	G8
Sibutu, *Phil.*	33	D5
Sibutu Passage, E. Indies	33	D5
Sibuyan, *Phil.*	33	B6
Sibuyan Sea, *Phil.*	33	B6
Sicamous, *Canada*	64	C5
Sichuan □, *China*	30	C5
Sicilia, *Italy*	20	F6
Sicily = Sicilia, *Italy*	20	F6
Sicuani, *Peru*	78	F4
Siddipet, *India*	36	K11
Sidéradougou, *Burkina Faso*	44	F4
Sîdi Barrâni, *Egypt*	45	B10
Sidi-bel-Abbès, *Algeria*	44	A4
Sidlaw Hills, *U.K.*	12	E5
Sidley, Mt., *Antarctica*	5	D14
Sidmouth, *U.K.*	11	G4
Sidmouth, C., *Australia*	54	A3
Sidney, *Canada*	64	D4
Sidney, *Mont., U.S.A.*	70	B2
Sidney, *N.Y., U.S.A.*	68	D8
Sidney, *Nebr., U.S.A.*	70	E3
Sidney, *Ohio, U.S.A.*	68	E3
Sidoarjo, *Indonesia*	33	G15
Sidon = Saydā, *Lebanon*	41	B4
Sidra, G. of = Surt, Khalīj, *Libya*	45	B8
Siedlce, *Poland*	17	B12
Sieg →, *Germany*	16	C4
Siegen, *Germany*	16	C5
Siem Reap, *Cambodia*	34	F7
Siena, *Italy*	20	C4
Sieradz, *Poland*	17	C10
Sierra Blanca, *U.S.A.*	73	L11
Sierra Blanca Peak, *U.S.A.*	73	K11
Sierra City, *U.S.A.*	72	G3
Sierra Colorada, *Argentina*	80	E3
Sierra Gorda, *Chile*	80	A3
Sierra Leone ■, *W. Afr.*	44	G3
Sífnos, *Greece*	21	F11
Sifton, *Canada*	65	C8
Sifton Pass, *Canada*	64	B3
Sighetu-Marmației, *Romania*	17	E12
Sighișoara, *Romania*	17	E13
Sigli, *Indonesia*	32	C1
Siglufjörður, *Iceland*	8	C4
Sigsig, *Ecuador*	78	D3
Sigtuna, *Sweden*	9	G17
Sigüenza, *Spain*	19	B4

Siguiri, *Guinea*	44	F3
Sigulda, *Latvia*	9	H21
Sigurd, *U.S.A.*	73	G8
Sihanoukville = Kompong Som, *Cambodia*	34	G7
Siikajoki →, *Finland*	8	D21
Siilinjärvi, *Finland*	8	E22
Sikar, *India*	36	F9
Sikasso, *Mali*	44	F3
Sikeston, *U.S.A.*	71	G10
Sikhote Alin, Khrebet, *Russia*	25	E14
Sikhote Alin Ra. = Sikhote Alin, Khrebet, *Russia*	25	E14
Síkinos, *Greece*	21	F11
Sikkani Chief →, *Canada*	64	B4
Sikkim □, *India*	37	F16
Sikotu-Ko, *Japan*	28	C10
Sil →, *Spain*	19	A2
Silchar, *India*	37	G18
Silcox, *Canada*	65	B10
Siler City, *U.S.A.*	69	H6
Silesia = Śląsk, *Poland*	16	C9
Silgarhi Doti, *Nepal*	37	E12
Silghat, *India*	37	F18
Silifke, *Turkey*	23	G5
Siliguri = Shiliguri, *India*	37	F16
Siling Co, *China*	30	C3
Silistra, *Bulgaria*	21	B12
Silivri, *Turkey*	21	D13
Siljan, *Sweden*	9	F16
Silkeborg, *Denmark*	9	H13
Sillajhuay, Cordillera, *Chile*	78	G5
Sillamäe, *Estonia*	9	G22
Siloam Springs, *U.S.A.*	71	G7
Silsbee, *U.S.A.*	71	K7
Šilute, *Lithuania*	9	J19
Silva Porto = Kuito, *Angola*	47	G3
Silver City, *Panama*	74	H14
Silver City, *N. Mex., U.S.A.*	73	K9
Silver City, *Nev., U.S.A.*	72	G4
Silver Cr. →, *U.S.A.*	72	E4
Silver Creek, *U.S.A.*	68	D6
Silver Lake, *U.S.A.*	72	E3
Silver Streams, *S. Africa*	48	D3
Silverton, *Colo., U.S.A.*	73	H10
Silverton, *Tex., U.S.A.*	71	H4
Silvies →, *U.S.A.*	72	E4
Simanggang, *Malaysia*	32	D4
Simard, L., *Canada*	62	C4
Simav, *Turkey*	21	E13
Simbirsk, *Russia*	22	D8
Simcoe, *Canada*	62	D3
Simcoe, L., *Canada*	62	D4
Simenga, *Russia*	25	C11
Simeria, *Romania*	17	F12
Simeulue, *Indonesia*	32	D1
Simferopol, *Ukraine*	23	F5
Sími, *Greece*	21	F12
Simikot, *Nepal*	37	E12
Simla, *India*	36	D10
Simmie, *Canada*	65	D7
Simojoki →, *Finland*	8	D21
Simojovel, *Mexico*	74	D6
Simonette →, *Canada*	64	B5
Simonstown, *S. Africa*	48	E2
Simpang, *Malaysia*	34	Q13
Simplon P., *Switz.*	16	E5
Simplon Pass = Simplon P., *Switz.*	16	E5
Simpson Desert, *Australia*	54	D2
Simrishamn, *Sweden*	9	J16
Simunjan, *Malaysia*	32	D4
Simushir, Ostrov, *Russia*	25	E16
Sinabang, *Indonesia*	32	D1
Sinadogo, *Somali Rep.*	40	F4
Sinai = Es Sînâ', *Egypt*	45	C11
Sinai, Mt. = Mûsa, G., *Egypt*	45	C11
Sinai Peninsula, *Egypt*	41	F2
Sinaloa de Levya, *Mexico*	74	B3
Sinan, *Burma*	44	B7
Sincelejo, *Colombia*	78	B3
Sinclair, *U.S.A.*	72	F10
Sinclair Mills, *Canada*	64	C4
Sincorá, Serra do, *Brazil*	79	F10
Sind □, *Pakistan*	36	F6
Sind Sagar Doab, *Pakistan*	36	D7
Sindangan, *Phil.*	33	C6
Sindangbarang, *Indonesia*	33	G12
Sines, *Portugal*	19	D1
Sines, C. de, *Portugal*	19	D1
Singa, *Sudan*	45	F11
Singapore ■, *Asia*	34	T16
Singapore, Straits of, *Asia*	34	T17
Singaraja, *Indonesia*	32	F5
Singida, *Tanzania*	46	E6
Singitikós Kólpos, *Greece*	21	D11
Singkaling Hkamti, *Burma*	37	G19
Singkawang, *Indonesia*	32	D3
Singleton, *Australia*	55	E5
Singleton, Mt., *N. Terr., Australia*	52	D5
Singleton, Mt., *W. Austral., Australia*	53	E2
Singora = Songkhla, *Thailand*	34	J6
Sinî □, *Egypt*	41	F2

Sinjai, *Indonesia*	33	F6
Sinjār, *Iraq*	38	B4
Sinkat, *Sudan*	45	E12
Sinkiang Uighur = Xinjiang Uygur Zizhiqu □, *China*	30	B3
Sinni →, *Italy*	20	D7
Sînnicolau Maré, *Romania*	17	E11
Sinnuris, *Egypt*	45	C11
Sinop, *Turkey*	23	F6
Sinsk, *Russia*	25	C13
Sint Niklaas, *Belgium*	15	C4
Sint Truiden, *Belgium*	15	D5
Sintang, *Indonesia*	32	D4
Sinton, *U.S.A.*	71	L6
Sintra, *Portugal*	19	C1
Siocon, *Phil.*	33	C6
Siófok, *Hungary*	17	E10
Sioma, *Zambia*	48	B3
Sion, *Switz.*	16	E4
Sioux City, *U.S.A.*	70	D6
Sioux Falls, *U.S.A.*	70	D6
Sioux Lookout, *Canada*	62	B1
Siping, *China*	31	B7
Sipiwesk L., *Canada*	65	B9
Sipura, *Indonesia*	32	E1
Siquijor, *Phil.*	33	C6
Sir Edward Pellew Group, *Australia*	54	B2
Sir Graham Moore Is., *Australia*	52	B4
Sira →, *Norway*	9	G12
Siracusa, *Italy*	20	F6
Sirajganj, *Bangla.*	37	G16
Sīrdān, *Iran*	39	B6
Sirdaryo = Syrdarya →, *Kazakhstan*	24	E7
Siret →, *Romania*	17	F14
Sirohi, *India*	36	G8
Sironj, *India*	36	G10
Síros, *Greece*	21	F11
Sirsa, *India*	36	E9
Sisak, *Croatia*	16	F9
Sisaket, *Thailand*	34	E8
Sishen, *S. Africa*	48	D3
Sisipuk L., *Canada*	65	B8
Sisophon, *Cambodia*	34	F7
Sisseton, *U.S.A.*	70	C6
Sīstān va Balūchestān □, *Iran*	39	E9
Sisters, *U.S.A.*	72	D3
Sitapur, *India*	37	F12
Siteki, *Swaziland*	49	D5
Sitges, *Spain*	19	D6
Sitía, *Greece*	21	G12
Sitoti, *Botswana*	48	C3
Sitka, *U.S.A.*	60	C6
Sittang Myit →, *Burma*	37	L20
Sittard, *Neths.*	15	C5
Sittwe, *Burma*	37	J18
Siuri, *India*	37	H15
Sīvand, *Iran*	39	D7
Sivas, *Turkey*	23	G6
Sivomaskinskiy, *Russia*	22	A11
Sivrihisar, *Turkey*	23	G5
Sîwa, *Egypt*	45	C10
Siwalik Range, *Nepal*	37	F13
Siwan, *India*	37	F14
Sizewell, *U.K.*	11	E9
Sjælland, *Denmark*	9	J14
Sjumen = Šumen, *Bulgaria*	21	C12
Skadarsko Jezero, *Montenegro, Yug.*	21	C8
Skaftafell, *Iceland*	8	D5
Skagafjörður, *Iceland*	8	D4
Skagastølstindane, *Norway*	9	F12
Skagen, *Denmark*	9	H14
Skagerrak, *Denmark*	9	H13
Skagway, *U.S.A.*	64	B1
Skala-Podilska, *Ukraine*	17	D14
Skala Podolskaya = Skala-Podilska, *Ukraine*	17	D14
Skalat, *Ukraine*	17	D13
Skåne, *Sweden*	9	J15
Skara, *Sweden*	9	G15
Skardu, *Pakistan*	36	B9
Skarzysko-Kamienna, *Poland*	17	C11
Skeena →, *Canada*	64	C2
Skeena Mts., *Canada*	64	B3
Skegness, *U.K.*	10	D8
Skeldon, *Guyana*	78	B7
Skellefte älv →, *Sweden*	8	D19
Skellefteå, *Sweden*	8	D19
Skelleftehamn, *Sweden*	8	D19
Skerries, The, *U.K.*	10	D3
Ski, *Norway*	9	G14
Skíathos, *Greece*	21	E10
Skibbereen, *Ireland*	13	E2
Skiddaw, *U.K.*	10	C4
Skien, *Norway*	9	G13
Skierniewice, *Poland*	17	C11
Skikda, *Algeria*	44	A6
Skipton, *Australia*	55	F3
Skipton, *U.K.*	10	D5
Skirmish Pt., *Australia*	54	A1
Skíros, *Greece*	21	E11
Skive, *Denmark*	9	H13
Skjálfandafljót →, *Iceland*	8	D5
Skjálfandi, *Iceland*	8	C5
Skoghall, *Sweden*	9	G15
Skole, *Ukraine*	17	D12
Skópelos, *Greece*	21	E10
Skopje, *Macedonia*	21	C9
Skövde, *Sweden*	9	G15
Skovorodino, *Russia*	25	D13

Skowhegan, *U.S.A.*	63	D6
Skownan, *Canada*	65	C9
Skull, *Ireland*	13	E2
Skunk →, *U.S.A.*	70	E9
Skuodas, *Lithuania*	9	H19
Skvyra, *Ukraine*	17	D15
Skye, *U.K.*	12	D2
Skykomish, *U.S.A.*	72	C3
Skyros = Skíros, *Greece*	21	E11
Slættaratindur, *Færoe Is.*	8	E9
Slagelse, *Denmark*	9	J14
Slamet, *Indonesia*	32	F3
Slaney →, *Ireland*	13	D5
Śląsk, *Poland*	16	C9
Slate Is., *Canada*	62	C2
Slatina, *Romania*	17	F13
Slaton, *U.S.A.*	71	J4
Slave →, *Canada*	64	A6
Slave Coast, *W. Afr.*	42	F4
Slave Lake, *Canada*	64	B6
Slave Pt., *Canada*	64	A5
Slavgorod, *Russia*	24	D8
Slavonski Brod, *Croatia*	21	B8
Slavuta, *Ukraine*	17	C14
Slavyanka, *Russia*	28	C5
Slavyansk = Slovyansk, *Ukraine*	23	E6
Slawharad, *Belarus*	17	B16
Sleaford, *U.K.*	10	E7
Sleaford B., *Australia*	55	E2
Sleat, Sd. of, *U.K.*	12	D3
Sleeper Is., *Canada*	61	C11
Sleepy Eye, *U.S.A.*	70	C7
Sleman, *Indonesia*	33	G14
Slemon L., *Canada*	64	A5
Slidell, *U.S.A.*	71	K10
Sliedrecht, *Neths.*	15	C4
Slieve Aughty, *Ireland*	13	C3
Slieve Bloom, *Ireland*	13	C4
Slieve Donard, *U.K.*	13	B6
Slieve Gullion, *U.K.*	13	B5
Slieve Mish, *Ireland*	13	D2
Slievenamon, *Ireland*	13	D4
Sligeach = Sligo, *Ireland*	13	B3
Sligo, *Ireland*	13	B3
Sligo □, *Ireland*	13	B3
Sligo B., *Ireland*	13	B3
Slite, *Sweden*	9	H18
Sliven, *Bulgaria*	21	C12
Slobodskoy, *Russia*	22	C9
Slobozia, *Romania*	17	F14
Slocan, *Canada*	64	D5
Slochteren, *Neths.*	15	A6
Slonim, *Belarus*	17	B13
Slough, *U.K.*	11	F7
Slovak Rep. ■, *Europe*	17	D10
Slovakia = Slovak Rep. ■, *Europe*	17	D10
Slovakian Ore Mts. = Slovenské Rudohorie, *Slovak Rep.*	17	D10
Slovenia ■, *Europe*	16	F8
Slovenija = Slovenia ■, *Europe*	16	F8
Slovenská Republika = Slovak Rep. ■, *Europe*	17	D10
Slovenské Rudohorie, *Slovak Rep.*	17	D10
Slovyansk, *Ukraine*	23	E6
Sluch →, *Ukraine*	17	C14
Sluis, *Neths.*	15	C3
Słupsk, *Poland*	17	A9
Slurry, *S. Africa*	48	D4
Slutsk, *Belarus*	17	B14
Slyne Hd., *Ireland*	13	C1
Slyudyanka, *Russia*	25	D11
Småland, *Sweden*	9	H16
Smalltree L., *Canada*	65	A7
Smara, *Morocco*	44	B3
Smartt Syndicate Dam, *S. Africa*	48	E3
Smeaton, *Canada*	65	C8
Smederevo, *Serbia, Yug.*	21	B9
Smidovich, *Russia*	25	E14
Smiley, *Canada*	65	C7
Smith, *Canada*	64	B6
Smith →, *Canada*	64	B3
Smith Arm, *Canada*	60	B7
Smith Center, *U.S.A.*	70	F5
Smith Sund, *Greenland*	4	B4
Smithburne →, *Australia*	54	B3
Smithers, *Canada*	64	C3
Smithfield, *S. Africa*	49	E4
Smithfield, *N.C., U.S.A.*	69	H6
Smithfield, *Utah, U.S.A.*	72	F8
Smiths Falls, *Canada*	62	D4
Smithton, *Australia*	54	G4
Smithtown, *Australia*	55	E5
Smithville, *U.S.A.*	71	K6
Smoky →, *Canada*	64	B5
Smoky Bay, *Australia*	55	E1
Smoky Falls, *Canada*	62	B3
Smoky Hill →, *U.S.A.*	70	F6
Smoky Lake, *Canada*	64	C6
Smøla, *Norway*	8	E13
Smolensk, *Russia*	22	D5
Smolikas, Óros, *Greece*	21	D9
Smolyan, *Bulgaria*	21	D11
Smooth Rock Falls, *Canada*	62	C3
Smoothstone L., *Canada*	65	C7
Smorgon = Smarhon, *Belarus*	17	A14
Smyrna = İzmir, *Turkey*	21	E12
Snæfell, *Iceland*	8	D6
Snaefell, *U.K.*	10	C3

Snæfellsjökull, *Iceland* 8 D2
Snake →, *U.S.A.* 72 C4
Snake I., *Australia* 55 F4
Snake L., *Canada* 65 B7
Snake Range, *U.S.A.* 72 G6
Snake River Plain, *U.S.A.* 72 E7
Snåsavatnet, *Norway* 8 D14
Sneek, *Neths.* 15 A5
Sneeuberge, *S. Africa* 48 E3
Snežka, *Europe* 16 C8
Snizort, L., *U.K.* 12 D2
Snøhetta, *Norway* 9 E13
Snow Hill, *U.S.A.* 68 F8
Snow Lake, *Canada* 65 C8
Snowbird L., *Canada* 65 A8
Snowdon, *U.K.* 10 D3
Snowdrift, *Canada* 65 A6
Snowdrift →, *Canada* 65 A6
Snowflake, *U.S.A.* 73 J8
Snowshoe Pk., *U.S.A.* 72 B6
Snowtown, *Australia* 55 E2
Snowville, *U.S.A.* 72 F7
Snowy →, *Australia* 55 F4
Snowy Mts., *Australia* 55 F4
Snyatyn, *Ukraine* 17 D13
Snyder, *Okla., U.S.A.* 71 H5
Snyder, *Tex., U.S.A.* 71 J4
Soahanina, *Madag.* 49 B7
Soalala, *Madag.* 49 B8
Soanierana-Ivongo, *Madag.* 49 B8
Soap Lake, *U.S.A.* 72 C4
Sobat, Nahr →, *Sudan* 45 G11
Sobolevo, *Russia* 25 D16
Sobradinho, Reprêsa de, *Brazil* 79 E10
Sobral, *Brazil* 79 D10
Soc Trang, *Vietnam* 34 H8
Soch'e = Shache, *China* 30 C2
Sochi, *Russia* 23 F6
Société, Is. de la, *Pac. Oc.* 57 J12
Society Is. = Société, Is. de la, *Pac. Oc.* 57 J12
Socompa, Portezuelo de, *Chile* 80 A3
Socorro, *Colombia* 78 B4
Socorro, *U.S.A.* 73 J10
Socotra, *Ind. Oc.* 40 E5
Soda, L., *U.S.A.* 73 J5
Soda Plains, *India* 36 B11
Soda Springs, *U.S.A.* 72 E8
Sodankylä, *Finland* 8 C22
Söderhamn, *Sweden* 9 F17
Söderköping, *Sweden* 9 G17
Södermanland, *Sweden* 9 G17
Södertälje, *Sweden* 9 G17
Sodiri, *Sudan* 45 F10
Sodo, *Ethiopia* 45 G12
Soekmekaar, *S. Africa* 49 C4
Soest, *Neths.* 15 B5
Sofia = Sofiya, *Bulgaria* 21 C10
Sofia →, *Madag.* 49 B8
Sofiya, *Bulgaria* 21 C10
Sofiysk, *Russia* 25 D14
Sōfu-Gan, *Japan* 29 K10
Sogamoso, *Colombia* 78 B4
Sogār, *Iran* 39 E8
Sogndalsfjøra, *Norway* 9 F12
Søgne, *Norway* 9 G12
Sognefjorden, *Norway* 9 F11
Soh, *Iran* 39 C6
Sohâg, *Egypt* 45 C11
Soignies, *Belgium* 15 D4
Soissons, *France* 18 B5
Sōja, *Japan* 29 G6
Sokal, *Ukraine* 17 C13
Söke, *Turkey* 21 F12
Sokhumi, *Georgia* 23 F7
Sokodé, *Togo* 44 G5
Sokol, *Russia* 22 C7
Sokółka, *Poland* 17 B12
Sokolo, *Mali* 44 F3
Sokołów Podlaski, *Poland* 17 B12
Sokoto, *Nigeria* 44 F6
Sol Iletsk, *Russia* 22 D10
Solano, *Phil.* 33 A6
Solapur, *India* 36 L9
Soledad, *U.S.A.* 73 H3
Soledad, *Venezuela* 78 B6
Solent, The, *U.K.* 11 G6
Solfonn, *Norway* 9 F12
Soligalich, *Russia* 22 C7
Soligorsk = Salihorsk, *Belarus* 17 B14
Solikamsk, *Russia* 22 C10
Solila, *Madag.* 49 C8
Solimões = Amazonas →, *S. Amer.* 79 C9
Solingen, *Germany* 15 C7
Sollefteå, *Sweden* 8 E17
Sóller, *Spain* 19 C7
Sologne, *France* 18 C4
Solok, *Indonesia* 32 E2
Solomon, N. Fork →, *U.S.A.* 70 F5
Solomon, S. Fork →, *U.S.A.* 70 F5
Solomon Is. ■, *Pac. Oc.* 56 H7
Solon, *China* 31 B7
Solon Springs, *U.S.A.* 70 B9
Solor, *Indonesia* 33 F6
Solothurn, *Switz.* 16 E4
Šolta, *Croatia* 20 C7
Solţānābād, *Khorāsān, Iran* 39 C8
Solţānābād, *Khorāsān, Iran* 39 B8

Solţānābād, *Markazī, Iran* 39 C6
Solunska Glava, *Macedonia* 21 D9
Solvay, *U.S.A.* 68 D7
Sölvesborg, *Sweden* 9 H16
Solvychegodsk, *Russia* 22 B8
Solway Firth, *U.K.* 10 C4
Solwezi, *Zambia* 47 G5
Sōma, *Japan* 28 F10
Soma, *Turkey* 21 E12
Somali Rep. ■, *Africa* 40 F4
Somalia = Somali Rep. ■, *Africa* 40 F4
Sombor, *Serbia, Yug.* 21 B8
Sombrerete, *Mexico* 74 C4
Sombrero, *Anguilla* 75 D12
Somers, *U.S.A.* 72 B6
Somerset, *Canada* 65 D9
Somerset, *Colo., U.S.A.* 73 G10
Somerset, *Ky., U.S.A.* 68 G3
Somerset □, *U.K.* 11 F5
Somerset East, *S. Africa* 48 E4
Somerset I., *Canada* 60 A10
Somerset West, *S. Africa* 48 E2
Somerton, *U.S.A.* 73 K6
Someş →, *Romania* 17 D12
Sommariva, *Australia* 55 D4
Somme →, *France* 18 A4
Somosierra, Puerto de, *Spain* 19 B4
Somport, Puerto de, *Spain* 18 E3
Son La, *Vietnam* 34 B7
Sondags →, *S. Africa* 48 E4
Sønderborg, *Denmark* 9 J13
Søndre Strømfjord, *Greenland* 61 B14
Sóndrio, *Italy* 20 A3
Sonepur, *India* 37 J13
Song Cau, *Vietnam* 34 F10
Songea, *Tanzania* 46 G7
Songhua Jiang →, *China* 31 B8
Songkhla, *Thailand* 34 J6
Songpan, *China* 30 C5
Sonipat, *India* 36 E10
Sonmiani, *Pakistan* 36 G5
Sono →, *Brazil* 79 E9
Sonora, *Calif., U.S.A.* 73 H3
Sonora, *Tex., U.S.A.* 71 K4
Sonora →, *Mexico* 74 B2
Sonsonate, *El Salv.* 74 E7
Soochow = Suzhou, *China* 31 C7
Sopi, *Indonesia* 33 D7
Sopot, *Poland* 17 A10
Sopron, *Hungary* 17 E9
Sop's Arm, *Canada* 63 C8
Sør-Rondane, *Antarctica* 5 D4
Sorata, *Bolivia* 78 G5
Sorel, *Canada* 62 C5
Soreq, N. →, *Israel* 41 D3
Sorgono, *Italy* 20 D3
Soria, *Spain* 19 B4
Sorkh, Kuh-e, *Iran* 39 C8
Soroca, *Moldova* 17 D15
Sorocaba, *Brazil* 80 A7
Sorochinsk, *Russia* 22 D9
Soroki = Soroca, *Moldova* 17 D15
Sorong, *Indonesia* 33 E8
Soroti, *Uganda* 46 D6
Sørøya, *Norway* 8 A20
Sørøysundet, *Norway* 8 A20
Sorrento, *Australia* 55 F3
Sorsele, *Sweden* 8 D17
Sorsogon, *Phil.* 33 B6
Sortavala, *Russia* 22 B5
Sortland, *Norway* 8 B16
Soscumica, L., *Canada* 62 B4
Sosnogorsk, *Russia* 22 B9
Sosnovka, *Russia* 25 D11
Sosnowiec, *Poland* 17 C10
Sosva, *Russia* 22 C11
Sotkamo, *Finland* 8 D23
Sotuta, *Mexico* 74 C7
Souanké, *Congo* 46 D2
Soúdhas, Kólpos, *Greece* 21 G11
Soufrière, *Lesotho* 49 D4
Soure, *Brazil* 79 D9
Souris, *Man., Canada* 65 D8
Souris, *P.E.I., Canada* 63 C7
Souris →, *Canada* 70 A5
Sousa, *Brazil* 79 E11
Sousel, *Brazil* 79 D8
Sousse, *Tunisia* 45 A7
South Africa ■, *Africa* 48 E3
South Aulatsivik I., *Canada* 63 A7
South Australia □, *Australia* 55 E2
South Baldy, *U.S.A.* 73 J10
South Bend, *Ind., U.S.A.* 68 E2
South Bend, *Wash., U.S.A.* 72 C2
South Boston, *U.S.A.* 69 G6
South Branch, *Canada* 63 C8
South Brook, *Canada* 63 C8
South Carolina □, *U.S.A.* 69 J5
South Charleston, *U.S.A.* 68 F5
South China Sea, *Asia* 32 C4
South Dakota □, *U.S.A.* 70 C5
South Downs, *U.K.* 11 G7
South East C., *Australia* 54 G4

South East Is., *Australia* 53 F3
South Esk →, *U.K.* 12 E5
South Foreland, *U.K.* 11 F9
South Fork →, *U.S.A.* 72 C7
South Gamboa, *Panama* 74 H14
South Georgia, *Antarctica* 5 B1
South Glamorgan □, *U.K.* 11 F4
South Haven, *U.S.A.* 68 D2
South Henik, L., *Canada* 65 A9
South Honshu Ridge, *Pac. Oc.* 56 E6
South Horr, *Kenya* 46 D7
South I., *N.Z.* 51 L3
South Invercargill, *N.Z.* 51 M2
South Knife →, *Canada* 65 B10
South Korea ■, *Asia* 31 C7
South Loup →, *U.S.A.* 70 E5
South Magnetic Pole, *Antarctica* 5 C9
South Milwaukee, *U.S.A.* 68 D2
South Molton, *U.K.* 11 F4
South Nahanni →, *Canada* 64 A4
South Natuna Is. = Natuna Selatan, Kepulauan, *Indonesia* 32 D3
South Orkney Is., *Antarctica* 5 C18
South Pagai, I. = Pagai Selatan, P., *Indonesia* 32 E2
South Pass, *U.S.A.* 72 E9
South Pittsburg, *U.S.A.* 69 H3
South Platte →, *U.S.A.* 70 E4
South Pole, *Antarctica* 5 E
South Porcupine, *Canada* 62 C3
South River, *Canada* 62 C4
South Ronaldsay, *U.K.* 12 C6
South Sandwich Is., *Antarctica* 5 B1
South Saskatchewan →, *Canada* 65 C7
South Seal →, *Canada* 65 B9
South Sentinel I., *India* 34 G2
South Shetland Is., *Antarctica* 5 C18
South Shields, *U.K.* 10 C6
South Sioux City, *U.S.A.* 70 D6
South Taranaki Bight, *N.Z.* 51 H5
South Thompson →, *Canada* 64 C4
South Twin I., *Canada* 62 B4
South Tyne →, *U.K.* 10 C5
South Uist, *U.K.* 12 D1
South West Africa = Namibia ■, *Africa* 48 C2
South West C., *Australia* 54 G4
South Yorkshire □, *U.K.* 10 D6
Southampton, *Canada* 62 D3
Southampton, *U.K.* 11 G6
Southampton, *U.S.A.* 68 E9
Southampton I., *Canada* 61 B11
Southbridge, *N.Z.* 51 K4
Southend, *Canada* 65 B8
Southend-on-Sea, *U.K.* 11 F8
Southern Alps, *N.Z.* 51 K3
Southern Cross, *Australia* 53 F2
Southern Hills, *Australia* 53 F3
Southern Indian L., *Canada* 65 B9
Southern Ocean, *Antarctica* 5 C6
Southern Pines, *U.S.A.* 69 H6
Southern Uplands, *U.K.* 12 F5
Southport, *Australia* 55 D5
Southport, *U.K.* 10 D4
Southport, *U.S.A.* 69 J6
Southwest C., *N.Z.* 51 M1
Southwold, *U.K.* 11 E9
Soutpansberg, *S. Africa* 49 C4
Sovetsk, *Kaliningd., Russia* 9 J19
Sovetsk, *Kirov, Russia* 22 C8
Sovetskaya Gavan, *Russia* 25 E15
Sovetskoye = Ketchenery, *Russia* 25 D14
Soweto, *S. Africa* 49 D4
Sōya-Kaikyō = La Perouse Str., *Asia* 28 B11
Sōya-Misaki, *Japan* 28 B10
Soyo, *Angola* 46 F2
Sozh →, *Belarus* 17 B16
Spa, *Belgium* 15 D5
Spain ■, *Europe* 19 B4
Spalding, *Australia* 55 E2
Spalding, *U.K.* 10 E7
Spalding, *U.S.A.* 70 E5
Spaniard's Bay, *Canada* 63 C9
Spanish, *Canada* 62 C3
Spanish Fork, *U.S.A.* 72 F8
Spanish Town, *Jamaica* 74 K17
Sparks, *U.S.A.* 72 G4
Sparta = Spárti, *Greece* 21 F10
Sparta, *Ga., U.S.A.* 69 J4
Sparta, *Wis., U.S.A.* 70 D9
Spartanburg, *U.S.A.* 69 H4
Spárti, *Greece* 21 F10
Spartivento, C., *Calábria, Italy* 20 F7
Spartivento, C., *Sard., Italy* 20 E3

Spassk Dalniy, *Russia* 25 E14
Spátha, Ákra, *Greece* 21 G10
Spatsizi →, *Canada* 64 B3
Spearfish, *U.S.A.* 70 C3
Spearman, *U.S.A.* 71 G4
Speers, *Canada* 65 C7
Speightstown, *Barbados* 74 P22
Spence Bay, *Canada* 60 B10
Spencer, *Idaho, U.S.A.* 72 D7
Spencer, *Iowa, U.S.A.* 70 D7
Spencer, *Nebr., U.S.A.* 70 D5
Spencer, *W. Va., U.S.A.* 68 F5
Spencer, C., *Australia* 55 F2
Spencer B., *Namibia* 48 D1
Spencer G., *Australia* 55 E2
Spences Bridge, *Canada* 64 C4
Spenser Mts., *N.Z.* 51 K4
Sperrin Mts., *U.K.* 13 B5
Spey →, *U.K.* 12 D5
Speyer, *Germany* 16 D5
Spirit Lake, *U.S.A.* 72 C5
Spirit River, *Canada* 64 B5
Spiritwood, *Canada* 65 C7
Spithead, *U.K.* 11 G6
Spitzbergen = Svalbard, *Arctic* 4 B8
Spjelkavik, *Norway* 9 E12
Split, *Croatia* 20 C7
Split L., *Canada* 65 B9
Spofford, *U.S.A.* 71 L4
Spokane, *U.S.A.* 72 C5
Spoleto, *Italy* 20 C5
Spooner, *U.S.A.* 70 C9
Sporyy Navolok, Mys, *Russia* 24 B7
Spragge, *Canada* 62 C3
Sprague, *U.S.A.* 72 C5
Sprague River, *U.S.A.* 72 E3
Spratly I., *S. China Sea* 32 C4
Spray, *U.S.A.* 72 D4
Spree →, *Germany* 16 B7
Sprengisandur, *Iceland* 8 D5
Spring City, *U.S.A.* 72 G8
Spring Mts., *U.S.A.* 73 H6
Spring Valley, *U.S.A.* 70 D8
Springbok, *S. Africa* 48 D2
Springdale, *Canada* 63 C8
Springdale, *Ark., U.S.A.* 71 G7
Springdale, *Wash., U.S.A.* 72 B5
Springer, *U.S.A.* 71 G2
Springerville, *U.S.A.* 73 J9
Springfield, *N.Z.* 51 K3
Springfield, *Colo., U.S.A.* 71 G3
Springfield, *Ill., U.S.A.* 70 F10
Springfield, *Mass., U.S.A.* 68 D9
Springfield, *Mo., U.S.A.* 71 G8
Springfield, *Ohio, U.S.A.* 68 F4
Springfield, *Oreg., U.S.A.* 72 D2
Springfield, *Tenn., U.S.A.* 69 G2
Springfontein, *S. Africa* 48 E4
Springhill, *Canada* 63 C7
Springhouse, *Canada* 64 C4
Springhurst, *Australia* 55 F4
Springs, *S. Africa* 49 D4
Springsure, *Australia* 54 C4
Springvale, *Queens., Australia* 54 C3
Springvale, *W. Austral., Australia* 52 C4
Springville, *N.Y., U.S.A.* 68 D6
Springville, *Utah, U.S.A.* 72 F8
Springwater, *Canada* 65 C7
Spur, *U.S.A.* 71 J4
Spurn Hd., *U.K.* 10 D8
Spuzzum, *Canada* 64 D4
Squamish, *Canada* 64 D4
Square Islands, *Canada* 63 B8
Squires, Mt., *Australia* 53 E4
Sragen, *Indonesia* 33 G14
Srbija = Serbia □, *Yugoslavia* 21 C9
Sre Umbell, *Cambodia* 34 G7
Srebrnica, *Bos.-H.* 21 B8
Sredinny Ra. = Sredinnyy Khrebet, *Russia* 25 D16
Sredinnyy Khrebet, *Russia* 25 D16
Sredne Tambovskoye, *Russia* 25 D14
Srednekolymsk, *Russia* 25 C16
Srednevilyuysk, *Russia* 25 C13
Śrem, *Poland* 17 B9
Sremska Mitrovica, *Serbia, Yug.* 21 B8
Sretensk, *Russia* 25 D12
Sri Lanka ■, *Asia* 36 R12
Srikakulam, *India* 37 K13
Srinagar, *India* 36 B9
Staaten →, *Australia* 54 B3
Stade, *Germany* 16 B5
Stadskanaal, *Neths.* 15 A6
Staffa, *U.K.* 12 E2
Stafford, *U.K.* 10 E5
Stafford, *U.S.A.* 71 G5
Staffordshire □, *U.K.* 10 E5
Staines, *U.K.* 11 F7
Stakhanov, *Ukraine* 23 E6
Stalingrad = Volgograd, *Russia* 23 E7
Staliniri = Tskhinvali, *Georgia* 23 F7
Stalino = Donetsk, *Ukraine* 23 E6

Stalinogorsk = Novomoskovsk, *Russia* 22 D6
Stalowa Wola, *Poland* 17 C12
Stalybridge, *U.K.* 10 D5
Stamford, *Australia* 54 C3
Stamford, *U.K.* 11 E7
Stamford, *Conn., U.S.A.* 68 E9
Stamford, *Tex., U.S.A.* 71 J5
Stamps, *U.S.A.* 71 J8
Stanberry, *U.S.A.* 70 E7
Standerton, *S. Africa* 49 D4
Standish, *U.S.A.* 68 D4
Stanford, *U.S.A.* 72 C8
Stanger, *S. Africa* 49 D5
Stanislav = Ivano-Frankivsk, *Ukraine* 17 D13
Stanke Dimitrov, *Bulgaria* 21 C10
Stanley, *Australia* 54 G4
Stanley, *N.B., Canada* 63 C6
Stanley, *Sask., Canada* 65 B8
Stanley, *Falk. Is.* 80 G5
Stanley, *Idaho, U.S.A.* 72 D6
Stanley, *N. Dak., U.S.A.* 70 A3
Stanley, *Wis., U.S.A.* 70 C9
Stanovoy Khrebet, *Russia* 25 D13
Stanovoy Ra. = Stanovoy Khrebet, *Russia* 25 D13
Stansmore Ra., *Australia* 52 D4
Stanthorpe, *Australia* 55 D5
Stanton, *U.S.A.* 71 J4
Staples, *U.S.A.* 70 B7
Stapleton, *U.S.A.* 70 E4
Star City, *Canada* 65 C8
Stara Planina, *Bulgaria* 21 C10
Stara Zagora, *Bulgaria* 21 C11
Starachowice, *Poland* 17 C11
Staraya Russa, *Russia* 22 C5
Starbuck I., *Kiribati* 57 H12
Stargard Szczeciński, *Poland* 16 B8
Staritsa, *Russia* 22 C5
Starke, *U.S.A.* 69 K4
Starkville, *Colo., U.S.A.* 71 G2
Starkville, *Miss., U.S.A.* 69 J1
Starogard Gdański, *Poland* 17 B10
Starokonstantinov = Starokonstyantyniv, *Ukraine* 17 D14
Starokonstyantyniv, *Ukraine* 17 D14
Start Pt., *U.K.* 11 G4
Staryy Chartoriysk, *Ukraine* 17 C13
Staryy Kheydzhan, *Russia* 25 C15
Staryy Oskol, *Russia* 22 D6
State College, *U.S.A.* 68 E7
Staten, I. = Estados, I. de Los, *Argentina* 80 G4
Statesboro, *U.S.A.* 69 J5
Statesville, *U.S.A.* 69 H5
Staunton, *Ill., U.S.A.* 70 F10
Staunton, *Va., U.S.A.* 68 F6
Stavanger, *Norway* 9 G11
Staveley, *N.Z.* 51 K3
Stavelot, *Belgium* 15 D5
Staveren, *Neths.* 15 B5
Stavern, *Norway* 9 G14
Stavropol, *Russia* 23 E7
Stawell, *Australia* 55 F3
Stawell →, *Australia* 54 C3
Steamboat Springs, *U.S.A.* 72 F10
Steele, *U.S.A.* 70 B5
Steelton, *U.S.A.* 68 E7
Steelville, *U.S.A.* 71 G9
Steen River, *Canada* 64 B5
Steenkool = Bintuni, *Indonesia* 33 E8
Steenwijk, *Neths.* 15 B6
Steep Pt., *Australia* 53 E1
Steep Rock, *Canada* 65 C9
Stefanie L. = Chew Bahir, *Ethiopia* 45 H12
Stefansson Bay, *Antarctica* 5 C5
Steiermark □, *Austria* 16 E8
Steinbach, *Canada* 65 D9
Steinfort, *Lux.* 15 E5
Steinkjer, *Norway* 8 D14
Steinkopf, *S. Africa* 48 D2
Stellarton, *Canada* 63 C7
Stellenbosch, *S. Africa* 48 E2
Stendal, *Germany* 16 B6
Steornabhaigh = Stornoway, *U.K.* 12 C2
Stepanakert = Xankändi, *Azerbaijan* 23 G8
Stephen, *U.S.A.* 70 A6
Stephens Creek, *Australia* 55 E3
Stephens I., *Canada* 64 C2
Stephenville, *Canada* 63 C8
Stephenville, *U.S.A.* 71 J5
Stepnoi = Elista, *Russia* 23 E7
Stepnyak, *Kazakhstan* 24 D8
Steppe, *Asia* 26 E7
Sterkstroom, *S. Africa* 48 E4
Sterling, *Colo., U.S.A.* 70 E3
Sterling, *Ill., U.S.A.* 70 E10
Sterling, *Kans., U.S.A.* 70 F5
Sterling City, *U.S.A.* 71 K4
Sterlitamak, *Russia* 22 D10
Stettin = Szczecin, *Poland* 16 B8
Stettiner Haff, *Germany* 16 B8
Stettler, *Canada* 64 C6
Steubenville, *U.S.A.* 68 E5

Stevens Point, *U.S.A.* 70 C10
Stevenson L., *Canada* 65 C9
Stewart, *B.C., Canada* 64 B3
Stewart, *N.W.T., Canada* 60 B6
Stewart, C., *Australia* 54 A1
Stewart, I., *Chile* 80 G2
Stewart I., *N.Z.* 51 M1
Stewiacke, *Canada* 63 C7
Steynsburg, *S. Africa* 48 E4
Steyr, *Austria* 16 D8
Steytlerville, *S. Africa* 48 E3
Stigler, *U.S.A.* 71 H7
Stikine →, *Canada* 64 B2
Stilfontein, *S. Africa* 48 D4
Stillwater, *N.Z.* 51 K3
Stillwater, *Minn., U.S.A.* 70 C8
Stillwater, *Okla., U.S.A.* 71 G6
Stillwater Range, *U.S.A.* 72 G4
Stilwell, *U.S.A.* 71 H7
Štip, *Macedonia* 21 D10
Stirling, *Australia* 54 B3
Stirling, *Canada* 64 D6
Stirling, *U.K.* 12 E5
Stirling Ra., *Australia* 53 F2
Stjernøya, *Norway* 8 A20
Stjørdalshalsen, *Norway* 8 E14
Stockerau, *Austria* 16 D9
Stockett, *U.S.A.* 72 C8
Stockholm, *Sweden* 9 G18
Stockport, *U.K.* 10 D5
Stockton, *Calif., U.S.A.* 73 H3
Stockton, *Kans., U.S.A.* 70 F5
Stockton, *Mo., U.S.A.* 71 G8
Stockton-on-Tees, *U.K.* 10 C6
Stoke on Trent, *U.K.* 10 D5
Stokes Bay, *Canada* 62 C3
Stokes Pt., *Australia* 54 G3
Stokes Ra., *Australia* 52 C5
Stokksnes, *Iceland* 8 D6
Stokmarknes, *Norway* 8 B16
Stolac, *Bos.-H.* 21 C7
Stolbovaya, *Russia* 25 C16
Stolbovoy, Ostrov, *Russia* 25 D17
Stolbtsy = Stowbtsy, *Belarus* 17 B14
Stolin, *Belarus* 17 C14
Stonehaven, *U.K.* 12 E6
Stonehenge, *Australia* 54 C3
Stonewall, *Canada* 65 C9
Stony L., *Canada* 65 B9
Stony Rapids, *Canada* 65 B7
Stony Tunguska = Podkamennaya Tunguska →, *Russia* 25 C10
Stora Lulevatten, *Sweden* 8 C18
Storavan, *Sweden* 8 D18
Stord, *Norway* 9 G11
Store Bælt, *Denmark* 9 J14
Store Creek, *Australia* 55 E4
Storm B., *Australia* 54 G4
Storm Lake, *U.S.A.* 70 D7
Stormberge, *S. Africa* 48 E4
Stormsrivier, *S. Africa* 48 E3
Stornoway, *U.K.* 12 C2
Storozhinets = Storozhynets, *Ukraine* 17 D13
Storozhynets, *Ukraine* 17 D13
Storsjön, *Sweden* 8 E16
Storuman, *Sweden* 8 D17
Storuman, sjö, *Sweden* 8 D17
Stoughton, *Canada* 65 D8
Stour →, *Here. & Worcs., U.K.* 11 E5
Stour →, *Kent, U.K.* 11 F9
Stour →, *Suffolk, U.K.* 11 F9
Stourbridge, *U.K.* 11 E5
Stout, L., *Canada* 65 C10
Stowbtsy, *Belarus* 17 B14
Stowmarket, *U.K.* 11 E9
Strabane, *U.K.* 13 B4
Strabane □, *U.K.* 13 B4
Strahan, *Australia* 54 G4
Stralsund, *Germany* 16 A7
Strand, *S. Africa* 48 E2
Stranda, *Møre og Romsdal, Norway* 9 E12
Stranda, *Nord-Trøndelag, Norway* 8 E14
Strangford L., *U.K.* 13 B6
Stranraer, *U.K.* 12 G3
Strasbourg, *Canada* 65 C8
Strasbourg, *France* 18 B7
Strasburg, *U.S.A.* 70 B4
Stratford, *Canada* 62 D3
Stratford, *N.Z.* 51 H5
Stratford, *Calif., U.S.A.* 73 H4
Stratford, *Tex., U.S.A.* 71 G3
Stratford-upon-Avon, *U.K.* 11 E6
Strath Spey, *U.K.* 12 D5
Strathalbyn, *Australia* 55 F2
Strathclyde □, *U.K.* 12 F4
Strathcona Prov. Park, *Canada* 64 D3
Strathmore, *Australia* 54 B3
Strathmore, *Canada* 64 C6
Strathmore, *U.K.* 12 E5
Strathnaver, *Canada* 64 C4
Strathpeffer, *U.K.* 12 D4
Strathroy, *Canada* 62 D3
Strathy Pt., *U.K.* 12 C4
Stratton, *U.S.A.* 70 F3
Straubing, *Germany* 16 D7
Straumnes, *Iceland* 8 C2
Strawberry Reservoir, *U.S.A.* 72 F8

121

Strawn, U.S.A. 71 J5
Streaky B., Australia .. 55 E1
Streaky Bay, Australia 55 E1
Streator, U.S.A. 70 E10
Streeter, U.S.A. 70 B5
Strelka, Russia 25 D10
Streymoy, Færøe Is. . 8 E9
Strezhevoy, Russia .. 24 C8
Strimón →, Greece . 21 D10
Strimonikós Kólpos,
  Greece 21 D11
Strómboli, Italy 20 E6
Stromeferry, U.K. .. 12 D3
Stromness, U.K. 12 C5
Stromsburg, U.S.A. . 70 E6
Strömstad, Sweden .. 9 G14
Strömsund, Sweden .. 8 E16
Stronsay, U.K. 12 B6
Stroud, U.K. 11 F5
Stroud Road, Australia 55 E5
Struer, Denmark 9 H13
Strumica, Macedonia . 21 D10
Struthers, Canada .. 62 C2
Struthers, U.S.A. ... 68 E5
Stryker, U.S.A. 72 B6
Stryy, Ukraine 17 D12
Strzelecki Cr. →,
  Australia 55 D2
Stuart, Fla., U.S.A. . 69 M5
Stuart, Nebr., U.S.A. . 70 D5
Stuart →, Canada .. 64 C4
Stuart Bluff Ra.,
  Australia 52 D5
Stuart L., Canada ... 64 C4
Stuart Ra., Australia 55 D1
Stull, L., Canada 62 B1
Stung Treng = Stoeng
  Treng, Cambodia 34 F8
Stupart →, Canada . 65 B10
Sturgeon B., Canada . 65 C9
Sturgeon Bay, U.S.A. 68 C2
Sturgeon Falls, Canada 62 C4
Sturgeon L., Alta.,
  Canada 64 B5
Sturgeon L., Ont.,
  Canada 62 B1
Sturgis, Mich., U.S.A. 68 E3
Sturgis, S. Dak., U.S.A. 70 C3
Sturt Cr. →, Australia 52 C4
Sturt Creek, Australia 52 C4
Stutterheim, S. Africa 48 E4
Stuttgart, Germany .. 16 D5
Stuttgart, U.S.A. 71 H9
Stykkishólmur, Iceland 8 D2
Styria = Steiermark □,
  Austria 16 E8
Suakin, Sudan 45 E12
Subang, Indonesia .. 33 G12
Subansiri →, India .. 37 F18
Subayhah, Si. Arabia 38 D3
Subi, Indonesia 32 D3
Subotica, Serbia, Yug. 21 A8
Success, Canada 65 C7
Suceava, Romania .. 17 E14
Suchan, Russia 28 C6
Suchou = Suzhou,
  China 31 C7
Süchow = Xuzhou,
  China 31 C6
Suck →, Ireland 13 C3
Sucre, Bolivia 78 G5
Sud, Pte., Canada ... 63 C7
Sud-Ouest, Pte. du,
  Canada 63 C7
Sudan, U.S.A. 71 H3
Sudan ■, Africa 45 E11
Sudbury, Canada 62 C3
Sudbury, U.K. 11 E8
Sûdd, Sudan 45 G11
Sudeten Mts. = Sudety,
  Europe 17 C9
Sudety, Europe 17 C9
Suðuroy, Færoe Is. ... 8 F9
Sudirman,
  Pegunungan,
  Indonesia 33 E9
Sueca, Spain 19 C5
Suez = El Suweis,
  Egypt 45 C11
Suez, G. of = Suweis,
  Khalîg el, Egypt .. 45 C11
Suffield, Canada 65 C6
Suffolk, U.S.A. 68 G7
Suffolk □, U.K. 11 E9
Sugar City, U.S.A. .. 70 F3
Sugluk = Salluit,
  Canada 61 B12
Suhâr, Oman 39 E8
Suhl, Germany 16 C6
Suihua, China 31 B7
Suir →, Ireland 13 D4
Sukabumi, Indonesia 33 G12
Sukadana, Kalimantan,
  Indonesia 32 E3
Sukadana, Sumatra,
  Indonesia 32 E3
Sukagawa, Japan ... 29 F10
Sukaraja, Indonesia . 32 E4
Sukarnapura =
  Jayapura, Indonesia 33 E10
Sukhona →, Russia . 22 C6
Sukhumi = Sokhumi,
  Georgia 23 F7
Sukkur, Pakistan ... 36 F6
Sukkur Barrage,
  Pakistan 36 F6
Sukumo, Japan 29 H6
Sukunka →, Canada 64 B4
Sula, Kepulauan,
  Indonesia 33 E7
Sulaiman Range,
  Pakistan 36 D6
Sūlār, Iran 39 D6
Sulawesi □, Indonesia 33 E6

Sulawesi Sea =
  Celebes Sea,
  Indonesia 33 D6
Sulima, S. Leone ... 44 G2
Sulina, Romania 17 F15
Sulitjelma, Norway .. 8 C17
Sullana, Peru 78 D2
Sullivan, Ill., U.S.A. .. 70 F10
Sullivan, Ind., U.S.A. . 68 F2
Sullivan, Mo., U.S.A. . 70 F9
Sullivan Bay, Canada . 64 C3
Sullivan I. = Lambi
  Kyun, Burma 34 G5
Sulphur, La., U.S.A. . 71 K8
Sulphur, Okla., U.S.A. 71 H6
Sulphur Pt., Canada . 64 A6
Sulphur Springs, U.S.A. 71 J7
Sulphur Springs
  Draw →, U.S.A. ... 71 J4
Sultan, Canada 62 C3
Sultanpur, India 37 F13
Sultsa, Russia 22 B8
Sulu Arch., Phil. ... 33 C6
Sulu Sea, E. Indies .. 33 C6
Suluq, Libya 45 B9
Sulzberger Ice Shelf,
  Antarctica 5 D10
Sumalata, Indonesia . 33 D6
Sumatera □, Indonesia 32 D2
Sumatra =
  Sumatera □,
  Indonesia 32 D2
Sumatra, U.S.A. 72 C10
Sumba, Indonesia ... 33 F5
Sumba, Selat,
  Indonesia 33 F5
Sumbawa, Indonesia . 32 F5
Sumbawa Besar,
  Indonesia 32 F5
Sumbe, Angola 46 G2
Sumburgh Hd., U.K. . 12 B7
Sumdeo, Indonesia . 33 G12
Sumen, Bulgaria 21 C12
Sumenep, Indonesia . 33 G15
Sumgait = Sumqayıt,
  Azerbaijan 23 F8
Summer L., U.S.A. ... 72 E3
Summerland, Canada . 64 D5
Summerside, Canada . 63 C7
Summersville,
  U.S.A. 68 F5
Summerville, Ga.,
  U.S.A. 69 H3
Summerville, S.C.,
  U.S.A. 69 J5
Summit Lake, Canada 64 C4
Summit Peak, U.S.A. . 73 H10
Sumner, U.S.A. 70 D8
Sumoto, Japan 29 G7
Sumperk, Czech. ... 17 D9
Sumqayıt, Azerbaijan . 23 F8
Sumter, U.S.A. 69 J5
Sumy, Ukraine 23 D5
Sun City, U.S.A. 73 K7
Sunagawa, Japan ... 28 C10
Sunart, L., U.K. 12 E3
Sunburst, U.S.A. 72 B8
Sunbury, Australia .. 55 F3
Sunbury, U.S.A. 68 E7
Sunda, Selat, Indonesia 32 F3
Sunda Is., Indonesia . 26 K13
Sunda Str. = Sunda,
  Selat, Indonesia .. 32 F3
Sundance, U.S.A. ... 70 C2
Sundarbans, The, Asia 37 J16
Sundargarh, India ... 37 H14
Sundays →
  Sondags →,
  S. Africa 48 E4
Sunderland, U.K. ... 10 C6
Sundre, Canada 64 C6
Sundridge, Canada .. 62 C4
Sundsvall, Sweden .. 9 E17
Sungai Patani, Malaysia 34 P13
Sungaigerong,
  Indonesia 32 E2
Sungailiat, Indonesia . 32 E3
Sungaipakning,
  Indonesia 32 D2
Sungaipenuh,
  Indonesia 32 E2
Sungaitiram, Indonesia 32 E5
Sungari = Songhua
  Jiang →, China .. 31 B8
Sungei Siput, Malaysia 34 Q14
Sungguminasa,
  Indonesia 33 F5
Sunghua Chiang =
  Songhua Jiang →,
  China 31 B8
Sunndalsøra, Norway . 9 E13
Sunnyside, Utah,
  U.S.A. 72 G8
Sunnyside, Wash.,
  U.S.A. 72 C3
Sunnyvale, U.S.A. ... 73 H2
Sunray, U.S.A. 71 G4
Suntar, Russia 25 C12
Suomenselkä, Finland 8 E21
Suomussalmi, Finland 8 D23
Suoyarvi, Russia ... 22 B5
Supai, U.S.A. 73 H7
Supaul, India 37 F15
Superior, Ariz., U.S.A. 73 K8
Superior, Mont., U.S.A. 72 C6
Superior, Nebr., U.S.A. 70 E5
Superior, Wis., U.S.A. 70 B8
Superior, L., U.S.A. . 62 C2
Suphan Buri, Thailand 34 E6
Supiori, Indonesia ... 33 E9
Sūq Suwayq, Si. Arabia 38 E3
Sūr, Lebanon 41 B4
Sur, Pt., U.S.A. 73 H3
Sura →, Russia 22 C8
Surabaja = Surabaya,
  Indonesia 33 G15

Surabaya, Indonesia . 33 G15
Surakarta, Indonesia . 33 G14
Surat, Australia 55 D4
Surat, India 36 J8
Surat Thani, Thailand . 34 H5
Suratgarh, India 36 E8
Sûre = Sauer →,
  Germany 15 E6
Surgut, Russia 24 C8
Suriapet, India 36 L11
Surigao, Phil. 33 C7
Surin, Thailand 34 E7
Surinam ■, S. Amer. . 79 C7
Surinam →
  Surinam ■, Surinam 79 C7
Suriname ■, Surinam 79 C7
Sûrmaq, Iran 39 D7
Surrey □, U.K. 11 F7
Surt, Libya 45 B8
Surt, Khalij, Libya .. 45 B8
Surtsey, Iceland 8 E3
Suruga-Wan, Japan . 29 G9
Susaki, Japan 29 H6
Süsangerd, Iran 39 D6
Susanino, Russia ... 25 D15
Susanville, U.S.A. .. 72 F3
Susquehanna →,
  U.S.A. 68 F7
Susques, Argentina . 80 A3
Sussex, Canada 63 C6
Sussex, U.S.A. 68 E8
Sussex, E. □, U.K. .. 11 G8
Sussex, W. □, U.K. .. 11 G7
Sustut →, Canada .. 64 B3
Susuman, Russia ... 25 C15
Susunu, Indonesia .. 33 E8
Susurluk, Turkey ... 21 E13
Sutherland, S. Africa . 48 E3
Sutherland, U.S.A. .. 70 E4
Sutherland Falls, N.Z. 51 L1
Sutherlin, U.S.A. ... 72 E2
Sutlej →, Pakistan . 36 E7
Sutton, U.S.A. 70 E6
Sutton →, Canada .. 62 A3
Sutton in Ashfield, U.K. 10 D6
Sutton →, Australia . 54 C4
Suttsu, Japan 28 C10
Suva, Fiji 51 D8
Suva Planina,
  Serbia, Yug. 21 C10
Suvorov Is. =
  Suwarrow Is.,
  Cook Is. 57 J11
Suwałki, Poland 17 A12
Suwannee →, U.S.A. 69 L4
Suwanose-Jima, Japan 29 K4
Suwarrow Is., Cook Is. 57 J11
Suwayq aş Şuqban,
  Iraq 38 D5
Suweis, Khalîg el,
  Egypt 45 C11
Suzdal, Russia 22 C7
Suzhou, China 31 C7
Suzu, Japan 29 F8
Suzu-Misaki, Japan . 29 F8
Suzuka, Japan 29 G8
Svalbard, Arctic ... 4 B8
Svappavaara, Sweden . 8 C19
Svartisen, Norway .. 8 C15
Svay Rieng, Cambodia 34 G8
Svealand □, Sweden . 9 G16
Sveg, Sweden 9 E16
Svendborg, Denmark . 9 J14
Sverdlovsk =
  Yekaterinburg, Russia 22 C11
Sverdrup Is., Canada . 4 B3
Svetlaya, Russia ... 28 A9
Svetlogorsk =
  Svyetlahorsk, Belarus 17 B15
Svetozarevo,
  Serbia, Yug. 21 C9
Svir →, Russia 22 B5
Svishtov, Bulgaria .. 21 C11
Svislach, Belarus ... 17 B13
Svobodnyy, Russia .. 25 D13
Svolvær, Norway ... 8 B16
Svyetlahorsk, Belarus 17 B15
Swabian Alps =
  Schwäbische Alb,
  Germany 16 D5
Swainsboro, U.S.A. . 69 J4
Swakopmund, Namibia 48 C1
Swale →, U.K. 10 C6
Swan Hill, Australia . 55 F3
Swan Hills, Canada . 64 C5
Swan L., Canada ... 65 C8
Swan River, Canada . 65 C8
Swanage, U.K. 11 G6
Swansea, Australia .. 55 E5
Swansea, U.K. 11 F4
Swartberge, S. Africa 48 E3
Swartmodder, S. Africa 48 D3
Swartruggens, S. Africa 48 D4
Swastika, Canada ... 62 C3
Swatow = Shantou,
  China 31 D6
Swaziland ■, Africa . 49 D5
Sweden ■, Europe .. 9 G16
Sweet Home, U.S.A. . 72 D2
Sweetwater, U.S.A. . 71 J4
Sweetwater →, U.S.A. 72 E10
Swellendam, S. Africa 48 E3
Świdnica, Poland ... 16 C9
Świdnik, Poland 17 C12
Świebodzin, Poland . 16 B8
Świecie, Poland 17 B10
Swift Current, Canada 65 C7
Swiftcurrent →,
  Canada 65 C7
Swilly, L., Ireland ... 13 A4
Swindle, I., Canada . 64 C3
Swindon, U.K. 11 F6
Świnemünde =
  Świnoujście, Poland 16 B8
Świnoujście, Poland . 16 B8

Świnoujście, Poland . 16 B8
Switzerland ■, Europe 16 E5
Swords, Ireland 13 C5
Sydney, Australia ... 55 E5
Sydney, Canada 63 C7
Sydney Mines, Canada 63 C7
Sydprøven, Greenland 4 C5
Sydra, G. of = Surt,
  Khalij, Libya 45 B8
Syktyvkar, Russia .. 22 B9
Sylacauga, U.S.A. .. 69 J2
Sylarna, Sweden ... 8 E15
Sylhet, Bangla. 37 G17
Sylt, Germany 16 A5
Sylvan Lake, Canada . 64 C6
Sylvania, U.S.A. 69 J5
Sylvester, U.S.A. ... 69 K4
Sym, Russia 24 C9
Synnott Ra., Australia 52 C4
Syracuse, Kans., U.S.A. 71 F4
Syracuse, N.Y., U.S.A. 68 D7
Syrdarya →
  Kazakhstan 24 E7
Syria ■, Asia 38 C3
Syul'dzhyukyor, Russia 25 C12
Syzran, Russia 22 D8
Szczecin, Poland ... 16 B8
Szczecinek, Poland . 17 B9
Szczytno, Poland ... 17 B11
Szechwan =
  Sichuan □, China . 30 C5
Szeged, Hungary ... 17 E11
Székesfehérvár,
  Hungary 17 E10
Szekszárd, Hungary . 17 E11
Szentes, Hungary ... 17 E11
Szolnok, Hungary .. 17 E11
Szombathely, Hungary 17 E9

T

Tabacal, Argentina ... 80 A4
Tabaco, Phil. 33 B6
Tābah, Si. Arabia ... 38 E4
Tabarka, Tunisia ... 44 A6
Tabas, Khorāsān, Iran 39 C9
Tabas, Khorāsān, Iran 39 C8
Tabatinga, Serra da,
  Brazil 79 F10
Tābāzīn, Iran 39 D8
Taber, Canada 64 D6
Tabibuga, Phil. 33 B6
Table B. = Tafelbaai,
  S. Africa 48 E2
Table B., Canada ... 63 B8
Table Mt., S. Africa . 48 E2
Tableland, Australia . 52 C4
Tabletop, Mt., Australia 54 C4
Tábor, Czech. 16 D8
Tabora, Tanzania ... 46 F6
Tabou, Ivory C. 44 H3
Tabrīz, Iran 38 B5
Tabuaeran, Pac. Oc. . 57 G12
Tabūk, Si. Arabia ... 38 D3
Tacheng, China 30 B3
Tacloban, Phil. 33 B6
Tacna, Peru 78 G4
Tacoma, U.S.A. 72 C2
Tacuarembó, Uruguay 80 C5
Tademaït, Plateau du,
  Algeria 44 C5
Tadjoura, Djibouti .. 40 E3
Tadmor, N.Z. 51 J4
Tadoule, L., Canada . 65 B9
Tadoussac, Canada . 63 C6
Tadzhikistan =
  Tajikistan ■, Asia . 24 F8
Taegu, S. Korea 31 C7
Taejŏn, S. Korea ... 31 C7
Tafalla, Spain 19 A5
Tafelbaai, S. Africa . 48 E2
Tafermaar, Indonesia 33 F8
Tafihān, Iran 39 D7
Taft, Iran 39 D7
Taft, Phil. 33 B7
Taft, Calif., U.S.A. .. 73 J4
Taft, Tex., U.S.A. ... 71 M6
Taga Dzong, Bhutan . 37 F16
Taganrog, Russia ... 23 E6
Tagbilaran, Phil. 33 C6
Tagish, Canada 64 A2
Tagish L., Canada ... 64 A2
Tagliamento →, Italy 20 B5
Taguatinga, Brazil .. 79 F10
Tagum, Phil. 33 C7
Tagus = Tejo →,
  Europe 19 C1
Tahakopa, N.Z. 51 M2
Tahan, Gunong,
  Malaysia 34 Q15
Tahat, Algeria 44 D6
Tāherī, Iran 39 E7
Tahiti, Pac. Oc. 57 J13
Tahoe, L., U.S.A. ... 72 G3
Tahoe City, U.S.A. .. 72 G3
Tahoua, Niger 44 F6
Tahta, Egypt 45 C11
Tahulandang, Indonesia 33 D7
Tahuna, Indonesia .. 33 D7
Taï, Ivory C. 44 G3
Taibei, Taiwan 31 D7
T'aichung = Taizhong,
  Taiwan 31 D7
Taieri →, N.Z. 51 M3
Taihape, N.Z. 51 H5
Tailem Bend, Australia 55 F2
Taimyr Peninsula =
  Taymyr, Poluostrov,
  Russia 25 B11
Tain, U.K. 12 D4
Tainan, Taiwan 31 D7

Taínaron, Ákra, Greece 21 F10
T'aipei = Taibei,
  Taiwan 31 D7
Taiping, Malaysia ... 34 Q13
Tairbeart = Tarbert,
  U.K. 12 D2
Taitao, Pen. de, Chile 80 F2
Taivalkoski, Finland . 8 D23
Taiwan ■, Asia 31 D7
Taïyetos Óros, Greece 21 F10
Taiyiba, Israel 41 C4
Taiyuan, China 31 C6
Taizhong, Taiwan ... 31 D7
Ta'izz, Yemen 40 E3
Tājābād, Iran 39 D7
Tājūrā, Libya 45 B7
Tajikistan ■, Asia .. 24 F8
Tajima, Japan 29 F9
Tajo = Tejo →,
  Europe 19 C1
Tajrīsh, Iran 39 C6
Tājūrā, Libya 45 B7
Tak, Thailand 34 D5
Takāb, Iran 38 B5
Takachiho, Japan ... 29 H5
Takada, Japan 29 F9
Takahagi, Japan 29 F10
Takaka, N.Z. 51 J4
Takamatsu, Japan .. 29 G7
Takaoka, Japan 29 F8
Takapuna, N.Z. 51 G5
Takasaki, Japan 29 F9
Takatsuki, Japan ... 29 G7
Takaungu, Kenya ... 46 E7
Takayama, Japan ... 29 F8
Take-Shima, Japan .. 29 J5
Takefu, Japan 29 G8
Takengon, Indonesia 32 D1
Takeo, Cambodia ... 34 G8
Takeo, Sa. del,
  Japan 29 H5
Tākestān, Iran 39 C6
Taketa, Japan 29 H5
Takikawa, Japan ... 28 C10
Takla →, Canada .. 64 B3
Takla Landing, Canada 64 B3
Takla Makan =
  Taklamakan Shamo,
  China 26 F12
Taklamakan Shamo,
  China 26 F12
Taku →, Canada ... 64 B2
Takum, Nigeria 44 G6
Tal Halāl, Iran 39 D7
Talara, Peru 78 D2
Talas, Kyrgyzstan ... 24 E8
Talaud, Kepulauan,
  Indonesia 33 D7
Talaud Is. = Talaud,
  Kepulauan, Indonesia 33 D7
Talavera de la Reina,
  Spain 19 C3
Talawana, Australia . 52 D3
Talayan, Phil. 33 C6
Talbot, C., Australia . 52 B4
Talbragar →, Australia 55 E4
Talca, Chile 80 D2
Talcahuano, Chile .. 80 D2
Talcher, India 37 J14
Taldy Kurgan =
  Taldyqorghan,
  Kazakhstan 24 E8
Taldyqorghan,
  Kazakhstan 24 E8
Tālesh, Iran 39 B6
Tālesh, Kūhhā-ye, Iran 39 B6
Tali Post, Sudan ... 45 G11
Talibon, Phil. 33 B6
Talihina, U.S.A. 71 H7
Taling Sung, Thailand 34 E5
Taliwang, Indonesia . 32 F5
Tall 'Asūr, West Bank . 41 D4
Tall Kalakh, Syria ... 41 A5
Talladega, U.S.A. ... 69 J2
Tallahassee, U.S.A. . 69 K3
Tallangatta, Australia 55 F4
Tallarook, Australia . 55 F4
Tallering Pk., Australia 53 E2
Tallinn, Estonia 9 G21
Tallulah, U.S.A. 71 J9
Talodi, Sudan 45 F11
Talsi, Latvia 9 H20
Taltal, Chile 80 B2
Taltson →, Canada . 64 A6
Talwood, Australia . 55 D4
Talyawalka Cr. →,
  Australia 55 E3
Tama, U.S.A. 70 E8
Tamala, Australia ... 53 E1
Tamale, Ghana 44 G4
Tamano, Japan 29 G6
Tamanrasset, Algeria 44 D6
Tamar →, U.K. 11 G3
Tamarang, Australia . 55 E5
Tamashima, Japan .. 29 G6
Tamaské, Niger 44 F6
Tambacounda, Senegal 44 F2
Tambelan, Kepulauan,
  Indonesia 32 D3
Tambellup, Australia 53 F2
Tambo, Australia ... 54 C4
Tambo de Mora, Peru 78 F3
Tambohorano, Madag. 49 B7
Tambora, Indonesia . 32 F5
Tambov, Russia 22 D7
Tambuku, Indonesia 33 G15
Tamburâ, Sudan ... 45 G10
Tâmchekkett, Mauritania 44 E2
Tamega →, Portugal 19 B1
Tamenglong, India .. 37 G18
Tamgak, Mts., Niger 44 E6
Tamil Nadu □, India 36 P10
Tammerfors =
  Tampere, Finland . 9 F20
Tammisaari, Finland . 9 F20

Tamo Abu,
  Pegunungan,
  Malaysia 32 D5
Tampa, U.S.A. 69 M4
Tampa B., U.S.A. ... 69 M4
Tampere, Finland ... 9 F20
Tampico, Mexico ... 74 C5
Tampin, Malaysia ... 34 S15
Tamrida = Qādib,
  Yemen 40 E5
Tamu, Burma 37 G19
Tamworth, Australia . 55 E5
Tamworth, U.K. 11 E6
Tana →, Kenya 46 E8
Tana →, Norway ... 8 A23
Tana, L., Ethiopia ... 45 F12
Tanabe, Japan 29 H7
Tanafjorden, Norway . 8 A23
Tanahbala, Indonesia 32 E1
Tanahgrogot, Indonesia 32 E5
Tanahjampea,
  Indonesia 33 F6
Tanahmasa, Indonesia 32 E1
Tanahmerah, Indonesia 33 F10
Tanakura, Japan 29 F10
Tanami, Australia ... 52 C4
Tanami Desert,
  Australia 52 C5
Tanana, U.S.A. 60 B4
Tanana →, U.S.A. . 60 B4
Tananarive =
  Antananarivo,
  Madag. 49 B8
Tánaro →, Italy 20 B3
Tanbar, Australia ... 54 D3
Tandag, Phil. 33 C7
Tandaué, Angola ... 48 B2
Tandil, Argentina ... 80 D5
Tandil, Sa. del,
  Argentina 80 D5
Tando Adam, Pakistan 36 G6
Tandou L., Australia . 55 E3
Tane-ga-Shima, Japan 29 J5
Taneatua, N.Z. 51 H6
Tanen Tong Dan,
  Burma 34 D5
Tanezrouft, Algeria . 44 D5
Tanga, Tanzania 46 F7
Tanganyika, L., Africa 46 F6
Tanger, Morocco ... 44 A3
Tangerang, Indonesia 33 G12
Tanggula Shan, China 30 C4
Tangier = Tanger,
  Morocco 44 A3
Tangkak, Malaysia .. 34 S15
Tangorin P.O., Australia 54 C3
Tangshan, China ... 31 C6
Tanimbar, Kepulauan,
  Indonesia 33 F8
Tanimbar Is. =
  Tanimbar,
  Kepulauan, Indonesia 33 F8
Tanjay, Phil. 33 C6
Tanjore = Thanjavur,
  India 36 P11
Tanjung, Indonesia . 32 E5
Tanjungbalai, Indonesia 32 D1
Tanjungbatu, Indonesia 32 D5
Tanjungkarang
  Telukbetung,
  Indonesia 32 F3
Tanjungpandan,
  Indonesia 32 E3
Tanjungpinang,
  Indonesia 32 D2
Tanjungpriok,
  Indonesia 33 G12
Tanjungredeb,
  Indonesia 32 D5
Tanjungselor, Indonesia 32 D5
Tannu-Ola, Russia .. 25 D10
Tanout, Niger 44 F6
Tanta, Egypt 45 B11
Tantung = Dandong,
  China 31 B7
Tanunda, Australia . 55 E2
Tanzania ■, Africa . 46 F6
Tanzilla →, Canada . 64 B2
Taolanaro, Madag. .. 49 D8
Taos, U.S.A. 73 H11
Taoudenni, Mali ... 44 D4
Taourirt, Morocco .. 44 B4
Tapa, Estonia 9 G21
Tapa Shan = Daba
  Shan, China 31 C5
Tapah, Malaysia ... 34 Q14
Tapajós →, Brazil .. 79 D8
Tapaktuan, Indonesia 32 D1
Tapanui, N.Z. 51 L2
Tapauá →, Brazil .. 78 E6
Tapeta, Liberia 44 G3
Tapi →, India 36 J8
Tapirapecó, Serra,
  Venezuela 78 C6
Tappahannock, U.S.A. 68 G7
Tapuaenuku, Mt., N.Z. 51 J4
Tapul Group, Phil. .. 33 C6
Taqiābād, Iran 39 C8
Taqtaq, Iraq 38 C5
Taquari →, Brazil .. 78 G7
Tara, Australia 55 D5
Tara, Russia 24 D8
Tara →,
  Montenegro, Yug. . 21 C8
Tara →, Russia 24 D8
Tarabagatay, Khrebet,
  Kazakhstan 24 E9
Tarābulus, Lebanon . 41 A4
Tarābulus, Libya ... 45 B7
Tarakan, Indonesia . 32 D5
Taralga, Australia ... 55 E4
Tarama-Jima, Japan . 29 M2
Taran, Mys, Russia . 9 J18
Taranaki □, N.Z. ... 51 H5

Tarancón, Spain	19	B4
Taranga Hill, India	36	H8
Táranto, Italy	20	D7
Táranto, G. di, Italy	20	D7
Tarapacá, Colombia	78	D5
Tararua Ra., N.Z.	51	J5
Tarashcha, Ukraine	17	D16
Tarauacá, Brazil	78	E4
Tarauacá →, Brazil	78	E5
Tarawera, N.Z.	51	H6
Tarawera L., N.Z.	51	H6
Tarazona, Spain	19	B5
Tarbat Ness, U.K.	12	D5
Tarbela Dam, Pakistan	36	B8
Tarbert, Strath., U.K.	12	F3
Tarbert, W. Isles, U.K.	12	D2
Tarbes, France	18	E4
Tarboro, U.S.A.	69	H7
Tarbrax, Australia	54	C3
Tarcoola, Australia	55	E1
Tarcoon, Australia	55	E4
Taree, Australia	55	E5
Tarfaya, Morocco	44	C2
Tarifa, Spain	19	D3
Tarija, Bolivia	80	A4
Tariku →, Indonesia	33	E9
Tarim Basin = Tarim Pendi, China	30	B3
Tarim He →, China	30	C3
Tarim Pendi, China	30	B3
Taritatu →, Indonesia	33	E9
Tarka →, S. Africa	48	E4
Tarkastad, S. Africa	48	E4
Tarkhankut, Mys, Ukraine	23	E5
Tarko Sale, Russia	24	C8
Tarkwa, Ghana	44	G4
Tarlac, Phil.	33	A6
Tarlton Downs, Australia	54	C2
Tarma, Peru	78	F3
Tarn →, France	18	E4
Tarnobrzeg, Poland	17	C11
Tarnów, Poland	17	C11
Tarnowskie Góry, Poland	17	C10
Taroom, Australia	55	D4
Taroudannt, Morocco	44	B3
Tarpon Springs, U.S.A.	69	L4
Tarragona, Spain	19	B6
Tarrasa, Spain	19	B7
Tarshiha = Me'ona, Israel	41	B4
Tarso Emissi, Chad	45	D8
Tarsus, Turkey	23	G5
Tartagal, Argentina	80	A4
Tartu, Estonia	9	G22
Tarţūs, Syria	38	C2
Tarumizu, Japan	29	J5
Tarutao, Ko, Thailand	34	J5
Tarutung, Indonesia	32	D1
Taseko →, Canada	64	C4
Tash-Kömür, Kyrgyzstan	24	E8
Tash-Kumyr = Tash-Kömür, Kyrgyzstan	24	E8
Tashauz = Dashhowuz, Turkmenistan	24	E6
Tashi Chho Dzong = Thimphu, Bhutan	37	F16
Tashkent = Toshkent, Uzbekistan	24	E7
Tashtagol, Russia	24	D9
Tasikmalaya, Indonesia	33	G13
Taskan, Russia	25	C16
Tasman B., N.Z.	51	J4
Tasman Mts., N.Z.	51	J4
Tasman Pen., Australia	54	G4
Tasman Sea, Pac. Oc.	56	L8
Tasmania □, Australia	54	G4
Tasu Sd., Canada	64	C2
Tatabánya, Hungary	17	E10
Tatar Republic = Tatarstan □, Russia	22	C9
Tatarbunary, Ukraine	17	F15
Tatarsk, Russia	24	D8
Tatarstan □, Russia	22	C9
Tateyama, Japan	29	G9
Tathlina L., Canada	64	A5
Tathra, Australia	55	F4
Tatinnai L., Canada	65	A9
Tatnam, C., Canada	65	B10
Tatra = Tatry, Slovak Rep.	17	D11
Tatry, Slovak Rep.	17	D11
Tatsuno, Japan	29	G7
Tatta, Pakistan	36	G5
Tatuí, Brazil	80	A7
Tatum, U.S.A.	71	J3
Tat'ung = Datong, China	31	B6
Tatvan, Turkey	23	G7
Tauern, Austria	16	E7
Taumarunui, N.Z.	51	H5
Taumaturgo, Brazil	78	E4
Taung, S. Africa	48	D3
Taungdwingyi, Burma	37	J19
Taunggyi, Burma	37	J20
Taungup, Burma	37	K19
Taungup Pass, Burma	37	K19
Taungup Taunggya, Burma	37	K18
Taunton, U.K.	11	F4
Taunton, U.S.A.	68	E10
Taunus, Germany	16	C5
Taupo, N.Z.	51	H6
Taupo, L., N.Z.	51	H5
Taurage, Lithuania	9	J20
Tauranga, N.Z.	51	G6
Tauranga Harb., N.Z.	51	G6
Taurianova, Italy	20	E7
Taurus Mts. = Toros Dağları, Turkey	23	G5
Tavda, Russia	24	D7
Tavda →, Russia	24	D7
Taveta, Tanzania	46	E7
Taveuni, Fiji	51	C9
Tavira, Portugal	19	D2
Tavistock, U.K.	11	G3
Tavoy, Burma	34	E5
Taw →, U.K.	11	F3
Tawas City, U.S.A.	68	C4
Tawau, Malaysia	32	D5
Tawitawi, Phil.	33	B6
Tay →, U.K.	12	E5
Tay, Firth of, U.K.	12	E5
Tay, L., Australia	53	F3
Tay, L., U.K.	12	E4
Tay Ninh, Vietnam	34	G9
Tayabamba, Peru	78	E3
Taylakova, Russia	24	D8
Taylakovy = Taylakova, Russia	24	D8
Taylor, Canada	64	B4
Taylor, Nebr., U.S.A.	70	E5
Taylor, Tex., U.S.A.	71	K6
Taylor, Mt., U.S.A.	73	J10
Taylorville, U.S.A.	70	F10
Taymá, Si. Arabia	38	E3
Taymyr, Oz., Russia	25	B11
Taymyr, Poluostrov, Russia	25	B11
Tayport, U.K.	12	E6
Tayshet, Russia	25	D10
Tayside □, U.K.	12	E5
Taytay, Phil.	33	B5
Taz →, Russia	24	C8
Taza, Morocco	44	B4
Tāzah Khurmātū, Iraq	38	C5
Tazawa-Ko, Japan	28	E10
Tazin →, Canada	65	B7
Tazovskiy, Russia	24	C8
Tbilisi, Georgia	23	F7
Tch'eng-tou = Chengdu, China	30	C5
Tchentlo L., Canada	64	B4
Tchibanga, Gabon	46	E2
Tch'ong-k'ing = Chongqing, China	30	D5
Tczew, Poland	17	A10
Te Anau, L., N.Z.	51	L1
Te Aroha, N.Z.	51	G5
Te Awamutu, N.Z.	51	H5
Te Kuiti, N.Z.	51	H5
Te Puke, N.Z.	51	G6
Te Waewae B., N.Z.	51	M1
Tea Tree, Australia	54	C1
Teague, U.S.A.	71	K6
Tebakang, Malaysia	32	D4
Tébessa, Algeria	44	A6
Tebicuary →, Paraguay	80	B5
Tebingtinggi, Indonesia	32	D1
Tecuci, Romania	17	F14
Tecumseh, U.S.A.	68	D4
Tedzhen = Tejen, Turkmenistan	24	F7
Tees →, U.K.	10	C6
Teesside, U.K.	10	C6
Tefé, Brazil	78	D6
Tegal, Indonesia	33	G13
Tegelen, Neths.	15	C6
Tegid, L. = Bala, L., U.K.	10	E4
Tegina, Nigeria	44	F6
Tegucigalpa, Honduras	74	E7
Tehachapi, U.S.A.	73	J4
Tehachapi Mts., U.S.A.	73	J4
Tehrān, Iran	39	C6
Tehuantepec, Mexico	74	D5
Tehuantepec, G. de, Mexico	74	D6
Tehuantepec, Istmo de, Mexico	74	D6
Teifi →, U.K.	11	E3
Teign →, U.K.	11	G4
Teignmouth, U.K.	11	G4
Tejen, Turkmenistan	24	F7
Tejo →, Europe	19	C1
Tekamah, U.S.A.	70	E6
Tekapo, L., N.Z.	51	K3
Tekeli, Kazakhstan	24	E8
Tekirdağ, Turkey	21	D12
Tekkali, India	37	K14
Tekoa, U.S.A.	72	C5
Tel Aviv-Yafo, Israel	41	C3
Tel Lakhish, Israel	41	D3
Tel Megiddo, Israel	41	C4
Tela, Honduras	74	D7
Telanaipura = Jambi, Indonesia	32	E2
Telavi, Georgia	23	F8
Telegraph Creek, Canada	64	B2
Telekhany = Tsyelyakhany, Belarus	17	B13
Telemark, Norway	9	G12
Teleng, Iran	39	E9
Teles Pires →, Brazil	78	E7
Telescope Pk., U.S.A.	73	H5
Telford, U.K.	10	E5
Télimélé, Guinea	44	F2
Telkwa, Canada	64	C3
Tell City, U.S.A.	68	G2
Tellicherry, India	36	P9
Telluride, U.S.A.	73	H10
Telom →, Malaysia	34	Q14
Telpos Iz, Russia	22	B10
Telsen, Argentina	80	E3
Telšiai, Lithuania	9	H20
Teluk Anson, Malaysia	34	Q14
Teluk Betung = Tanjungkarang Telukbetung, Indonesia	32	F3
Teluk Intan = Teluk Anson, Malaysia	34	Q14
Telukbutun, Indonesia	32	D3
Telukdalem, Indonesia	32	D1
Tema, Ghana	44	G5
Temanggung, Indonesia	33	G14
Temax, Mexico	74	C7
Temba, S. Africa	49	D4
Tembeling →, Malaysia	34	Q14
Teme →, U.K.	11	E5
Temecula, U.S.A.	73	K5
Temerloh, Malaysia	34	R15
Temir, Kazakhstan	24	E6
Temirtau, Kazakhstan	24	D8
Temirtau, Russia	24	D9
Témiscaming, Canada	62	C4
Temma, Australia	54	G3
Temora, Australia	55	E4
Tempe, U.S.A.	73	K8
Tempe Downs, Australia	52	D5
Temple, U.S.A.	71	K6
Temple B., Australia	54	A3
Templemore, Ireland	13	D4
Templeton →, Australia	54	C2
Temuco, Chile	80	D2
Temuka, N.Z.	51	L3
Tenaha, U.S.A.	71	K7
Tenali, India	36	L12
Tenasserim, Burma	34	F5
Tenasserim □, Burma	34	F5
Tenby, U.K.	11	F3
Tenda, Col di, France	20	D7
Tendaho, Ethiopia	40	E3
Tenerife, Canary Is.	44	C1
Teng →, Burma	34	B5
Tengah □, Indonesia	33	E6
Tengah Kepulauan, Indonesia	32	F5
Tengchong, China	30	D4
Tenggara □, Indonesia	33	E6
Tenggarong, Indonesia	32	E5
Tengiz, Ozero = Chelkar Tengiz, Solonchak, Kazakhstan	24	E7
Tengiz, Ozero, Kazakhstan	24	D7
Tenkasi, India	36	Q10
Tenke, Zaïre	46	G5
Tenkodogo, Burkina Faso	44	F4
Tennant Creek, Australia	54	B1
Tennessee □, U.S.A.	69	H2
Tennessee →, U.S.A.	68	G1
Tennille, U.S.A.	69	J4
Tenom, Malaysia	32	C5
Tenryū-Gawa →, Japan	29	G8
Tent L., Canada	65	A7
Tenterfield, Australia	55	D5
Teófilo Otoni, Brazil	79	G10
Tepa, Indonesia	33	F7
Tepic, Mexico	74	C4
Teplice, Czech.	16	C7
Ter →, Spain	19	A7
Ter Apel, Neths.	15	B7
Téra, Niger	44	F5
Teraina, Kiribati	57	G11
Téramo, Italy	20	C5
Terang, Australia	55	F3
Terebovlya, Ukraine	17	D13
Terek →, Russia	23	F8
Terengganu □, Malaysia	34	Q16
Teresina, Brazil	79	E10
Terewah, L., Australia	55	D4
Terhazza, Mali	44	D3
Teridgerie Cr. →, Australia	55	E4
Termez = Termiz, Uzbekistan	24	F7
Términi Imerese, Italy	20	F5
Termiz, Uzbekistan	24	F7
Térmoli, Italy	20	C6
Ternate, Indonesia	33	D7
Terneuzen, Neths.	15	C3
Terney, Russia	25	E14
Terni, Italy	20	C5
Ternopil, Ukraine	17	D13
Ternopol = Ternopil, Ukraine	17	D13
Terowie, N.S.W., Australia	55	E4
Terowie, S. Austral., Australia	55	E2
Terrace, Canada	64	C3
Terrace Bay, Canada	62	C2
Terracina, Italy	20	D5
Terralba, Italy	20	E3
Terranova = Ólbia, Italy	20	D3
Terrassa = Tarrasa, Spain	19	B7
Terre Haute, U.S.A.	68	F2
Terrebonne B., U.S.A.	71	L9
Terrell, U.S.A.	71	J6
Terrenceville, Canada	63	C9
Terrick Terrick, Australia	54	C4
Terry, U.S.A.	70	B2
Terschelling, Neths.	15	A5
Teruel, Spain	19	B5
Tervola, Finland	8	C21
Teryaweyna L., Australia	55	E3
Teshio, Japan	28	B10
Teshio-Gawa →, Japan	28	B10
Tesiyn Gol →, Mongolia	30	A4
Teslin, Canada	64	A2
Teslin →, Canada	64	A2
Teslin L., Canada	64	A2
Tessalit, Mali	44	D5
Tessaoua, Niger	44	F6
Test →, U.K.	11	F6
Tetachuck L., Canada	64	C3
Tetas, Pta., Chile	80	A2
Tete, Mozam.	47	H6
Teterev →, Ukraine	17	C16
Teteven, Bulgaria	21	C11
Tethul →, Canada	64	A6
Tetiyev, Ukraine	17	D15
Teton →, U.S.A.	72	C8
Tétouan, Morocco	44	A3
Tetovo, Macedonia	21	C9
Tetuán = Tétouan, Morocco	44	A3
Tetyukhe Pristan, Russia	28	B7
Teuco →, Argentina	80	B4
Teulon, Canada	65	C9
Teun, Indonesia	33	F7
Teutoburger Wald, Germany	16	B5
Tévere →, Italy	20	D5
Teverya, Israel	41	C4
Teviot →, U.K.	12	F6
Tewantin, Australia	55	D5
Tewkesbury, U.K.	11	F5
Texada I., Canada	64	D4
Texarkana, Ark., U.S.A.	71	J8
Texarkana, Tex., U.S.A.	71	J7
Texas, Australia	55	D5
Texas □, U.S.A.	71	K5
Texas City, U.S.A.	71	L7
Texel, Neths.	15	A4
Texhoma, U.S.A.	71	G4
Texline, U.S.A.	71	G3
Texoma, L., U.S.A.	71	J6
Tezpur, India	37	F18
Tezzeron L., Canada	64	C4
Tha-anne →, Canada	65	A10
Tha Nun, Thailand	34	H5
Thaba Putsoa, Lesotho	49	D4
Thabana Ntlenyana, Lesotho	49	D4
Thabazimbi, S. Africa	49	C4
Thai Hoa, Vietnam	34	C8
Thai Nguyen, Vietnam	34	B8
Thailand ■, Asia	34	D6
Thailand, G. of, Asia	34	G6
Thakhek, Laos	34	D8
Thal, Pakistan	36	C7
Thala La, Burma	37	E20
Thallon, Australia	55	D4
Thame →, U.K.	11	F6
Thames, N.Z.	51	G5
Thames →, Canada	62	D3
Thames →, U.K.	11	F8
Thane, India	36	K8
Thanet, I. of, U.K.	11	F9
Thang Binh, Vietnam	34	E10
Thangoo, Australia	52	C3
Thangool, Australia	54	C5
Thanh Hoa, Vietnam	34	C8
Thanh Pho Ho Chi Minh = Phanh Bho Ho Chi Minh, Vietnam	34	G9
Thanjavur, India	36	P11
Thar Desert, India	36	F7
Tharad, India	36	G7
Thargomindah, Australia	55	D3
Tharrawaddy, Burma	37	L19
Tharthār, Mileh, Iraq	38	C4
Tharthār, W. ath →, Iraq	38	C4
Thásos, Greece	21	D11
Thatcher, Ariz., U.S.A.	73	K9
Thatcher, Colo., U.S.A.	71	G2
Thaton, Burma	37	L20
Thaungdut, Burma	37	G19
Thayer, U.S.A.	71	G9
Thayetmyo, Burma	37	K19
Thazi, Burma	37	J20
The Alberga →, Australia	55	D2
The Coorong, Australia	55	F2
The Dalles, U.S.A.	72	D3
The English Company's Is., Australia	54	A2
The Frome →, Australia	55	D2
The Grampians, Australia	55	F3
The Great Divide = Great Dividing Ra., Australia	54	C4
The Hague = 's-Gravenhage, Neths.	15	B4
The Hamilton →, Australia	55	D2
The Macumba →, Australia	55	D2
The Neales →, Australia	55	D2
The Officer →, Australia	53	E5
The Pas, Canada	65	C8
The Rock, Australia	55	F4
The Salt L., Australia	55	E3
The Stevenson →, Australia	55	D2
The Warburton →, Australia	55	D2
Thebes = Thívai, Greece	21	E10
Thedford, U.S.A.	70	E4
Theebine, Australia	55	D5
Thekulthili L., Canada	65	A7
Thelon →, Canada	65	A8
Theodore, Australia	54	C5
Thermaïkós Kólpos, Greece	21	D10
Thermopolis, U.S.A.	72	E9
Thermopylae P., Greece	21	E10
Thessalon, Canada	62	C3
Thessaloníki, Greece	21	D10
Thessaloníki, Gulf of = Thermaïkós Kólpos, Greece	21	D10
Thetford, U.K.	11	E8
Thetford Mines, Canada	63	C5
Theunissen, S. Africa	48	D4
Thevenard, Australia	55	E1
Thibodaux, U.S.A.	71	L9
Thicket Portage, Canada	65	B9
Thief River Falls, U.S.A.	70	A6
Thiel Mts., Antarctica	5	E16
Thiers, France	18	D5
Thies, Senegal	44	F1
Thika, Kenya	46	E7
Thikombia, Fiji	51	B9
Thimphu, Bhutan	37	F16
Thionville, France	18	B7
Thíra, Greece	21	F11
Thirsk, U.K.	10	C6
Thistle I., Australia	55	F2
Thívai, Greece	21	E10
þjórsá →, Iceland	8	E3
Thlewiaza →, Man., Canada	65	B8
Thlewiaza →, N.W.T., Canada	65	A10
Thoa →, Canada	65	A7
Thomas, Okla., U.S.A.	71	H5
Thomas, W. Va., U.S.A.	68	F6
Thomas, L., Australia	55	D2
Thomaston, U.S.A.	69	J3
Thomasville, Ala., U.S.A.	69	K2
Thomasville, Ga., U.S.A.	69	K3
Thomasville, N.C., U.S.A.	69	H5
Thompson, Canada	65	B9
Thompson, U.S.A.	73	G9
Thompson →, Canada	64	C4
Thompson →, U.S.A.	70	F8
Thompson Falls, U.S.A.	72	C6
Thompson Landing, Canada	65	A6
Thompson Pk., U.S.A.	72	F2
Thomson's Falls = Nyahururu, Kenya	46	D7
Thon Buri, Thailand	34	F6
Þórisvatn, Iceland	8	D4
Thornaby on Tees, U.K.	10	C6
Thornbury, U.K.	10	C6
Þórshöfn, Iceland	8	C6
Thouin, C., Australia	52	D2
Thrace, Turkey	21	D12
Three Forks, U.S.A.	72	D8
Three Hills, Canada	64	C6
Three Hummock I., Australia	54	G3
Three Lakes, U.S.A.	70	C10
Three Points, C., Ghana	44	H4
Three Rivers, Australia	53	E2
Three Rivers, U.S.A.	71	L5
Three Sisters, U.S.A.	72	D3
Throssell, Australia	53	E3
Throssell Ra., Australia	52	D3
Thubun Lakes, Canada	65	A6
Thuin, Belgium	15	D4
Thule, Greenland	4	B4
Thun, Switz.	16	E4
Thunder B., U.S.A.	68	C4
Thunder Bay, Canada	62	C2
Thung Song, Thailand	34	H5
Thunkar, Bhutan	37	F17
Thüringer Wald, Germany	16	C6
Thurles, Ireland	13	D4
Thurloo Downs, Australia	55	D3
Thursday I., Australia	54	A3
Thurso, Canada	62	C4
Thurso, U.K.	12	C5
Thurston I., Antarctica	5	D16
Thutade L., Canada	64	B3
Thylungra, Australia	55	D3
Thysville = Mbanza Ngungu, Zaïre	46	F2
Tia, Australia	55	E5
Tian Shan, China	30	B3
Tianjin, China	31	C6
Tianshui, China	30	C5
Tiaret, Algeria	44	A5
Tiassalé, Ivory C.	44	G4
Tibati, Cameroon	45	G7
Tiber = Tévere →, Italy	20	D5
Tiber Reservoir, U.S.A.	72	B8
Tiberias = Teverya, Israel	41	C4
Tiberias, L. = Yam Kinneret, Israel	41	C4
Tibesti, Chad	45	D8
Tibet = Xizang □, China	30	C3
Tibni, Syria	38	C3
Tibooburra, Australia	55	D3
Tiburón, Mexico	74	B2
Tîchît, Mauritania	44	E3
Ticino →, Italy	20	B3
Ticonderoga, U.S.A.	68	D9
Tidaholm, Sweden	9	G15
Tiddim, Burma	37	H18
Tidjikja, Mauritania	44	E2
Tidore, Indonesia	33	D7
Tiel, Neths.	15	C5
Tiel, Senegal	44	F1
Tielt, Belgium	15	D3
Tien Shan, Asia	26	E11
Tien-tsin = Tianjin, China	31	C6
T'ienching = Tianjin, China	31	C6
Tientsin = Tianjin, China	31	C6
Tierra Amarilla, U.S.A.	73	H10
Tierra de Campos, Spain	19	A3
Tierra del Fuego, I. Gr. de, Argentina	80	G3
Tiétar →, Spain	19	C3
Tieyon, Australia	55	D1
Tiffin, U.S.A.	68	E4
Tiflis = Tbilisi, Georgia	23	F7
Tifton, U.S.A.	69	K4
Tifu, Indonesia	33	E7
Tighina, Moldova	17	E15
Tigil, Russia	25	D16
Tignish, Canada	63	C7
Tigre →, Peru	78	D4
Tigris = Dijlah, Nahr →, Asia	38	D5
Tigyaing, Burma	37	H20
Tîh, Gebel el, Egypt	45	C11
Tijuana, Mexico	74	A1
Tikamgarh, India	36	G11
Tikhoretsk, Russia	23	E7
Tikrīt, Iraq	38	C4
Tiksi, Russia	25	B13
Tilamuta, Indonesia	33	D6
Tilburg, Neths.	15	C5
Tilbury, Canada	62	D3
Tilbury, U.K.	11	F8
Tilden, Nebr., U.S.A.	70	D6
Tilden, Tex., U.S.A.	71	L5
Tilichiki, Russia	25	C17
Till →, U.K.	10	B5
Tillabéri, Niger	44	F5
Tillamook, U.S.A.	72	D2
Tillsonburg, Canada	62	D3
Tílos, Greece	21	F12
Tilpa, Australia	55	E3
Tilsit = Sovetsk, Russia	9	J19
Tilt →, U.K.	12	E5
Timagami L., Canada	62	C3
Timanskiy Kryazh, Russia	22	A9
Timaru, N.Z.	51	L3
Timbedgha, Mauritania	44	E3
Timber Lake, U.S.A.	70	C4
Timboon, Australia	55	F3
Timbuktu = Tombouctou, Mali	44	E4
Timimoun, Algeria	44	C5
Timișoara, Romania	17	F11
Timmins, Canada	62	C3
Timok →, Serbia, Yug.	21	B10
Timon, Brazil	79	E10
Timor, Indonesia	33	F7
Timor □, Indonesia	33	F7
Timor Sea, Ind. Oc.	52	B4
Tinaca Pt., Phil.	33	C7
Tindouf, Algeria	44	C3
Tingo Maria, Peru	78	E3
Tinjoub, Algeria	44	C3
Tinkurrin, Australia	53	F2
Tinnevelly = Tirunelveli, India	36	Q10
Tinogasta, Argentina	80	B3
Tínos, Greece	21	F11
Tintinara, Australia	55	F3
Tioman, Pulau, Malaysia	34	S17
Tipongpani, India	37	F19
Tipperary, Ireland	13	D3
Tipperary □, Ireland	13	D4
Tipton, U.K.	11	E5
Tipton, Calif., U.S.A.	73	H4
Tipton, Ind., U.S.A.	68	E2
Tipton, Iowa, U.S.A.	70	E9
Tiptonville, U.S.A.	71	G10
Tīrān, Iran	39	C6
Tirana, Albania	21	D8
Tiranë = Tirana, Albania	21	D8
Tiraspol, Moldova	17	E15
Tirat Karmel, Israel	41	C3
Tire, Turkey	21	E12
Tirebolu, Turkey	23	F6
Tiree, U.K.	12	E2
Tîrgovişte, Romania	17	F13
Tîrgu-Jiu, Romania	17	F12
Tîrgu Mureş, Romania	17	E13
Tirich Mir, Pakistan	36	A7
Tírnăveni, Romania	17	E13
Tírnavos, Greece	21	E10
Tírodi, India	36	J11
Tirol □, Austria	16	E6
Tirso →, Italy	20	E3
Tiruchchirappalli, India	36	P11
Tirunelveli, India	36	Q10
Tirupati, India	36	N11
Tiruppur, India	36	P10
Tiruvannamalai, India	36	N11
Tisa →, Serbia, Yug.	21	B9
Tishomingo, U.S.A.	71	H6
Tisza = Tisa →, Serbia, Yug.	21	B9
Tit-Ary, Russia	25	B13
Titicaca, L., S. Amer.	78	G5
Titograd = Podgorica, Montenegro, Yug.	21	C8
Titov Veles, Macedonia	21	D9
Titova-Mitrovica, Serbia, Yug.	21	C9

Titovo Užice, Serbia, Yug. . 21 C8
Titule, Zaïre . 46 D5
Titusville, Fla., U.S.A. . 69 L5
Titusville, Pa., U.S.A. . 68 E6
Tivaouane, Senegal . 44 F1
Tiverton, U.K. . 11 G4
Tivoli, Italy . 20 D5
Tizi-Ouzou, Algeria . 44 A5
Tiznit, Morocco . 44 C3
Tjeggelvas, Sweden . 8 C17
Tjirebon = Cirebon, Indonesia . 33 G13
Tjörn, Sweden . 9 G14
Tlaxcala, Mexico . 74 D5
Tlaxiaco, Mexico . 74 D5
Tlell, Canada . 64 C2
Tlemcen, Algeria . 44 B4
Tmassah, Libya . 45 C8
Toad →, Canada . 64 B4
Toamasina, Madag. . 49 B8
Toamasina □, Madag. . 49 B8
Toay, Argentina . 80 D4
Toba, Japan . 29 G8
Toba Kakar, Pakistan . 36 D6
Tobago, W. Indies . 74 R21
Tobelo, Indonesia . 33 D7
Tobermorey, Australia 54 C2
Tobermory, Canada . 62 C3
Tobermory, U.K. . 12 E2
Tobin, L., Australia . 52 D4
Tobin L., Canada . 65 C8
Toboali, Indonesia . 32 E3
Tobol, Kazakhstan . 24 D7
Tobol →, Russia . 24 D7
Toboli, Indonesia . 33 E6
Tobolsk, Russia . 24 D7
Tobruk = Tubruq, Libya 45 B9
Tobyl = Tobol →, Russia . 24 D7
Tocantinópolis, Brazil . 79 E9
Tocantins □, Brazil . 79 F9
Tocantins →, Brazil . 79 D9
Toccoa, U.S.A. . 69 H4
Tochigi, Japan . 29 F9
Tochigi □, Japan . 29 F9
Tocopilla, Chile . 80 A2
Tocumwal, Australia . 55 F4
Tocuyo →, Venezuela 78 A5
Todd →, Australia . 54 C2
Todeli, Indonesia . 33 E6
Todenyang, Kenya . 46 D7
Todos os Santos, B. de, Brazil . 79 F11
Tofield, Canada . 64 C6
Tofino, Canada . 64 D3
Tofua, Tonga . 51 D11
Tōgane, Japan . 29 G10
Togba, Mauritania . 44 E2
Togian, Kepulauan, Indonesia . 33 E6
Togliatti, Russia . 22 D8
Togo ■, W. Afr. . 44 G5
Tōhoku □, Japan . 28 E10
Toinya, Sudan . 45 G10
Tojikiston = Tajikistan ■, Asia . 24 F8
Tojo, Indonesia . 33 E6
Tōjō, Japan . 29 G6
Tokachi-Dake, Japan . 28 C11
Tokachi-Gawa →, Japan . 28 C11
Tokala, Indonesia . 33 E6
Tōkamachi, Japan . 29 F9
Tokanui, N.Z. . 51 M2
Tokar, Sudan . 45 E12
Tokara-Rettō, Japan . 29 K4
Tokarahi, N.Z. . 51 L3
Tokashiki-Shima, Japan 29 L3
Tokelau Is., Pac. Oc. . 56 H10
Tokmak, Kyrgyzstan . 24 E8
Toko Ra., Australia . 54 C2
Tokong, Malaysia . 34 P13
Tokoro-Gawa →, Japan . 28 B12
Tokuno-Shima, Japan . 29 L4
Tokushima, Japan . 29 G7
Tokushima □, Japan . 29 H7
Tokuyama, Japan . 29 G5
Tōkyō, Japan . 29 G9
Tolaga Bay, N.Z. . 51 H7
Tolbukhin = Dobrich, Bulgaria . 21 C12
Toledo, Spain . 19 C3
Toledo, Ohio, U.S.A. . 68 E4
Toledo, Oreg., U.S.A. . 72 D2
Toledo, Wash., U.S.A. . 72 C2
Toledo, Montes de, Spain . 19 C3
Tolga, Algeria . 44 B6
Toliara, Madag. . 49 C7
Toliara □, Madag. . 49 C8
Tolima, Colombia . 78 C3
Tolitoli, Indonesia . 33 D6
Tolleson, U.S.A. . 73 K7
Tolo, Zaïre . 46 E3
Tolo, Teluk, Indonesia . 33 E6
Toluca, Mexico . 74 D5
Tom Burke, S. Africa . 49 C4
Tom Price, Australia . 52 D2
Tomah, U.S.A. . 70 D9
Tomahawk, U.S.A. . 70 C10
Tomakomai, Japan . 28 C10
Tomar, Portugal . 19 C1
Tomaszów Mazowiecki, Poland . 17 C10
Tombé, Sudan . 45 G11
Tombigbee →, U.S.A. 69 K2
Tomboctou, Mali . 44 E4
Tombstone, U.S.A. . 73 L8
Tombua, Angola . 48 B1
Tomelloso, Spain . 19 C4
Tomingley, Australia . 55 E4
Tomini, Indonesia . 33 D6

Tomini, Teluk, Indonesia . 33 E6
Tomkinson Ras., Australia . 53 E4
Tommot, Russia . 25 D13
Tomnavoulin, U.K. . 12 D5
Tomorit, Albania . 21 D9
Tomsk, Russia . 24 D9
Tonalea, U.S.A. . 73 H8
Tonantins, Brazil . 78 D5
Tonasket, U.S.A. . 72 B4
Tonbridge, U.K. . 11 F8
Tondano, Indonesia . 33 D6
Tonekābon, Iran . 39 B6
Tonga ■, Pac. Oc. . 51 D11
Tonga Trench, Pac. Oc. 56 J10
Tongaat, S. Africa . 49 D5
Tongareva, Cook Is. . 57 H12
Tongatapu, Tonga . 51 E11
Tongchuan, China . 31 C5
Tongeren, Belgium . 15 D5
Tonghua, China . 31 B7
Tongking, G. of = Tonkin, G. of, Asia . 30 E5
Tongobory, Madag. . 49 C7
Tongoy, Chile . 80 C2
Tongres = Tongeren, Belgium . 15 D5
Tongsa Dzong, Bhutan 37 F17
Tongue, U.K. . 12 C4
Tongue →, U.S.A. . 70 B2
Tonk, India . 36 F9
Tonkin = Bac Phan, Vietnam . 34 A8
Tonkin, G. of, Asia . 30 E5
Tonlé Sap, Cambodia . 34 F8
Tono, Japan . 28 E10
Tonopah, U.S.A. . 73 G5
Tønsberg, Norway . 9 G14
Tooele, U.S.A. . 72 F7
Toompine, Australia . 55 D3
Toonpan, Australia . 54 B4
Toora, Australia . 55 F4
Toora-Khem, Russia . 25 D10
Toowoomba, Australia 55 D5
Top-ozero, Russia . 22 A5
Topeka, U.S.A. . 70 F7
Topki, Russia . 24 D9
Topley, Canada . 64 C3
Topock, U.S.A. . 73 J6
Topol'čany, Slovak Rep. 17 D10
Topolobampo, Mexico 74 B3
Toppenish, U.S.A. . 72 C3
Toraka Vestale, Madag. 49 B7
Torata, Peru . 78 G4
Torbalı, Turkey . 21 E12
Torbay, Canada . 63 C9
Torbay, U.K. . 11 G4
Tordesillas, Spain . 19 B3
Torgau, Germany . 16 C7
Torhout, Belgium . 15 C3
Tori-Shima, Japan . 29 J10
Torino, Italy . 20 B2
Torit, Sudan . 45 H11
Tormes →, Spain . 19 B2
Tornado Mt., Canada . 64 D6
Torne älv →, Sweden 8 D21
Torneå = Tornio, Finland . 8 D21
Torneträsk, Sweden . 8 B18
Tornio, Finland . 8 D21
Tornionjoki →, Finland . 8 D21
Tornquist, Argentina . 80 D4
Toro, Cerro del, Chile . 80 B3
Toro, Pta., Panama . 74 H14
Toroníios Kólpos, Greece . 21 D10
Toronto, Australia . 55 E5
Toronto, Canada . 62 D4
Toronto, U.S.A. . 68 E5
Toropets, Russia . 22 C5
Tororo, Uganda . 46 D6
Toros Dağları, Turkey . 23 G5
Torquay, Canada . 65 D8
Torquay, U.K. . 11 G4
Tôrre de Moncorvo, Portugal . 19 B2
Torre del Greco, Italy . 20 D6
Torrejón de Ardoz, Spain . 19 B4
Torrelaveja, Spain . 19 A3
Torremolinos, Spain . 19 D3
Torrens, L., Australia . 55 E2
Torrens Cr. →, Australia . 54 C4
Torrens Creek, Australia . 54 C4
Torrente, Spain . 19 C5
Torreón, Mexico . 74 B4
Torres, Mexico . 74 B2
Torres Strait, Australia 56 H6
Torres Vedras, Portugal 19 C1
Torrevieja, Spain . 19 D5
Torrey, U.S.A. . 73 G8
Torridon, L., U.K. . 12 D3
Torrington, Conn., U.S.A. . 68 E9
Torrington, Wyo., U.S.A. . 70 D2
Tórshavn, Færoe Is. . 8 E9
Tortosa, Spain . 19 B6
Tortosa, C. de, Spain . 19 B6
Toruń, Poland . 17 B10
Tory I., Ireland . 13 A3
Tosa, Japan . 29 H6
Tosa-Shimizu, Japan . 29 H6
Tosa-Wan, Japan . 29 H6
Toscana □, Italy . 20 C4
Toshkent, Uzbekistan . 24 E7

Tostado, Argentina . 80 B4
Tosu, Japan . 29 H5
Toteng, Botswana . 48 C3
Totma, Russia . 22 C7
Totnes, U.K. . 11 G4
Totten Glacier, Antarctica . 5 C8
Tottenham, Australia . 55 E4
Tottori, Japan . 29 G7
Tottori □, Japan . 29 G7
Touba, Ivory C. . 44 G3
Toubkal, Djebel, Morocco . 44 B3
Tougan, Burkina Faso 44 F4
Touggourt, Algeria . 44 B6
Tougué, Guinea . 44 F2
Toul, France . 18 B6
Toulepleu, Ivory C. . 44 G3
Toulon, France . 18 E6
Toulouse, France . 18 E4
Toummo, Niger . 45 D7
Toungoo, Burma . 37 K20
Touraine, France . 18 C4
Tourane = Da Nang, Vietnam . 34 D10
Tourcoing, France . 18 A5
Touriñán, C., Spain . 19 A1
Tournai, Belgium . 15 D3
Tournon, France . 18 D6
Tours, France . 18 C4
Touwsrivier, S. Africa . 48 E3
Towada, Japan . 28 D10
Towada-Ko, Japan . 28 D10
Towamba, Australia . 55 F4
Towanda, U.S.A. . 68 E7
Towang, India . 37 F17
Tower, U.S.A. . 70 B8
Towerhill Cr. →, Australia . 54 C3
Towner, U.S.A. . 70 A4
Townsend, U.S.A. . 72 C8
Townshend I., Australia 54 C5
Townsville, Australia . 54 B4
Towson, U.S.A. . 68 F7
Toya-Ko, Japan . 28 C10
Toyah, U.S.A. . 71 K3
Toyahvale, U.S.A. . 71 K3
Toyama, Japan . 29 F8
Toyama □, Japan . 29 F8
Toyama-Wan, Japan . 29 F8
Toyohashi, Japan . 29 G8
Toyokawa, Japan . 29 G8
Toyonaka, Japan . 29 G7
Toyooka, Japan . 29 G7
Toyota, Japan . 29 G8
Tozeur, Tunisia . 44 B6
Trá Lí = Tralee, Ireland 13 D2
Trabzon, Turkey . 23 F6
Tracadie, Canada . 63 C7
Tracy, Calif., U.S.A. . 73 H3
Tracy, Minn., U.S.A. . 70 C7
Trafalgar, C., Spain . 19 D2
Trail, Canada . 64 D5
Trainor L., Canada . 64 A4
Tralee, Ireland . 13 D2
Tralee B., Ireland . 13 D2
Tramore, Ireland . 13 D4
Tran Ninh, Cao Nguyen, Laos . 34 C7
Tranås, Sweden . 9 G16
Trancas, Argentina . 80 B3
Trang, Thailand . 34 J5
Trangahy, Madag. . 49 B7
Trangan, Indonesia . 33 F8
Trangie, Australia . 55 E4
Trani, Italy . 20 D7
Tranoroa, Madag. . 49 C8
Transantarctic Mts., Antarctica . 5 E12
Transcaucasia = Zakavkazye, Asia . 23 F7
Transcona, Canada . 65 D9
Transilvania, Romania 17 E12
Transilvanian Alps = Carpaţii Meridionali, Romania . 17 F13
Transvaal = Transvaal, Romania . 17 E12
Transylvanian Alps = Romania . 6 F10
Trápani, Italy . 20 E5
Trapper Pk., U.S.A. . 72 D6
Traralgon, Australia . 55 F4
Trasimeno, L., Italy . 20 C5
Trat, Thailand . 34 F7
Traun, Austria . 16 D8
Traveller's L., Australia 55 E3
Travemünde, Germany 16 B6
Travers, Mt., N.Z. . 51 K4
Traverse City, U.S.A. . 68 C3
Travnik, Bos.-H. . 21 B7
Trayning, Australia . 53 F2
Trébbia →, Italy . 20 B3
Třebíč, Czech. . 16 D8
Trebinje, Bos.-H. . 21 C8
Trebonne, Australia . 54 B4
Tredegar, U.K. . 11 F4
Tregaron, U.K. . 11 E4
Tregrosse Is., Australia 54 B5
Treherne, Canada . 65 D9
Treinta y Tres, Uruguay 80 C6
Trelew, Argentina . 80 E3
Trelleborg, Sweden . 9 J15
Tremonton, U.S.A. . 72 F7
Tremp, Spain . 19 A6
Trenche →, Canada . 62 C5
Trenčín, Slovak Rep. . 17 D10
Trenggalek, Indonesia 33 H14
Trenque Lauquen, Argentina . 80 D4
Trent →, U.K. . 10 D7
Trento, Italy . 20 A4
Trenton, Canada . 62 D4
Trenton, Mo., U.S.A. . 70 E8

Trenton, N.J., U.S.A. . 68 E8
Trenton, Nebr., U.S.A. 70 E4
Trenton, Tenn., U.S.A. 71 H10
Trepassey, Canada . 63 C9
Tres Arroyos, Argentina 80 D4
Três Corações, Brazil . 79 H9
Três Lagoas, Brazil . 79 H8
Tres Montes, C., Chile 80 F1
Tres Puentes, Chile . 80 B2
Tres Puntas, C., Argentina . 80 F3
Três Rios, Brazil . 79 H10
Treviso, Italy . 20 B5
Triabunna, Australia . 54 G4
Tribulation, C., Australia . 54 B4
Tribune, U.S.A. . 70 F4
Trichinopoly = Tiruchchirappalli, India . 36 P11
Trichur, India . 36 P10
Trida, Australia . 55 E4
Trier, Germany . 16 D4
Trieste, Italy . 20 B5
Triglav, Slovenia . 16 E7
Trikkala, Greece . 21 E9
Trikora, Puncak, Indonesia . 33 E9
Trim, Ireland . 13 C5
Trincomalee, Sri Lanka 36 Q12
Trindade, I., Atl. Oc. . 2 F8
Trinidad, Bolivia . 78 F6
Trinidad, Colombia . 78 B4
Trinidad, Cuba . 75 C9
Trinidad, Uruguay . 80 C5
Trinidad, U.S.A. . 71 G2
Trinidad, I., Argentina 80 D4
Trinidad & Tobago ■, W. Indies . 74 S20
Trinity, Canada . 63 C9
Trinity, U.S.A. . 71 K7
Trinity →, Calif., U.S.A. . 72 F2
Trinity →, Tex., U.S.A. 71 L7
Trinity B., Canada . 63 C9
Trinity Range, U.S.A. . 72 F4
Trinkitat, Sudan . 45 E12
Trion, U.S.A. . 69 H3
Tripoli = Tarābulus, Lebanon . 41 A4
Tripoli = Tarābulus, Libya . 45 B7
Tripolis, Greece . 21 F10
Tripp, U.S.A. . 70 D6
Tripura □, India . 37 H17
Tristan da Cunha, Atl. Oc. . 2 F9
Trivandrum, India . 36 Q10
Trnava, Slovak Rep. . 17 D9
Trochu, Canada . 64 C6
Trodely I., Canada . 62 B4
Troglav, Croatia . 20 C7
Troilus, L., Canada . 62 B5
Trois-Pistoles, Canada 63 C6
Trois-Rivières, Canada 62 C5
Troitsk, Russia . 24 D7
Troitsko Pechorsk, Russia . 22 B10
Trölladyngja, Iceland . 8 D5
Trollhättan, Sweden . 9 G15
Trollheimen, Norway . 8 E13
Tromelin I., Ind. Oc. . 35 F4
Tromsø, Norway . 8 B18
Tronador, Argentina . 80 E2
Trøndelag, Norway . 8 D14
Trondheim, Norway . 8 E14
Trondheimsfjorden, Norway . 8 E14
Troon, U.K. . 12 F4
Tropic, U.S.A. . 73 H7
Trossachs, The, U.K. . 12 E4
Trostan, U.K. . 13 A5
Trotternish, U.K. . 12 D2
Troup, U.S.A. . 71 J7
Trout →, Canada . 64 A5
Trout L., N.W.T., Canada . 64 A4
Trout L., Ont., Canada 65 C10
Trout Lake, U.S.A. . 63 C2
Trout River, Canada . 63 C8
Trouville-sur-Mer, France . 18 B4
Trowbridge, U.K. . 11 F5
Troy, Turkey . 21 E12
Troy, Ala., U.S.A. . 69 K3
Troy, Idaho, U.S.A. . 72 C5
Troy, Kans., U.S.A. . 70 F7
Troy, Mo., U.S.A. . 70 F9
Troy, Mont., U.S.A. . 72 B6
Troy, N.Y., U.S.A. . 68 D9
Troy, Ohio, U.S.A. . 68 E3
Troyes, France . 18 B6
Trucial States = United Arab Emirates ■, Asia . 39 F7
Trudovoye, Russia . 28 C6
Trujillo, Honduras . 74 D2
Trujillo, Peru . 78 E3
Trujillo, Spain . 19 C3
Trujillo, U.S.A. . 71 H2
Trujillo, Venezuela . 78 B4
Truk, Pac. Oc. . 56 G6
Trumann, U.S.A. . 71 H9
Trumbull, Mt., U.S.A. . 73 H7
Trundle, Australia . 55 E4
Trung-Phan, Vietnam . 34 D10
Truro, Canada . 63 C7
Truro, U.K. . 11 G2
Truskavets, Ukraine . 17 D12
Truslove, Australia . 53 F3
Truth or Consequences, U.S.A. . 73 K10
Trutnov, Czech. . 16 C8

Tryon, U.S.A. . 69 H4
Tsaratanana, Madag. . 49 B8
Tsaratanana, Mt. de, Madag. . 49 A8
Tsarevo = Michurin, Bulgaria . 21 C12
Tsau, Botswana . 48 C3
Tselinograd = Aqmola, Kazakhstan . 24 D8
Tsetserleg, Mongolia . 30 B5
Tshabong, Botswana . 48 D3
Tshane, Botswana . 48 C3
Tshela, Zaïre . 46 E2
Tshesebe, Botswana . 49 C4
Tshikapa, Zaïre . 46 F4
Tshofa, Zaïre . 46 F5
Tshwane, Botswana . 48 C3
Tsigara, Botswana . 48 C4
Tsihombe, Madag. . 49 D8
Tsimlyansk Res. = Tsimlyanskoye Vdkhr., Russia . 23 E7
Tsimlyanskoye Vdkhr., Russia . 23 E7
Tsinan = Jinan, China 31 C6
Tsineng, S. Africa . 48 D3
Tsinghai = Qinghai □, China . 30 C4
Tsingtao = Qingdao, China . 31 C7
Tsinjomitondraka, Madag. . 49 B8
Tsiroanomandidy, Madag. . 49 B8
Tsivory, Madag. . 49 C8
Tskhinvali, Georgia . 23 F7
Tsna →, Russia . 22 D7
Tsodilo Hill, Botswana 48 B3
Tsolo, S. Africa . 49 E4
Tsomo, S. Africa . 49 E4
Tsu, Japan . 29 G8
Tsu L., Canada . 64 A6
Tsuchiura, Japan . 29 F10
Tsugaru-Kaikyō, Japan 28 D10
Tsumeb, Namibia . 48 B2
Tsumis, Namibia . 48 C2
Tsuruga, Japan . 29 G8
Tsurugi-San, Japan . 29 H7
Tsuruoka, Japan . 28 E9
Tsushima, Gifu, Japan 29 G8
Tsushima, Nagasaki, Japan . 29 G4
Tsyelyakhany, Belarus 17 B13
Tual, Indonesia . 33 F8
Tuam, Ireland . 13 C3
Tuamotu Arch. = Tuamotu Is., Pac. Oc. 57 J13
Tuamotu Is., Pac. Oc. 57 J13
Tuamotu Ridge, Pac. Oc. . 57 K14
Tuao, Phil. . 33 A6
Tuapse, Russia . 23 F6
Tuatapere, N.Z. . 51 M1
Tuba City, U.S.A. . 73 H8
Tuban, Indonesia . 33 G15
Tubarão, Brazil . 80 B7
Tūbās, West Bank . 41 C4
Tubau, Malaysia . 32 D4
Tübingen, Germany . 16 D5
Tubruq, Libya . 45 B9
Tubuai Is., Pac. Oc. . 57 K12
Tucacas, Venezuela . 78 A5
Tuchodi →, Canada . 64 B4
Tucson, U.S.A. . 73 K8
Tucumcari, U.S.A. . 71 H3
Tucupita, Venezuela . 78 B6
Tucuruí, Brazil . 79 D9
Tucuruí, Rêpresa de, Brazil . 79 D9
Tudela, Spain . 19 A5
Tudmur, Syria . 38 C3
Tudor, L., Canada . 63 A6
Tuen, Australia . 55 D4
Tugela →, S. Africa . 49 D5
Tuguegarao, Phil. . 33 A6
Tukangbesi, Kepulauan, Indonesia . 33 F6
Tukarak I., Canada . 62 A4
Tukayyid, Iraq . 38 D5
Tükrah, Libya . 45 B9
Tuktoyaktuk, Canada . 60 B6
Tukums, Latvia . 9 H20
Tukuyu, Tanzania . 46 F6
Tula, Mexico . 74 C5
Tula, Russia . 22 D6
Tulancingo, Mexico . 74 C5
Tulare, U.S.A. . 73 H4
Tulare Lake Bed, U.S.A. 73 J4
Tularosa, U.S.A. . 73 K10
Tulbagh, S. Africa . 48 E2
Tulcán, Ecuador . 78 C3
Tulcea, Romania . 17 F15
Tulchyn, Ukraine . 17 D15
Tüleh, Iran . 39 C7
Tulemale L., Canada . 65 A9
Tuli, Indonesia . 33 E6
Tuli, Zimbabwe . 47 J5
Tulia, U.S.A. . 71 H4
Tülkarm, West Bank . 41 C4
Tullahoma, U.S.A. . 69 H2
Tullamore, Australia . 55 E4
Tullamore, Ireland . 13 C4
Tulle, France . 18 D4
Tullibigeal, Australia . 55 E4
Tullow, Ireland . 13 D5
Tully, Australia . 54 B4
Tulmaythah, Libya . 45 B9
Tulmur, Australia . 54 C3
Tulsa, U.S.A. . 71 G7
Tulsequah, Canada . 64 B2
Tulua, Colombia . 78 C3
Tulun, Russia . 25 D11

Tulungagung, Indonesia . 32 F4
Tum, Indonesia . 33 E8
Tumaco, Colombia . 78 C3
Tumatumari, Guyana . 78 B7
Tumba, Sweden . 9 G17
Tumba, L., Zaïre . 46 E3
Tumbarumba, Australia 55 F4
Túmbes, Peru . 78 D2
Tumby Bay, Australia . 55 E2
Tumeremo, Venezuela 78 B6
Tumkur, India . 36 N10
Tummel, L., U.K. . 12 E5
Tump, Pakistan . 36 F3
Tumpat, Malaysia . 34 N15
Tumu, Ghana . 44 F4
Tumucumaque, Serra, Brazil . 79 C8
Tumut, Australia . 55 F4
Tumwater, U.S.A. . 72 C2
Tunbridge Wells = Royal Tunbridge Wells, U.K. . 11 F8
Tuncurry, Australia . 55 E5
Tunduru, Tanzania . 46 G7
Tundzha →, Bulgaria 21 C11
Tunga Pass, India . 37 E19
Tungabhadra →, India 36 M11
Tungaru, Sudan . 45 F11
Tungsten, Canada . 64 A3
Tunguska, Nizhnyaya →, Russia . 25 C9
Tunica, U.S.A. . 71 H9
Tunis, Tunisia . 44 A7
Tunisia ■, Africa . 44 B6
Tunja, Colombia . 78 B4
Tunnsjøen, Norway . 8 D15
Tunungayualok I., Canada . 63 A7
Tunuyán →, Argentina . 80 C3
Tunxi, China . 31 D6
Tuolumne, U.S.A. . 73 H3
Tuoy-Khaya, Russia . 25 C12
Tūp Āghāj, Iran . 38 B5
Tupelo, U.S.A. . 69 H1
Tupik, Russia . 25 D12
Tupinambaranas, Brazil 78 D7
Tupiza, Bolivia . 80 A3
Tupper, Canada . 64 B4
Tupper Lake, U.S.A. . 68 C8
Tupungato, Cerro, S. Amer. . 80 C3
Túquerres, Colombia . 78 C3
Tura, Russia . 25 C11
Turabah, Si. Arabia . 38 D4
Tūrān, Iran . 39 C8
Turan, Russia . 25 D10
Turayf, Si. Arabia . 38 D3
Turda, Romania . 17 E12
Turek, Poland . 17 B10
Turfan = Turpan, China 30 B3
Tūrgovishte, Bulgaria . 21 C12
Turgutlu, Turkey . 21 E12
Turia →, Spain . 19 C5
Turiaçu, Brazil . 79 D9
Turiaçu →, Brazil . 79 D9
Turin = Torino, Italy . 20 B2
Turin, Canada . 64 D6
Turkana, L., Africa . 46 D7
Turkestan = Türkistan, Kazakhstan . 24 E7
Turkey ■, Eurasia . 23 G6
Turkey Creek, Australia 52 C4
Türkistan, Kazakhstan 24 E7
Turkmenistan ■, Asia . 24 F6
Turks & Caicos Is. ■, W. Indies . 75 C10
Turku, Finland . 9 F20
Turlock, U.S.A. . 73 H3
Turnagain →, Canada 64 B3
Turnagain, C., N.Z. . 51 J6
Turneffe Is., Belize . 74 D7
Turner, Australia . 52 C4
Turner, U.S.A. . 72 B9
Turner Pt., Australia . 54 A1
Turner Valley, Canada 64 C6
Turnhout, Belgium . 15 C4
Turnor L., Canada . 65 B7
Türnovo = Veliko Tŭrnovo, Bulgaria . 21 C11
Turnu Măgurele, Romania . 17 G13
Turnu Roşu, P., Romania . 17 F13
Turon, U.S.A. . 71 G5
Turpan, China . 30 B3
Turriff, U.K. . 12 D6
Tursāq, Iraq . 38 C5
Turtle Head I., Australia 54 A3
Turtle L., Canada . 65 C7
Turtle Lake, N. Dak., U.S.A. . 70 B4
Turtle Lake, Wis., U.S.A. . 70 C8
Turtleford, Canada . 65 C7
Turukhansk, Russia . 25 C9
Tuscaloosa, U.S.A. . 69 J2
Tuscany = Toscana □, Italy . 20 C4
Tuscola, Ill., U.S.A. . 68 F1
Tuscola, Tex., U.S.A. . 71 J5
Tuscumbia, U.S.A. . 69 H2
Tuskar Rock, Ireland . 13 D5
Tuskegee, U.S.A. . 69 J3
Tuticorin, India . 36 Q11
Tutóia, Brazil . 79 D10
Tutong, Brunei . 32 D4
Tutrakan, Bulgaria . 21 B12
Tutshi L., Canada . 64 B2
Tuttle, U.S.A. . 70 B5
Tuttlingen, Germany . 16 E5
Tutuala, Indonesia . 33 F7

Tutuila, Amer. Samoa 51 B13
Tuva □, Russia 25 D10
Tuvalu ■, Pac. Oc. 56 H9
Tuxpan, Mexico 74 C5
Tuxtla Gutiérrez, Mexico 74 D6
Tuy, Spain 19 A1
Tuy Hoa, Vietnam 34 F10
Tuya L., Canada 64 B2
Tuyen Hoa, Vietnam 34 D9
Tūysarkān, Iran 39 C6
Tuz Gölü, Turkey 23 G5
Ţūz Khurmātū, Iraq 38 C5
Tuzla, Bos.-H. 21 B8
Tver, Russia 22 C6
Tweed →, U.K. 12 F7
Tweed Heads, Australia 55 D5
Tweedsmuir Prov. Park, Canada 64 C3
Twentynine Palms, U.S.A. 73 J5
Twillingate, Canada 63 C9
Twin Bridges, U.S.A. 72 D7
Twin Falls, U.S.A. 72 E6
Twin Valley, U.S.A. 70 B6
Twisp, U.S.A. 72 B3
Two Harbors, U.S.A. 70 B9
Two Rivers, U.S.A. 68 C2
Twofold B., Australia 55 F4
Tyachiv, Ukraine 17 D12
Tychy, Poland 17 C10
Tyler, U.S.A. 67 D7
Tyler, Minn., U.S.A. 70 C6
Tyler, Tex., U.S.A. 71 J7
Tynda, Russia 25 D13
Tyne →, U.K. 10 C6
Tyne & Wear □, U.K. 10 C6
Tynemouth, U.K. 10 B6
Tyre = Sūr, Lebanon 41 B4
Tyrifjorden, Norway 9 F14
Tyrol = Tirol □, Austria 16 E6
Tyrrell →, Australia 55 F3
Tyrrell, L., Australia 55 F3
Tyrrell Arm, Canada 65 A9
Tyrrell L., Canada 65 A7
Tyrrhenian Sea, Medit. S. 20 E5
Tysfjorden, Norway 8 B17
Tyulgan, Russia 22 D10
Tyumen, Russia 24 D7
Tywi →, U.K. 11 F3
Tywyn, U.K. 11 E3
Tzaneen, S. Africa 49 C5
Tzukong = Zigong, China 30 D5

U

U.S.A. = United States of America ■, N. Amer. 66 C7
Uanda, Australia 54 C3
Uarsciek, Somali Rep. 40 G4
Uato-Udo, Indonesia 33 F7
Uatumã →, Brazil 78 D7
Uaupés, Brazil 78 D5
Uaupés →, Brazil 78 C5
Ubá, Brazil 79 H10
Ubaitaba, Brazil 79 F11
Ubangi = Oubangi →, Zaïre 46 E3
Ubauro, Pakistan 36 E6
Ube, Japan 29 H5
Ubeda, Spain 19 C4
Uberaba, Brazil 79 G9
Uberlândia, Brazil 79 G9
Ubombo, S. Africa 49 D5
Ubon Ratchathani, Thailand 34 E8
Ubort →, Belarus 17 B15
Ubundu, Zaïre 46 E5
Ucayali →, Peru 78 D4
Uchi Lake, Canada 65 C10
Uchiura-Wan, Japan 28 C10
Uchur →, Russia 25 D14
Ucluelet, Canada 64 D3
Uda →, Russia 25 D14
Udaipur, India 36 G8
Udaipur Garhi, Nepal 37 F15
Uddevalla, Sweden 9 G14
Uddjaur, Sweden 8 D17
Udgir, India 36 K10
Udhampur, India 36 C9
Udi, Nigeria 44 G6
Udine, Italy 20 A5
Udmurtia □, Russia 22 C9
Udon Thani, Thailand 34 D7
Udupi, India 36 N9
Ueda, Japan 29 F9
Uedineniya, Os., Russia 4 B12
Uele →, Zaïre 46 D4
Uelen, Russia 25 C19
Uelzen, Germany 16 B6
Ufa, Russia 22 D10
Ufa →, Russia 22 D10
Ugab →, Namibia 48 C1
Ugalla →, Tanzania 46 F6
Uganda ■, Africa 46 D6
Ugie, S. Africa 49 E4
Uglegorsk, Russia 25 E15
Ugljane, Croatia 16 E8
Ugolyak, Russia 25 C13
Ugûn Mûsa, Egypt 41 F1
Uhrichsville, U.S.A. 68 E5
Uibhist a Deas = South Uist, U.K. 12 D1
Uibhist a Tuath = North Uist, U.K. 12 D1
Uíge, Angola 46 F2
Uinta Mts., U.S.A. 72 F8

Uitenhage, S. Africa 48 E4
Uithuizen, Neths. 15 A6
Uji-guntō, Japan 29 J4
Ujjain, India 36 H9
Ujung Pandang, Indonesia 33 F5
Uka, Russia 25 D17
Uke-Shima, Japan 29 K4
Ukerewe I., Tanzania 46 E6
Ukhrul, India 37 G19
Ukhta, Russia 22 B9
Ukiah, U.S.A. 72 G2
Ukmerge, Lithuania 9 J21
Ukraine ■, Europe 23 E5
Ukwi, Botswana 48 C3
Ulaanbaatar, Mongolia 25 E11
Ulaangom, Mongolia 30 A4
Ulan Bator = Ulaanbaatar, Mongolia 25 E11
Ulan Ude, Russia 25 D11
Ulcinj, Montenegro, Yug. 21 D8
Ulco, S. Africa 48 D3
Ulefoss, Norway 9 G13
Ulhasnagar, India 36 K8
Uladulla, Australia 55 F5
Ullapool, U.K. 12 D3
Ullswater, U.K. 10 C5
Ulm, Germany 16 D5
Ulmarra, Australia 55 D5
Ulonguè, Mozam. 47 G6
Ulricehamn, Sweden 9 H15
Ulster □, U.K. 13 B5
Ulubat Gölü, Turkey 21 D13
Uludağ, Turkey 21 D13
Ulungur He →, China 30 B3
Uluru = Ayers Rock, Australia 53 E5
Ulutau, Kazakhstan 24 E7
Ulverston, U.K. 10 C4
Ulverstone, Australia 54 G4
Ulya, Russia 25 D15
Ulyanovsk = Simbirsk, Russia 22 D8
Ulyasutay, Mongolia 30 B4
Ulysses, U.S.A. 71 G4
Umala, Bolivia 78 G5
Uman, Ukraine 17 D16
Umaria, India 37 H12
Umarkot, Pakistan 36 G6
Umatilla, U.S.A. 72 D4
Umba, Russia 22 A5
Umbrella Mts., N.Z. 51 L2
Ume älv →, Sweden 8 E19
Umeå, Sweden 8 E19
Umera, Indonesia 33 E7
Umkomaas, S. Africa 49 E5
Umm ad Daraj, J., Jordan 41 C4
Umm al Qaywayn, U.A.E. 39 E7
Umm al Qittayn, Jordan 41 C5
Umm Bāb, Qatar 39 E6
Umm Bel, Sudan 45 F10
Umm el Fahm, Israel 41 C4
Umm Lajj, Si. Arabia 38 E3
Umm Ruwaba, Sudan 45 F11
Umnak I., U.S.A. 60 C3
Umniati →, Zimbabwe 47 H5
Umpang, Thailand 34 D5
Umpqua →, U.S.A. 72 E1
Umtata, S. Africa 49 E4
Umuarama, Brazil 79 H8
Umzimvubu = Port St. Johns, S. Africa 49 E4
Umzinto, S. Africa 49 E5
Una →, Bos.-H. 16 F9
Unalaska, U.S.A. 60 C3
Uncia, Bolivia 78 G5
Uncompahgre Peak, U.S.A. 73 G10
Underbool, Australia 55 F3
Ungarie, Australia 55 E4
Ungarra, Australia 55 E2
Ungava B., Canada 61 C13
Ungava Pen., Canada 61 C12
Ungeny = Ungheni, Moldova 17 E14
Ungheni, Moldova 17 E14
União da Vitória, Brazil 80 B5
Unimak I., U.S.A. 60 C3
Union, Miss., U.S.A. 71 J10
Union, Mo., U.S.A. 70 F9
Union, S.C., U.S.A. 69 H5
Union, Mt., U.S.A. 73 J7
Union City, Pa., U.S.A. 68 E6
Union City, Tenn., U.S.A. 71 G10
Union Gap, U.S.A. 72 C3
Union Springs, U.S.A. 69 J3
Uniondale, S. Africa 48 E3
Uniontown, U.S.A. 68 F6
Unionville, U.S.A. 70 E8
United Arab Emirates ■, Asia 39 F7
United Kingdom ■, Europe 7 E5
United States of America ■, N. Amer. 66 C7
Unity, Canada 65 C7
Unnao, India 37 F12
Unst, U.K. 12 A8
Unuk →, Canada 64 B2
Uozu, Japan 29 F8
Upata, Venezuela 78 B6
Upemba, L., Zaïre 46 F5
Upernavik, Greenland 4 B5
Upington, S. Africa 48 D3
Upolu, W. Samoa 51 A13
Upper Alkali Lake, U.S.A. 72 F3

Upper Arrow L., Canada 64 C5
Upper Foster L., Canada 65 B7
Upper Hutt, N.Z. 51 J5
Upper Klamath L., U.S.A. 72 E3
Upper Lake, U.S.A. 72 G2
Upper Musquodoboit, Canada 63 C7
Upper Red L., U.S.A. 70 A7
Upper Sandusky, U.S.A. 68 E4
Upper Volta = Burkina Faso ■, Africa 44 F4
Uppland, Sweden 9 F17
Uppsala, Sweden 9 G17
Upstart, C., Australia 54 B4
Upton, U.S.A. 70 C2
Ur, Iraq 38 D5
Uracara, Brazil 78 D7
Urakawa, Japan 28 C11
Ural = Zhayyq →, Kazakhstan 23 E9
Ural, Australia 55 E4
Ural Mts. = Uralskie Gory, Eurasia 22 C10
Uralla, Australia 55 E5
Uralsk = Oral, Kazakhstan 22 D9
Uralskie Gory, Eurasia 22 C10
Urandangi, Australia 54 C2
Uranium City, Canada 65 B7
Uranquinty, Australia 55 F4
Urawa, Japan 29 G9
Uray, Russia 24 C7
Urban, Ill., U.S.A. 68 E1
Urbana, Ohio, U.S.A. 68 E4
Urbino, Italy 20 C5
Urbión, Picos de, Spain 19 A4
Urcos, Peru 78 F4
Urda, Kazakhstan 23 E8
Urdzhar, Kazakhstan 24 E9
Ure →, U.K. 10 C6
Ures, Mexico 74 B2
Urfa = Sanliurfa, Turkey 23 G6
Urganch, Uzbekistan 24 E7
Urgench = Urganch, Uzbekistan 24 E7
Uribia, Colombia 78 A4
Urk, Neths. 15 B5
Urla, Turkey 21 E12
Urmia = Orūmīyeh, Iran 38 B5
Urmia, L. = Orūmīyeh, Daryācheh-ye, Iran 38 B5
Uroševac, Serbia, Yug. 21 C9
Uruana, Brazil 79 G9
Urubamba, Peru 78 F4
Urubamba →, Peru 78 F4
Uruçuí, Brazil 79 E10
Uruguai →, Brazil 80 B5
Uruguaiana, Brazil 80 B5
Uruguay ■, S. Amer. 80 C5
Uruguay →, S. Amer. 80 C5
Urumchi = Ürümqi, China 24 E9
Ürümqi, China 24 E9
Urup, Os., Russia 25 E16
Usa →, Russia 22 A10
Uşak, Turkey 23 G4
Usakos, Namibia 48 C2
Usedom, Germany 16 B8
Ush-Tobe, Kazakhstan 24 E8
Ushakova, Os., Russia 4 A12
Ushant = Ouessant, I. d', France 18 B1
Ushibuka, Japan 29 H5
Ushuaia, Argentina 80 G3
Ushumun, Russia 25 D13
Usk →, U.K. 11 F5
Üsküdar, Turkey 23 F4
Uslar, Germany 16 C5
Usman, Russia 22 D6
Usoke, Tanzania 46 F6
Usolye Sibirskoye, Russia 25 D11
Uspallata, P. de, Argentina 80 C3
Uspenskiy, Kazakhstan 24 E8
Ussuri →, Asia 28 A7
Ussuriysk, Russia 25 E14
Ussurka, Russia 28 B6
Ust-Aldan = Batamay, Russia 25 C13
Ust Amginskoye = Khandyga, Russia 25 C14
Ust-Bolsheretsk, Russia 25 D16
Ust Chaun, Russia 25 C18
Ust'-Ilga, Russia 25 D11
Ust Ilimpeya = Yukti, Russia 25 C11
Ust-Ilimsk, Russia 25 D11
Ust Ishim, Russia 24 D8
Ust-Kamchatsk, Russia 25 D17
Ust-Kamenogorsk = Öskemen, Kazakhstan 24 E9
Ust-Karenga, Russia 25 D12
Ust Khayryuzovo, Russia 25 D16
Ust-Kut, Russia 25 D11
Ust Kuyga, Russia 25 C14
Ust Maya, Russia 25 C14
Ust-Mil, Russia 25 D14
Ust Muya, Russia 25 D12
Ust-Nera, Russia 25 C15
Ust-Nyukzha, Russia 25 D13
Ust Olenek, Russia 25 B12
Ust-Omchug, Russia 25 C15
Ust Port, Russia 24 C9
Ust Tsilma, Russia 22 A9
Ust-Tungir, Russia 25 D13

Ust Urt = Ustyurt, Plateau, Asia 24 E6
Ust Usa, Russia 22 A10
Ust Vorkuta, Russia 24 C7
Ústí nad Labem, Czech. 16 C8
Ustica, Italy 20 E5
Ustinov = Izhevsk, Russia 22 C9
Ustye, Russia 25 D10
Ustyurt, Plateau, Asia 24 E6
Usu, China 30 B3
Usuki, Japan 29 H5
Usumacinta →, Mexico 74 D6
Usumbura = Bujumbura, Burundi 46 E5
Uta, Indonesia 33 E9
Utah □, U.S.A. 72 G8
Utah, L., U.S.A. 72 F8
Ute Creek →, U.S.A. 71 H3
Utena, Lithuania 9 J21
Utete, Tanzania 46 F7
Uthai Thani, Thailand 34 E6
Utiariti, Brazil 78 F7
Utica, U.S.A. 68 D8
Utik L., Canada 65 B9
Utikuma L., Canada 64 B5
Utrecht, Neths. 15 B5
Utrecht □, Neths. 15 B5
Utrera, Spain 19 D3
Utsjoki, Finland 8 B22
Utsunomiya, Japan 29 F9
Uttar Pradesh □, India 36 F11
Uttaradit, Thailand 34 D6
Uttoxeter, U.K. 10 E6
Uummannarsuaq = Farvel, Kap, Greenland 4 D5
Uusikaarlepyy, Finland 8 E20
Uusikaupunki, Finland 9 F19
Uva, Russia 22 C9
Uvalde, U.S.A. 71 L5
Uvinza, Tanzania 46 F6
Uvira, Zaïre 46 E5
Uvs Nuur, Mongolia 30 A4
Uwajima, Japan 29 H6
Uyandi, Russia 25 C15
Uyuni, Bolivia 78 H5
Uzbekistan ■, Asia 24 E7
Uzen, Kazakhstan 23 F9
Uzerche, France 18 D4
Uzh →, Ukraine 17 C16
Uzhgorod = Uzhhorod, Ukraine 17 D12
Uzhhorod, Ukraine 17 D12
Uzunköprü, Turkey 21 D12

V

Vaal →, S. Africa 48 D3
Vaal Dam, S. Africa 49 D4
Vaalwater, S. Africa 49 C4
Vaasa, Finland 8 E19
Vác, Hungary 17 E10
Vacaville, U.S.A. 72 G3
Vach = Vakh →, Russia 24 C8
Vadodara, India 36 H8
Vadsø, Norway 8 A23
Vaduz, Liech. 16 E5
Værøy, Norway 8 C15
Vågar, Færoe Is. 8 E9
Vågsfjorden, Norway 8 B17
Vahsel B., Antarctica 5 D1
Vaigach, Russia 24 B6
Vakh →, Russia 24 C8
Val d'Or, Canada 62 C4
Val Marie, Canada 65 D7
Valahia, Romania 17 F13
Valandovo, Macedonia 21 D10
Valcheta, Argentina 80 E3
Valdayskaya Vozvyshennost, Russia 22 C5
Valdepeñas, Spain 19 C4
Valdés, Pen., Argentina 80 E4
Valdez, U.S.A. 60 B5
Valdivia, Chile 80 D2
Valdosta, U.S.A. 69 K4
Valdres, Norway 9 F13
Vale, U.S.A. 72 E5
Valença, Brazil 79 F11
Valença do Piauí, Brazil 79 E10
Valence, France 18 D6
Valencia, Spain 19 C5
Valencia, Venezuela 78 A5
Valencia □, Spain 19 C5
Valencia, G. de, Spain 19 C6
Valencia de Alcántara, Spain 19 C2
Valencia Harbour, Ireland 13 E1
Valencia I., Ireland 13 E1
Valenciennes, France 18 A5
Valentim, Sa. do, Brazil 79 E10
Valentin, Russia 28 C7
Valentine, Nebr., U.S.A. 70 D4
Valera, Venezuela 78 B4
Valga, Estonia 9 H22
Valier, U.S.A. 72 B7
Valjevo, Serbia, Yug. 21 B8
Valka, Latvia 9 H21
Valkeakoski, Finland 9 F20
Valkenswaard, Neths. 15 C5
Vall de Uxó, Spain 19 C5
Valladolid, Mexico 74 C7
Valladolid, Spain 19 B3

Vatomandry, Madag. 49 B8
Vatra-Dornei, Romania 17 E13
Vättern, Sweden 9 G16
Vaughn, Mont., U.S.A. 72 C8
Vaughn, N. Mex., U.S.A. 73 J11
Vaupés = Uaupés →, Brazil 78 C5
Vauxhall, Canada 64 C6
Vava'u, Tonga 51 D11
Vawkavysk, Belarus 17 B13
Växjö, Sweden 9 H16
Vaygach, Ostrov, Russia 24 C6
Vechte →, Neths. 15 B6
Vedea →, Romania 17 G13
Veendam, Neths. 15 A6
Veenendaal, Neths. 15 B5
Vefsna →, Norway 8 D15
Vega, Norway 8 D14
Vega, U.S.A. 71 H3
Veghel, Neths. 15 C5
Vegreville, Canada 64 C6
Vejer de la Frontera, Spain 19 D3
Vejle, Denmark 9 J13
Velddrif, S. Africa 48 E2
Velebit Planina, Croatia 16 F8
Vélez, Colombia 78 B4
Vélez Málaga, Spain 19 D3
Vélez Rubio, Spain 19 D4
Velhas →, Brazil 79 G10
Velika Kapela, Croatia 16 F8
Velikaya →, Russia 22 C4
Velikaya Kema, Russia 28 B8
Veliki Ustyug, Russia 22 B8
Velikiye Luki, Russia 22 C5
Veliko Tŭrnovo, Bulgaria 21 C11
Velikonda Range, India 36 M11
Velletri, Italy 20 D5
Vellore, India 36 N11
Velsen-Noord, Neths. 15 B4
Velsk, Russia 22 B7
Velva, U.S.A. 70 A4
Venado Tuerto, Argentina 80 C4
Vendée □, France 18 C3
Vendôme, France 18 C4
Venézia, Italy 20 B5
Venézia, G. di, Italy 20 B5
Venezuela ■, S. Amer. 78 B5
Venezuela, G. de, Venezuela 78 A4
Vengurla, India 36 M8
Venice = Venézia, Italy 20 B5
Venkatapuram, India 37 K12
Venlo, Neths. 15 C6
Vennesla, Norway 9 G12
Venraij, Neths. 15 C5
Ventana, Sa. de la, Argentina 80 D4
Ventersburg, S. Africa 48 D4
Venterstad, S. Africa 48 E4
Ventnor, U.K. 11 G6
Ventotene, Italy 20 D5
Ventoux, Mt., France 18 D6
Ventspils, Latvia 9 H19
Venturi →, Venezuela 78 C5
Ventura, U.S.A. 73 J4
Venus B., Australia 55 F5
Vera, Argentina 80 B4
Vera, Spain 19 D5
Veracruz, Mexico 74 D5
Veraval, India 36 J7
Verbánia, Italy 20 B3
Vercelli, Italy 20 B3
Verdalsøra, Norway 8 E14
Verde →, Argentina 80 E3
Verden, Germany 16 B5
Verdigre, U.S.A. 70 D5
Verdun, France 18 B6
Vereeniging, S. Africa 49 D4
Vérendrye, Parc Prov. de la, Canada 62 C4
Verga, C., Guinea 44 F2
Vergemont Cr. →, Australia 54 C3
Verín, Spain 19 B2
Verkhnevilyuysk, Russia 25 C13
Verkhneye Kalinino, Russia 25 D11
Verkhniy Baskunchak, Russia 23 E8
Verkhnyaya Amga, Russia 25 D13
Verkhoyansk, Russia 25 C14
Verkhoyansk Ra. = Verkhoyanskiy Khrebet, Russia 25 C13
Verkhoyanskiy Khrebet, Russia 25 C13
Verlo, Canada 65 C7
Vermilion →, Alta., Canada 65 C6
Vermilion →, Qué., Canada 62 C5
Vermilion, B., U.S.A. 71 L9
Vermilion Bay, Canada 65 D10
Vermilion Chutes, Canada 64 B6
Vermillion, U.S.A. 70 D6
Vermont □, U.S.A. 68 D9
Vernal, U.S.A. 72 F9
Verner, Canada 62 C3
Verneukpan, S. Africa 48 E3
Vernon, Canada 64 C5
Vernon, U.S.A. 71 H5
Vero Beach, U.S.A. 69 M5

Véroia

Véroia, *Greece* 21 D10
Verona, *Italy* 20 B4
Versailles, *France* 18 B5
Vert, C., *Senegal* 44 F1
Verulam, *S. Africa* 49 D5
Verviers, *Belgium* 15 D5
Veselovskoye Vdkhr., *Russia* 23 E7
Vesoul, *France* 18 C7
Vesterålen, *Norway* 8 B16
Vestfjorden, *Norway* 8 C15
Vestmannaeyjar, *Iceland* 8 E3
Vestspitsbergen, *Svalbard* 4 B8
Vestvågøy, *Norway* 8 B15
Vesuvio, *Italy* 20 D6
Vesuvius, Mte. = Vesuvio, *Italy* 20 D6
Veszprém, *Hungary* 17 E9
Vetlanda, *Sweden* 9 H16
Vetlugu →, *Russia* 24 D5
Vettore, Mte., *Italy* 20 C5
Veurne, *Belgium* 15 C2
Veys, *Iran* 39 D6
Vezhen, *Bulgaria* 21 C11
Viacha, *Bolivia* 78 G5
Viamão, *Brazil* 80 C6
Viana, *Brazil* 79 D10
Viana do Alentejo, *Portugal* 19 C2
Viana do Castelo, *Portugal* 19 B1
Vianópolis, *Brazil* 79 G9
Viaréggio, *Italy* 20 C4
Vibank, *Canada* 65 C8
Vibo Valéntia, *Italy* 20 E7
Viborg, *Denmark* 9 H13
Vicenza, *Italy* 20 B4
Vich, *Spain* 19 B7
Vichy, *France* 18 C5
Vicksburg, *Mich., U.S.A.* 68 D3
Vicksburg, *Miss., U.S.A.* 71 J9
Viçosa, *Brazil* 79 E11
Victor, *India* 36 J7
Victor, *U.S.A.* 70 F2
Victor Harbor, *Australia* 55 F2
Victoria, *Canada* 64 D4
Victoria, *Chile* 80 D2
Victoria, *Guinea* 44 F2
Victoria, *Malaysia* 32 C5
Victoria, *Seychelles* 35 E4
Victoria, *Kans., U.S.A.* 70 F5
Victoria, *Tex., U.S.A.* 71 L6
Victoria □, *Australia* 55 F3
Victoria →, *Australia* 52 C4
Victoria, Grand L., *Canada* 62 C4
Victoria, L., *Africa* 46 E6
Victoria, L., *Australia* 55 E3
Victoria Beach, *Canada* 65 C9
Victoria de Durango, *Mexico* 74 C4
Victoria Falls, *Zimbabwe* 47 H5
Victoria Harbour, *Canada* 62 D4
Victoria I., *Canada* 60 A8
Victoria Ld., *Antarctica* 5 D11
Victoria Res., *Canada* 63 C8
Victoria River Downs, *Australia* 52 C5
Victoria Taungdeik, *Burma* 37 J18
Victoria West, *S. Africa* 48 E3
Victoriaville, *Canada* 63 C5
Victorica, *Argentina* 80 D3
Victorville, *U.S.A.* 73 J5
Vicuña, *Chile* 80 C2
Vidalia, *U.S.A.* 69 J4
Vidin, *Bulgaria* 21 C10
Vidisha, *India* 36 H10
Vidzy, *Belarus* 9 J22
Viedma, *Argentina* 80 E4
Viedma, L., *Argentina* 80 F2
Vien Pou Kha, *Laos* 34 B6
Vienna = Wien, *Austria* 16 D9
Vienna, *U.S.A.* 71 G10
Vienne, *France* 18 D6
Vienne →, *France* 18 C4
Vientiane, *Laos* 34 D7
Vierzon, *France* 18 C5
Vietnam ■, *Asia* 34 C9
Vigan, *Phil.* 33 A6
Vigévano, *Italy* 20 B3
Vigia, *Brazil* 79 D9
Vigo, *Spain* 19 A1
Vijayawada, *India* 37 L12
Vik, *Iceland* 8 E4
Vikeke, *Indonesia* 33 F7
Viking, *Canada* 64 C6
Vikna, *Norway* 8 D14
Vikulovo, *Russia* 24 D8
Vila da Maganja, *Mozam.* 47 H7
Vila de João Belo = Xai-Xai, *Mozam.* 49 D5
Vila do Bispo, *Portugal* 19 D1
Vila do Chibuto, *Mozam.* 49 C5
Vila Franca de Xira, *Portugal* 19 C1
Vila Gomes da Costa, *Mozam.* 49 C5
Vila Machado, *Mozam.* 47 H6
Vila Nova de Gaia, *Portugal* 19 B1
Vila Real, *Portugal* 19 B2
Vila Real de Santo António, *Portugal* 19 D2
Vila Velha, *Brazil* 79 H10
Vilaine →, *France* 18 C2
Vilanandro, Tanjona, *Madag.* 49 B7
Vilanculos, *Mozam.* 49 C6
Vileyka, *Belarus* 17 A14
Vilhelmina, *Sweden* 8 D17
Vilhena, *Brazil* 78 F6
Viliga, *Russia* 25 C16
Viliya →, *Lithuania* 9 J21
Viljandi, *Estonia* 9 G21
Vilkitskogo, Proliv, *Russia* 25 B11
Vilkovo = Vylkove, *Ukraine* 17 F15
Villa Ahumada, *Mexico* 74 A3
Villa Ângela, *Argentina* 80 B4
Villa Bella, *Bolivia* 78 F5
Villa Bens = Tarfaya, *Morocco* 44 C2
Villa Cisneros = Dakhla, *W. Sahara* 44 D1
Villa Colón, *Argentina* 80 C3
Villa de María, *Argentina* 80 B4
Villa Dolores, *Argentina* 80 C3
Villa Hayes, *Paraguay* 80 A5
Villa María, *Argentina* 80 C4
Villa Mazán, *Argentina* 80 B3
Villa Montes, *Bolivia* 80 A4
Villa Ocampo, *Argentina* 80 B5
Villacarrillo, *Spain* 19 C4
Villach, *Austria* 16 E7
Villagarcía de Arosa, *Spain* 19 A1
Villaguay, *Argentina* 80 C5
Villahermosa, *Mexico* 74 D6
Villajoyosa, *Spain* 19 C5
Villalba, *Spain* 19 A2
Villanueva, *U.S.A.* 73 J11
Villanueva de la Serena, *Spain* 19 C3
Villanueva y Geltrú, *Spain* 19 B6
Villarreal, *Spain* 19 C5
Villarrica, *Chile* 80 D2
Villarrica, *Paraguay* 80 B5
Villarrobledo, *Spain* 19 C4
Villavicencio, *Colombia* 78 C4
Villaviciosa, *Spain* 19 A3
Villazón, *Bolivia* 80 A3
Ville-Marie, *Canada* 62 C4
Ville Platte, *U.S.A.* 71 K8
Villena, *Spain* 19 C5
Villeneuve-d'Ascq, *France* 18 A5
Villeneuve-sur-Lot, *France* 18 D4
Villiers, *S. Africa* 49 D4
Villingen-Schwenningen, *Germany* 16 D5
Villisca, *U.S.A.* 70 E7
Vilna, *Canada* 64 C6
Vilnius, *Lithuania* 9 J21
Vilvoorde, *Belgium* 15 D4
Vilyuy →, *Russia* 25 C13
Vilyuysk, *Russia* 25 C13
Viña del Mar, *Chile* 80 C2
Vinaroz, *Spain* 19 B6
Vincennes, *U.S.A.* 68 F2
Vindelälven →, *Sweden* 8 E18
Vindeln, *Sweden* 8 D18
Vindhya Ra., *India* 36 H10
Vineland, *U.S.A.* 68 F8
Vinh, *Vietnam* 34 C8
Vinita, *U.S.A.* 71 G7
Vinkovci, *Croatia* 21 B8
Vinnitsa = Vinnytsya, *Ukraine* 17 D15
Vinnytsya, *Ukraine* 17 D15
Vinton, *Iowa, U.S.A.* 70 D8
Vinton, *La., U.S.A.* 71 K8
Virac, *Phil.* 33 B6
Virago Sd., *Canada* 64 C2
Viramgam, *India* 36 H8
Virden, *Canada* 65 D8
Vire, *France* 18 B3
Vírgenes, C., *Argentina* 80 G3
Virgin →, *Canada* 65 B7
Virgin →, *U.S.A.* 73 H6
Virgin Is. (British) ■, *W. Indies* 75 D12
Virgin Is. (U.S.) ■, *W. Indies* 75 D12
Virginia, *S. Africa* 48 D4
Virginia, *U.S.A.* 70 B8
Virginia □, *U.S.A.* 68 G7
Virginia Beach, *U.S.A.* 68 G8
Virginia City, *Mont., U.S.A.* 72 D8
Virginia City, *Nev., U.S.A.* 72 G4
Virginia Falls, *Canada* 64 A3
Virginiatown, *Canada* 62 C4
Viroqua, *U.S.A.* 70 D9
Virovitica, *Croatia* 20 B7
Virton, *Belgium* 15 E5
Virudunagar, *India* 36 Q10
Vis, *Croatia* 20 C7
Visalia, *U.S.A.* 73 H4
Visayan Sea, *Phil.* 33 B6
Visby, *Sweden* 9 H18
Viscount Melville Sd., *Canada* 4 B2
Visé, *Belgium* 15 D5
Višegrad, *Bos.-H.* 21 C8
Viseu, *Brazil* 79 D9
Viseu, *Portugal* 19 B2
Vishakhapatnam, *India* 37 L13
Viso, Mte., *Italy* 20 B2
Visokoi I., *Antarctica* 5 B1
Vistula = Wisła →, *Poland* 17 A10
Vitebsk = Vitsyebsk, *Belarus* 22 C5
Viterbo, *Italy* 20 C5
Viti Levu, *Fiji* 51 C7
Vitigudino, *Spain* 19 B2
Vitim, *Russia* 25 D12
Vitim →, *Russia* 25 D12
Vitória, *Brazil* 79 H10
Vitoria, *Spain* 19 A4
Vitória da Conquista, *Brazil* 79 F10
Vitsyebsk, *Belarus* 22 C5
Vittória, *Italy* 20 F6
Vittório Véneto, *Italy* 20 B5
Vivero, *Spain* 19 A2
Vize, *Turkey* 21 D12
Vizianagaram, *India* 37 K13
Vjosa →, *Albania* 21 D8
Vlaardingen, *Neths.* 15 C4
Vladikavkaz, *Russia* 23 F7
Vladimir, *Russia* 22 C7
Vladimir Volynskiy = Volodymyr-Volynskyy, *Ukraine* 17 C13
Vladivostok, *Russia* 25 E14
Vlieland, *Neths.* 15 A4
Vlissingen, *Neths.* 15 C3
Vlóra, *Albania* 21 D8
Vltava →, *Czech.* 16 D8
Vogelkop = Doberai, Jazirah, *Indonesia* 33 E8
Vogelsberg, *Germany* 16 C5
Voghera, *Italy* 20 B3
Vohibinany, *Madag.* 49 B8
Vohimarina, *Madag.* 49 A9
Vohimena, Tanjon' i, *Madag.* 49 D8
Vohipeno, *Madag.* 49 C8
Voi, *Kenya* 46 E7
Voiron, *France* 18 D6
Voisey B., *Canada* 63 A7
Vojmsjön, *Sweden* 8 D17
Vojvodina □, *Serbia, Yug.* 21 B9
Volborg, *U.S.A.* 70 C2
Volcano Is. = Kazan-Rettō, *Pac. Oc.* 56 E6
Volchayevka, *Russia* 25 E14
Volda, *Norway* 9 E12
Volga →, *Russia* 23 E8
Volga Hts. = Privolzhskaya Vozvyshennost, *Russia* 23 D8
Volgodonsk, *Russia* 23 E7
Volgograd, *Russia* 23 E7
Volgogradskoye Vdkhr., *Russia* 23 D8
Volkhov →, *Russia* 22 B5
Volkovysk = Vawkavysk, *Belarus* 17 B13
Volksrust, *S. Africa* 49 D4
Vollenhove, *Neths.* 15 B5
Volochanka, *Russia* 25 B10
Volodymyr-Volynskyy, *Ukraine* 17 C13
Vologda, *Russia* 22 C6
Vólos, *Greece* 21 E10
Volovets, *Ukraine* 17 D12
Volozhin = Valozhyn, *Belarus* 17 A14
Volsk, *Russia* 22 D8
Volta →, *Ghana* 44 G5
Volta, L., *Ghana* 44 G5
Volta Redonda, *Brazil* 79 H10
Voltaire, C., *Australia* 52 B4
Volterra, *Italy* 20 C4
Volturno →, *Italy* 20 D5
Volvo, *Australia* 55 E3
Volzhskiy, *Russia* 23 E7
Vondrozo, *Madag.* 49 C8
Voorburg, *Neths.* 15 B4
Vopnafjörður, *Iceland* 8 D6
Voríai Sporádhes, *Greece* 21 E10
Vorkuta, *Russia* 22 A11
Vormsi, *Estonia* 9 G20
Voronezh, *Russia* 22 D6
Voroshilovgrad = Luhansk, *Ukraine* 23 E6
Voroshilovsk = Alchevsk, *Ukraine* 23 E6
Vorovskoye, *Russia* 25 D16
Võrts Järv, *Estonia* 9 G22
Võru, *Estonia* 9 H22
Vosges, *France* 18 B7
Voss, *Norway* 9 F12
Vostok I., *Kiribati* 57 J12
Votkinsk, *Russia* 22 C9
Votkinskoye Vdkhr., *Russia* 22 C10
Vouga →, *Portugal* 19 B1
Vozhe Ozero, *Russia* 22 B6
Voznesenka, *Russia* 25 D10
Voznesensk, *Ukraine* 23 E5
Voznesenye, *Russia* 22 B6
Vrangelya, Ostrov, *Russia* 25 B19
Vranje, *Serbia, Yug.* 21 C9
Vratsa, *Bulgaria* 21 C10
Vrbas →, *Bos.-H.* 20 B7
Vrede, *S. Africa* 49 D4
Vredefort, *S. Africa* 48 D4
Vredenburg, *S. Africa* 48 E2
Vredendal, *S. Africa* 48 E2
Vršac, *Serbia, Yug.* 21 B9
Vryburg, *S. Africa* 48 D3
Vryheid, *S. Africa* 49 D5
Vught, *Neths.* 15 C5
Vukovar, *Croatia* 21 B8
Vulcan, *Canada* 64 C6
Vulcan, *Romania* 17 F12
Vulcan, *U.S.A.* 68 C2
Vulcaneşti, *Moldova* 17 F15
Vulcano, *Italy* 20 E6
Vulkaneshty = Vulcaneşti, *Moldova* 17 F15
Vung Tau, *Vietnam* 34 G9
Vyatka = Kirov, *Russia* 24 D5
Vyatka →, *Russia* 22 C9
Vyatskiye Polyany, *Russia* 22 C9
Vyazemskiy, *Russia* 25 E14
Vyazma, *Russia* 22 C5
Vyborg, *Russia* 22 B4
Vychegda →, *Russia* 22 B8
Vychodné Beskydy, *Europe* 17 D11
Vyg-ozero, *Russia* 22 B5
Vylkove, *Ukraine* 17 F15
Vynohradiv, *Ukraine* 17 D12
Vyrnwy, L., *U.K.* 10 E4
Vyshniy Volochek, *Russia* 22 C5
Vyshzha = imeni 26 Bakinskikh Komissarov, *Turkmenistan* 23 G9
Vyškov, *Czech.* 17 D9
Vytegra, *Russia* 22 B6

W

W.A.C. Bennett Dam, *Canada* 64 B4
Wa, *Ghana* 44 F4
Waal →, *Neths.* 15 C5
Wabakimi L., *Canada* 62 B2
Wabana, *Canada* 63 C9
Wabasca, *Canada* 64 B6
Wabash, *U.S.A.* 68 E3
Wabash →, *U.S.A.* 68 G1
Wabeno, *U.S.A.* 68 C1
Wabigoon L., *Canada* 65 D10
Wabowden, *Canada* 65 C9
Wabuk Pt., *Canada* 62 A2
Wabush, *Canada* 63 B6
Wabuska, *U.S.A.* 72 G4
Waco, *U.S.A.* 71 K6
Waconichi, L., *Canada* 62 B5
Wad Banda, *Sudan* 45 F10
Wad Hamid, *Sudan* 45 E11
Wâd Medanî, *Sudan* 45 F11
Wadayama, *Japan* 29 G7
Waddeneilanden, *Neths.* 15 A5
Waddenzee, *Neths.* 15 A5
Wadderin Hill, *Australia* 53 F2
Waddington, Mt., *Canada* 64 C3
Waddy Pt., *Australia* 55 C5
Wadena, *Canada* 65 C8
Wadena, *U.S.A.* 70 B7
Wadesboro, *U.S.A.* 69 H5
Wadhams, *Canada* 64 C3
Wādī as Sīr, *Jordan* 41 D4
Wadi Halfa, *Sudan* 45 D11
Wadsworth, *U.S.A.* 72 G4
Wafrah, *Si. Arabia* 38 D5
Wageningen, *Neths.* 15 C5
Wager B., *Canada* 61 B11
Wager Bay, *Canada* 61 B10
Wagga Wagga, *Australia* 55 F4
Waghete, *Indonesia* 33 E9
Wagin, *Australia* 53 F2
Wagon Mound, *U.S.A.* 71 G2
Wagoner, *U.S.A.* 71 G7
Wah, *Pakistan* 36 C8
Wahai, *Indonesia* 33 E7
Wahiawa, *U.S.A.* 66 H15
Wâḥid, *Egypt* 41 E1
Wahoo, *U.S.A.* 70 E6
Wahpeton, *U.S.A.* 70 B6
Waiau →, *N.Z.* 51 K4
Waibeem, *Indonesia* 33 E8
Waigeo, *Indonesia* 33 E8
Waihi, *N.Z.* 51 G5
Waihou →, *N.Z.* 51 G5
Waikabubak, *Indonesia* 33 F5
Waikari, *N.Z.* 51 K4
Waikato →, *N.Z.* 51 G5
Waikerie, *Australia* 55 E2
Waikokopu, *N.Z.* 51 H6
Waikouaiti, *N.Z.* 51 L3
Waimakariri →, *N.Z.* 51 K4
Waimate, *N.Z.* 51 L3
Wainganga →, *India* 36 K11
Waingapu, *Indonesia* 33 F6
Wainwright, *Canada* 65 C6
Wainwright, *U.S.A.* 60 A3
Waiouru, *N.Z.* 51 H5
Waipara, *N.Z.* 51 K4
Waipawa, *N.Z.* 51 H6
Waipiro, *N.Z.* 51 H7
Waipu, *N.Z.* 51 F5
Waipukurau, *N.Z.* 51 J6
Wairakei, *N.Z.* 51 H6
Wairarapa, L., *N.Z.* 51 J5
Wairoa, *N.Z.* 51 H6
Waitaki →, *N.Z.* 51 L3
Waitara, *N.Z.* 51 H5
Waitsburg, *U.S.A.* 72 C5
Waiuku, *N.Z.* 51 G5
Wajima, *Japan* 29 F8
Wajir, *Kenya* 46 D8
Wakasa, *Japan* 29 G7
Wakasa-Wan, *Japan* 29 G7
Wakatipu, L., *N.Z.* 51 L2
Wakaw, *Canada* 65 C7
Wakayama, *Japan* 29 G7
Wakayama-ken □, *Japan* 29 H7
Wake Forest, *U.S.A.* 69 H6
Wake I., *Pac. Oc.* 56 F8
Wakefield, *N.Z.* 51 J4
Wakefield, *U.K.* 10 D6
Wakefield, *U.S.A.* 70 B10
Wakeham Bay = Maricourt, *Canada* 61 C12
Wakema, *Burma* 37 L19
Wakkanai, *Japan* 28 B10
Wakkerstroom, *S. Africa* 49 D5
Wakool, *Australia* 55 F3
Wakool →, *Australia* 55 F3
Wakre, *Indonesia* 33 E8
Wakuach L., *Canada* 63 A6
Wałbrzych, *Poland* 16 C9
Walbury Hill, *U.K.* 11 F6
Walcha, *Australia* 55 E5
Walcheren, *Neths.* 15 C3
Walcott, *U.S.A.* 72 F10
Wałcz, *Poland* 16 B9
Waldburg Ra., *Australia* 52 D2
Walden, *U.S.A.* 72 F10
Waldport, *U.S.A.* 72 D1
Waldron, *U.S.A.* 71 H7
Wales □, *U.K.* 11 E4
Walgett, *Australia* 55 E4
Walgreen Coast, *Antarctica* 5 D15
Walhalla, *Australia* 55 F4
Walhalla, *U.S.A.* 65 D9
Walker, *U.S.A.* 70 B7
Walker L., *Man., Canada* 65 C9
Walker L., *Qué., Canada* 63 B6
Walker L., *U.S.A.* 72 G4
Walkerston, *Australia* 54 C4
Wall, *U.S.A.* 70 C3
Walla Walla, *U.S.A.* 72 C4
Wallabadah, *Australia* 54 B3
Wallace, *Idaho, U.S.A.* 72 C6
Wallace, *N.C., U.S.A.* 69 H7
Wallace, *Nebr., U.S.A.* 70 E4
Wallaceburg, *Canada* 62 D3
Wallachia = Valahia, *Romania* 17 F13
Wallal, *Australia* 55 D4
Wallal Downs, *Australia* 52 C3
Wallambin, L., *Australia* 53 F2
Wallaroo, *Australia* 55 E2
Wallasey, *U.K.* 10 D4
Wallerawang, *Australia* 55 E5
Wallhallow, *Australia* 54 B2
Wallis & Futuna, Is., *Pac. Oc.* 56 J10
Wallowa, *U.S.A.* 72 D5
Wallowa Mts., *U.S.A.* 72 D5
Wallsend, *Australia* 55 E5
Wallsend, *U.K.* 10 C6
Wallula, *U.S.A.* 72 C4
Wallumbilla, *Australia* 55 D4
Walmsley, L., *Canada* 65 A7
Walney, I. of, *U.K.* 10 C4
Walnut Ridge, *U.S.A.* 71 G9
Walsall, *U.K.* 11 E6
Walsenburg, *U.S.A.* 71 G2
Walsh, *U.S.A.* 71 G3
Walsh →, *Australia* 54 B3
Walsh P.O., *Australia* 54 B3
Walterboro, *U.S.A.* 69 J5
Walters, *U.S.A.* 71 H5
Waltham Station, *Canada* 62 C4
Waltman, *U.S.A.* 72 E10
Walvisbaai, *Namibia* 48 C1
Wamba, *Zaïre* 46 D5
Wamego, *U.S.A.* 70 F6
Wamena, *Indonesia* 33 E9
Wamulan, *Indonesia* 33 E7
Wana, *Pakistan* 36 C6
Wanaaring, *Australia* 55 D3
Wanaka, *N.Z.* 51 L2
Wanaka L., *N.Z.* 51 L2
Wanapiri, *Indonesia* 33 E9
Wanapitei L., *Canada* 62 C3
Wanbi, *Australia* 55 E3
Wandarrie, *Australia* 53 E2
Wandel Sea = McKinley Sea, *Arctic* 4 A7
Wandoan, *Australia* 55 D4
Wang Saphung, *Thailand* 34 D6
Wangal, *Indonesia* 33 F8
Wanganella, *Australia* 55 F3
Wanganui, *N.Z.* 51 H5
Wangaratta, *Australia* 55 F4
Wangary, *Australia* 55 E2
Wangerooge, *Germany* 16 B4
Wangiwangi, *Indonesia* 33 F6
Wanless, *Canada* 65 C8
Wanxian, *China* 31 C5
Wapakoneta, *U.S.A.* 68 E3
Wapato, *U.S.A.* 72 C3
Wapawekka L., *Canada* 65 C8
Wapikopa L., *Canada* 62 B2
Wapsipinicon →, *U.S.A.* 70 E9
Warangal, *India* 36 L11
Waratah, *Australia* 54 G4
Waratah B., *Australia* 55 F4
Warburton, *Vic., Australia* 55 F4
Warburton, *W. Austral., Australia* 53 E4
Warburton Ra., *Australia* 53 E4
Ward, *N.Z.* 51 J5
Ward →, *Australia* 55 D4
Ward Cove, *U.S.A.* 64 B2
Warden, *S. Africa* 49 D4
Wardha, *India* 36 J11
Wardha →, *India* 36 K11
Wardlow, *Canada* 64 C6
Ware, *Canada* 64 B3
Warialda, *Australia* 55 D5
Wariap, *Indonesia* 33 E8
Warkopi, *Indonesia* 33 E8
Warley, *U.K.* 11 E6
Warm Springs, *U.S.A.* 73 G5
Warman, *Canada* 65 C7
Warmbad, *Namibia* 48 D2
Warmbad, *S. Africa* 49 C4
Warnambool Downs, *Australia* 54 C3
Warner, *Canada* 64 D6
Warner Mts., *U.S.A.* 72 F3
Warner Robins, *U.S.A.* 69 J4
Waroona, *Australia* 53 F2
Warracknabeal, *Australia* 55 F3
Warragul, *Australia* 55 F4
Warrawagine, *Australia* 52 D3
Warrego →, *Australia* 55 E4
Warrego Ra., *Australia* 54 C4
Warren, *Australia* 55 E4
Warren, *Ark., U.S.A.* 71 J8
Warren, *Mich., U.S.A.* 68 D4
Warren, *Minn., U.S.A.* 70 A6
Warren, *Ohio, U.S.A.* 68 E5
Warren, *Pa., U.S.A.* 68 E6
Warrenpoint, *U.K.* 13 B5
Warrensburg, *U.S.A.* 70 F8
Warrenton, *S. Africa* 48 D3
Warrenton, *U.S.A.* 72 C2
Warrenville, *Australia* 55 D4
Warri, *Nigeria* 44 G6
Warrina, *Australia* 55 D2
Warrington, *U.K.* 10 D5
Warrington, *U.S.A.* 69 K2
Warrnambool, *Australia* 55 F3
Warroad, *U.S.A.* 70 A7
Warsa, *Indonesia* 33 E9
Warsaw = Warszawa, *Poland* 17 B11
Warsaw, *U.S.A.* 68 E3
Warszawa, *Poland* 17 B11
Warta →, *Poland* 16 B8
Warthe = Warta →, *Poland* 16 B8
Waru, *Indonesia* 33 E8
Warwick, *Australia* 55 D5
Warwick, *U.K.* 11 E6
Warwick, *U.S.A.* 68 E10
Warwickshire □, *U.K.* 11 E6
Wasatch Ra., *U.S.A.* 72 F8
Wasbank, *S. Africa* 49 D5
Wasco, *Calif., U.S.A.* 73 J4
Wasco, *Oreg., U.S.A.* 72 D3
Waseca, *U.S.A.* 70 C8
Wasekamio L., *Canada* 65 B7
Wash, The, *U.K.* 10 E8
Washburn, *N. Dak., U.S.A.* 70 B4
Washburn, *Wis., U.S.A.* 70 B9
Washim, *India* 36 J10
Washington, *D.C., U.S.A.* 68 F7
Washington, *Ga., U.S.A.* 69 J4
Washington, *Ind., U.S.A.* 68 F2
Washington, *Iowa, U.S.A.* 70 E9
Washington, *Mo., U.S.A.* 70 F9
Washington, *N.C., U.S.A.* 69 H7
Washington, *Pa., U.S.A.* 68 E5
Washington, *Utah, U.S.A.* 73 H7
Washington □, *U.S.A.* 72 C3
Washington, Mt., *U.S.A.* 68 C10
Washington I., *U.S.A.* 68 C2
Wasian, *Indonesia* 33 E8
Wasior, *Indonesia* 33 E8
Waskaganish, *Canada* 62 B4
Waskaiowaka, L., *Canada* 65 B9
Waskesiu Lake, *Canada* 65 C7
Wassenaar, *Neths.* 15 B4
Wasserkuppe, *Germany* 16 C5
Waswanipi, *Canada* 62 C4
Waswanipi, L., *Canada* 62 C4
Watangpone, *Indonesia* 33 E6
Water Park Pt., *Australia* 54 C5
Water Valley, *U.S.A.* 71 H10
Waterberge, *S. Africa* 49 C4
Waterbury, *U.S.A.* 68 E9
Waterbury L., *Canada* 65 B8
Waterford, *Ireland* 13 D4
Waterford □, *Ireland* 13 D4
Waterford Harbour, *Ireland* 13 D5
Waterhen L., *Man., Canada* 65 C9
Waterhen L., *Sask., Canada* 65 C7
Waterloo, *Belgium* 15 D4
Waterloo, *Canada* 62 D3
Waterloo, *S. Leone* 44 G2
Waterloo, *Ill., U.S.A.* 70 F9
Waterloo, *Iowa, U.S.A.* 70 D8
Watersmeet, *U.S.A.* 70 B10
Waterton-Glacier International Peace Park, *U.S.A.* 72 B7
Watertown, *N.Y., U.S.A.* 68 D8
Watertown, *S. Dak., U.S.A.* 70 C6
Watertown, *Wis., U.S.A.* 70 D10
Waterval-Boven, *S. Africa* 49 D5
Waterville, *Maine, U.S.A.* 63 D6

Worcester

Waterville, Wash., U.S.A. 72 C3
Watervliet, U.S.A. 68 D9
Wates, Indonesia 33 G14
Watford, U.K. 11 F7
Watford City, U.S.A. 70 B3
Wathaman →, Canada 65 B8
Watheroo, Australia 53 F2
Watkins Glen, U.S.A. 68 D7
Watling I. = San Salvador, Bahamas 75 C10
Watonga, U.S.A. 71 H5
Watrous, Canada 65 C7
Watrous, U.S.A. 71 H2
Watsa, Zaïre 46 D5
Watseka, U.S.A. 68 E2
Watson, Australia 53 F5
Watson, Canada 65 C8
Watson Lake, Canada 64 A3
Watsonville, U.S.A. 73 H3
Wattiwarriganna Cr. →, Australia 55 D2
Watuata = Batuata, Indonesia 33 F6
Watubela, Kepulauan, Indonesia 33 E8
Watubela Is. = Watubela, Kepulauan, Indonesia 33 E8
Waubay, U.S.A. 70 C6
Waubra, Australia 55 F3
Wauchope, Australia 55 E5
Wauchula, U.S.A. 69 M5
Waugh, Canada 65 D9
Waukarlycarly, L., Australia 52 D3
Waukegan, U.S.A. 68 D2
Waukesha, U.S.A. 68 D1
Waukon, U.S.A. 70 D9
Wauneta, U.S.A. 70 E4
Waupaca, U.S.A. 70 C10
Waupun, U.S.A. 70 D10
Waurika, U.S.A. 71 H6
Wausau, U.S.A. 70 C10
Wautoma, U.S.A. 70 C10
Wauwatosa, U.S.A. 68 D2
Wave Hill, Australia 52 C5
Waveney →, U.K. 11 E9
Waverley, N.Z. 51 H5
Waverly, Iowa, U.S.A. 70 D8
Waverly, N.Y., U.S.A. 68 D7
Wavre, Belgium 15 D4
Wâw, Sudan 45 G10
Wâw al Kabīr, Libya 45 C8
Wawa, Canada 62 C3
Wawanesa, Canada 65 D9
Waxahachie, U.S.A. 71 J6
Way, L., Australia 53 E3
Wayabula Rau, Indonesia 33 D7
Wayatinah, Australia 54 G4
Waycross, U.S.A. 69 K4
Wayne, Nebr., U.S.A. 70 D6
Wayne, W. Va., U.S.A. 68 F4
Waynesboro, Ga., U.S.A. 69 J4
Waynesboro, Miss., U.S.A. 69 K1
Waynesboro, Pa., U.S.A. 68 F7
Waynesboro, Va., U.S.A. 68 F6
Waynesburg, U.S.A. 68 F5
Waynesville, U.S.A. 69 H4
Waynoka, U.S.A. 71 G5
Wazirabad, Pakistan 36 C9
We, Indonesia 32 C1
Weald, The, U.K. 11 F8
Wear →, U.K. 10 C6
Weatherford, Okla., U.S.A. 71 H5
Weatherford, Tex., U.S.A. 71 J6
Weaverville, U.S.A. 72 F2
Webb City, U.S.A. 71 G7
Webster, S. Dak., U.S.A. 70 C6
Webster, Wis., U.S.A. 70 C8
Webster City, U.S.A. 70 D8
Webster Green, U.S.A. 70 F9
Webster Springs, U.S.A. 68 F5
Weda, Indonesia 33 D7
Weda, Teluk, Indonesia 33 D7
Weddell I., Falk. Is. 80 G4
Weddell Sea, Antarctica 5 D1
Wedderburn, Australia 55 F3
Wedgeport, Canada 63 D6
Wee Waa, Australia 55 E4
Weed, U.S.A. 72 F2
Weemelah, Australia 55 D4
Weenen, S. Africa 49 D5
Weert, Neths. 15 C5
Weiden, Germany 16 D7
Weifang, China 31 C6
Weimar, Germany 16 C6
Weipa, Australia 54 A3
Weir →, Australia 55 D4
Weir →, Canada 65 B10
Weir River, Canada 65 B10
Weiser, U.S.A. 72 D5
Wejherowo, Poland 17 A10
Wekusko L., Canada 65 C9
Welbourn Hill, Australia 55 D1
Welch, U.S.A. 68 G5
Welkom, S. Africa 48 D4
Welland, Canada 62 D4
Welland →, U.K. 10 E7
Wellesley Is., Australia 54 B2
Wellin, Belgium 15 D5
Wellingborough, U.K. 11 E7
Wellington, Australia 55 E4
Wellington, Canada 62 D4
Wellington, N.Z. 51 J5
Wellington, S. Africa 48 E2
Wellington, Shrops., U.K. 10 E5
Wellington, Somst., U.K. 11 G4
Wellington, Colo., U.S.A. 70 E2
Wellington, Kans., U.S.A. 71 G6
Wellington, Nev., U.S.A. 72 G4
Wellington, Tex., U.S.A. 71 H4
Wellington, I., Chile 80 F1
Wellington, L., Australia 55 F4
Wells, U.K. 11 F5
Wells, Minn., U.S.A. 70 D8
Wells, Nev., U.S.A. 72 F6
Wells, L., Australia 53 E3
Wells Gray Prov. Park, Canada 64 C4
Wells-next-the-Sea, U.K. 10 E8
Wellsboro, U.S.A. 68 E7
Wellsville, Mo., U.S.A. 70 F9
Wellsville, N.Y., U.S.A. 68 D7
Wellsville, Ohio, U.S.A. 68 E5
Wellsville, Utah, U.S.A. 72 F8
Wellton, U.S.A. 73 K6
Wels, Austria 16 D8
Welshpool, U.K. 11 E4
Wem, U.K. 10 E5
Wemindji, Canada 62 B4
Wenatchee, U.S.A. 72 C3
Wenchi, Ghana 44 G4
Wenchow = Wenzhou, China 31 D7
Wendell, U.S.A. 72 E6
Wendesi, Indonesia 33 E8
Wendover, U.S.A. 72 F6
Wenlock →, Australia 54 A3
Wenshan, China 30 D5
Wensu, China 30 B3
Wentworth, Australia 55 E3
Wenut, Indonesia 33 E8
Wenzhou, China 31 D7
Weott, U.S.A. 72 F2
Wepener, S. Africa 48 D4
Werda, Botswana 48 D3
Werder, Ethiopia 40 F4
Weri, Indonesia 33 E8
Werra →, Germany 16 C5
Werribee, Australia 55 F3
Werrimull, Australia 55 E3
Werris Creek, Australia 55 E5
Wersar, Indonesia 33 E8
Weser →, Germany 16 B5
Wesiri, Indonesia 33 F7
Wesley Vale, U.S.A. 73 J10
Wesleyville, Canada 63 C9
Wessel, C., Australia 54 A2
Wessel Is., Australia 54 A2
Wessington, U.S.A. 70 C5
Wessington Springs, U.S.A. 70 C5
West, U.S.A. 71 K6
West B., U.S.A. 71 L10
West Baines →, Australia 52 C4
West Bank □, Asia 41 C4
West Bend, U.S.A. 68 D1
West Bengal □, India 37 H15
West Beskids = Západné Beskydy, Europe 17 D10
West Branch, U.S.A. 68 C3
West Bromwich, U.K. 11 E5
West Cape Howe, Australia 53 G2
West Chester, U.S.A. 68 F8
West Columbia, U.S.A. 71 L7
West Des Moines, U.S.A. 70 E8
West Falkland, Falk. Is. 80 G4
West Fjord = Vestfjorden, Norway 8 C15
West Frankfort, U.S.A. 70 G10
West Glamorgan □, U.K. 11 F4
West Helena, U.S.A. 71 H9
West Ice Shelf, Antarctica 5 C7
West Memphis, U.S.A. 71 H9
West Midlands □, U.K. 11 E6
West Monroe, U.S.A. 71 J8
West Nicholson, Zimbabwe 47 J5
West Palm Beach, U.S.A. 69 M5
West Plains, U.S.A. 71 G9
West Point, Ga., U.S.A. 69 J3
West Point, Miss., U.S.A. 69 J1
West Point, Nebr., U.S.A. 70 E6
West Point, Va., U.S.A. 68 G7
West Pt. = Ouest, Pte., Canada 63 C7
West Pt., Australia 55 F2
West Road →, Canada 64 C4
West Rutland, U.S.A. 68 D9
West Schelde = Westerschelde →, Neths. 15 C3
West Siberian Plain, Russia 26 C11
West Sussex □, U.K. 11 G7
West-Terschelling, Neths. 15 A5
West Virginia □, U.S.A. 68 F5
West-Vlaanderen □, Belgium 15 D3
West Wyalong, Australia 55 E4
West Yellowstone, U.S.A. 72 D8
West Yorkshire □, U.K. 10 D6
Westall Pt., Australia 55 E1
Westbrook, Maine, U.S.A. 69 D10
Westbrook, Tex., U.S.A. 71 J4
Westbury, Australia 54 G4
Westby, U.S.A. 70 A2
Westerland, Germany 9 J13
Western Australia □, Australia 53 E2
Western Cape □, S. Africa 48 E3
Western Ghats, India 36 N9
Western Isles □, U.K. 12 D1
Western Sahara ■, Africa 44 D2
Western Samoa ■, Pac. Oc. 51 A13
Westernport, U.S.A. 68 F6
Westerschelde →, Neths. 15 C3
Westerwald, Germany 16 C4
Westhope, U.S.A. 70 A4
Westland Bight, N.Z. 51 K3
Westlock, Canada 64 C6
Westmeath □, Ireland 13 C4
Westminster, U.S.A. 68 F7
Westmorland, U.S.A. 73 K6
Weston, Malaysia 32 C5
Weston, Oreg., U.S.A. 72 D4
Weston, W. Va., U.S.A. 68 F5
Weston I., Canada 62 B4
Weston-super-Mare, U.K. 11 F5
Westport, Ireland 13 C2
Westport, N.Z. 51 J3
Westport, U.S.A. 72 C1
Westray, Canada 65 C8
Westray, U.K. 12 B6
Westree, Canada 62 C3
Westville, Ill., U.S.A. 68 E2
Westville, Okla., U.S.A. 71 G7
Westwood, U.S.A. 72 F3
Wetar, Indonesia 33 F7
Wetaskiwin, Canada 64 C6
Wetteren, Belgium 15 D3
Wetzlar, Germany 16 C5
Wewoka, U.S.A. 71 H6
Wexford, Ireland 13 D5
Wexford □, Ireland 13 D5
Wexford Harbour, Ireland 13 D5
Weyburn, Canada 65 D8
Weyburn L., Canada 64 A5
Weymouth, Canada 63 D6
Weymouth, U.K. 11 G5
Weymouth, C., Australia 54 A3
Whakatane, N.Z. 51 G6
Whale →, Canada 63 A6
Whale Cove, Canada 65 A10
Whales, B. of, Antarctica 5 D12
Whalsay, U.K. 12 A7
Whangamomona, N.Z. 51 H5
Whangarei, N.Z. 51 F5
Whangarei Harb., N.Z. 51 F5
Wharfe →, U.K. 10 D6
Wharfedale, U.K. 10 C5
Wharton, U.S.A. 71 L6
Wheatland, U.S.A. 70 D2
Wheaton, U.S.A. 70 C6
Wheeler, Oreg., U.S.A. 72 D2
Wheeler, Tex., U.S.A. 71 H4
Wheeler →, Canada 65 B7
Wheeler Pk., N. Mex., U.S.A. 73 H11
Wheeler Pk., Nev., U.S.A. 73 G6
Wheeling, U.S.A. 68 E5
Whernside, U.K. 10 C5
Whidbey I., U.S.A. 64 D4
Whiskey Gap, Canada 64 D6
Whiskey Jack L., Canada 65 B8
Whistleduck Cr. →, Australia 54 C2
Whitby, U.K. 10 C7
White →, Ark., U.S.A. 71 J9
White →, Ind., U.S.A. 68 F2
White →, S. Dak., U.S.A. 70 D5
White →, Utah, U.S.A. 72 F9
White, L., Australia 52 D4
White B., Canada 63 B8
White Bear Res., Canada 63 C8
White Bird, U.S.A. 72 D5
White Butte, U.S.A. 70 B3
White City, U.S.A. 70 F6
White Cliffs, Australia 55 E3
White Deer, U.S.A. 71 H4
White Hall, U.S.A. 70 F9
White Horse, Vale of, U.K. 11 F6
White I., N.Z. 51 G6
White L., U.S.A. 71 L8
White Mts., Calif., U.S.A. 73 H4
White Mts., N.H., U.S.A. 67 B12
White Nile = Nil el Abyad →, Sudan 45 E11
White Otter L., Canada 62 C1
White Pass, Canada 64 B1
White River, Canada 62 C2
White River, S. Africa 49 D5
White River, U.S.A. 70 D4
White Russia = Belarus ■, Europe 17 B14
White Sea = Beloye More, Russia 22 A6
White Sulphur Springs, Mont., U.S.A. 72 C8
White Sulphur Springs, W. Va., U.S.A. 68 G5
Whitecliffs, N.Z. 51 K3
Whitecourt, Canada 64 C5
Whiteface, U.S.A. 71 J3
Whitefish, U.S.A. 72 B6
Whitefish L., Canada 65 A7
Whitefish Point, U.S.A. 68 B3
Whitegull, L., Canada 63 A7
Whitehall, Mich., U.S.A. 68 D2
Whitehall, Mont., U.S.A. 72 D7
Whitehall, N.Y., U.S.A. 68 D9
Whitehall, Wis., U.S.A. 70 C9
Whitehaven, U.K. 10 C4
Whitehorse, Canada 64 A1
Whitemark, Australia 54 G4
Whitemouth, Canada 65 D9
Whitesboro, U.S.A. 71 J6
Whiteshell Prov. Park, Canada 65 C9
Whitetail, U.S.A. 70 A2
Whiteville, U.S.A. 69 H6
Whitewater, U.S.A. 68 D1
Whitewater Baldy, U.S.A. 73 K9
Whitewater L., Canada 62 B2
Whitewood, Australia 54 C3
Whitewood, Canada 65 C8
Whitfield, Australia 55 F4
Whithorn, U.K. 12 G4
Whitianga, N.Z. 51 G5
Whitmire, U.S.A. 69 H5
Whitney, Canada 62 C4
Whitney, Mt., U.S.A. 73 H4
Whitstable, U.K. 11 F9
Whitsunday I., Australia 54 C4
Whittlesea, Australia 55 F4
Whitwell, U.S.A. 69 H3
Wholdaia L., Canada 65 A8
Whyalla, Australia 55 E2
Whyjonta, Australia 55 D3
Wiarton, Canada 62 D3
Wibaux, U.S.A. 70 B2
Wichita, U.S.A. 71 G6
Wichita Falls, U.S.A. 71 J5
Wick, U.K. 12 C5
Wickenburg, U.S.A. 73 K7
Wickepin, Australia 53 F2
Wickham, C., Australia 54 F3
Wicklow, Ireland 13 D5
Wicklow □, Ireland 13 D5
Wicklow Hd., Ireland 13 D5
Widgiemooltha, Australia 53 F3
Widnes, U.K. 10 D5
Wieluń, Poland 17 C10
Wien, Austria 16 D9
Wiener Neustadt, Austria 16 E9
Wierden, Neths. 15 B6
Wiesbaden, Germany 16 C5
Wigan, U.K. 10 D5
Wiggins, Colo., U.S.A. 70 E2
Wiggins, Miss., U.S.A. 71 K10
Wight, I. of □, U.K. 11 G6
Wigtown, U.K. 12 G4
Wigtown B., U.K. 12 G4
Wilber, U.S.A. 70 E6
Wilberforce, C., Australia 54 A2
Wilburton, U.S.A. 71 H7
Wilcannia, Australia 55 E3
Wildrose, U.S.A. 70 A3
Wildspitze, Austria 16 E6
Wildwood, U.S.A. 68 F8
Wilge →, S. Africa 49 D4
Wilhelm II Coast, Antarctica 5 C7
Wilhelmshaven, Germany 16 B5
Wilhelmstal, Namibia 48 C2
Wilkes-Barre, U.S.A. 68 E8
Wilkesboro, U.S.A. 69 G5
Wilkie, Canada 65 C7
Wilkinson Lakes, Australia 53 E5
Willamina, U.S.A. 72 D2
Willandra Billabong Creek →, Australia 55 E4
Willapa B., U.S.A. 72 C2
Willard, N. Mex., U.S.A. 73 J10
Willard, Utah, U.S.A. 72 F7
Willcox, U.S.A. 73 K9
Willemstad, Neth. Ant. 75 E11
Willeroo, Australia 52 C5
William →, Canada 65 B7
William Creek, Australia 55 D2
Williambury, Australia 53 D2
Williams, Australia 53 F2
Williams, U.S.A. 73 J7
Williams Lake, Canada 64 C4
Williamsburg, Ky., U.S.A. 69 G3
Williamsburg, Va., U.S.A. 68 G7
Williamson, U.S.A. 68 G4
Williamsport, U.S.A. 68 E7
Williamston, U.S.A. 69 H7
Williamstown, Australia 55 F3
Williamsville, U.S.A. 71 G9
Willis Group, Australia 54 B5
Williston, S. Africa 48 E3
Williston, Fla., U.S.A. 69 L4
Williston, N. Dak., U.S.A. 70 A3
Williston L., Canada 64 B4
Willits, U.S.A. 72 G2
Willmar, U.S.A. 70 C7
Willow Bunch, Canada 65 D7
Willow L., Canada 64 A5
Willow Lake, U.S.A. 70 C6
Willow Springs, U.S.A. 71 G8
Willowlake →, Canada 64 A4
Willowmore, S. Africa 48 E3
Willows, Australia 54 C4
Willows, U.S.A. 72 G2
Willowvale = Gatyana, S. Africa 49 E4
Wills, L., Australia 52 D4
Wills Cr. →, Australia 54 C3
Wills Point, U.S.A. 71 J7
Willunga, Australia 55 F2
Wilmette, U.S.A. 68 D2
Wilmington, Australia 55 E2
Wilmington, Del., U.S.A. 68 F8
Wilmington, Ill., U.S.A. 68 E1
Wilmington, N.C., U.S.A. 69 H7
Wilmington, Ohio, U.S.A. 68 F4
Wilpena Cr. →, Australia 55 E2
Wilsall, U.S.A. 72 D8
Wilson, U.S.A. 69 H7
Wilson →, Queens., Australia 55 D3
Wilson →, W. Austral., Australia 52 C4
Wilson Bluff, Australia 53 F4
Wilsons Promontory, Australia 55 F4
Wilton, U.K. 11 F6
Wilton, U.S.A. 70 B4
Wilton →, Australia 54 A1
Wiltshire □, U.K. 11 F6
Wiltz, Lux. 15 E5
Wiluna, Australia 53 E3
Wimmera →, Australia 55 F3
Winburg, S. Africa 48 D4
Wincanton, U.K. 11 F6
Winchester, Idaho, U.S.A. 72 C5
Winchester, Ind., U.S.A. 68 E3
Winchester, Ky., U.S.A. 68 G3
Winchester, Tenn., U.S.A. 69 H2
Winchester, Va., U.S.A. 68 F6
Wind →, U.S.A. 72 E9
Wind River Range, U.S.A. 72 E9
Windau = Ventspils, Latvia 9 H19
Windber, U.S.A. 68 E6
Windermere, L., U.K. 10 C5
Windfall, Canada 64 C5
Windflower L., Canada 64 A5
Windhoek, Namibia 48 C2
Windom, U.S.A. 70 D7
Windorah, Australia 54 D3
Window Rock, U.S.A. 73 J9
Windrush →, U.K. 11 F6
Windsor, Australia 55 E5
Windsor, N.S., Canada 63 D7
Windsor, Nfld., Canada 63 C8
Windsor, Ont., Canada 62 D3
Windsor, U.K. 11 F7
Windsor, Colo., U.S.A. 70 E2
Windsor, Mo., U.S.A. 70 F8
Windsor, Vt., U.S.A. 68 D9
Windsorton, S. Africa 48 D3
Windward Is., W. Indies 74 P20
Windy L., Canada 65 A8
Winefred L., Canada 65 B6
Winfield, U.S.A. 71 G6
Wingate Mts., Australia 52 B5
Wingen, Australia 55 E5
Wingham, Australia 55 E5
Wingham, Canada 62 D3
Winifred, U.S.A. 72 C9
Winisk, Canada 62 A2
Winisk →, Canada 62 A2
Winisk L., Canada 62 B2
Wink, U.S.A. 71 K3
Winkler, Canada 65 D9
Winlock, U.S.A. 72 C2
Winneba, Ghana 44 G4
Winnebago, U.S.A. 70 D7
Winnebago, L., U.S.A. 68 D1
Winnecke Cr. →, Australia 52 C5
Winnemucca, U.S.A. 72 F5
Winnemucca L., U.S.A. 72 F4
Winner, U.S.A. 70 D5
Winnett, U.S.A. 72 C9
Winnfield, U.S.A. 71 K8
Winnibigoshish, L., U.S.A. 70 B7
Winning, Australia 52 D1
Winnipeg, Canada 65 D9
Winnipeg →, Canada 65 C9
Winnipeg, L., Canada 65 C9
Winnipeg Beach, Canada 65 C9
Winnipegosis, Canada 65 C9
Winnipegosis L., Canada 65 C9
Winnsboro, La., U.S.A. 71 J9
Winnsboro, S.C., U.S.A. 69 H5
Winnsboro, Tex., U.S.A. 71 J7
Winokapau, L., Canada 63 B7
Winona, Minn., U.S.A. 70 C9
Winona, Miss., U.S.A. 71 J10
Winooski, U.S.A. 68 C9
Winschoten, Neths. 15 A7
Winslow, U.S.A. 73 J8
Winston-Salem, U.S.A. 69 G5
Winter Garden, U.S.A. 69 L5
Winter Haven, U.S.A. 69 M5
Winter Park, U.S.A. 69 L5
Winters, U.S.A. 71 K5
Winterset, U.S.A. 70 E7
Winterswijk, Neths. 15 C6
Winterthur, Switz. 16 E5
Winthrop, Minn., U.S.A. 70 C7
Winthrop, Wash., U.S.A. 72 B3
Winton, Australia 54 C3
Winton, N.Z. 51 M2
Winton, U.S.A. 69 G7
Wirral, U.K. 10 D4
Wirrulla, Australia 55 E1
Wisbech, U.K. 10 E8
Wisconsin □, U.S.A. 70 C10
Wisconsin →, U.S.A. 70 D9
Wisconsin Dells, U.S.A. 70 D10
Wisconsin Rapids, U.S.A. 70 C10
Wisdom, U.S.A. 72 D7
Wishaw, U.K. 12 F5
Wishek, U.S.A. 70 B5
Wisła →, Poland 17 A10
Wismar, Germany 16 B6
Wisner, U.S.A. 70 E6
Witbank, S. Africa 49 D4
Witdraai, S. Africa 48 D3
Witham →, U.K. 10 D7
Withernsea, U.K. 10 D8
Witney, U.K. 11 F6
Witnossob →, Namibia 48 D3
Witten, Germany 15 C7
Wittenberg, Germany 16 C7
Wittenberge, Germany 16 B6
Wittenoom, Australia 52 D2
Wkra →, Poland 17 B11
Wlingi, Indonesia 33 H15
Włocławek, Poland 17 B10
Włodawa, Poland 17 C12
Wodonga, Australia 55 F4
Wokam, Indonesia 33 F8
Wolf →, Canada 64 A2
Wolf Creek, U.S.A. 72 C7
Wolf L., Canada 64 A2
Wolf Point, U.S.A. 70 A2
Wolfe I., Canada 62 D4
Wolfsberg, Austria 16 E8
Wolfsburg, Germany 16 B6
Wolin, Poland 16 B8
Wollaston, Is., Chile 80 H3
Wollaston L., Canada 65 B8
Wollaston Pen., Canada 60 B8
Wollogorang, Australia 54 B2
Wollongong, Australia 55 E5
Wolmaransstad, S. Africa 48 D4
Wolseley, Australia 55 F3
Wolseley, Canada 65 C8
Wolseley, S. Africa 48 E2
Wolstenholme, C., Canada 58 C12
Wolvega, Neths. 15 B6
Wolverhampton, U.K. 11 E5
Wonarah, Australia 54 B2
Wondai, Australia 55 D5
Wongalarroo L., Australia 55 E3
Wongan Hills, Australia 53 F2
Wongawol, Australia 53 E3
Wonosari, Indonesia 33 G14
Wŏnsan, N. Korea 31 C7
Wonthaggi, Australia 55 F4
Woocalla, Australia 55 E2
Wood Buffalo Nat. Park, Canada 64 B6
Wood Is., Australia 52 C3
Wood L., Canada 65 B8
Wood Lake, U.S.A. 70 D4
Woodah I., Australia 54 A2
Woodanilling, Australia 53 F2
Woodburn, Australia 55 D5
Woodenbong, Australia 55 D5
Woodend, Australia 55 F3
Woodgreen, Australia 54 C1
Woodland, U.S.A. 72 G3
Woodlands, Australia 52 D2
Woodpecker, Canada 64 C4
Woodridge, Canada 65 D9
Woodroffe, Mt., Australia 53 E5
Woodruff, Ariz., U.S.A. 73 J8
Woodruff, Utah, U.S.A. 72 F8
Woods, L., Australia 54 B1
Woods, L., Canada 63 B6
Woods, L. of the, Canada 65 D10
Woodstock, Queens., Australia 54 B4
Woodstock, W. Austral., Australia 52 D2
Woodstock, N.B., Canada 63 C6
Woodstock, Ont., Canada 62 D3
Woodstock, U.K. 11 F6
Woodstock, U.S.A. 70 D10
Woodsville, U.S.A. 68 C9
Woodville, N.Z. 51 J5
Woodville, U.S.A. 71 K7
Woodward, U.S.A. 71 G5
Woolamai, C., Australia 55 F4
Woolgoolga, Australia 55 E5
Woombye, Australia 55 D5
Woomera, Australia 55 E2
Woonsocket, R.I., U.S.A. 68 E10
Woonsocket, S. Dak., U.S.A. 70 C5
Wooramel, Australia 53 E1
Wooramel →, Australia 53 E1
Wooroloo, Australia 53 F2
Wooster, U.S.A. 68 E5
Worcester, S. Africa 48 E2
Worcester, U.K. 11 E5

Worcester

Worcester, U.S.A. 68 D10
Workington, U.K. 10 C4
Worksop, U.K. 10 D6
Workum, Neths. 15 B5
Worland, U.S.A. 72 D10
Worms, Germany 16 D5
Wortham, U.S.A. 71 K6
Worthing, U.K. 11 G7
Worthington, U.S.A. 70 D7
Wosi, Indonesia 33 E7
Wou-han = Wuhan, China 31 C6
Wour, Chad 45 D8
Wousi = Wuxi, China 31 C7
Wowoni, Indonesia 33 E6
Woy Woy, Australia 55 E5
Wrangel I. = Vrangelya, Ostrov, Russia 25 B19
Wrangell, U.S.A. 60 C6
Wrangell I., U.S.A. 64 B2
Wrangell Mts., U.S.A. 60 B5
Wrath, C., U.K. 12 C3
Wray, U.S.A. 70 E3
Wrekin, The, U.K. 10 E5
Wrens, U.S.A. 69 J4
Wrexham, U.K. 10 D4
Wright, Canada 64 C4
Wright, Phil. 33 B7
Wrightson Mt., U.S.A. 73 L8
Wrigley, Canada 60 B7
Wrocław, Poland 17 C9
Września, Poland 17 B9
Wu Jiang →, China 30 D5
Wubin, Australia 53 F2
Wuhan, China 31 C6
Wuhsi = Wuxi, China 31 C7
Wuhu, China 31 C6
Wukari, Nigeria 44 G6
Wuliaru, Indonesia 33 F8
Wuluk'omushih Ling, China 30 C3
Wulumuchi = Ürümqi, China 24 E9
Wum, Cameroon 44 G7
Wunnummin L., Canada 62 B2
Wuntho, Burma 37 H19
Wuppertal, Germany 16 C4
Wuppertal, S. Africa 48 E2
Wurung, Australia 54 B3
Würzburg, Germany 16 D5
Wusuli Jiang = Ussuri →, Asia 28 A7
Wutongqiao, China 30 D5
Wuwei, China 30 C5
Wuxi, China 31 C7
Wuxing, China 31 C7
Wuyi Shan, China 31 D6
Wuzhong, China 30 C5
Wuzhou, China 31 D6
Wyaaba Cr. →, Australia 54 B3
Wyalkatchem, Australia 53 F2
Wyandotte, U.S.A. 68 D4
Wyandra, Australia 55 D4
Wyangala Res., Australia 55 E4
Wyara, L., Australia 55 D3
Wycheproof, Australia 55 F3
Wye →, U.K. 11 F5
Wyemandoo, Australia 53 E2
Wymondham, U.K. 11 E7
Wymore, U.S.A. 70 E6
Wynbring, Australia 55 E1
Wyndham, Australia 52 C4
Wyndham, N.Z. 51 M2
Wyndmere, U.S.A. 70 B6
Wynne, U.S.A. 71 H9
Wynnum, Australia 55 D5
Wynyard, Australia 54 G4
Wynyard, Canada 65 C8
Wyola, L., Australia 53 E5
Wyoming □, U.S.A. 72 E10
Wyong, Australia 55 E5
Wytheville, U.S.A. 68 G5

X

Xai-Xai, Mozam. 49 D5
Xainza, China 30 C3
Xangongo, Angola 48 B2
Xankändi, Azerbaijan 23 G8
Xánthi, Greece 21 D11
Xapuri, Brazil 78 F5
Xau, L., Botswana 48 C3
Xenia, U.S.A. 68 F4
Xhora, S. Africa 49 E4
Xhumo, Botswana 48 C3
Xi Jiang →, China 31 D6
Xiaguan, China 30 D5
Xiamen, China 31 D6
Xi'an, China 31 C5
Xiang Jiang →, China 31 D6
Xiangfan, China 31 C6
Xiangtan, China 31 D6
Xianyang, China 31 C5
Xiao Hinggan Ling, China 31 B7
Xichang, China 30 D5
Xieng Khouang, Laos 34 C7
Xigazê, China 30 D3
Xinavane, Mozam. 49 D5
Xing'an, China 31 D6
Xingu →, Brazil 79 D8
Xining, China 30 C5
Xinjiang Uygur Zizhiqu □, China 30 B3
Xinxiang, China 31 C6
Xique-Xique, Brazil 79 F10
Xisha Qundao = Hsisha Chuntao, Pac. Oc. 32 A4
Xixabangma Feng, China 37 E14
Xizang □, China 30 C3
Xuanhua, China 31 B6
Xuzhou, China 31 C6

Y

Yaamba, Australia 54 C5
Yaapeet, Australia 55 F3
Yabelo, Ethiopia 45 H12
Yablonovy Ra. = Yablonovyy Khrebet, Russia 25 D12
Yablonovyy Khrebet, Russia 25 D12
Yabrūd, Syria 41 B5
Yacheng, China 31 E5
Yacuiba, Bolivia 80 A4
Yadgir, India 36 L10
Yadkin →, U.S.A. 69 H5
Yagodnoye, Russia 25 C15
Yagoua, Cameroon 46 B3
Yahk, Canada 64 D5
Yahuma, Zaïre 46 D4
Yaita, Japan 29 F9
Yakima, U.S.A. 72 C3
Yakima →, U.S.A. 72 C3
Yakovlevka, Russia 28 B6
Yaku-Shima, Japan 29 J5
Yakutat, U.S.A. 60 C6
Yakutia = Sakha □, Russia 25 C13
Yakutsk, Russia 25 C13
Yala, Thailand 34 N14
Yalbalgo, Australia 53 E1
Yalboroo, Australia 54 C4
Yalgoo, Australia 53 E2
Yalinga, C.A.R. 45 G9
Yalleroi, Australia 54 C4
Yalobusha →, U.S.A. 71 J9
Yalong Jiang →, China 30 D5
Yalova, Turkey 21 D13
Yalta, Ukraine 23 F5
Yalutorovsk, Russia 24 D7
Yam Ha Melaḥ = Dead Sea, Asia 41 D4
Yam Kinneret, Israel 41 C4
Yamada, Japan 29 H5
Yamagata, Japan 28 E10
Yamagata □, Japan 28 E10
Yamaguchi, Japan 29 G5
Yamaguchi □, Japan 29 G5
Yamal, Poluostrov, Russia 24 B8
Yamal Pen. = Yamal, Poluostrov, Russia 24 B8
Yamanashi □, Japan 29 G9
Yamantau, Gora, Russia 22 D10
Yamba, N.S.W., Australia 55 D5
Yamba, S. Austral., Australia 55 E3
Yambah, Australia 54 C1
Yambarran Ra., Australia 52 C5
Yâmbiô, Sudan 45 H10
Yambol, Bulgaria 21 C12
Yamdena, Indonesia 33 F8
Yame, Japan 29 H5
Yamethin, Burma 37 J20
Yamma-Yamma, L., Australia 55 D3
Yamoussoukro, Ivory C. 44 G3
Yampa →, U.S.A. 72 F9
Yampi Sd., Australia 52 C3
Yampil, Moldova 17 D15
Yampol = Yampil, Moldova 17 D15
Yamuna →, India 37 G12
Yamzho Yumco, China 30 D4
Yana →, Russia 25 B14
Yanac, Australia 55 F3
Yanagawa, Japan 29 H5
Yanai, Japan 29 H6
Yanaul, Russia 22 C10
Yanbu 'al Baḥr, Si. Arabia 38 F3
Yancannia, Australia 55 E3
Yanco Cr. →, Australia 55 F4
Yandal, Australia 53 E3
Yandanooka, Australia 53 E2
Yandaran, Australia 54 C5
Yandoon, Burma 37 L19
Yangambi, Zaïre 46 D4
Yangch'ü = Taiyuan, China 31 C6
Yangon = Rangoon, Burma 37 L20
Yangquan, China 31 C6
Yangtze Kiang = Chang Jiang →, China 31 C7
Yangzhou, China 31 C6
Yanhee Res., Thailand 34 D5
Yanji, China 31 B7
Yankton, U.S.A. 70 D6
Yanna, Australia 55 D4
Yanqi, China 30 B3
Yantabulla, Australia 55 D4
Yantai, China 31 C7
Yanykurgan, Kazakhstan 24 E7
Yao, Chad 45 F8
Yaoundé, Cameroon 44 H7
Yap I., Pac. Oc. 56 G5
Yapen, Indonesia 33 E9
Yapen, Selat, Indonesia 33 E9
Yappar →, Australia 54 B3
Yaqui →, Mexico 74 B2
Yar-Sale, Russia 24 C8
Yaraka, Australia 54 C3
Yaransk, Russia 22 C8
Yardea P.O., Australia 55 E2
Yare →, U.K. 11 E9
Yaremcha, Ukraine 17 D13
Yarensk, Russia 22 B8
Yarí →, Colombia 78 D4
Yarkand = Shache, China 30 C2
Yarkhun →, Pakistan 36 A8
Yarmouth, Canada 63 D6
Yarmūk →, Syria 41 C4
Yaroslavl, Russia 22 C6
Yarqa, W. →, Egypt 41 F2
Yarra Yarra Lakes, Australia 53 E2
Yarraden, Australia 54 A3
Yarraloola, Australia 52 D2
Yarram, Australia 55 F4
Yarraman, Australia 55 D5
Yarranvale, Australia 55 D4
Yarras, Australia 55 E5
Yarrowmere, Australia 54 C4
Yartsevo, Russia 25 C10
Yasawa Group, Fiji 51 C7
Yaselda, Belarus 17 B14
Yasinski, L., Canada 62 B4
Yasinya, Ukraine 17 D13
Yasothon, Thailand 34 E8
Yass, Australia 55 E4
Yatağan, Turkey 21 F13
Yates Center, U.S.A. 71 G7
Yathkyed L., Canada 65 A9
Yatsushiro, Japan 29 H5
Yauyos, Peru 78 F3
Yavari →, Peru 78 D4
Yavatmal, India 36 J11
Yavne, Israel 41 D3
Yavoriv, Ukraine 17 D12
Yavorov = Yavoriv, Ukraine 17 D12
Yawatahama, Japan 29 H6
Yayama-Rettō, Japan 29 M1
Yazd, Iran 39 D7
Yazd □, Iran 39 D7
Yazoo →, U.S.A. 71 J9
Yazoo City, U.S.A. 71 J9
Yding Skovhøj, Denmark 9 J13
Ye Xian, China 31 C6
Yealering, Australia 53 F2
Yebyu, Burma 37 M21
Yecla, Spain 19 C5
Yedintsy = Edinița, Moldova 17 D14
Yeeda, Australia 52 C3
Yeelanna, Australia 55 E2
Yegros, Paraguay 80 B5
Yehuda, Midbar, Israel 41 D4
Yei, Sudan 45 H11
Yekaterinburg, Russia 22 C11
Yekaterinodar = Krasnodar, Russia 23 E6
Yelanskoye, Russia 25 C13
Yelarbon, Australia 55 D5
Yelets, Russia 22 D6
Yelizavetgrad = Kirovohrad, Ukraine 23 E5
Yell, U.K. 12 A7
Yell Sd., U.K. 12 A7
Yellow Sea, China 31 C7
Yellowhead Pass, Canada 64 C5
Yellowknife, Canada 64 A6
Yellowknife →, Canada 64 A6
Yellowstone →, U.S.A. 70 B3
Yellowstone L., U.S.A. 72 D8
Yellowstone National Park, U.S.A. 72 D8
Yellowtail Res., U.S.A. 72 D9
Yelsk, Belarus 17 C15
Yelvertoft, Australia 54 C2
Yemen ■, Asia 40 E3
Yenangyaung, Burma 37 J19
Yenbo = Yanbu 'al Baḥr, Si. Arabia 38 F3
Yenda, Australia 55 E4
Yenice, Turkey 21 E12
Yenisey →, Russia 24 B9
Yeniseysk, Russia 25 D10
Yeniseyskiy Zaliv, Russia 24 B9
Yenyuka, Russia 25 D13
Yeo, L., Australia 53 E3
Yeola, India 36 J9
Yeovil, U.K. 11 G5
Yeppoon, Australia 54 C5
Yerbent, Turkmenistan 24 F6
Yerbogachen, Russia 25 C11
Yerevan, Armenia 23 F7
Yerilla, Australia 53 E3
Yermak, Kazakhstan 24 D8
Yermakovo, Russia 25 D13
Yermo, U.S.A. 73 J5
Yerofey Pavlovich, Russia 25 D13
Yeropol, Russia 25 C17
Yershov, Russia 23 D8
Yerushalayim = Jerusalem, Israel 41 D4
Yes Tor, U.K. 11 G4
Yeso, U.S.A. 71 H2
Yessey, Russia 25 C11
Yeu, I. d', France 18 C2
Yevpatoriya, Ukraine 23 E5
Yeysk, Russia 23 E6
Yezd = Yazd, Iran 39 D7
Yi 'Allaq, G., Egypt 41 E2
Yiannitsa, Greece 21 D10
Yibin, China 30 D5
Yichang, China 31 C6
Yichun, China 31 B7
Yilehuli Shan, China 31 A7
Yinchuan, China 30 C5
Yindarlgooda, L., Australia 53 F3
Yingkou, China 31 B7
Yining, China 24 E9
Yinmabin, Burma 37 H19
Yinnietharra, Australia 52 D2
Yishan, China 30 D5
Yíthion, Greece 21 F10
Yiyang, China 31 D6
Yli-Kitka, Finland 8 C23
Ylitornio, Finland 8 C20
Ylivieska, Finland 8 D21
Ynykchanskiy, Russia 25 C14
Yoakum, U.S.A. 71 L6
Yog Pt., Phil. 33 B6
Yogyakarta, Indonesia 33 G14
Yoho Nat. Park, Canada 64 C5
Yokadouma, Cameroon 46 D2
Yokkaichi, Japan 29 G8
Yoko, Cameroon 45 G7
Yokohama, Japan 29 G9
Yokosuka, Japan 29 G9
Yokote, Japan 28 E10
Yola, Nigeria 45 G7
Yonago, Japan 29 G6
Yonaguni-Jima, Japan 29 M1
Yonezawa, Japan 28 F10
Yong Peng, Malaysia 34 T16
Yonibana, S. Leone 44 G2
Yonkers, U.S.A. 68 E9
Yonne →, France 18 B5
York, Australia 53 F2
York, U.K. 10 D6
York, Ala., U.S.A. 69 J1
York, Nebr., U.S.A. 70 E6
York, Pa., U.S.A. 68 F7
York, C., Australia 54 A3
York, Kap, Greenland 4 B4
York Sd., Australia 52 B4
Yorke Pen., Australia 55 E2
Yorkshire Wolds, U.K. 10 D7
Yorkton, Canada 65 C8
Yorktown, U.S.A. 71 L6
Yornup, Australia 53 F2
Yoron-Jima, Japan 29 L4
Yos Sudarso, Pulau, Indonesia 33 F9
Yosemite National Park, U.S.A. 73 H4
Yoshkar Ola, Russia 22 C8
Yotvata, Israel 41 F4
Youbou, Canada 64 D4
Youghal, Ireland 13 E4
Youghal B., Ireland 13 E4
Young, Australia 55 E4
Young, Canada 65 C7
Younghusband, L., Australia 55 E2
Younghusband Pen., Australia 55 F2
Youngstown, Canada 65 C6
Youngstown, U.S.A. 68 E5
Yoweragabbie, Australia 53 E2
Yozgat, Turkey 23 G5
Ypres = Ieper, Belgium 15 D2
Ypsilanti, U.S.A. 68 D4
Yreka, U.S.A. 72 F2
Ysleta, U.S.A. 73 L10
Ystad, Sweden 9 J15
Ysyk-Köl, Ozero, Kyrgyzstan 24 E8
Ythan →, U.K. 12 D7
Ytyk Kyuyel, Russia 25 C14
Yu Jiang →, China 31 D6
Yu Shan, Taiwan 31 D7
Yuan Jiang →, China 31 D6
Yuba City, U.S.A. 72 G3
Yūbari, Japan 28 C10
Yūbetsu, Japan 28 B11
Yucatán □, Mexico 74 C7
Yucatán, Canal de, Caribbean 74 C7
Yucatán, Península de, Mexico 74 D7
Yucatan Str. = Yucatán, Canal de, Caribbean 74 C7
Yucca, U.S.A. 73 J6
Yuci, China 31 C6
Yudino, Russia 24 D7
Yuendumu, Australia 52 D5
Yugoslavia ■, Europe 21 B9
Yukon →, U.S.A. 60 B3
Yukon Territory □, Canada 60 B6
Yukti, Russia 25 C11
Yukuhashi, Japan 29 H5
Yule →, Australia 52 D2
Yuma, Ariz., U.S.A. 73 K6
Yuma, Colo., U.S.A. 70 E3
Yumen, China 30 C4
Yundamindra, Australia 53 E3
Yungas, Bolivia 78 G5
Yunnan □, China 30 D5
Yunta, Australia 55 E2
Yur, Russia 25 D14
Yurgao, Russia 24 D9
Yuribei, Russia 24 B8
Yurimaguas, Peru 78 E3
Yuryung Kaya, Russia 25 B12
Yushu, China 30 C4
Yuxi, China 30 D5
Yuzawa, Japan 28 E10
Yuzhno-Sakhalinsk, Russia 25 E15
Yvetot, France 18 B4

Z

Zaandam, Neths. 15 B4
Zabaykalsk, Russia 25 E12
Zabid, Yemen 40 E3
Zābol, Iran 39 D9
Zābolī, Iran 39 E9
Zabrze, Poland 17 C10
Zacapa, Guatemala 74 E7
Zacatecas, Mexico 74 C4
Zacoalco, Mexico 74 C4
Zadar, Croatia 16 F8
Zadetkyi Kyun, Burma 34 H5
Zafarqand, Iran 39 C7
Zafra, Spain 19 C2
Żagań, Poland 16 C8
Zagazig, Egypt 45 B11
Zāgheh, Iran 39 C6
Zagorsk = Sergiyev Posad, Russia 22 C6
Zagreb, Croatia 16 F9
Zāgros, Kūhhā-ye, Iran 39 C6
Zagros Mts. = Zāgros, Kūhhā-ye, Iran 39 C6
Zāhedān, Fārs, Iran 39 D7
Zāhedān, Sīstān va Balūchestān, Iran 39 D9
Zahlah, Lebanon 41 B4
Zaïre ■, Africa 46 E4
Zaïre →, Africa 46 F2
Zaječar, Serbia, Yug. 21 C10
Zakamensk, Russia 25 D11
Zakavkazye, Asia 23 F7
Zakhodnaya Dzvina = Daugava →, Latvia 9 H21
Zākhū, Iraq 38 B4
Zákinthos, Greece 21 F9
Zakopane, Poland 17 D10
Zalaegerszeg, Hungary 17 E9
Zalău, Romania 17 E12
Zaleshchiki = Zalishchyky, Ukraine 17 D13
Zalew Wiślany, Poland 17 A10
Zalingei, Sudan 45 F9
Zalishchyky, Ukraine 17 D13
Zambeze →, Africa 47 H7
Zambezi = Zambeze →, Africa 47 H7
Zambezi, Zambia 47 G4
Zambia ■, Africa 47 G5
Zamboanga, Phil. 33 C6
Zamora, Mexico 74 D4
Zamora, Spain 19 B3
Zamość, Poland 17 C12
Zanaga, Congo 46 E2
Zandvoort, Neths. 15 B4
Zanesville, U.S.A. 68 F4
Zangābād, Iran 38 B5
Zanjān, Iran 39 B6
Zanjān □, Iran 39 B6
Zante = Zákinthos, Greece 21 F9
Zanthus, Australia 53 F3
Zanzibar, Tanzania 46 F7
Zaouiet El-Kala = Bordj Omar Driss, Algeria 44 C6
Zaouiet Reggane, Algeria 44 C5
Zap Suyu = Kabīr, Zab al →, Iraq 38 C4
Zapadnaya Dvina, Russia 24 D4
Zapadnaya Dvina = Daugava →, Latvia 9 H21
Západné Beskydy, Europe 17 D10
Zapala, Argentina 80 D2
Zapata, U.S.A. 71 M5
Zapolyarnyy, Russia 22 A5
Zaporizhzhya, Ukraine 23 E6
Zaporozhye = Zaporizhzhya, Ukraine 23 E6
Zaragoza, Spain 19 B5
Zarand, Kermān, Iran 39 D8
Zarand, Markazī, Iran 39 C6
Zaranj, Afghan. 36 D2
Zarasai, Lithuania 9 J22
Zāreh, Iran 39 C6
Zarembo I., U.S.A. 64 B2
Zaria, Nigeria 44 F6
Zarneh, Iran 38 C5
Zarqā' →, Jordan 41 C4
Zarrīn, Iran 39 C7
Zaruma, Ecuador 78 D3
Żary, Poland 16 C8
Zarzis, Tunisia 45 B7
Zashiversk, Russia 25 C15
Zaskar Mts., India 36 C10
Zastron, S. Africa 48 E4
Zavāreh, Iran 39 C7
Zavitinsk, Russia 25 D13
Zavodovski, I., Antarctica 5 B1
Zawiercie, Poland 17 C10
Zāyā, Iraq 38 C5
Zayarsk, Russia 25 D11
Zaysan, Kazakhstan 24 E9
Zaysan, Oz., Kazakhstan 24 E9
Zayü, China 30 D4
Zbarazh, Ukraine 17 D13
Zdolbuniv, Ukraine 17 C14
Zduńska Wola, Poland 17 C10
Zeballos, Canada 64 D3
Zebediela, S. Africa 49 C4
Zeebrugge, Belgium 15 C3
Zeehan, Australia 54 G4
Zeeland □, Neths. 15 C3
Zeerust, S. Africa 48 D4
Zefat, Israel 41 C4
Zeil, Mt., Australia 52 D5
Zeila, Somali Rep. 40 E3
Zeist, Neths. 15 B5
Zeitz, Germany 16 C7
Zelenograd, Russia 22 C6
Zelenogradsk, Russia 9 J19
Zelzate, Belgium 15 C3
Zémio, C.A.R. 46 C5
Zemun, Serbia, Yug. 21 B9
Zenica, Bos.-H. 21 B7
Žepce, Bos.-H. 21 B8
Zeya, Russia 25 D13
Zeya →, Russia 25 D13
Zêzere →, Portugal 19 C1
Zghartā, Lebanon 41 A4
Zgorzelec, Poland 16 C8
Zhabinka, Belarus 17 B13
Zhailma, Kazakhstan 24 D7
Zhambyl, Kazakhstan 24 E8
Zhangaqazaly, Kazakhstan 24 E7
Zhangjiakou, China 31 B6
Zhangye, China 30 C5
Zhangzhou, China 31 D6
Zhanjiang, China 31 D6
Zhanyi, China 30 D5
Zhaotong, China 30 D5
Zhashkiv, Ukraine 17 D16
Zhayyq →, Kazakhstan 23 E9
Zhdanov = Mariupol, Ukraine 23 E6
Zhejiang □, China 31 D7
Zheleznodorozhny, Russia 22 B9
Zheleznogorsk-Ilimskiy, Russia 25 D11
Zhengzhou, China 31 C6
Zhetiqara, Kazakhstan 24 D7
Zhezqazghan, Kazakhstan 24 E7
Zhigansk, Russia 25 C13
Zhilinda, Russia 25 C12
Zhitomir = Zhytomyr, Ukraine 17 C15
Zhlobin, Belarus 17 B16
Zhmerinka = Zhmerynka, Ukraine 17 D15
Zhmerynka, Ukraine 17 D15
Zhodino = Zhodzina, Belarus 17 A15
Zhodzina, Belarus 17 A15
Zhokhova, Ostrov, Russia 25 B16
Zhongdian, China 30 D4
Zhumadian, China 31 C6
Zhupanovo, Russia 25 D16
Zhytomyr, Ukraine 17 C15
Zīārān, Iran 39 B6
Zibo, China 31 C6
Zielona Góra, Poland 16 C8
Zierikzee, Neths. 15 C3
Zigey, Chad 45 F8
Zigong, China 30 D5
Ziguinchor, Senegal 44 F1
Žilina, Slovak Rep. 17 D10
Zillah, Libya 45 C8
Zima, Russia 25 D11
Zimbabwe ■, Africa 47 H5
Zimnicea, Romania 17 G13
Zinder, Niger 44 F6
Zion National Park, U.S.A. 73 H7
Zipaquirá, Colombia 78 C4
Zitundo, Mozam. 49 D5
Ziway, L., Ethiopia 45 G12
Zlatograd, Bulgaria 21 D11
Zlatoust, Russia 22 C10
Zlin, Czech. 17 D9
Zlītan, Libya 45 B7
Zmeinogorsk, Kazakhstan 24 D9
Znojmo, Czech. 16 D9
Zobeyrī, Iran 38 C5
Zolochev = Zolochiv, Ukraine 17 D13
Zolochiv, Ukraine 17 D13
Zomba, Malawi 47 H7
Zongo, Zaïre 46 D3
Zonguldak, Turkey 23 F5
Zorra I., Panama 74 H14
Zorritos, Peru 78 D2
Zouar, Chad 45 D8
Zouérate, Mauritania 44 D3
Zoutkamp, Neths. 15 A6
Zrenjanin, Serbia, Yug. 21 B9
Zuetina = Az Zuwaytīnah, Libya 45 B9
Zufar, Oman 40 D5
Zug, Switz. 16 E5
Zugspitze, Germany 16 E6
Zuid-Holland □, Neths. 15 C4
Zuidhorn, Neths. 15 A6
Zula, Eritrea 45 E12
Zumbo, Mozam. 47 H6
Zungeru, Nigeria 44 G6
Zuni, U.S.A. 73 J9
Zunyi, China 30 D5
Zurbātīyah, Iraq 38 C5
Zürich, Switz. 16 E5
Zutphen, Neths. 15 B6
Zuwārah, Libya 45 B7
Zūzan, Iran 39 C8
Zverinogolovskoye, Russia 24 D7
Zvishavane, Zimbabwe 47 J6
Zvolen, Slovak Rep. 17 D10
Zwettl, Austria 16 D8
Zwickau, Germany 16 C7
Zwolle, Neths. 15 B6
Zwolle, U.S.A. 71 K8
Zymoetz →, Canada 64 C3
Żyrardów, Poland 17 B11
Zyryan, Kazakhstan 24 E9
Zyryanka, Russia 25 C16
Zyryanovsk = Zyryan, Kazakhstan 24 E9
Żywiec, Poland 17 D10

WORLD : REGIONS IN THE NEWS

Maps show the situation in May 1995

MOLDOVA
FORMER YUGOSLAVIA
THE CAUCASUS
THE NEAR EAST
ECUADOR AND PERU

THE BREAK UP OF YUGOSLAVIA
The former country of Yugoslavia comprised six republics. In 1991 Slovenia and Croatia declared independence. Bosnia-Herzegovina followed in 1992 and Macedonia in 1993. Yugoslavia now comprises the remaining two republics, Serbia and Montenegro.

YUGOSLAVIA
Population : 10,763,000 (Serb 62.6%, Albanian 16.5%, Montenegrin 5%, Hungarian 3.3%, Muslim 3.2%)
Serbia
Population : 5,824,211 (Serb 87.7%) excluding the former autonomous provinces of Kosovo and Vojvodina
Kosovo
Population : 1,956,196 (Albanian 81.6%, Serb 9.9%)
Vojvodina
Population : 2,014,000 (Serb 56.8%, Hungarian 16.9%)
Montenegro Population : 615,035 (Montenegrin 61.9%, Muslim 14.6%, Albanian 6.6%)
CROATIA
Population : 4,504,000 (Croat 78.1%, Serb 12.2%)
SLOVENIA
Population : 1,942,000 (Slovene 88%, Croat 3%, Serb 2%)
MACEDONIA (F.Y.R.O.M.)
Population : 2,142,000 (Macedonian 64%, Albanian 21.7%, Turkish 5%, Romanian 3%, Serb 2%)
BOSNIA - HERZEGOVINA
Population : 3,527,000 (Muslim 49%, Serb 31.2%, Croat 17.2%)

Civil war between Serbs and other ethnic groups continues in Bosnia-Herzegovina. The large scale map on the left shows the situation in early 1995.

FORMER YUGOSLAVIA
0   50   100   150   200 km

–·–·– International boundaries
–·–·– Republic boundaries
– – – Province boundaries
⊚ Capital cities

BOSNIA-HERZEGOVINA
0   50   100 km

Under Croatian control
Under Serbian control
Under Muslim control

THE NEAR EAST
0   25   50km

RUSSIA
North Ossetia
Population : 695,000 (Ossetian 53%, Russian 29%, Chechen 5.2%, Ingush 5% [expelled in 1992])
Chechenia
Population : 1,308,000 (Chechen and Ingush 70.7%, Russian 23.1%)
Neighbouring **Ingushetia** (now split from Chechenia)
Population : 250,000 (mainly Ingush)
GEORGIA
Population : 5,450,000 (Georgian 70.1%, Armenian 8.1%, Russian 6.3%, Azerbaijani 5.7%, Ossetian 3%, Greek 2%, Abkhazian 2%)
Abkhazia
Population : 537,500 (Georgian 45.7%, Abkhazian 17.8%, Armenian 14.6%, Russian 14.3%)
Ajaria
Population : 382,000 (Georgian 82.8%, Russian 7.7%, Armenian 4%)
South Ossetia
Population : 99,800 (Ossetian 66.2%, Georgian 29%)
ARMENIA
Population : 3,548,000 (Armenian 93.3%, Azerbaijani 2.6%)
Nagorno-Karabakh
Population : 192,400 (Armenian 76.9%, Azerbaijani 21.5%)
AZERBAIJAN
Population : 7,472,000 (Azerbaijani 82.7%, Russian 5.6%, Armenian 5.6%, Lezgin 2.4%)
Naxçivan
Population : 300,400 (Azerbaijani 95.9%)

THE CAUCASUS
0   100   200 km

–·–·– International boundaries
–·–·– Republic boundaries

Georgia, Armenia and Azerbaijan achieved independence in 1991. Abkhazia, Ajaria and South Ossetia seek independence from Georgia. Chechenia has been trying to break away from Russia since 1991, but Russia has resisted with military force. Hostility also continues between Armenia and Azerbaijan over the enclave of Nagorno-Karabakh.

ISRAEL Population : 5,458,000 (inc. East Jerusalem and Jewish settlers in the areas under Israeli administration. (Jewish 82%, Arab Muslim 13.8%, Arab Christian 2.5%, Druze 1.7%)

West Bank Population : 973,500 (Palestinian Arabs 97% [of whom Arab Muslim 85%, Jewish 7%, Christian 8%])

Gaza Strip Population : 658,200 (Arab Muslim 98%)

JORDAN Population : 5,198,000 (Arab 99% [of whom about 50% are Palestinian Arab])

–·–·– 1949 Armistice Line
– – – 1974 Cease-fire Lines

Efrata ● Main Jewish settlements in the West Bank and Gaza Strip

Halhul □ Main Palestinian Arab towns in the West Bank and Gaza Strip

MOLDOVA
0   50   100   150 km

Separatist regions

Population : 4,420,000 (Moldovan 64.5%, Ukrainian 13.9%, Russian 14%, Gagauzi 3.5%, Jewish 2%, Bulgarian 2%)

ECUADOR AND PERU
0   100   200 km

– – – – 1995 disputed border

Disputed territory allocated to Peru in 1942

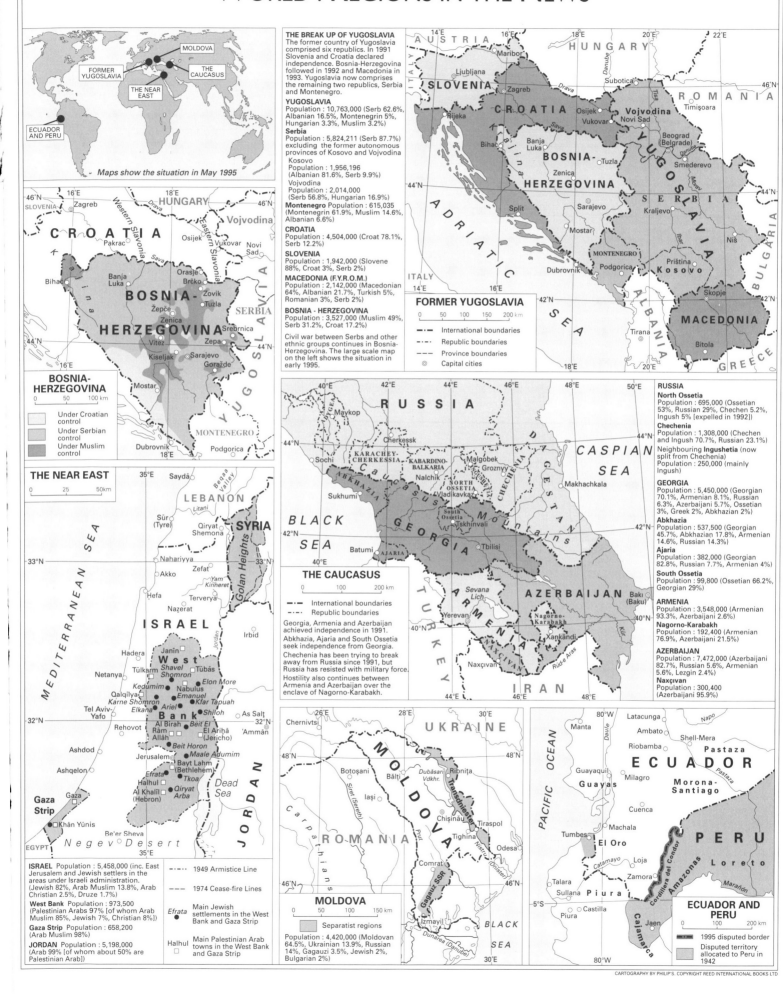

KEY TO WORLD MAP PAGES

NORTH
AMERICA

4

Arctic Circle

60-61

8

64-65

62-63

14

72-73   70-71   68-69

ATLANTIC

OCEAN

Tropic of Cancer

66

74-75

PACIFIC
OCEAN
56-57

Equator

AFRICA

78-79

SOUTH
AMERICA

Tropic of Capricorn

PACIFIC OCEAN

80